The First Century of the
INTERNATIONAL JOINT COMMISSION

CANADIAN HISTORY AND ENVIRONMENT SERIES

SERIES EDITOR: Alan MacEachern

ISSN 1925-3702 (Print) ISSN 1925-3710 (Online)

The Canadian History & Environment series brings together scholars from across the academy and beyond to explore the relationships between people and nature in Canada's past.

Alan MacEachern, Founding Director
NiCHE: Network in Canadian History & Environment
Nouvelle initiative canadienne en histoire de l'environnement
http://niche-canada.org

No. 1 · *A Century of Parks Canada, 1911–2011*
Edited by Claire Elizabeth Campbell

No. 2 · *Historical GIS Research in Canada*
Edited by Jennifer Bonnell and Marcel Fortin

No. 3 · *Mining and Communities in Northern Canada: History, Politics, and Memory*
Edited by Arn Keeling and John Sandlos

No. 4 · *Canadian Countercultures and the Environment*
Edited by Colin M. Coates

No. 5 · *Moving Natures: Mobility and the Environment in Canadian History*
Edited by Ben Bradley, Jay Young, and Colin M. Coates

No. 6 · *Border Flows: A Century of the Canadian-American Water Relationship*
Edited by Lynne Heasley and Daniel Macfarlane

No. 7 · *Ice Blink: Navigating Northern Environmental History*
Edited by Stephen Bocking and Brad Martin

No. 8 · *Animal Metropolis: Histories of Human-Animal Relations in Urban Canada*
Edited by Joanna Dean, Darcy Ingram, and Christabelle Sethna

No. 9 · *Environmental Activism on the Ground: Small Green and Indigenous Organizing*
Edited by Jonathan Clapperton and Liza Piper

No. 10 · *The First Century of the International Joint Commission*
Edited by Daniel Macfarlane and Murray Clamen

UNIVERSITY OF CALGARY
Press

The First Century of the
INTERNATIONAL JOINT COMMISSION

EDITED BY
DANIEL MACFARLANE
and **MURRAY CLAMEN**

Canadian History and Environment Series
ISSN 1925-3702 (Print) ISSN 1925-3710 (Online)

© 2020 Daniel Macfarlane and Murray Clamen

University of Calgary Press
2500 University Drive NW
Calgary, Alberta
Canada T2N 1N4
press.ucalgary.ca

This book is available as an ebook which is licensed under a Creative Commons license. The publisher should be contacted for any commercial use which falls outside the terms of that license.

Library and Archives Canada Cataloguing in Publication

Title: The first century of the International Joint Commission / edited by Daniel Macfarlane and Murray Clamen.
Names: Macfarlane, Daniel, 1979- editor. | Clamen, Murray, editor.
Series: Canadian history and environment series ; no. 10. 1925-3702
Description: Series statement: Canadian history and environment series, 1925-3702 ; no. 10 | Includes bibliographical references and index.
Identifiers: Canadiana (print) 20190228504 | Canadiana (ebook) 20190228555 | ISBN 9781773851075 (softcover) | ISBN 9781773851082 (Open Access PDF) | ISBN 9781773851099 (PDF) | ISBN 9781773851105 (EPUB) | ISBN 9781773851112 (Kindle)
Subjects: LCSH: International Joint Commission—History. | LCSH: International rivers. | LCSH: International lakes. | LCSH: Canada—Boundaries—United States. | LCSH: United States—Boundaries—Canada.
Classification: LCC HD1694.A2 F57 2020 | DDC 341.4/4—dc23

The University of Calgary Press acknowledges the support of the Government of Alberta through the Alberta Media Fund for our publications. We acknowledge the financial support of the Government of Canada. We acknowledge the financial support of the Canada Council for the Arts for our publishing program.

This book has been published with the help of a grant from the Canadian Federation for the Humanities and Social Sciences, through the Awards to Scholarly Publications Program, using funds provided by the Social Sciences and Humanities Research Council of Canada.

  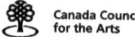 

Copyediting by Ryan Perks
Cover image: Aerial View of Niagara Falls and Vicinity, 2018. Photograph by Daniel Macfarlane.
Cover design, page design, and typesetting by Melina Cusano

CONTENTS

Illustrations	ix
Foreword	xiii
Gordon W. Walker and Lana Pollack	
Acknowledgements	xvii
Introduction	1
Murray Clamen and Daniel Macfarlane	

Section 1: Beginnings

1	From IWC to BWT: Canada-US Institution Building, 1902–1909	35
	David Whorley	
2	Construction of a Keystone: How Local Concerns and International Geopolitics Created the First Water Management Mechanisms on the Canada-US Border	71
	Meredith Denning	

Section 2: From Coast to Coast

3	The International Joint Commission and Water Quality in the Bacterial Age	115
	Jamie Benidickson	

4   The Boundary Waters Treaty and the International Joint   143
    Commission in the St. Mary–Milk Basin
    B. Timothy Heinmiller

5   The International Joint Commission and Hydro-power   165
    Development on the Northeastern Borderlands, 1945–1970
    James Kenny

6   A Square Peg: The Lessons of the Point Roberts Reference,   195
    1971–1977
    Kim Richard Nossal

7   The International Joint Commission and Mid-continent   215
    Water Issues: The Garrison Diversion, Red River, Devils
    Lake, and the Northwest Area Water Supply Project
    Norman Brandson and Allen Olson

8   The International Joint Commission's Unique and Colourful   239
    Role in Three Projects in the Pacific Northwest
    Richard Moy and Jonathan O'Riordan

Section 3: Great Lakes–St. Lawrence Basin

9   The International Joint Commission and Great Lakes   285
    Water Levels
    Murray Clamen and Daniel Macfarlane

10 The International Joint Commission and Air Pollution: 313
    A Tale of Two Cases
    Owen Temby and Don Munton

11	Origin of the Great Lakes Water Quality Agreement: Concepts and Structures	347
	Jennifer Read	
12	The Great Lakes Remedial Action Plan Program: A Historical and Contemporary Description and Analysis	367
	Gail Krantzberg	
13	The International Joint Commission and the Evolution of the Great Lakes Water Quality Agreement: Accountability, Progress Reporting, and Measuring Performance	395
	Debora VanNijnatten and Carolyn Johns	

Section 4: Legacies

14	From "Stakeholder to Rights-Holder": Re-examining the Role of Indigenous Peoples in the International Joint Commission as the Third Sovereign	433
	Frank Ettawageshik and Emma S. Norman	
15	The Boundary Waters Treaty, the International Joint Commission, and the Evolution of Transboundary Environmental Law and Governance	457
	Noah D. Hall, A. Dan Tarlock, and Marcia Valiante	
16	The Importance of the International Joint Commission	483
	John Kirton and Brittaney Warren	
17	The International Joint Commission: Continually Evolving Approaches to Conflict Resolution	507
	Ralph Pentland and Ted R. Yuzyk	

Conclusion 529
Murray Clamen and Daniel Macfarlane

Appendices 549
    APPENDIX 1: Boundary Waters Treaty 551
    APPENDIX 2: The Clinton-Gibbons Draft, 1907 565
    APPENDIX 3: List of IJC Commissioners 573

Selected Bibliography 577
Contributors 589
Index 597

ILLUSTRATIONS

FIG. 0.1	Canada-US border watersheds. Used with permission of the IJC.	4
FIG. 0.2	Current logo of the IJC. Used with permission of the IJC.	6
FIG. 0.3	Watersheds covered in this book. J. Glatz, Western Michigan University Libraries.	13
FIG. 2.1	American population of lower Great Lakes watershed, 1840–1920. Created by author.	74
FIG. 2.2	Demographic change in Southern Ontario, 1871–1921. Created by author.	74
FIG. 2.3	Value added in manufacturing, US side of Lake Erie, 1899–1914. Created by author.	75
FIG. 2.4	Iron ore received at US ports on Lake Erie, 1892–1903. Created by author.	75
FIG. 4.1	Map of the St. Mary–Milk watershed. J. Glatz, Western Michigan University Libraries.	144
FIG. 5.1	The two-pool Passamaquoddy tidal power project. Source: *Report to the International Joint Commission by the International Passamaquoddy Engineering Board* (October 1959), p. 7.	176

FIG. 5.2	Location of proposed Passamaquoddy tidal and Rankin Rapids hydro developments. Source: *Report to the International Joint Commission by the International Passamaquoddy Engineering Board* (October 1959), p. 3.	178
FIG. 6.1	Map of Point Roberts. J. Glatz, Western Michigan University Libraries.	197
FIG. 7.1	Map of water issues discussed in this chapter. Used with permission of the Government of Manitoba.	216
FIG. 8.1	Skagit River Basin and Ross Lake. J. Glatz, Western Michigan University Libraries.	242
FIG. 8.2	High Ross Dam Reservoir compared to the existing Ross Dam Reservoir. J. Glatz, Western Michigan University Libraries.	245
FIG. 8.3	The Columbia River Basin. J. Glatz, Western Michigan University Libraries.	254
FIG. 8.4	Crown of the Continent Eco-region. J. Glatz, Western Michigan University Libraries.	262
FIG. 8.5	Location of the proposed Sage Creek coal mine within the Flathead River Basin. J. Glatz, Western Michigan University Libraries.	264
FIG. 9.1	Map of the St. Lawrence Seaway. Map by Eric Leinberger, used with the permission of UBC Press.	290-91
FIG. 9.2	St. Lawrence Seaway lock across from Montreal. Used with the permission of Library and Archives Canada.	292
FIG. 9.3	Proposed Niagara Remedial Works. Library and Archives Canada.	297

Fig. 9.4	Niagara waterscape. Map by Rajiv Ravat, Anders Sandberg, and Daniel Macfarlane.	298
Fig. 10.1	Detroit–St. Clair River area. IJC, *Transboundary Air Pollution: Detroit and St. Clair River Areas*, p. ii.	325
Fig. 11.1	Trudeau and Nixon signing the GLWQA. Used with permission of the Canadian Press.	348
Fig. 12.1	Location and status of the Areas of Concern. Used with permission of Binational.net.	368
Fig. 12.2	RAP review process for delisting AOCs. Created by author.	373
Fig. 12.3	Collingwood Harbour. Created by author.	375
Fig. 12.4	Presque Isle Bay case study. Created by author.	376
Fig. 12.5	Severn Sound case study. Created by author.	382
Fig. 13.1	Areas of Concern in the 1987 GLWQA (2018). Used with the permission of Environment and Climate Change Canada.	409
Fig. 13.2	Beneficial Use Impairments in the 1987 GLWQA.	410
Fig. 13.3	Objectives set for the 1972, 1978, and 1987 versions of the GLWQA. Created by authors.	411
Fig. 13.4	Performance assessment, accountability, and reporting mechanisms in the 1972, 1978, and 1987 versions of the GLWQA. Created by authors.	412
Tab. 13.1	State of the Great Lakes 2017. Created by authors.	419

FIG. 17.1	Diversion system for St. Mary–Milk Rivers. Image used with the permission of the IJC.	512
FIG. 17.2	Devils Lake annual peak water levels. Image used with the permission of the IJC.	514
FIG. 17.3	Existing diversions in the Great Lakes basin. Image used with the permission of the IJC.	516
FIG. 17.4	Adaptive management cycle. Image used with the permission of the IJC.	518
FIG. 17.5	Harmonized data sets for Souris River basin. Image used with the permission of the IJC.	522

FOREWORD

As former chairs of our respective national sections and with a total of eighteen years of service on the International Joint Commission (IJC), we read *The First Century of the International Joint Commission* with the delight of discovery, and with the pleasant familiarity that comes from encountering old stories in a new light. Long-time IJC insider Murray Clamen, who for years spoke to us of the need for a history of the IJC, and historian Daniel Macfarlane have recruited a decidedly diverse team of highly qualified contributors to provide an unsparingly honest history of this frequently misunderstood binational treaty organization.

We commend Clamen and Macfarlane for taking on the task of assembling the fantastic story of the IJC. Only two books dedicated to the IJC have preceded this 2019 assessment, the most recent of which marked the commission's seventieth birthday, forty years back. The interim period has provided time to re-evaluate the early decades of the IJC's history and to observe its continuing evolution. In the face of changing natural and political climates, the authors elucidate the sometimes "messy" relationships among the impacted provinces and states, as well as between the two federal governments and engaged stakeholders.

In reading *First Century* we are reminded of the particularities of the approximately 140 government references and applications submitted to IJC under the Boundary Waters Treaty, including the singularly significant standing reference created by four iterations of the Great Lakes Water Quality Agreement. As practitioners of the treaty we are particularly pleased that this book offers a deeper dive into the challenges of making the treaty work for multiple interests in both countries. We have lived the treaty and know that many IJC consensus decisions have been realized, not in an entirely pristine, politics-free environment, but rather in the context of vocal expressions of national, regional, local, business, and environmental interests.

We have oft seen the Boundary Waters Treaty likened to a marriage in which each party comes with only one vote—or to be more precise in this case, each party comes with three votes—each side needing the other to accomplish anything. The only way forward is for sufficient numbers from both sides of the border to favour a particular resolution of the challenge before them. As commissioners we have often thought that the federal governments would do well to engage the IJC's services more frequently. But as *First Century* points out, national and sub-national politics sometimes intervene to deny the IJC a potentially positive role in resolving knotty binational issues. Increasingly, however, even when the IJC is not granted a new reference, the commission's binational, basin-wide boards are meeting to resolve water level and flow issues, and, more recently, to address water quality issues as well. Now in the face of climate change challenges, the IJC is supporting collaborations among its inter-basin boards and increasingly supporting adaptive management principles. In every case the IJC is providing a platform for ongoing forums that draw disparate interests into science-based, solution-focused binational discussions.

The IJC has laboured in relative obscurity for more than a century, rarely generating more than passing reference in the media. Few people within the watershed areas—tens of millions of people—can identify the meaning of the initials "IJC," or even the full name for which they stand. And yet border issues, especially border water issues, rank very high in the minds of the public. As commissioners, we found that the IJC is most likely to make occasional headlines when a well-considered, science-based decision disappoints a player looking for a bigger slice of the interest pie. That the IJC generates few headlines could well be seen as an indication of client satisfaction.

We are pleased to have readers of *First Century* informed that the consensus decisions we and our predecessors on the IJC have reached were often preceded by substantive, multi-faceted, and indeed difficult discussions that were nevertheless critically informed by a significant investment in relevant science and engineering, and most often marked by the Boundary Waters Treaty's high-minded bipartisan perspective. As commissioners' decisions are often not easy ones, this book can only be an asset to those who will come after us in the IJC community, for they will be better informed by the IJC's history and will benefit from this discriminating analysis of the treaty's performance.

Gordon W. Walker, QC
IJC Commissioner 1992–95 and 2013–18 and
Canada Section Chair 2014–18

Lana Pollack
IJC Commissioner and US Section Chair 2010–19

ACKNOWLEDGEMENTS

We would like to begin by thanking the contributors to this book for their hard work. We need to acknowledge the financial support of a Social Sciences and Humanities Research Council of Canada (SSHRC) Connection grant which funded a conference in 2017 in Ottawa that brought together this book's contributors. That conference went so smoothly because of the efforts of Jamie Benidickson (University of Ottawa) and Greg Donaghy (Global Affairs Canada). We want to thank the editors and staff with whom we worked at the University of Calgary Press, especially: Helen Hajnoczky, Brian Scrivener, Keyan Zhang, and Melina Cusano. We thank Alan MacEachern, the editor of the Canadian History and Environment series, for his enthusiastic encouragement as well as his feedback. This series is done in conjunction with the Network in Canadian History and Environment (NiCHE), which continues to be the hub for Canadian environmental history.

We appreciate the support of the IJC and its various officials and staff members who provided valuable feedback but gave us the necessary space to produce an objective study, especially Paul Allen, David Fay, Nick Heisler, and Sarah Lobrichon. In their roles as IJC chairs, Lana Pollock and Gordon Walker offered thoughts at the 2017 conference and then supplied the Foreword to this book. We thank Lynne Heasley for her insights, and Jason Glatz for creating many fantastic maps on short notice. Three graduate students from the Faculty of Law, University of Ottawa, Alex Geddes, Angela Lee and Alexandre Lillo, provided administrative and research assistance in connection with the conference. Their support was greatly appreciated, as well as the further contribution of Alex Geddes and Angela Lee in preparing the index to this volume. We would like to heartily tip our hat to the two external reviewers who provided constructive and positive feedback that made this a better book (if only all peer reviews processes could be so pleasant). Both Murray and Daniel thank the *Journal of Policy Research* for allowing them to reprint parts of their 2015 article, "The International Joint Commission, Water Levels, and Transboundary Governance in the Great Lakes," in their chapter in this volume.

Murray would like to thank the many commissioners and colleagues he worked with at the IJC over the years in both the Canadian and US Sections, and the Great Lakes Regional Office from whom he learned to appreciate the interdisciplinary aspects of water management and the uniqueness of the Canada-US relationship. Specifically he would like to honour and thank Canadian commissioner and chair Leonard Legault for appointing him as Secretary of the Canadian Section and making it possible to participate in direct discussions and deliberations of commissioners. It is essential to note the support of his family, especially wife Jill, for all the times he travelled away from home during his career with the IJC, and their encouragement to complete this book. Daniel would like to thank his home department and institution, the Institute of the Environment and Sustainability at Western Michigan University. Most importantly, he thanks his family for their love and support: Jen, Elizabeth, and Lucas.

Murray Clamen and Daniel Macfarlane

Introduction

Murray Clamen and Daniel Macfarlane

It was the summer of 2008 and the commissioners of the International Joint Commission (IJC) and their cadre of advisers were meeting to discuss the next steps in the evolving process of revising the plan of regulation for Lake Ontario and the upper St. Lawrence River. This regulation plan has long been one of the IJC's most controversial activities, since different interests want very different water regimes: some property owners want levels kept low, while the shipping and hydro-power sectors benefit from higher water flows; environmentalists, meanwhile, hope that the lake and upper portions of the river can be regulated in a way that allows for more natural fluctuations.

In summer 2008 the IJC had just completed an extensive public consultation process of ten public information sessions and ten formal public hearings on a proposed new regulation plan called Plan 2007, which had evolved from a five year, US$20 million study by a binational team of experts. Heading into these public sessions, commissioners and their advisers were confident they had found a new plan that would satisfy most of the diverse stakeholders in this important watershed by bringing in new environmental values, assisting recreational boaters, and preserving all the existing benefits to hydro-power, commercial navigation, and riparians that had been created when the original St. Lawrence Power Project had been approved by the IJC in the 1950s. However, the proposed plan was widely criticized by almost all who attended the public sessions, either for not providing sufficient environmental benefits or for not preserving enough of the existing benefits.

As the commissioners and their staff debated these unanticipated results, some commissioners were so discouraged they wanted to halt the process completely and continue with the current regulation plan (Plan 1958D), even though they knew it was not performing satisfactorily. Feelings in the room were quite high as other commissioners and IJC officials knew the opportunity to make a significant change in regulation was before them and they wanted to continue and find a new plan of regulation. As various ideas were batted around, someone suggested that a new, smaller working group composed solely of senior representatives of the federal and provincial governments and IJC advisers might be able to resurrect Plan 2007 and develop a slightly better version. That working group, which was eventually accepted by the governments, met several times starting in December 2009. It ultimately came up with Plan Bv7, which the IJC—after further consultation, deliberations, and refinement—developed as a new proposal called Plan 2014.[1]

In the summer of 2013, the IJC invited public comment and convened public hearings on the proposed Plan 2014. More than 5,500 comments were received in total. This included 206 oral testimonies at the twelve hearings and public teleconferences; over 3,500 signatures on four different petitions; more than 700 postcards and form letters; and nearly 1,000 written website, email, and unique letter responses. This latter group of responses ranged from short endorsements or rejections of Plan 2014 to formal responses from local governments, governmental departments, and non-governmental organizations.[2]

Although there was opposition, there seemed to be generally strong support for the new plan. After more than fifteen years of intensive analysis and extensive consultation (serious talks about a new regulation plan dated back at least to the 1990s) with governments, experts, Lake Ontario and St. Lawrence River interests, and the public, the IJC concluded Plan 2014 should be implemented as soon as possible, and recommended as much in their June 2014 report to the two federal governments. On 6 December 2016, the governments of Canada and the United States agreed with the IJC's December 2016 Supplementary Order of Approval and the proposed regulation plan in accordance with certain undertakings, as outlined in their letter of concurrence.[3] Part of the delay, on both sides, in achieving government agreement was the complexity of interests involved and the range of government departments and agencies that needed to be consulted and give their individual concurrences. In December the commissioners signed the Supplementary Order implementing Plan 2014, which went into effect in January 2017.

A few months later, however, the Lake Ontario-St. Lawrence system experienced record-setting flooding stemming from natural causes. Riparian owners were up in arms because of the extensive damage to their property, especially on the south shore of Lake Ontario. Some politicians, such as New York governor Andrew Cuomo, irresponsibly used the matter for partisan purposes and began attacking the IJC. Then, in spring 2019, Lake Ontario levels surpassed even those of 2017. Consequently, there is very strong pressure to reopen the method of regulation for the upper St. Lawrence River.

This Lake Ontario-St. Lawrence regulation saga is just one of the most recent episodes in a history of ups and downs for the IJC. It illustrates the challenges faced regularly by the IJC in trying to predict natural forces, use engineering structures to provide some control, balance interests upstream and downstream, and address both water quantity and quality, as well as air pollution and other transborder environmental issues—all while adhering to the principles enshrined in the Boundary Waters Treaty of 1909. The IJC also faces many political challenges. While the commission does much of its work in obscurity, away from the glare of the media spotlight, when it comes to certain hot-button topics (such as regulation of Lake Ontario and the upper St. Lawrence River) different constituents are often diametrically opposed about outcomes and water levels, and they aren't afraid to make their complaints public. The IJC has to balance a range of interests, some of which are narrow but loud and well-funded, since making technically and scientifically sound choices often benefits some more than others. When advocating for a policy position, commissioners must be ever cognizant of how far they can go without alienating the federal governments, other levels of government, and various stakeholders; adjudicating between the sometimes competing interests of two sovereign federal nations is challenging. The IJC can technically only deal with environmental issues referred to it by the federal governments, which

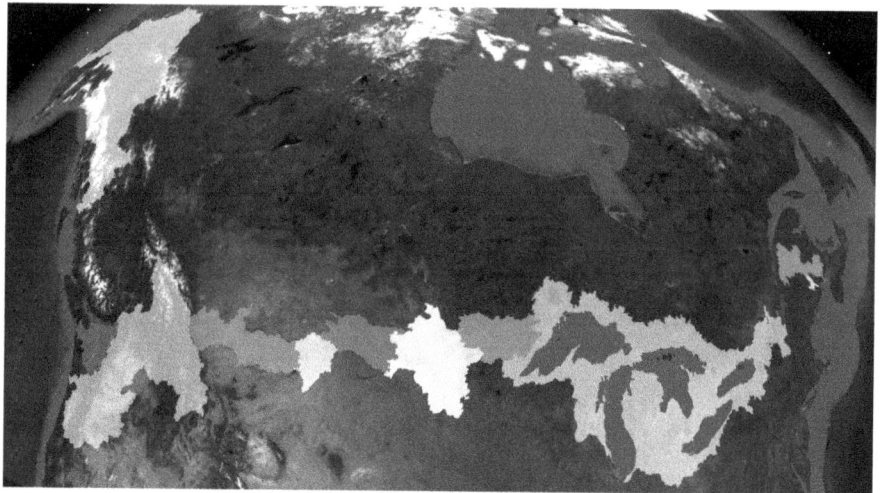

FIGURE 0.1. Canada-US border watersheds. Used with permission of the IJC.

puts limits on the commission's ability to be proactive—even though anticipation is a best practice when it comes to dealing with ecological issues.

The contributors to this edited collection take up these challenges, and many others. We collectively examine important aspects of the history of the IJC and the 1909 Boundary Waters Treaty (whose formal title is the Treaty Between the United States and Great Britain Relating to Boundary Waters, and Questions Arising Between the United States and Canada) over the first century of its existence, and we explain how this unique organization came to be, how it was supposed to work, and how it has actually worked for more than a hundred years. We have brought together leading scholars on the IJC in a consciously multidisciplinary way, so that hydraulic engineers, water resources professionals, and policy practitioners can ideally get as much from this volume as historians, lawyers, and political scientists. Not only have we amassed an impressive roster of contributors, we have attempted, as much as possible, to cover various thematic and geographic aspects: water quality and quantity, air pollution, past and future, east and west, etc. As editors, we are very satisfied with the chronological, geographic, thematic, and disciplinary breadth of this collection, with the various contributions providing a history of the IJC that is both wide and deep.

The Boundary Waters Treaty and the IJC

Canada and the United States share a particularly fluid border: around 150 waterbodies comprising about 40 per cent of the 8,800 kilometre international frontier. In the early twentieth century, boundary water issues such as the Chicago Diversion, sharing the waters of the St. Mary and Milk Rivers in the Western Prairies, and dividing the hydroelectric generating capacity of Niagara Falls and the St. Lawrence River, led to the creation of an institution called the International Waterways Commission (IWC). In 1906 and 1907 the IWC made a series of recommendations calling on Canada and the United States to adopt principles of law governing uses of international waters along the border and to create an international body with authority to study and regulate the use of these waters. In the ensuing negotiations, Canada wanted a powerful body, while the United States sought a weaker one; the eventual result was a compromise. The Boundary Waters Treaty (BWT) was signed on 11 January 1909 by James Bryce, the British ambassador to the United States, and by Elihu Root, the US secretary of state.

Securing the agreement was a significant coup for Canada, since it resulted in the much more powerful United States agreeing to a commission within which the two countries were equal. Though Great Britain technically signed the treaty for Canada, the Canadian government did much of the negotiating, and it was therefore an important nation-building step for Canada. Among other features, the BWT settled the outstanding water issues mentioned in the previous paragraph (aside from the Chicago Diversion) and brought about the creation of the IJC, which held its first meeting in Washington, DC, on 10 January 1912.

The BWT was a pioneering piece of water resource management. The treaty was also an initial step in the rapprochement that characterized Canadian-American eco-politics for most of the twentieth century. The IJC is the key to the regime established by the 1909 treaty. It is a unique kind of international institution that combines interstate and supranational functions. As an adaptable governance form, it has evolved over time

FIGURE 0.2. Current logo of the IJC. Used with permission of the International Joint Commission.

(both as an organization and the way it has been used and approached), and it has increasingly incorporated transnational policy networks, public feedback, and scientific/engineering expertise. It has succeeded in providing a framework and ground rules that have, for the most part, prevented or resolved bilateral disputes over boundary and transboundary waters for over a century. It has been said that the dispute-settlement and conflict-avoidance philosophies enshrined in the BWT were far more sophisticated than perhaps any comparable piece of bilateral machinery then existing in Western society. As one former Canadian IJC chairman pointed out, its pioneering anti-pollution obligations fashioned a multiple-use instrument that went beyond any similar measures in other countries and perhaps even beyond the full appreciation of the draftsmen themselves; even the use of the word "pollution" was novel at the time.[4] That said, the commission's focus on pollution was intermittent, for aside of some studies on the connecting channels of the Great Lakes, until after the Second World War the IJC was much more concerned about issues dealing with navigation, hydro-power, and apportioning each country's share of boundary waters.

The BWT, which is reproduced in full in Appendix 1, notably granted equal navigation access to the waters covered by the treaty—including Lake Michigan for Canadian citizens and flag vessels—and regulations were adopted concerning water diversions and changes to water levels. Essentially, any changes in the level of a boundary water needed agreement through the IJC (or a special agreement between the federal governments, which was the case for the St. Lawrence, Niagara, and Columbia Rivers in the early Cold War, though the IJC still had to approve the construction and maintenance of any resulting infrastructure that affected boundary waters). The BWT outlined an order of precedence for how border waters could be used: 1) for domestic and sanitary purposes; 2) for navigation; and 3) for power and irrigation. However, no reference was made to industrial, recreational, or environmental uses, though these were recognized and incorporated over time, particularly in the quarter-century after the Second World War. The treaty assigned the IJC four categories of function that it was expected to discharge, which can be summarized as *administrative* (articles v and vi): directing the measurement and division of the waters of the Niagara River and the St. Mary–Milk Rivers; *quasi-judicial* (articles iii, iv, and viii): passing on applications for permission to use, divert, or obstruct treaty waters (commission approval with relevant conditions is typically given in an Order of Approval, which the commission then monitors for compliance); *investigative* (article ix): examining and making recommendations on any differences arising along the common boundary (these investigations are called "references" and recommendations are non-binding); and *arbitral* (article x): making binding decisions with respect to *any* questions arising between the two countries, regardless of whether it was a boundary question—a function that has never been used.[5] A fifth function, *monitoring*, is arguably implicit in the text of the BWT, achieving formal function status beginning in the 1970s through the IJC's involvement in the Great Lakes Water Quality Agreement (GLWQA) and the International Air Quality Advisory Board.

The 1909 treaty established the IJC as a six-member body in which there is parity between Canada and the United States (i.e., three commissioners per nation, with one commissioner from each section serving as chair). The IJC is not an arm of government and commissioners are technically independent from the government that appointed them. The IJC is meant to deliberate as a joint, collegial body that normally acts by consensus and seeks win-win solutions in the common interest of both countries. Commissioners are supported in their work by two section offices in Ottawa and Washington, DC (the Secretariat) and, since the signing of the Great Lakes Water Quality Agreement in 1972, by a Great Lakes Regional Office in Windsor, Ontario, which supports the work of the commission's Great Lakes water quality and science advisory boards. The staffs in Ottawa and Washington currently total about thirty individuals, and there are about the same number of permanent employees in Windsor.

Much of the commission's work, which takes place in transboundary watersheds from coast to coast, is performed by international boards or task forces. Boards of control are appointed to report on compliance with orders while study or advisory boards assist in references. Commissioners select and appoint board members to serve in their personal and professional capacity, much like the commissioners themselves. Board members are often senior officials of state, provincial, or federal agencies, and are able to contribute financial and human resources to the work of the IJC (although this is less often the case in current times); the departments are, however, in no way bound by the opinion of a board member. Trust, which is crucial to the effective operation of the IJC, is arguably the most important aspect of the commission's operation.

The BWT provided for public-input mechanisms, such as public hearings that take place in the area concerned (rather than just in national and provincial/state capitals), so that locals affected by a particular docket—each separate issue the IJC deals with, whether a reference or application, is given a docket number—could have their voice heard, which was significant in the early twentieth century. That said, initially the IJC was only responsible to the various levels of government. However, the "spirit" of the treaty has evolved (particularly after the signing of the Great Lakes Water Quality Agreement) in such a way that the commission also came to see itself as responsible to other public authorities, as well as the public itself. The 1909 treaty has been amended only once: the third, fourth, and fifth paragraphs of article v were terminated when the Niagara River Diversion Treaty of 1950 was signed. Concerns about developments around Niagara Falls (as well as interpretations of article vi concerning the St. Mary–Milk) led both countries to seriously consider amending the treaty in the 1910s, and at that time the BWT, and thus the IJC, was almost abandoned. That the treaty would persist and the IJC become an important institution was not a foregone conclusion; the BWT could well have ended up as an agreement that merely solved some specific disputes before being jettisoned after a half-decade or so.

The IJC has historically been limited in its ability to go beyond the wishes of the two federal governments. The commission's reports are advisory, not binding, and, with some exceptions (e.g., under the GLWQA standing reference), the IJC cannot initiate investigations, since the federal governments must initiate references (though this is changing somewhat with the advent of international watershed boards). By convention, both federal governments need to agree to a reference in order for it to move forward, though according to the BWT either government *could* technically submit a unilateral reference (indeed, at various points in the past there were concerns that such a reference might be forthcoming, such as in the Passamaquoddy case in the 1950s). When it came to investigations under article ix, historically both nations have agreed to the requests of the other. To be fair, it is likely that the treaty and the IJC would never have been achieved if the treaty's drafters had been more ambitious and included stronger enforcement capabilities.

Any person or interest who wishes to use, divert, or obstruct boundary or transboundary waters must submit an application to the government within whose territorial jurisdiction such use, diversion, or obstruction is contemplated. This requirement in effect allows the governments to determine whether a particular project falls within those provisions of the BWT requiring approval by the IJC. This guidance also applies to existing structures that may not be compliant with the BWT. The IJC then acts as a quasi-judicial body by deciding whether these projects can be built and, if so, under what conditions (which are contained in an IJC Order of Approval).

The BWT distinguishes between projects built in boundary waters that form the border, waters flowing from boundary waters, and waters flowing across the boundary. In particular, article ii deals with jurisdiction and control over the use and diversion of waters that subsequently flow across the boundary or into boundary waters. Articles iii and iv set out requirements for binational approval, either by the governments or the IJC, for: 1) certain projects in boundary waters that would affect levels or flows in the other country; and 2) certain projects in transboundary rivers or in waters flowing from boundary waters that would raise levels across the boundary in the upstream country. In cases where the IJC is asked to provide approval, the commission must follow certain principles that have been agreed to by Canada and the United States as set out in article viii: each country shall have equal and similar rights in the use of boundary waters on its own side of the border; an order of precedence shall be observed among municipal, navigation, power, and irrigation uses; and where obstructions in one country will raise the natural level in the other country, the commission "shall require, as a condition of its approval thereof, that suitable and adequate provision, approved by it, be made for the protection and indemnity of all interests on the other side of the line which may be injured thereby."

Of the 50 cases handled by the commission prior to 1944, 39 were applications for approval of specific works under the quasi-judicial power of article viii, while only 11 were references under article ix, the investigative function. During the second half of the twentieth century, the ratio was reversed: between 1944 and 1979 there were 35 references and 20 applications,[6] while between 1979 and 2017 there were 16 references and 3 applications. However, the IJC has been very busy since 2000 reviewing its Orders of Approval for Lake Superior and Lake Ontario.

The number and type of references varies considerably over time and depends on various factors, including natural phenomena such as floods and droughts; project proposals that might affect water levels, flows, or quality; and to some extent the political climate at the national and sub-national levels, and particularly whether there exists concurrence that the IJC is the appropriate organization to address the concerns related to these factors. These points are noted and discussed elsewhere in this volume. The commission is funded by the United States and Canada directly through the two national section offices, subject to the normal appropriations procedures of each country. The US commissioners are appointed by the president and subject to confirmation by the US Senate, while Canadian commissioners are appointed by the governor in council (in practice this is done by the prime minister). Terms of office vary but initial appointments are typically for three or four years and can be extended.

The IJC in History

Political scientists, international relations scholars, geographers, legal scholars, and water resources scholars have produced most of the academic research and writing on the IJC—and scholars from those fields are well represented in this volume. The IJC has received little focused attention from historians, however, particularly in those areas where the IJC is very relevant: Canada-US relations, borderlands, and environmental history.[7] An animating purpose of this collection is that a sustained historical perspective can bring fresh insights on the first century of the BWT and the IJC. Moreover, we equally hope that this collection can be a valuable tool for present and future border environmental governance and policy-making.

Monographs, or lengthy studies, focused on the IJC are few and far between. The earliest book-length analysis, *The International Joint Commission between the United States of America and the Dominion of Canada*, was published in 1932 by Chirakairkan Joseph Chacko.[8] Chacko fits the historiographical trend identified above in that he was a law scholar. But, given that he was based in the United States, Chacko bucked what has been another major historiographical trend: the tendency of Canadians—in both government and academia—to pay more attention to the IJC than their American counterparts. Chacko was followed several decades later by L. M. Bloomfield and Gerald F. FitzGerald's *Boundary Waters Problems of Canada and the United States* (1958), though this volume was, much like Chacko's, predominantly a legal compendium of IJC activities to date.[9]

N. F. Dreisziger, whose 1974 PhD dissertation was about the BWT's creation, is one of the few historians to focus on the IJC's origins.[10] Dreisziger also contributed to *The International Joint Commission Seventy Years On*, which was published in 1981.[11] Stemming from a 1979 conference, this brief collection has been the pre-eminent academic text on the IJC, combining expert contributions from both inside and outside the commission, including from the likes of William Willoughby, who had recently published *The Joint Organizations of Canada and the United States*, and Maxwell Cohen, who as a former Canadian chairman of the IJC spilled a good deal of ink discussing the commission.[12] In many ways this present volume sees itself as the successor to that 1981 book. Providing some continuity, three of the authors from that 1981 volume are contributors to this book. Other lengthy publications that should be mentioned here are the 2001 memoir *The Making of a Conservative Environmentalist* by former US Section chair Gordon Durnil, and the 2008 special symposium issue of the *Wayne Law Review* commemorating the centennial of the BWT.[13]

The lack of book-length studies on the IJC may speak to the propensity of many social scientists to disseminate their research results through journal articles. Since the BWT's inception a range of scholars have written articles and book chapters about particular events, issues, or cases that involved the treaty or commission—e.g., the Chicago Diversion, navigation on the St. Lawrence River, hydro-power on the Niagara and Columbia Rivers, water pollution in the Detroit River, air pollution from the Trail Smelter, among others.[14] If one spends the copious amounts of time necessary to identify and collect all these writings produced over the course of the last century, a substantial body of literature on the IJC can be amassed. But these publications often do not speak to each other across disciplinary divides: for example, the legal scholars were often interested in water law or natural resource precedents (and thus more interested in historical dimensions), whereas political scientists and international relations scholars understandably paid more attention to the current/future policy and governance implications.

The number of academics directly addressing the IJC has proliferated in the last few decades because of rising interest in environmental issues in general, and transboundary environmental issues in particular. For example, the Great Lakes Water Quality Agreements of 1972 and 1978, and subsequent additions to the 1978 GLWQA, were central to the growth in interest in the IJC. At the same time, the rise of other binational and multilateral transboundary governance mechanisms that don't include the IJC or that give it a reduced role—e.g., 1991 Canada-US Air Quality Agreement, the IJC's decreasing role in the GLWQA, the Great Lakes–St. Lawrence River Water Basin Resources Compact and the companion international agreement—suggests the policy "submergence" of the IJC since the 1980s.[15] Granted, contributors to this volume point out that the IJC played an invaluable role in creating many of the aforementioned transboundary mechanisms and institutions. Nonetheless, the question undoubtedly remains as to why these separate processes arose when the

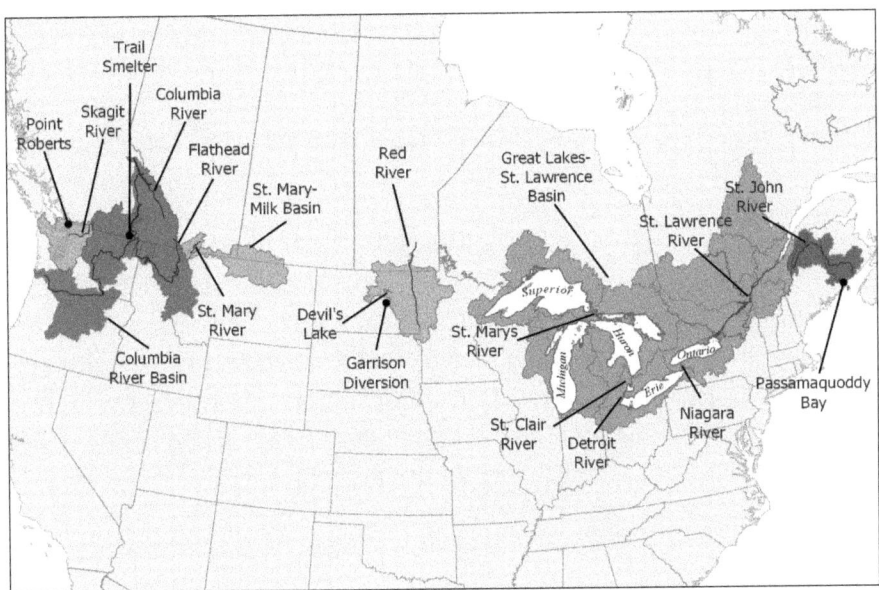

FIGURE 0.3. Watersheds covered in this book. J. Glatz, Western Michigan University Libraries.

IJC already existed. The proliferation of cross-border governance processes since the 1960s has undercut the IJC as the primary arbiter and mechanism of transborder governance—but the IJC has also arguably done its most important work, or at least has been publicly recognized as such, precisely in the post-1960s period.

Framing Questions

As the editors of this book, we began soliciting contributions in 2016, and almost all of the contributors we approached agreed to come on board. Most of the chapters in this volume were then presented at a conference in Ottawa in September 2017, funded by a Connection Grant from the Social Sciences and Humanities Research Council of Canada, which proved an invaluable tool for identifying and expanding on connections and coherence. Even before the conference, we tasked the various contributors with addressing some common themes. These framing questions included the following: Is the BWT/IJC a pioneering model of bilateral environmental co-operation? Is there evidence that other institutions and countries have looked to the IJC as a model? Does the IJC have such a limited mandate, or has its role been so circumscribed, that it is has been of limited importance for much of the past century? Is there a "myth of the IJC" that exaggerates its importance, and if so, what contributes to that myth? What have been the IJC's major accomplishments, and its major failures?

A survey of the extant literature reveals disparate and competing interpretations of the BWT's and IJC's saliency. As an organization the IJC has been lauded as a pioneering model of bilateral environmental co-operation, which should be extended to other Canada-US issues, and indeed exported to other nations.[16] Others contend that it is more important symbolically and for "legitimacy building" than it is in directly shaping policy. Still others deem the commission irrelevant and powerless outside the wishes of the two federal governments.[17] Between those opposing poles, there are more measured assessments recognizing both positive and negative aspects of the BWT and IJC. For example, consider the following:

> The Boundary Waters Treaty of 1909 and the treaty's vehicle for implementation, the International Joint Commission, have built a foundation that has underlain bilateral environmental relations between Canada and the United States. . . . Touted world-wide as a unique model of what can be accomplished by two nations with sufficient will, the treaty and the commission have long been respected for their unusual spirit of collegiality, for their long record of sound scientific and technical findings; for the unique nature of their organization and approaches; and, perhaps most significantly, for their success in conflict avoidance. Recognition on all of these grounds is justified, though a caveat is in order: the commission's task under the treaty has been narrow and specialized; its work has been relegated to noncontroversial areas where there was already diplomatic recognition that agreement could be achieved and most of its efforts, especially in recent years, have led to nonbinding recommendations that the two governments can (and often

do) ignore. Hence the work of this in many respects admirable treaty and vehicle is confined and its impact limited.[18]

The IJC has had a higher profile in Canada—but even that is mostly limited to the Great Lakes–St. Lawrence basin, outside of some particular border hotspots.[19] Are there significant differences in the national and ideological outlooks of Canadians and Americans, and between the commissioners from each country? There is certainly a tendency on the part of Canadians to extol the virtues of the IJC. This is partly because the BWT can be regarded as an extremely important part of the smaller nation's grappling with the North Atlantic triangle and the American empire. In that sense, the BWT could be considered a peace treaty.[20] Another overarching question our contributors address is the extent to which the IJC is key to the Canadian-American relationship, either symbolically or practically. A case can be made that the BWT was one of the key steps in fostering the spirit of rapprochement that characterized northern North American relations in the early twentieth century, establishing a pattern of co-operation that has continued ever since while establishing a basis for direct Canadian-American relations that removed the British middleman. Did the IJC establish a pattern of pragmatic "functionalism" in bilateral relations that would come to full fruition after the Second World War?[21] Or is this part of the "myth" of the IJC, fed by a "propaganda campaign aimed at bolstering the Commission's image," in which the IJC "gradually acquired attributes and power it never really possessed"?[22] There is probably some truth to speculation that self-servingly lecturing the rest of the world about the need to follow the BWT/IJC model harmonizes with Canada's smug self-image as a power broker, middle power, and peacekeeper.

Since historical knowledge about the IJC before the 1950s is rather incomplete, there is a tendency on the part of many contemporary commentators to read history backwards and to assume that the IJC operated much the same in its first half-century as it has in its second. Many of the positive virtues attributed to the IJC—equality; common vision and common objectives; different scales of action; strong scientific foundation; active community participation; good governance mechanisms in the form of accountability and adaptability; partnerships; binationalism[23]—are more apparent in the post-1960s period, and these positive assessments do not necessarily apply equally to the first half-century, when the IJC was finding its feet and evolving. This volume shows that the IJC's behaviour, role, and function has indeed evolved and changed over time. The IJC's narrative arc has often been presented as one of intergenerational stability, but in a number of respects this arc doesn't match the historical record. Drawing from some of our previous research on the IJC and the Great Lakes, we asked the contributors to respond to, and argue for or against, the following historical periodization: an initial half-century of mixed results, followed by a period, lasting from the 1940s to the 1960s, of partisan politics resulting in large-scale endeavours with dubious environmental impacts, followed by a period of more noticeable success up to the 1990s, and then a period of marginalization continuing into the twenty-first century.[24]

Some further fleshing out of that periodization might be helpful for the reader. Both the originators and the first members of the IJC assumed that the commission's quasi-judicial role would be much more important than its investigative role, and for three decades this assumption seemed correct.[25] The IJC was initially reluctant to settle legal issues and establish precedents, but generally adopted pragmatic solutions. Up to about the Great Depression, high-calibre officials were not often appointed to the IJC; those with relevant experience were often treated to patronage appointments or their various positions created conflicts of interest (though such conflicts were quite standard at the time in North America, and patronage appointments still happen). Take C. A. McGrath, for example, who was chairman of the Canadian Section of the IJC from 1914 to 1935. Not only was McGrath largely a patronage appointment by Robert Borden after McGrath lost his seat in the 1911 federal election, but while serving on the IJC he was also the chairman of the Hydro-Electric Power Commission of Ontario between 1926 and 1931. This was a clear conflict-of-interest scenario.

In addition, over its first half-century of existence there were numerous cases where the IJC did not operate smoothly, such as when the Canadian and US sides of the IJC split along national lines; when the respective federal governments ignored the IJC's recommendations; or when the IJC failed to make a timely recommendation or made a flawed recommendation. Up to about the time of the Second World War, the IJC focused mainly on apportioning water resources. A number of large-scale water control megaprojects, during which the politicization of the IJC was apparent, characterized the two postwar decades.[26] Then, beginning with such notable successes as addressing Great Lakes water pollution, the IJC transitioned into a period in which it successfully dealt with a wide range of issues. However, at the tail end of the twentieth century, the role of the IJC was increasingly circumscribed by the two federal governments, at least in part because of perceptions that the IJC had engaged in policy overreach and/or was too activist in the post-1970 period (e.g., the IJC called out the federal government for insufficient support for the GLWQA, and in chapter 10 of this volume Temby and Munton point out several other cases where the IJC was perceived by government as overly activist). This may well be linked to the increase in multi-level environmental-governance approaches, which can potentially serve to marginalize a national-level organization like the IJC, but which also provided new opportunities that the IJC has moved to embrace (such as the International Watersheds Initiative). But it should be noted that environmental governance, and the cumulative impact of pollution and human activities, has become much more complex over the last half-century, making the IJC's job today inherently more complicated.

The IJC has displayed elements of both a capacity-building and a regulatory institution: soliciting for public input, helping shape consensus, and collaborating widely. Yet it has regulatory functions that involve a gatekeeper role when it comes to approving project applications and handling references, and a role in implementation oversight.[27] In the context of key North American transboundary governance themes and theories, the IJC is an example of "fragmented bilateralism."[28] Without the consent of the Canadian and American federal governments, the IJC has little legal and regulatory capacity, as it has no enforcement mechanism, though it can use its reputation and symbolic authority to influence environmental issues. (That said, in theory at least, once the IJC passes an Order of Approval it retains continuing jurisdiction over it such that its provisions, once accepted by the applicant, are not appealable, even by governments.) The IJC has wielded technocratic expertise and has been successful in framing scientific information with policy applicability; though that is a trend that was less noticeable during the first half of its existence, when it dealt largely with applications rather than references.[29]

During and after our 2017 conference in Ottawa, additional focal themes emerged. One of the overarching questions that became apparent was the difference between the IJC on paper (i.e., what the BWT technically prescribes) and the IJC in reality (i.e., the IJC's approach is partially dictated by convention). Put another way, even though the BWT has not changed since 1909 (aside from several of the Niagara provisions), the "spirit" of the treaty has evolved. The outlooks of specific provinces and states also emerged as a factor—for example, Ontario has frequently asked the federal government to refer matters to the IJC, while British Columbia has, since the commission's report on the Flathead Reference, been adverse to IJC involvement in its border-water affairs. Thus, on the surface, the ways in which the IJC actually operates (e.g., only the federal governments can ask the IJC to undertake a reference under the BWT) would appear to counter the "sub-state actor hypothesis." On the other hand, it is apparent that provinces and states, such as Ontario and New York, have played key roles in the evolution of major issues related to the IJC and have membership on various engineering and scientific boards within the IJC. Moreover, subnational actors, such as activist organizations, have since the 1950s inspired or contributed to IJC investigations, a trend which is only increasing in the twenty-first century.[30]

The IJC as a Model?

Is the IJC a model? And if so, for whom? Canadian officials have on numerous occasions urged other nations to copy the BWT/IJC, such as in the League of Nations, debates about the post–First World War European settlement, or Middle Eastern water disputes. In a similar vein, it is clear that over the years many foreign dignitaries and experts from myriad nations came to North America to inspect IJC-sanctioned projects and meet with IJC officials; but few, if any, of them went back to their home countries and actually applied the BWT/IJC model to their activities.[31] There are cases where scholars from outside of Canada have promoted the BWT and IJC as something worthy of emulation—for example, the IJC has been lauded in United Nations publications.[32] Nonetheless, given the limited extent of these "model" examples, this collection suggests that it is probably time to retire the trope of the BWT/IJC as a direct model.

That is not to say that the BWT/IJC hasn't been an indirect model, or that elements of the treaty and commission shouldn't be a model in the future. The longevity of both the treaty and the commission helped prove the viability of not just transboundary environmental governance mechanisms, but joint commissions in general, potentially paving the way for similar agreements and institutions. For example, it is possible to conjecture that the creation of such bodies as the Permanent Joint Board of Defense were partly based on the IJC. There are certainly cases where specific recommendations or findings of the IJC have been highly valued, such as in the Trail Smelter arbitration, the Garrison Diversion, and Red River flooding. Moreover, there are ways that the IJC should be a model that are often overlooked. Many of the IJC's reports, such as on water supplies, natural cycles, and consumptive usage in the Great Lakes basin, are heralded as seminal studies. Theo Colborn's groundbreaking studies on endocrine disruptors, as a further example, came out of work commissioned by the IJC.[33] And, in a connected vein, the GLWQA was arguably the first large-scale policy application of the ecosystem principle. Thus, the IJC might be considered a model for incorporating science into policy.

Nonetheless, the findings showcased in this volume might suggest that the IJC worked primarily because of its specific North American context, and thus can't really be imported whole cloth by other water borders around the world. But we can consider what aspects of the BWT/IJC specifically were most responsible for its successes. Was it the terms of the BWT itself and the resulting institutional structure of the IJC? Was it the unique Canadian-American relationship (or, in a chicken-and-egg scenario, did the IJC help foster comity in the relationship)? Was it the unique geographic setting—in other words, the fact that across the length of the whole shared border neither country is the predominant upstream or downstream riparian? How much do individual personalities and leadership styles contribute to the operation of the commission?

Going back to the origins of the IJC, the various contributors to this collection look at the key steps and driving factors in the process that created the BWT. Was the treaty a progressive, anticipatory step in international environmental law and governance—or actually a fairly pragmatic, conservative approach meant to allow the two nations to co-operatively exploit, rather than protect, their shared water resources? Looking at water quantity and control for dams, irrigation, and navigation—as a number of contributors to this volume do—this would appear to be the case. But on the axis of water quality and pollution, which a set of chapters in these pages address, there is evidence that from the beginning the IJC was at least somewhat concerned with protecting public health (protecting ecological health would come later on). Over time, pollution emerged as one of the commission's primary concerns. The last line of article iv of the BWT reads: "It is further agreed that the waters herein defined as boundary waters and waters flowing across the boundary shall not be polluted on either side to the injury of health or property on the other." This may well have been a reluctant compromise that did not have the backing of the majority of those involved in the crafting of the accord, but it has turned out to be perhaps the most important legacy of the treaty.

It is apparent that the IJC operates differently along a resource axis—that is, whether it is dealing with water quantity or quality, or air pollution. It also operates along a geographic axis. During the 2017 workshop these different axes led several participants to aver that the IJC essentially has two different regimes, particularly after the implementation of the GLWQAs: it acts like a treaty institution in the Great Lakes, but elsewhere like a binational organization.

Moreover, cutting across both resource and geographic axes, and running like a thread though the IJC's 122 (and counting) dockets, are thematic issues like science and colonialism. The IJC's application of objective and cutting-edge science in policy has been exemplary, and is one of those areas where the IJC should be considered a model. But expertise can easily be turned to imperialist ends. Water resource development in North America has often taken place at the disproportionate expense of Indigenous Peoples because of the propensity for dams to be placed at water sites frequented by Indigenous communities, which were considered expendable and their use of waterways unproductive compared to hydro installations or irrigation works. The IJC has undoubtedly been a part of the settler-colonial apparatus. A number of our chapters touch on the relationship between the IJC and Indigenous communities, with one chapter in particular focusing on that relationship. It should be noted that in May 2019 Henry Lickers was appointed to the Canadian Section of the IJC, making him the first Indigenous commissioner.

A strong case can be made that the BWT does directly address the potential transboundary harms stemming from taking and diverting boundary waters. From a legal perspective, it is worth asking: Does the BWT and IJC create a legal foundation for co-operation and a duty to avoid harm? And, if the answer is in the affirmative, when and to what extent did avoidance of harm extend past human interests and to ecological interests?[34] Several leading legal scholars grapple with such questions, as well as the issue of the infamous Harmon Doctrine: US attorney general Judson Harmon's 1895 opinion, originally made about American water flows into Mexico, holding that the upstream country is absolutely sovereign over those parts of international watercourses within its borders. It is worth pointing out that the BWT and IJC would not likely have succeeded if the United States had not abandoned its initial insistence on the Harmon Doctrine. Perhaps the United States did so in this instance because spatial reality indicated that application of the doctrine vis-à-vis Canada would not often be beneficial stateside.

Scholars of Canadian-American relations and borderlands, particularly historians, need to take better cognizance of the IJC. In the early Cold War period, the IJC was heavily involved in shaping some of the issues key to the general bilateral relationship, such as the St. Lawrence Seaway and Power Project, the Columbia River Treaty, and the GLWQA. But there is also an irony in that the era during which the federal governments most trusted the IJC was also the era of the commission's most overt partisanship, and the period when it created what are now recognized as ecologically harmful projects. Thus, the IJC's visibility may be a double-edged sword: the more the IJC is perceived as relevant, the greater the chance it might be used for partisan purposes. The history of the IJC would, on the one hand, affirm claims that the Canadian-American relationship is a unique or special one within the context of international affairs; at the same time, delving into the intricate workings of IJC issues, it appears that linkage politics were frequently deployed by both nations.[35]

If the bar of success for the IJC is to avoid significant state-to-state conflict over border resources, then the IJC has been quite successful. But the argument has been made that the IJC is generally only given relatively unimportant issues to handle, except where the federal governments are in agreement about what they want to result. The federal governments have often avoided using the IJC in the second half of the twentieth century when they didn't think the commission would provide an answer they would like. According to some, the IJC was a place to send a problem so that it could be defused, but at times it may also have been used as a place to bury a problem or provide political cover. And the federal governments have also often disregarded the IJC's conclusions or recommendations. Moreover, as has been mentioned, some of the IJC's major accomplishments are, in hindsight, quite unsustainable, and the IJC has been guilty in the past of promoting an engineering mindset in which nature should be controlled and commodified.

We could certainly measure the IJC against the wishes of its creators and the BWT itself—but this is only fruitful to a limited extent since institutions evolve and change over time. A frequently used method of measuring the success of the IJC is statistical evaluation. For example, the IJC has successfully approved 49 applications, with no action or deferred action on 6 applications, while 6 were withdrawn or had technical concerns. This 80 per cent success rate is impressive, though less so when compared to the more grandiose claims about the IJC. We often hear that the IJC has only in a few cases made non-unanimous decisions, and has virtually never split along national lines. A 2006 presentation made by a former US Section chair included a slide showing that in only 2 per cent of all cases resolved by the IJC did the commissioners split on national lines.[36] But this is an extremely misleading, if not outright false, statistic. For one thing, many controversial cases were kept out of the IJC's ambit (a recent example is Devils Lake). For another, it only measures cases resolved: when cases weren't resolved, it was sometimes precisely because of such Canada-US splits. In other cases, commissioners agreed to go along with a unanimous recommendation more or less for the sake of saying that it was unanimous, or resigned or were replaced when they objected. Moreover, unanimous approval of a project at the commissioner level might cover up the fact that on-the-ground engineering decisions for that project splintered along politicized national lines.[37]

Moreover, these statistics don't indicate whether the federal governments effectively implemented or funded the commission's recommendations—

in many cases they did not, although this is generally not the fault of the IJC. It is clear that IJC appointees sometimes also saw the writing on the wall, so to speak, censoring themselves or changing their decisions in advance to correspond with the political wishes of Ottawa and Washington. Thus, it is important to be objective about the IJC. One could selectively put together a resume of the IJC's activities from examples in this book that cast the commission in quite a poor light. Exaggerating what the IJC can do is counterproductive because it undermines trust in the commission and creates unrealistic expectations.

Though the IJC was intended to be apolitical, its members are appointed by the prime minister and president, and this process involves some inherent politicization. As many contributions to this volume show, a number of issues have become politicized within the IJC.[38] This politicization was most pronounced in the early Cold War period and was epitomized by General A. G. L. McNaughton, the Canadian chairman who pushed for solutions based on Canadian nationalism. McNaughton was selected for the IJC by the St. Laurent government precisely because he would prioritize Canadian self-interest in a period—the 1950s and '60s—when the issues before the IJC were also top diplomatic concerns between the Canadian and American governments.

Chapter Organization

The contributors to this volume bring a variety of different perspectives and backgrounds. One of the two editors, Murray Clamen, is a water resources engineer who spent three decades in the IJC—as an engineering adviser from 1977 to 1997, and secretary of the Canadian Section from 1997 to 2011—while his co-editor, Daniel Macfarlane, is an academic historian and political ecologist who has spent many years in the archives researching IJC projects, primarily those in the Great Lakes–St. Lawrence basin. Many of the contributing authors come from academic backgrounds, including political science, history, and law, while several contributors are policy practitioners who have direct experience with the IJC.

The volume has been divided into four sections. Section 1 looks at the creation of the 1909 BWT and the IJC. David Whorley addresses Canadian and US actions from the creation of the IWC through to the finalization of the BWT, which demonstrate how institutional creation and change can be a messy, complex, and not entirely predictable affair. Whorley describes one of the treaty drafts that, though ultimately not accepted, would have created quite a different treaty and commission. Meredith Denning explores why this cornerstone treaty and commission were created in 1909, rather than earlier or later, and why they took the forms that they did.

Section 2 looks at various cases in which the IJC has been involved from coast to coast (though with the exception of one chapter, this section excludes the Great Lakes–St. Lawrence basin) and which have contributed significantly to its history and the history of Canada and the United States. Jamie Benidickson writes about the IJC's fourth docket, showing that although the IJC's earliest pollution reference did not resolve the water quality challenges of the early twentieth century, the initiative contributed significantly to greater awareness of bacterial contamination of boundary waters and potential responses. Timothy Heinmiller provides a focused study of the historic St. Mary–Milk Rivers apportionment, how it evolved over the twentieth century, and what issues are at play today. Allen Olson and Norman Brandson look at some of the most important references (and a non-reference) over the last forty years in the middle of the continent—i.e., the Prairie/Plains region—and how the conclusions and recommendations have played, and continue to play, such an important role for the IJC in those watersheds. Richard Moy and Jonathan O'Riordan provide a comprehensive study of the role of the IJC in the Far West with respect to the Columbia, Flathead, and Skagit Rivers. Kim Richard Nossal looks at one of the so-called failures of the IJC, the Point Roberts Reference, and suggests why it failed and how it could have been successful (and how that failure brings into sharper relief the success of the IJC). The history of the IJC and hydro-power development in the northeastern borderlands is the subject of James Kenney's chapter, which shows that while the IJC investigations did not result in a tangible international megaproject on the East Coast, they did play an important role in shaping the orientation of New Brunswick's power utility.

Section 3 focuses on one region—the Great Lakes–St. Lawrence basin—which has had the central role in the history of the IJC's water management activities. The editors of this volume, Murray Clamen and Daniel Macfarlane, provide a historical survey of the evolution of the

IJC's transboundary water governance in the Great Lakes basin over the course of the twentieth century, with a focus on water quantity (diversions, canals, hydroelectric developments, remedial works, etc.). Owen Temby and Don Munton provide a unique chapter on the role of the IJC in the field of transboundary air pollution, from the landmark Trail Smelter case to the various studies in the Great Lakes. Jennifer Read traces the evolution of ideas and structures incorporated into the GLWQA from the initial pollution reference in 1912 through to the GLWQA's conclusion, noting important antecedents to the agreement in the commission's early days. Gail Krantzberg discusses the creation of the Areas of Concern, the Remedial Action Plan, and the Lakewide Action Management Plan processes—novel and significant experiments in collaborative management that have had mixed results to date. Deborah VanNijnatten and Carolyn Johns take a critical look at the role of the IJC over the course of successive revisions to the GLWQA in 1978 and 1987, wherein the commission was given a more supportive role (and additional help in the form of advisory boards), but it also became enmeshed in monitoring and reporting on the commitments made by both governments in the agreement.

Section 4 takes a long view of the history of the BWT and the IJC. Frank Ettawageshik and Emma Norman examine the involvement of Indigenous communities in the IJC process using several historical case studies, including the establishment of the International Watershed Initiative in 2000. The chapter by Noah Hall, Dan Tarlock, and Marcia Valiante shows how the treaty and the commission have played an important role in the evolution of transboundary environmental law and governance, both in North America and globally. John Kirton and Brittany Warren argue that the treaty and the commission embodied, entrenched, and expanded several of Canada's six distinctive national values. In their chapter, Ralph Pentland and Ted Yuzyk suggest that the commission's success relates both to its formal functions and also to a number of other attributes that have appeared over the past century, but which are continuing to change. Clamen and Macfarlane's concluding chapter offers insights about what the historical lessons can teach us about the IJC and its future.

It is our hope that this book will make a contribution to the analysis of water management in Canada and the United States, to the environmental and water history of both countries, and to environmental policy, law, and governance in North America. As we approach the end of the second decade of the twenty-first century, water is being talked and written about more and more by media, politicians, academics, entrepreneurs, and society in general. It is now a truism to say that water is the new oil. While such an observation is meant to highlight the importance of water, it is also a misnomer, since oil is not central to life and ecological health in the same way that water is (and comparing water to oil risks commodifying the former). There is no getting around the fact that "water is life," and there is a pressing need for more, rather than less, education and awareness of all things related to this most precious resource. The end result of this book, we hope, will not just be awareness of an institution that has existed since 1909 and is a key part of the Canadian-American relationship, but a greater understanding of water and border environmental issues, and a desire to ensure politicians and decision-makers appreciate water's importance now and in the years to come. Along the way some very valuable lessons about institution building, dispute prevention and resolution, and international water law and governance have been learned, some of which may be applicable to other organizations, and even countries, around the globe.

Notes

1   On the evolution of the method of regulation see Murray Clamen and Daniel Macfarlane, "Plan 2014: The Historical Evolution of Lake Ontario-St. Lawrence River Regulation," *Canadian Water Resources Journal / Revue canadienne des ressources hydriques* vol. 43, no. 4 (December 2018): 416–31.

2   International Joint Commission, "Lake Ontario-St. Lawrence River Plan 2014: A Report to the Governments of Canada and the United States by the International Joint Commission (June 2014), http://www.ijc.org/files/tinymce/uploaded/LOSLR/IJC_LOSR_EN_Web.pdf.

3   International Joint Commission, "Supplementary Order of Approval 2016 (International Joint Commission in the Matter of the Regulation of Lake Ontario)" (December 2016), https://ijc.org/en/loslrb/who/orders.

4   Maxwell Cohen, "The Commission From the Inside," in *The International Joint Commission Seventy Years On*, ed. Richard Spencer, John Kirton, and Kim Richard Nossal (Toronto: Centre For International Studies, University of Toronto, 1981), 108.

5   William Willoughby, "Expectations and Experience, 1909–1979," in Spencer, Kirton, and Nossal, *The International Joint Commission Seventy Years On*.

6   Ibid.

7   To be fair, legal scholars in particular often bring a nuanced and sophisticated historical analysis to bear. Part of the reason that the IJC has been ignored by historians is that the general importance of environmental diplomacy to the Canada-US relationship has also been ignored by historians. See Daniel Macfarlane, "Natural Security: Canada-US Environmental Diplomacy" in *Undiplomatic History: Rethinking Canada in the World*, ed. Asa McKercher and Phil Van Huizen (Montreal: McGill-Queen's University Press, 2019). In addition to the sources already mentioned or cited elsewhere in this introduction, the historical scholarship on the IJC includes Alan O. Gibbons, "Sir George Gibbons and the Boundary Waters Treaty of 1909," *Canadian Historical* Review 34, no. 2 (June 1953): 124–38; Harriet Eleanor Whitney, "Sir George C. Gibbons and the Boundary Waters Treaty of 1909" (PhD diss., Michigan State University, 1968); Alvin Gluek, "The Lake Carriers Association and the Origins of the International Waterways Commission," *Inland Seas* (Q.J. Great Lakes Historical Society) 36, no. 4 (1980): 236–45; Peter Neary, "Grey, Bryce, and the Settlement of Canadian American Differences, 1905–11," *Canadian Historical Review* 49 (1968): 357–80; Joseph T. Jockel and Alan M. Schwartz, "The Changing Role of the Canada-United States International Joint Commission," *Environmental Review* 8, no. 3 (Autumn 1984): 236–51; Jennifer Read, "Addressing 'A quiet horror': The Evolution of Ontario Pollution Control Policy in the International Great Lakes, 1909–1972," (PhD diss., University of Western Ontario, 1999); Kurkpatrick Dorsey, *The Dawn of Conservation Diplomacy: U.S.-Canadian Wildlife Protection Treaties in the Progressive Era* (Seattle: University of Washington Press, 1998); Brittany Flaherty, Raul Pacheco-Vega, and Judy Isaac-Renton, "Moving Forward in Canada-United States transboundary water management: an analysis of historical and emerging concerns," *Water International* (36:7); 924–936; Daniel Macfarlane, "Fluid Relations: Hydro Developments, the International Joint Commission, and Canada-US Border Waters," in *Towards Continental Environmental Policy? North American Transnational Environmental Networks and Governance*, ed. Peter Stoett and Owen Temby (Albany: SUNY Press, 2017); Lynne Heasley and Daniel Macfarlane, eds., *Border Flows: A Century of the Canadian-American Water Relationship* (Calgary: NiCHE-University of Calgary Press Environmental History Series, 2016); Daniel Macfarlane, " 'A Completely Man-Made and Artificial Cataract': The Transnational Manipulation of Niagara Falls," *Environmental History* 18, no. 4 (October 2013): 759–84; John D. Wirth, *Smelter Smoke in North America: The Politics of Transborder Pollution* (Lawrence: University of Kansas Press, 2000); Meredith Denning, "Connections and Consensus: Changing Goals for Transnational Water Management on Lake Erie and Lake Ontario, 1900-1972" (PhD Dissertation: Georgetown University, 2018); Shannon Stunden Bower, *Wet Prairie: People, Land, and Water in Agricultural Manitoba* (Vancouver: UBC Press, 2011); Nancy Langston, *Sustaining Lake Superior: An Extraordinary Lake in a Changing World* (New Haven, CN: Yale University Press, 2017); Jamie Benidickson, *Leveling the Lake: Transboundary Resource Management in the Lake of the Woods Watershed* (Vancouver: UBC Press, 2019).

8   J. C. Chacko, *The International Joint Commission between the United States of America and the Dominion of Canada* (New York: Columbia University Press, 1932).

9   L. M. Bloomfield and G. F. FitzGerald, *Boundary Waters Problems of Canada and the United States* (Toronto: Carswell, 1958). The IJC in the specific context of the Great Lakes is featured in Don Courtney Piper, *The International Law of the Great Lakes: A*

Study of Canadian-United States Cooperation (Durham, NC: Duke University Press, 1967). The IJC is discussed to varying degrees, though generally not enough, in the various survey histories of Canadian-American relations.

10   N. F. Dreisziger, "The International Joint Commission of the United States and Canada, 1895-1920: A Study in Canadian-American Relations" (PhD diss., University of Toronto, 1974). Though it wasn't subsequently released as a book, many of the chapters in this dissertation became journal articles; see for example N. F. Dreisziger, "The Great Lakes in United States-Canadian Relations: The First Stock-Taking," *Inland Seas* (Q.J. Great Lakes Historical Society) 28, no. 4 (1972): 259-71; "The Campaign to Save Niagara Falls and the Settlement of United States-Canadian Differences, 1906-1911," *New York History* 55, no. 4 (October 1974): 437-58.

11   Spencer, Kirton, and Nossal, *The International Joint Commission Seventy Years On*.

12   William Willoughby, *The Joint Organizations of Canada and the United States* (Toronto: University of Toronto Press, 1979).

13   Gordon Durnil, *The Making of a Conservative Environmentalist* (Bloomington: Indiana University Press, 2001). The contributions to the Boundary Waters Treaty Centennial Symposium are reprinted in a theme issue of the *Wayne Law Review* 54, no. 4 (Winter 2008).

14   For a list of publications on the IJC up to 1966 see F. J. E. Jordan, *An Annotated Digest of Materials Relating to the Establishment and Development of the International Joint Commission* (Ottawa: Report Prepared for the Canadian Section of the International Joint Commission, August 1966).

15   For more on the composition and backgrounds of IJC appointees see Brooks, "The Promise and Limits of an Ambitious Model."

16   A. D. P. Heeney, a former member of the IJC, is one of the most notable proponents of expanding the IJC's functions; See A. D. P. Heeney and Livingston Merchant, *Canada and the United States: Principles for Partnership* (Washington, DC: Department of State, 1965), and A. D. P. Heeney, *Along the Common Frontier: The International Joint Commission* (Toronto: Canadian Institute for International Affairs, 1967). For a list of nine key reason for the enduring success of the IJC, see Willoughby, *The Joint Organizations of Canada and the United States*, 52-58; see also Kim Richard Nossal's chapter in this volume for this list.

17   Some others include David LeMarquand, "The International Joint Commission and Changing Canada-United States Boundary Relations," *Natural Resources Journal* 33 (1993): 59-91; Alan Schwartz, "The Management of Shared Waters," in *Bilateral Ecopolitics: Continuity and Change in Canadian-American Environmental Relations*, ed. Peter Stoett and Philippe LePrestre (New York: Routledge, 2006).

18   Kenneth M. Curtis and John E. Carroll, *Canadian-American Relations: The Promise and the Challenge* (Toronto: D.C. Heath and Company, 1983), 27-8.

19   It should be pointed out that the IJC has a negative profile on the south shore of Lake Ontario because of the history there of riparian flooding due to natural causes (though this reputation is arguably undeserved). Stephen Brooks notes that "most volumes of the Canadian Institute of International Affairs longstanding 'Canada in World Affairs'

series make only brief and passing mention of the IJC. In no annual issue of Carleton University's prestigious 'Canada Among Nations' series, between 1996 and 2016, is there a single mention of the IJC, despite the fact that every year there are chapters devoted to aspects of Canada-US relations. On the other side of the border, leading textbooks on American foreign policy make no or only passing mention of the IJC." Brooks also looked at mentions of the IJC in the *New York Times* as a proxy for the public relevance of the IJC, with the 1950s being the decade in which the IJC was mentioned the most. See Brooks, "The Promise and Limits of an Ambitious Model," 40, 45.

20 Gordon Walker, "The Boundary Water Treaty 1909—A Peace Treaty?," *Canada-US Law Journal* 170 (2015): 1–17.

21 Robert Bothwell, *Your Country, My Country: A Unified History of the United States and Canada* (Toronto: Oxford University Press, 2015). According to A. D. P. Heeney, within the Canadian Department of External Affairs "the commission was highly regarded both by senior officials such as O. D. Skelton and John Read as well as by more junior colleagues who had a good deal to do with the references to the commission over the years." A. D. P. Heeney, *The Things That are Ceasar's: Memoirs of a Canadian Public Servant* (Toronto: University of Toronto Press, 1973), 183.

22 Dreisziger, "The International Joint Commission of the United States and Canada, 1895–1920," 380–1.

23 Marcia Valiante, "Management of the North American Great Lakes," in *Management of Transboundary Rivers and Lakes*, ed. O. Varis, C. Tortajada, and A. K. Biswas (Berlin: Springer, 2008), 258–60.

24 Murray Clamen and Daniel Macfarlane, "The International Joint Commission, Water Levels, and Transboundary Governance in the Great Lakes," *Journal of Policy Research* 32, no. 1 (January 2015): 40–59.

25 Willoughby, "Expectations and Experience, 1909–1979."

26 For a study on the selection of IJC members see William R. Willoughby, "The Appointment and Removal of Members of the International Joint Commission," *Canadian Public Administration* 12, no. 3 (Sept. 1969): 411–26.

27 From a political theory perspective, we suggest that the IJC moved from a bureaucratic to a post-bureaucratic model (though it could be said to blend the two categories and retain aspects of the bureaucratic model).

28 S. P. Mumme and P. Duncan, "The Commission for Environmental Cooperation and environmental management in the Americas," *Journal of Interamerican Studies and World Affairs* 39, no. 4 (1997): 41–62.

29 The approach employed in this study ultimately aligns with the "rational-legal authority" approach stemming from the constructivist camp of international relations theory. In line with this theory, the IJC theoretically has a great deal of autonomy and has developed its own bureaucratic culture and internal processes, and it has gained a reputation among many for effectiveness, expertise, and impartiality because of these processes. As such, it wields symbolic and tangible power to frame issues, orient problems, and identify actors and solutions (often holding itself up as the impartial repository of expertise). See M. Barnett and M. Finnemore, *Rules for the World:*

International Organizations in Global Politics (Ithaca, NY: Cornell University Press, 2004); F. Biermann and B. Siebenhuner, eds., *Managers of Global Change: The Influence of International Environmental Bureaucracies* (Cambridge, MA: MIT Press, 2009).

30 See for example Noah D. Hall, "Toward A New Horizontal Federalism: Interstate Water Management in the Great Lakes Region," *Colorado Law Review* 77 (2006): 405–56, and Daniel Macfarlane, "Watershed Decisions: The St. Lawrence Seaway and Sub-National Water Diplomacy," *Canadian Foreign Policy Journal* 21, no. 3 (2015): 212–23.

31 There is at least one minor example of other Canadians employing the BWT as a model: the 2009 amendment to the 1981 Canada-US Pacific Albacore Tuna Treaty. In fact, the BWT's article IX was used as a model for this 2009 treaty's dispute resolution mechanism by a negotiating delegation that included David Whorley, who was then at the Department of Foreign Affairs and International Trade, and who is a contributor to this volume.

32 Canadian-US boundary waters management is commonly regarded as one of the most successful ventures of international co-operation in the world according to a UN publication *Management of International Water Resources: Institutional and Legal Aspects. Report of panel of experts on legal and institutional implications of water resources development* (New York: United Nations Publication St/ESA/5, 1975). A. Dan Tarlock, a contributor to this collection, was also a contributor to the UN Economic Commission for Europe's 2015 report "Water and Climate Change Adaptation in Transboundary Basins: Lessons Learned and Good Practices," which cites the Great Lakes Compact and IJC's work as a example of good practice. A copy of this report is available at https://www.unece.org/fileadmin/DAM/env/water/publications/WAT_Good_practices/ece.mp.wat.45.pdf. Our thanks to Stephen Brooks for pointing out several publications that promote the IJC/BWT: Zigurds Zile, *Binational land resource management for the Great Lakes area: Powers of the International Joint Commission* (Canada-US University Seminar Great Lakes Management Series, no.1, 1974); J. Isaac and H. Shuval, eds., *Water and Peace in the Middle East*, 1st ed. (Amsterdam: Elsevier Science, 1994), vol. 58: 237–8; Clive Lipchin, Eric Pallant, Danielle Saranga, and Allyson Amster, eds., *Integrated Water Resources Management and Security in the Middle East* (New York: Springer, 2007), 226–8.

33 Theo Colborn, Dianne Dumanoski, and John Peterson Myers, *Our Stolen Future: Are We Threatening Our Fertility, Intelligence, and Survival? A Scientific Detective Story* (New York: Plume, 1997).

34 Daniel Macfarlane and Noah Hall, "Transborder Water Management and Governance in the Great Lakes-St. Lawrence Basin," in Brooks and Olive, eds., *Transboundary Environmental Governance*.

35 Daniel Macfarlane, " 'Caught Between Two Fires': St. Lawrence Seaway and Power Project, Canadian-American Relations, and Linkage," *International Journal* 67, no. 2 (Summer 2012): 465–82.

36 Cited in Brooks, "The Promise and Limits of an Ambitious Model," 30. See also Dennis Schornack, "The International Joint Commission: A Case Study in the Management of International Waters" (paper presented at the Rosenberg International Forum on Water Policy, Banff, AB, 10 September 2006).

37 See Daniel Macfarlane, *Negotiating a River: Canada, the US, and the Creation of the St. Lawrence Seaway* (Vancouver: UBC Press, 2014); see also the chapter 9 in this volume.

38 To provide just one example, Jane Elder, formerly the Sierra Club Midwest representative, stated in a 1998 interview: "Look at the International Joint Commission. There was a body that was considered to be learned, independent—and *useful*. Their scientific reports were groundbreaking for the Great Lakes. They drove the agenda. But in the last ten years the IJC has become a very different animal. It's extremely politicized, in terms of appointees. Industry has discovered it. So the instruments have changed." Cited in William Ashworth, *Great Lakes Journey: A New Look at America's Freshwater Coast* (Detroit: Wayne State University Press, 2000), 63.

SECTION 1

BEGINNINGS

From IWC to BWT: Canada-US Institution Building, 1902–1909

David Whorley

The Treaty Between the United States and Great Britain Relating to Boundary Waters and Questions Arising Between the United States and Canada (the Boundary Waters Treaty for short) is the principal instrument framing Canadian-US relations regarding the two countries' shared fresh water.[1] While formally an Anglo-American agreement, the Boundary Waters Treaty (BWT) is, and was recognized at the time of its development as, essentially a Canada-US arrangement, involving direct negotiations between Canadian and US officials and establishing an international institution that would have exclusively Canadian and US membership. In this respect, Glazebrook accurately observed many years ago that "the process of negotiation, so largely direct between Canadians and Americans, foreshadowed an essential characteristic of the new commission."[2] In place now for over a century, the BWT and the International Joint Commission (IJC) have proven to be durable and useful instruments for helping to prevent and resolve disagreements over shared Canadian and US waters.

The purpose of this chapter is to sketch the origins of the BWT and the IJC, with particular emphasis on the predecessor institution, the International Waterways Commission (IWC). In undertaking such a review, this chapter seeks to understand the process of institutional development between Canada and the United States concerning the management of their shared waterways by applying a framework on the use, modification, and creation of international organizations (IOs) as supplied by Jupille and Snidal and subsequently applied by Jupille, Mattli, and Snidal.[3] Along the way, the chapter reviews a lesser-known treaty option that was briefly on the table for consideration, the Clinton-Gibbons draft of 1907. As will be seen, the BWT is certainly not the agreement that Canadian and US negotiators set out to develop. The original trajectory of negotiations momentarily pointed toward a more comprehensive and authoritative IO, a binational commission that would have enjoyed a very broad set of decisive powers as initially envisioned. In the end, Canada and the United States opted for a more limited agreement, one that altered the institutional landscape but in doing so did not wholly reject the more modest nature of the IWC. On the contrary, the eventual institutional arrangement at which the parties arrived in 1909 demonstrates notable continuity with this predecessor IO.

Canadian and US actions, from the creation of the IWC through to the finalization of the BWT, demonstrate how institution creation and change can be a messy, complex, and not entirely predictable affair. Given the durability, utility, and steadfast presence of the BWT, there may be some temptation to think that the arrival of something like it was in some way inevitable. In the event, the process of moving from problem identification to institution construction did not proceed in a straight line leading inescapably to the BWT and the IJC, but rather progressed through a number of quite different iterations involving changing conceptions of institutional scope and authority in response to growing tensions over shared Canada-US waterways. The benefits as well as the limitations and risks revealed by earlier stages of institutional development in the form of the IWC and the 1907 Clinton-Gibbons draft contributed to the eventual practicality, flexibility, and longevity of the BWT.

Causes for IO Creation

Irritants at different locations along the international boundary eventually led actors on the Canadian and US sides to recognize the need for a mechanism to help manage shared waters. Dreisziger identifies a suite of Canada-US water-related tensions at the end of the nineteenth and beginning of the twentieth centuries that focused attention and ultimately led to the creation of an arrangement on all shared waters.[4] Along with the stresses discussed below and the attendant interests involved, the BWT and its predecessor, the IWC, were shaped by a set of ideas in good currency at the time. In this case, ideas related to conservation, itself part of a broader suite of ideas that contributed to Progressive-Era thought, were salient.[5] This chapter is not intended to retrace the history and influence of the Progressive movement or the role of conservationism within it in the early twentieth century. Nonetheless, Canadian and US efforts to build an effective cross-border institution for preventing and resolving water conflict owe something to these ideas.

Conservationism

Like progressivism itself, US conservationism in the late nineteenth and early twentieth centuries was multi-stranded, characterized by the sometimes uneasy cohabitation of utilitarians, favouring the efficient use of natural resources, and preservationists, more committed to the protection of nature for itself on aesthetic grounds.[6] These strands of conservationist thought are sometimes caricatured as falling under two camps led by their respective champions: Gifford Pinchot, chief US forester and an important influence in natural resource conservation and protection in the Roosevelt era, for the utilitarians (sometimes simply termed "conservationists"); and John Muir, founder of the Sierra Club, for the preservationists. This simplified characterization tends to mask a more subtle interplay of ideas between the two streams of thought, something perhaps as complex as the relationship between Pinchot and Muir themselves who, though friends and one-time allies in the conservationist movement, ultimately broke over differing views about natural resource protection and use.[7] Regarding conservationism, Stradling points out that the term "does double (and conflicting) duty—signifying both a movement to promote efficient use and the preservation movement that struggled against that use."[8] Hays describes the conflict between preservationists and conservationists at the time as "between those who favored resource development and others who argued that wild areas and wildlife should be preserved from commercial use," differing views that "pervaded a great number of resource incidents during and after the Roosevelt administration, and led to mutual suspicion, scorn and distrust. Each group claimed the banner of true conservationism and accused the other of being false standard bearers of the gospel."[9]

For his part, Theodore Roosevelt was influenced by both streams of thought—and was a friend of both Pinchot and Muir—in a presidency that embraced the protection of natural resources.[10] In a 1908 address to open the Conference on the Conservation of Natural Resources, Roosevelt set out the challenge he saw facing the United States, and pointed toward a more utilitarian frame of reference, by observing that "the wise use of all of our natural resources, which are our national resources as well, is the great material question today. . . . The enormous consumption of these resources and the threat of imminent exhaustion of some of them, due to reckless and wasteful use, once more call for common effort, common action."[11] He also pointed out that "we have thoughtlessly, and to a large degree unnecessarily, diminished the resources upon which not only our prosperity but the prosperity of our children must always depend."[12] Facing the end of the US frontier, and the prospect of natural resource limitation and depletion, Roosevelt saw the efficient use of natural resources, and national efficiency in general, as nothing short of a patriotic duty.[13] Similarly, Pinchot defined natural resource conservation as embracing development to deliver "the greatest good to the greatest number for the longest time."[14] These views, while perhaps not recognizable as current-day sustainable development, do bear a certain, if distant, family resemblance.

For its part, the BWT is principally directed toward the establishment of rational rules and a predictable system for dispute resolution in the use of an important resource shared by two countries. Viewed from this perspective, the treaty clearly owes something to the utilitarian stream of Progressive-Era conservationist thought. Putting in place a system of rules for the use of shared resources supports rational and efficient resource development, something that is not feasible when the rights and obligations of the parties are unclear. However, the BWT is also animated by preservationist elements, as is seen perhaps most clearly in the protections afforded Niagara Falls, where both hydroelectric development and the need to protect the natural beauty of the Falls for themselves are present.

The St. Mary and Milk Rivers

Pressure for irrigation in the semi-arid region of Southern Alberta and Montana was an important and early driver for some form of cross-border water arrangement, in particular for the waters of the St. Mary and Milk Rivers (see Heinmiller in this volume). Both rivers originate in Montana and flow north into Alberta. The St. Mary River is part of the Saskatchewan-Nelson system in the Hudson Bay basin. In contrast, the Milk River is a tributary of the Missouri River, part of Gulf of Mexico drainage. The Milk River runs through Southern Alberta for approximately 160 kilometers (about 100 miles) before re-entering Montana.[15] US plans to divert the relatively more abundant and reliable waters of the St. Mary River into the Milk River to irrigate the lower Milk River basin had existed since the 1870s.[16] In 1891, the US Department of Agriculture conducted an assessment of the two rivers and concluded that the United States had the right to divert waters from the St. Mary provided that the water was not appropriated by Canada.[17] Canadian Interior Department officials responded with their own water survey "of a canal to divert the water from the St. Mary River . . . with the object of creating a vested right on our side of the International Boundary, before Americans divert the waters of this stream on their side of the line."[18]

In 1895, stemming in part from the international competition for St. Mary River water, a resolution supported by Canadian and Mexican delegates to the United States International Irrigation Congress, held in Albuquerque, New Mexico, called for the creation of a trilateral commission to adjudicate international water disputes arising between Mexico, the United States, and Canada. This resolution echoed earlier calls by Canadian interests for diplomatic efforts with the United States to protect access to St. Mary River water.[19] Though an 1896 Canadian expression of interest to co-operate with the United States in developing an international commission to resolve transboundary water disputes was not taken up,[20] the need for some form of international agreement to address at least the challenges related to these rivers eventually came to be acknowledged by both sides. While the St. Mary–Milk River diversion was among the first projects to be authorized by the US Reclamation Act of 1902, US officials, recognizing the international challenges they faced on these rivers, were reluctant to start construction until an international agreement setting out respective rights to the waters on both sides of the border was put in place.[21] In the end, the St. Mary and Milk Rivers would find a place in the BWT.

The Great Lakes

Elsewhere, actions on the Great Lakes also contributed to the sense that Canada and the United States required an international agreement on shared waterways (see Clamen and Macfarlane on Great Lakes–St. Lawrence basin water quantity in this volume). The diversion of Lake Michigan water into the Mississippi River via a canal near Chicago to address that city's sanitation needs, and pressure for hydro-power generation at Niagara Falls and Sault Ste. Marie, all underlined the need for something to facilitate cross-border co-operation.

The city of Chicago had long struggled with challenges related to sanitary sewage disposal. Until the construction of a diversion canal that carried the city's sewage away from Lake Michigan, Chicago discharged its sewage into that lake, which was also the city's water supply, an arrangement that contributed to substantial public health problems related to water-borne illnesses.[22] In 1889, the Illinois legislature passed legislation for the construction of a canal to reverse the flow of the south branch of the Chicago River into the Des Plaines River in order to convey the city's sewage away from Lake Michigan, across the Great Lakes basin boundary and into the Mississippi River, in the Gulf of Mexico drainage system.[23] Construction was completed in 1899 and the canal was operational in 1900. While built to discharge 283 cubic metres of water per second (10,000 cubic feet per second), due to US federal concerns about the speed of flow and possible effects on navigation, by 1902 the US secretary of war had reduced the maximum discharge permitted to 165 cubic metres per second (5,830 cubic feet per second).[24] The discharge of Chicago's sewage was of obvious and immediate concern to downstream recipients of the water, but Canadian reaction to the diversion was slow to develop, notwithstanding the conclusions of a report prepared for the Canadian Department of Marine and Fisheries that the Chicago Diversion would depress lake levels by between 12.5 centimetres (about 5 inches) and 19 centimetres (about 7.5 inches).[25] Nonetheless, concern about drawdown by the Chicago Diversion and the potential impacts on power and navigation in the Great Lakes would play their parts in shaping the eventual international arrangement between Canada and the United States.

At Sault Ste. Marie, where the St. Marys River connects Lakes Huron and Superior, from an early date both sides had navigation channels in place to circumvent the St. Marys rapids. The first canal was constructed by the North West Company in 1797–8.[26] The structure was destroyed by US troops during the War of 1812 and eventually rebuilt in 1816. Further navigational improvements around the rapids took place on both sides through the middle and late nineteenth century.[27] However, it was plans for hydro-power generation by both Canada and the United States in the 1880s that helped to spur an international waterways agreement. In 1898, the US Army Corps of Engineers reviewed a submission by the Michigan Lake Superior Power Company to the US government for the diversion of 906 cubic metres per second (32,000 cubic feet per second) of water through a power canal for hydro generation and the construction of compensating works in the St. Marys River. Significantly, the officer responsible for the review, Colonel G. J. Lydecker, observed, among other things, that the compensating works proposed would be partially in Canadian waters, and went on to suggest that both the Canadian and US governments should approve such projects that would modify the volume of discharge of Lake Superior waters. Noting the potential for harm to navigation stemming from reduced lake levels, Lydecker recommended the creation of an international commission made up of Canadian and US representatives to investigate and consider the legal and technical matters in such cases and to make recommendations to the governments regarding such projects. Finally, he advised that no projects be approved until his report's recommendations were adopted.[28]

Along with competition to develop hydro generation at Sault Ste. Marie, the politics of hydroelectric generation at Niagara Falls also helped to bring about an international agreement on shared waterways as Canada and the United States sought to develop the Falls. At the same time, growing concerns about the need to protect the Falls from the ravages of overdevelopment for commercial purposes helped to advance the idea that an international arrangement was needed to protect their natural uniqueness. In this respect, the eventual BWT reveals the influence of both utilitarianism (as we saw, involving the efficient use of natural resources for the future) and preservationism, related to the aesthetic value of nature, elements that progressives believed should be permanently preserved and protected from economic exploitation and despoliation through the excesses of unbridled individualism.[29] In the mid-1880s, both Canada and the United States moved to defend Niagara Falls by creating reservations to protect the area from unsightly commercial and industrial establishments. In 1896, however, the commissioners in New York began to press for federal protection of the Niagara River itself. As companies in New York and Ontario sought to withdraw water from above the Falls, people concerned about preserving their natural beauty grew increasingly alarmed.[30]

While intended to be only a synopsis of the pressures underlying the creation of a cross-border waterways arrangement, this brief survey helps to explain the eventual—though by no means inevitable—arrival of the current agreement. The parties were not obliged in any way to come up with an international organization or a treaty to resolve their problems over shared waterways, and they certainly did not set out to create the BWT. Decisions to co-operate or engage in the risky business of institution building must be understood by the principal actors as rational, promising superior outcomes to non-co-operation or ad hoc co-operation. In the case of Canada and the United States at the turn of the century, the points of tension along the border were perceived by the parties as sufficient to warrant the challenges of building a cross-border water institution. That institution was not, however, the IJC.

The Way We Were

Created by the US Rivers and Harbors Act of 1902, the IWC was the predecessor organization to the IJC. Operating from 1905 to 1915,[31] it differed from the eventual IJC in a number of respects. First, the commission was not based on a treaty, but rather US legislation. Specifically, the Rivers and Harbors Act called upon the US president

> to invite the government of Great Britain to join in the formation of an international commission to be composed of

three members from the United States and three who shall represent the interests of the Dominion of Canada, whose duty it shall be to investigate and report upon the conditions and uses of the waters adjacent to the boundary lines between the United States and Canada, including all of the waters of the lakes and rivers whose natural outlet is by the River Saint Lawrence to the Atlantic Ocean, also upon the maintenance and regulation of suitable levels, and also upon the effect upon the shores of these waters and the structures thereon, and upon the interests of navigation by reason of the diversion of these waters from or change in their natural flow; and, further, to report upon the necessary measures to regulate such diversion, and to make such recommendations for improvements and regulations as shall best subserve the interests of navigation in the said waters.[32]

Second, the commission's scope was limited to the Great Lakes–St. Lawrence system, at least in the US view. Canada interpreted the scope as described in the 1902 legislation to be non-restrictive with respect to the Great Lakes and the St. Lawrence River, believing that the commission's scope could, and should, have included all international waters shared between Canada and the United States. The IWC had fewer powers than the IJC, being limited strictly to investigative and recommendatory roles, having none of the IJC's administrative, quasi-judicial, or arbitral powers. Finally, it remained ambiguous as to whether the commission was permanent, something that posed obvious problems related to ongoing commission oversight of any regulations developed in response to various international waterways problems. Nonetheless, the IWC would mark an important and foundational stage in the management and resolution of Canada-US water issues, and the experience gained under this earlier IO would influence the development of the subsequent BWT and the IJC.

The establishment of the IWC, and later the BWT, can be usefully discussed in the terms of a framework developed by Jupille and Snidal setting out conditions under which actors, primarily states, operating under conditions of bounded rationality, may pursue one of a variety of options around co-operation. They may decide to: 1) use an existing international organization; 2) select between multiple IOs; 3) engage in institutional change; or 4) create a new institution. Jupille and Snidal outline a general decision sequence in which states decide whether to co-operate to resolve a given issue. A decision to co-operate—that is, not to engage in unilateralism—leads to a question of whether to engage in ad hoc co-operation or the use of an institution. If an institutional approach is preferred, the parties must next determine whether there is an existing "focal organization" available,[33] and whether it might be satisfactory for resolving the particular dispute. If the focal organization is satisfactory, the parties will simply choose to use it, while a finding that it is unsatisfactory leads to a further decision over whether to alter the organizational landscape. If the actors decide not to alter the existing landscape, and assuming there are multiple IOs available for potential use, they will select one as the locus for resolving their problem. Should the parties decide to alter the organizational landscape, they must then decide between modifying an existing institution and creating a new one.[34] Later, Jupille, Mattli, and Snidal named this repertoire of actions the USCC framework for the options of use, selection, change, and creation.[35]

In the context of growing cross-border water tensions, while there was some emerging acceptance of the need for some sort of Canada-US cooperative arrangement, no obvious focal organization existed for that purpose. It was not the case that the institutional field was utterly barren at the time, though it is clear that British and US cross-border water interests had focused nearly exclusively on navigational concerns. Those concerns are reflected in various treaties, including the Treaty of Paris (1783), the Jay Treaty (1794), the Webster-Ashburton Treaty (1842), the Northwest Boundary Treaty (1846), and the Treaty of Washington (1871).[36] While none of these agreements created a focal organization for the purposes of helping to resolve Canada-US cross-border water disputes, Britain and the United States had, at least, firmly institutionalized the principle of free navigation in shared international waters, a norm that would continue to be included in subsequent Canada-US water arrangements.

The creation of the IWC, then, is an example of international organization building where no focal institution is available or seems appropriate for the task. The main alternative for co-operation available at the time to Canada and the United States was likely that of ad hoc co-operation—that is, non-institutionalized, bilateral co-operation in the absence of an IO. Canadian actors sought to avoid non-institutionalized approaches to addressing cross-border water issues with the United States for fear that results over the longer run would be to Canada's disadvantage.[37] In Jupille and Snidal's framework, institutional creation is the most risky and costly of the options described. They note that, because "institutional creation is difficult and costly, actors will pursue it only when the stakes are high."[38] The brief synopsis of the various Canada-US cross-border water challenges provided above supports the view that a set of substantial issues required resolution, something that seems to have justified for both parties the choice to take on the costs and risks of IO building.

While Canada eventually decided to participate in a binational commission with the United States under US legislation, the Canadian side of the IWC never fully reconciled itself to a commission whose scope was limited to the Great Lakes and the St. Lawrence River. In March 1905, the Canadian IWC chairman and commissioners met to discuss topics they wished to propose to their US counterparts for the IWC's consideration. Those matters included the waters of the Columbia River; the St. Mary and Milk Rivers; the waters and streams emptying into the Rainy River; the Saint John River and tributaries in New Brunswick and Maine; the St. Croix River between Maine and New Brunswick; and those of the Great Lakes and the St. Lawrence River. The range of this work was indicative of Canada's wider sense of what the commission's jurisdiction should have been.[39]

At a meeting of the commission in May 1905, the US side presented a letter from the acting US attorney general confirming for US commissioners that the wording of the River and Harbors Act, " 'including all of the waters of the lakes and rivers whose natural outlet is by the River St. Lawrence to the Atlantic Ocean' [were] intended as a limitation to what precedes them."[40] The Canadian side's approach of accepting the limited mandate while pressing for its modifications accurately reflected the prime minister's views as communicated to the first Canadian chairman of the IWC, James Mabee. In June 1905, Prime Minister Laurier wrote to Mabee that "it would be of no use to persist in our contention, and the Government therefore are of the opinion that the commissioners had better proceed even in this limited way." However, in the next sentence the prime minister revealed his continued interest in addressing issues beyond the Great Lakes–St. Lawrence system: "At the same time, the Canadian Commissioners would do well to call the attention of the Commission to the conditions of things which exist on the River St. John, and the necessity of prompt joint action there."[41]

Over its relatively brief existence, the IWC carried out a wide range of useful and important work that dealt not only with shared Canada-US waters, but also international boundary delineation, the latter eventually being carried out under a separate treaty.[42] Along with boundary delineation work that would continue after the commencement of the BWT, the IWC considered and made recommendations to the Canadian and US governments on matters that included: diversion of waters at Sault Ste. Marie; operation and impact of the Chicago Diversion; the use and apportionment of waters at Niagara Falls; construction of regulatory works on the Richelieu River; construction of the Detroit River tunnel; regulation of Lake Erie levels; tunnel and inlet pier construction for the city of Buffalo's waterworks; and construction of a diversion for power generation affecting Rainy River and Lake of the Woods. While the IWC carried out groundbreaking work to help Canada and the United States address cross-border water issues, one of the more interesting plotlines of this period involves the continued pressure to expand the IWC's jurisdiction, in essence an effort at incremental IO change.

In February 1906, reporting to George C. Gibbons, the new chairman of the Canadian side following Mabee's appointment to the Ontario bench, Canadian commissioner Louis Coste summarized a conversation with Canada's minister of public works: "Mr. Hyman is of the opinion that the full Commission should investigate all questions touching international waterways—agree if we can—and report fully to the two Governments facts, causes and effects, and suggest rules, regulations, even treaties—in a word—suggest a policy."[43] At the IWC's meeting in Toronto in early March, a window began to open for Canada to expand commission jurisdiction when the US chairman of the IWC presented a letter from the US secretary of state suggesting the possibility of a treaty for the use of waters at Niagara Falls:

It seems desirable, therefore, to press forward the negocia-tion [*sic*] for such an agreement without any avoidable delay. May I ask you to ascertain whether the Joint Commission is now prepared to make such a report as may furnish the basis upon which the State Department and the [British] Ambassador may take up and proceed with the negociation?[44]

Niagara Falls seems to have represented for the United States a distinct kind of water issue, one in which not only powerful competing interests existed for the use of the resource on both sides of the border, but that included a pressing need to protect the unique beauty of the Falls themselves, a powerful public idea and something that offered leverage to the Canadian side. While the Canadians might have shared US views about the beauty of Niagara Falls, they also understood the Falls as part of a broader suite of water challenges, something that contributed to their sense that a general arrangement was needed for the settlement of all Canada-US water issues, including Niagara.

Late March 1906 found the Canadian side working up a set of strategic resolutions for presentation to their US counterparts for adoption that attempted to take advantage of the opening presented by the US interest in a separate treaty for Niagara Falls. While the resolutions touched on the Falls, their broader intent was for a comprehensive deal on all shared Canada-US waters. Accordingly, the draft Canadian resolutions began: "Whereas in the opinion of the Commission it is desirable that the whole question of uses and diversions of water adjacent to the boundary line between the United States and Canada should be settled by a treaty between the United States and Great Britain."[45] The points that followed outlined broad principles, specifically: the paramountcy of water for navigation and the allowance for diversions for domestic purposes and the service of locks; allotment in equal proportion for diversions for uses that did not affect navigation; a declaration that diversions such as that at Chicago would be "wrong in principle" and prohibited in the future; limitation of flows at Chicago to 10,000 cubic feet per second; the importance of the scenic beauty of Niagara Falls and their value in power generation; and limitations on Canadian and US diversions at Niagara Falls and tributary waters.[46]

In April 1906, in advance of the approaching IWC meeting, the Canadian side shared its resolutions with its US counterparts, including US commissioner George Clinton. On April 17, Gibbons received a sympathetic review of the resolutions from Clinton: "I received a copy of the resolutions and find that the general principles announced in them is in accordance with my ideas and I believe with those of [US chairman] Colonel Ernst and [US commissioner] Mr. Wisner."[47] Similarly, in his response to the Canadian secretary of the IWC, Clinton expressed similar personal views, noting "the general principles enunciated seem to be proper and within our jurisdiction." He closed by saying "you will understand that I am simply giving my personal opinion and that this is not an official letter."[48]

Gibbons presented a slightly modified set of resolutions at the 26–28 April 1906 meeting of the IWC. The reaction of US chairman Ernst differed somewhat to that of Commissioner Clinton. Ernst objected to the resolutions on the grounds that they "went beyond the jurisdiction conferred upon the American members and beyond the scope of their functions."[49] Gibbons pressed the case, indicating that "the Canadian Section was not prepared to recommend a treaty covering Niagara Falls alone, but desired that all other questions arising on the boundary waters should be considered at the same time."[50] The Canadian side's efforts to engage US interest in Niagara Falls as part of a broader and more formal waterways arrangement made some tentative headway by getting their ideas before the Canadian and US governments. On April 28, the IWC sought to agree on a report on Niagara Falls with the US chairman expressing his side's interest in joint action on them, while the Canadian side continued "to express the strong view that all matters referred to in the resolutions presented by them at the meeting 26th inst. should be dealt with as a whole."[51] The eventual binational report to the governments, issued 3 May 1906, outlined the importance of the Falls, set limits for diversions on the Canadian and US sides, set a maximum discharge for the Chicago drainage canal, and recommended that these measures be reflected in a treaty. The report went on to note, among other things, that while the Canadian Section concurred with the above measures, any treaty dealing with Niagara Falls "should also establish the principles applicable to all diversions or uses of water adjacent to the international boundary and of all streams which flow across the boundary."⁵² There followed the Canadian resolutions and the US side's opinion that they fell outside of the commission's legislated scope.

It is worth observing that the historical record shows some openness from the US side regarding Canada's interest in expanding the commission's scope. As it was, the US attorney general's interpretation of the US legislation simply amounted to a binding constraint on the US commissioners. As seen, US commissioner Clinton was sympathetic, at least on a personal level, to the objective of expanded scope for the IWC. Regarding the Canadian resolutions, Clinton wrote to US chairman Ernst urging "some intimation from the Secretary of State as to his views regarding the extent to which it would be proper for us to go, in laying down principles which will apply to other boundary waters than those included in the St. Lawrence system."⁵³ Clinton's particular willingness to engage on the question of scope can also be seen in his report to US colleagues at an October 1905 meeting of the US side, during which he summarized his earlier meeting with Secretary of War Taft. Clinton had raised Canada's expectations around scope expansion for the IWC, to which Taft responded with an endorsement of the US attorney general's views on jurisdiction, though he added that he felt the jurisdictional limits would be extended or further clarified, a position that may well have contributed to Clinton's receptivity to Canada's views.⁵⁴ Finally, the US side's December 1906 progress report pointed out that

> the Canadian government has from the beginning desired that the Commission should consider all questions which may arise concerning the international waters from the Atlantic to the Pacific. To enable the American members to do this, further legislation by Congress is necessary. It would seem proper to comply with the wishes of the Canadian government in this respect.⁵⁵

All of this to say that while the Canadian commissioners certainly pressed actively to have the IWC's scope expanded, it was also the case that the US side had not foreclosed on the matter but was awaiting higher-level direction that could enable the IWC to address it. As it was, the US side felt unable to disregard the US attorney general's interpretation of the legislation, a reasonable enough position.

Annus Mirabilis

Canadian pressure to expand the IWC's scope and formally adopt a set of general principles for governing the use of shared Canadian and US waters was showing some results in the spring of 1906. That year would prove to be an important one in putting the two countries on track for negotiations over what would eventually be the BWT. The United States found itself agreeing to a modest expansion in the commission's scope, if on an apparently ad hoc basis, when faced with the challenge of an application from the Minnesota Canal and Power Company to divert waters that fell outside of Great Lakes–St. Lawrence River drainage. The US decision to include in this case waters from the Hudson Bay basin within the IWC's scope would contribute substantially to the cause of a broader treaty that embedded core principles for the management of all international waterways.

The project proposed to divert water from the Birch Lake basin in Minnesota for power generation, something with implications for the Rainy River and the Lake of the Woods. The intention was to divert about 17 cubic metres of water per second (600 cubic feet per second) to generate some 22,400 kilowatts (30,000 electrical horse power). In its joint report, the commission noted it had been slowed in taking up the matter due to, among other things, the fact that its jurisdiction "had been placed in some doubt by the construction given by the Government of the United States to the Act of Congress under which the Commission was organized," but that the jurisdictional hurdle had been removed with a supporting referral from the US secretary of war.[56] In May 1906, US Secretary of State Elihu Root, responding to pressure to see the IWC take up the proposal, had written to the secretary of war to request that referral.[57] With this seemingly small action, the US government had agreed that expanding the commission's scope was possible after all. The incremental step of modifying the scope of an existing IO would lead to a key commission report on the Minnesota Canal and Power Company, one that made a number of important contributions to advancing a broader treaty.

In its examination of the case, the commission was clear that the project would offend both the letter and the spirit of the Webster-Ashburton Treaty in light of the impact expected on navigable waterways. It also ventured into useful analysis of national rights to use water, finding that international law had established that "the exercise of sovereign power over waters within the jurisdiction of a country, cannot be questioned." But it went on to outline its sense that "it would seem that comity would require that, in the absence of necessity, the sovereign power should not be exercised to the injury of a friendly nation or of its citizens or subjects, without the consent of that nation."[58] The report's recommendations noted that

> as questions involving the same principles and difficulties, liable to create friction, hostile feelings and reprisals, are liable to arise between the two countries, the Commission would recommend that a treaty be entered into which shall settle the rules and principles upon which all such questions may be peacefully and satisfactorily determined as they arise.[59]

That treaty, it declared

> should define the uses to which international waters may be put by either country without the necessity of adjustment in each instance by treaty, and would respectfully suggest that such uses should be declared to be: (a) Use for domestic and sanitary purposes. (b) Service of locks used for navigation purposes. (c) The right to navigate.[60]

Finally, the IWC recommended that the proposed treaty "should prohibit the permanent diversion of navigable streams which cross the international boundary or which form a part thereof, except upon adjustment of the rights of all parties concerned by a permanent commission and with its consent."[61]

As 1906 drew to an end, both Canada and the United States were moving to start negotiations on a waterways treaty that would embody certain principles under a permanent commission, principles based on the earlier Canadian proposals, here transformed into joint recommendations from the IWC. In December of that year, Secretary of State Root forwarded Chandler Anderson—a New York lawyer who advised the State Department and would come to play a decisive role in the eventual BWT—the Canadian resolutions from the May 1906 IWC report on Niagara Falls for review.[62] While Anderson expressed certain reservations about some of Canada's proposals, he noted that

> It would seem to be desirable that a commission should be appointed to deal with all the questions arising with respect to the use of boundary waters and waters tributary thereto and flowing therefrom on both sides of the line, and that the authority of such commission should be limited to the applications of principles agreed upon by treaty.[63]

On the Canadian side, George Gibbons pressed Prime Minister Laurier to move forward with treaty negotiations, to which Laurier agreed. Clinton and Gibbons were assigned lead roles for the United States and Canada, respectively, in developing a new arrangement for the purposes of addressing Canada-US international water issues.[64]

With the decision to proceed with treaty negotiations, Canada and the United States had ended one stage of their relationship as it pertained to cross-border waterways institution building and entered another. In Jupille and Snidal's terms, in launching the IWC the parties had decided to engage in institution building in the absence of an obvious focal organization for taking up matters pertaining to shared waterways. However, as seen, IO creation and change can be complex and untidy. In this case, Canada accepted the offer to participate in the establishment of an IO with whose terms of reference it did not fully agree, but which proved a serviceable enough arena in which to pursue its objectives as they pertained to shared waters with the United States and whose mandate constraints it sought to modify. That is, in some respects, the IWC period demonstrates a mix of the various modes outlined by Jupille and Snider. It was first and foremost a clear example of IO building, but that stage was followed very quickly by efforts at IO change, seen in pressure to expand the organization's scope, at least by the Canadians. When viewed in terms of Jupille and Snidal's framework, the decision to include within the IWC's scope work that pertained to the Hudson Bay basin looks like a satisfactory IO—at least from the US point of view—being employed in a novel way in an area that until that point had been beyond its formal competence. The parties engaged in satisficing behaviour by modifying an existing IO that had developed a certain stock of credibility as an emerging focal organization. The employment of the IWC in this modestly innovative means of ad hoc scope expansion is a variety of incremental change to the institutional landscape, but, critically, one that would help to enable larger changes that were not fully predictable when the US secretary of state made his request to the secretary of war to refer the Minnesota Canal and Power Company to the IWC.

Throughout, the IWC was not a passive object, but rather played an important role in its own change. Jupille and Snidal note that "IOs themselves might be active players in processes of institutional change. In some cases, IOs may position themselves in new areas of operations. This may result from a desire to expand organizational goals . . . or from a 'battle of ideas' within the IO where internal norm entrepreneurs successfully redefine an organization's purpose."[65] The IWC, its relative newness at the time notwithstanding, seems to have exemplified this process.

It is not the intention of this chapter to retell the details of the negotiations that led to the specifics of the current treaty (see Denning in this volume) or to review its structure in any detail. Yet even at the distance of more than a century, it remains perhaps a debatable point as to whether the BWT negotiations were an example of IO change or more fundamental IO creation. It is suggested here that, in its final form, the BWT is better viewed as an incremental alteration on the then-existing institutional landscape occupied by the IWC, and less the creation of a wholly new IO.[66] However, the window was briefly open for something quite different from the IWC, and was set out in the 1907 Clinton-Gibbons draft treaty. In the end, though, the BWT and the IJC emerged as elements in a more modest bilateral arrangement, one that shares much with the predecessor focal organization. The next section introduces and briefly reviews the surprising 1907 Clinton-Gibbons draft.

Notes on a Road Not Taken

In the process of creating a new waterways treaty, a draft arrangement was briefly considered that differed markedly from the eventual BWT, and was a product of considerable deliberation by the Canadian and US negotiators Gibbons and Clinton. It is intriguing to review the Clinton-Gibbons draft (see Appendix 2 for the full text) and compare it to the final 1909 treaty as it contains elements for a more authoritative set of institutional arrangements, more binding outcomes, and an international commission with a greater decision-making role than the eventual IJC.[67]

Gibbons and Clinton signed off on the draft on 24 September 1907 before forwarding it to Secretary of State Root and Prime Minister Laurier. The draft agreement makes an international commission the central decision-making and advisory body for all matters of difference pertaining to a wide range of subjects, boundary waters among them, and, unlike the eventual BWT, might have established a positive obligation for the parties to make referrals to it. The draft is brief, containing only seven articles, but its scope is broad. Article i declares that Canada and the United States seek to settle all matters existing or which may arise concerning

> the use and diversion of boundary waters of the United States and Canada, and in relation to the protection of fisheries therein, the improvement of navigable channels, the location of the boundary line, the construction of new channels for navigation, the improvement and maintenance of levels therein, and the protection of the banks and shores of such waters.

The draft also expresses the parties' desire that navigation rules and the rules for signal lights for vessels in boundary waters be uniform and that boundary water uses, including power, should be "regulated by joint rules of the United States and the Dominion of Canada, and that such rules must be enforced by joint action of both countries." Article v provides specific directions to the international commission on boundary delineation through Lakes Ontario, Erie, St. Clair, and Huron, and connecting waters.

Unlike the BWT, the Clinton-Gibbons draft makes no explicit distinction between waters that lay along the border and waters that flow across it—a major difference. Both types are simply termed "boundary waters," which are defined in article iv as including "Lake Superior, Michigan, Huron including Georgian Bay, St. Clair, Erie and Ontario; the connecting and tributary waters of said lakes, the river St. Lawrence from its source to the ocean; the Columbia River and all rivers and streams which cross the boundary line between the Dominion of Canada and the United States, and their tributaries." The draft includes a prohibition on transboundary pollution similar to that found in the 1909 treaty, an element of some foresight. Clinton notes in his cover letter to Root transmitting the 1907 draft that the anti-pollution language was inserted "to take care of cases which are likely to arise in the future when the North West becomes more densely populated." He then adds with a note of caution, "perhaps the language is too strong."[68]

As in the BWT, navigation is the paramount application for boundary waters, save for domestic and sanitary uses. The hierarchy of uses set out in the BWT is absent, though the central importance of navigation compared to power and irrigation is maintained along with the commitment that navigable boundary waters shall remain forever free for navigation.[69] In instances where the use of power generation is permitted in waters that lay along the border, the primacy of navigation is upheld and "as far as possible, the right to use one half of the surplus waters available for power purposes shall be preserved to each country, its citizens or subjects." Similarly, for instances where diversion of boundary waters for irrigation is permitted, navigation retains its priority, though unlike the power generation provisions of article iv no clear allocation formula is provided for the balance, only that "the rights of each country affected and of its citizens and subjects be equitably protected."

Article iv of the Clinton-Gibbons draft makes specific mention of diversions related to Niagara Falls, limiting diversions from the Niagara River and Lake Erie of more than 524 cubic metres per second (18,500 cubic feet per second) by the United States, and 1019 cubic metres per second (36,000 cubic feet per second) by Canada. Here, Lake Erie is included within the scope of source waters for diversion, whereas in the

BWT, Lake Erie is mentioned only in terms of the objective of not appreciably affecting the lake's level.

The international commission outlined in the Clinton-Gibbons draft differs noticeably from the IJC. Article i of the draft declares that the parties, in seeking to settle questions existing or arising pertaining to the wide range of matters covered in the article (noted above), deem it wise "that a permanent international commission be appointed with full powers in the premises: therefore the high contracting parties agree that all such questions and matters as they may arise shall be referred by them to a commission to consist of six commissioners, three appointed by the President of the United States, and three by his Britannic Majesty." In requiring that all matters as they arise be referred to the commission, article i, in addition to laying out a wide range of matters for potential consideration by the commission, might also have created a positive obligation for the parties to refer matters of difference, something that is not the case with the BWT.

Article iii of the 1907 draft treaty further delineates the international commission's decision-making authority, noting that "the commission shall have the power to consider and determine all questions and matters related to the subject specified in Article I which may be referred to it by the High Contracting Parties," perhaps suggesting some discretion on the part of the parties in making referrals to the commission. On the other hand, it is entirely possible to read article iii as supportive of a positive obligation on the parties to refer under article i and conferring on the commission the power to "consider and determine" once a matter has been mandatorily referred to it. Whether article iii moderates the article i obligation of the parties to refer matters as they may arise, what is clear is that the commission's role was not to be confined to reviewing, reporting, and recommending, as was the case for the IWC. Clinton and Gibbons intended the commission to decide questions of difference on a wide range of matters.

The second part of article iii speaks again to the decision-making role of the commission, along with its enforcement powers:

> The decision of the Commission upon matters submitted to it shall be enforced by the High Contracting Parties; and for

the purpose of enforcing any rules and regulations, which may be adopted by the Commission, pursuant to the powers conferred upon it by this treaty, the Commission may exercise such police powers as may be vested in it by concurrent legislation of the United States and the Dominion of Canada.

Commissioners under the Clinton-Gibbons draft are required to work impartially and "decide, to the best of their judgment and according to justice and equity, without feeling, favor or affection to their country, on all matters as shall be laid before them," similar to the provisions of the BWT.

Notably, and in contrast to the IJC, the draft agreement drives the commission toward decision-making even in cases where a majority of commissioners is unable to reach agreement. Article ii declares that "the majority of commissioners shall have power to render a decision, but in case a majority do not agree, the commission shall select an arbitrator or arbitrators to whom the matters of difference may be referred and whose decision shall be final." For matters outside of those covered in article i, article vi provides for similar arbitral appointment for matters referred to the commission for decision. The BWT retains a vestigial element of the Clinton-Gibbons provisions for an arbitral backstop in its unused—and probably unusable—article x. There is capacity for the IJC to receive referrals from the parties on matters beyond the scope of the treaty's article ix referral provisions. Article x directs the parties to refer to an "umpire" matters of difference on which the commission is unable to decide. Whatever else it might be, article x is peripheral to the main work of the IJC, and was probably destined to be so with its high barriers to use. In contrast, the arbitral backstop measures in the Clinton-Gibbons draft pertained to the core decision-making areas of the commission. The commission that begins to emerge in the Clinton-Gibbons draft would certainly have been something of a departure from the IWC, one with broad powers of decision and with arbitral backstop provisions to ensure resolution of questions. When viewed in terms of Jupille and Snidal's framework the new commission would have been a substantial alteration to the institutional landscape indicative of a rejection of the IWC.

On 15 October 1907 the US State Department forwarded the Clinton-Gibbons draft to Chandler Anderson—encountered earlier—for review and comment. His subsequent extensive recommendations to Secretary of State Root, based on his concerns about the scope and authorities set out in the draft document, substantially shaped the eventual treaty. Anderson's review and subsequent role as lead negotiator for the United States—replacing Clinton in this capacity—arguably did more than any other individual intervention to fashion a number of core elements of the BWT as we have come to know them. In making this claim, it is not the intention here to diminish the undeniably important role that George Gibbons played in helping to bring about a comprehensive waterways treaty between Canada and the United States, a view expressed by, among others, Elihu Root. On this point Whitney notes about Gibbons that "of all those connected with the events leading to the final Boundary Waters Treaty, it was he who showed the greatest dedication to the adoption of principles to govern water use in a treaty with a permanent joint commission to apply them."[70]

However, it was nevertheless Anderson's decisive intervention in late 1907 that perhaps more than anything else transformed the Clinton-Gibbons draft into the BWT. His efforts and successes with the BWT were things for which Anderson apparently felt under appreciated. In 1910, Anderson expressed some frustration in response to a congratulatory letter he received about the completion of the BWT from Charles Henry Butler, a lawyer and the reporter of decisions of the Supreme Court of the United States. In his reply, Anderson informs Butler "that Mr. Root always refers to this treaty as the Anderson-Gibbons Treaty," and notes further he was "much interested, but not altogether surprised" to learn "that in Canada Mr. Gibbons is receiving entire credit for it. As a matter of fact the original treaty was prepared by me without consultation with Mr. Gibbons, and after being submitted to Mr. Root was forwarded to Gibbons without change." Anderson goes on to belittle Gibbons's role further in his reply to Butler.[71] However unattractive Anderson's bitterness might seem, his asperity may be, in retrospect, understandable in light of the plaudits given to Gibbons, and Anderson's own publicly under-recognized role in fashioning the BWT. Root was, himself, in fact, well aware of Anderson's central role in the resolution of a range of Anglo-American matters, and recognized his contributions in a letter to him in 1909 as Root was preparing to leave the State Department to take up his role as US Senator for New York:

> Before leaving the office of Secretary of State, I wish to express to you the very high estimate which I put upon the service you have rendered to the country in the negotiations relating to the numerous questions between the United States and the British colonies in North America. The successful conclusion of which has been reached in the negotiation upon the many widely different questions which existed would have been impossible if it had not been for your industry, clearness of vision and sound judgment.[72]

It is useful to review Anderson's report on the Clinton-Gibbons draft briefly given his impact on the final treaty.

Anderson's December 1907 paper to the State Department is directed primarily toward reducing the scope of the Clinton-Gibbons draft and curtailing the authority of the international commission. He found that "the extent of the jurisdiction proposed to be conferred upon this international commission is in some ways without precedent." Anderson advised the elimination of fisheries and boundary demarcation from the scope of the treaty since these matters were already under treaty negotiation elsewhere. He expressed concern about the judicial authority that was proposed for the commission, pointing out a development he viewed as worrying, believing that the judicial functions

> show a notable departure from the course heretofore followed by this Government in delegating by treaty judicial powers to an international commission. In such treaties it has been customary to limit the exercise of the judicial powers of such a Commission to some particular question already at issue and involving matters not wholly within the jurisdiction of either of the parties to the treaty, or over which neither of the parties alone had undisputed control.[73]

The problems for Anderson lay in the fact that the Clinton-Gibbons draft would extend authority of the international commission over waters that were entirely within the United States, and within the competence of state and federal authorities to manage, and that the draft treaty was open-ended in granting the commission the power to decide on all matters of difference that might arise in the future.

With respect to the jurisdictional concern, Anderson noted that waters flowing across the boundary and waters tributary to boundary waters were wholly within the jurisdiction of the individual parties. Similarly he found that improvement of navigable channels, construction of new channels, and riverbank and shoreline protection for boundary waters as set out in the draft treaty were all matters for exclusive jurisdiction. He recommended that the authority of the international commission be confined to the uses of contiguous boundary waters—that is, waters that lay along the international border, as would be subsequently defined in the BWT. On this point Anderson drew a connection to the Chicago drainage canal and the St. Mary and Milk Rivers, noting that if such waters were to fall under the broad classification of boundary waters, as set out in the Clinton-Gibbons draft, "the right of exclusive control over them would be lost and Canadian consent to the diversion of them would be necessary." Overall, given the scope of the Clinton-Gibbons draft, Anderson observed that it was "unlikely that the approval of the Senate would be given to a treaty delegating to an international commission such unrestricted powers over matters wholly within the borders of the United States."[74] The US Senate had long guarded its authorities and prerogatives pertaining to advice and consent with respect to treaties under article ii, section 2 of the US Constitution, and had demonstrated some enthusiasm for amending international agreements.[75]

Anderson also expressed concerns about the extent of the commission's discretion, since it would be under-constrained by the terms of the proposed agreement. He noted that in addition to the oath of office that commissioners would be required to take, the only other provisions of the treaty that would guide the commissioners in making decisions were found in the series of principles contained in the draft, though he believed that these principles fell short in this respect. As seen, they tended to focus on the centrality of navigational uses in boundary waters, non-interference with natural flow to the injury of the other party, and a requirement for equitable treatment where diversions for irrigation are allowed. In Anderson's view, the draft treaty did not establish sufficient guiding principles and therefore left "the commissioners free to adopt their own ideas of justice and equity in the decision of questions arising thereon, which practically amounts to a power to legislate." He urged that principles to guide the international commission not be left to the discretion of the commission itself but rather be agreed to in advance by the parties and incorporated in the treaty, and he was particularly interested in an order of precedence for various uses of boundary waters.[76]

Anderson's views decisively influenced the outlook of the US government, particularly those of Secretary of State Root. The eventual BWT differentiated between boundary waters and waters flowing across the boundary (with limited roles for the IJC with respect to the latter), made provision for special agreements by the parties, and clarified the obligations around referrals. The IJC's judicial function is limited to uses, diversions, and obstructions in boundary waters. The BWT's article x arbitral powers for matters falling outside of the article ix referral provisions have never been engaged, and would be challenging to use even if the parties were ever to be so inclined given that, among other things, their use would require the advice and consent of the US Senate and approval from the Canadian governor in council.

In the 1907 draft, the negotiators took IO creation in a direction that simply was not feasible for the US government, suggesting that Clinton seemed to misjudge the intentions of the State Department and the political space that was available for him to work within. It is interesting to compare Clinton's sanguine outlook about the power of the commission described in the draft text to the somewhat alarmed response from Anderson. In a letter to Root, Clinton observes:

> The decisions of the commission will, therefore, necessarily be the law of the land, so far as they do not contravene acts of Congress or the rights of individuals protected by the Constitution. Nevertheless, the action of Congress would be necessary from time to time to enable the commission to perform its duties, and the questions which may come

> before the commission may be of such a nature as to require legislation to enforce them. It would seem to me that such a treaty, being an international obligation, can hardly be ignored by Congress and the legislation necessary to preserve the good faith of the United States, by carrying out the decisions of the commission, will be forthcoming, almost as a matter of course.[77]

In retrospect, the United States was ultimately more interested in IO modification rather than more comprehensive redesign and construction efforts, something it viewed as unnecessarily risky. As expressed by Anderson, the US concerns centred on the extensive power of the new organization, loss of US sovereignty, and the potentially unfavourable and/or unpredictable distributional consequences that could have resulted for the United States. Jupille and Snidal point out that "actors must also be willing to tolerate the potentially substantial risk of opening the Pandora's Box of institutional creation, unmoored as it is from existing institutions."[78] On this point, in reviewing the Clinton-Gibbons draft, Anderson moved forcefully in essentially urging the secretary of state to slam that box shut and drive toward a more limited treaty, something with a greater resemblance to the status quo arrangement under the IWC.

Conclusion

While not the destination initially intended by Canadian and US negotiators, in light of the BWT's subsequent record, the change in direction was perhaps no bad thing for the two countries. Anderson's intervention can be seen as a prudent move that has, on reflection, benefited both Canada and the United States. In its relative modesty, the BWT shares much with the IWC, and it is here that the distinction between institutional change and institutional creation becomes murky, a point allowed by Jupille and Snidal.[79] The experience of arriving at a more modest international arrangement demonstrates some of the potential risks involved in IO creation. In this case the United States found itself flirting briefly with the prospects of a powerful and under-constrained international commission and what it viewed as unacceptable risks to sovereignty. It moved accordingly to mitigate those risks by seeking to fashion a more limited agreement.

There are clear continuities between the BWT and the IWC, including substantial scope for discretion by the parties and more-limited commission powers. Yet the two organizations are different. The IJC is certainly vested with broader authorities compared to its predecessor IO, but it is by no means the powerful decision-making commission at the heart of the 1907 Clinton-Gibbons draft. In the end, the BTW and its commission seem more like the products of incremental changes that built upon the experience of the IWC era rather than a substantial rejection of it. While the IJC is a less powerful and far-reaching commission than that contemplated in 1907, with its reduced authorities and protections for sovereignty of the parties, the IJC, like the IWC before it, instantiates the important feature of flexibility.

More than a century after the current treaty was fashioned, it is difficult to say that something like the Clinton-Gibbons draft, with its broad scope and stronger commission, would have rendered better service or enjoyed the same longevity as the BWT. A more authoritative commission framed primarily as a decision-making organization with a broad mandate, and that obliged the parties to refer questions to it for binding resolution might well have been able to render a decision that satisfied a particular interest to a water dispute at any particular moment. However, it seems doubtful that such an IO would necessarily have been better than the current arrangement, particularly if a goal is to promote stable and amicable relations in the resolution of disputes over the longer run. It seems more probable that something like the Clinton-Gibbons draft, if adopted, would have failed long ago, probably after imposing an unacceptable loss on one of the parties in a polarizing win-lose outcome, though such speculative history is a perilous undertaking and always open to question.

This brief review of the institutional choices that brought Canada and the United States eventually to the BWT also points to the fact that the people involved mattered, and that different principal actors would probably have brought about different outcomes. Again, the perils of speculative history notwithstanding, we can ask: What outcomes might have emerged had Canada's first chairman of the IWC, James Mabee, not been appointed to the bench, thereby creating an opportunity for the arrival of

George Gibbons? Would Mabee have been as determined as Gibbons in pressing for a comprehensive waterways treaty? Similarly, on the US side the shift from Clinton to Anderson in the role of lead negotiator perhaps did more than any other single thing to bring about the now-familiar features of the BWT.

In the Minnesota Canal and Power Company case, the IWC noted the friendly nature of the Canada-US relationship and that a waterways treaty should emerge from this circumstance. Canada and the United States continue to enjoy the benefits of a long and peaceful relationship, one that is perhaps without equal in the world. As Thompson and Randall note, "no other pair of neighbors can claim as successful and mutually prosperous relationship as has evolved between the United States and Canada over the past two hundred years. The countries share not only a continent but also an interwoven culture, political, and economic heritage."[80] It is perhaps specifically because of this closeness that a modest and flexible arrangement like the BWT has been able to function as well as it has. The treaty is both symptomatic of the friendly binational relationship and an ongoing contributor to its continuation.

While the temptation to create a stronger or more authoritative institution may persist for some, the IJC has over the course of its long life become a key focal organization for helping to prevent and resolve Canada-US water conflicts. Nonetheless, it may be possible to imagine again incremental change to the current BWT/IJC arrangement. However, short of a crisis, and with the stock of credibility that resides in the commission and the treaty, it is difficult to envisage the parties embarking on a major alteration to the institutional landscape in the foreseeable future.

Notes

1. The views expressed in this chapter do not necessarily reflect those of the Government of Canada.
2. George P. de T. Glazebrook, *Canadian External Relations: An Historical Study to 1914* (London: Oxford University Press, 1942), 254.
3. Joseph Jupille and Duncan Snidal, "The Choice of International Institutions: Cooperation, Alternatives and Strategies" (Paper presented at the annual meeting of

the American Political Science Association, Washington, DC, September 2005). Jupille, Walter Mattli, and Snidal subsequently applied the framework comprehensively in *Institutional Choice and Global Commerce* (Cambridge: Cambridge University Press, 2013).

4   N. F. Dreisziger, "The International Joint Commission of the United States and Canada: A Study in Canadian-American Relations" (PhD diss., University of Toronto, 1974).

5   Robert H. Wiebe, *The Search for Order, 1877–1920* (New York: Hill and Wang, 1967).

6   Kurkpatrick Dorsey, *The Dawn of Conservation Diplomacy: U.S. Canadian Wildlife Protection Treaties in the Progressive Era* (Seattle: University of Washington Press, 1998).

7   Char Miller, *Gifford Pinchot and the Making of Modern Environmentalism* (Washington, DC: Island Press, 2001), 132–41.

8   David Stradling, *Conservationism in the Progressive Era: Classic Texts* (Seattle: University of Washington Press, 2004), 13.

9   Samuel P. Hays, *Conservation and the Gospel of Efficiency: The Progressive Conservation Movement, 1890–1920* (Pittsburgh: University of Pittsburgh Press, 1959), 189.

10 Douglas Brinkley, *The Wilderness Warrior: Theodore Roosevelt and the Crusade for America* (New York: Harper Collins, 2009).

11 Theodore Roosevelt, *Address of President Roosevelt at the Opening of the Conference on the Conservation of Natural Resources at the White House, Wednesday Morning, May 13, 1908 at 10:30 O'Clock* (n.p.: Adamant Media Corporation, 2007), 17.

12 Ibid., 24.

13 Ibid., 47.

14 Gifford Pinchot. "The Fight for Conservation" in *Conservationism in the Progressive Era: Classic Texts*, ed. David Stradling (Seattle: University of Washington Press, 2004), 22.

15 The International Joint Commission, *International St. Mary–Milk Rivers Administrative Measures Task Force: Report to the International Joint Commission* (April 2006), 10, https://ijc.org/en/media/1532.

16 R. Halliday and G. Faveri, "The St. Mary and Milk Rivers: The 1921 Order Revisited," *Canadian Water Resources Journal* 32, no. 1 (2007): 77–9.

17 Dreisziger, "The International Joint Commission of the United States and Canada," 17.

18 Ibid., 19.

19 Ibid., 17–24.

20 Ibid., 24.

21 Donald J. Pisani, *Water and American Government: The Reclamation Bureau, National Water Policy and the West, 1902–1935* (Berkeley: University of California Press, 2002), 14–15.

22 Stanley A. Changnon and Joyce M. Changnon "History of the Chicago Diversion and Future Implications," *Journal of Great Lakes Research* 22, no. 1 (1996): 100–18. It should be noted here that the figure of ninety thousand deaths often attributed to an outbreak of waterborne diseases in Chicago in 1885 is apocryphal. The correction was set out by Libby Hill of Northeastern Illinois University in "The Making of an Urban Legend," *Chicago Tribune*, 29 July 2007. On 22 August 2007, the *Tribune* issued something of a belated clarification regarding its contributions to the legend over the years, noting that "outbreaks of killer diseases truly did play havoc with Chicago and its people: stockyards runoff, water-borne sewage, spoiled food and lethal bugs variously brought dysentery, smallpox, diphtheria, influenza and other contagions to the city. Chicago did not, though, suffer deaths of Black Plague proportion in 1885." The author is grateful to an anonymous reviewer of this chapter for drawing his attention to the contested death toll.

23 Dreisziger, "The International Joint Commission of the United States and Canada," 26–7.

24 Changnon and Changnon "History of the Chicago Diversion," 105.

25 Dreisziger, "The International Joint Commission of the United States and Canada," 28–9.

26 William R. Willoughby, *The St. Lawrence Seaway: A Study in Politics and Diplomacy* (Madison: University of Wisconsin Press, 1961), 8.

27 Ibid., 32–5, 50–1.

28 Dreisziger, "The International Joint Commission of the United States and Canada," 32–3.

29 Michael McGerr, *A Fierce Discontent: The Rise and Fall of the Progressive Movement in America* (Oxford: Oxford University Press, 2003), 164–5.

30 Dreisziger, "The International Joint Commission of the United States and Canada," 35–6; Daniel Macfarlane, "'A Completely Man-Made and Artificial Cataract': The Transnational Manipulation of Niagara Falls," *Environmental History* 18, no. 4 (October 2013): 759-784.

31 While the legislation dates from 1902, the work of the commission did not begin until 1905 due to delays on the Canadian side. The IWC's final meeting was 29–30 April 1915 in Buffalo, New York.

32 US River and Harbors Act, 13 June1902, ch. 1079, §4, 32 Stat. 373.

33 A focal institution is in essence an existing and obvious "go-to" organization. According to Jupille and Snidal, it is a feature of status quo conditions in which an IO exists that is "widely accepted as the 'natural' forum for dealing with a particular cooperation problem. This may be for reasons of habit, cognitive limitation, socialization . . . organizational culture, or simply a generic satisficing decision style." Jupille and Snidal, "The Choice of International Institutions," 13.

34 Ibid., 15.

35 Joseph Jupille, Walter Mattli, and Duncan Snidal, *Institutional Choice and Global Commerce* (Cambridge: Cambridge University Press, 2013), 19.

36   L. M. Bloomfield and Gerald F. Fitzgerald, *Boundary Water Problems of Canada and the United States* (Toronto: Carswell, 1958), 2–7.

37   Reflecting on his concerns about more ad hoc approaches to Canada-US transboundary water co-operation, Gibbons explained to Laurier in February 1908 that "what we did not want and could not stand was that one principle should be applied to [the United States'] advantage through the pressure of their politicians in one place, and another principle to equal advantage in another." Letter to Sir Wilfrid Laurier, 11 Feburary 1908, George Christie Gibbons fonds, MG30E71 vol. 3, Library and Archives Canada, Ottawa.

38   Jupille and Snidal, "The Choice of International Institutions," 37.

39   International Waterways Commission, "Minutes of the Proceedings of the Meeting Held by the Canadian Section of the International Waterways Commission, March 7, 1905," George Christie Gibbons fonds, MG30E71, vol 15, Library and Archives Canada, Ottawa.

40   International Waterways Commission, "Memorandum of Proceedings at Preliminary Meeting of the International Waterways Commission, Held at Washington D.C., May 25, 1905," George Christie Gibbons fonds, MG30-E71, volume 14, Library and Archives Canada, Ottawa.

41   International Waterways Commission, "Minutes of the Proceedings of the International Waterways Commission, June 14, 1905," George Christie Gibbons fonds MG30E71, vol. 14, Library and Archives Canada, Ottawa.

42   In April 1908, the US secretary of state and the British ambassador to the United States signed the Treaty Between the United States and the United Kingdom Concerning the Boundary Between the United States and the Dominion of Canada from the Atlantic Ocean to the Pacific Ocean. Article 4 of that treaty directed the IWC "to ascertain and accurately re-establish" the Canada-US boundary from where the 45th parallel intersects the St. Lawrence River to the western shore of Lake Superior. See International Boundary Commission, "Treaty Between the United States and the United Kingdom Concerning the Boundary Between the United States and the Dominion of Canada from the Atlantic Ocean to the Pacific Ocean," available at http://www.internationalboundarycommission.org/uploads/treaties/treaty%20of%20 1908%20(english).pdf.

43   "Letter from Coste to Gibbons," February 1906, George Christie Gibbons fonds, MG30E71 volume 15, Library and Archives Canada, Ottawa.

44   International Waterways Commission, "Minutes of the Proceedings of the Meeting Held by the International Waterways Commission, March 6, 7, 1906," George Christie Gibbons fonds, MG30E71 vol 10, Library and Archives Canada, Ottawa.

45   International Waterways Commission, "Minutes of the Proceedings of the Meeting Held by the Canadian Section of the International Waterways Commission, March 23, 1906," George Christie Gibbons fonds, MG30E71, vol 10, Library and Archives Canada, Ottawa.

46   Ibid.

47 International Waterways Commission, "Minutes of the Proceedings of the Meeting Held by the International Waterways Commission, April 26–28, 1906," Records of the US Section of the International Water Ways Commission, RG 76, 76.2.6, Box 2. US National Archives, College Park, MD.

48 International Waterways Commission, "Letter from George Clinton to Thomas Coté," 16 April 1906, George Christie Gibbons fonds, MG30E71 vol 1. Library and Archives Canada, Ottawa.

49 International Waterways Commission, "Minutes of Meetings, April 26–28, 1906, Held at the Office of the American Section, 328 Federal Building, Buffalo, N.Y," Records of the US Section of the International Water Ways Commission, RG 76, 76.2.6, Box 2. US National Archives, College Park, MD.

50 Ibid.

51 Ibid.

52 Parliament of Canada, Sessional Papers, 1906. Paper 19c, "From the International Waterways Commission on Conditions at Niagara Falls, and their recommendations in relation thereto."

53 International Waterways Commission, "Minutes of Meeting: American Section International Waterways Commission, April 25, 1906," appendix J. Records of the US Section of the International Water Ways Commission RG 76, 76.2.6, Box 1. US National Archives, College Park, MD.

54 International Waterways Commission, "Minutes of Meeting, American Section, International Waterway Commission, October 28, 1905," Records of the US Section of the International Water Ways Commission RG 76, 76.2.6, Box 1. US National Archives, College Park, MD.

55 International Waterways Commission, *Second Progress Report, December 1, 1906*. Records of the US Section of the International Water Ways Commission RG 76, 76.2.6, Box 2. US National Archives, College Park, MD.

56 International Waterways Commission, "Report of the International Waterways Commission Upon the Application of the Minnesota Canal and Power Company of Duluth, Minnesota, for Permission to Divert Certain Waters in the State of Minnesota from the Boundary Waters Between the United States and Canada." Records of the US Section of the International Water Ways Commission RG 76, 76.2.6, Box 12. US National Archives, College Park, MD.

57 "Letter from Secretary of State Root to Secretary of War Taft, May 14, 1906." Records of the US Section of the International Waterways Commission RG 76,76.2.6, US National Archives, College Park MD.

58 International Waterways Commission, "Minnesota Canal and Power Company." Records of the US Section of the International Water Ways Commission RG 76, 76.2.6, Box 12. US National Archives, College Park, MD. "Letter from Secretary of State Root to Secretary of War Taft, May 14, 1906." Records of the US Section of the International Waterways Commission RG 76,76.2.6, US National Archives, College Park MD.

59 Ibid.

60 Ibid.

61 Ibid.

62 Anderson had some familiarity with Anglo-American matters pertaining to Canada. In 1903 he had been assistant counsel for the Alaska Boundary Tribunal. From 1905 to 1910 he served as a legal advisor for the State Department on Anglo-American negotiations of Canadian questions. He would go on to be the US agent for the North Atlantic coast fisheries arbitration in 1910, followed by counsel for the State Department 1910 from 1913, then arbitrator for American-British pecuniary claims. He continued in this way, taking on a series of high-profile international positions, throughout his career. Chandler Anderson died on 2 August 1936.

63 Chandler Anderson, "Letter to Elihu Root," 28 December 1906. Chandler P. Anderson Papers, 1894-1953, Office File, Box 13. United States Library of Congress.

64 F. J. E. Jordan, "An Annotated Digest of Materials Relating to the Establishment and Development of the International Joint Commission," 12–19, https://ijc.org/sites/default/files/A69.pdf.

65 Jupille and Snidal, "The Choice of International Institutions," 35.

66 It will be noted that the IJC was of course a separate organization from the IWC and that, therefore, the existence of two separate organizations at the end of the day is an argument in support of the view that the arrival of the IJC was an instance of IO creation, and not simply change. However, the negotiators were aware that a new treaty would likely lead to the effective end of the IWC as the new treaty and IO would be in conflict with the US law that established the IWC. Clinton expressed this point of view to Root in September 1907 noting that "I think, after very careful consideration that the existence of the treaty commission [in the Clinton-Gibbons draft] necessarily negatives the continuance of the International Waterways Commission, inasmuch as there would certainly be conflicts of jurisdiction." This situation meant that the IWC was never likely to be a site for substantial organizational modification given the legal constraints posed by the Rivers and Harbors Act of 1902. It is argued here that the arrival of a new IO in the form of the IJC is still an example of IO change rather than IO creation if one looks to the substantive roles of the IJC and its predecessor commission, which, while different, demonstrate considerable continuity. Letter, Clinton to Root 25 September 1907. Chandler P. Anderson Papers, Office File 1894-1953, Box 12. US Library of Congress.

67 There is a methodological challenge that may be raised in treating the 1907 draft as though it were final treaty text and holding it to that standard. The draft text contains certain ambiguities that might have been clarified en route to finalization, had the Clinton-Gibbons draft proceeded further. However, it should also be allowed that plenty of final texts have been ambiguous, sometimes deliberately so. Nonetheless, the 1907 draft as we have it should be taken seriously as a sincere effort by the negotiators to craft a viable treaty to respond to challenges as they understood them at the time. Among other things, doing so offers an opportunity to observe the less-than-straightforward route the parties took in reaching the eventual BWT, what elements from the draft survived, and what got left on the cutting room floor.

68 Clinton to Root, September 25, 1907. Chandler P. Anderson Papers, Office File 1894-1953, Box 13. US Library of Congress.

69 Some copies of the September 1907 Clinton-Gibbons draft declare that navigable boundary waters "shall be for free *from* navigation by the citizens and subjects of both countries" (italics mine)—a typographical error.

70 Harriet E. Whitney, "Sir George Gibbons and the Boundary Waters Treaty" (PhD diss., Michigan State University, 1968), 104.

71 Chandler Anderson. Letter to Charles Henry Butler. 9 May 1910. Chandler P. Anderson papers. Office File, Box 14. US Library of Congress.

72 Elihu Root. Letter to Anderson. 26 January 1909. Chandler P. Anderson papers. General Correspondence, Box 4. US Library of Congress.

73 Chandler Anderson, "Boundary Waters. Report on Draft Treaty by George Clinton and George C. Gibbons of the International Waterways Commission," 1907, Chandler P. Anderson Papers, Office File, Box 13. US Library of Congress.

74 Ibid.

75 The Hay-Paunceforte Treaty (1901) related to the construction of an isthmian canal (ultimately the Panama Canal), the Hay-Bond Treaty (1902) on Newfoundland reciprocity, and the Hay-Herbert Treaty (1903) on delineating the Alaska-Canada boundary, among others, had all experienced concessions to the US Senate. Ronald Reter, "President Theodore Roosevelt and the Senate's 'Advice and Consent' to Treaties," *The Historian* 44, no 2 (August 1982): 483–504.

76 Anderson, "Boundary Waters. Report on Draft Treaty by George Clinton and George C. Gibbons on the International Waterways Commission," 1907, Chandler P. Anderson Papers, Office File, Box 13, US Library of Congress.

77 Clinton to Root, September 25, 1907. US Library of Congress, Chandler P. Anderson Papers, Office Files, 1896-1933, Box 13.

78 Jupille and Snidal, "The Choice of International Institutions," 38.

79 Ibid., 19.

80 John Herd Thompson and Stephen J. Randall, *Canada and the United States: Ambivalent Allies*, 4th ed. (Athens: University of Georgia Press, 2008), 333.

Construction of a Keystone: How Local Concerns and International Geopolitics Created the First Water Management Mechanisms on the Canada-US Border

Meredith Denning

In 1909, the United States and Britain (on behalf of Canada) signed the Boundary Waters Treaty into existence. Part of the treaty established the International Joint Commission, the very first permanent, joint institution for managing fresh water along the Canada-US border. The treaty also resolved several urgent water disputes affecting the Great Lakes and laid out an order of priorities for water usage along the boundary. The Boundary Waters Treaty and the International Joint Commission have been central to all subsequent attempts to control the quality, quantity, and flow of water along the US-Canada border.

The overarching theme of this chapter is to analyze the historical context in which these unique water management mechanisms came into existence. Why were this foundational treaty and this influential commission created in 1909, rather than earlier or later? Why did they take the forms that they did? The answers lie in two very different sets of events: rapid transformations in water use around the Great Lakes and shifts in global geopolitics.

At the turn of the twentieth century, rapid industrialization, urbanization, and intensification of resource extraction around the Great Lakes provoked disputes over transboundary water use between Canada and the United States. The existing methods for resolving these disputes were extremely inefficient and, in Canada, had little legitimacy. The general public and elected officials at all levels saw the need for a better way to manage the disputes that mushroomed as more people tried to generate hydro-electricity, expand canals and harbours, and divert water to growing cities and farms. At the same time, global shifts in military and economic power were changing relations between Canada, Britain, and the United States, bringing American and Canadian policy-makers into closer conversation. Once officials from the two North American countries began to communicate more directly, they were able to produce a durable solution to the boundary waters disputes fairly rapidly: the Boundary Waters Treaty to settle the existing disputes, and the International Joint Commission to address future problems amicably.

First, a brief overview of the economic development of the Great Lakes region will demonstrate how quickly and completely land use and water use changed there during the last decades of the nineteenth century. Second, an examination of the water disputes of the later nineteenth century shows how they were closely related to this intensification of human activity and how businessmen, investors, and local officials in the Great Lakes region pressed their governments to resolve these problems, raising their concerns at the highest levels.

Then, a brief excursion into the geopolitics of the British Empire will examine the diplomatic roadblocks that prevented the proliferating water disputes in the Great Lakes from being addressed as they arose. It took time and changes in personnel before British officials in North America decided that helping the Canadians deal directly with the United States would serve their interests, but once that occurred, the negotiations for the Boundary Waters Treaty proceeded more rapidly. Direct Canadian-American communication was crucial to the process, even though most of the negotiators were motivated by a desire to prevent boundary waters issues from impinging on British-American relations.

Finally, a close analysis of the treaty-making process demonstrates that the coalescence of these two trends—local pressure for clear solutions to the new water disputes and diplomatic pressure to facilitate Anglo-American rapprochement—produced an unusually equitable treaty and a practical joint institution.

The Great Lakes Region Becoming a "Hearth of Industry"

A brief survey of the region's economic history clarifies why a set of high-profile disputes arose around the Great Lakes in the last years of the nineteenth century, in places that had been farming communities and deep wilderness only decades before. The expansion and intensification of human activity in the Great Lakes at the end of the nineteenth century was part of a global transition from a coal-and-steam energy regime to the even more energetic petroleum and natural gas regime.[1] Many areas of economic activity grew rapidly, including but not limited to: mining, logging, agriculture, fishing, petroleum refining, and the production of iron, steel, pulp and paper, electrical equipment, and chemicals. As resource extraction and industrialization accelerated throughout the region, transportation networks expanded to move raw materials to workshops and to market, spurring construction of railroads, roads, ships, harbour facilities, and communications infrastructure. This also drew regions producing raw materials into closer contact with population centres around the Great Lakes.

This wide-ranging economic development was accompanied by demographic change and urbanization; the growth of cities and towns relative to rural areas was as impressive as the rapid overall population growth. The following graphs are intended to give a quantitative sample of the changes the region underwent during this formative period. The first two graphs depict population growth in the Lake Erie and Lake Ontario watersheds, the third and fourth graphs show the extremely rapid growth of industry in a very short time. The fourth graph, showing deliveries of ore mined north of Lake Huron and Lake Superior more than doubling in ten years, hints at the massive increases in demand for raw materials and in shipping capacity around the Great Lakes.

FIGURE 2.1. American population of lower Great Lakes watershed, 1840–1920.

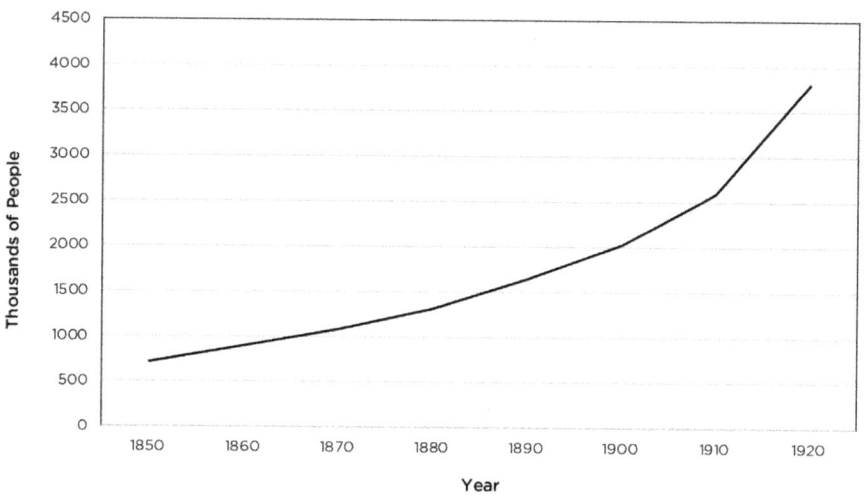

FIGURE 2.2. Demographic change in Southern Ontario, 1871–1921.

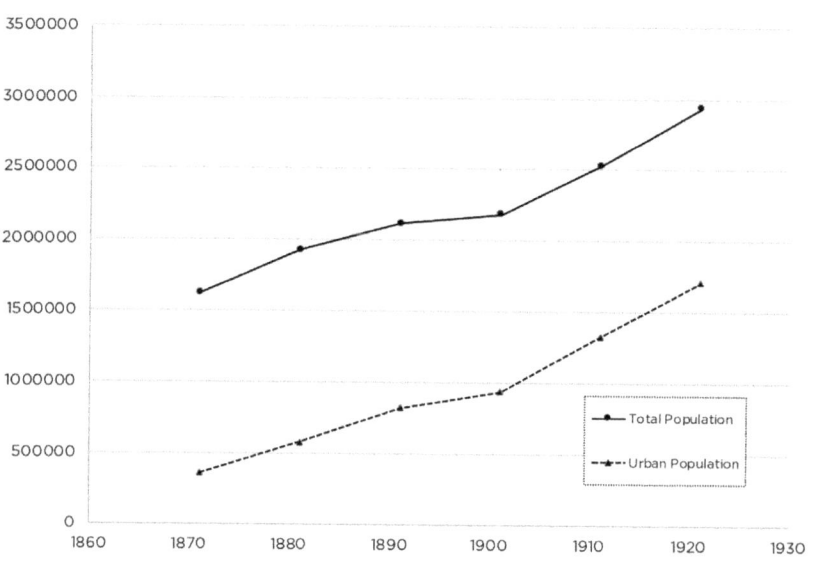

FIGURE 2.3. Value added in manufacturing, US side of Lake Erie, 1899–1914.

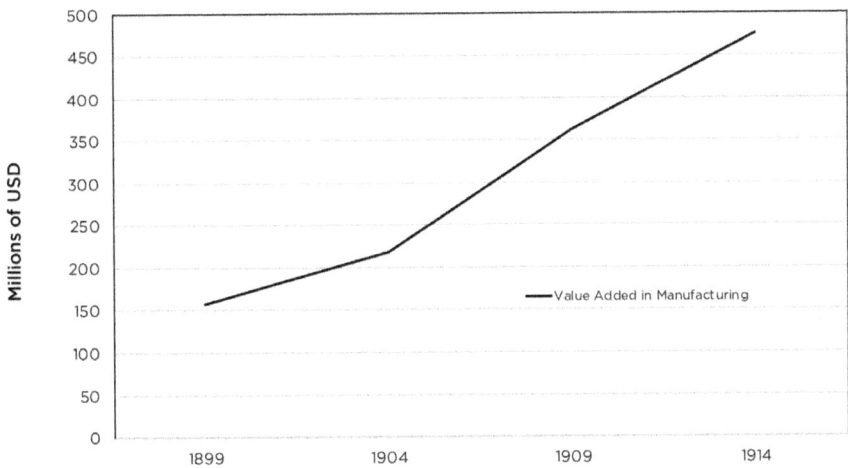

FIGURE 2.4. Iron ore received at US ports on Lake Erie, 1892–1903.

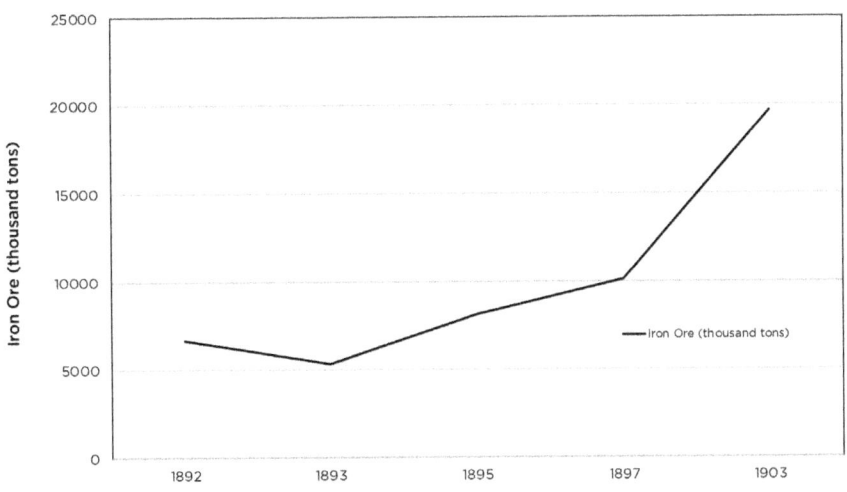

After the US Civil War ended in 1865, the most quickly growing parts of American industry slowly shifted from the Eastern Seaboard to Pennsylvania and the Midwest, and steel production became more valuable than iron production.[2] Investors from the Eastern Seaboard, including well-known Progressive-Era captains of industry like J. P. Morgan, expanded their holdings westward.[3] Oil and gas were quickly becoming the industrial fuels of choice, making the coalfields of eastern Pennsylvania less important to manufacturers.[4] Cleveland and Pittsburgh were the first western hubs of the rapidly expanding iron and steel industries, followed quickly by Chicago, Detroit, Buffalo, and a host of smaller cities.

North of the border during the same period, British and American citizens, with a few Canadians, invested heavily to get raw and partially finished materials from the Canadian hinterlands to American, Commonwealth, and international markets. In particular, American demand for iron ore drove a remarkably fast set of investments in extraction and transportation infrastructure on Lake Superior and Lake Huron.[5]

At the same time, many industries accompanied the iron and steel mills to the growing cities of the Great Lakes, where proximity to oil fields, ore deposits, and cheap hydroelectricity facilitated metallurgy and chemical refining. A Minneapolis newspaper described a steelworks being built at Sault Ste. Marie in typically glowing terms, referring to the entrepreneur heading the group of Michigan and Ontario financiers there as a "Western Cecil Rhodes."[6] Canadian-American joint ventures and "branch plants" in Canada were common ways for American industrial firms to establish themselves in Canada, circumventing the restrictive laws governing transboundary corporations at the time.[7] Food processing, paper milling, and small manufacturing grew rapidly in Southern Ontario cities like Hamilton, Windsor, and Toronto. Economic historians refer to this period as the "Laurier Boom," after Prime Minister Wilfrid Laurier (1896–1911).[8] Historians of the United States chronicle the same trends on a larger scale, though the histories of the Gilded Age and Progressive Era in the United States addressed the period's social inequities earlier and in greater detail than the Canadian histories.[9]

The aggressive resource extraction, industrialization, and growing population of these years drove massive changes in land use throughout the Great Lakes region. These included urbanization, deforestation, and the drainage of wetlands as farms expanded, and railroads, canals, harbours, roads, and bridges were installed. While these changes were lauded near-unanimously at the time, they also had drastic environmental implications and created powerful new incentives for people to own and control water resources, which gave rise to new conflicts.

How were these changes linked to politics and international diplomacy? During this period of extremely fast and comprehensive growth, new investment opportunities abounded. Americans, Canadians, and Britons with investments in water infrastructure on the Great Lakes took an understandably avid interest in political decisions affecting the waterscape. Citizens of all three countries promoted ideas for infrastructure by lobbying their governments, by publishing in the popular and professional presses, and by forming civil groups like the St. Lawrence Seaway Association, the Lake Carriers Association, the Deep Waterways Association, and the Lake Erie Fishermen's Association. The enthusiasm for new transportation infrastructure financed several expansions of the Welland Canal around Niagara Falls, enlarged the St. Lawrence River canals, and dredged the channels at Sault Ste Marie. Other well-publicized schemes of the era included pressing for a St. Lawrence seaway, an enlarged Lakes-to-Hudson River canal system, and a Lakes-to-Gulf waterway.[10] Investors were equally pleased to buy stock in companies developing the hydroelectric capacity of the rivers flowing into the lakes, near cities that would use the electricity.[11] Around the Great Lakes basin, the governments of cities, counties, states, and provinces spent tax revenue and issued bonds to build harbour facilities and to ensure predictable water levels for the convenience of shipping and hydroelectricity by dredging, damming, and draining marshes. In other parts of Canada and the United States, this was a period of rapid growth and dramatic change, but only on Lake Erie and Lake Ontario were capitalists and citizens constantly obliged to make allowance for the international boundary in order to profit from the new opportunities.

The Canadian, British, and American governments of the day were in favour of development. Occasionally, fishermen and conservationists protested the impact of all these changes on local biota, and occasionally residents complained about the sounds, smells, and dangers associated with new manufacturing and resource extraction.[12] However, by and large the local, provincial, state, national, and imperial governments in northern North America regarded it as their responsibility to facilitate these changes to foster "progress" that would make their citizens wealthier, healthier, and more numerous. Although environmental historians have begun to analyze the ecological impact of this period of intense growth, most of the existing histories accept it as uncritically as the policy-makers of the time.[13] This chapter will not detail these many, many exercises in political manoeuvring, but it will show how the quick pace of economic development contributed to water disputes and drew high-level political attention to the countries' shared hydrology. Never before had North Americans tried to share the boundary waterways while simultaneously building new industries, founding new cities, and tapping new energy sources.

Proliferating Disputes, Escalating Concern

Although no policy-makers of the day explicitly stated it, diplomatic historians recognize a direct link between the proliferation of water disputes in the late nineteenth century and the rapid industrialization and urbanization on both sides of the border at that time.[14] As water disputes began to represent an increasingly large proportion of Canada-US conflicts, the need for a straightforward way to address them became pressing. Examining the four disputes that received the most political attention will demonstrate how little institutional capacity existed to address water conflicts and why citizens of both countries were anxious to settle them.

One of the longest-lasting, most acrimonious disputes in the history of the Great Lakes began in 1900 when the Sanitary District of Chicago opened a canal to move the city's disease-laden sewage away from its drinking water supply in Lake Michigan by diverting a massive quantity of water out of the Great Lakes and into the Mississippi River watershed.[15] The diversion lowered the upper Great Lakes by approximately six inches, and because many of Lake Michigan's harbours are very shallow, this was enough to impair navigation. The Chicago Sanitary District did not consult the other jurisdictions bordering the Great Lakes before building the canal, and it refused to change its plans despite vehement private and public protests on both sides of the border.[16] When the diversion began, Canadian shipping interests were extremely upset by the lower water levels on the lakes and in the St. Lawrence River. For the next two decades, they protested to their federal, provincial, and local governments, via British diplomats in the United States, and in the popular press.[17] South of the border, various American groups protested and then filed lawsuits to shut down the canal or reduce its flow.[18] The federal War Department filed suit because the new canal created a current in Chicago Harbour that prevented ships from safely accessing the docks, which were strategic assets.[19] Only the War Department's lawsuit produced any results: in 1929, the Supreme Court ruled that the sanitary canal had to diminish its diversion.[20] However, in the years leading up to the creation of the Boundary Waters Treaty, these legal proceedings were in full swing and everyone with a financial or political interest in the Great Lakes was eager to know what kind of a precedent the Chicago Diversion would set. Would drastic, unilateral changes to the shared hydrology be permitted or prevented?

At the same time, other problems were emerging as Canadians and Americans began to alter the flow of transboundary rivers to build hydroelectric power plants on both the Rainy and Niagara Rivers. In 1904, the Minnesota Canal and Power Company proposed to construct reservoirs on Birch Lake, which was tributary to the boundary waters of the Rainy Lake/Lake of the Woods system.[21] The state, local, and provincial governments in the watershed were not empowered to decide how a power company could use a boundary tributary, and so they referred the question to the federal governments. Canada objected that the proposed dams would create lower water levels downstream, thus harming navigation and violating the 1842 Webster-Ashburton Treaty.[22] The issue remained unresolved while the company's shareholders waited impatiently. In the case of the Niagara River, unresolved questions centred on two issues: first, how to divide the rights to develop hydroelectric power at Niagara Falls, and second, whether or not to try to preserve the Falls as a "natural wonder" while developing their enormous power generation potential.[23] The topic was widely covered because the Falls were a popular tourist destination.[24] (See the chapter by Clamen and Macfarlane in this volume for a more detailed discussion of Niagara and other water quantity issues in the Great Lakes–St. Lawrence basin).

A newspaper report on the Lake Carriers Association's lobbying of Congress mentions many of the competing interests involved in these disputes, and shows how closely linked all of the various issues were:

> Cleveland, Feb. 10 [1900]. A delegation of twenty of the most prominent vessel owners on the great lakes will start for Washington Monday, accompanied by Harvey D. Goulder, the attorney of the Lake Carriers' association. The object is to induce congress to take steps towards the formation with Canada of an international commission, which shall consider all matters affecting the water outlets of the lakes. The reasons why they are active at this time are the completion of the Chicago drainage canal, the completion of the Soo [Sault Ste. Marie] power canal and the proposed building of a dam in the Niagara river.[25]

The report also shows that citizens around the lakes were publicly calling on their governments to manage their waters co-operatively.

Finally, farther west, a pressing and intractable dispute emerged over water for irrigation in the St. Mary and Milk River system between Montana and the North-West Territories (in present-day Alberta and Saskatchewan). The location's hydrology is unusual, in that Canada and the United States are both upstream and downstream users of the two rivers.[26] When American farmers and land speculators began to lobby their government to build irrigation canals to divert water from the St. Mary River to the Milk River in the 1890s, Canadians protested that such canals would deprive settlers along the St. Mary River of irrigation water.[27] When it began to seem likely that Montana would receive federal funds for the project, the Canadian federal government undertook a well-publicized survey of the two watersheds on their side of the border, as Timothy Heinmiller describes in his chapter in this volume. The implication of the survey was that if the Americans diverted the St. Mary water to the Milk River, Canadians would divert it back through another canal on their side of the Milk River. Press coverage from the period indicates that this subtext was widely understood.[28] By 1904, this pre-emptive canal, locally known as "the Spite Ditch," was completed but not in use. The American

State Department complained to the British government about it, while local boosters on both sides protested that the other country's developers were trying to ruin their settlements.[29] It was all too easy for policy-makers in Ottawa and Washington to envision the tension erupting into violent conflict.

These four disputes over sanitation, hydroelectricity, and irrigation provide ample proof of how much trouble Canadians and Americans were having as they tried, in reasonably good faith, to share the water resources along their boundary. Whether they were investors, farmers, ranchers, sanitary engineers, health officials, or fishermen, the need for co-operative water management was abundantly clear to people living in the Great Lakes region.

There were several attempts to address these emerging water problems before the negotiations for the Boundary Waters Treaty began. In general, they show how little institutional capacity existed to resolve this kind of tension during this period: there were no established procedures, no budget, no technical experts, and not much political momentum. For example, in 1895, an International Irrigation Conference attended by Canadians, Americans, and Mexicans recommended that the United States, Mexico, and Canada form a commission to settle boundary waters questions. A full year later, when the Canadian cabinet finally replied that it was willing to consider the idea, the United States did not even respond.[30] The United States and Britain created the Joint High Commission in 1898 to address that idea and a long list of other Canadian-American disputes, but it dissolved after less than two years with no results.[31]

The United States Congress raised the issue of boundary waters disputes again in June of 1902, passing a Rivers and Harbors Act, which requested the president to invite the British government to form a commission to investigate "the conditions and uses" of the Great Lakes, to report on how diversions affected navigation interests there, and to recommend improvements.[32] The widespread dissatisfaction with the Chicago Diversion was one of the reasons for this: opponents of the diversion wanted a well-researched case to bolster their lawsuits, and proponents wanted an end to the protests. President Roosevelt made the invitation, and the British Foreign Office conveyed it to Prime Minister Laurier in Ottawa, who consented nearly twelve months later, in April 1903.[33] The

International Waterways Commission (IWC) was created and the United States named its commissioners on 2 October 1903. However, the Canadian government chose to let the IWC remain incomplete that autumn, after a dispute over the Alaska boundary put a damper on its relations with Britain and the United States.

By the turn of the century, interested legislators and jurists were attempting to address the multiplying water disputes, without much success. To understand the solution that did emerge, it is important to understand the relationships between Canada, the United States, and Britain.

Canada, Britain, and the Changing Empire

As the twentieth century began, British and Canadian policy-makers were responding to the geopolitics of the day, trying to manage Canada's budding nationalist movement, the rising power of the United States in global affairs, and the roiling tensions that would ignite the First World War. While these men (for they were, without exception, men) thought little of the environmental consequences of their policies, their decisions produced the negotiations for the Boundary Waters Treaty, which has had a profound impact on some of North America's largest waterways.

Between Canada's Confederation in 1867 and the start of the First World War in 1914, most of its external affairs were disputes or trade arrangements with the United States, the messy business of sharing a huge border. Boundary disputes ranged from housekeeping details like salvage fees for shipwrecks on the Great Lakes, to much more politically and commercially important differences over the Alaskan boundary, North Atlantic fishing rights, use and delineation of boundary waters, and pelagic sealing. Prime Minister Wilfrid Laurier's governments (1896–1911), like every one of their successors and predecessors, monitored Canada's interests vis-à-vis the United States closely. Canada was a small, new, relatively poor nation with deep internal divisions, and it wanted to conduct trade and settle disputes as favourably as possible, without loss of sovereignty or national unity. Canadians during this period wanted a strong economy and they elected Laurier's Liberals repeatedly to further that agenda. Laurier famously declared that if the nineteenth century had been America's century, the twentieth century belonged to Canada. His government tried to foster domestic industry, settle the northern and western parts of the country, and promote economic development. The Great Lakes region was the centre of these development policies, and the disputes with the United States over dams and diversions were preventing them from being fully realized.

Unfortunately, these Canadian priorities were represented in London and Washington by Britons with very British goals.[34] The Dominion of Canada had become formally independent from Britain with an Act of Parliament in 1867, but its independence had some limits. In the last decades of the nineteenth century, the Dominion of Canada was internally self-governing, and was slowly becoming responsible for some aspects of its trade and defence. However, all international diplomacy was conducted by the British Foreign Service on Canada's behalf. The Foreign and Colonial Offices corresponded with the governor general of Canada, a titled British subject who communicated with the Canadian prime minister and other politicians and civil servants. Officially, Canadians did not even speak for themselves to the British government. Furthermore, the British government refused to allow its embassy in Washington to keep Canadian attachés or spokesmen.

The Foreign Office valued smooth Anglo-American relations over good deals for Canadians and its position became more and more clear as the European security environment degraded in the decades preceding the First World War. As economic and military competition intensified between Britain, the United States, and Wilhelmine Germany in the later decades of the nineteenth century, the British government felt less and less secure. During this period, Britain's foreign policy vis-à-vis the United States shifted toward determined rapprochement. The British government saw alliances as a cheap way to protect its increasingly expensive empire and the increasingly vulnerable British Isles, and hoped that a sturdy Anglo-American friendship would remove the need to provide for defence against the United States and perhaps ensure help in the case of a Continental war or German invasion. In the interests of warmer relations, the British government made a number of conciliatory gestures toward the United States between 1870 and 1905. These included settling naval claims from the American Civil War, yielding to US preferences in a South American border dispute, supporting the Americans in the

Spanish-American War (1898), and giving the United States sole control over the Panama Canal in 1901 (instead of sharing control with Britain as agreed in an earlier treaty). None of these gestures impinged heavily on Canada.

However, the same considerations of imperial and domestic defence that drove the British to cultivate the United States also influenced intra-imperial relations. As the cost of maintaining the British Empire grew and the European security environment became more volatile, British and Canadian imperialists argued for a more centralized empire and more Canadian military spending. Some argued that centralization and joint defence would give the Dominions more influence in British foreign policy, while others simply hoped that they would make the empire safer. Prime Minister Lord Salisbury's governments (1885–6, 1886–92, 1895–1902) pressed for centralization and for Canada and the other Dominions to develop the military capacity to support Britain and defend themselves. The Canadian militia system was somewhat revised between the Boer War and the First World War, and British naval commitments on the Pacific and Atlantic coasts of Canada were greatly reduced during this period.

The official Canadian response to British requests for help with imperial defence was wary because Prime Minister Wilfrid Laurier knew that most French Canadians and some English Canadians were nationalists, opposed to greater imperial unity. After an intense debate, Canada sent a small number of volunteers to the second Boer War (1899–1902) in South Africa. The same politically risky balancing act was required when the colonial secretary asked Laurier to form a navy. Canada had no use for a navy and had many more pressing expenses, but the question was hotly contested. For the most part, Prime Minister Laurier resisted London's ongoing pressure, maintaining what one journalist of the time called "the policy of the 'everlasting no.' "[35] The impracticality of having one diplomatic service represent two diverging sets of interests became increasingly obvious, colouring Canadian and British attitudes throughout the negotiation of the Boundary Waters Treaty.

The Young American Empire

American foreign policy in the late nineteenth century was much less conflicted. After the American Civil War (1861–5), the United States conducted its international affairs with increasing confidence. The Monroe Doctrine became a central tenet of American foreign policy, asserting the supremacy of American over European interests in the Western Hemisphere. As the nineteenth century ended, the United States was in fine fettle, with a trade surplus, growing GDP, and more activist foreign policies.[36] Under Presidents Harrison (1889–93) and Cleveland (1885–9, 1894–7), the United States took a proprietary interest in Nicaragua, Hawaii, Brazil, Venezuela, and Cuba. In 1898, President McKinley fought and won the Spanish-American War, which was a relatively uncomplicated victory for the country, compared to the divisions engendered by the American Civil War.

With victory over Spain came responsibility for the spoils of war: the United States took over the Spanish overseas colonies of Puerto Rico, Guam, Cuba, and the Philippines. These colonial acquisitions were politically incongruous for the United States, which prided itself on its rebellious origin and pointedly eschewed overseas commitments.[37] President McKinley and his vice-president, Theodore Roosevelt, were determined to be enlightened imperialists, bringing civilization and liberty to the Caribbean and Pacific islands and independence to Cuba. In 1899, President McKinley asked Elihu Root, a prominent New York lawyer and Republican with no military experience, to administer the new conquests.[38] Serving as secretary of war from 1899 until 1904, and as secretary of state from 1904 to 1909, Root was a key figure in all negotiations with Canada and Britain.

The Crucial Lessons of the Alaska Boundary Dispute

One short answer to the question, "Why were the Boundary Waters Treaty and the International Joint Commission created in 1909?" could be, "Because the Alaska Boundary Award occurred in 1903." The political fallout from the award produced important changes in British policy, which in turn dictated the conditions for the negotiation of the Boundary Waters Treaty three years later. Many of the same people played important roles in both processes. Having outlined the broad strokes of American, British, and Canadian relations at the turn of the twentieth century, a close look at the Alaska Boundary Award illustrates how these relationships interacted to obstruct conflict resolution in North America.

The Alaska boundary dispute was longstanding: the exact Canadian-American border had never been satisfactorily delineated after the American purchase of Alaska from the Russian government in 1867. (Alaska became an official territory in 1912 and a state in 1959.) This ambiguity did not matter to either country until a gold rush erupted near the border between the purchased land of Alaska and the Canadian Yukon Territory in the 1890s. Suddenly, access to the ports in the Alaska Panhandle became valuable and both Prime Minister Laurier and the new American president, Theodore Roosevelt, claimed them. Since the American interpretation of the boundary had "a strong case arising out of use and occupation," Roosevelt saw no reason to be tactful.[39] Encouraged by prosperity and conscious of anti-American sentiment among Canadians, Laurier also refused to compromise.[40] There are useful parallels between the gold rush and the rapid growth of the Great Lakes region that explain this dispute's political significance. The United States and Canada associated national interest with their citizens' gold mining ventures, and they tried to protect them in the same way that they championed their people over questions of power generation and water diversion along the border.

Attempts to negotiate failed, and in 1903 the United States, Britain, and Canada agreed to refer the Alaska boundary dispute to a six-member panel of arbitration with three Americans, two Canadians, and one Briton. The British assured Laurier that the American panelists would be impartial, but in fact they were all personally loyal to Roosevelt, and two were well known for their anti-British rhetoric.[41] The third appointee was Elihu Root, who was a well-respected jurist but also the serving secretary of war. Laurier believed that the Americans and the British were both pushing him to agree to an unfair arbitration, while the British accepted the biased American appointments because they were more interested in maintaining good Anglo-American relations than in the outcome of the dispute.[42]

On 20 October 1903, the British panelist, Lord Alverstone, sided with the three American panelists against the Canadians, and the Alaska Boundary Tribunal ruled in favour of the United States. The British government approved the verdict and exchanged ratifications with the United States, not bothering to formally notify Laurier about the decision until after the fact.⁴³ This cavalier treatment did at least as much damage to British-Canadian relations as the actual decision. The detrimental effect of the Alaska boundary dispute on Canadian-American and Canadian-British relations should not be underestimated. The Canadian members of the tribunal refused to sign the decision and wrote a scathing public letter explaining their dissent. The Canadian Parliament, press, and general public were incensed by what they saw as Britain's betrayal, and Prime Minister Laurier was as angry as the rest.⁴⁴ British indifference deprived Canadians of their only way to defend their interests with respect to the United States, and the Alaska award convinced Laurier that he needed to change the way Canadian-American relations were conducted.⁴⁵ However, rather than start an immediate foreign policy revolution, with all its attendant political risks, he awaited developments. His first biographer noted,

> Nothing was more foreign to Sir Wilfrid's ruling bias than to urge any policy on general and theoretical grounds; not until a concrete issue arose would the demand for wider powers be renewed. When the occasion did arise, in the Waterways treaty with the United States . . . Canada's control over foreign relations was to be quietly, un-dogmatically but surely and steadily advanced.⁴⁶

Given Canada's relative weakness and the political difficulties inherent in any change of the diplomatic status quo, this was a practical choice.

The Alaska boundary dispute forced the British to choose between Canada and the United States, and although the choice was not difficult, the cost was high: the overwhelming Canadian recriminations seemed likely to impede imperial defence planning. The following year, determined not to repeat the episode, the Colonial Office refused to consider addressing a Canadian-American dispute directly, "[because] we should get no thanks for taking the initiative."[47] More constructively, the Colonial and Foreign Offices also decided to consult Canada before taking any action in matters involving Canadian interests in the future.[48] After the debacle of 1903, Canada and Britain came to the same conclusion: the next North American dispute had to be handled very differently. This evolution was not immediately apparent, but during the negotiation of the Boundary Waters Treaty, it gradually became clear that Britain was giving Canada much more control over its relationships.

The Alaska boundary dispute did not have nearly as much of an effect on the United States. The United States government was appreciative of Britain's sustained interest in good relations, while their view of Canada as a weak if vocal neighbour was left unchanged.[49]

Exploratory Discussions and the Decision to Focus on Boundary Waters

Between 1905 and 1910, policy-makers established a new Canada-Britain-US working relationship, concluded a set of treaties based on North American collaboration, and created the International Joint Commission, an institution based on direct Canada-US communication. Given the furor over Alaska, this rather abrupt reversal demands explanation. What changed, and why?

First, as key personnel in British government posts in North America changed, the new appointees approached Canada-US issues differently than their predecessors had done, reflecting the changing balance of their empire's interests in North America and the growing urgency of Britain's need for allies in a possible war with Germany. The first prominent British official to employ the new, hands-off approach was Earl Grey, who arrived in Ottawa in 1904 to replace his brother-in-law as the governor general of Canada.[50] As governor general, Albert Grey handled all of Canada's communications with the United States and Britain. Letters and telegrams came directly to his office, and he either answered them or forwarded them to Prime Minister Laurier, who acted as his own foreign minister. Many governors general simply passed their correspondence along, but Earl Grey took a more involved attitude. One historian characterized him as "constitutionally incapable of playing the role of figurehead."⁵¹ Grey was an ardent imperialist with little interest in defending Canadian interests for their own sake. However, he was creative enough to realize that British-American harmony required sound British-Canadian and Canadian-American relationships, and he used his post to improve them.⁵²

As soon as he arrived, Grey began to lobby Prime Minister Laurier to improve Canadian-American relations. First, he asked the prime minister to appoint commissioners to the International Waterways Commission, which had been formally set up two years previously and then left in abeyance after the Alaskan controversy. After a few months, Laurier did as Grey asked, and for the first time, the political and economic concerns of the Great Lakes region and the global anxieties of the British Empire began to interact vis-à-vis boundary waters. The commission had a very limited mandate, but its reports laid the groundwork for the actual Boundary Waters Treaty.

Although not empowered to take concrete action, the IWC's meetings were the first mechanism by which the concerns of interest groups from the Great Lakes reached the briefing books and memos of the people who handled foreign policy for the United States, Britain, and Canada. Their ideas reached a rarified audience of cabinet-level officials and their staffs, and many later became policy. (For a detailed description of the IWC's work and an analysis of how it exemplified cultural trends such as progressivism and conservationism, see David Whorley's chapter in this volume.)

The career of the IWC's Canadian chairman, George Gibbons, is an excellent example of the pressure that Canadians living around the Great Lakes brought to bear on their prime minister and Parliament during the late nineteenth and early twentieth centuries. Gibbons was a commercial lawyer and businessman from the agricultural town of London, Ontario. In addition to his legal practice, he was founder and president of the London and Western Trusts Company, the president of the City Gas Company of London, and director of the London Life Insurance Company. Though never elected, he was a well-known Liberal organizer and fundraiser, recognized in his day as a privileged and capable professional man.⁵³ Gibbons and his peers used their political connections and business "pull" to raise their concerns about the Chicago Diversion, the need for a good power-sharing deal at Niagara, and the federal government's duty to safeguard Canadian interests. (Frank Ettawageshik and Emma Norman's chapter in this volume analyzes the evolution of First Nations and Native American involvement with the International Joint Commission, and illuminates how some Great Lakes residents have been able to influence transboundary water policy over the course of the twentieth century while others have not.)

After activating the IWC, governor general Grey began to make encouraging official gestures to the United States. He visited New York in March 1906 and invited the secretary of state, Elihu Root, to Ottawa—events generally cited by diplomatic historians as the first public signs of a more positive tone in Canadian-American relations after the Alaskan controversy. They were certainly symbolic, but the launch of the IWC was just as public and much more significant in the long run.

While diplomatic historians have described the origins of the Boundary Waters Treaty and the actual treaty-making process in great detail, they have rarely devoted much time to examining the domestic or local factors that influenced the leaders of the United States or Canada. Much of the admirably detailed secondary literature was written by Canadian historians and ex-diplomats who placed the treaty in the context of that industrious period of British/Canadian-American relations.[54] This is unsurprising, given its importance to Canadian foreign policy and the fact that the treaties made in the first decade of the twentieth century between the United States and Britain regarding Canada were catalysts for reorganization in Ottawa. Though the period was far from uneventful for American diplomats, it has not drawn the same scholarly attention because the treaty did not reshape the State Department in any fundamental way. This chapter attempts to connect those carefully drawn accounts of treaty drafts and negotiations to their larger motivations. In particular, it asks, Why did President Roosevelt and Prime Minister Laurier regard the boundary waters disputes as important? It also aims to ground analysis of the policies in the material reality of the history of the Great Lakes, to connect the reader to the rapidly industrializing, densely settled places where residents were simultaneously creating and reacting to massive environmental changes, and discussing how best to cope with them together.

The Beginnings of Direct Communication

Governor General Grey also began to correspond directly with Secretary Root about "cleaning the slate," as he phrased it. Their exchange produced a list of Canadian-American disputes that the secretary of state presented to the British ambassador in Washington on 3 May 1906. It was the first comprehensive catalogue of disagreements since the Joint High Commission had adjourned in 1898.[55] The list had sixteen items, of which half were related to marine and freshwater management, and four to the Great Lakes.[56] The ambassador sent Root's list to Canada for comment through official diplomatic channels. The fate of that list, "[an] important document, which was destined to be the touchstone of Canadian-American diplomacy for the next five years," was a perfect illustration of the impractical arrangements that hindered the Canadian-American working relationship.[57] It took *seven months* for the list to go from Washington to the Foreign Office, and thence to the Colonial Office, Governor General Grey, Prime Minister Laurier, and for Laurier's unencouraging reply to reach Secretary Root. (At this time, a privately posted letter took less than a week to go between the capitals.) After seeing the need for direct communication so vividly demonstrated, Governor General Grey asked the Foreign Office to add a Canadian attaché to Britain's Washington embassy.[58] The idea was rejected, but Grey began to write directly to the State Department, and Britain's government seems to have been pragmatic enough to wink at this bending of the rules.

Communication was also hindered by the British ambassador to Washington, Sir Mortimer Durand, who either did not see or did not choose to act upon the coalescence of Canadian and British interests that Grey perceived. In April 1906, President Roosevelt wrote to his own ambassador in London that "[Durand] seems to have a brain of about eight-guinea-pig power. Why, under Heaven the English keep him here I do not know."[59] Roosevelt and his cabinet took no interest in Durand, and the Boundary Waters Treaty did not become possible until his more sympathetic successor arrived the following year. In January 1907, Lord James Bryce took over as the British ambassador. He was unusually well qualified for his post because he had travelled widely in the United States, had published a book about the country, and had a personal network in Washington that included Elihu Root and other members of the foreign-policy elite.[60] As he became more familiar with his embassy, Bryce realized that much of its business was focused purely on Canadian-American interaction. He held the same view of Canadian-American relations as Grey: that the resolution of their local, "parochial" differences would be an indirect way to improve British-American relations and, like Grey, corresponded directly with Ottawa and received no complaints from London about it. Their pragmatic attitude was legitimated by, and is indicative of, larger changes of opinion within the British press, policy elite, and electorate.

In 1907, there came a particularly concrete example of these shifting British policies: Root and Bryce both visited Ottawa at Earl Grey's invitation, to meet Prime Minister Laurier and to talk informally about US-Canada disputes. The Foreign Office's instructions to the governor general demonstrate its new wish to facilitate, rather than direct, Canadian-American dialogue: Grey was ordered to avoid saying or doing anything "which would imply the intervention of His Majesty's government in the discussion."[61] It was very rare for cabinet-level American officials to go to Ottawa, and the press credited Bryce with being the first British ambassador to visit Ottawa in an official capacity.[62] These exchanges were also a clear demonstration of the pressures that Canadians and Americans had brought to bear upon Roosevelt and Laurier. Without significant domestic incentive, it is unlikely that their governments or the British government would have made these unusual efforts. By 1907, then, the bitterness of the Alaskan controversy had dissipated, the list of North American disputes was clear, and all three parties knew each other's positions.

Setting an Agenda

Both the form and substance of the Boundary Waters Treaty are the product of an extended period of negotiations in which Canadian, British, and American officials all had vital roles. The speed of the negotiations and the detailed attention paid to them by the secretary of state and the Canadian prime minister show how seriously both countries regarded the boundary waters issues. To appreciate Canada's effort in achieving this efficient result, it is essential to understand just how little bureaucratic capacity the Dominion had. Although official correspondence moved more quickly under Bryce and Grey, no one in Canada kept a precise record of the dialogue because there was no filing system. Prime Minister Laurier acted as his own foreign minister, but the additional work was onerous, and when he did not respond promptly to letters or cables, negotiations had to wait. Canadian public servants noticed this deficiency and a senior bureaucrat, Joseph Pope, had been arguing for the creation of a department of external affairs since 1900.

After visiting Ottawa in 1907, Ambassador Bryce argued that it would be best to start with the most easily resolved items. He hoped that removing the "lesser irritants" would "sweeten and soften the feeling between the two countries" before tackling the more controversial problems.[63] With that plan in mind, Bryce and Grey tried to decide which of the most pressing disputes would be the easiest to resolve: the North Atlantic fisheries, boundary waters, or pelagic sealing disputes? Of the three, boundary waters seemed to offer the best chance of success. The North Atlantic fisheries dispute was very old and convoluted, and it involved Britain and the colony of Newfoundland as well as the United States. The pelagic sealing dispute was complicated by intricate questions of compensation for Canadian sealers. Conversely, the boundary waters disputes were relatively new and bilateral rather than tri- or quadrilateral. Boundary waters also seemed attractive because the IWC's recommendations on the subject were recent and practical.

In May 1907, the Canadian, British, and American governments asked the heads of the International Waterways Commission's two sections, Canadian George Gibbons and American George Clinton, to draw up a draft boundary waters treaty (see Appendix 2). The normal procedure for the period would have been for the British Embassy in Washington to draft it, but Gibbons and Clinton were a safe bet to test a new approach. They had been working together as co-chairs of the IWC for three years, they were intimately familiar with the relevant disputes, and both had legal training. In addition, George Gibbons was devoted to the topic as a resident of the region most affected, as a member of Laurier's Liberal Party, and as a Canadian nationalist. Given the public pressure that Laurier faced to get a good deal after the Alaska award, those loyalties made Gibbons a better representative than any Englishman. The fact that a Canadian and an American produced the first blueprint of a treaty for settling boundary waters issues is a testament to the change in official thinking after 1903.

Comparing Drafts, Comparing Objections

With the presentation of the first Clinton-Gibbons draft in September 1908, the negotiation of the Boundary Waters Treaty began in earnest. Bryce kept the British government apprised, but the dealings were essentially American-Canadian, rather than trilateral. The Clinton-Gibbons draft stipulated freedom of navigation for all citizens throughout the Great Lakes and St. Lawrence system, specifically prohibited the diversion of boundary waters except for domestic sanitation or navigation canals, and prohibited diversions or obstructions of boundary waters that would cause injury to public or private interests in the other country. This last provision was a direct response to the furor over whether or not the Sanitary District of Chicago could legally divert so much water that it affected shipping. It aimed to reassure people around the Great Lakes that their livelihoods and investments would be insulated from such drastic, unilateral changes in the future. According to Gibbons and Clinton's draft, where diversion would not injure navigation, public interests, or private interests, each country was entitled to half of the water in streams crossing the boundary.[64] This clause was a crucial clarification for hydroelectric power companies and for the municipalities and industries that wanted to buy electricity.

Analyzing the two sides' initial objections to the draft treaty provides a picture of how lawmakers regarded environmental management and reflects the concerns of local stakeholder groups around the Great Lakes. For the American State Department, the central problem was whether and how much Americans' freedom of action should be constrained, while the Canadians sought clear guidelines for management, to offset their comparative poverty and military weakness.

The State Department's lawyers argued that the transboundary commission outlined in the treaty would compromise private citizens' control of their property, states' control of their territory vis-à-vis the federal government and foreign countries, and the nation's autonomy.[65] The lingering rancour and domestic lawsuits over the Chicago Diversion figured prominently in their analysis. They also objected that the guidelines for commissioners were inadequate, while Secretary Root was apparently reluctant to commit to a definite course of action in the relatively young policy area of hydroelectricity.[66] Finally, Root did not want to have a single set of water management principles for every case, which was precisely what George Gibbons and the Canadian government did want.

The Canadians believed that their citizens would only be treated equitably in disputes with Americans if the treaty laid out such clear rules that the imbalance of power would not be a factor. George Gibbons and Prime Minister Laurier agreed that "there is only one way in which we will get fair play . . . that is by a permanent joint Commission."[67] Laurier was concerned that he would be accused of selling his country to the Americans if the final treaty was not clearly beneficial to Canada. In addition, Laurier wanted the new treaty to address the detrimental effect of the Chicago canal on water levels in the Great Lakes, as well as the other site-specific disputes. Finessing Canada's determination to secure equal treatment despite the power imbalance was a consistently difficult part of the negotiations.

In late winter 1908, the Americans proposed creating a Joint Commission of Inquiry that would do nothing more than provide reports and recommendations.[68] Without the judicial and arbitral functions that the Clinton-Gibbons draft envisioned, the Commission of Inquiry posed no threats to sovereignty, and Anderson and Root thought it would be relatively simple to get it through the Senate. Laurier rejected the proposal and sent Gibbons to Washington to negotiate. The Canadian lawyer convinced Secretary Root to agree that management principles were a good idea, though Root insisted that the Senate would never accept them. In return for this concession, Gibbons reported to Laurier that he "urged the view that . . . we were not very particular what the principles were as long as they were uniformly applied."[69] Judging from his correspondence with Laurier, Gibbons was quite ready to accommodate the American preference for territorial sovereignty, best exemplified by the extreme Harmon Doctrine applied to the US-Mexican border. (Attorney General Harmon had argued in 1906 that because the United States had sovereignty over the Rio Grande within its own territory, no international law could impose an obligation upon the United States to share the water with Mexico.[70]) The geography of the Canada-US border, where the two countries are both upstream and downstream water users, as well as joint tenants of watersheds bisected by the boundary, may have made it easier to contemplate this solution. The chapter in this volume by Hall, Tarlock, and Valiante explores whether the Boundary Waters Treaty can be presented as a compromise between two different self-interested legal views—absolute territorial integrity (Canada) as opposed to absolute territorial sovereignty (US)—but the Canadian negotiators do not appear to have been committed to either. Instead, Gibbons and Laurier were determined to achieve a treaty that would protect Canadian interests in the same way and to the same extent as it did American interests. During their meetings early in 1908, Root and Gibbons did not come to any conclusions, and the treaty project seemed stalled. Policy-makers in both countries regarded future water disputes as a near-certainty, but disagreed about the best way to plan for them.

Persistence and Progress

Some of the disputes could not wait. In the spring of 1908, rather than abandon their negotiations, as they had done in earlier years, the Canadian and US governments demonstrated their new commitment to dispute resolution and the urgency of the situation by moving forward on several other fronts. After two weeks of intensive consultation in February, they agreed to assign two people to confer on the St. Mary and Milk River irrigation dispute.[71] They also made progress on the North Atlantic fisheries dispute, concluded two minor boundary-delineation treaties, and signed the Inland Fisheries Treaty, hoping to prevent a repetition of the bitter disputes that had troubled the North Atlantic by creating a common understanding about freshwater fishing. Under the Inland Fisheries Treaty, the United States and Canada agreed to set up an International Fisheries Commission to draft a set of "uniform and common regulations for the protection and preservation of the food fishes of the boundary waters" within six months. The broad scope and short duration of the commissioners' assignment prevented them from accomplishing much, and the treaty was abandoned, unratified, in 1914, but it did contribute to better Canadian-American and Anglo-American relations in 1908.

Encouraged by the signature of the new treaties and spurred by the pressing disputes, George Gibbons joined Ambassador Bryce in Washington in late spring 1908 to urge Root to settle all remaining boundary waters issues with a single treaty. Given the British government's repeated refusals to hire an actual Canadian attaché, Gibbons's recurring presence there is striking. Bryce valued his work and the Foreign Office in London either tolerated or ignored the innovation.[72] Ambassador Bryce's chargé d'affaires also felt that American prejudices favoured Canada, writing that, "there is ever yet a hereditary and traditional desire to give the [British] lion's ear a tweak or his tail a little twist."[73] The perceived willingness of the Americans to deal more generously with a weak neighbour than with a strong empire may seem odd, but it appears in the archival record regularly. The attitude may be related to how boundary waters negotiations fit into Elihu Root's larger policy of strengthening the United States' relations with countries in the Western Hemisphere. During his tenure, he cultivated relationships in Central and South America and promoted the Pan-American Union as a tool for good relations in the Western Hemisphere. The Roosevelt administration seems to have regarded Canada more warmly as a neighbour in the New World rather than as a part of a European empire.

In any case, the British Embassy believed that the water disputes and the need for an Anglo-American alliance were pressing enough to disregard protocol, and George Gibbons went back to Washington.[74] Over the course of three days, he convinced the State Department to accept a treaty with explicitly stated principles for water use and a permanent commission to enforce them. Furthermore, Root agreed that one of his most valued assistants, Chandler Anderson, would work with Gibbons to write another draft treaty. These coups made Gibbons's reputation as a negotiator.[75] The assignment of Anderson elevated the treaty to a higher level of official attention, and the June discussions started a definitive new set of talks.

The Final Draft and Informal Arrangements

Gibbons and Anderson achieved a draft by mid-autumn.[76] It was, in general terms and in most details, the Boundary Waters Treaty. It bore a much closer resemblance to the Clinton-Gibbons draft treaty than to the Root-Anderson proposal, with clearly defined management precepts, and a decisive role for a permanent international institution, the International Joint Commission.

In their draft, transboundary waters (which flowed across the boundary or were tributary to boundary waters) stayed under national jurisdiction, but in article ii, citizens of the United States and Canada were granted the right to claim damages for injury caused by water use in the other country.[77] The negotiators fully expected that companies and individuals would manage their conflicts by suing each other under this clause, sparing the United States, Britain, and Canada from having to adjudicate between them. The draft treaty also set out an order of precedence for the use of boundary waters: domestic and sanitary uses were listed as the first, most important use, for the benefit of waterside communities. Navigation was the second priority because it seemed, "more important to the general welfare of the country" than hydroelectric power and irrigation. Hydroelectricity and irrigation came last because, Anderson explained, "[they] benefit only a very limited number."[78] The order of precedence was intended to benefit the greatest possible number of people, so as to secure maximum political support for the treaty.

Gibbons and Anderson also included a general arbitration clause, which empowers the International Joint Commission to act as an arbitrator between Canada and the United States on any topic, if both countries request it. The United States and Britain had concluded an arbitration agreement in 1908 that applied to Canada through Britain, but this arbitration mechanism was exclusive to Canada and the United States. From a British standpoint, this reduced the chances of another acrimonious tribunal like Alaska, and for North Americans, it provided a more direct way to address grievances and conflicts. Altogether, these clauses and tools represent a serious effort to address the institutional gap that had become so apparent as Americans and Canadians intensified their impact on the Great Lakes basin and other boundary waters.

Since they had successfully negotiated a broad treaty structure, Laurier and Root told Gibbons and Anderson to move on to the more difficult task of settling the existing water disputes. In the end, the disputes about the Chicago Diversion and the Rainy River were addressed informally and are not mentioned in the final Boundary Waters Treaty. Because the American government was suing the Chicago Sanitary District, and because the State Department believed that putting a clause about the Chicago Diversion into the treaty would prevent its ratification and further politicize the contentious lawsuit, the Canadians agreed to leave diversions from Lake Michigan out of the treaty.[79] In return for this concession, Secretary Root proposed to accept a smaller share of the water at the Niagara River, which was carefully allocated under article v of the Boundary Waters Treaty, thus disposing of another site-specific dispute.[80]

Anderson and Gibbons also made a quiet deal to solve the Rainy River dispute. The central question was whether the United States could legally grant the Minnesota Power Company's request to divert water from the tributary of a boundary river. Under the Webster-Ashburton Treaty of 1842, the river was to be "free and open" to all citizens of both countries for navigation, and the proposed power dam would interfere with that navigation. In return for Canada giving up its objections to the dam, Gibbons got article ii, the reciprocal damages clause.[81] He apparently decided that the Rainy River was an acceptable loss, arguing that the new treaty would do a better job of protecting Canadian interests in diversion disagreements than Webster-Ashburton.

The last point to settle was the St. Mary and Milk Rivers, where rival canal-builders had nearly come to blows over scarce irrigation water. Article vi of the Boundary Waters Treaty sets out a highly technical management system for the St. Mary and Milk Rivers and their tributaries in Montana, Alberta, and Saskatchewan. The clause stipulated that the two rivers "were to be treated as one and the total available water was to be divided equally over all but not in respect to each stream."[82] A Canadian and an American were to be assigned to measure and apportion the available water for each growing season. The accredited officers, as they are known, have been a linchpin of the region's agriculture ever since. The annual determinations are often contentious, and may be expected to become more volatile as climate change proceeds, but a century of painstaking calculations kept these two watersheds from being a worse problem. Anderson and Gibbons submitted their final draft to Secretary Root and Prime Minister Laurier on 3 December 1908.

The Home Stretch: Formal Acceptance and Ratification

With the treaty drafted and all of the site-specific disputes resolved, the formal acceptance processes could begin in each country. Laurier approved the treaty draft in January 1909 before sending it to the British Foreign Office, where administrative staff changed the language of the treaty to reflect Canada's formal, subordinate diplomatic relationship with Britain.[83] For example, every reference to "the Government of Canada," was replaced with "the High Contracting Party" (i.e., Great Britain).[84] The British government had no interest in altering the terms of the treaty, but neither did it have any intention of ceding its imperial prerogatives. The new Canada-US co-operation that had grown so quickly between 1906 and 1909 was strictly operational, not official, but it was just as crucial to transboundary environmental management as the treaty itself. That collaboration, coupled with local pressure for a reliable regulatory environment around the rapidly developing Great Lakes and British anxiety for an American rapprochement, were the driving forces behind the Boundary Waters Treaty.

After the treaty text was approved, British officials settled down to await the outcome of the North American ratification processes. In the United States, the Senate Foreign Affairs Committee and then the rest of the chamber had to vote in favour of the treaty, and in the Canadian-British case, it meant convincing Prime Minister Laurier to recommend ratification to Westminster.

Elihu Root was correct when he predicted that the Senate would oppose the Boundary Waters Treaty. Powerful constituents were paying close attention and the Senate Foreign Relations Committee raised a number of objections to the treaty that echoed the complaints of the executive branch: basically, they saw the treaty as a threat to states' rights and national sovereignty.[85] However, the most inconvenient objection was raised by Senator Smith of Michigan, whose constituency included several companies invested in hydroelectric power generation along the boundary. He argued that the principle of equal division of boundary waters interfered with the proprietary rights of Michigan citizens in the St. Mary's River at Sault Ste. Marie, where the river's flow was greater on the American side than the Canadian side. On February 15, Smith proposed a "rider," or amendment to the treaty, stating that,

> Nothing in this treaty shall be construed as affecting, or changing, any existing territorial or riparian rights in the water, or right of the owners of the lands under, on either side of the international boundary . . . [and] that nothing in the treaty shall be construed to interfere with the drainage of wet swamp and overflowed lands into streams flowing into boundary waters.[86]

This amendment was a blatant effort to safeguard local interests. Part of the land along the St. Mary's River at Sault Ste. Marie was shortly to be expropriated by the US government for a shipping channel, and the owners of the plot hoped that they would get a better price for it if their riparian rights were unchanged.[87] Smith's rider is an excellent example of how much the advancing development of hydroelectricity, the accelerating transformation of shorelines and wetlands, and expectation of greater development around the Great Lakes was changing transboundary management at this time. As steam-, coal-, and gas-powered engineering equipment made it possible to harness rivers more cheaply and easily, the boundary streams in the already industrialized Great Lakes were becoming even more valuable.

As the committee discussed the treaty and proposed amendment, it attracted a lot of media interest. Under the headline "Two Senators Almost Come to Blows," one newspaper noted that the debate "was the liveliest tilt seen in the Senate in many days."[88] Debate over Smith's amendment was as heated in Ottawa as in Washington.[89] The Senate leaked the text of the Boundary Waters Treaty, and Canadian newspapers picked it up. Laurier faced loud demands for a debate in the House of Parliament, but, as the Colonial Office unhelpfully reminded him, the Canadian legislators were prohibited from debating the treaty until it was officially released.

Wealthy, well-connected people expected to make money by altering the hydrology of the boundary waters, and the public debate around the treaty was largely about whose interests would be helped or hurt. In this context, the principles of usage as set out in the treaty (domestic and sanitary use, then navigation, then hydroelectricity and irrigation) had unprecedented weight. Secretary Root wrote to Laurier and Gibbons several times during the debate to reassure them, explaining that despite the amendment, "I am perfectly satisfied that the rights of Canada will be exactly the same. . . . The very large private interests involved are apparently afraid of some occult meaning and effect of any words they don't devise themselves."[90] However, Canadians were concerned about being bullied out of their share of the water by British indifference or American strength.[91]

Despite Root's best efforts to prevent it, the Senate Foreign Relations Committee approved the treaty with Smith's amendment. It passed the Senate in late February 1909. After this ratification, the treaty could not be substantially altered. The British government waited to submit the treaty to Parliament until Laurier gave his approval. To convince the Canadian prime minister that the Smith rider did not hurt his country's interests, proponents of the treaty presented him with favourable opinions from a variety of policy-makers, including the US attorney general, the Canadian justice minister and the minister of public works, Gibbons, Bryce, Grey, the chief astronomer, and all six IWC commissioners.

Despite this litany of affirmation, Laurier studied the treaty for a full year. He engaged a private engineer for an outside opinion and corresponded with Canadian companies that expected to profit from the boundary waters.[92] While the Boundary Waters Treaty awaited ratification, the disputes it was designed to settle remained unresolved.[93] The urgency of the existing problems and the likelihood of their multiplication may have helped push Laurier to a decision. He finally approved the Boundary Waters Treaty, which was ratified in London and then signed into action on 13 May 1910 in Washington, DC.

Conclusion

The old saying that "an ounce of prevention is worth a pound of cure" seems particularly apt in the context of the Boundary Waters Treaty. After thirty years of failed attempts to cure Canadian-American disputes, the treaty was a labouriously built remedy that finally included a measure of prevention in the International Joint Commission. Under its terms, the St.

Mary–Milk and Niagara disputes were resolved, while the tensions over development on the Rainy River and the Chicago Diversion were defused informally during the negotiation process.

In the aftermath of the Alaska Boundary Award of 1903, British policy-makers and the Canadian government recognized that Britain could no longer conduct Canada's political relations with the United States without encountering serious conflicts of interest. While the governments of the United States, Britain, and Canada began to realize the need to change their style of diplomacy, North Americans were looking for ways to resolve their proliferating boundary waters disputes.

Between 1906 and 1910, the direct Canada-US negotiation process and the practically bilateral treaty that it produced improved relations between Canada and Britain, Canada and the United States, and Britain and the United States. All three governments were encouraged by the creation of the International Joint Commission to look after a policy area that was prone to disputes. Referring to the International Joint Commission's potential role as an arbitration mechanism, Elihu Root, writing to George Gibbons in 1910, remarked that "the public has no adequate conception of the tremendous scope and importance of the thing which has been done as a preventative of controversy in the future."[94]

In retrospect, it is ironic that policy-makers in all three countries were so excited by the possibilities inherent in the International Joint Commission's expandable mandate. Politicians and early historians of Canadian-American affairs hoped that the article x arbitration clause would make the new commission into a "miniature Hague Tribunal," where Canada-US disputes could be solved judicially.[95] In fact, the arbitration clause has never been used. Legal and institutional historians of the Boundary Waters Treaty have tended to evaluate the performance of the International Joint Commission and its potential role in contemporary Canada-US relations rather than focusing on the Boundary Waters Treaty in its historical context, and this literature has been, on balance, more critical of the commission than the diplomatic historiography. For example, early legal scholars noted the "fairly obvious tendency to treat membership in the commission as a suitable reward for political services, a criterion of selection not entirely calculated to guarantee that impartiality, training, and knowledge required for the objective adjudication of burning issues," as well as the disinclination to use the Boundary Waters Treaty's arbitration clause.[96] However, legal experts also valued the treaty and the International Joint Commission for the precedents they set and for their inclusion of universally applicable principles for water management.

In September 1907, George Gibbons predicted that if the Boundary Waters Treaty got through the Senate, it would be "the best thing that ever happened to this country and . . . the only way of preventing friction between ourselves and the Mother County as well as between Great Britain and the United States."[97] His prediction turned out to be reasonably accurate: the treaty improved all three relationships, and the process of making it indirectly encouraged the development of Canadian foreign policy mechanisms, which filled a gap that had impeded the three countries' smooth relations. In 1909, a bill to form the Department of External Affairs was introduced and passed Ottawa's Parliament with very little fanfare, making Canadian external communications faster and better organized. Governor General Grey was upset by the bill because he did not want his post to be superseded by a purely Canadian unit.[98] His worries were fully justified—Canadian historians regard the creation of the Department of External Affairs as an important step toward foreign policy autonomy.

Despite its undeniably positive influences, it is equally true that the International Joint Commission's work during the twentieth century would please someone with Chandler Anderson's objections about sovereignty and jurisdiction. Because the US and Canadian governments hold the organization's purse strings and appoint the commissioners, the International Joint Commission's independence only goes so far. The powerful interests at stake have made it impossible for politicians to hand over as much control to the commission as its creators envisioned. The tension between its broad mandate and its actual activities has perhaps contributed to the perception of the International Joint Commission as a deceptive creation—an unreliable "myth" as described by Clamen and Macfarlane in the introduction to this volume—but it has also enabled the institution to change and grow as goals for water management have evolved on both sides of the border.

The dramatic changes that humans made to the Great Lakes watershed in the early twentieth century—industrialization, urbanization, hydroelectric development, and transportation infrastructure, to name a few—interacted with shifting calculations of national and imperial self-interest on the global stage, and one result of this concatenation was the Boundary Waters Treaty of 1909 and the creation of the International Joint Commission. These uniquely North American tools brought the people living around the Great Lakes closer to control over the treaties that governed their boundary waters.

Notes

1. For a global overview of this process, see John R. McNeill, *Something New Under the Sun* (London: Allen Lane, 2000). For a description of how this process played out on Lake Erie, see Jon Wlasiuk, *Refining Nature: Standard Oil and the Limits of Efficiency* (Pittsburgh: University of Pittsburgh Press, 2017), intro. and ch. 1, esp. 40–9.

2. Kenneth Warren, *The American Steel Industry, 1850–1970: A Geographical Interpretation* (Pittsburgh, PA: University of Pittsburgh Press, 1988), 109–32.

3. "Mr. Morgan Wants It: Definite Offer Made for Stock of American Shipbuilding Company, Control of the Great Lakes Would Thus be Assured," *Minneapolis Journal*, 16 August 1902, 1.

4. William T. Hogan, *Economic History of the Iron and Steel Industry in the United States* (Lexington, MA: Heath, 1971), 328.

5. Warren, *The American Steel Industry*, 116, and William R. Wightman, *The Land Between: Northwestern Ontario Resource Development, 1800 to the 1990s* (Toronto: University of Toronto Press, 1997), 118–23.

6. "Two Big Furnaces: Clergue, the Western Cecil Rhodes, to Outdo Previous Effort," *Minneapolis Journal*, 18 February 1901, 1, and "What Clergue is Doing at the Soo: Modern Steel Worlds with Electrical Power Furnished by New Canals—Associate Industries of Wonderful Character," *Minneapolis Journal*, 31 August 1901, 18.

7. Michael Bliss, *Northern Enterprise: Five Centuries of Canadian Business* (Toronto: McClelland and Stewart, 1987), 285–8.

8. "Starting in 1896, the beginning of an inflationary cycle for most of the advanced industrial world, the boom reached its apogee during the first Canadian merger wave that began in 1909, only to die out with the world-wide recession of 1913." Gregory Marchildon, *Profits and Politics: Beaverbrook and the Gilded Age of Canadian Finance* (Toronto: University of Toronto Press, 1996), 7.

9. Two excellent monographs dealing with the environment of the Great Lakes during this period are William Cronon's *Nature's Metropolis* (New York: W. W. Norton, 1991) and Harold Platt's *Shock Cities* (Chicago: University of Chicago Press, 2005). For the broader history of this period, see also Elizabeth Sanders, *Roots of Reform* (Chicago: University of Chicago Press, 1999), Alan Trachtenberg, *The Incorporation of*

America (New York: Hill and Wang, 1982) and Richard Bensel, *The Political Economy of American Industrialization, 1877–1900* (Cambridge: Cambridge University Press, 2000).

10   For a comprehensive history of the development of the St. Lawrence River for shipping, see William Willoughby, *The St. Lawrence Waterway* (Madison: University of Wisconsin Press, 1961) and Daniel Macfarlane, *Negotiating a River* (Vancouver: UBC Press, 2014). For an example of contemporary coverage of the Lakes-to-Gulf waterway, see "Oppose Lake to Gulf Waterway," *New York Daily Tribune*, 17 January 1908, 2, and "Shall Chicago be a Seaport? Plans for a Ship Canal from Gulf to Great Lakes" *The Sun* (New York), 2 September 1907, 7.

11   For example, the Niagara River, the Rainy River, and the St. Lawrence River.

12   Archives Canada, RG 23, box 436, file 702-4-2(1), 702-4-3 through 9, 11-13 (2) covering complaints from residents of Southern Ontario to the federal Department of Fisheries, 1914–53. See also Margaret Beattie Bogue, *Fishing the Great Lakes: An Environmental History, 1783–1933* (Madison: University of Wisconsin Press, 2000), 279–96.

13   Recent studies of environmental change around the Great Lakes during this period include Jonathan Wlasiuk, "A Company Town on Common Waters: Standard Oil in the Calumet," *Environmental History*, 19 (October 2014): 687–713; Bogue, *Fishing the Great Lakes*; and Harold Platt, "Chicago, the Great Lakes, and the Origins of Federal Urban Environmental Policy," *Journal of the Gilded Age and Progressive Era* 1, no. 2 (April 2002): 122–53.

14   For example, Peter Neary noted that the question of boundary water use "had been brought to the fore by rapid industrialization at the turn of the century on both sides of the border." See Neary, "Grey, Bryce and the Settlement of Canadian-American Differences, 1905–1911," *Canadian Historical Review* 49, no. 4 (December 1968): 359.

15   When it opened, the canal removed ten thousand cubic feet per second, lowering Lakes Huron, Erie, Ontario, and Michigan by approximately six inches and hindering navigation. See Maurice O. Graff, "The Lake Michigan Water Diversion Controversy: A Summary Statement," *Journal of the Illinois State Historical Society* 34, no. 4 (December 1941): 453–71, and Jacob Austin "Canadian-United States Practice and Theory Respecting the International Law of International Rivers: A Study of the History and Influence of the Harmon Doctrine," *Canadian Bar Review* 37, no. 3 (1959): 416.

16   The downstream city of St. Louis even filed a lawsuit while the canal was still under construction, to no avail. For contemporary coverage, see "Chicago Drainage Canal Open," *New York Tribune*, 3 January 1900, 1. See also "What Chicago Talks Of: Drainage Canal Not an Entire Success—How Taxpayers Were Deluded," *New York Daily Tribune*, 22 January 1900, 3.

17   Austin, "Canadian-United States Practice and Theory," 416–17. See also Hildegard Willman, "The Chicago Diversion from Lake Michigan," *Canadian Bar Review* 10, no. 9 (1932): 575–83. For contemporary coverage, see "Canada's Waterways Must Not Be Sacrificed for Chicago Drainage," *The Globe* (Toronto), 27 June 1906. See also "The Chicago Canal: Canada's Case Has Not Been Fairly Stated," *The Globe* (Toronto), 24 October 1906, and "Chicago Scheme Stoutly Opposed," *The Globe* (Toronto), 28 March 1912.

18 Graff, "The Lake Michigan Water Diversion Controversy," 453–71. For contemporary coverage, see "Decision Hits the Canal: Supreme Court of United States Rules Against Sanitary Board and State of Illinois" *True Republican* (Sycamore, IL), 2 February 1901.

19 Cornelius Lynde, "The Controversy Concerning the Diversion of Water from Lake Michigan by the Sanitary District of Chicago," *Illinois Law Review* 25, no. 3 (1930): 243–60. See also Austin, "Canadian-United States Practice and Theory," 416.

20 "Chicago Victor over St. Louis: Supreme Court Decide Illinois Drainage Canal Does Not Harm Missouri," *Minneapolis Journal*, 19 February 1906, 1. See also, J. Q. Dealey, "The Chicago Drainage Canal and St. Lawrence Development," *American Journal of International Law* 23, no. 2 (April 1929): 307–28.

21 "Power Scheme Gives Offense: Watershed of the Rainy River Would Be Tapped," *Minneapolis Journal*, 17 March 1904, 1. See also "Rainy River is to Have Power Plant: This is One of the Chief Items of Development in Canadian Northwest," *St. Paul Globe*, 25 June 1904. See also "Great Developments at Koochiching Falls," *The Appeal* (Saint Paul, MN), 29 April 1905. For legal history, see Patricia K. Wouters, "Allocation of the Non-Navigational Uses of International Watercourses: Efforts at Codification and the Experience of Canada and the United States," *Canadian Yearbook of International Law* (1992): 56.

22 Wouters, "Allocation of the Non-Navigational Uses of International Watercourses," 313. The Webster-Ashburton Treaty required the river system to be "free and open" to navigation.

23 William Griffin, "A History of the Canadian-United States Boundary Waters treaty of 1909," *University of Detroit Law Journal* 37, no. 1 (1959): 78. See also Daniel Macfarlane, " 'A Completely Man-Made and Artificial Cataract': The Transnational Manipulation of Niagara Falls," *Environmental History* 18, no. 4 (October 2013): 859–84.

24 For contemporary press coverage, see "Almost Ready to Harness Niagara: Contract Let to Furnish Buffalonians with Motive Power," *Scranton Tribune* (PA), 29 August 1896, 5. See also "To Harness Up Niagara: The Gigantic Scheme Soon to Be Put In Effect at a Cost of Three Million Dollars," *Democratic Press* (Ravenna, OH), 14 June 1888, 1; "Niagara Falls in Danger: Time Coming When Commercialism May Destroy Great Cataract," *Hocking Sentinel* (Logan, OH), 27 April 1905; "Utilizing Niagara: Capitalists Who Propose to Divert Water from the Mighty Falls," *The News-Herald* (Hillsboro, OH), 22 September 1886; "Niagara River Power: How it is Proposed to Utilize it at Buffalo," *Springfield Daily Republic* (OH), 11 February 1888, 2; "Curbing the Falls: The Tunnel for Turbine Wheels at Niagara Nearly Finished," *Pittsburgh Dispatch*, 17 January 1892, 3; "To Preserve Niagara Falls: Report of American Side of International Commission," *The Sun* (New York), 25 March 1906, 6; "Preserve Niagara Falls: Secretary Taft urged to Save its Scenic Beauty," *The Sun* (New York), 27 November 1906, 7; "Niagara Falls Bill: Measure Likely to Pass, House Commits Reports One to Restrict Diversion of Water," *New York Daily Tribune*, 3 June 1906, 12; and "Another Raid on Niagara Falls," *The Globe* (Toronto), 29 May 1911.

25 "Lake Carriers Active: Will Send a Delegation to Washington Monday," *St. Paul Globe*, 11 February 1900, 9.

26   The Milk River flows northward across the border before looping back into Montana, while the St. Mary River begins in Montana and flows north into Alberta.

27   M. E. Wolfe, "The Milk River: Deferred Water Policy Transitions in an International Waterway," *Natural Resources Journal* 32, no. 1 (Winter 1992): 66. For contemporary coverage, see "Reclaim Arid Lands: This the Subject of Secretary Maxwell's Address to Commercial Bodies," *St. Paul Globe*, 11 March 1900, 8; "Funds for Irrigation: Eight Million Dollars Available for Reclaiming Arid Lands," *Minneapolis Journal*, 16 August 1902, 1; "Montana's Reclamation: The St. Mary Irrigation Project—An Ingenious Method of Changing a River's Course," *St. Paul Globe*, 1 July 1902; "Big Irrigation Project: Explanation of the Proposed St. Mary Division Canal," *Scranton Tribune* (PA), 19 April 1902, 5; "Irrigation by the Great Milk," *Minneapolis Journal*, 24 March 1903, 1.

28   "Water Scheme Miffs Canada: How It May Retaliate on the United States," *Minneapolis Journal*, 10 May 1905. See also "Supply Water for Canadian Users: Plan is Devised to Remove International Difficulty over Irrigation," *St. Paul Globe*, 29 April 1905, 1 and 5.

29   Wolfe, "The Milk River," 67; see also N. F. Dreisziger, "Wrangling over the St. Mary and Milk," *Alberta History* 28, no 2 (1980): 6–15.

30   Privy Council Order 3465, 8 January 1896, Canadian government. Quoted in F. J. E. Jordan, *An Annotated Digest of Materials Relating to the Establishment and Development of the International Joint Commission* (Prepared for internal use of the Canadian Section of the International Joint Commission, Ottawa, ON, 1967), 1.

31   O. D. Skelton, *The Life and Letters of Sir Wilfrid Laurier* (Toronto: McClelland and Stewart, 1965), 2: 360. See also Alvin Gluek, "Pilgrimages to Ottawa: Canadian-American Diplomacy, 1903–1913," in *Canadian Historical Association Papers* (Ottawa: Canadian Historical Association, 1969), 65–83.

32   Quoted in Gluek, "Pilgrimages to Ottawa," 1–2.

33   Privy Council Minutes, 27 April 1903, Canadian government. Quoted in Jordan, *Annotated Digest*, 3.

34   See John Hilliker, *Canada's Department of External Affairs, Volume 1: The Early Years, 1909–1946* (Montreal: McGill-Queen's University Press, 1990).

35   Norman Hillmer and John Granatstein, *Empire to Umpire* (Toronto: Irwin, 2000), 17.

36   For a good overview of the period, see George C. Herring, *From Colony to Superpower: US Foreign Relations Since 1776* (New York: Oxford University Press, 2008), 303–24.

37   Ibid., 691.

38   Account of the conversation, given by Elihu Root in a speech to the New York County Lawyers' Association on 13 March 1915. Quoted in Phillip Jessup, *Elihu Root* (Hamden, CT: Archon Books, 1968), 1: 215.

39   Norman Hillmer and John Granatstein, *For Better or For Worse: Canada and the United States into the Twenty-first Century* (Toronto: Nelson, 2005), 31–2.

40   Hillmer and Granatstein, *Empire to Umpire*, 25.

41   Gluek, "Pilgrimages to Ottawa," 66.

42 Laurier cable, quoted in Joseph Schull, *Laurier: The First Canadian* (Toronto: MacMillan, 1965), 431. The British government named the Lord Chief Justice Alverstone and two Canadian Supreme Court judges, Sir Louis Jette and Douglas Armour, as their panelists. Mr. Armour died before the tribunal convened, and was replaced by A. B. Aylesworth, a Toronto lawyer who later became Wilfrid Laurier's minister for justice and his advisor during the negotiation of the Boundary Waters Treaty.

43 Gluek, "Pilgrimages to Ottawa," 66–7.

44 Hillmer and Granatstein, *Empire to Umpire*, 26.

45 Gluek, "Pilgrimages to Ottawa," 68.

46 Skelton, *Sir Wilfrid Laurier*, 2: 159–60, and Hilliker, *Canada's Department of External Affairs*, 26.

47 Gluek, "Pilgrimages to Ottawa," p 68–9.

48 Mary E. Hallett, "The 4th Earl Grey as Governor General of Canada, 1904–1911," (PhD diss., University of London, King's College, 1970), 215. See also Neary, "Grey, Bryce and the Settlement of Canadian-American Differences," 380.

49 Hillmer and Granatstein, *For Better or For Worse*, 35–6.

50 The governor general of Canada acts as Canada's head of state on behalf of the British king or queen. Before the First World War, this job included handling political relationships in addition to the ceremonial duties that continue to the present day, such as signing bills into laws and opening Parliament in Ottawa.

51 Neary, "Grey, Bryce and the Settlement of Canadian-American Differences," 358, and Hallett, "The 4th Earl Grey," 215.

52 Neary, "Grey, Bryce and the Settlement of Canadian-American Differences," 358, and Hallett, "The 4th Earl Grey," 215.

53 Peter Neary, "Gibbons, Sir George Christie," *Dictionary of Canadian Biography*, vol. 14 (University of Toronto/Université Laval, 2003), http://www.biographi.ca/en/bio/gibbons_george_christie_14E.html.

54 Including, but not limited to L. M. Bloomfield and Gerald Fitzgerald, *Boundary Waters Problems of Canada and the United States: The International Joint Commission 1912-1958* (Toronto: Carswell, 1958); Robert Bothwell, *Canada and the United States: The Politics of Partnership* (New York: Twayne Publishers, 1992); John Bartlett Brebner, *North Atlantic Triangle: The Interplay of Canada, the United States and Great Britain* (Toronto: Ryerson Press, 1945); Gerald Craig, *The United States and Canada* (Cambridge, MA: Harvard University Press, 1968); G. Glazebrook, *A History of Canadian External Relations* (Toronto: Oxford University Press, 1950); Alan O. Gibbons, "Sir George Gibbons and the Boundary Waters Treaty of 1909," *Canadian Historical Review* 34, no. 2 (June 1953): 124–38; Gluek, "Pilgrimages to Ottawa," 65–83; A. D. P. Heeney, "Along the Common Frontier: The International Joint Commission," *Behind the Headlines* 26, no. 5 (July 1967); Hugh L. Keenleyside, *Canada and the United States: Some Aspects of the History of the Republic and the Dominion* (New York:

Alfred A. Knopf, 1929); Neary, "Grey, Bryce and the Settlement of Canadian-American Differences."

55 Neary, "Grey, Bryce and the Settlement of Canadian-American Differences," 358.

56 Durand to Grey, enclosure. 3 May 1906. Governor General Grey Correspondence. Governor General's Office. Vol. 93, File 192A, 294–316, Library and Archives Canada (LAC).

57 Neary, "Grey, Bryce and the Settlement of Canadian-American Differences," 358.

58 Ibid., and Hallett, "The 4th Earl Grey," 242.

59 T. R. Roosevelt to Whitelaw Reid, 28 April 1906. Quoted in Gluek, "Pilgrimages to Ottawa," 2.

60 Neary, "Grey, Bryce and the Settlement of Canadian-American Differences," 363.

61 Lord Elgin to Earl Grey, 14 January 1907. Quoted in Hallett, "The 4th Earl Grey," 222–3.

62 Ibid., 226.

63 Foreign Office Memo 414/199, Bryce to Sir Edward Grey, 9 April 1907. Quoted in Neary, "Grey, Bryce and the Settlement of Canadian-American Differences," 364.

64 Draft Treaty, 1907. Pp. 129636–129644, Vol. 480, Laurier Papers, 1907, Ottawa, Ontario. Quoted in Jordan, *Annotated Digest*, 27.

65 Article ii of Clinton-Gibbons draft treaty, 1907, quoted in Jordan, *Annotated Digest*, 27; Anderson memo, December 1907, quoted in Jordan, *Annotated Digest*, 42–3.

66 Anderson memo, December 1907. Quoted in Jordan, *Annotated Digest*, 42–3.

67 Gibbons to Laurier, 15 February 1907. Quoted in William Harbaugh, *The Life and Times of Theodore Roosevelt* (New York: Collier, 1963), 127; also quoted in Neary, "Grey, Bryce and the Settlement of Canadian-American Differences," 368–9.

68 Dispatch from Bryce to Earl Grey, 3 February 1908. Quoted in Jordan, *Annotated Digest*, 53.

69 Gibbons to Laurier, 8 January 1908, quoted in Jordan, *Annotated Digest*, 51; Gibbons to Laurier, 11 February 1908, quoted in Gibbons, "Sir George Gibbons and the Boundary Waters Treaty of 1909," 131–2.

70 William Griffin, "A History of the Canadian-United States Boundary Waters treaty of 1909," *University of Detroit Law Journal* 37, no. 1 (October 1959): 77.

71 Laurier's cabinet chose the chief astronomer, Dr. W. F. King, who had extensive experience with surveying and border delineation, and the Americans appointed Mr. Newell, from the Bureau of Reclamation. See Jordan, *Annotated Digest*, 60.

72 Dispatch, Bryce to Lord Grey, 8 June 1908. Quoted in Jordan, *Annotated Digest*, 65.

73 Howard to Earl Grey, 13 August 1908. Quoted in Jordan, *Annotated Digest*, 74.

74 Memoranda for Mr. Root, 13 June 1908. Quoted in Jordan, *Annotated Digest*, 67.

75 Grey to Crewe. Quoted in Hallett, "The 4th Earl Grey," 233–4.

76   Jordan, *Annotated Digest*, 69–71. The points they decided to include were described as follows: "freedom of navigation on the Great Lakes system, principles of international law governing the obstruction and diversion of boundary and transboundary waters, appointment of a permanent commission to consider and decide cases involving application of the principles, provision for the same body to act as an advisory board in respect to any matters in dispute arising with regard to property rights of any kind between the two countries, and creation of the same body as a permanent board of arbitration to which by consent of both countries any matter of dispute might be referred for final decision."

77   Letter from Anderson to Root, 2 June 1908. Quoted in Jordan, *Annotated Digest*, 77n115.

78   Letter from Anderson to Root, 26 August 1908. Quoted in Jordan, *Annotated Digest*, 76.

79   Austin, "Canadian-United States Practice and Theory," 416.

80   Graff, "The Lake Michigan Water Diversion Controversy," 457.

81   Jordan, *Annotated Digest*, 92, and Gibbons to Laurier, 16 December 1908. Paraphrased and quoted in Jordan, *Annotated Digest*, 89–90.

82   Jordan, *Annotated Digest*, 93–4.

83   Ibid., 96.

84   Ibid.

85   Ibid., 100.

86   Text of treaty, *The International Joint Commission and the Boundary Waters Treaty of 1909* [pamphlet] (Ottawa: International Joint Commission, 1997), 14.

87   Neary, "Grey, Bryce and the Settlement of Canadian-American Differences," 375.

88   Anonymous clipping, 1909. Chandler Anderson Papers, Manuscript Room, Library of Congress, Washington, DC.

89   "Canada Humiliated Over Treaty: Laurier Irritates at Publicity of Waterway Convention Before He Had Copy," *New York Daily Tribune*, 27 January 1909, 4.

90   Letter, Root to Gibbons, 2 March 1909. Laurier Papers, CA 153654, LAC.

91   Neary, "Grey, Bryce and the Settlement of Canadian-American Differences," 376.

92   Shaugnessy to Pugsley, 4 March 1910. Quoted in Gibbons, "Sir George Gibbons and the Boundary Waters Treaty," 134.

93   In the spring of 1910, Gibbons and the other Canadian members of the International Waterways Commission observed irritably to Laurier that the issue of power development on the St. Lawrence River at Cornwall, Ontario, would be much easier to settle if the Boundary Waters Treaty were in force. See Gibbons to Laurier, 2 March 1910. Quoted in Gibbons, "Sir George Gibbons and the Boundary Waters Treaty," 133.

94   Root to Gibbons, 16 May 1910. Quoted in Gibbons, "Sir George Gibbons and the Boundary Waters Treaty," 138.

95   Jordan, *Annotated Digest*, 127.

96 Including but not limited to Philip Anisman, "Water Pollution Control in Canada," *Ottawa Law Review* 5, no. 2 (1972): 342–410; Jacob Austin, "Canadian-United States Practice and Theory Respecting the International Law of International Rivers: A Study of the History and Influence of the Harmon Doctrine," *Canadian Bar Review* 37, no. 3 (September 1959): 391–443; Richard Bilder, "Controlling Great Lakes Pollution: A Study in United States-Canadian Environmental Cooperation," *Michigan Law Review* 70, no. 3 (January 1972): 469–556; P. E. Corbett, *The Settlement of Canadian-American Disputes: A Critical Study of Methods and Results* (Toronto: Ryerson Press, 1937); Stephane Rousell, *The North American Democratic Peace: Absence of War and Security Institution-Building in Canada-US Relations, 1867–1958* (Montreal and Kingston: McGill-Queen's University Press, 2004); William Griffin, "A History of the Canadian-United States Boundary Waters treaty of 1909," *University of Detroit Law Journal* 37, no. 1 (October 1959): 76–95; Macdonald, Gerald L. Morris, and Douglas M. Johnston, eds., *Canadian Perspectives on International Law and Organization* (Toronto: University of Toronto Press, 1974), 522–43; G. V. La Forest, "Boundary Problems in the East," in *Canada-United States Treaty Relations*, ed. David R. Deener (Durham, NC: Duke University Press, 1963), 28–50; Don Courtney Piper, *The International Law of the Great Lakes: A study of Canadian-United States Co-operation* (Durham, NC: Duke University Press, 1967); Robert Spencer, John Kirton, and Kim Richard Nossal, eds., *The International Joint Commission Seventy Years On* (Toronto: Centre for International Studies, 1981); M. H. Wershof, "Notes on the Jurisprudence of the International Joint Commission" (Prepared for the International Joint Commission, 1975).

97 Gibbons to Laurier, 24 September 1907. Laurier Papers. CA 129648-129649, LAC.

98 Quoted in Hallett, "The 4th Earl Grey," 252.

SECTION 2

FROM COAST TO COAST

The International Joint Commission and Water Quality in the Bacterial Age

Jamie Benidickson

Nineteenth-century belief in the capacity of running water to purify itself largely alleviated contemporary anxiety about the detrimental impacts from municipal sewage discharges. This comforting misconception persisted as an obstacle to reform when the International Joint Commission (IJC) conducted its first major pollution inquiry between 1912 and 1918.[1] As the new institution explored its innovative mandate, efforts to enhance water quality were thus significantly hampered by the perception that sewage was essentially a local nuisance or inconvenience accompanying vital municipal waste-water removal. Yet while water-based displacement of untreated municipal sewage substantially improved the living conditions of upstream residents, epidemics remained rampant as the nineteenth century drew to a close,[2] prompting no less a figure than former US president Theodore Roosevelt to argue in 1910 that "civilized people should be able to dispose of sewage in a better way than by putting it into drinking water."[3] To move beyond the rhetoric of "a better way," however, would require new and affordable treatment methodologies capable of securing institutional approval and ideally backstopped by an effective framework for enforcement. The search for that cluster of supporting conditions constituted Docket No. 4 of the IJC's official agenda. Although the IJC's first boundary waters pollution reference (1912–18) did not resolve the water quality challenges of the early twentieth century, this bilateral initiative contributed significantly to greater awareness of bacterial contamination and potential responses. It did so on the basis of a substantial investigative effort involving extensive institutional collaboration and widespread community involvement along much of the Canada–United States border and beyond.

The Bacteriological Background

Ground-breaking scientific advances—notably bacteriological insights derived after the 1870s from the work of Louis Pasteur and Robert Koch—conferred substantial authority on public health officials, who were quick to question reassuring assumptions derived from the work of their forerunners in chemistry. As the new bacteriological era got underway, health officials set out to advance a water quality agenda consistent with the contagionist theory of the transmission of disease, even attempting to reshape local legal environments through new forms of regulation. These interventions, by no means welcomed by municipal leaders, involved a vigorous campaign to eliminate untreated discharges of civic wastes. The effort intermittently transferred debate from the local to the state, provincial, or national level. By the era of the First World War, senior public health officials on both sides of the Canada–United States border even spearheaded an ultimately unsuccessful international initiative to safeguard communities around the Great Lakes and along boundary waters.

By the late nineteenth century, popular and professional opinion in Europe and North America had begun to associate water quality in some way with disease, and public agencies were frequently established to assume responsibility for municipal water supplies. Yet, with the bacteriological transmission of disease still not well understood, linkages remained speculative.

The efforts of newly empowered public health officials focused on the vaguely characterized realm of "nuisance." One Canadian official, for example, circulated a questionnaire concerning nuisances attributed to industrial activity in 1886. Dr. Peter Bryce, who had previously investigated the public health implications of sawdust, now inquired into the number and extent of slaughterhouses, dairies, and cheese factories, as well as piggeries. Breweries and distilleries were also to be tallied up, and special attention paid to cattle byres in the vicinity of the distilleries. Moreover, Bryce asked: "Are any of your streams polluted by town or city sewage; and if so, what is the extent of this pollution?"[4] But he could offer no guidance as to any standard relevant to the assessment.

In the same year, a Massachusetts State Health Commission, having examined the condition of inland waters, advocated a permanent body to assume responsibility. The designated state guardians of inland waters would be expected to familiarize themselves with the actual conditions bearing upon the relationship of water pollution and purity to public health. They were to address all remediable pollution and, through advice to cities, towns, and manufacturing concerns, to "use every means in their power to prevent further vitiation." In sum, the agency's function would be "to guard the public interest and the public health in its relation with water, whether pure or defiled." The ultimate goal, "which must never be abandoned," was that means might eventually be found to redeem and preserve all the waters of the state.[5] The shift away from the wishful thinking of such comparatively rudimentary investigation and exhortation came quickly in the wake of important discoveries regarding the transmission of typhoid.

Traceable to one home upstream from Plymouth, Pennsylvania, typhoid had led in 1885 to the deaths of 114 of the town's 8,000 inhabitants. Nearly a thousand more experienced but survived the disease.[6] Newark, Jersey City, Louisville, Cincinnati, and Philadelphia were among other American cities to encounter first-hand the ravages of late-nineteenth-century typhoid, whose transmission was facilitated by bacteria-contaminated sewerage and misunderstanding. For North Americans, much learning was derived from the experience along the Merrimack River, one of the three major waterways that Massachusetts legislators had chosen to exempt from pollution control measures in the 1870s.

Contemporary professional opinion had supported the decision to exempt the Merrimack. Health officials calculated—or assumed—that, by virtue of dilution and distance, the river would purify itself between points of waste-water discharge and water intake sites. Indeed, they embraced an even more mischievous doctrine—the notion of beneficial contamination—whereby certain industrial wastes actually accelerated natural processes: "The sewage of Lowell is diluted with from 600 to 1,000 times its volume of water, and then flows a dozen miles to Lawrence, much of the refuse from the mills acting as a precipitant and disinfectant to it."[7] However comforting it must have been to imagine mill refuse as an antidote to the effects of sewage, beneficial contamination was a mirage. In little more than a decade, deaths from typhoid spiked dramatically in communities along the Merrimack. First in Lowell and shortly thereafter in Lawrence, whose water intake was nine miles downstream from the former community's sewage discharge, the toll of victims mounted. Investigation of the higher rates of illness and death along unprotected rivers produced "remarkably conclusive evidence of the river water supply being the direct cause of the epidemics."[8]

William Thompson Sedgwick, recently appointed as the first head of biology at the Massachusetts Institute of Technology, was recruited to investigate.[9] Sedgwick's meticulous observations established the point of origin for the outbreak in the privies of the neighbouring community of North Chelmsford, and traced the passage of the typhoid bacillus "down the river and over the falls" along the Merrimack into Lowell's water supply.[10] His report on Lowell was unequivocal about sewage practices and disease. Lowell and Lawrence, he declared, "have constantly distributed to their citizens water, unpurified, drawn from a stream originally pure but now grossly polluted with the crude sewage of several large cities and towns."[11]

Experimental work at Lawrence then helped to reveal how sewage might be purified.[12] The essential conditions, as explained to the Massachusetts State Board of Health, involved "very slow motion of very thin films of liquid over the surface of particles having spaces between them sufficient to allow air to be continually in contact with the films of liquid." Here, bacteria did their work, with the consequence that during an experiment conducted over several months, the intermittent filtration process over gravel stones removed 97 per cent of the organic nitrogenous matter, a large part of which was in solution, as well as 99 per cent of the bacteria. These organic matters were oxidized or burned, so that the resulting effluent contained only 3 per cent of the decomposable organic matter of the sewage.[13] By the early 1900s, twenty-three Massachusetts towns and cities had adopted intermittent filtration sewage treatment plants to encourage bacterial decomposition.[14]

The importance of supplementing traditional chemical analysis of water with bacterial research had been firmly placed on the agenda by the pioneering bacteriological inquiries of Louis Pasteur and the subsequent investigations of Robert Koch. The former's microbial studies in the context of beer, wine, and vinegar production were soon followed in 1883 by Koch's investigation of a possible linkage between a distinctive "comma shaped" organism and the spread of cholera.[15] Very shortly thereafter, the etiology of typhoid and its relationship to sewage in waterways was more clearly understood: coliform bacteria, prevalent in human and animal feces, though not ordinarily found in water, signalled fecal pollution and indicated the possible presence of pathogenic organisms.[16] New biological insights, gathering support from the 1880s onwards, led to the recognition that germs, rather than noxious smells, putrefaction, or miasmas, were responsible for many diseases. Nonetheless, miasmas and their cousin, sewer gas, retained their status as treacherous foes for many years.[17]

Even where the new contagionist principles were acknowledged, the implications encountered resistance. A number of US courts had shown a singular reluctance to impose preventive obligations on private water supply companies. In 1891, for example, Pennsylvania water companies were relieved of the obligation to respond to new knowledge even though the court recognized that typhoid fever was "produced by a specific typhoid germ existing in the excreta of a person sick with that disease, which, being deposited in a stream, multiplies so that it contaminates the body of the water and reproduces the disease in the persons who drink it." A few years earlier, another Pennsylvania court had sharply lowered the performance bar: "Even comparatively pure water is hard to be obtained in large quantities, for in populous sections of the country where waterworks are most needed, neither rivers nor small streams can be kept entirely free of sewage." To the court, these were matters of "common observation" requiring no substantiation from experts; "purity" would thus be interpreted pragmatically to mean "wholesome, ordinarily pure." To put its dismissal of specialist opinion still more bluntly, the court emphasized: "We must use [pure] as it is used by the world at large and not in the abstract or chemical sense." In no other way would it be possible to attain the court's chosen outcome of ensuring that a water company charter would remain "economically valuable."[18] But alongside economic considerations and financial constraints, sewage treatment faced governmental and institutional obstacles.

State Policy, Local Funding, and Someone Else's Health

As one early twentieth-century summary of governmental responsibilities for waste management commented: "The interest of the city is to get rid of its waste; the state sees to it that one municipality does not commit a nuisance upon others."[19] Following the Massachusetts example, state and provincial boards of health dominated by medical practitioners and public health professionals began to emerge.[20] National health organizations sprang up: the American Public Health Association in 1872, followed within a decade by the short-lived US National Board of Health, a response of the federal government to yellow fever devastating Memphis, New Orleans, and the Mississippi Valley. In Britain, the Public Health Act of 1875, with its requirements for local boards of health, represented a pivotal accomplishment. Equivalent institutions appeared in Canada.

Yet both in Britain and North America, controversy persisted about the appropriate location of responsibility for water quality. In 1882 a legislative committee in Ontario determined that the water supply was being polluted by privies in three-quarters of the eighty municipalities that responded to its inquiries. Remedial efforts were virtually non-existent and disease was widespread. The committee called for a provincially appointed board of health.[21] This body repeatedly encountered municipal penny-pinching in its efforts to persuade local councils to act systematically and methodically in dealing with the sewage of their burgeoning populations. In Toronto, where health officials had responsibility for sanitary conditions affecting nearly a hundred thousand people, civic leaders allocated a mere five hundred dollars to the local board of health.[22] The situation was not unlike that in Massachusetts a few years earlier, when nuisances such as polluted water and contaminated food were also accepted as the responsibility of town and city governments whose commitment was at best uneven.[23]

Yet as health officials assumed the role of the public "conscience" for water quality, their efforts remained grounded in the common law of nuisance. Law offered a few gratifying successes, but was equally a source of frustration, thanks to its preoccupation with property rights and procedural preconditions. Legislation greatly extended—indeed, formally created—the authority that health officials exercised over water. Simultaneously, it constrained that authority within broader norms.

Ontario health officials were initially encouraged by successes in the courts. In 1884 they reported enthusiastically: "The reading of the law has been so clear that verdicts against offenders have been obtained and remedies have been effected."[24] But early successes were short-lived. Waves of individual offenders were dishearteningly common in certain communities, and public health professionals soon grew sceptical of the legal process. It seemed excruciatingly difficult to establish nuisance at trial—"not only whether this or that condition is *injurious to the public health*, but whether it is *materially offensive to the senses*, or interferes with the *enjoyment of life and property*." Health officials lost confidence in the capacity of juries to reach decisions that they—as experts—would consider appropriate: "To make the question of whether a man with senses rendered obtuse is or is not nauseated by a smell a criterion of the existence or absence of a nuisance is as crude as was trial by fire in old Saxon times, since the guilt or innocence of the accused was tested by his power to endure pain."[25]

In reviewing American law on inland water pollution for the United States Geological Survey in 1905, Edwin B. Goodell found that despite uneven levels of "public enlightenment as to the deleterious effects of water pollution" there was no shortage of statutory initiatives to alleviate the problem.[26] These he presented in three rough categories. In the first, represented by seventeen states, Goodell could ascertain "no sense of the general desirability of pure natural waters, but only a desire to prevent certain acts recognized as criminal in intent or as likely to injure special groups of persons whom the legislature desires to protect."[27] These jurisdictions had simply enacted prohibitions, albeit often accompanied by the threat of imprisonment, for wrongs related to the offence of knowingly or wilfully depositing noxious, poisonous, or offensive matter in or near water supplies, springs, wells, or reservoirs. Judging from the frequency with which specific prohibitions appear, dead animals were particularly adept at finding their way into the sources of water supply.

A further twenty states had gone somewhat further in protecting their water supplies. In this second grouping, prohibitions similar to those in Goodell's first category were often supplemented by greater detail—concern about contamination of ice supplies, for example. In addition, a number of these states had conferred modest regulatory authority over water pollution on boards of health, occasionally funding enforcement actions or the operation of laboratory facilities. A few states required permits for the discharge of waste water, some even insisting that sewage be treated before effluent could be released.

Eight states—New York, Minnesota, and Pennsylvania alongside the Great Lakes, plus Connecticut, Massachusetts, New Hampshire, New Jersey, and Vermont—constituted Goodell's third category. He credited these jurisdictions with "stringent methods to enforce the right of their citizens to unpolluted natural waters."[28] Their enactments, he anticipated, would control pollution so as "eventually to prevent all danger to public health." Refinements adopted in these states served to encourage regular water quality investigation and reporting. Authorizations to enter premises subject to public health regulations or considered possible sources of pollution were also commonly granted. Some states—New Jersey, for example—provided for sewerage districts or boards with supervisory responsibility over permits, treatment facilities, and the means of financing the costs of infrastructure. Remedial measures and the prevention of pollution were also addressed.[29]

For its part, in 1906 Ontario promulgated a more sternly worded general prohibition on a province-wide basis: "No garbage, excreta, manure, vegetable or animal matter or filth shall be discharged into or be deposited in any of the lakes, rivers, streams or other waters in Ontario, or on the shores or banks thereof."[30] In a later revision of the Public Health Act (PHA) that further fortified the public health arsenal, officials were empowered to develop regulations for preventing pollution in the province's lakes, rivers, streams, and other inland waters.[31] Perhaps most significantly, for purposes of the PHA, "nuisance" was redefined to pertain to more than inconvenience or aesthetic sensibilities: "any condition . . . which is or may become injurious to health or prevent or hinder in any manner the suppression of disease."[32]

Regulatory measures against those whose actions threatened public welfare was undoubtedly an important alternative to the procedural and financial pitfalls of private litigation—or to formal criminal prosecutions in which technical and evidentiary requirements might prove insurmountable. But, as public health officials increasingly recognized, prohibitions against pollution were no more self-enforcing than the Ten Commandments. Indeed, the paradoxical coexistence of permissive regulations alongside prohibitions risked undermining the authority of the latter. As judges and other officials considered prohibitions and regulations on the front lines in local communities, the practical and symbolic significance of legislative measures were publicly tested, and anomalies in enforcement exposed.

Other incidents more positively suggested the potential of a determined environmental and public health bureaucracy to pursue its objectives—when supported by the judiciary and the legislature. In 1914, Dr. John W. S. McCullough, who was by this time actively associated with research for the IJC, put Ontario residents on notice that anyone contravening the pollution provisions of the *PHA* would be "prosecuted to the full extent of the law."[33]

Frederick A. Dallyn, sanitary engineer for the Public Board of Health (PBH), believed the time was ripe for the province to suggest collaborative ways for municipalities to handle their sewage as well as improve their water supply. Smaller municipalities were "keenly concerned" about the situation, he urged, but, as they lacked local engineers, could take no steps to assess the practicality of remedial alternatives. Assuming that the province would take some initiative, Dallyn outlined further issues to be considered. Would the PBH be content to discuss generalities and ultimately to generate a little business for consulting engineers, or would it wish to furnish each municipality with a plan and a general cost estimate, either at no charge or on the basis of some formula for cost recovery? Given provincial support, Dallyn argued, the engineering department might (without waiting for civic initiatives) collaborate with local health officers to campaign for improved sewers, treatment facilities, the extension of water supply systems, and water purification processes—especially in smaller municipalities.

Unwillingness to address the challenge of treating sewage was not confined to smaller communities. Many major centres had a less than sterling record when it came to dealing responsibly with residential, commercial, and industrial wastes.[34] Nor was it entirely clear that local public health administrators could actually influence or accomplish sewage treatment to the degree that sanitary officials might have wished. The challenges were quickly compounded on a scale that affected entire watersheds in North America, including the Great Lakes and boundary waters, although the magnitude of the public health and environmental challenge to international watersheds was not yet widely recognized or acknowledged. Indeed, influential commentators occasionally even denied the need for intervention.

Wastes Unlimited in Boundary Waters

Allen Hazen, a prominent and experienced engineering consultant, dismissed sewage treatment in 1914 as a viable contributor to public health: "The Great Lakes are so large, and the dilution and time intervals and exposure to sun and air are so great that there is no chance of infection being carried from one of the great cities to another."[35] The sewage of Detroit, he categorically insisted, was harmless to Cleveland, while sewage from Cleveland posed no threat whatsoever to Buffalo. Perhaps Hazen was unaware of the extent to which the Detroit and Niagara Rivers were being exploited for waste disposal purposes in the late nineteenth century. Perhaps he had not heard of the barges of municipal waste that were being towed out by the Detroit Sanitation Company for dumping near Amherstburg, Ontario, emboldening Canadian customs officials to arrest the perpetrators. With a similar approach to waste management by Buffalo meeting the same fate,[36] mounting expressions of concern from both sides of the border encouraged the United States and Canadian governments to contemplate water supply and sewage treatment on a bilateral basis.

When it was finally assigned to the IJC, the public health challenge presented by bacterial water contamination was continental in scope and without any obvious means of resolution. The challenge was evident enough in comparative typhoid mortality rates. These exposed a sharp contrast between the overall incidence in Canada and the United States (35.5 and 46.0 per 100,000, respectively) and the vastly more satisfactory results then being achieved in much of Europe. Even the worst European experience, in Hungary (28.3) and Italy (35.2), was better than the North American record. In the assessment of George Whipple, author of *The Microscopy of Drinking Water*, the overall situation in the United States as of 1907 saw cities with "reasonably good water supplies" reach a typhoid fever death rate of around 20 per 100,000. In communities whose supplies were "more or less contaminated" the rate rose up to 40 or 60.[37] A good many communities around the Great Lakes suffered substantially higher rates.

Powerful voices were being raised against the flood of sewage. Charles Evans Hughes, New York State's influential governor, had risen to prominence through his exposure of malpractice in gas utilities and insurance companies. Turning his energies to water quality, Hughes proclaimed in 1909—the date of the Boundary Waters Treaty—that the state could "no longer afford to permit the sewage of our cities and our industrial wastes to be poured into our watercourses." Roosevelt's previously quoted remarks pursued the same theme as he emphasized before a Buffalo audience the importance of protecting the quality of the Great Lakes. His prescription was directly linked to imperatives of public health when he proclaimed that "We must keep the water supply unpolluted and to do that you must see that it is not polluted in the source."[38] An American expert similarly questioned presumptions about the security of water supplies in the bacteriological era: "He who says that a polluted river will purify itself in the course of several miles reckons with an unknown force which will probably fail him at the critical time."[39] The Canadian equivalent was represented in a series of articles by T. Aird Murray, a Canadian civil engineer who endeavoured to call attention to the extent of the public health crisis attributable to contaminated water supplies.[40]

Against rapidly evolving scientific opinion, Canada and the United States took advantage of the newly created IJC to put water pollution on the international agenda. In 1912 the neighbouring countries specifically asked the newly established commission to investigate the location, extent, and causes of boundary water pollution that was injurious to public health and rendered the affected waters unfit for domestic or other uses. Remedies were requested, whether involving the construction and operation of suitable drainage canals or treatment plants. The inquiry also encompassed potential preventive measures to make the waters of the Great Lakes sanitary and suitable for domestic and other uses, so as to fulfill treaty obligations. The parties had agreed that boundary waters and waters flowing across the boundary would not be polluted on either side to the injury of health or property on the other. Although the original terms of reference appeared to invite "an investigation of all boundary waters as ... defined in the treaty without regard to the present or future transboundary effect of their pollution on either side," the two national governments subsequently determined to confine the scope of the inquiry to transboundary pollution. Either way, this was a tall order, the scale of which was perhaps not fully realized even after the eventual completion of the inquiry's work in 1918.

A preparatory conference in Buffalo, held on 17 December 1912, brought together representatives of the Canadian and US federal governments, as well as provincial and state officials from Ontario, Quebec, Illinois, Minnesota, New York, and Ohio. The Buffalo gathering identified a research agenda, which Dr. Allan J. McLaughlin of the United States Public Health Service would oversee as chief sanitary expert and director of fieldwork. Among the Canadian participants, Dr. J. W. S. McCullough and Dr. John A. Amyot of the Ontario Board of Public Health were named as consultants to the undertaking. By September 1913, the scope of the investigation had been determined, and arrangements formulated to examine the Niagara River; the Detroit River and connecting waterways from Lake Huron to Lake Erie; the St. Mary's River; the St. Lawrence River from Lake Ontario to the point where it departs from the boundary; and a portion of the St. John River.[41]

At this point, more than seven million people lived along the boundary waters, from Lake of the Woods between Ontario and Minnesota on the west, to the St. John River flowing between New Brunswick and Maine in the east. Extensive pollution, signalled by the presence of certain micro-organisms in water samples, was common in centres of population.[42]

The research program involved analysis of about 18,000 samples taken from 1,500 locations and reviews of the historic incidence of certain diseases, accompanied by an elaborate program of interviews and correspondence. In concluding what they described as the most extensive investigation and bacteriological examination ever made in the world, the commissioners presented their preliminary findings in 1914. In the absence of comprehensive information establishing historic baselines, the report's authors made comparative references to conditions in other jurisdictions. However, the use of these horizontal benchmarks—perhaps the best or most persuasive indicators that might have been obtained—had the effect of establishing standards already far removed from pre-industrial conditions on the lakes. Pollution was therefore being defined against a baseline or norm that appeared already to take for granted a significant level of contamination from human activity.

Addressing the effects of pollution on public health, the commissioners indicated that—apart from public water supplies—the sanitary and climatic conditions of cities and towns around the Great Lakes were much better than national averages, and infinitely better than those pertaining in the filthy, overcrowded, and often impoverished cities of Europe. Yet despite such advantages, excessive rates of typhoid fever persisted in Great Lakes communities. The explosive epidemics sometimes seen in the region were said to be without parallel in the European context. While death rates attributed to typhoid fever averaged less than 5 per 100,000 in the large cities of Northern Europe, where water supplies—often underground—enjoyed better protection, the Great Lakes inquiry revealed disturbingly high impacts in many North American communities. Between 1910 and 1912, the death rate per 100,000 ranged from 15 in Detroit to well over 100 in many centres, and it skyrocketed to over 300 in Ashland, Wisconsin.[43] As generalized in the context of the IJC's final report in 1918, "the intolerable condition of boundary waters from a sanitary standpoint"[44] was widely acknowledged. The situation was "generally chaotic, everywhere perilous and in some cases disgraceful."[45]

The IJC's advisors advanced a straightforward explanation directly implicating untreated sewage in the public health crisis: "The greatest single factor in this avoidable and remediable pollution is the sewage discharged without restriction or treatment of any kind by the municipalities situated on the boundary waters."[46] The situation at the Niagara River illustrated this crucial finding. On the American side, a population of roughly 615,000 (including 100,000 rural residents and more than 500,000 in the cities of Lackawanna, Buffalo, Tonawanda, North Tonawanda, and Niagara Falls), occupying approximately 2,000 square miles, discharged raw sewage directly into the river above the Falls.[47] The waters below the Falls were dangerously polluted, affecting municipalities on both the Canadian and American sides. Buffalo, a city of 460,000 people, was the most important contributor to Niagara River pollution. This city discharged all its sewage in an untreated state into the river above the intakes of the public water supplies of all the downstream communities.[48] The researchers' analysis of this popular tourist mecca was clear in its assessment of the implications: they rejected the popular impression that the action of the Falls purified sewage. "It simply mixes it more thoroughly with the water; it does not remove it or its danger. The pollution below the Falls is gross."[49]

The Canadian situation had yet to be addressed in detail by sanitary experts, but at Niagara-on-the-Lake researchers reported "the injurious effects of the pollution from the upper cities on the river have been seriously felt." These findings were in marked contrast to the assessment gratuitously offered by British engineer James Mansergh in an 1896 report on Toronto's water supply. Mansergh had quoted the highly regarded Dr. Edward Frankland on the quality of the Niagara River at the entrance to Lake Ontario: "The water of the Niagara River as it enters Lake Ontario is of excellent quality, for, although it has received the sewage of Buffalo and other places, the immense volume of water with which this is mixed renders its effect upon the chemical, as distinguished from the bacteriological character of the water, inappreciable." Yet Mansergh had added an essential caution that was taking some time to register with municipal officials around the Great Lakes: "The bacteriological condition of the water intended for dietetic purposes is probably of greater importance than its chemical composition."[50]

There was no particular reason apart from size to single out individual municipalities for critical comment, since the expert investigators had quite categorically concluded that "Every municipality, without exception, in the area investigated of the Great Lakes and their connecting rivers, avails itself of the opportunity to discharge its sewage untreated into these international waterways. This is the largest factor in their pollution."[51] For purposes of the final report to the national governments, the IJC explained that "The present international situation is not the result of any desire on the part of the inhabitants of either country to ignore international obligations either of comity or of law, but is the outcome of the failure on the part of the urban communities in each country, respectively, to recognize from a sanitary standpoint any right in other communities to river waters, especially communities on their own side of the boundary line."[52] In general terms, therefore, the problem confronting the IJC involved finding ways to alter long-established and accepted practices whose unintended adverse consequences were largely experienced by others.

As early as its interim report, the IJC offered up success stories as examples for other communities to follow: Cleveland saw its typhoid death rate fall to single digits—7 per 100,000 after 1912—while Erie, Pennsylvania, recorded equally positive improvements. The interim report then advanced a finding with immense and continuing significance for future water-quality management: rather than treating sewage—the outflow—communities such as Erie and Cleveland had taken advantage of new chemical or mechanical procedures to treat water prior to consumption. These means would increasingly expose a gulf between the protection of human health and the preservation of the natural environment.[53]

Dr. McLaughlin, in his advisory capacity, expressed the opinion that a sewage-oriented campaign would be futile: "The source of Detroit's water supply is polluted," he declared, "and the attempt to purify is ineffectual."[54] The Tonawandas and Lockport suffered an even more intemperate dressing-down: the residents of Tonawanda and North Tonawanda "still drink sewage-polluted water, expending their energies in a fruitless effort to improve sewerage conditions in the Upper Niagara River instead of protecting themselves by treating their own water supplies." The town of Lockport drew water from the same source, and, "in spite of repeated warnings and advice," followed the same course as the Tonawandas. In forty-eight hours and at a cost of under a thousand dollars, Dr. McLaughlin insisted, a plant could be installed to treat the water supply with hypochlorite of lime. Treatment costs would be less than fifty cents per million gallons. Even if it were later decided to construct a filtration plant, temporary arrangements of this nature were vital to save lives in the interim: "There is no excuse for delay in making the temporary installation."[55]

The priority accorded human health in these circumstances was by no means surprising, and where modest expenditures would allow civic officials to deal quickly and effectively with the threat of typhoid—after several promptings in the case of the Tonawandas—McLaughlin's rebuke was well-deserved. But emphasis on remedial water treatment in the immediate interests of human health, rather than a comprehensive preventive alternative, also signalled official acknowledgement within much of the medical community that, despite Roosevelt's vision of civilization, the flushing of untreated municipal wastes would not readily be curtailed at the start of the twentieth century.

A notable exception to the investigation's initial recommendation to forsake sewage discharge controls in favour of drinking water treatment—and a direct rejoinder to Allen Hazen's broad assurance that the water supplies of Great Lakes communities were entirely secure from each other's sewage—concerned vessels plying the Great Lakes. The scale of the phenomenon and its potential contribution to the contamination of the Great Lakes was apparent from the fact that in 1912 alone twenty-six thousand vessels passed through the Detroit River. These and other vessels navigating the Great Lakes and connecting waterways annually transported a population of at least fifteen million. The sewage these vessels discharged indiscriminately along their routes—and in harbours—contributed materially to pollution in both countries.[56] Even ballast was problematic, since some vessels took on water ballast before leaving port and discharged it just before entering the port of destination. There was therefore a danger of polluted water being discharged near the intake of a city water supply in an otherwise uncontaminated harbour.[57] And, of course, passengers themselves were at risk, for even though lake vessels were supposed to fill their drinking tanks in mid-lake—ostensibly far removed from sources of pollution—the distance that pollution travelled from shore made it difficult to find unpolluted areas. "There is excellent evidence," the commissioners noted, "to show that vessels frequently fill their tanks from polluted sources."[58] Officials on the American side conducted a survey of lake vessels to determine whether any were equipped with holding tanks or other retaining devices. Without exception they were not so equipped; the sewage outlet pipes from these lake vessels discharged directly into the water.[59]

As chief sanitary officer of the 1912 international investigation, Dr. McLaughlin had perhaps not entirely abandoned sewage treatment as a public health measure, but rather recognized that it would not likely come about through the ad hoc initiatives of individual communities. He argued, as British and Canadian authorities were also inclined to observe, that a more encompassing authority was essential: "The problem of pollution of interstate and international waters is so broad and affects so many interests that it necessitates for its equitable and efficient handling a central directing authority independent of local influences and prejudices."[60] The 1918 final report built upon this insight in its recommendation for institutional reform, a proposal—ultimately unsuccessful—for the IJC itself to receive authority to make the required "rules, regulations, directions and orders."[61]

It was becoming increasingly urgent on both sides of the Canada-US border to ascertain which level of government was most suited to respond effectively to the distinctive and growing challenges of controlling water pollution. Each of the existing options—local, national, or the intermediate-level jurisdictions of state or provincial governments—had plausible claims. Local governments have always asserted a degree of responsiveness to community sentiment greater than state, regional, or provincial jurisdictions might offer, while the latter have tended to insist that the remoteness of national institutions disqualifies them from involvement in activities and services intimately associated with the preferences and well-being of individual communities. From the perspective of problem-solving and effectiveness, however, the calibre of personnel and access to financial resources—purse-string politics—have sometimes favoured national-level initiatives.

Whereas in the United Kingdom tension between local and national institutions was perpetuated in philosophical considerations and deeply rooted traditions, in the North American federations the potential for inter-jurisdictional controversy and uncertainty was embedded in constitutional documents. As a new generation of public health issues came to prominence, national governments were forced to reflect on their potential contributions and responsibilities, and the jurisdictional basis for any actions they might contemplate. When pollution concerns of the Progressive Era coincided with the formation of the US Public Health

Service in 1912, Congress authorized the new institution to study the problem. The PHS established a Center for Pollution Studies in Cincinnati, although its mandate was congressionally confined to navigable waters. Despite the absence of any powers to compel abatement, the PHS enjoyed considerable success persuading state and local authorities to adopt water treatment along uniform standards.[62] Thus it came about that interstate transport provided the leverage on which federal regulation of drinking water quality oriented around bacterial standards was introduced in the United States.[63]

Navigable waters and transportation also grounded federal water quality initiatives in Canada, where the public health implications of sewage discharges were widely apparent. Within a decade of the first US federal drinking water quality standards, the Canadian government followed suit with bacterial quality standards for drinking water and water used for culinary purposes on vessels engaged in inter-provincial and international transport.[64] Yet authority over navigable waters was ultimately too limited a basis on which to proceed against the ever-increasing volume of sewage and industrial waste pouring into Canadian waterways.

The IJC's wartime quest for a satisfactory resolution of the uncertain local-state-national allocation of will and capacity in relation to sewage pollution resulted in an array of sophisticated diplomatic suggestions designed to safeguard public health at a cost that would appear affordable and without ruffling municipal feathers. Accordingly, it was recommended that all sewage destined for boundary waters should receive some purification, "and [that] the degree of such treatment is to be determined in a large measure by the limits of safe loading of a water-purification plant."[65] In the commission's words, "to the extent that is consistent with a proper degree of autonomy by the urban communities interested, all boundary waters should be subject to regulations prescribed by . . . some authority clothed with the necessary power."[66] From a cost perspective, though, "sewage treatment requirements must not be made so excessive and unreasonable as to involve the cities and towns along these waters in an expenditure entirely unjustifiable."[67]

The strength and persistence of reservations against sewage treatment contributed to the eventual abandonment of the IJC's early anti-pollution initiative.[68] It is noteworthy nonetheless that the 1912–18 pollution reference—notably its formulation of scientific guidance—stimulated both binational and multi-level intergovernmental exchange, a precedent if not a model for subsequent water quality protection initiatives.

National Default and International Failure

Campaigns for national action against sewage contamination were intermittently underway on both sides of the border alongside the IJC inquiry. In 1910, as President Roosevelt was calling for action in the United States, Canadian senator Napoléon Belcourt, an Ottawa resident, called on Parliament to declare that "our noble rivers shall no longer be made the receptacles of the raw sewage of the country."[69] His proposal was diverted to Canada's newly created Commission of Conservation, which recommended a modified version. Although passed by the Senate, the measure—a prohibition against contaminating navigable water in Canada, subject to specifically authorized exemptions—was not considered in the House of Commons because of the unexpected dissolution of Parliament.

Over the years, Belcourt's advocacy of national anti-pollution measures was vigorous and wide-ranging. He turned to history, and Roman law in particular, for the principle that water "is a natural commodity provided by the law of creation for the use of man." "Consequently," Belcourt argued, putting his claim on a very high plane, "the individual and the public as well, have an inalienable and indefeasible right to pure water."[70] But the senator's proposition never became a rallying cry.[71] Belcourt furnished evidence that stringent legislative provisions had been implemented to this effect in European jurisdictions. And, lest apprehension about the practical challenges deter action, he offered a brief inventory of successful—ostensibly even profitable—sewage treatment procedures.[72]

Outside Parliament, Aird Murray promoted government action along the lines of Belcourt's initiatives. Murray voiced the concern that isolated provincial actions would never achieve more than localized responses based on local interests, and that many aspects of the pollution problem would be ignored: "For example the province of Ontario may have the most stringent laws relative to water pollution, and after putting its house in order would be yet dependent upon the action taken by the province of Quebec relative to the pollution of the Ottawa river whose banks are interprovincial."⁷³ Similarly, referring to the United States, he wrote, "while one state may have drastic laws with reference to river pollution, the adjoining state may have none."⁷⁴ Action at the national level, on the other hand, offered attractions: standardized information could be assembled, neglected problems of interprovincial pollution could be addressed, and the array of questions associated with Canada-US boundary waters could be effectively confronted.⁷⁵

Despite the apparent attractions, critics showed no hesitation. Senator McSweeney voiced a strong reservation, inquiring on behalf of the city of Moncton, New Brunswick, whether that community would be put to great expense by the far-ranging proposal. Moncton was by then well accustomed to discharging its sewage into the Petitcodiac River, confident in the capacity of this tidal waterway to flush municipal waste thirty miles into the Bay of Fundy, whence it would be swept into the ocean.⁷⁶ Exemptions were available under the proposed amendment, Belcourt assured his senatorial colleagues, but the expression of doubt was underway. Other senators queried the constitutional authority of the federal government to enact the proposed measure, imagining it to fall more appropriately within provincial jurisdiction. The suggestion was made that the criminal law, statutorily codified in Canada in 1892, was a more suitable location for a prohibition of the sort envisaged. But it was the measure's practical implications that occasioned the most doubt.

Perhaps established communities could be spared, one senator reflected, if the proposed measure could be confined to new localities. Having satisfied himself that Montreal could not possibly prevent its own sewage from accumulating along the St. Lawrence waterfront, Senator Casgrain advanced the self-interested proposition that "it would be a great improvement if in all the new places being constantly established above Montreal such a system were adopted."⁷⁷ The *Sanitary Review* was thus fully vindicated in its assessment of Montreal as "a hygienic disgrace to civilization."⁷⁸

A former Canadian prime minister, Sir Mackenzie Bowell, expressed the opinion that the Belcourt proposal as drafted was too wide in its implications to be carried out. By way of example he described the circumstances of his own community on the Moira River, which flowed to Lake Ontario's Bay of Quinte. The Moira, he explained, extended some hundreds of miles to the north along a course into which twenty or more villages of various sizes emptied their sewage. Numerous other communities along tributary creeks and branches similarly discharged wastes that descended the Moira to the very navigable Bay of Quinte. The proposed legislation, Bowell protested, "provides that if a dead horse is thrown into the river a hundred miles north of its outlet, or sewage from any of the towns or villages upstream is deposited in the waters running into the Bay of Quinte, then the operation of this law could be invoked, because the River Moira empties into the Bay of Quinte."[79] The former prime minister thus emerges as a stalwart defender of the right to throw dead horses and discharge sewage into rivers against the inalienable right to pure water championed by Belcourt. To this end Bowell invoked "scientific treatises" purportedly establishing "very clearly that once sewage is emptied into a running stream, after it has travelled a certain distance it purifies itself."[80]

Belcourt had at least one strong ally in the person of Senator James Lougheed, who seems to have appreciated both the promise and the limitations of his colleague's proposal. While by no means a panacea, Belcourt's measure struck Lougheed as an initiative that had "set public opinion in motion." Something useful might result to address a tragic state of affairs, he said: "all our public streams, provincial and inter-provincial are becoming practically the great sewers of the Dominion." Municipalities, he observed, find it cheaper in their attempts to avoid indebtedness, "to empty their sewers into the streams which run by their doors, than to adopt some scientific method which possibly will cost more, for the purpose of cremating or otherwise destroying the sewage of that community." Concerted national action, Lougheed concluded, was essential to confront the intolerable situation that had developed: "We seem to have concluded that nature has placed those streams by our doors to carry off our sewage, and notwithstanding the fact that the community requires pure water, yet we will reject the best methods of purification and take the consequences. It seems to me we have reached that stage."[81]

Napoléon Belcourt's campaign against pollution of navigable waters during the 1912–15 period coincided with work on the IJC reference, and it encountered comparable obstacles. Municipalities resisted expenditures on sewage treatment where the benefits seemed to accrue to the neighbours. Other municipal critics, notably in coastal communities blessed with the apparent infinity of the undrinkable oceans, rejected national sewage treatment measures as irrelevant to their circumstances, and found amenable parliamentary allies. Constitutional reservations persisted, while the boldness of the flushing constituency reached new heights: Montreal senator Henry Cloran maintained that Canada's geography provided "rivers and lakes large enough to contain all the refuse that the inhabitants of the country could discharge into them, without danger of contagion to the people."[82] A blessed country indeed.

To the extent that Belcourt's proposal had actually secured a sufficient number of allies, even including government supporters, to sustain active interest in Canadian pollution legislation applicable to navigable waters, that pressure dissipated with anticipation of the IJC's final report on boundary water pollution. The desire to avoid inconsistent action, the virtues of being more fully informed, and the significance of simple courtesy or respect for the commission's efforts all counselled delay. Unfortunately, the IJC did not report in 1915 as expected, nor in 1916, nor the year after that. Only in September 1918 did the product of over half a decade of scientific and engineering research, public consultations, and vigorous deliberations emerge from the IJC.[83]

Whether a sincere interest in receiving the findings of the IJC's work, as opposed to the availability of a convenient source of delay, had caused Canadian authorities to set aside the Belcourt initiative is of some interest. Evidently the commission considered the delay unnecessary or merely opportunistic, for it cited the disinclination of governmental authorities at all levels to take responsible action as grounds for endowing yet another jurisdiction with authority over Great Lakes waters and effluent quality, and would have assigned that responsibility to itself.[84]

In relatively short order—that is, by March 1919—the two national governments agreed to call upon the IJC to formulate a convention or to draft concurrent legislation for the purpose of conferring such authority as would be necessary to remedy existing pollution problems. In completing this assignment the following year, the commission proposed a draft treaty that would allow it to investigate sources of pollution on its own initiative while leaving enforcement matters to be addressed on the basis of national legislation.[85] That the fledgling IJC was prepared to assert this level of autonomy over its own potential mandate was indeed remarkable.

Intermittent international negotiations throughout the twenties finally lapsed completely in 1929, to some degree in consequence of other preoccupations triggered by the Great Depression. At the end of the decade, though, health officials still imagined that some basic treatment standard would be adopted for international waters and that the example would inspire communities elsewhere to do the right thing. Only a collective initiative, it was now assumed (in a manner that foreshadowed twenty-first-century global climate policy), could overcome the natural inclination of communities to defer significant local measures in the interests of a wider constituency until they were confident that their efforts would be reciprocated. "So many of our municipalities are located on international waters where similar conditions exist on both sides that there is a distinct tendency to make no move until assurance is given that other offenders will follow the same course." A committee representing communities bordering on international waters had already been formed. It had agreed upon sedimentation as a minimum treatment at such time as treatment might be considered necessary. Ideally, such an example "should have an excellent effect on inland centres where conditions are generally more acute by lack of sufficient dilution water."[86] But time, as we know, then passed.

Conclusion

The IJC's early experience with pollution exhibited a number of notable features. Firstly, of course, the pollution reference addressed a subject whose innovative inclusion in the Boundary Waters Treaty had been something of a struggle. Agreement on the reference, thus, in and of itself, suggests some softening of previous resistance, possibly in the face of prominent calls from both sides of the border, for action. The pollution reference also coincided with important advances in scientific and professional understandings of the role of bacteria in public health. This experience foreshadows future examples of the transboundary influence of experts in fostering a shared outlook. The researchers, by all accounts, collaborated effectively and with a common purpose in mind and offered a valuable illustration of the potential for scientific deliberations to stimulate discussion, if not to resolve policy challenges.

Clearly, if the reference coincided with a new understanding of waterborne diseases, there was no comparable clarity in relation to potential solutions ranging from protecting natural water sources through treating public drinking water supplies. The latter approach ultimately carried the day. This in turn allows us to highlight another feature of the early pollution era, a period focused clearly on public health rather than environmental quality more generally. Later water quality considerations (addressed in several other chapters in this volume) were almost entirely absent from early twentieth-century deliberations apart from passing references to recreational enjoyment of boundary waters and to fishing.

The IJC's boldness or assertiveness in offering itself as a formal source of regulatory authority concerning standards is also notable. The attractions and the pitfalls of such a role are a further aspect of the legacy of the IJC's first water quality inquiry, and should be noted alongside important contributions to capacity-building that resulted from pioneering investigative work, the active exchange of comparative research findings, and the engagement of officials from all levels of government.

Notes

1. International Joint Commission, *Final Report of the International Joint Commission on the Pollution of Boundary Waters Reference* (Ottawa and Washington, DC: Government Printing Bureau, 1918), 27; hereafter "1918 Pollution Reference."

2. J. A. Hassan, "The Growth and Impact of the British Water Industry in the Nineteenth Century," *Economic History Review* 39 (2nd Series) (1983): 531 at 543.

3. Joel A. Tarr, Terrie Yosie, and James McCurley, "Disputes Over Water Quality Policy: Professional Cultures in Conflict, 1900-1917," *American Journal of Public Health* 70 (1980): 427. See also "Mr Roosevelt and the People," *Outlook* 96 (1910): 1, as quoted in Joel A. Tarr, "Environmental Risk in Historical Perspective," in *The Social and Cultural Construction of Risk: Essays on Risk Selection and Perception*, ed. Branden B. Johnson and Vincent T. Covello (Dordrecht, NL: D. Reidel, 1987), 317 at 320; "The Pollution of Lakes and Rivers," *Outlook* 96 (1910): 144-5.

4. Ontario Archives, Provincial Board of Health, RG62 Series B4, Scrapboooks, Item 32, 1884, "Sawdust Survey," PH Bryce, Secretary; Ontario Archives, RG 62B4, Scrapbooks, Item 56, 10 May 1886.

5. As quoted by C. -E. A. Winslow, "Pioneers of Sewage Disposal in New England," in *Modern Sewage Disposal*, ed. Langdon Pearse (New York: Federation of Sewage Works Associations, 1938), 276 at 279.

6   Donald J. Pisani, "Fish Culture and the Dawn of Concern over Water Pollution in the United States," *Environmental Review* 8, no. 2 (1984): 24.

7   Health Committee of the Massachusetts Board of Health, "Lunacy and Charity," quoted in Barbara Gutmann Rosenkrantz, *Public Health and the State* (Cambridge, MA: Harvard University Press, 1972), 81.

8   Ontario, Provincial Board of Health *Annual Report, 1892*, 50.

9   John Duffy, *The Sanitarians: A History of American Public Health* (Urbana and Chicago: University of Illinois Press, 1990) 176, 194, 201–2.

10 "Report of Sedgewick's presentation to the Lowell Water Board," 9 January 1891, available through the University of Massachusetts at Lowell, Center for Lowell History, available at https://uml.worldcat.org/title/report-upon-the-sanitary-condition-of-the-water-supply-of-lowell-mass-presented-to-the-water-board-of-lowell-april-10-1891/oclc/55483004?referer=di&ht=edition.

11 Quoted in Rosencrantz, *Public Health and the State*, 105.

12 Ibid.

13 Quoted in C.-E. A. Winslow and Earle B. Phelps, "The Purification of Boston Sewage," (Washington, DC: United States Geological Service, 1906), 37.

14 Ibid., 39.

15 Keith Vernon, "Pus, Sewage, Beer and Milk: Microbiology in Britain, 1870–1940," *History of Science* 28, no. 3 (1990): 289.

16 Joel A. Tarr, "Industrial Wastes and Public Health: Some Historical Notes, Part 1, 1876–1932," *American Journal of Public Health* 75, no. 9 (1985): 1059 at 1060.

17 Duffy, *The Sanitarians*, 129, 187.

18 Earl Finbar Murphy, *Water Purity: A Study in Legal Control of Natural Resources* (Madison: University of Wisconsin, 1961), 29–30.

19 Henry Bixby Hemenway, *Legal Principles of Public Health Administration* (Chicago: T. H. Flood, 1914), 684.

20 45 Vict. (1882), c. 29.

21 J. E. Hodgetts, *From Arm's Length to Hands-On: The Formative Years of Ontario's Public Service, 1867–1940*, (Toronto: University of Toronto Press for the Ontario Historical Studies Series, 1995), 20–1.

22 Ibid., 14.

23 Rosenkrantz, *Public Health and the State*, 52.

24 Ontario, Provincial Board of Health *Annual Report, 1884*, 15, 22, 26.

25 Ibid., 22.

26 Edwin B. Goodell, "A Review of the Laws Forbidding Pollution of Inland Waters in the United States" (Washington, DC: United States Geological Survey, Department of the Interior, Water-Supply and Irrigation Paper No. 152, 1905), 32.

27 Ibid., 33.

28 Ibid., 73.

29 Ibid., 107, 109.

30 Charges were laid under the Public Health Act 2 George V, c. 58, s. 91. The prohibition was introduced to Ontario law by the Statute Law Amendment Act, 1906 6 Edward VII S.O. c. 19, assented to 14 May 1906.

31 S.O. 1912 c.58 s.8(o).

32 S.O. 1912 c.58 s.73.

33 See, for example, *Re Waterloo Local Board of Health. Campbell's Case* (1918), 44 OLR 338.

34 Michele Dagenais, *Montreal et l'eau: une histoire environnementale* (Montreal: Boréal, 2011); Nancy B. Boucher and Ken Cruikshank, *The People and the Bay: a social and environmental history of Hamilton Harbour* (Vancouver: UBC Press, 2016).

35 Allen Hazen, *Clean Water and How to Get It*, 2nd ed. (New York: John Wiley, 1914), 31.

36 Margaret Beattie Bogue, *Fishing the Great Lakes: An Environmental History, 1783–1933*, (Madison: University of Wisconsin Press, 2000), 144–5.

37 George C. Whipple, *The Value of Pure Water* (New York: John Wiley and Sons, 1907), 36.

38 "Mr Roosevelt and the People," 1.

39 Marshall Ora Leighton, *Sewage Pollution in the Metropolitan Area near New York City and its Effect on Inland Water Resources* (Washington, DC: US Government Printing Office, 1902), 10.

40 T. Aird Murray, *The Prevention of the Pollution of Canadian Surface Waters* (Ottawa: Commission of Conservation, 1912). The three articles reproduced in this pamphlet originally appeared in the Toronto *Globe*, 30 December 1911 and early January 1912.

41 IJC, Progress Report of the IJC on the Reference by the United States and Canada in "The Pollution of Boundary Waters," 16 January 1914, 2–7; henceforth "1914 Progress Report."

42 For a description of the use of "indicator" organisms to detect contamination, see D. Krewski, J. Babus, D. Butler-Jones, C. Haas, J. Isaac-Renton, K. J. Roberts, and M. Sinclair, "Managing Heath Risks from Drinking Water," *Journal of Toxicology and Environmental Health* 65 (2002): 1635 at 1692–5.

43 IJC, 1914 Progress Report, 14. During at least one of the three years preceding the reference (1910–12), a death rate (per 100,000) of over 300 was registered in Ashland, Wisconsin; of 109 in Marquette, Michigan; of 196 in Port Huron, Michigan; of 194 in Niagara Falls, New York; of 190 in Erie, Pennsylvania; and above 50 in the Michigan communities of Alpena, Bay City, and Sault Ste. Marie, as well as in Duluth, Minnesota, and Sandusky, Ohio. The Ontario side produced equally alarming numbers—330 in Sault Ste. Marie; 179 in Port Arthur; 134 in Sarnia; 86 in Niagara Falls; 63 in Brockville; and 55 and 57 in Windsor and Walkerville, respectively. Even comparatively fortunate

Great Lakes cities such as Detroit, where the rate had never fallen below 15, and in 1913 had a rate of above 30, were operating at levels of typhoid that would not be tolerated in Europe.

44 IJC, 1918 Pollution Reference, 39.
45 Ibid., 31.
46 IJC, 1914 Progress Report, 12.
47 The exception was Lackawanna, which discharged its water through Smoke's Creek a mile and a half above the head of the river.
48 IJC, 1914 Progress Report, 8.
49 Ibid., 45.
50 James Mansergh, *The Water Supply of the City of Toronto, Canada* (Westminster, 1896), 19.
51 IJC, 1914 Progress Report, 21.
52 IJC, 1918 Pollution Reference, 48.
53 IJC, 1914 Progress Report, Appendix, 354.
54 Ibid., 353.
55 Ibid., 356.
56 Ibid., 3.
57 Ibid., 7–8.
58 Ibid., 12.
59 Jamie Benidickson, *The Culture of Flushing: A Social and Legal History of Sewage* (Vancouver: UBC Press, 2007).
60 Writing in the US Public Health Service Annual Report 41–41 (1913), as quoted in L. B. Dworsky, "Assessing North America's Management of its Transboundary Waters," *Natural Resources Journal* 33 (1993): 427.
61 IJC, 1918 Pollution Reference, 50, 52.
62 John Capper, Garrett Power, and Frank R. Shivers Jr., *Chesapeake Waters: Pollution, Public Health and Public Opinion, 1607–1972* (Centreville, MD: Tidewater Publishers, 1983), 97. See also William L. Andreen, "The Evolution of Water Pollution Control in the United States—State, Local and Federal Efforts, 1789–1972, Part II," *Stanford Environmental Law Journal* 22 (2003): 222–3; N. William Hines, "Nor Any Drop to Drink: Public Regulation of Water Quality, Part III: The Federal Effort," *Iowa Law Review* 52 (1967): 804–5.
63 The initial US Treasury Department standard specified a maximum limit of 2 B. coli per 100 c.c. George W Fuller, "Relations Between Sewage Disposal and Water Supply are Changing," *Engineering New-Record*, 5 April 1917, 12.

64 B. Grover and D. Zussman, *Safeguarding Canadian Drinking Water* (Ottawa: Inquiry on Federal Water Policy, Research Paper No. 4, 1985); Frank Quinn, "The Evolution of Federal Water Policy," *Canadian Water Resources Journal* 10 (1985): 21 at 25.

65 IJC, 1918, 36.

66 Ibid., 48.

67 Ibid., 36.

68 For a more comprehensive review of the challenges of introducing sewage treatment, see Benidickson, *The Culture of Flushing*.

69 Senate of Canada, Debates 2 March 1910, 349.

70 Senate of Canada, Debates 2 March 1910, 335.

71 The Boundary Waters Treaty had put domestic uses at the top of its hierarchy, and distinguished sanitation.

72 Senate of Canada, Debates 2 March 1910, 342.

73 Murray, *Pollution of Canadian Surface Waters*, 7.

74 Ibid., 8.

75 Ibid., 6.

76 Senate of Canada, Debates 2 March 1910, 341 (Senator McSweeney).

77 Senate of Canada, Debates, 3 March 1910, 352–3 (Senator Casgrain).

78 *Canadian Engineer* 16 (16 April 1909): 527.

79 Senate of Canada, Debates, 3 March 1901, 370.

80 Ibid.

81 Senate of Canada, Debates, 3 March 1910, 371–2.

82 Jennifer Read, "Water Pollution Management in the Great Lakes Basin, 1900–1930" (paper presented to Themes and Issues in North American Environmental History Conference, April 1998), 9. See also Jennifer Read, " 'A Sort of Destiny': The Multi-Jurisdictional Response to Sewage Pollution in the Great Lakes, 1900–1930," *Scientia canadensis* 55 (1999): 103–29.

83 *Final Report of the International Joint Commission on the Pollution of Boundary Waters Reference* (Ottawa and Washington, DC: Government Printing Bureau, 1918).

84 Read, "Water Pollution Management in the Great Lakes Basin," 14–15.

85 F. J. E. Jordan, "Great Lakes Pollution: A Framework for Action," *Ottawa Law Review* 5 (1971): 65 at 69.

86 Provincial Board of Health *Annual Report, 1929*, 49.

# The Boundary Waters Treaty and the International Joint Commission in the St. Mary–Milk Basin

B. Timothy Heinmiller

The St. Mary and Milk River basins, shared by Alberta, Saskatchewan, and Montana in the Western Prairies, have a long history of international conflict and co-operation. In fact, as mentioned in the introductory chapter of this book, international conflict in the St. Mary–Milk was one of the motivating factors in the negotiation of the Boundary Waters Treaty (BWT) in 1909, and part of the BWT is specifically dedicated to managing conflicts in the basin. The root of conflict in the St. Mary–Milk has to do with the region's endemic water scarcity and the heavy demands placed on it by water users, particularly irrigators, on both sides of the border. Article VI of the BWT addresses this conflict by establishing an international water apportionment, dividing the waters of the St. Mary–Milk between the two countries sharing it. Quite quickly, the apportionment became the centrepiece of conflict management in the St. Mary–Milk and administering the apportionment became the International Joint Commission's (IJC) most important function in the basin.

However, the article VI apportionment was introduced over a hundred years ago, so it is important to examine how successful it has been in managing conflict thus far, and whether it will be sustainable in the future. An examination of the historical record suggests that the apportionment

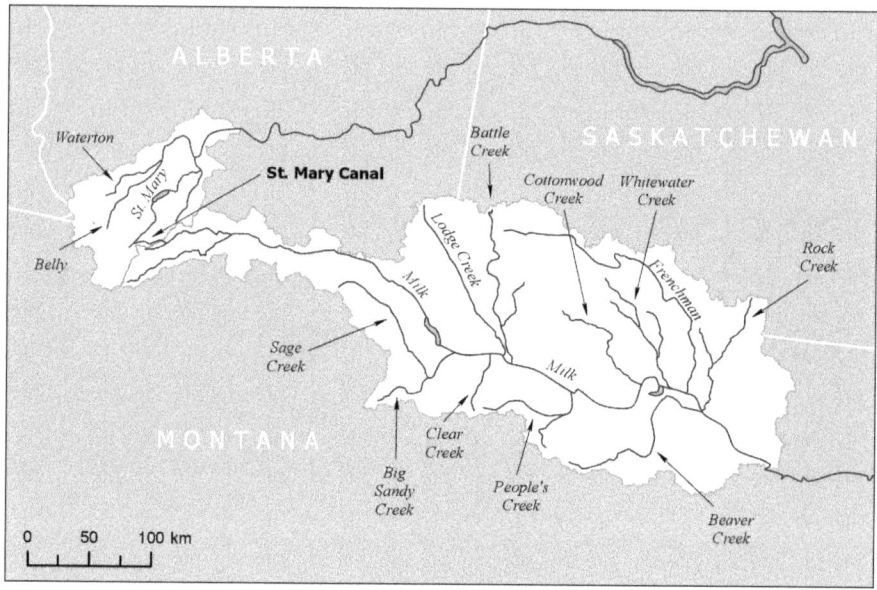

FIGURE 4.1. Map of the St. Mary–Milk watershed. J. Glatz, Western Michigan University Libraries.

has been successful in containing—but not resolving—water use conflicts in the St. Mary–Milk. That is, the apportionment has prevented many conflicts from getting out of hand, but it has not resolved these conflicts entirely. Looking forward, many of these simmering conflicts are likely to resurface, and could become more intractable, as the effects of climate change take hold. Climate change is expected to increase water scarcity in the St. Mary–Milk, so the demands on the basin, and the pressures on the governments sharing it, are likely to be even more acute in the apportionment's second century than in its first.

This chapter examines the history (and future) of St. Mary–Milk conflict management in five sections. The first section describes the hydrology of the St. Mary–Milk, its economic uses, and its international upstream-downstream dynamics. The second section recounts the importance of the St. Mary–Milk in the negotiation of the BWT and the central role of the article vi apportionment in the management of international conflicts in the basin. Section three examines a range of historical conflicts in the basin, noting the general trend toward conflict containment, but not resolution. The fourth section describes the most likely effects of climate change and projects how the changing climate could impact ongoing water conflicts in the region. The final section summarizes the analysis and speculates on the apportionment's future.

The St. Mary–Milk Basin(s)

The St. Mary and Milk are naturally separate and adjacent river basins that, technologically and politically, have been joined as one.[1] The St. Mary basin originates in Montana and flows northward into Alberta, where it forms part of the larger Saskatchewan-Nelson basin that empties into Hudson's Bay. The Milk basin, just east of the St. Mary, also rises in Montana and flows into Alberta before turning southward, re-entering Montana, and joining the Missouri River, which, eventually, drains into the Gulf of Mexico. The two basins are separate in their natural hydrology, but close in their geographical proximity, particularly in their respective headwaters in northwestern Montana and southwestern Alberta. Early in the twentieth century, canals linking the two basins were built in both Montana and Alberta, allowing water to be diverted between them, and empowering their users to treat them as, essentially, a single basin. This inter-basin marriage was then formalized in article vi of the BWT, which explicitly and purposefully provided for the two basins to be governed as a single hydrological unit.[2] Since then, it has been impossible to separate the two basins, especially in their international governance.

Some of the reasons for connecting the two basins had to do with their natural characteristics. In terms of natural river flows, the St. Mary is far larger than the Milk. The median annual flow of the St. Mary River, at the international border, is 771,300 dam^3 compared to 149,400 dam^3 for the Milk.[3] The flows of the St. Mary are also more reliable than the Milk, as the St. Mary's flows range 106 per cent from the median while the Milk's flows range 220 per cent.[4] The St. Mary's flows are more reliable because part of its source is glacial melt from the Rocky Mountains, which is available every year, while the Milk relies entirely on snowmelt and rainfall run-off, which varies with the changing weather. The larger size and higher reliability of the St. Mary prompted plans to connect it with the Milk, the objective being to augment the Milk's flows with St. Mary water to increase both the size and the reliability of the Milk.

Other reasons for connecting the St. Mary and Milk Rivers were related to their human uses, particularly agricultural irrigation, which is the largest user of water in the basin by far. The St. Mary–Milk is situated in the semi-arid Prairie region, where precipitation is scarce (500 mm or less per year) and highly variable.[5] In order to put more land into production and to grow higher-value crops, irrigation is very important on both sides of the border. However, irrigation requires a voracious use of water, so large-scale irrigation puts heavy demands on the basin's rivers. In Montana, irrigation development has concentrated in the eastern part of the Milk and, to support this irrigation, a canal was completed in 1917 to divert St. Mary's water into the Milk.[6] In Alberta, large-scale irrigation development has concentrated in the Lethbridge Plains of the St. Mary basin, with only a few, smaller irrigation projects in its portion of the Milk.[7] It is important to note that both Montana and Alberta covet the upstream flows of the St. Mary River, the former to support irrigation in the Milk and the latter to support irrigation in the downstream portion of the St. Mary. This political-economic dynamic has been fundamentally important in shaping how the St. Mary–Milk has been developed and, ultimately, how it has been governed.

In addition to the St. Mary and Milk Rivers, there are a number of smaller international rivers in the basin also worth mentioning. For example, the Waterton and Belly Rivers are located just west of the St. Mary. These rivers originate in Montana and flow into Alberta, where they join up with the St. Mary to help form the Oldman River. In the Milk basin, there are a number of rivers and creeks that originate in the Cypress Hills of Alberta and Saskatchewan and form tributaries of the Milk. These rivers are known as the Eastern Tributaries, and include such notable bodies as the Frenchman River, Poplar River, Battle Creek, Lodge Creek, and Sage Creek.[8] The Waterton and Belly Rivers, and the Eastern Tributaries, are all smaller than the St. Mary and Milk Rivers, but their political-economic dynamics are largely the same: irrigation is the dominant water use, and there is considerable competition among water users on both sides of the border to capture scarce water resources.[9]

Overall, international governance of the St. Mary–Milk is characterized by scarcity, zero-sum competition, and offsetting upstream-downstream dynamics. As a semi-arid region, water is naturally scarce in the St. Mary–Milk and heavy demands are placed on its rivers, particularly from agricultural irrigation. Since irrigation is a consumptive use of water, the water taken by some irrigators leaves less for others, giving the competition to secure water a zero-sum dynamic. This dynamic also plays out at the international level, particularly with respect to the St. Mary headwaters, which are sought-after by irrigators in both countries.[10] Even more interesting are the offsetting upstream-downstream dynamics in the basin. The main irrigation areas in both Alberta and Montana are situated in locations downstream of the others: Alberta's irrigation areas are downstream of Montana on the St. Mary, and Montana's irrigation areas are downstream of Alberta on the Milk. This makes each jurisdiction's irrigation areas vulnerable to unilateral actions (and retaliations) by the other, creating a sort of "mutually assured destruction" situation that creates underlying incentives for co-operation. This has played a big role in the governance of the St. Mary–Milk and was a key factor in the negotiation of the BWT itself.

The St. Mary–Milk in the Formation of the BWT

International controversy over the appropriation and use of the St. Mary–Milk dates to the early 1890s. Around this time, officials in both the US Department of Agriculture and the Canadian Ministry of the Interior realized that the waters of the St. Mary could be diverted to support large-scale irrigation in the region. On the US side of the border, a proposal was developed to build a canal from St. Mary Lake to the Milk River that would divert St. Mary water into the Milk. The diverted water would flow northward through Canadian territory until it re-entered the United States, where it could be tapped by American irrigators on the eastern part of the Milk. Since the Milk River naturally flowed in a deep channel, the river had plenty of capacity for additional water, and it was believed that the deep channel would make it impossible for the Canadians to divert this water for their own purposes as it flowed through their territory. On the Canadian side of the border, irrigation boosters were developing plans for large-scale irrigation on the Lethbridge Plains, and these plans substantially relied on the availability of St. Mary water. "As there was not enough water in the St. Mary to satisfy the needs of all the lands on both sides of the border a controversy arose over who should have the right to use the waters."[11]

Further complicating matters was the prevalence of the Harmon Doctrine in the United States at this time. The Harmon Doctrine, named after former US attorney general Judson Harmon, was developed during a conflict between the United States and Mexico over the waters of the Rio Grande. Under the Harmon Doctrine, the United States asserted that, as the upstream jurisdiction, it had absolute sovereignty over the waters of the Rio Grande; could dispose of these waters as it wished; and had no obligation to allow any of these waters to flow into Mexico. In effect, the Harmon Doctrine claimed unilateral control of waters for upstream jurisdictions.[12] On the St. Mary, the United States was the upstream jurisdiction, so many Americans called for the application of the Harmon Doctrine there as well. The United States was also a downstream jurisdiction on the Milk, but, since it was believed that the Canadians could not divert water out of the deep Milk channel, any upstream advantaged enjoyed by Canada on the Milk was effectively negated.[13] So, for much of the 1890s and into the early 1900s, it looked like the St. Mary–Milk controversy might be addressed unilaterally by the United States through its application of the Harmon Doctrine.

However, as the St. Mary–Milk controversy continued, a number of factors pushed the US and Canadian governments toward co-operation rather than confrontation. First, the canal diverting water from the St. Mary to the Milk in Montana did not materialize as quickly as first expected. The eventual St. Mary Canal did not become fully operational until 1917, leaving time for the governments to resolve their differences before the development pressures on the St. Mary became overwhelming. Second, the belief that the Canadians could not divert water out of the Milk proved false. Just such a canal was approved by the Canadian government and completed in 1903, allowing Canadian irrigators to reclaim any St. Mary water diverted into the Milk. This negated the upstream advantage enjoyed by the United States, made it almost impossible for them to apply the Harmon Doctrine, and provided strong incentives to reach some kind of negotiated settlement.[14] Third, as negotiations progressed, the St. Mary–Milk controversy became linked with other cross-border water disputes, particularly those stemming from the development of hydroelectric power generation facilities on the St Mary's[15] and Niagara Rivers in the Great Lakes basin.[16] With this linkage, the negotiations over the St. Mary–Milk evolved into negotiations for a general treaty over Canada-US shared waters, as described by Whorley and Denning in their respective contributions to this volume.

By 1905, the United States, having moved away from unilateralism, expressed a desire to reach a mutually agreeable solution on the St. Mary–Milk. The two countries appointed representatives to an International Waterways Commission, which investigated the various cross-border water disputes and recommended measures to address them. In its April 1906 report, the commission made a couple of key recommendations with regard to the St. Mary–Milk. First, it suggested that each country should be able to divert "in equal quantities" from rivers crossing the international border.[17] This, in effect, recommended an international apportionment of the waters of the St. Mary–Milk that should be based on the principle of equal sharing. Second, the commission recommended the creation of a "permanent joint commission" that would allow the countries to deal more effectively with their cross-border water disputes than the current ad hoc approach.[18] This was particularly important in the St. Mary–Milk, where some sort of international body would be needed to oversee the international apportionment and manage disputes arising from it. Negotiations over a general water treaty ensued for another three years, but the principles espoused by the International Waterways Commission are clearly reflected in the eventual design of the BWT.

Article vi of the BWT is so specific to the St. Mary–Milk, and so unlike the other articles in the treaty, that Mitchner describes it as "almost a treaty within a treaty."[19] Essentially, article vi fleshes out the apportionment recommended by the International Waterways Commission. It states that the two rivers "are to be treated as one stream for the purposes of irrigation and power, and the waters thereof shall be apportioned equally between the two countries, but in making such equal apportionment more than half may be taken from one river and less than half from the other by either country so as to afford a more beneficial use to each."[20] During the irrigation season, which lasts from April to October, article vi also established a US prior appropriation of 500 cubic feet per second (cfs) on the Milk and a Canadian prior appropriation of 500 cfs on the St. Mary, and guaranteed that the United States could use the Milk to convey water diverted from the St. Mary, without undue Canadian interference. Thus, the apportionment was meant to be equitable in aggregate, but Canada was granted measures to support irrigation development in the lower St. Mary basin and the United States was granted measures to support irrigation development in the lower Milk basin, reflecting the areas of major irrigation development in each country. Article vi further established that the entire apportionment arrangement would be jointly overseen by water administrators from both countries, a provision that would eventually result in the creation of an international administrative panel—known as the accredited officers—which still functions to this day.[21]

As Whorley points out in his chapter, the St. Mary–Milk and Niagara Rivers are the only waterways with specific provisions in the BWT, and only the St. Mary–Milk, through article vi, is subject to apportionment. Dividing the waters of the St. Mary–Milk was an important step in managing international conflict in the basin, and the apportionment approach was in keeping with practices utilized in other transboundary river basins in the arid and semi-arid parts of western North America and southeastern Australia.[22] However, the article vi apportionment did not end conflict in the basin once and for all. Instead, article vi became the institutional framework through which further conflicts in the St. Mary–Milk were played out, and its main effect has been to contain conflict in the basin rather than resolving it, as over a century of experience with the treaty can attest.

Managing Conflicts Under the BWT

Within only a few years of the BWT's completion, Canada-US disagreements about the interpretation of article vi began to surface and became so severe that they put the treaty itself in jeopardy. In 1913, the IJC appointed two of its commissioners, Henry Powell of Canada and Obadiah Gardner of the United States, to a special committee to investigate apportionment-related disputes in the St. Mary–Milk. The two commissioners toured the basin and recommended that public hearings be held before the IJC issued an order clarifying the interpretation of article vi.[23] The public hearings were held between 1915 and 1921, at various locations both inside and outside of the basin, and, during this period, the IJC issued a number of provisional orders dividing the St. Mary–Milk waters during irrigation seasons. Despite these efforts, the conflict threatened to spin out of control as the US government claimed that it would ignore any IJC ruling that did not favour its interpretation of the article vi apportionment.[24]

The conflicts of interpretation essentially boiled down to two issues: 1) the locations at which the apportionment should be measured; and 2) the reconciliation of the countries' prior appropriations with the principle of equal sharing.[25] In order to divide the waters of the St. Mary–Milk, the countries needed to agree on locations at which the river flows would be measured and apportioned. While the United States argued that the apportionments should take place where the rivers crossed the international border, Canada argued that the apportionments should take place much further upstream, closer to the rivers' respective sources, before any water had been lost to evaporation, absorption, or diversion. Canada pushed for this interpretation because it would secure it a larger share of the basin's water. On the other question, both countries agreed that Canada should receive its 500 cfs prior appropriation from the St. Mary and that the United States should receive its 500 cfs prior appropriation from the Milk before the remaining river flows were divided between the two countries. However, after the initial 500 cfs prior appropriations were met, Canada argued that the waters of the St. Mary and Milk should be divided equally between the two countries, while the United States argued that the next 500 cfs on each river should go to the lower-prioritized countries, as a sort of balancing measure, with equal division of river flows only thereafter. The United States took this position because it would provide its irrigators with more water from the St. Mary in the driest years.

The conflict over the interpretation of article vi intensified with the completion of the St. Mary Canal in 1917, which placed more demands on the basin's waters, and the IJC finally issued an order in October 1921 clarifying its interpretation of the apportionment. The commissioners crafted a compromise that essentially accepted the American position on the locations at which the apportionment should be measured and the

Canadian position on the reconciliation of the prior appropriations with the principle of equal sharing. Under the 1921 order, all international rivers in the St. Mary–Milk basin, including the Eastern Tributaries, would be apportioned at the international border. During the irrigation season, each country would receive its respective prior appropriation, and river flows beyond these levels would be divided equally. In especially dry years, when river flows were low and meeting the prior appropriations would create hardships in the lower-prioritized countries, the prior appropriations were reduced to three-quarters of the available flows, to ensure that the lower-prioritized countries received at least a small amount of water. The order also touched on the apportionment of the Eastern Tributaries, which, because there were no established prior appropriations, were to be divided equally between the two countries.[26] Neither country was entirely satisfied with the 1921 order and, much like article vi itself, the order has become part of the institutional framework for managing international conflict in the St. Mary–Milk.

The most dissatisfaction has been expressed by Montana, which has repeatedly claimed that the 1921 order violates the principle of equal sharing in article vi because, in aggregate, it provides more water to Canada than the United States.[27] Historic flow records show that, indeed, Canada has consistently received more water from the St. Mary–Milk than has the United States. However, whether this is attributable to the 1921 order, to a lack of storage capacity in Montana, or to other factors remains controversial.[28] Nevertheless, between 1928 and 1932, Montana brought its concerns about the order before the IJC no less than four times. In 1932, the IJC voted on whether to reopen the order and—for the first time in its history—the commissioners split along national lines, with the American commissioners voting in favour and the Canadian commissioners voting against. The stalemate meant that there was no mandate to reopen the order, so it remained in force as the status quo, establishing a sort of uneasy truce in the St. Mary–Milk conflict, a truce that persisted for the rest of the twentieth century.

The persistence of this truce, and one of the main reasons that article vi and the 1921 order have succeeded in containing conflict in the St. Mary–Milk, has to do with the work of the accredited officers. The accredited officers is an international panel of water administrators that monitors flows in the St. Mary–Milk and reports on compliance with the international apportionment: three of its members come from the Canadian government and three from the US government.[29] The creation of such an international oversight panel was provided for in article vi of the BWT, and the 1921 order elaborated further on its responsibilities.[30]

The accredited officers are very important in the St. Mary–Milk because they work to manage small international water conflicts before they can become big ones. For example, the accredited officers report on apportionment compliance every fifteen or sixteen days, a time span known as a balancing period. If an upstream country has diverted too much water during a balancing period, this creates a water deficit owing to the downstream country whose treaty entitlement has not been met. Standard practice of the accredited officers is to have any water deficit from one balancing period be made up in the next balancing period, thereby fulfilling treaty requirements without creating an international incident.[31] The accredited officers are also empowered to trade off water deficits between rivers in the St. Mary–Milk basin if the trade-offs are acceptable to both countries and can facilitate treaty compliance.[32] In this way, and others, the accredited officers have a degree of flexibility and discretion in monitoring and implementing the apportionment, and they have used this to make the apportionment work for both countries and to manage and contain conflicts.

Despite the general success of the accredited officers, Montana's underlying resentment of the 1921 order has remained, and the state continues to challenge it. In 2003–4, Montana's governor requested that the IJC reopen the order on the grounds that it violated the principle of equal sharing by providing more water to Canada. In response, the IJC held public meetings in the basin during the summer of 2004 and appointed an Administrative Measures Task Force to review the order's implementation.[33] The task force recommended a number of changes to the way the St. Mary–Milk apportionment is administered, and it encouraged the governments of Alberta and Montana to work more closely on St. Mary–Milk governance issues. Alberta and Montana followed up by launching the joint Water Management Initiative in early 2009, and since then Alberta and Montana officials have met over a dozen times to discuss St. Mary–Milk issues.[34] Nevertheless, the order itself was not reopened or amended, so it is unlikely that the underlying source of Montana's grievance has been addressed.

As intimated above, other, smaller rivers in the St. Mary–Milk basin have also been subject to international apportionment, and the situations on these rivers are similar to those on the St. Mary and Milk Rivers themselves: difficult and protracted zero-sum conflicts that the BWT and the 1921 order have contained but not permanently resolved.

Take, for example, the Waterton and Belly Rivers (also discussed by Pentland and Yuzyk in their chapter in this volume), which lie west of the St. Mary, originating in Montana and flowing northward into Alberta's Oldman River. In the late 1940s, the Canadian government, through its Prairie Farm Rehabilitation Administration, undertook irrigation development in the Waterton and Belly sub-basins that would appropriate most of the water available from these rivers. Since most of the land in Montana's portion of the Waterton and Belly was not amenable to cropping, the Canadian government expected little resistance from the United States. However, the United States objected to the Canadian appropriations on the grounds that it could, at some point, divert these rivers to remote areas more suitable to agriculture, and it argued that it should receive compensation for Canada's over-appropriation, in the form of additional water from the St. Mary. Canada rejected this position and the matter was referred to the IJC in 1948.[35] After two years of investigations and hearings, the commissioners were unable to reach consensus, but instead split along national lines and issued separate reports to their governments. This is the only instance in the history of the IJC in which separate reports have been submitted. Ultimately, no satisfactory resolution to the Waterton-Belly conflict was found: Canada went ahead with its irrigation development and further escalation was avoided only because the terrain on the American side of the border made retaliatory action prohibitively difficult.[36]

On Sage Creek, a small, closed stream[37] originating in the Cypress Hills of southeastern Alberta and terminating just across the border in Montana, international conflict over apportionment also came to a stalemate. Conflict erupted in the mid-1940s when ranchers on the American side of the border complained that the flow of Sage Creek was being unduly interrupted on the Canadian side. The matter was referred to the IJC for investigation, and the commission issued a report recommending a formal apportionment for the stream and the construction of a dam to serve the water users in the area. However, both governments rejected the IJC's recommendations as financially unviable, so the IJC resorted to working informally with water users on both sides of the border in an effort to contain the conflict.[38]

On the Eastern Tributaries of the Milk, apportionment is also an issue in the three largest streams: Lodge Creek, Battle Creek, and the Frenchman River. Apportionment of these rivers is covered by the 1921 order, which, in the absence of any specified prior appropriations on these streams, called for them to be apportioned equally between the two countries. Formal apportionment began in 1937 on the Frenchman River, in 1957 on Battle Creek, and in 1961 on Lodge Creek. The other notable Eastern Tributaries, which include the Woodpile, East Fork Battle, Lyons, Whitewater, Rock, and McEachern Creeks, do not have apportionments because they are not heavily used on the Canadian side of the border, and they have not prompted complaint from the American side.[39] Presumably, these streams and any other Eastern Tributaries would also be governed by the principle of equal sharing if cross-border appropriation conflicts were to emerge.

Overall, in the St. Mary–Milk basin, the BWT and the IJC have been tasked with managing difficult, zero-sum water apportionment issues, and, though they have succeeded in containing these conflicts, in most cases they have not been able to resolve them. Montana remains unsatisfied with the 1921 order on the apportionment of the St. Mary and Milk Rivers, and no agreement on apportioning the Waterton River, the Belly River, or Sage Creek has been reached. The apportionment of the Eastern Tributaries appears to be more settled, but there remain a number of unapportioned streams in this area that could be a source of conflict. The difficulties faced by the IJC in managing St. Mary–Milk apportionment conflicts are illustrated by the splits among the IJC commissioners with respect to the St. Mary and Milk Rivers in 1932 and the Waterton and Belly Rivers in 1950. Such splits have been exceedingly rare in the history of the IJC, and it is telling that they have been most prevalent on apportionment issues in the St. Mary–Milk.

Despite these challenges, international water conflict has not escalated out of control, and neither country has significantly defected from the BWT. The offsetting international upstream-downstream dynamics surely have something to do with this, as each country knows that the other can retaliate if it takes damaging unilateral action on any one river. However, it is also clear that both countries see something of great value in the treaty that is worth preserving. Close co-operation, particularly through the accredited officers, has been good for irrigation development in the basin, facilitating the irrigation of 247,600 hectares in the Canadian lower St. Mary, 3,480 hectares in the Canadian Milk, 13,800 hectares in the Canadian Eastern Tributaries, and 44,500 hectares in the American Milk.[40] Both countries are unwilling to put the international water governance regime that underpins this development at risk by allowing any single water conflict to destroy it. Moreover, more than a century of close co-operation has created a network of contacts and trust ties between water administrators on both sides of the border, which has also helped to contain escalating conflicts. So, although the BWT has not resolved water conflicts in the St. Mary–Milk, it has effectively contained them, which may be the most that can be reasonably expected in a basin characterized by intractable, zero-sum water apportionment issues.

A Changing Climate

In their second century, the BWT and the IJC now face a new water governance challenge in the St. Mary–Milk basin: climate change. Most climate change models predict that the Prairie region will become warmer and its precipitation patterns more erratic as climate change accelerates, with important implications for the region's rivers and how they are governed.

The predicted effects of climate change in the St. Mary–Milk are manifold. As the region becomes warmer and its precipitation patterns more erratic, it is likely to experience more frequent extreme weather events, such as intense floods and prolonged droughts. Higher winter temperatures are predicted to cause more winter precipitation to fall as rain rather than snow, which is highly problematic for farmers because much of the water will run off during the winter months when it cannot be used for irrigation, rather than staying around as snowpack and feeding the rivers during the spring melt.[41] There is also evidence that the St. Mary River, which has part of its source in the Rocky Mountains, will experience a long-term decline in flows due to melting glaciers and reduced winter snows. Furthermore, higher summer temperatures, while increasing the potential growing season for farmers, will also increase evaporation rates, creating more demand for water at times when available supplies are likely to be at their lowest.[42] Overall, the median water supply in the St. Mary–Milk is expected to decline as a result of climate change, creating a number of new challenges for the international river apportionments in the basin.

These climate change effects must also be considered in light of the St. Mary–Milk's current state of use, which can best be described as "full allocation." While the governments of Canada and the United States are responsible for the international governance of the basin, the governments of Alberta and Montana are responsible for allocating water entitlements in the basin, and these governments have decided (individually) that most of their respective portions of the St. Mary–Milk have reached the point of full allocation. Full allocation means that such a large volume of water entitlements has already been allocated that the rivers do not have enough remaining flows to support additional entitlements. As a result, Alberta closed the St. Mary, Waterton, and Belly Rivers to new water licence applications in the late 1970s and closed its portion of the Milk River in 1985.[43] Similarly, Montana closed part of its portion of the Milk basin in 1991.[44] At full allocation, there is very little "extra" water in the St. Mary–Milk system, so if the median water supply declines as a result of climate change, there is unlikely to be enough water to support all existing uses. In other words, current development levels in the basin—particularly current irrigation levels—may not be sustainable in the context of climate change, and this is likely to create new challenges in the international governance of the basin.

For example, consider the projected long-term decline in St. Mary River flows. The melting and eventual disappearance of the Rocky Mountain glaciers that feed the St. Mary River is problematic because both countries rely heavily on this water. The St. Mary is the largest river in the basin and it has the most reliable flows, due, in part, to the glacial melt that provides part of its source. The main irrigation areas on both sides of the border rely on this water and its disappearance creates a considerable problem for them. As the St. Mary's flows decline and become more erratic, both the US and Canadian governments are likely to face pressure to secure access to the dwindling flows, but there simply may not be enough water available to support existing development. This is not only a zero-sum conflict, but a zero-sum conflict with existing development at stake, which is likely to be more intractable than the zero-sum conflicts faced in the past. Moreover, Montana is already dissatisfied with the existing apportionment under the 1921 order, and it may be particularly motivated to correct what it views as a past injustice. So, a simmering conflict that has been contained thus far could boil over into something more substantial, challenging the very basis of the international apportionment in the St. Mary–Milk.

As the effects of climate change take hold, it may also be necessary to revisit the apportionment's focus on the irrigation season from April to October. Both article vi and the 1921 order establish apportionment arrangements that apply only during the irrigation season, and, in a basin where there is no winter irrigation and little winter run-off, this makes sense. However, in a warming climate, more winter precipitation is expected to fall as rain and there is likely to be more winter run-off, so water users may try to capture and store this winter run-off for later use, possibly to the detriment of other users. Therefore, it may make sense to extend the St. Mary–Milk apportionment provisions year-round, but doing so will likely require the reopening of both article vi and the 1921 order to international negotiation, since the irrigation season restrictions are entrenched in both. Although extending the apportionment provisions year-round seems like a relatively simple change in itself, reopening article vi and the 1921 order to negotiation could provide an opportunity for long-contained conflicts to come to the fore, so it could be quite difficult to achieve, in practice.

The effects of climate change could spark other international water conflicts in the St. Mary–Milk, as well. In a hotter, drier climate, governments and water users may turn to previously untapped or underutilized rivers to support development. The United States, for example, may decide that the cost of diverting the Belly and Waterton Rivers is worthwhile in the context of declining St. Mary flows, and any such diversions would create serious problems for downstream irrigators in Canada, where the rivers are already fully allocated. Or, Canada may decide to increase diversions from the Milk or its Eastern Tributaries, creating all sorts of problems for American irrigators downstream in the eastern Milk. If river flows become less reliable and more erratic, governments may also turn to the construction (or expansion) of dams to increase storage capacity and provide more control over flows. Canadian residents on the Milk River, for example, have revived calls for the construction of an on-stream dam on the Milk to reduce their vulnerability.[45] Related to this is the declining state of existing infrastructure, particularly the large siphons in Montana that carry diverted water from the St. Mary to the Milk. The siphons have been operating for over a century, and though they have been repeatedly patched over the years, they will soon need replacement.[46] The siphons are a key point of vulnerability in the St. Mary–Milk system, and could spark international conflict if the Americans responsible for operating and maintaining them fail to do so and downstream Canadians are seriously impacted by this failure.

Finally, there is the state of riverine environments in the St. Mary–Milk and their further decline in the context of climate change. It is important to understand that the apportionment in the St. Mary–Milk divides the waters between Canada and the United States; riverine environments were not part of the apportionment and were treated as an afterthought. In fact, in the era when article vi and the 1921 order were introduced, water left in rivers was regarded as wasted water, and full allocation of rivers was a desired objective. This has had a tremendous environmental impact on the rivers in the St. Mary–Milk basin. Heavy use of these rivers has destroyed fish, fowl, and wildlife habitat, increased the concentration of water pollutants, altered river flow patterns, channelized rivers, interrupted fish spawning, and caused a loss of biodiversity. The environmental damage wrought in the St. Mary–Milk is illustrated in recent water quality assessments by the US Environmental Protection Agency, which found that a very high number of the river branches in the St. Mary–Milk basin were impaired, meaning that water quality conditions were so poor that one or more water uses could not be supported.[47] Climate change is likely to make things worse environmentally, and this could be a flashpoint of cross-border conflict. Since the late 1990s, the IJC has introduced an International Watersheds Initiative, in an effort to introduce ecosystem-based governance in international water basins that addresses environmental problems. The initiative has yet to take hold in the St. Mary–Milk, but it could provide a path forward in addressing the basin's pressing environmental issues.[48]

In short, many of the conflicts that have thus far been contained under the BWT could become increasingly difficult to contain in the context of climate change. As the St. Mary–Milk basin becomes warmer and its median water supply declines, the zero-sum nature of apportionment is amplified, and conflicts become more difficult to resolve. This is especially true given the powerful vested interests on both sides of the border that have come to rely on the basin's waters. So, many of the twentieth-century conflicts that were contained but unresolved could become even more intractable in the twenty-first century, creating unprecedented challenges to the BWT, the IJC, and the partner governments.

Conclusion

Over the first hundred-plus years of its existence, the international apportionment of the St. Mary–Milk has been successful in containing international water conflicts in the basin. Given the difficult, zero-sum nature of these conflicts, this containment is no small achievement. However, containment means that these conflicts have been prevented from escalating out of control; it does not mean that these conflicts have been permanently resolved. In fact, many unresolved conflicts remain in the St. Mary–Milk, and the effects of climate change could very well bring these conflicts to the fore in the not-so-distant future: Montana is still aggrieved about the 1921 order, and a decline in St. Mary flows could inflame this grievance further; the Waterton, Belly, and Sage Rivers still have no formal apportionment even though Canada uses them heavily and the United States covets them; the Eastern Tributaries could face additional water use pressures on both sides of the border; the 1921 order may need updating to accommodate a new climate and hydrology in the basin; and the entire apportionment arrangement could face reform to halt the continued deterioration of the basin's riverine environments and wetlands. Clearly, the challenges facing the IJC and the partner governments in the St. Mary–Milk are formidable.

Moving forward, it seems likely that the governments of Alberta and Montana will play a crucial role. Most of the governance challenges in the St. Mary–Milk stem from the heavy development (or overdevelopment) of the basin's waters and, due to the design of Canadian and American federalism, provincial and state governments have important responsibilities in this area. These governments are responsible for the issuance of water entitlements, play a major role in irrigation development and support, and have important powers of environmental regulation. Therefore, any substantive efforts to address water use and overuse in the St. Mary–Milk will necessarily involve the sub-national governments in the basin, and there is already some evidence that things are moving in this direction. For example, the Administrative Measures Task Force recommended that Alberta and Montana engage in greater coordination on St. Mary–Milk issues, and the two governments followed up on this recommendation by signing the joint Water Management Initiative in 2009. Thus, while the first century of the St. Mary–Milk apportionment was characterized by international governance dominated by the two national governments, the second century of the apportionment is likely to be characterized by multi-level governance involving both the national and sub-national governments of the basin, all of which play important roles in containing St. Mary–Milk conflicts.

Notes

1. There is some disagreement as to whether the St. Mary–Milk should be described as one basin or two. Since the basins have been hydrologically connected, and they are treated as one hydrological system in the BWT, I refer to the St. Mary–Milk as a single basin while acknowledging that, naturally, they are two separate basins.
2. Boundary Waters Treaty, (1909).
3. R. Halliday and G. Faveri, "The St. Mary and Milk Rivers: The 1921 Order Revisited," *Canadian Water Resources Journal* 32, no. 1 (2007): 77.
4. Ibid.
5. Environment Canada, "Section 2: Annual Statistics: Canada's Physical Environment," *Human Activity and the Environment: Annual Statistics 2007 and 2008*, http://www.statcan.gc.ca/pub/16-201-x/2007000/5212638-eng.htm.
6. E. Alyn Mitchner, *The Development of Western Waters* (Edmonton: Department of History, University of Alberta, 1973); William J. Simonds, "The Milk River Project,

Bureau of Reclamation History Program," http://www.usbr.gov/dataweb/html/milkrive.html#Milk.

7   Mitchner, *The Development of Western Waters*; Prairie Farm Rehabilitation Administration, *History of Irrigation in Western Canada* (Ottawa: Government of Canada, 1982).

8   International Joint Commission, "The Accredited Officers of the St. Mary-Milk Rivers—Members," http://ijc.org/en_/aosmmr/Members.

9   Halliday and Faveri, "The St. Mary and Milk Rivers: The 1921 Order Revisited."

10 B. Timothy Heinmiller, "The Boundary Waters Treaty and Canada-US Relations in Abundance and Scarcity," *Wayne Law Review* 54, no. 4 (2008): 1499–1524.

11 Mitchner, *The Development of Western Waters*, 110–11.

12 Stephen McCaffrey, "The Harmon Doctrine One Hundred Years Later: Buried, Not Praised," *Natural Resources Journal* 36, no. 4 (1996): 965–1007.

13 Mitchner, *The Development of Western Waters*, 112–14.

14 Ibid., 123

15 To clarify, the St. Mary River is shared between Montana and Alberta, while the St. Mary's River connects Lake Superior with Lake Huron.

16 Nandor F. Dreisziger, "Dreams and Disappointments," in *The International Joint Commission Seventy Years On*, ed. Robert Spencer, John Kirton, and Kim Richard Nossal (Toronto: Centre for International Studies, 1981), 8–23.

17 International Waterways Commission, *Joint Report of the International Waterways Commission* (1906).

18 Ibid.

19 Mitchner, *The Development of Western Waters*, 133.

20 Boundary Waters Treaty (1909).

21 Ibid.

22 B. Timothy Heinmiller, "Multilevel Governance and the Politics of Environmental Water Recoveries," in *Multilevel Environmental Governance: Managing Water and Climate Change in Europe and North America*, ed. Inger Weibust and James Meadowcroft (Cheltenham, UK: Edward Elgar, 2014), 58–79.

23 Mitchner, *The Development of Western Waters*, 135–6.

24 William R. Willoughby, "Expectations and Experiences" in *The International Joint Commission Seventy Years On*, ed. Robert Spencer, John Kirton, and Kim Richard Nossal (Toronto: Centre for International Studies, 1981), 24–42.

25 Halliday and Faveri, "The St. Mary and Milk Rivers: The 1921 Order Revisited," 80.

26 International Joint Commission, *In the Matter of the Measurement and Apportionment of the Waters of the St. Mary and Milk Rivers and their Tributaries in the United States and Canada* (1921).

27 Lawrence S. Dolan, "Comment on 'The St. Mary and Milk Rivers: The 1921 Order Revisited,' by R. Halliday and G. Faveri," *Canadian Water Resources Journal* 32, no. 4 (2007): 335–8.

28 Ibid.

29 International Joint Commission, "The Accredited Officers of the St. Mary-Milk Rivers—Members."

30 The accredited officers effectively function as an IJC international board for the St. Mary–Milk, similar to the IJC boards that operate in the other Canada-US basins, even though it is not labelled as a "board."

31 Halliday and Faveri, "The St. Mary and Milk Rivers: The 1921 Order Revisited," 87.

32 Ibid.

33 Ibid., 82.

34 Nigel Bankes and Elizabeth Bourget, "Apportionment of the St. Mary and Milk Rivers," in *Water Without Borders? Canada, the United States and Shared Waters*, ed. Emma S. Norman, Alice Cohen, and Karen Bakker (Toronto: University of Toronto Press, 2013), 170–3.

35 Louis M. Bloomfield and Gerald F. Fitzgerald, *Boundary Water Problems of Canada and the United States: The International Joint Commission* (Toronto: Carswell, 1958), 177–80.

36 Willoughby, "Expectations and Experiences," 24–42; Prairie Farm Rehabilitation Administration, *History of Irrigation in Western Canada*.

37 A closed stream is one that is not connected with a larger river basin. In this case, Sage Creek is in the area considered to be part of the Milk basin, but it does not connect with the Milk River.

38 Bloomfield and Fitzgerald, *Boundary Water Problems of Canada and the United States*, 174–5.

39 International Joint Commission, "The Accredited Officers of the St. Mary-Milk Rivers—Members."

40 Halliday and Faveri, "The St. Mary and Milk Rivers: The 1921 Order Revisited," 84.

41 James Byrne, Stefan Kienzle, and David Sauchyn, "Prairie Water and Climate Change" in *The New Normal—The Canadian Prairies in a Changing Climate*, ed. David Sauchyn, Harry Diaz, and Suren Kulshreshtha (Regina: Canadian Plains Research Centre, 2010), 61–79.

42 J. P. Barnett, J. C. Adam, and D. P. Lettenmaier, "Potential Impacts of a Warming Climate on Water Availability in Snow-Dominated Regions," *Nature* 438 (2005): 303–9

43 B. Timothy Heinmiller, *Water Policy Reform in Southern Alberta: An Advocacy Coalition Approach* (Toronto: University of Toronto Press, 2016), 14; Halliday and Faveri, "The St. Mary and Milk Rivers: The 1921 Order Revisited," 81

44 Ibid.

45 Barb Glen, "Water Infrastructure Well Past Its Prime," *The Western Producer* (Saskatoon), 25 August 2016.

46 Paul Azevedo, "The Need to Rehabilitate the St. Mary Facilities 2004," https://www.kobo.com/us/en/the-need-to-rehabilitate-the-st-mary-facilities-electronic-resource.

47 United States Environmental Protection Agency, *Montana Water Quality Assessment Report*, https://archive.org/details/41888D1D-8C7C-40D5-A91C-AE7530597FC7/page/n7.

48 Murray Clamen, "The IJC and Transboundary Water Disputes: Past, Present, and Future," in *Water Without Borders? Canada, the United States, and Shared Waters*, ed. Emma S. Norman, Alice Cohen, and Karen Bakker (Toronto: University of Toronto Press, 2013), 70–8; International Joint Commission, "International Watersheds Initiative–History," https://www.ijc.org/en/what/iwi/history.

The International Joint Commission and Hydro-power Development on the Northeastern Borderlands, 1945-1970

James Kenny

As other contributors to this collection have noted, during the early Cold War the International Joint Commission (IJC) played a key role in the development of high-profile Canadian-American megaprojects on the St. Lawrence, Niagara, and Columbia Rivers. Less well known is the IJC's role in studying potential hydro projects along international waterways in the northeastern borderlands of New Brunswick and Maine.[1] Throughout the 1950s and '60s the IJC, working with the US Army Corps of Engineers and public and private utilities, studied the hydroelectric possibilities of the full development of the international St. John River, as well as an ambitious and novel plan to develop tidal power in Passamaquoddy Bay. While both countries supported the former IJC reference, the impetus for the tidal study came exclusively from the United States, which, at least initially, used the reference to address domestic political problems. Canadian officials, who had significant reservations about the project, eventually agreed to participate after weighing the possible consequences of a negative response for other continental projects. While the St. John River and Passamaquoddy Bay investigations were initially discrete they were eventually combined into a much more ambitious TVA-style project that would provide electricity to New England and Maritime Canadian markets, and which proponents saw as an eastern counterpart to the Columbia River developments. Brief addition to the sentence: Although the St. John River investigation resulted in the negotiation of a draft treaty in the 1960s, the two international projects eventually came to naught, both because of concerns about their economic feasibility (especially in the case of tidal power) and environmental impact, and because of heavy lobbying by American private power utilities that opposed the federal government's role in any power development. While the IJC investigations did not result in a tangible international megaproject in northeastern North America, they did play an important role in shaping the "high modernist" orientation of New Brunswick's power utility, as well as its planning capacity, and they contributed to a more general understanding of rivers as economic units.[2] Moreover, the St. John-Passamaquoddy case study confirms the observations of scholars of the St. Lawrence–Niagara and Columbia developments regarding the intense politicization and partisanship of the IJC during the early Cold War era.[3]

Investigating FDR's "Green Dream": The First Passamaquoddy Reference, 1948-50

The IJC's attention was drawn to the Passamaquoddy region in the late 1940s in response to an ambitious plan to generate hydroelectricity by harnessing the Bay of Fundy's tides, which are the highest in the world. Passamaquoddy Bay is an inlet located at the entrance to the Bay of Fundy through which runs the international border (see Figure 5.1). Most of the bay is located within Canada but Maine's Washington County forms the western boundary. While higher tides occur elsewhere in the Bay of Fundy, Passamaquoddy Bay's tides are significantly large, ranging from eighteen to twenty-six feet. In the early 1920s hydroelectric engineer Dexter P. Cooper, who summered at Campobello Island (located at the mouth of Passamaquoddy Bay), began promoting a plan to develop an international tidal hydroelectric project in the bay. Cooper's ambitious and expensive plan (it was to cost $100 million) called for the damming of both the international Passamaquoddy Bay and neighbouring Cobscook

Bay, located entirely in Maine. At high tide, water from the Bay of Fundy would pass through dams at the mouth of Passamaquoddy dam and be held there until low tide, when the entrapped waters would be released through a dam into Cobscook Bay, which had been kept at the low tide level. The head resulting from the difference between the high and low tide levels would generate electricity.[4]

Despite the assistance of his Campobello neighbour, Franklin Delano Roosevelt (who was himself fascinated by the project), Cooper had difficulty persuading private investors of the project's feasibility. Moreover, the Canadian and New Brunswick governments, whose support was crucial, were concerned about the project's impact on the region's rich sardine and herring industries. A joint Canadian-American study concluded in 1933 that the sardine industry inside the dam would be "obliterated," but was inconclusive on the impact to the larger herring industry in the Bay of Fundy. Canadian officials were therefore unwilling to support the project. Undaunted, Cooper turned his attention to developing a smaller, all-American tidal power project on Cobscook Bay. Although both the Federal Power Commission and the Army Corps of Engineers concluded that the project was uneconomical, Cooper was able to leverage his friendship with Roosevelt, who by this time occupied the White House, for some measure of federal support. In 1935 Roosevelt made available $10 million of Public Works Administration funds to begin construction on earthen dams and a village to house workers. However, the project was short-lived as a sceptical Congress refused to authorize further spending on Quoddy, as the project had become popularly known.[5]

By the late 1940s both FDR and Cooper were gone but a new generation of boosters in Maine and New England revived the two-pool international scheme. These supporters, who included Maine senators Owen Brewster and Margaret Chase Smith, emphasized the regional development benefits that would accrue from locating the project in a poverty-stricken region of Washington County. They, and local business leaders, also situated Quoddy firmly in the Cold War context, arguing that this project would provide a reliable and predictable source of electricity that could be mobilized for both military and civilian purposes. This call had particular resonance in the New England region, where the cost of electricity was reportedly 23 per cent higher than in the rest of the country due to reliance on antiquated thermal plants and underdeveloped hydro sites.[6]

While appeals to American national security were perhaps convincing to some, it was ultimately old-fashioned politics that kick-started Quoddy and brought it to the attention of the IJC. Faced with heavy lobbying from Maine, and wanting to shore up support for the upcoming federal election, President Harry Truman, in 1948, promised the Maine congressional group that the United States would initiate a reference to the IJC on the matter. However, this was a diplomatically fraught promise, as Truman had not consulted Canadian officials in advance. Moreover, US State Department officials were well aware that there was significant opposition to Quoddy in Canada because of the project's potential impact on the herring and sardine fisheries (largely based on the Canadian side).[7] State Department officials tried to assuage these concerns by proposing that Canada join in a more "innocuous" reference, asking the IJC to determine the cost and requirements for a full-scale feasibility study of tidal power. There was little enthusiasm for the watered-down reference in Ottawa. In addition to long-standing concerns about the project's feasibility and its impact on the fisheries, External Affairs officials contended that the work proposed in the reference was of a minor nature and should be conducted at a lower level by an informal committee.[8] Canadian officials were also irked by the informal intervention of A. O. Stanley, chairman of the US Section of the IJC, before an official reference had been made. Pressured by Maine political and business interests, Stanley wrote a long letter to a senior External Affairs official, complaining that Canada was dragging its heels.[9] Stanley believed that Canadian reticence was based on a misunderstanding of the meaning of a reference under article ix of the treaty. According to Stanley, Canada had no choice but to join the reference because "under Article IX all such matters [of dispute] <u>SHALL</u> be so referred [to the IJC] 'for examination and report whenever *either* Government shall request that such questions or matters of difference be so referred.' " He recognized Canadian concerns about Quoddy but noted also that an investigation under article ix was non-binding (as opposed to an article x investigation).[10] Privately, Canadian External Affairs officials complained that the eighty-one-year-old Stanley, whom they described uncharitably as "a meddlesome old man," had no business intervening on the question of whether or not a reference was made. However, concerned about the possible diplomatic fallout of making an official complaint, they chose to remain quiet on the issue.[11] The actions of Stanley and the Truman administration more generally led External Affairs minister Louis St. Laurent to confide to his cabinet colleagues that it was "regrettable that the IJC should be misused and involved in US political issues." However, the Truman administration had backed itself into a corner and could not retreat. External Affairs ultimately agreed to join the reference, fearing that a negative response would "force the United States into a unilateral reference, and this precedent might be followed by the US government in more important cases." Behind closed doors, though, Canadian officials made known to American diplomats their unhappiness with how Canada was "virtually forced" into participating in the reference for domestic political reasons.[12]

When, in October 1950, the IJC reported that, although technically possible, Quoddy's economic feasibility would have to be assessed in a $3.9 million comprehensive study, Canadian External Affairs officials were forced again to consider a diplomatic response to a project that did not appear to be in Canada's interests.[13] Most Canadian officials were opposed to participating in another study, but they were also concerned about rejecting an American overture for a joint reference to the IJC, particularly considering that Canada had already declined to participate in two recent references. When, in the heat of another election season in 1952, the United States government formally asked Canada to participate, External Affairs Minister Pearson, after consulting all interested departments, politely declined, citing a number of factors. First, previous studies by both American and Canadian organizations had concluded that the project was uneconomical compared to other forms of electricity, especially thermal and traditional hydroelectric. Second, there was no evidence that there were markets for higher priced Quoddy power in New Brunswick or Maine, and the cost of transmitting power to "adjacent areas" was too costly. Third, there were untapped hydroelectric resources on the St. John, Pennobscot, and Kennebec Rivers that "could be developed at a rate closely paralleling increases in demand for power." Fourth, New Brunswick needed to develop lower-cost electricity (compared to tidal power) with which it could attract industry. Finally, Pearson highlighted the potential impact of tidal dams on the region's sardine and herring fisheries. Given these factors, Canada declined to join in a reference to the IJC, but diplomatically signaled that it was open to reconsideration if new information should emerge.[14]

Columbia River in Reverse? The St. John River Reference, 1950-4

At the same time that it was trying to avoid participation in a full study of Quoddy, the Canadian government was a very active participant in another—and soon to be related—investigation of international water resources in New Brunswick and Maine: the St. John River. This large international waterway begins in Maine and winds its way briefly through Quebec and then through New Brunswick, before emptying into the Bay of Fundy at St. John. Historically, the river had been used as a source of food and a means of transportation by Indigenous Peoples and, later by European settlers and sawmill operators (who used it to transport logs). However, in the immediate postwar period state planners in New Brunswick, working through a provincial Resources Development Board (RDB), looked to the river as a potential source of hydroelectric power that could be used to attract industry to the have-not province. An RDB-commissioned study identified promising hydroelectric sites at Tobique, Beechwood, and Mactaquac. However, there were impediments to hydro development. As a "flashy river," the St. John was subject to large seasonal fluctuations in flow and this made producing power on a "run of river" basis a questionable proposition. The creation of upriver storage in Maine or Quebec would, however, create a steady flow and thereby optimize hydro developments downstream.[15] Quebec was uninterested and New Brunswick's attempt to negotiate a satisfactory arrangement with its southern neighbour yielded no results.[16] This prompted New Brunswick premier John B. McNair, at the behest of RDB chairman H. J. Rowley, to ask the Canadian federal government to refer the question of hydroelectric development on the river to the IJC. Rowley saw the St. John reference as an eastern equivalent of the ongoing Columbia River investigations, only in reverse: while American authorities were asking for upriver storage in

British Columbia to facilitate hydro development in Washington State, up-river storage along the Maine portion of the St. John would provide hydro opportunities downstream in New Brunswick. Rowley advised McNair that "we might at this time most opportunely introduce the St. John River watershed question and balance the West against East with respect to reciprocal agreements." Since Maine was also amenable to the investigation, in 1950 the United States joined Canada in a reference asking the IJC to investigate possible conservation and regulation projects along the upper St. John River (in Quebec and Maine) with a view to developing hydroelectric power along the "Rhine of North America."[17]

The survey was carried out under the auspices of a St. John River Engineering Board (SJREB), formed in October 1950 and composed of representatives of the US Army Corps of Engineers, the US Geological Survey, and the Canadian federal Departments of Resources and Development and Public Works. Although the title of the IJC reference suggested a broad look at water resources in the St. John River basin, the SJREB acknowledged that its principal focus was identifying the river's hydroelectric potential as well as the most promising sites for storage and generating stations. To do this the board established a working group which, in turn, created a series of sub-committees to address particular issues, most notably the location of possible sites for hydro development and "use and distribution," which focused on projected demand for electricity in the region. These two investigations—the former led by the Corps of Engineers and the latter by Maine utilities—involved consultation and co-operation with a wide range of interests, including private and public power companies, corporations that utilized Maine and New Brunswick's forest resources, engineering consultants, and Canadian and American government departments, including the province's public power utility, the New Brunswick Electric Power Corporation (NBEPC).[18]

In 1950 the NBEPC was a small utility, dependent on thermal power and with little expertise in hydroelectricity. Indeed, the only significant hydroelectric power facility, located at Grand Falls, was privately owned by Gatineau Power, and focused on servicing the pulp and paper companies located in the northern part of the province. The NBEPC was also a conservative organization, focused on incremental growth based on demand. However, in 1948 the province began an organizational review designed to modernize the utility and improve engineering expertise. The utility began to embrace the idea of developing the province's hydroelectric resources, and this made upriver storage an important preoccupation. The participation of utility engineers on the IJC Engineering Working Group would play an important role in the utility's modernization. Newly appointed chief engineer J. L. Feeney and a young electrical engineer, Reg Tweeddale, played a very active role in the IJC investigations. They were particularly interested in the identification of potential sites for hydro development, and they were influential in having the IJC investigation expanded, in 1952, from a consideration of upriver storage only to the entire river system above tidewater.[19] This provided an opportunity to mobilize the SJREB's expertise to evaluate promising sites downriver in New Brunswick, especially Beechwood, Morrill, and Hawkshaw.

The SJREB's interim report, submitted to the IJC in April 1953 after two years of study, made five major conclusions. First, demand for electricity in the St. John River basin was predicted to increase significantly over the next decade and both Maine and New Brunswick would be unable to meet this demand with existing generating facilities. Second, the most promising site for upriver storage was in the Rankin Rapids region in northern Maine, where the river's elevation was highest. The Corps of Engineers proposed the construction of a 5,900-foot-long dam, a reservoir of 48,000 acres that would inundate largely unpopulated forestlands, and a generating station with installed capacity of 230,000 kilowatts (kw). Total cost of the development was estimated to be $80 million.[20] Third, while the development of generating facilities was considered "practical" on six downstream sites (two of which were on tributaries of the St. John), a $26 million, 102,000 kw facility at Beechwood had the best cost-benefit assessment on a run-of-river basis.[21] Fourth, Canadian and American interests should consider cross-border interconnections and perhaps, in the long term, a regional power pool. Finally, compared to existing thermal plants, hydro development was judged to be the most economical way to meet demand for power. However, the SJREB report was ultimately cautious on the question of comprehensive river development. In assessing future demands it focused only on local consumption, putting aside any possible use at "distant load centers." Consequently, it saw little reason to assess what full development might look like. "The hydroelectric power potential of the area under reference is so large in relation to existing and potential demand growth that it would be unrealistic to contemplate the full development of the basin at this time."[22] The IJC's interim report, issued in January 1954, reiterated this point, noting that, should conditions change, the IJC would consider firm proposals by American or Canadian interests on a case-by-case basis. If upriver storage were to be developed in the future, the two countries would have to agree on equitable compensation. However, implicitly acknowledging the delicate ongoing discussions regarding the Columbia River (where optimum storage sites were located in Canada), the IJC cautioned that any decisions on the St. John River "should not necessarily be regarded as precedents in the consideration and disposition of other headwater-benefits situations in the basin or in other river basins lying partly in Canada and partly in the United States."[23]

Although the IJC's recommendations regarding hydro development on the St. John River were very modest, the investigation had important impacts on the Canadian side of the border. The IJC's favourable assessment of Beechwood gave the project legitimacy; the NBEPC and the New Brunswick provincial government began construction shortly thereafter and used the IJC interim report to great effect in obtaining financing from the Canadian federal government.[24] At an organizational level, the IJC experience contributed greatly to the modernization of New Brunswick's public power utility. Working closely with much more experienced counterparts in the US Army Corps of Engineers and other power utilities, young engineers, such as Reg Tweeddale, established a network of professional relationships and personal friendships that would be influential when the utility planned development of future generation projects. In later years Tweeddale commented also on how much the NBEPC engineers learned about storage and the sequencing of large-scale hydro developments from the IJC investigation.[25] They were also heavily influenced by the belief—common in continental hydro-power circles at this time—that the provision of cheap power was the key to economic development. Tweeddale's embrace of this concept can be observed in a letter to the NBEPC chairman: "The economic salvation of the Province depends in large measure on greater production.... And this will only come from the most extensive use of electric power as applied to our industrial life and the development of our resources."[26] The IJC experience also encouraged

NBEPC engineers to view rivers, first and foremost, through the lens of hydroelectric development. The engineers commented on other uses of the river (log drives, recreation, fishing, etc.), but these were all dismissed as of secondary importance to power development. This perception informed the utility's increasingly high-modernist approach to the river, which culminated in the 1960s in the construction of the Mactaquac hydroelectric facility.[27] Finally, the engineering studies clearly identified Rankin Rapids as the best site for a major upriver storage and power facility. While no immediate action was recommended, the site in northern Maine would play a key role in a new IJC investigation of Quoddy.[28]

An Offer Impossible to Refuse: The Passamaquoddy Reference, 1956–61

Despite Canada's initial reluctance to participate in a full IJC study of tidal power, a small group of New England politicians and business interests continued to lobby the American government to push for a reference on Quoddy throughout the 1950–6 period. Maine senators Margaret Chase Smith and Owen Brewster, supported, notably, by their Massachusetts colleague John F. Kennedy, regularly put forward resolutions calling for federal action on the reference.[29] The Eisenhower administration initially showed little interest in Quoddy, but would later use it as a negotiating chip in a Senate debate over the authorization of American participation in the St. Lawrence Seaway project. Faced with a close vote, the Eisenhower administration successfully wooed seven New England senators to support the St. Lawrence development by promising funding for a full IJC study.[30] When, in 1956, the United States again asked Canada to participate in another IJC reference, the federal cabinet felt it had little choice but to go along. While most Canadian officials felt that the project was both uneconomical and harmful to Canadian fishing interests, they feared that the United States would proceed with a unilateral reference to the IJC, thereby establishing "an unfortunate precedent." They also worried that a negative response might have a detrimental effect on sensitive discussions regarding the Columbia and St. Lawrence developments. However, given its concerns, the Canadian government advised the United States that it would only contribute its share of the fisheries studies (approximately $150,000); the United States agreed to cover the $3 million associated with the engineering and other aspects of the study.[31] The August 1956 reference (Docket 72) asked the IJC to determine the cost and economic feasibility of "developing the international tidal power potential of Passamaquoddy Bay in the State of Maine and the Province of New Brunswick." Equally important, the IJC was to investigate a long-standing concern: the impact of a tidal dam on the region's fisheries. It was also clearly stated that participation in the reference did not "imply commitment regarding the eventual construction of the project."[32]

The IJC established an International Passamaquoddy Fisheries Board (IPFB), composed of three marine biologists and the owner of a sardine cannery in Eastport, Maine, to explore the controversial fisheries issue. Since the 1920s most had agreed that a tidal power project would destroy the Passamaquoddy Bay's sardine industry, but later studies by Canadian fisheries scientists suggested that herring stocks outside the bay might also be affected by oceanographic changes caused by tidal dams. This was because the unique circulation of water in the bay created excellent feeding opportunities that drew almost all young herring in the region to Passamaquoddy.[33] The IPFB, however, presented a much sunnier assessment. After three years of study, it concluded that, while the proposed tidal dam would change oceanographic features within Passamaquoddy and Cobscook Bays (in particular, surface temperature would be more variable and salinities lowered), the herring fishery would be largely unaffected both inside and outside the bays. IPFB members were confident that herring could move through the dam gates when they were opened. Some fisheries inside the dam, such as haddock, winter flounder, and clams, would be negatively affected, but this would be offset by predicted increases in lobster and striped bass. The IPFB also had faith that the installation of a fish passageway would permit the continued presence of anadromous species, such as Atlantic salmon.[34]

An International Passamaquoddy Engineering Board (IPEB) was established to examine the project's feasibility, including the optimum project design, the impact of Quoddy on regional and national economies in Canada and the United States, existing and projected demand for power, and the competitiveness of the cost of tidal power compared to other

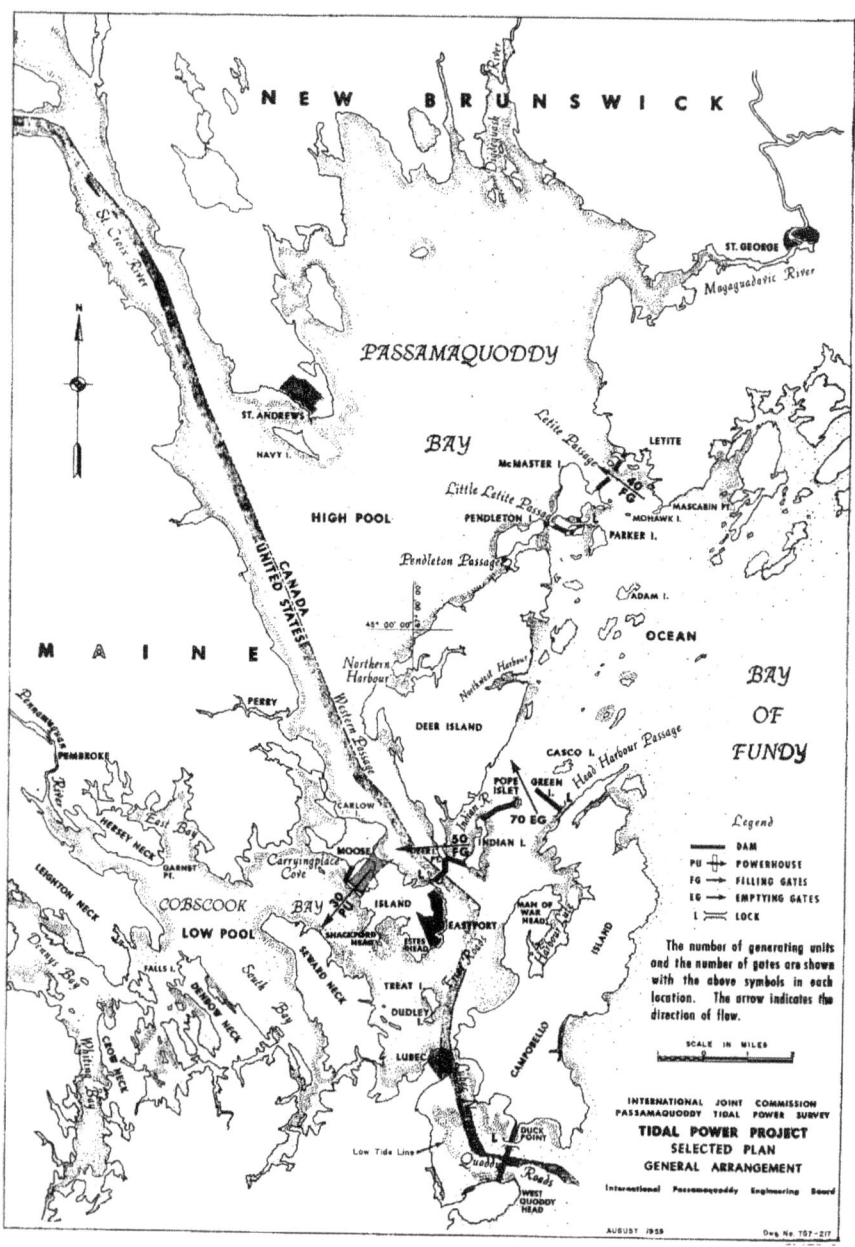

FIGURE 5.1. The two-pool Passamaquoddy tidal power project. Source: *Report to the International Joint Commission by the International Passamaquoddy Engineering Board* (October 1959), p. 7.

forms of power generation.³⁵ The IPEB recommended a two-pool design, similar to Cooper's original plan, with Passamaquoddy Bay as the high pool and Cobscook Bay as the low pool. The project would include 35,700 linear feet of earthen tidal dams, 90 filling gates, 4 navigation locks, and a power station containing 30 generating units producing 10,000 kw each for a maximum generating capacity of 300,000 kw and 90,000 kw of dependable power. It was estimated that the tidal project alone would produce 1.843 million kwh (kilowatt hours) annually and that the total cost of the project would be $532.1 million, including interest during the construction phase (see Figure 5.1).³⁶ It soon became clear, though, that the tidal power complex was not economically feasible by any conventional cost-benefit calculation. To compensate, the IPEB broadened its scope of analysis to include companion projects that would provide supplemental base-load power to offset the daily change of tides, which did not always coincide with peak periods of energy consumption. The Corps of Engineers considered a number of options, including thermal generation and pumped storage (by which water entering the tidal reservoir during non-peak periods would be pumped into a larger storage basin and, later, released through turbines when required). But the most attractive option was development of hydropower on the upper St. John River at Rankin Rapids, the site identified by the corps in its investigations earlier in the decade. The corps proposed the development of a large storage reservoir (2.8 million acre-feet of storage capacity) and generating station that would provide base load power. Taken together, Quoddy-Rankin Rapids could provide "555,000 kilowatts of dependable capacity and 3,063 million kilowatt hours of average annual generation." The Engineering Board highlighted other advantages of this hydro megaproject, which was estimated to cost $687.7 million, including interest. Not only would upriver storage "increas[e] substantially the usefulness of the [St. John] river for downstream use" in New Brunswick, but the engineers predicted that the tidal project would create recreational benefits and also draw tourists to the region to observe this engineering wonder.³⁷

On the key question of economic feasibility, the IPEB gave an equivocal endorsement of the Quoddy–St. John development. Contrary to previous analyses, which had found Passamaquoddy to be uneconomical, it concluded that the combined project could produce power at a competitive cost and that there would be sufficient demand in Maine and New

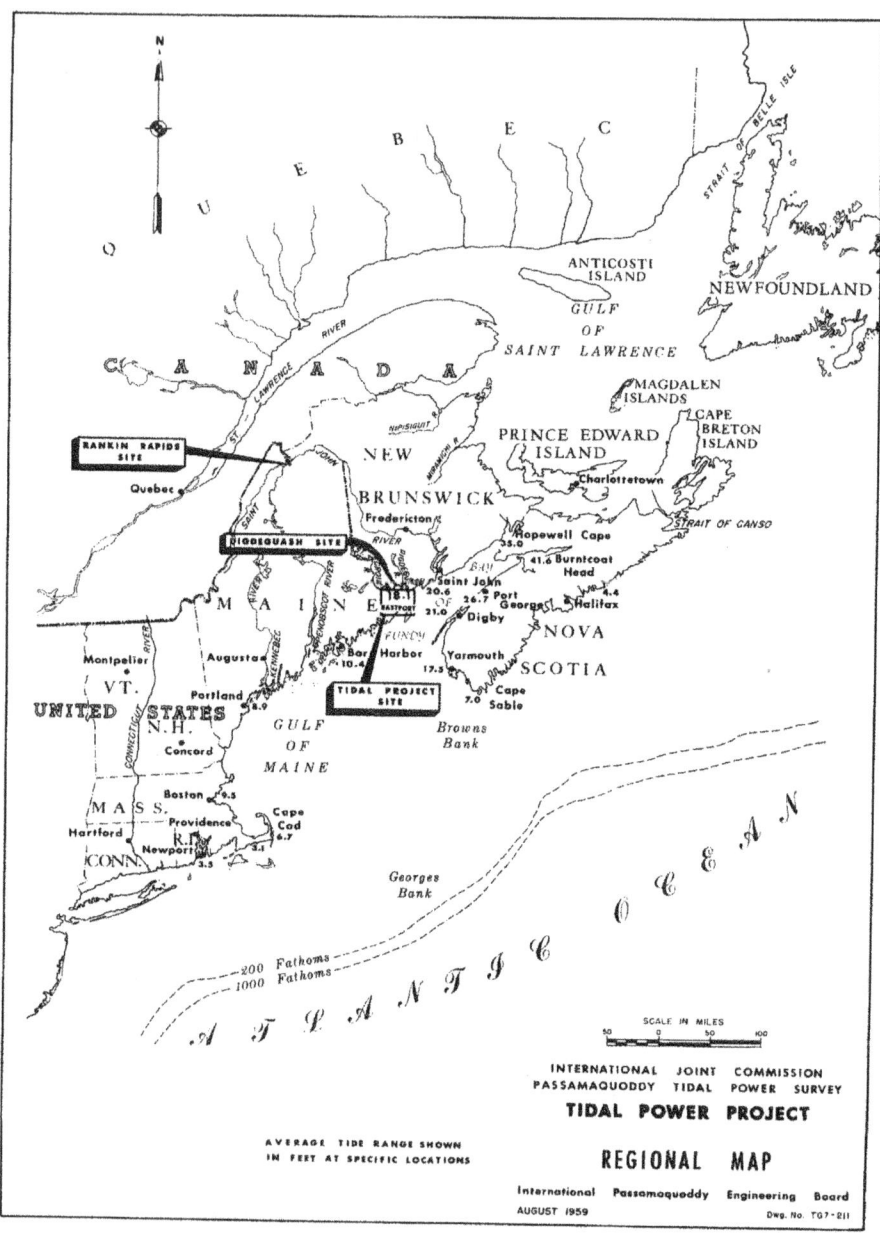

FIGURE 5.2. Location of proposed Passamaquoddy tidal and Rankin Rapids hydro developments. Source: *Report to the International Joint Commission by the International Passamaquoddy Engineering Board* (October 1959), p. 3.

Brunswick for the additional power. Despite this fact, the board found that Canadian participation in the project on a shared-cost basis could not be economically justified. However, due to a number of factors, including lower interest rates and economic spin-offs from construction, the board found that the US government was justified in pursuing the combined project entirely on its own.

The IPEB's interest in combining Quoddy with the Rankin Rapids development—and thereby going beyond its strict terms of reference—is explained in part by the personal interest in the project of retired lieutenant-general Samuel D. Sturgis, chairman of the US Section of the Engineering Board. Sturgis, former chief of the Corps of Engineers, had a long history with the project dating back to the 1930s, when he was in charge of building a village to accommodate tidal project workers (before the all-American project was canceled). In an address to the Washington County Chamber of Commerce shortly after he had been appointed to the IPEB in 1956, he referred to the tidal power project as both an engineering and a "humanitarian" challenge, emphasizing the importance of "priming the economic pump" of poor areas, such as Washington County, through public works. He recognized that in the 1930s the project had been rushed, without adequate surveys, in order to address the severe unemployment in the region. He welcomed the opportunity to conduct a more comprehensive survey and promised to "leave no stone unturned that can produce satisfactory evidence and support of the economic feasibility" of Quoddy.[38] In linking tidal power with the development of conventional hydro-power on the upper St. John River, the IPEB had found a way to make Quoddy more economically palatable.

The Quoddy–St. John linkage caught the imagination of Maine's tidal power proponents. Governor Edmund Muskie, who since the mid-1950s had been Quoddy's most passionate defender, saw the hydro-power project as a way to develop power and help rehabilitate two very poor regions of his state—Washington and Aroostook Counties. Others, such as Democratic congressman James Oliver, saw an opportunity to create New England's first publically funded TVA-style, multi-purpose development. "It is not difficult to envision the economic potential of the developed kilowatts of electrical energy, inherent in this project. Tens of thousands of industrial jobs in basic industry resulting from these installed kilowatts will transform these relatively stagnant areas, economically speaking, into live, vibrant and forward-moving communities, contributing with their great productive activities to the growing and expanding economy which we, in the North American continent, must have in the last half of the 20th Century." Quoddy–St. John was a nothing less than a project of modernity. Oliver encouraged the IJC to follow the example of international co-operation exhibited in the development of the St. Lawrence Seaway. "Put the natural resources, which Quoddy and the St. John River represent, to work, by harnessing them for use, and you . . . will have a tremendous contribution to the future survival of all of us, as free people." Then, in a fit of Cold War rhetorical excess, he concluded: "If we allow ourselves to become bogged down in the legislative quibblings and puny economic thinking and inhibitions in this instance we shall, indeed, become more vulnerable to our communistic competition with its goal of conquest of the free world."[39]

Not all New Englanders were pleased with the Engineering Board's inclusion of Rankin Rapids in the Quoddy discussion. Preservationists were particularly concerned that the creation of the large storage dam would inundate and destroy the valley surrounding the Allagash River, a tributary of the St. John. Richard Judd has shown how, in the postwar period, the Allagash Valley was prized by outdoorspeople as one of the few areas of "wilderness" left in the eastern United States. (Of course, as Judd shows, this was not a "pristine" wilderness; although there were few people in the area, forest companies had harvested the area for a century, leaving a significant human footprint.[40]) As the IJC's interest in Rankin Rapids became widely known, conservation organizations mobilized opposition to the project and, by the late 1950s, the campaign to save the Allagash became a *cause célèbre* for the modern American wilderness movement, which emphasized "the liberating effects of wildness on the human spirit" and celebrated natural rivers as symbols of "unfettered nature." Local conservation organizations and prominent national wilderness advocates, such as Supreme Court justice William O. Douglas, who penned a book on Maine's wilderness that highlighted the Allagash,[41] joined with large landowners in the region (mostly the forest products industries) against the Rankin Rapids plan and for the creation of an Allagash wilderness waterway. The US Department of Interior's Fish and Wildlife Service also had concerns. In a report submitted to the IPEB it concluded that the Rankin Rapids dam would, in addition to inundating a prized recreational area, eliminate some fish species (brook trout), introduce new ones (yellow perch), and destroy wildlife habitat. Because of the devastating impact of the proposed Rankin Rapids dam, it encouraged the IJC to instead consider a two-dam alternative at Big Rapids and Lincoln School, which would have a much smaller impact on the Allagash.[42] In arguing for the preservation of the Allagash, the Fish and Wildlife Service's report cited the projected population increase in the cities along the Eastern Seaboard over the next two decades. This expansion increased the importance of "high-quality wilderness recreation" for people looking to escape urban life. "In [the] eastern United States, this northwestern section of Maine is the only remaining wilderness area of its type . . . which can supply this demand."[43] It is perhaps notable that the IPEB, too, cited population expansion to justify the development of Rankin Rapids; however, where conservationists saw increased recreational requirements arising from urbanization, the engineers saw increased electrical demand. Regardless, the IPEB's final report made only passing mention of the Fish and Wildlife Service's concerns, and it contained no discussion of the Big Rapids–Lincoln School alternative.

In carrying out its investigation, the IJC made little effort at public consultation. After the studies by the Fisheries and Engineering Boards were completed, they were made public and the IJC organized a single day of public hearings in April 1960. The Quoddy–Rankin Rapids proposal was endorsed by a number of those who appeared, including the Maine congressional delegation and Sumner Pike, chairman of the Maine Governor's Committee on Quoddy. While Pike acknowledged that the Big Rapids–Lincoln site would preserve more of the Allagash, Rankin Rapids would produce more power and was therefore "the logical choice." Others appearing before the IJC disagreed. Roland Cobb, commissioner of inland fisheries for Maine, stated that he had received "over 1000 letters and telegrams" favoring Big Rapids–Lincoln. This would "preserve the Allagash for the future, and still supply enough firming power for 'Quoddy." James Briggs, of the Natural Resources Council and a state senator, declared himself "violently and unalterably opposed to Rankin Rapids" and questioned "why dams have to be built on all available water courses."

He also chastised the IJC for ignoring the Fish and Wildlife Service's report. Canadian representation at the hearing was small. The NBEPC's Reg Tweeddale welcomed plans to develop the upper St. John River, but diplomatically avoided the Rankin Rapids–Big Rapids controversy. However, he did note that there was no Canadian interest in Quoddy, given the IPEB's conclusion that the tidal power development was uneconomical for Canada. The fisheries, too, remained a sore point for Canadian interests. Charlotte County MP Allan McLean, owner of the largest sardine operation in the world, was sceptical of the Fisheries Board's conclusion that the herring industry would be unaffected by Quoddy. "The fishing industry and the power project could not live together."[44]

The IJC's final report, issued two years late, in April 1961, accepted the IPEB's finding that Quoddy was technically feasible but took issue with the conclusion that the combined tidal-river hydroelectric project was economically feasible for the United States.[45] The commissioners pointed out "an economic fallacy in the concept of . . . a combination project"—namely that Quoddy needed Rankin Rapids to be considered feasible. All studies had shown tidal power, on its own, to be uneconomical (and by a significant margin), while the upper St. John development was assessed as having a strong cost-benefit ratio. Combining the two projects muddied the true economic worth of Quoddy.[46] It also revisited the costs of competitive forms of energy and found that modern thermal plants would produce a lower unit cost of power than would tidal power. However, the report did suggest that the storage-hydro development at Rankin Rapids, if publically built (and therefore qualified for lower government financing), could provide power at a lower rate than other competitors and had the added bonus of enhancing downriver developments. The commissioners acknowledged that other factors could be considered in assessing the project's feasibility, such as "the conservation of fossil fuel resources and the provision of employment opportunities in economically depressed areas," but that Quoddy was not feasible using conventional economic practices. Tidal power, they concluded, should be viewed "as a long range possibility having better prospects when other less costly energy resources available in the area are exhausted."[47]

Friends in High Places: Ignoring the IJC and Revisiting Quoddy, 1961–5

But Quoddy still had high-profile supporters. As early as 1952, during his first Senate campaign, John F. Kennedy had championed the project. As president, he remained enthusiastic, seeing the hydroelectric project as strategically important for New England and as a symbol of "our greater scientific society." "Man only needs to exercise his ingenuity," he stated in 1963, "to convert the ocean's surge into a national asset."[48] So it is not surprising that the new president immediately asked his interior secretary, Stewart Udall, to reconsider the IJC's negative feasibility assessment in May 1961, taking into consideration "what changes in fuel, engineering and financing cost might result in making the project economically feasible." Udall, also a fervent Quoddy believer, reported, in July 1963, that the combined Quoddy–St. John River development was both "desirable and economically feasible," provided that the project was enlarged significantly.[49] Originally conceived by the IJC as a project servicing Maine and New Brunswick, Quoddy–St. John was now conceptualized as a $670 million regional power supply for a New England–Maritime power grid (now possible due to developments in electrical transmission). The capacity of the Quoddy facility was to be increased from 300,000 kw to 1 million kw and would now provide peaking power only for between one and three hours per day. An expanded hydro development on the St. John River, to which Quoddy would be connected, would provide base load power during off-peak periods. The revised plan also addressed the public concerns that the Rankin Rapids development would inundate the Allagash River Valley by choosing a new high dam site at Dickey, not far from Big Rapids, that would be complemented with a re-regulating dam downstream at Lincoln School.[50] Moreover, both Quoddy and Dickey-Lincoln were to be developed as TVA-style, multi-purpose developments, with recreational facilities (it was predicted that tourists would flock to the region to observe this "engineering marvel") and flood control capacity on the St. John River, which would enhance the value of downstream power facilities in New Brunswick. The revised project's economic feasibility was also calculated using non-unconventional cost-benefit factors, including recreational and regional development benefits,[51] and utilizing a hundred-year amortization period.[52] Kennedy liked what he heard and, in short order, instructed Udall and the Corps of Engineers to conduct more detailed engineering studies in preparation for the project's construction. He also asked the State Department to approach Canada regarding the negotiation of a St. John River treaty.

Udall's report gave new life to Quoddy. Supporters, including the interior secretary and Edmund Muskie, who was now a US senator, took every opportunity to highlight the project's benefits. As a multi-purpose megaproject on international waters, Quoddy-Dickey would be built and managed by public authorities as a TVA-style project, the first in New England. "It's time the people of the United States invested in a New England project," Udall told reporters.[53] More importantly, the project would generate much-needed employment in two very poor regions. Kennedy, too, took every opportunity to promote the project. Indeed, just weeks before his assassination he flew over Quoddy with reporters in tow, to inspect the site.[54] Over the next two years, the Department of the Interior and the US Army Corps of Engineers conducted further economic, geological, and engineering studies through a Passamaquoddy–Saint John River Study Committee. In August 1964 the committee confirmed the findings contained in Udall's 1963 report and encouraged the quick authorization of both Dickey-Lincoln and Quoddy.[55]

However, within a year the tidal development was dead. With the assassination of President Kennedy in November 1963, Quoddy lost its most influential supporter. His successor, Lyndon Johnson, did not have the same history with or attachment to the project, and he found it easy to cancel when rising interest rates and costs again raised feasibility questions in the mid-1960s. Moreover, New England private power interests launched a concerted—and effective—campaign against the publically funded Quoddy–St. John scheme, arguing that they could provide power more efficiently and that Udall had overestimated Quoddy's benefits and underestimated its costs.[56] Udall argued otherwise, contending in April 1965 that the United States needed to be a leader in tidal power development; the project's uniqueness meant that it should not be "put on the procrustean bed of regular water projects. It should be considered as a separate, unique, project with rules of its own as far as cost-benefit ratio is concerned because a tidal project will have a perpetual life."[57] However, by August 1965, the interior secretary had to admit defeat, concluding in a report to President Johnson that, under existing conditions, Quoddy was no longer economically feasible.[58]

However, the proposed development on the upper St. John River remained attractive. In July 1965 Johnson announced his support for Dickey-Lincoln and shortly thereafter Congress authorized the project in the 1965 Flood Control Act and allocated funds to the Corps of Engineers to begin design of the project. Also, the State Department initiated formal negotiations with Canada for an international St. John River treaty.[59] Negotiations were fairly far advanced before they were abandoned due to changing circumstances in the United States. In response to intense lobbying against public power at Dickey-Lincoln by a coalition of private power companies and representatives from oil- and coal-producing states, Congress cancelled funding for the project in 1967.[60]

Canadian interests in Ottawa and Fredericton watched the ongoing American debates over Quoddy–St. John in the 1960s with great interest. From the outset, Canadian officials had been reluctant to participate in the IJC reference, as they saw few advantages to Quoddy. The power generated would be too expensive for the New Brunswick market (something the 1961 IJC report confirmed) and there were other hydroelectric opportunities to exploit on the Canadian part of the St. John River, such as Mactaquac (which was completed in 1968). Moreover, others argued that, if Canada was going to pursue tidal power, all-Canadian sites with higher tides on the Bay of Fundy might be more promising. Finally, few Canadian fishers were comforted by the IJC Fisheries Board's conclusion that the impact of tidal dams on herring would be minimal. (One fish processor noted that the "power project has been a verdict of death hanging over the sardine industry for the last 40 years.") Nevertheless, the New Brunswick government was intrigued by the linkage of Quoddy with the development of storage and power dams on the upper St. John River. By the early 1960s, the NBEPC was planning the development of a number of hydro facilities on the St. John River. A federal-provincial study of the river, conducted during the 1958–60 period, concluded that upstream storage would be beneficial but not crucial to the NBEPC's hydro development plans.[61]

However, the real prize associated with Quoddy–St. John, especially after it was reinvented by Udall, was integration into a northeastern North

American transmission grid. While the NBEPC had originally focused on meeting consumer and industrial demand within the province, in the mid-1960s utility managers began to consider export markets as the path for growth. A continental power grid in the Northeast was therefore very desirable.[62] Consequently, NBEPC's Reg Tweeddale encouraged federal External Affairs officials to be receptive to American overtures to open St. John River treaty negotiations and to not be publically dismissive of Quoddy. While the province had little interest in tidal power, it was willing to support American construction if it also led to the full development of the St. John River and the creation of an international power grid.[63] A federal Department of Trade and Commerce official also cautioned his colleagues on a Sub-committee on the Passamaquoddy Project to tread carefully on the issue as it was but "one element of a vast power picture of tremendous importance to the economic as well as political relations between both countries. Repercussions from Passamaquoddy would be felt in Quebec and Labrador."[64] As we have noted already, Quoddy was eventually found to be uneconomical but, until that point, it remained a delicate issue in continental power politics.

Conclusion

While the IJC's postwar investigations of Passamaquoddy tidal power and the St. John River did not result in international megaprojects, such as the St. Lawrence Seaway or the Columbia River hydro developments, they are nonetheless significant. First, the interest in these very different projects reflects a continental, if not global, concern for developing the electrical potential of waterways during the early Cold War, a period when Western governments worried about access to power for both strategic and consumer purposes. The St. John River—and, later, St. John–Quoddy—offered the possibility of a northeastern complement to the planned developments in the Pacific Northwest. Quoddy also had its own caché in the Cold War context: supporters, such as President Kennedy, believed that the successful completion of the project would demonstrate American scientific and engineering supremacy. Second, the Quoddy case, like the Columbia and St. Lawrence investigations taking place at the same time, demonstrates the degree to which the IJC had become politicized during this era. Disparate cross-border issues were linked at the level of domestic politics and diplomacy. Although the Canadian government had determined early on that it had little to gain from the tidal power proposal, both the Truman and Eisenhower administrations used the promise of an IJC reference as a political bargaining chip to win support from New Englanders. Concerned that a negative response to American overtures for a Quoddy reference would negatively impact other continental water projects, Canadian officials felt that they had little choice but to participate. Third, the IJC studies also had a profound impact on the electrical power regime in New Brunswick. Emboldened by their experience working shoulder-to-shoulder on these investigations with North America's leading electrical engineers (such as the US Army Corps of Engineers) and public power organizations (such as the American Public Power Association), the NBEPC developed both engineering expertise and a vision for itself. Between 1950 and 1970, the public utility grew dramatically and became the dominant actor in Maritime power generation. The St. John River investigation, in particular, also informed the organization's increasingly high-modernist view of both the river and hydroelectric megaprojects, manifested most clearly in the Mactaquac project. Finally, in both cases, the IJC contributed to a conceptualization of the waterways, first and foremost, as potential sources of power. Engineering expertise was dispatched to understand how power production could be optimized and engineering problems overcome. The waterways were understood in terms of the cost of power they could produce and the direct and indirect benefits they could contribute to local and national economies. The fact that both projects were to be located in poor regions on both sides of the border only heightened this emphasis on economic impact. In the economic calculation of waterway value, "nature" was often de-emphasized. This is perhaps best illustrated in the International Passamaquoddy Engineering Board's choice of the Rankin Rapids dam site—which would flood the Allagash Valley—because of its superior storage and hydro-generation potential.[65] Thus, while there are few physical testaments to its work in the Northeast during the 1945–70 period, the IJC nonetheless played an important role in shaping the ways in which utilities viewed both themselves and the natural environment.

Notes

1. On the more high-profile developments on the St. Lawrence and Columbia Rivers, see, for instance, Daniel Macfarlane, *Negotiating a River: Canada, the US, and the Creation of the St. Lawrence Seaway* (Vancouver: UBC Press, 2014), and Barbara Cosens, ed., *The Columbia River Treaty Revisited: Transboundary River Governance in the Face of Uncertainty* (Corvalis, OR: Oregon State University Press, 2012).

2. The IJC's role in investigating international waterways in northeastern North America during the postwar era has not been explored in any detail. The St. John River reference is discussed briefly in R. A. Young, "Planning for Power: The New Brunswick Electric Power Commission in the 1950s," *Acadiensis* 12, no. 1 (Autumn 1982): 73–99; Andrew G. Secord, "Megaprojects in Maritime Canada: A Case Study of the New Brunswick Electric Power Commission" (PhD thesis, University of Sussex, 1992); and James L. Kenny and Andrew Secord, "Public Power for Industry: A Re-examination of the New Brunswick Case, 1940-1960," *Acadiensis* 30, no. 2 (Spring 2001): 84–108. An earlier reference to the IJC regarding the construction of a dam on the St. John River at Grand Falls is briefly examined in Christopher S. Beach, "Electrification and Underdevelopment in New Brunswick: The Grand Falls Project, 1896-1930," *Acadiensis* 23, no. 1 (Autumn 1993): 60–85.

3. Macfarlane, *Negotiating a River*; Daniel Macfarlane, "Dam the Consequences: Hydropolitics, Nationalism, and the Niagara-St. Lawrence Projects," in *Border Flows: A Century of the Canadian-American Water Relationship*, ed. Lynne Heasley and Daniel Macfarlane (Calgary: University of Calgary Press, 2016), 123–50; Jeremy Mouat, "The Columbia Exchange: A Canadian Perspective on the Negotiation of the Columbia River Treaty, 1944-1964," in Cosens, ed., *The Columbia Treaty Revisited*, 14–42.

4. LAC, RG20 Vol.865 File 42-9 Water Use Policy/ Projects – Passamaquoddy Tidal Project, "The Passamaquoddy Tidal Power Project," 29 May 1948.

5. Walter E. Lowrie, "Roosevelt and the Passamaquoddy Bay Tidal Power Project," *The Historian* 31, no. 1 (November 1968): 64–89.

6. PANB Flemming Papers RS415 N4g Passamaquoddy Engineering Board, The Campaign for the Passamaquoddy Tidal Power Survey (Some Decisive Work); LAC, RG25 Vol 4275 File 10011-40 FP Vol. 2 Memorandum: Passamaquoddy Tidal Power Project, 22 January 1953.

7. LAC, RG25 Vol 4275 File 10011-40 FP Vol. 2 Memorandum: Passamaquoddy Tidal Power Project, 22 January 1953A.G. Huntsman, "Tidal Power and the Fisheries," LAC RG25 Col. 4724 File 1011-40 Pt. 1 Passamaquoddy Tidal Project, 1948–50.

8. LAC, External Affairs RG25 Vol. 4274 File 10011-40 Pt. 1 Passamaquoddy Tidal Project, 1948–50, Memorandum for Cabinet: Passamaquoddy Tidal Power Project by Louis S. St. Laurent, 8 October 1948; PANB Flemming Papers RS415 N4g Passamaquoddy Engineering Board, The Campaign for the Passamaquoddy Tidal Power Survey (Some Decisive Work).

9. A Democrat from Kentucky, Stanley had served as governor and in both the US House of Representatives and Senate before being appointed to the IJC by Republican president Herbert Hoover in 1930. Although his position on the IJC was in theory

non-partisan, it seems that he was in contact with Democratic politicians from Maine. On the political nature of IJC appointments, see William R. Willoughby, "The Appointment and Removal of Members of the International Joint Commission," *Canadian Public Administration* 12, no. 3 (Sept. 1969): 411–26.

10 LAC RG25 Vol. 4724 File 1011-40 Pt. 1 Passamaquoddy Tidal Project, 1948–50 A. O. Stanley to Kenneth Burbridge, 24 August 1948. In an appended document entitled "Construction of Article IX," Stanley provided a lengthy interpretation of the distinction between articles ix and x of the Boundary Waters Treaty.

11 LAC RG25 Vol. 4724 File 1011-40 Pt. 1 Passamaquoddy Tidal Project, 1948–50, Memorandum for Mr. Eberts: Senator Stanley and the Passamaquoddy Question, 30 August 1948. On the historical use of article ix references, especially the tendency of the US and Canadian governments to accede to one another's requests for such investigations, see William R. Willoughby, "Expectations and Experience," in *The International Joint Commission Seventy Years On*, ed. Robert Spencer, John Kirton, and Kim Richard Nossal (Toronto: Centre for International Studies University of Toronto, 1981), 24–42.

12 LAC, External Affairs RG25 Vol. 4274 File 10011-40 Pt. 1 Passamaquoddy Tidal Project, 1948–50, Memorandum for Cabinet: Passamaquoddy Tidal Power Project by Louis S. St. Laurent, 8 October 1948; PANB Flemming Papers RS415 N4g Passamaquoddy Engineering Board, The Campaign for the Passamaquoddy Tidal Power Survey (Some Decisive Work).

13 LAC, External Affairs RG25 Vol. 4275 File 10011-40 FP Vol. 2 Pt. 2 Report of the IJC on an International Passamaquoddy Tidal Power Project. A subsequent review conducted by the US Army Corps of Engineers concluded that the investigation would cost $3 million.

14 Long concerned about the sardine fisheries inside the bay, Canadian fisheries scientists now worried that the impact could also be felt more widely. Recent studies indicated that the majority of young herring "hatched in neighbouring areas, enter Passamaquoddy Bay, remain there for the first year of their life to take advantage of especially favourable food conditions (only a relatively small portion being taken as sardines), and . . . [later] move outside the bays to form the basis of the large herring industry." LAC, External Affairs RG25 Vol. 4275 File 10011-40 FP Vol. 2 pt. 2 Note No. 66, 11 March 1953; Minutes of Interdepartmental Meeting on the Passamaquoddy Tidal Power Project, 23 January 1953; Stewart Bates to Under-Secretary of State, External Affairs, 26 January 1953.

15 PANB RS415 High John Flemming Papers N4e3, "Storage on and regulation of the Saint John River: The interest of the Province of New Brunswick in the above, as submitted to the International Joint Commission at Ottawa," 4 October 1950, p.6. In contrast to run-of-river hydroelectricity, which relies almost exclusively on the natural elevation and flow of the river to produce electricity, conventional hydroelectricity involves the construction of large storage dams that impound and then release water in a controlled manner through turbines to generate electricity. These storage dams often result in the large-scale flooding of lands and habitats.

16 PANB RS414 F4a2, H. J. Rowley to J. B. McNair, 15 October 1946; Kenny and Secord, "Public Power for Industry," 94–5.

17 PANB RS414 F4a2, McNair Papers, H. J. Rowley to J. McNair, 10 April 1946; PANB RS414 C11, McNair to Louis St. Laurent, 8 December 1948.

18 Robert Andrew Young, "Development, Planning and Participation in New Brunswick: 1945–1975" (DPhil thesis, Oxford University, 1979), 131–3.

19 Ibid., 133; International Joint Commission, *Interim Report to the Governments of the United States and Canada on the Water Resources of the Saint John River Basin (Docket 63)*, 27 January 1954, 1–2.

20 PANB RS 415, N4-e-3-IJC, Saint John River Engineering Board, "Water Resources of the Saint John River Basin: Quebec – Maine – New Brunswick. Interim Report to the International Joint Commission Under the Reference of 7 July 1952" (6 April 1953), 58, 98. The Rankin Rapids site was considered so ideal that the corps did not survey other upriver storage sites, although it did assess storage potential on some tributaries of the St. John River.

21 Ibid., 117. The ISJREB considered these facilities as discrete run-of-river basis projects and did not consider how upriver storage at Rankin Rapids would impact generating capacity.

22 Ibid., 113–14.

23 International Joint Commission, "Interim Report on the Water Resources of the Saint John River Basin, Quebec, Maine and New Brunswick," 27 January 1954, 5–6. Nevertheless, Reg Tweeddale recalled in later years that A. G. L. McNaughton, chair of the Canadian Section of the IJC, was very anxious to negotiate a deal for Eastern Canada similar to what was being proposed on the Columbia to mitigate criticism of the Western proposal and "to show that the formula was fair." PANB, interview of R. E. Tweeddale by David Folster, 15 January 2000, Transcript 1, p.7.

24 Kenny and Secord, "Public Power for Industry," 103–5; Young, "Planning for Power."

25 Reg Tweeddale, interview by Janet Toole, October 2000, transcript, MC 2923, PANB; Kenny and Secord, "Engineering Modernity," 8.

26 Tweeddale to J. L. Feeney, 30 July 1951, cited in Young, "Development, Planning and Participation," 134.

27 James L. Kenny and Andrew Secord, "Engineering Modernity: Hydroelectric Development in New Brunswick, 1945–1970," *Acadiensis* 39, no. 1 (Winter/Spring 2010): 3–26. Originally conceived by James C. Scott, "high modernism" refers to an ideology, which was particularly influential between 1930 and 1970, that emphasized scientific and bureaucratic planning to control and shape the natural environment and society in order to achieve social and economic progress. See James C. Scott, *Seeing Like a State: How Certain Schemes to Improve the Human Condition Have Failed* (New Haven, CT: Yale University Press, 1998). High modernism has been widely used by scholars to describe the technocratic, bureaucratic, and political consensus surrounding hydroelectric megaprojects in Canada and elsewhere. For example, see Daniel Macfarlane, "Negotiating High Modernism: The St. Lawrence Seaway and Power

Project," in *Made Modern: Science and Technology in Canadian History*, ed. Edward Jones-Imhotep and Tina Adcock (Vancouver: UBC Press, 2018), and Tina Loo and Meg Stanley, "An Environmental History of Progress: Damming the Peace and Columbia Rivers," *Canadian Historical Review* 92, no. 3 (2011): 399–427.

28 Throughout the 1950s and '60s, A. G. L. McNaughton, chairman of the Canadian Section of the IJC, was a strong advocate for the full development of the St. John River. He saw it as a natural complement to the proposed Columbia River projects. See, for instance, NARA College Park RG59 File 611.42311/11-354, Minutes of IJC Semi-annual Meeting, Ottawa, ON, 8 October 1954; Tweeddale, interview by David Folster, tape 1, p. 7.

29 Report of the Committee on Foreign Affairs on S.J. Res. 12A, Resolution requesting the Secretary of State to Arrange for the IJC, US and Canada, to Conduct a Survey of the Proposed Passamaquoddy Tidal Project, 14 July 1955.

30 "Passamaquoddy Revival Part of Seaway Deal," *Boston Herald*, 22 January 1954.

31 LAC, RG2 Acc 90-91/154 Box 100 File W-10-8 Water Resources and Development – Passamaquoddy Tidal Power Project, 1953-59, "Memorandum to Cabinet: Passamaquoddy Tidal Power Project," 19 March 1956.

32 *Report of the International Joint Commission on the International Passamaquoddy Tidal Project*, April 1961, 1–2.

33 LAC RG25 Col. 4724 File 1011-40 Pt. 1 Passamaquoddy Tidal Project, 1948–50, A. G. Huntsman, "Tidal Power and the Fisheries."

34 *Report of the International Joint Commission United States and Canada on the Passamaquoddy Tidal Power Project*, April 1961, Section C, 16–17.

35 The Engineering Board subsequently established an Engineering Committee to oversee detailed studies conducted largely by the US Corps of Engineers, the US Federal Power Commission, and various Canadian government agencies.

36 The International Joint Commission Tidal Power Project, Washington-Ottawa, April 1961, Section B Investigation of the International Engineering Board, 7–8.

37 The International Joint Commission Passamaquoddy Tidal Power Project, Washington-Ottawa, April 1961, Section B Investigation of the International Engineering Board, 9–14.

38 PANB H.J. Flemming Fonds RS 415 N4g Passamaquoddy Engineering Project Remarks by Lt. Gen Samuel D. Sturgis, Jr ... Before the Washington County Chamber of Commerce, Eastport, Me, 7 December 1956.

39 PANB H.J. Flemming Fonds RS 415 N4g Passamaquoddy Engineering Project Statement of Hon. James C. Oliver ... for Submission to the International Joint Commission (undated).

40 Richard W. Judd, " 'A Last Chance for Wilderness': Defining the Allagash Wilderness Waterway, 1959–1966," *Maine History* 40, no. 1 (Spring 2001): 1–20; Judd and Christopher S. Beach, *Natural States: The Environmental Imagination in Maine, Oregon, and the Nation* (Washington, DC: Resources for the Future, 2003), ch. 3.

41 William O. Douglas, *My Wilderness: East to Katahdin* (Garden City, NY: Doubleday, 1961). On Douglas's role in American conservation, see Adam O. Sowards, *The Environmental Justice: William O. Douglas and American Conservation* (Corvallis: Oregon State University Press, 2009).

42 The alternative location was identified in the report of the New England-New York Inter-Agency Committee in 1956. It called for the construction of a high dam at Big Rapids, located upstream from the Allagash, and a low dam at Lincoln School, downriver from Rankin Rapids. NARA Boston RG22 Box 13 Project Files Rankin Rapids, 1959–68, John S. Gottschalk to Gen S. D. Sturgis, Jr., 1 October 1959; US Department of the Interior Fish and Wildlife Service, "Substantiating Data for A Report on Fish and Wildlife Resources in Relation to the Rankin Rapids Dam and Reservoir, St. John River, Maine," September 1959.

43 NARA Boston RG22 Box 13 Project Files Rankin Rapids, 1959–68, "Substantiating Data for A Report on Fish and Wildlife Resources in Relation to the Rankin Rapids Dam and Reservoir, St. John River, Maine," September 1959, 32–4.

44 *Report of the International Joint Commission on the Passamaquoddy Tidal Power Project*, Washington-Ottawa, April 1961, 18; NARA Boston RG22 Box 13 Project Files Rankin Rapids, 1959–68, Mark Abelson (acting chairman, Northeast Field Committee, Department of Interior) to John B. Bennett, 26 April 1960; Edwin H. Robinson to Supervisor, Concord Area Office, 25 April 1960.

45 *Report of the International Joint Commission on the Passamaquoddy Tidal Power Project*, Washington-Ottawa, April 1961, 19–20. The IPEB re-examined the Big Rapids–Lincoln site and concluded that, while it would reduce inundation of the Allagash Valley, the alternative site would produce less power than Rankin Rapids and cost 20 per cent more.

46 *Report of the International Joint Commission on the Passamaquoddy Tidal Power Project*, Washington-Ottawa, April 1961, 26–7. The IJC final report paid more attention to concerns about the Rankin Rapids site than did the IPEB report. Nevertheless, when discussing St. John River developments, it focused on Rankin Rapids.

47 *Report of the International Joint Commission on the Passamaquoddy Tidal Power Project*, Washington-Ottawa, April 1961, 17–30 and 35.

48 John F. Kennedy, "Remarks in Response to a Report on the Passamaquoddy Tidal Power Project," 16 July 1963, John F. Kennedy Presidential Library and Museum, https://www.jfklibrary.org/asset-viewer/archives/JFKWHA/1963/JFKWHA-206-002/JFKWHA-206-002; on Kennedy's earlier support, see NARA College Park RG59 A1 5388 Box 3, St. John River Treaty Negotiations Sen. Edmund Muskie's Letter to Maine, June 1961.

49 Stung by the IJC's "harsh" handling of the IPEB's report, the Corps of Engineers eagerly participated in the review. NARA Boston RG77 Box 59 1517-08 Passamaquoddy Tidal Power BGen, Seymour A. Potter, Jr. to Lt. Gen. S. D. Sturgis, Jr., USA (Rtd.) 18 May 1961.

50 By this time, the federal Department of Interior and Maine state government, encouraged by well-organized preservationist organizations, were also considering

51   a number of options to preserve the Allagash region. Eventually, in 1966, the state established the Allagash Wilderness Waterway.

51   The counties in which these developments would be located—Washington and Aroostook—were among the poorest regions in Maine.

52   Quoddy's feasibility was also improved by the planned use of a more efficient turbine that was to be used at the world's only tidal power facility, in LaRance, France. Stewart Udall, Secretary Department of the Interior, *The International Passamaquoddy Tidal Power Project and Upper Saint John River Hydroelectric Power Development: Report to President John F. Kennedy*, July 1963, 8–11.

53   "Quoddy Sound Project, Udall Informs Maine," *Lewiston-Auburn Sun*, 3 August 1963. The project was to be built by the US Army Corps of Engineers and operated by the Federal Power Commission.

54   "President Going All Out to Back Quoddy," *Portland Press Herald*, 18 October 1963.

55   Passamaquoddy-Saint John River Study Committee, *Supplement to July 1963 Report The International Passamaquoddy Tidal Power Project and Upper Saint John River Hydroelectric Power Development*, August 1964.

56   Canada's Consulate General in Boston reported regularly on the efforts by private power companies to discredit Quoddy–St. John. See, for instance, LAC RG20 Vol. 865 File 42-9 Water Use Policy/ Projects – Passamaquoddy Tidal Project, Consulate General, Boston to Under-secretary of State, External Affairs, 7 February 1964. This report included a copy of a card, entitled "Electrifacts of Interest to You," that the Boston Edison Company sent to its customers and in which the utility outlined its objections to Quoddy. See also, "Passamaquoddy's cost estimates ebb and flow," *Engineering News Record*, 17 October 1963.

57   LAC, RG20 Vol. 865 File 42-9 Water Use Policy/ Projects – Passamaquoddy Tidal Project Telex – Canadian Embassy in Washington to External, 2 April 1965.

58   Stewart L. Udall, Secretary US Department of the Interior, *Report to President Lyndon B. Johnson, Conservation of the Natural Resources of New England The Passamaquoddy Tidal Power Project and Upper Saint John River Hydroelectric Development*, July 1965, 6–7.

59   Using the Columbia River Treaty as a model, negotiators crafted a draft agreement that would see the United States and Canada share downstream benefits of upriver storage on a 50/50 basis, and a commitment was made to create a Maritime–New England power grid.

60   NARA Boston RG77 Box 59 File 1517-08 Passamaquoddy Tidal Power, John Wm Leslie to David O. Wilkinson, 8 October 1971. Despite the lack of appropriation, Dickey-Lincoln remained a congressionally "authorized project."

61   *Effects of Storage on Power Generation in New Brunswick, Report of the Saint John River Board* (Fredericton, NB: Queen's Printer, June 1960). The American section of the IPEB watched this investigation closely. One member lamented that the report's calculation of downstream benefits from Rankin Rapids storage was "disappointingly low." NARA Boston RG77 Box 70-28/15/10-5, Letter to Lt. Gen. Sturgis, 19 April 1961.

62 Andrew G. Secord, "NB Power 1967–72: Constructing the Export Dream," *Journal of New Brunswick Studies* 10 (Fall 2018): 3–20.

63 LAC RG20 Vol. 865 File 42-9, Water Use Policy and Projects Passamaquoddy Tidal Project, USA Division to Mr. Ritchie re: Talk with Mr. Reginald Tweeddale, November 1963; LAC RG20 Vol. 865 File 42-10 Water Use Policy and Projects – St. John River, NB Minutes of a Meeting with Reg Tweeddale, General Manager NBEPC, 17 November 1964.

64 LAC RG20 Vol. 865 File 42-9, Water Use Policy/ Projects – Passamaquoddy Tidal Project, Meeting of the Sub-Committee on the Passamaquoddy Project, 19 November 1964.

65 Muskie would continue to champion both Quoddy and Dickey-Lincoln; indeed, in the midst of the energy crisis in the 1970s both projects would again be given federal consideration. Quoddy was again found economically unfeasible and Dickey-Lincoln again fell victim to a strong private power lobby and a stricter environmental assessment regime, which highlighted negative ecological costs associated with the flooding of the upper St John River Valley.

A Square Peg: The Lessons of the Point Roberts Reference, 1971–1977

Kim Richard Nossal

Most assessments of the International Joint Commission (IJC) as an international institution designed to resolve disputes between Canada and the United States have a distinctly positive ring to them. This is not by accident: in over a century of operation, the IJC has a long and sustained record of successfully defusing and resolving disputes involving boundary waters that have arisen along the 8,891-kilometre border between the two countries. By contrast, the number of institutional "failures" during this period is exceedingly limited.

One of those rare failures was Docket 92R, an investigation into the social and economic conditions at Point Roberts, an American exclave located south of Vancouver that was cut off by the 49th parallel from the rest of the United States. As a result of the increasing problems faced by the residents of Point Roberts in the late 1960s because of their isolation from the rest of the United States, the two governments decided in April 1971 to refer the question of Point Roberts to the IJC for study and recommendations for the alleviation of these problems. The scope of the reference was unprecedented: never before had the IJC been asked to study and make recommendations on a social, political, and economic cross-border issue. Beginning in 1971, the IJC established an advisory panel, the International Point Roberts Board, which began to undertake a study. In October 1973 the board was ready to report: it recommended to the IJC that the problems created by Point Roberts's isolation be solved with the creation of a conservation and recreation area in the Gulf–San Juan Islands–Point Roberts area that would in essence turn Point Roberts and an equivalent area in Canada along Boundary Bay into a binational park, with exact powers to be determined through a treaty to be negotiated by the two federal governments. While this wide-ranging proposal had the support of conservation groups in the area, the proposal to transform the status of Point Roberts from American territory to a binational forum generated such opposition in Point Roberts and the Washington state legislature that the IJC decided to discontinue work on the reference. Eventually the reference was terminated in 1977 without the IJC having made any recommendations to the two governments—an unprecedented end to an IJC reference. As Paul Muldoon has put it, "the reference represents one of the few 'black marks' on the otherwise impeccable record of the IJC."[1]

It is perhaps because the IJC has been such a successful institution that much of the analysis of this institution focuses on the reasons for its success, while relatively little attention is paid to the causes of the IJC's few failures. Yet in an institution's failures we can sometimes see the reasons for its success. Thus the purpose of this chapter is to look at the Point Roberts reference in order to draw lessons about why the IJC has been so successful. How do we understand what caused this "black mark"? Did the Point Roberts reference fail because it went well outside the bounds of the IJC's more common mandate—boundary waters? Was it the case, as one Point Roberts official noted in 1971, that "the square peg of Point Roberts fails to fit any of the conventional round holes"?[2] I will argue that the reference failed not because the IJC was embarking into a radically new area of jurisdiction. After all, while the area might have been new, in the sense that the IJC had never before examined social, economic, and political problems relating to the border, it was not at all outside the formal jurisdiction of the IJC, as some have argued.[3] Rather, I will suggest that much of the failure of this reference can be attributed to the failure of the International Point Roberts Board, and the commission itself, to follow some of the key factors that had been so crucial for the success of other references given to the IJC. If Point Roberts was a "square peg," the solution lay in finding square holes. As we will see, that did not occur.

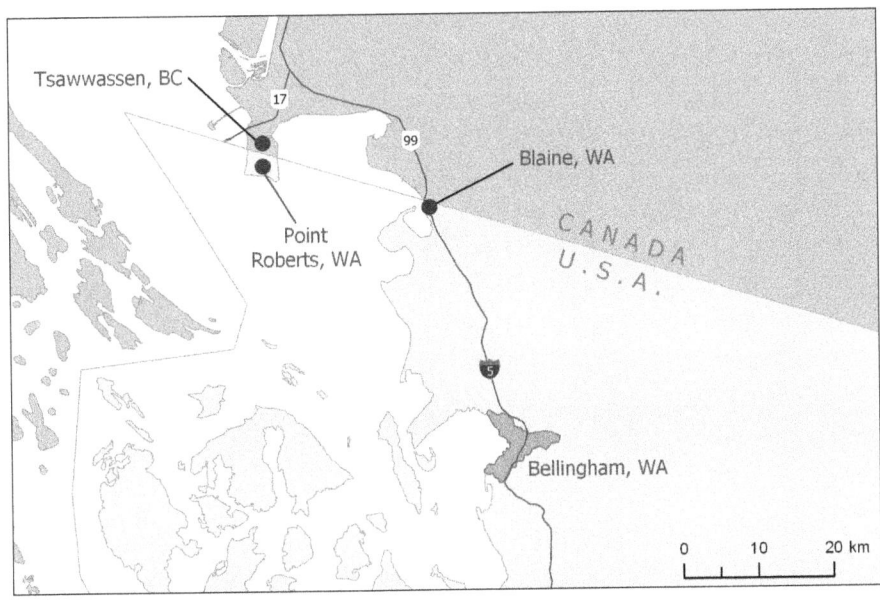

FIGURE 6.1. Map of Point Roberts. J. Glatz, Western Michigan University Libraries.

Explaining the IJC's "Success"

The IJC is widely seen as a successful binational institution in the Canadian-American relationship. Participants in the process have not been hesitant to express this view. Looking back on the IJC's first decade, Lawrence J. Burpee, who served as the Canadian secretary of the IJC from 1912 until his death in 1946, declared it a "successful experiment in international relations," noting that it was "a sort of international safety-valve" that helped settle thorny cases between the two neighbours.[4] Writing sixty years later, on the seventieth anniversary of the signing of the Boundary Waters Treaty, John W. Holmes, a former assistant under-secretary of state for external affairs in Ottawa, echoed Burpee's assessment, pronouncing the IJC "a successful experiment in coping with the ambiguities of an inescapable but unequal relationship."[5] In 2005, one of Burpee's successors as Canadian secretary, Murray Clamen, expressed a similar view, writing that "The IJC has helped to transform a vast potential source of conflict into a model of binational environmental cooperation."[6] It should be noted that the view of the IJC as a successful institution is also reflected on the American side of the line. For example, speaking to an IJC event in October 2016, the US ambassador to Canada, Bruce Heyman, heralded the commission's "long, productive history," noting that "people around the world look to the IJC organization as a model for how to work together."[7]

What accounts for this success? Explanations have focused on different elements. Perhaps the most important was the evolution of a long-term institutional culture that essentially denationalized the process of evaluating the applications and references that are the main parts of the IJC's work. This culture formed very early on, as Burpee's description in 1919 makes clear:

> The Commissioners have not approached these questions as two distinct groups of national representatives, each jockeying for advantage for its own side, but rather as members of a single tribunal, anxious to harmonize differences between the two countries, and to render decisions which would do substantial justice to all legitimate interests on both sides of the boundary, and particularly to those of the common people.[8]

A similar view was expressed forty-five years later by A. D. P. Heeney, the chair of the Canadian Section of the IJC from 1962 to 1970. In 1966, he wrote that the IJC's commissioners have tended not to serve as advocates "striving for national advantage under instruction from their respective governments, but as members of a single body seeking solutions to common problems, in the common interest."[9] This formulation was repeated in the commission's response to the 1997 request for proposals for meeting the environmental challenges of the twenty-first century.[10]

Likewise, examining the role of the IJC in the case of the Garrison Diversion project in the late 1970s, Garth O. Makepeace argued that the success of the IJC also depended on two further, and related, factors. First, the IJC developed and maintained strong links to bureaucratic agencies along the length of the border at the federal, state/provincial/territorial, and municipal levels, which gave the commission authority on the highly technical issues involving transboundary waters. This encouraged norms of consensus and common-goal decision-making that in turn undergirded the broader institutional culture.[11]

To these explanations we need to add the nature of the tasks assigned to the IJC by both countries' governments. If, as Ralph Pentland and Adele Hurley have argued, "the effectiveness of the IJC is a question of politics. The IJC is only effective when both governments want it to be,"[12] then we need to be mindful of why both governments have been willing to allow the IJC to be effective. I have argued elsewhere that a key explanation for the success of the commission was its limited and relatively low-stakes responsibilities: "The higher the stakes, the more incentive both governments would have had to handle high-priority issues through normal diplomatic channels. Had that been the case, it is likely that the IJC would have been allowed to slip into . . . obscurity. . . . The IJC has managed to thrive by serving limited and relatively unimportant interests."[13] In other words, one of the keys to the IJC's success lies in its parochial mandate.

However, the clearest appraisal of the IJC's success was made in the late 1970s by William R. Willoughby, a historian whose work focused on Canadian-American binational institutions. Willoughby enumerated nine key reasons for the enduring success of the IJC: the long-standing support of both federal governments; the independence that those governments permitted the IJC to enjoy; the decision to create a permanent institution rather than an ad hoc agency; the decision to structure the commission without an umpire from an impartial third country; the legal equality enshrined in the Boundary Waters Treaty of 1909 that established the commission; the reliance on expertise drawn from governments on both sides of the border; the IJC's embrace of pragmatic procedures that involve local residents on both sides of the line; the good judgement of the commissioners in embracing recommendations that attract political support; and the politico-cultural commonality of the two countries that belong to the institution. Willoughby also allowed that "there has also, no doubt, been more than a modicum of luck in the IJC's success."[14]

To what extent do we see these determinants of success in other references undertaken by the IJC reflected in the Point Roberts reference? To answer this question, we now turn to an examination of Point Roberts and the 1971 reference.

Point Roberts

Point Roberts is an American community located at the southern tip of the Tsawwassen Peninsula, south of Vancouver (see Figure 6.1). Although it is part of Whatcom County, in the state of Washington, Point Roberts is cut off from the rest of the United States by land because the 49th parallel intersects the peninsula. While there is a grass-runway airpark and a sizeable marina, there are no scheduled air services between Point Roberts and the United States, and no ferry service. Point Roberts is a very small community, both in area and population. It is just 12 square kilometres (5 square miles, or 3,000 acres) in area; the 2010 census indicated that there were 1,314 permanent residents in 678 households, out of a total of more than 2,000 housing units, most of which are unoccupied for much of the year. During the summer months, the population of Point Roberts swells to over 4,500, mostly vacationing Canadians.

The exclave of Point Roberts was created when the United Kingdom and the United States settled a protracted conflict over the northwestern border with the Treaty of Oregon. That treaty, signed in June 1846, established that the line of demarcation would run along the 49th parallel "to the middle of the channel which separates the continent from Vancouver's Island."[15] The British and American negotiators meeting in Washington had little detailed knowledge of West Coast geography, and had no idea that the wording they embraced would create an exclave in what was to become Boundary Bay. The Anglo-American boundary commission that was created in 1856 to locate and mark this boundary was well aware of the issue that had been unwittingly created; indeed, by some accounts,[16] the British, anticipating the problems that would be created by running the line to the middle of the Strait of Georgia and cutting off the southern tip of Point Roberts from the rest of the United States, proposed to the American side that the twelve square kilometres of the peninsula be left in British hands, and that an appropriate land swap be effected elsewhere in compensation. The proposal went nowhere, however, since any deviation from the treaty would have required reopening negotiations, and the boundary commission was facing a far more pressing issue: how to demarcate the boundary through the islands at the southern end of the Georgia Strait given the imprecise wording of the treaty vis-à-vis those islands.[17] As a result, the issue of Point Roberts was set aside and in 1857 surveying work was begun on the western edge of the peninsula. In 1861-2 the British erected an impressive stone obelisk—that still stands today—on the cliffs on the western side of Point Roberts to mark the initial point in the Canada-US border along the 49th parallel.[18]

The creation of an international boundary had a marked impact on human settlement on Point Roberts. Traditionally, the peninsula had been used by numerous Coast Salish Aboriginal peoples, particularly the Lummi and the Tsawwassen, for seasonal salmon fishing. However, the demarcation of the international boundary, which coincided with the Fraser Canyon gold rush, brought that to an end. Members of the Tsawwassen First Nation, whose traditional lands included the Fraser River, the Gulf Islands, and Point Roberts, were excluded from their seasonal fishing grounds in Point Roberts by the new boundary. And by the time that the surveying had begun in the late 1850s, the Lummi Nation, which had migrated seasonally around the Lummi Peninsula, the San Juan Islands, and Point Roberts, had been forcibly relocated along with other Northwest coastal tribes by the US government under the Point Elliott Treaty of 1855.

In the immediate aftermath of the establishment of the boundary, a small town was established on Point Roberts in 1857 to supply miners working the gold rush, but was abandoned when the gold rush ended in 1858. In 1859, Point Roberts was designated as a military and lighthouse reserve, and it remained largely uninhabited until the 1890s, when it began to be settled by squatters.

While Point Roberts had a precarious economic existence in the first half of the twentieth century, in the post-1945 period, the nature of the community changed. Washington state law was much more liberal than in British Columbia: the drinking age was lower, the bars remained open later, one could buy alcohol on Sunday, and pornographic movies and magazines were readily available. The construction of a tunnel under the Fraser River in 1959 made it easier for those in Vancouver to visit Point Roberts.[19] And the relaxation of Washington state law in 1953 to allow Canadians to purchase property in Washington increased the numbers of Canadians who purchased vacation property in Point Roberts. By the end of the 1960s, Canadians had come to dominate the Point: in 1969, only 132 of the 326 permanent residents were US citizens; there were 151

Canadians, 19 dual citizens, and 24 citizens of other countries. Of the 1,600 owners of real property in Point Roberts, 85 per cent were Canadians.[20] In the summer months, the population of Point Roberts would soar to 3,500.

The British concerns in the 1850s that this exclave would experience difficulties were prescient. Once Point Roberts was increasingly settled over the course of the twentieth century, the impact of geographic separation manifested itself in a number of different ways. While there were primary schools in Point Roberts, middle- and high-school students had to cross the border four times during the day and drive forty minutes each way to schools in Blaine. Law enforcement was problematic because the only way someone arrested on Point Roberts could be moved to trial was by air or sea, since moving an accused by land would involve extradition proceedings in Canada. Likewise, skilled tradespeople from the United States avoided Point Roberts because a customs escort was needed to move their tools and material through Canada. Anything moved from the mainland United States to Point Roberts required bonded trucks or other special arrangements. There was no hospital, and permanent residents of Point Roberts did not have access to doctors, dentists, pharmacists, or veterinarians, and American health-care insurers refused to pay for health care provided across the border in Canada. Moreover, Washington state law did not allow Canadian medical professionals to practise in Point Roberts.

The transformation of Point Roberts into a vacation destination for Canadians in the 1960s had a major impact on the demand for essential services, such as electricity and telephone, but in particular water for drinking and sewage. The Point had no fresh water supply other than ground wells. In the late 1960s, just seven wells were providing water for drinking water, and two of them had run dry by 1970. While water supplies for drinking were trucked in from Blaine at massive expense, there was no ability to construct a sewage system without a secure supply of water. Whatcom County suspended all new building on Point Roberts, but there was little willingness on either side of the border to fix this growing problem. None of the authorities on the American side—Whatcom County, the state of Washington, or the federal government in DC—were willing to allocate the considerable funds to provide services to a community of three hundred, only half of whom were American citizens. By the same token, all the governments on the Canadian side—the municipality of Delta, the

BC government, and the Canadian federal government—took the view that since Point Roberts was American territory, it was the responsibility of American governments to provide essential services. Moreover, because it was Canadian policy in the 1960s not to export water, governments on the Canadian side refused to provide water to Point Roberts.

In 1970, the two governments decided to give the issue to the IJC. As Munton notes, it was not clear whether Ottawa and Washington were moved to do so "out of sincerity, curiosity, or desperation."[21] But on 21 April 1971, the IJC was asked to undertake a study of the problems created by the border, and to recommend solutions to those problems.

The Point Roberts reference was undertaken under article ix of the Boundary Waters Treaty. While we commonly refer to the agreement signed in 1909 as the Boundary Waters Treaty, its formal title is "Treaty between the United States and Great Britain Relating to Boundary Waters, and Questions Arising between Canada and the United States." Article ix permits the two governments to use the IJC process more widely:

> Any other questions or matters of difference arising between them involving the rights, obligations, or interests of either in relation to the other or to the inhabitants of the other, along the common frontier between the United States and the Dominion of Canada, shall be referred from time to time to the International Joint Commission for examination and report.[22]

Before the Point Roberts reference, article ix had been invoked five times on issues that did not pertain exclusively to boundary water flow levels and uses. The first was in 1920, when the IJC was asked to examine a number of questions about navigation and hydroelectricity generation on the St. Lawrence River. Three focused on air pollution: the ill-fated Trail Smelter reference of 1928, and two others on air pollution in the Detroit-Windsor/Port Huron–Sarnia area of the Great Lakes (all of which are covered in the chapter in this volume by Owen Temby and Don Munton). The fifth reference focused on enhancing the beauty of the American Falls at Niagara (see chapter 9 in this volume).[23] Thus, while the reference on Point Roberts was unprecedented in that it asked the IJC to study and make recommendations on social, political, and economic matters rather than transboundary waters or air pollution, it was not at all outside the "questions arising" remit of the Boundary Waters Treaty.

The reference to the IJC enumerated several specific problems: the application of customs laws and regulations; regulations relating to employment; the adequacy of medical services for residents of Point Roberts; arrangements for the supply of electricity and telephone service; and the issue of law enforcement.[24] The reference, however, made no mention of the problem of water supply.

In keeping with standard IJC practice, the commission established an advisory board, the International Point Roberts Board, which began its work in November 1971. After holding hearings in Vancouver and Point Roberts in December 1971, the board conducted an investigation of the different elements of the reference, and issued a report in October 1973. The board found that the problems that the two governments had identified were quite minor compared to the problems that had emerged in the course of its work. Indeed, while the board had been undertaking its work, some changes to legislation in the United States had already alleviated some problems. For example, in 1972 changes to social security regulations provided that Americans in Point Roberts would be entitled to hospital insurance benefits if they went to a hospital in Canada. And in 1973, Washington State amended its health-care legislation, allowing Canadian physicians to respond to emergencies and make house calls.[25]

The board concluded that far more significant than the problems identified by the two federal governments in the 1971 reference was a matter that had not even been mentioned. As the report put it, among the most "fundamental problems" was the issue of resources:

> Point Roberts is both physically removed from the United States mainland and a natural part of a dormitory and recreational suburb of Vancouver. It does not have sufficient natural resources such as water to support the existing population and weekend visitors let alone any future development. The required natural resources must come from outside the Point.

However, because it was clear that none of the three levels of government on the US side was willing to provide those resources, given the tiny number of Americans on Point Roberts, the board concluded that the "logical" source of the resources necessary for the Point was Canada. But the board noted that governments on the Canadian side—municipal, provincial, or federal—would be willing to provide those resources "*only* if they also have a voice in the question of land use patterns and population densities on Point Roberts."[26]

As a result of the clear logjam that arose from the unwillingness of any of the governments to co-operate in resolving the "little" problems of Point Roberts, the board decided to propose a broad and holistic solution. The 1973 report recommended that Canada and the United States create a giant international park of some eight thousand square kilometres that would include the main islands in the Strait of Georgia and the Salish Sea—from Gabriola Island in the north to Whidbey Island in the south. "Concept B," as it was called, envisaged a conservation and recreation area that would incorporate existing communities and parks. The international park and conservation system was to be administered by what the board called a "binational forum" of three Canadians and three Americans appointed by their governments. Point Roberts and a comparably sized area of Canadian territory would serve as the headquarters of the park.

It is clear that the board had in mind the binational park that had been created just six years before on the East Coast. Franklin Delano Roosevelt had owned a summer retreat on Campobello Island in New Brunswick. When Roosevelt's spouse, Eleanor Roosevelt, died in 1962, the family deeded the property to the governments of the United States and Canada jointly so that an international park could be created to memorialize Roosevelt. The two governments negotiated an international treaty, signed in January 1964 by Prime Minister Lester B. Pearson and President Lyndon B. Johnson, outlining the governance of this international park, creating a six-person commission, and agreeing on the funding and running of the park, which opened in August 1964.[27]

However, creating an international park of eleven square kilometres from a property that belonged to a single family was fundamentally unlike the Concept B that was being proposed by the International Point Roberts Board in 1973. Concept B involved thousands of acres of land, several thousand property owners, and numerous municipal jurisdictions. However, the Concept B plan lacked any details about funding or the possible impact on private property values within the proposed park. Moreover, the 1973 report did not explain precisely how an international park would solve the very particular problems faced by Point Roberts residents. Nor did the report explain why the grand design envisaged in Concept B was the only solution. Most importantly of all, however, neither the board nor the IJC had the resources necessary for a comprehensive communications strategy for releasing the report to the community or publicizing the rationale behind Concept B. Copies of the report were only available at local libraries or by formal request from the IJC. As a result, most people had to rely on newspaper articles for their information about the proposal.[28]

When public hearings were held in Point Roberts in December 1973 and in Vancouver in early 1974, the reaction of the community was overwhelmingly negative. While some conservation and environmental groups welcomed the proposal for the creation of an international park, many residents of Point Roberts—and other jurisdictions affected by the proposal—expressed strong opposition to the "binational forum" that was being proposed; a common concern was that the appointed commissioners would be responsible to the national governments that appointed them, rather than to local residents.

During the public hearings on the report, the board was criticized for having paid insufficient attention to local views. Some critics argued that while the board had contacted a number of agencies in the national capitals about customs or other matters, it had not consulted local groups or municipalities, particularly those municipalities—such as San Juan County, a cluster of some four hundred islands in the Salish Sea on the American side of the line—proposed to be incorporated into the new international park. One of the reasons for this was that the board was severely understaffed: only the US side had a secretary, and there were no resources for the development of a communications strategy. Moreover, at the time that the Point Roberts reference was being undertaken, the IJC commissioners had a number of other, more pressing issues vying for their attention, including the Great Lakes pollution and the Skagit River references.

As the full extent of the opposition to the report became evident, the IJC directed the advisory board to engage in further consultations with the affected municipalities, which lead to a supplemental report to the IJC in September 1974. By this time, however, the board recognized that there was even less desire for co-operation among local levels of government for a solution. As a result, the board recommended to the commission that further work would be useless: "the job [the board] was given cannot be carried further until the various local and regional authorities agree that bi-national cooperation is required."[29] The board also recommended that the IJC not recommend Concept B to the federal governments in Ottawa and Washington. This report brought matters to a standstill, and no further work was done on the reference. In a final report to the governments, issued on 16 August 1977, the IJC informed the two governments that it was officially terminating its work under the reference: "until such time as the local jurisdictions have reached some sort of accommodation concerning the Point Roberts question, there is little the Commission can do in this matter."[30]

Aftermath

Today, more than forty years after the termination of the reference, Point Roberts is a thriving community. To be sure, some of the inconveniences that prompted the Canadian and United States governments to submit the reference in 1971 remain. School children beyond third grade still have to make the long, 86-kilometre round trip to Blaine, crossing the border four times a day. The deputy sheriff in what locals describe as "America's best gated community"[31] still has to transport anyone arrested for a crime to the county seat for trial by boat or plane. Medical services are still limited: while there is a health-care clinic, urgent care and more complex procedures still require a trip to Canada or to Blaine. But the Point Roberts economy is much more robust than it was in the late 1960s. Not only is the real estate market strong because of the high cost of property in Vancouver, but cross-border shopping for gasoline and groceries contributes significantly to the local economy. There is also an active parcel-receiving industry for Canadians who find it cheaper and more convenient to maintain a US shipping address than to have goods shipped across the border. The Point

Roberts marina is one of the largest employers; 95 per cent of the vessels there are registered to Canadians.[32]

The key to the transformation was water. During the reference period, the board had recommended that, because no American government would fund a water pipeline across Boundary Bay to Point Roberts from an American point, a water solution should be negotiated between Point Roberts and governments on the Canadian side. And on the Canadian side, there was strong opposition to bulk water removals: indeed, the NDP government of Dave Barrett, in power between 1972 and 1975, enacted legislation prohibiting bulk water removals. However, the negotiations recommended by the board were nonetheless undertaken, and in August 1987, ten years after the reference was terminated, the Point Roberts Water District finally signed an agreement with the Greater Vancouver Water District for an allotment of 840,000 gallons of water each day, to be provided from a reservoir in Delta.[33] With a steady and reasonably priced supply of water from the Lower Mainland, most of the problems that had given rise to the reference in 1971 have since disappeared.

Analysis

It can be argued that the failure of the Point Roberts reference had a deep structural cause: the positions and policies of the local and regional governments constituted a significant impediment to meaningful action on the problems of Point Roberts. All three levels of governments on the American side of the line had little interest in spending the large sums of money that would be necessary to provide US-based services for the small number of residents of Point Roberts (and the even smaller number of American citizens). Likewise, governments on the Canadian side, particularly the British Columbia provincial government and local municipalities that bordered Point Roberts, had little interest in providing services and resources such as water to American territory when these governments would be given no say in how Point Roberts was governed, much less any of the tax revenue. Stalemate was the inevitable result.

However, in the way that it pursued the reference, the IJC made this stalemate more pronounced. In particular, in three areas the IJC did not do in the Point Roberts reference what it generally did in other references and applications—the "causes of success" enumerated above. First, the advisory board was not given enough resources to involve locals as effectively as the IJC tended to do in other areas. Willoughby notes that "particularly important has been [the IJC's] custom of going to the people instead of requiring them to come to it; its affording all persons an opportunity to be heard."[34] The International Point Roberts Board did not have a member from the Point, which increased suspicions among locals that the IJC was a distant bureaucratic mechanism intent on destroying the Point Roberts community (suspicions that were for many confirmed when the board issued its Concept B proposal). This initial problem was exacerbated by the lack of resources available for a comprehensive communications strategy when the 1973 report was finally rolled out.

Second, both Willoughby and Makepeace focus on the importance of bureaucratic expertise in shaping the IJC's success: the ability of the IJC to draw on bureaucratic expertise from agencies on both sides of the border and from different levels of government that gives the commission both authenticity and authority. In the Point Roberts case, there was little involvement by bureaucrats from the surrounding localities. While the board conducted a vigorous study of the questions posed in the reference by approaching federal departments and local hydroelectric utilities, it was clear that there was little buy-in from township and county planners.

The fact that officials and experts from localities around Point Roberts were not deeply involved in the process contributed to a third problem. In Willoughby's view, one factor in the IJC's success "has been the good judgement it has shown in its orders and recommendations in taking into account local and regional requirements."[35] It is possible that had local planners from neighbouring municipalities on both sides of the border been more deeply involved in the work of the board, it might not have been quite as seized with the idea of trying to solve the Point Roberts problem by reaching for a giant holistic "fix." Certainly it can be argued that Concept B and its proposal to create a massive, eight-thousand-square-kilometre international park—from Gabriola Island near Nanaimo, British Columbia, in the north to Whidbey Island near Everett, Washington, in the south—did not reflect a *politically* sensitive judgement; there was little recognition that the model uppermost in the minds of the board—the

Roosevelt Campobello International Park—had such little applicability to the Point Roberts case.

In short, if we think counterfactually about the Point Roberts reference, might it have worked out differently had the IJC carefully followed its usual practices? In others words, what if the commission and the advisory board had involved local residents from the start? What if the board had consulted more broadly with local municipal bureaucracies? What if the board had had the good judgement to recognize that the solution that it had embraced—the international conservation and recreation area—was simply too large and indigestible given the multitude of interests involved? What if the board had had the good judgement to recognize that the Roosevelt Campobello International Park model it was using had been successful because it was infinitely less complex? What if the board had recognized that the IJC tends to be successful when its focus remains parochial?[36]

The most intriguing counterfactual question, however, involves the issue that the IJC has been so successful in dealing with in other references: water. One of the significant contributions made by the International Point Roberts Board was to demonstrate clearly that the concerns raised by both national governments in the reference in 1971 were in fact of minor concern, and that the real issue that confronted Point Roberts was water and the impossibility of meeting steadily increasing demand for water with the slowly failing ground wells. Having correctly identified the real problem, what would have resulted had the board—and the commission itself—fixed firmly on the issue of water, and defined access to water from the Lower Mainland as a "square hole" into which the Point Roberts peg might have been more readily fitted? What if the IJC had concentrated its recommendations to the two governments on the importance of overcoming the obstacles to getting appropriate supplies of water to Point Roberts? For, as the subsequent history of the Point demonstrated so clearly, once the water supply was fixed, all other problems became infinitely more manageable.

Conclusion: A Square Peg?

Some have suggested that the Point Roberts reference demonstrates the difficulty of going beyond the "usual" mandate of the IJC. "One wonders,"

William Willoughby noted, "whether the governments were not ill-advised when they asked the IJC to recommend a solution to the difficult problem of Point Roberts."[37] Likewise, as a commissioner confided to Don Munton in 1979, "the IJC as an institution was not ready for Point Roberts... we were simply not equipped to deal with it."[38] It is true, as Paul Muldoon notes, that the unusual nature of the reference took the IJC out of its traditional boundary water comfort zone: "Stripped of its traditional technical basis for resolving disputes, the IJC was asked to play a role more closely akin to that of a political body."[39]

However, I have argued in this chapter that this transboundary issue, while it might have been unprecedented, was well within the ambit of the 1909 treaty. Point Roberts may have been a "square peg" in a historical repertoire of "round hole" boundary waters cases. But it is not at all clear that had the IJC organized itself for this reference in the same way that it organized boundary waters references, the outcome would not have been different. The "causes of success" that we identify with so much of the IJC's operations could well have been embraced in the case of Point Roberts. Had the IJC structured the International Point Roberts Board to be more representative of local interests; had the board been more willing to bring local bureaucracies into the process; and had the board been more realistic and parochial, it may well have embraced a square hole into which the Point Roberts peg might have been fitted.

Notes

The author wishes to thank Jim Chandler, who served as secretary of the International Point Roberts Board in the mid-1970s, for his assistance during the research for this chapter.

1. Paul Robert Muldoon, "The International Joint Commission and Point Roberts: A Venture into a New Area of Concern" (MA thesis, McMaster University, 1983), 195.

2. Arthur Finch, secretary of the Point Roberts Harbor Committee, November 1971, quoted in Muldoon, "The International Joint Commission and Point Roberts," 92.

3. See, for example, Don Munton, "Paradoxes and Prospects," in *The International Joint Commission Seventy Years On*, ed. Robert Spencer, John Kirton, and Kim Richard Nossal (Toronto: Centre for International Studies, University of Toronto, 1981), 79.

4   Lawrence J. Burpee, "A Successful Experiment in International Relations," address to Victorian Club of Boston, 17 February 1919 (Ottawa: King's Printer, 1919), 13; available at https://archive.org/stream/cihm_82189.

5   John W. Holmes, "Introduction: The IJC and Canada-United States Relations," in Spencer, Kirton, and Nossal, eds., *International Joint Commission Seventy Years On*, 3.

6   Murray Clamen, "The International Joint Commission : A Model for Inter-American Cooperation ?" *VertigO: la revue électronique en sciences de l'environnement* 2 (September 2005), http://vertigo.revues.org/1885.

7   US Mission to Canada, "Ambassador Heyman's Remarks at the International Joint Commission Reception," Ottawa, 24 October 2016, https://ca.usembassy.gov/ambassador-heymans-remarks-international-joint-commission-reception/.

8   Burpee, "Successful Experiment," 8.

9   Quoted in William R. Willoughby, *The Joint Organizations of Canada and the United States* (Toronto: University of Toronto Press, 1979), 55.

10 International Joint Commission, "The IJC and the 21st Century: Response of the IJC to a Request by the Governments of Canada and United States for Proposals on How To Best Assist Them to Meet the Environmental Challenges of the 21st Century," Ottawa and Washington, n.d. [1997?].

11 Garth O. Makepeace, "The International Joint Commission: Determinants of Success" (MA thesis, University of British Columbia, 1980), 73–7.

12 Ralph Pentland and Adele Hurley, "Thirsty Neighbours: A Century of Canada-US Transboundary Water Governance," in *Eau Canada: The Future of Canadian Waters*, ed. Karen Bakker (Vancouver: UBC Press, 2007), 163–81; quotation at 177.

13 Kim Richard Nossal, "Institutionalization and the Pacific Settlement of Interstate Conflict: The Case of Canada and the International Joint Commission," *Journal of Canadian Studies* 18, no. 4 (Winter 1983–4), 75–87; quotation at 85.

14 Willoughby, *Joint Organizations*, 52–8.

15 Article 1, Treaty between Her Majesty and the United States, for the Settlement of the Oregon Boundary; American version: 1846, 9 Stat. 869; Treaty Series 120, https://www.loc.gov/law/help/us-treaties/bevans/b-gb-ust000012-0095.pdf.

16 Derek Hayes, *Historical Atlas of British Columbia and the Pacific Northwest* (Vancouver: Douglas & McIntyre, 1999), 161; see also Elizabeth Tower, *Over the Back Fence: Conflicts on the United States/Canadian Border from Maine to Alaska* (Anchorage: Publication Consultants, 2009).

17 According to article 1, the demarcation line would continue from the middle of the Georgia Strait "thence southerly through the middle of the said channel, and of Fuca's straits to the Pacific Ocean," a wording that made no provision for the many islands in the Salish Sea between the Georgia Strait and the Strait of Juan de Fuca.

18 United States Geological Survey, *Survey of the Northwestern Boundary of the United States, 1857–1861*, by Marcus Baker (Washington, 1900), 16–19. See also Richard

U. Goode, "The Northwestern Boundary between the United States and Canada," *American Geographical Survey* 32, no. 5 (1900), 465–70.

19 See Julian V. Minghi, "Point Roberts, Washington: Boundary Problems of an American Exclave," in *Borderlines and Borderlands: Political Oddities at the Edge of the Nation-State*, ed. Alexander C. Diener and Joshua Hagen (Lanham, MD: Rowman & Littlefield), 173–89.

20 Muldoon, "The International Joint Commission and Point Roberts," 109–10.

21 Munton, "Paradoxes and Prospects," 79.

22 Treaty between the United States and Great Britain Relating to Boundary Waters, and Questions Arising Between the United States and Canada [Boundary Waters Treaty], 11 January 1909, article ix—Appendix 1 of this book, or https://www.ijc.org/en/who/mission/bwt. See also William R. Willoughby, "Expectations and Experience, 1909–1979," in Spencer, Kirton, and Nossal, eds., *International Joint Commission Seventy Years On*, 35–8.

23 Down to 1971, the article ix references that did not pertain purely to boundary water levels and uses were: Docket 17R St Lawrence River—Navigation/Hydro Power (1920); Docket 25R, Trail Smelter (1928); Docket 61R, Windsor-Detroit Ship's Smoke (1949); Docket 85R, Port Huron-Sarnia/Detroit-Windsor (1966); and Docket 86R, American Falls (1967). After the Point Roberts reference in 1971, there were two further article ix references that did not pertain to boundary waters: Docket 99R, Air Quality—Detroit-Windsor/Port Huron-Sarnia (1975), and Docket 112R, Air Quality Agreement (1991), which asked the IJC to help monitor and implement the Canada-United States Air Quality Agreement of 1991 that had brought the long-running acid rain dispute to an end. While the Trail Smelter fumes reference is often classified as a failure, Temby and Munton persuasively argue in their chapter in this volume that the Trail case was one of the major success stories of the IJC in its first century of operations. In August 1928, the two governments asked the IJC to investigate a case of air pollution, and determine the extent to which property in Washington State was being damaged by fumes from a smelter operated by Consolidated Mining and Smelting Company (Cominco) in Trail, British Columbia. In this case, the IJC split along national lines and the United States government rejected the IJC report. See International Joint Commission, Docket 25R, at https://www.ijc.org/en/25r; see also D. H. Dinwoodie, "The Politics of International Pollution Control: The Trail Smelter Case," *International Journal* 27, no. 1 (1971–2), 219–35; and Martijn van de Kerkhof, "The Trail Smelter Case Re-examined: Examining the Development of National Procedural Mechanisms to Resolve a Trail Smelter Type Dispute," *Utrecht Journal of International and European Law* 27, no. 73 (2011), 68–83. For the case in comparative perspective, see John D. Wirth, *Smelter Smoke in North America: The Politics of Transborder Pollution* (Lawrence: University Press of Kansas, 2000).

24 International Joint Commission, Supplemental Report of the International Point Roberts Board, 15 September 1974, http://www.ijc.org/files/publications/ID418.pdf, 1.

25 Muldoon, "The International Joint Commission and Point Roberts," 153.

26 Supplemental Report of the International Point Roberts Board, 15 September 1974, 2.

27 Agreement between the Government of the United States of America and the Government of Canada relating to the Establishment of the Roosevelt Campobello International Park, in United States, Department of State, *United States Treaties and Other International Agreements,* vol. 15, pt. 2 (Washington: US Government Printing Service, 1964), 1504–7. See also Jonas Klein, *Beloved Island: Franklin & Eleanor and the Legacy of Campobello* (Forest Dale, VT: Paul S. Eriksson, 2000), epilogue.

28 Muldoon, "The International Joint Commission and Point Roberts," 171.

29 Supplemental Report of the International Point Roberts Board, 15 September 1974, 33.

30 Quoted in Muldoon, "The International Joint Commission and Point Roberts," 184.

31 Lauren Kramer, "Point Roberts: A Mini-Getaway in America's Best Gated Community," *Bellingham Insider Blogs,* 15 February 2016, https://www.bellingham.org/insider-blogs/point-roberts-a-mini-getaway-in-americas-best-gated-community/.

32 Tristin Hopper, "Point Roberts, Washington: A Little Slice of the U.S., Only Accessible through Canada," *National Post* (Toronto), 27 February 2012.

33 See Patrick Forest, "Inter-Local Water Agreements: Law, Geography and NAFTA," *Les Cahiers de droit* 51, no. 3–4 (2010): 749–99.

34 Willoughby, *Joint Organizations,* 56.

35 Ibid., 57.

36 Nossal, "Institutionalization and the Pacific Settlement of Interstate Conflict."

37 Willoughby, *Joint Organizations,* 59.

38 Quoted in Munton, "Paradoxes and Prospects," 80.

39 Muldoon, "The International Joint Commission and Point Roberts," 216.

7

The International Joint Commission and Mid-continent Water Issues: The Garrison Diversion, Red River, Devils Lake, and the Northwest Area Water Supply Project

Norman Brandson and Allen Olson

From the Atlantic to the Pacific, Canada–United States water relations have been shaped by the unique geography of the nine principal transboundary watersheds subject to the Boundary Waters Treaty (BWT). The states of Minnesota and North Dakota and the province of Manitoba share three of these watersheds: Manitoba and Minnesota (along with Ontario) the Rainy River basin; Manitoba and North Dakota (along with Saskatchewan) the Souris River basin; and all three share the Red River basin. The Red rises at the confluence of the Otter Tail and Bois de Sioux Rivers at the extreme southeast corner of North Dakota. Flowing northward it marks the Minnesota–North Dakota boundary, crossing the international border into Manitoba through the largest city in the basin, Winnipeg, its delta emptying into the south end of Lake Winnipeg. The topography of this northern Great Plains basin is largely tabletop flat, where elevation differences are measured in inches or fractions of inches rather than feet. Minnesota, known as the land of ten thousand lakes, is not generally water deficient; nor is Manitoba, with major rivers flowing

215

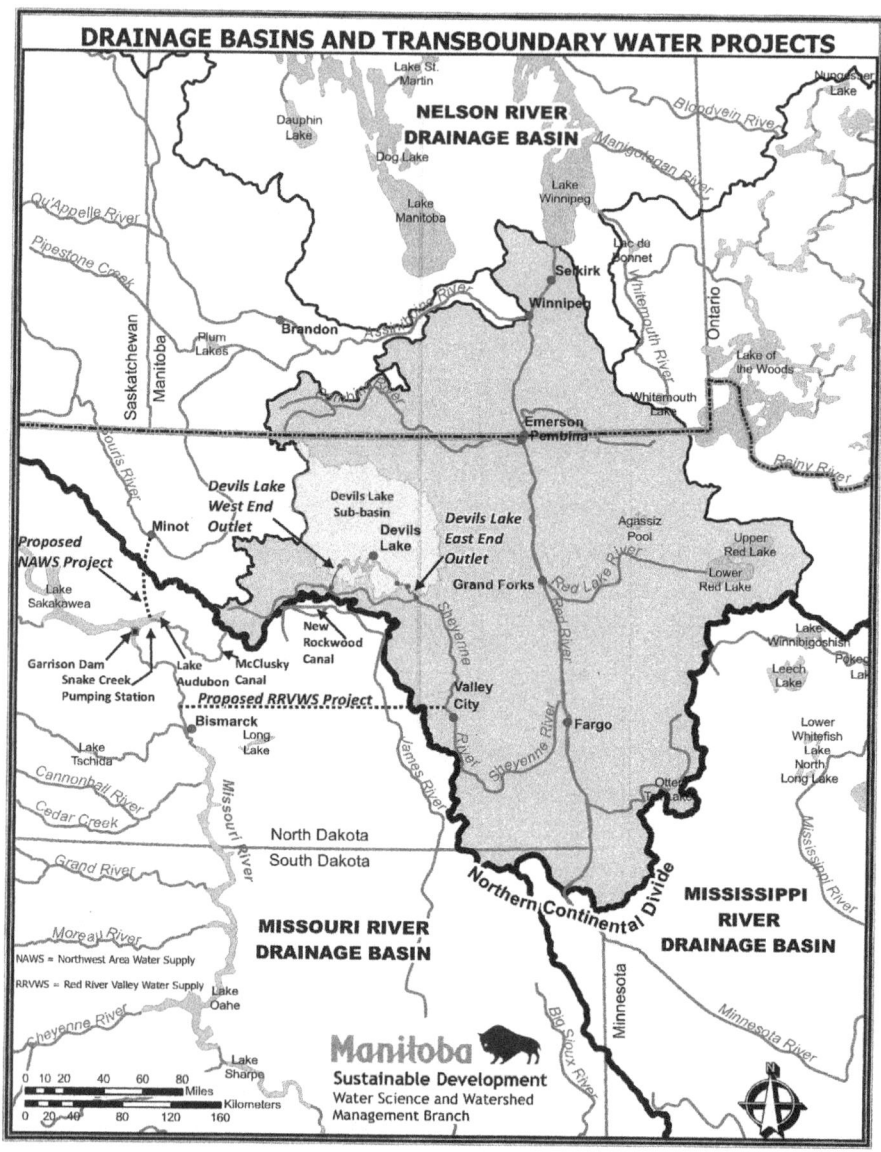

FIGURE 7.1. Map of water issues discussed in this chapter. Used with permission of the Government of Manitoba.

in from both east and west and an abundance of Prairie lakes. However there is a dearth of surface water in that portion of the basin west of the Red in North Dakota.

We will look at four cases in this region that neatly illustrate some of the strengths and weaknesses of both the BWT and the International Joint Commission (IJC), as well as how both the document and the institution are evolving over time. The first case (Garrison Diversion) examines what may be the last serious use of the treaty's dispute-resolution mechanism, an IJC reference to examine a proposed diversion of Missouri River water into the Red and hence the Hudson Bay drainage; an IJC study reference (Red River Flooding) that galvanized action after the largest Red River flood in over a century; and two more recent water disputes (Devils Lake and the Northwest Area Water Supply Project) that could have been referred to the IJC but were dealt with by alternative means.

The authors of this chapter were direct participants in many aspects of these four case studies: Governor Olson was an elected official in North Dakota and Norman Brandson was a senior official in the Manitoba government. Although supporting references are provided for most of the salient points of each case, the authors have called on first-hand experience and personal recollection to paint a full picture.

Garrison Diversion

The dream of building a water system to make productive the rich but arid farmland of eastern North Dakota is over one hundred years old, first mentioned at the state's Constitutional Convention in 1889. Beginning then and down through the years, the source of supply for such a system was seen as the Missouri River; but it really wasn't until the completion of the Garrison dam on the Missouri in 1953, which created the Lake Sakakawea reservoir, that the dream started to shift toward reality. In 1955 North Dakota created the Garrison Diversion Conservancy District,[1] a twenty-five county political subdivision authorized to raise funds to advance a project to divert water from Lake Sakakawea through a series of canals and natural streams to eastern and northern North Dakota. Most of the water was intended for distribution for irrigation but there was also a domestic and municipal component as well as some envisaged fish and wildlife benefits. It was clear at that time that North Dakota would require substantial federal funding for such a massive project. It was duly forthcoming as Congress authorized in 1965 the construction of the Garrison Diversion Unit (GDU).[2]

As construction proceeded on various components of the GDU—dependent on annual Congressional appropriations it was clearly going to take several years to fully complete—the Government of Manitoba began to have some concerns that this project would link two continental watersheds that had not been so connected for several millennia.[3] Because of their isolation from one another they had developed distinct ecosystems with different and perhaps incompatible species of fish, micro-organisms, fish pathogens, and so forth. There was concern that the return flows from irrigation could wash both artificial (pesticides, fertilizers) and natural (sulfates and other soil constituents) contaminants into the Red River and hence into Canadian waters; perhaps more seriously, these flows, as well as spills and flows from the system's conveyances, could bring damaging organisms not natural to the Red River/Hudson Bay basin, causing irreversible harm to the basin's ecology, in violation of article iv of the BWT.

It appears that the governments of Canada and the United States approached article ix of the BWT—the investigative functions of the IJC—and its use for dispute resolution with some caution. Although an *aide-mémoire* was developed as the basis of discussion between the two governments in 1970, it wasn't until 1975, with construction of GDU works proceeding apace, that it was agreed to refer what had clearly become a "dispute" between Manitoba and North Dakota to the IJC under article ix. Although there are instances of references stretching out over long periods of time, the commission was charged with reporting to the governments within one year, and they did so.[4]

The commission's work, given its tight time deadline, was based on existing information. Several technical teams were assembled with Manitoba, Minnesota, and North Dakota contributing personnel. Their work was directed by the International Garrison Diversion Study Board, established by the commission to provide technical advice. Eight public hearings were held throughout the basin with an accompanying public involvement program, somewhat advanced for its time. The commission considered the implications of the final proposed GDU (some parts of which had already been constructed) on Canadian waters based on the reports of its technical committees as well as feedback received through its public involvement process. The commissioners made three recommendations to the governments: first, that those parts of the GDU that would convey water into the Red River basin not be built at this time because of the threat of transferring harmful invasive species into Canadian waters; second, that "if and when the governments of Canada and the United States *agree* that methods have been *proven* that will *eliminate the risk* of biota transfer, or if the question of biota transfer is *agreed* to be no longer a matter of concern" (emphasis added) then the portion of the GDU conveying water into the waters flowing into Canada can proceed provided that a number of conditions outlined by the IJC are met; and third, that the two countries negotiate water quality agreements for the Red and Souris Rivers. This latter recommendation was not unanimous. (A separate opinion was filed by one of the Canadian commissioners recommending that the setting of water quality objectives should be extended to all transboundary tributaries of the two rivers.) It is the second recommendation that became Manitoba's mantra whenever it has been faced with potential inter-basin transfers of water into the watershed of the Red.

It is remarkable that the IJC was able to reach consensus rather than simply dividing on national lines, agreeing that a significant portion of the GDU not be built given that this was such a large undertaking backed by the Government of the United States. It is intended that commissioners approach their duties objectively without partisanship and the outcome of the Garrison reference, accepted by the national governments, offers proof that this ideal can actually be achieved in practice. In 1981, in the wake of the IJC report, the US-Canada Consultative Group (CG) of senior officials was established to initiate discussions concerning the conditions that might satisfy the IJC's second recommendation, and in 1983 a Joint Technical Committee (JTC) was established to assist the CG.[5] Ultimately the group was unable to agree on the type, location, and degree of water treatment that might satisfy Canadian concerns.

Dreams die hard, however, and the Garrison report—the second recommendation outlined above—did envisage circumstances under which the GDU or some future project to divert Missouri River water into the Red River basin might be acceptable. Less than ten years after the IJC report,

Congress passed the Garrison Diversion Reformulation Act,[6] which refocused the project on diverting Missouri water into the Red River Valley for municipal, rural, and industrial uses, substantially reducing the irrigation component. Federal funds continued to flow to the Garrison Diversion Conservancy District. Over time further modifications virtually eliminated the irrigation component, and in 2000 Congress authorized under the Dakota Water Resources Act[7] a "new" project, dropping the name "Garrison Diversion Unit" in favour of the Red River Valley Water Supply Project (RRVWSP), even though the federally funded Garrison Diversion Conservancy District remained (and remains) in existence.

The project would divert Lake Sakakawea water over the divide into the Red River Valley using most of the previously constructed GDU works, but unlike the original project would include measures (unspecified) to eliminate or at least mitigate the risk of invasive species transfer. Much has changed since the 1977 IJC report: massive irrigation projects using imported water have fallen out of favour; there is much more experience and better science concerning invasive species than was available to the IJC in the mid-seventies; water treatment technology has also advanced since then; both national governments seem reluctant to employ article ix of the BWT to resolve disputes, preferring instead ad hoc negotiations that may preserve the principles of the BWT while not formally falling under its provisions; and attitudes in both North Dakota and Manitoba have changed.

In the case of North Dakota the advent of shale oil and gas development has turned a state long dependent on the inflow of federal dollars into an economic powerhouse much more aggressive in solving its water problems without the necessity of federal aid. In Manitoba the emphasis has shifted from "no diversions ever" to insisting that the IJC's second Garrison recommendation still holds but that it is time to look at ways in which it might be possible to agree on measures for such diversions, as per the work of the CG and the JTC, that might eliminate invasive species risk; and that the IJC can play a useful role, not in "resolving a dispute" but in providing objective technical advice under article ix as it has on many occasions to the benefit of both countries (for example, see other chapters in this volume on Great Lakes water quality and the Columbia River Treaty). Four decades later the Garrison Diversion lives.

As this case illustrates, it is not always easy to reconcile the legitimate water needs of upstream interests with the principle of no harm to downstream neighbours. The BWT has worked, more or less, because the national governments have been able to take the larger view: reign in water aspirations in one basin and realize them in another—the greatest good for the greatest number. However, both countries are federations in which the sub-national governments have their own significant powers and also exert considerable influence on the national government. So when a state or province feels that they have lost, have had their aspirations curtailed because of the BWT, they are not likely to be mollified knowing their fellow citizens in another BWT basin have won. The RRVWSP project continues to be advanced by North Dakota.[8] Preliminary environmental analyses have been prepared and a detailed design is forthcoming. Having strongly disagreed with the results of the original GDU reference, the state adamantly opposes a future reference on this successor project. Overcoming the zero-sum, win-lose approach that was inadvertently triggered by the 1977 Garrison report will require compromise. It remains to be seen whether or not the BWT and the IJC can play a meaningful role to support compromise in the Red River basin.

Red River

The three largest cities on the Red River—Fargo-Moorhead, Grand Forks–East Grand Forks, and Winnipeg—were all incorporated about the same time (1874–5). For the next seventy-five years, although the Red experienced occasional spring flooding—and was a mere trickle during the drought of the Great Depression—there were no catastrophic basin-wide events. That changed in 1950, when the river spilled over its banks and, because of the valley's flat terrain, created a flood plain several miles wide. A good portion of the city of Winnipeg was inundated, triggering what is still the largest evacuation in Canadian history, partly due to the coincident flood peak of the Assiniboine River that joins the Red at Winnipeg. This led to the construction of the Greater Winnipeg Floodway, completed in 1968, which is an open channel capable of diverting part of the river around the city.[9] There were also major valley floods in 1968, 1969, 1978, 1979, 1989, and 1996, although none of the magnitude of the mid-century event. The 1996 flood caused significant agricultural damage and was followed by a wet summer, leaving the ground saturated; and the winter of 1996-7 saw above-average snowfall in the basin. To complete the perfect storm, warm weather in the basin in early April 1997 was followed by a major snowstorm. The Red River Valley contained far more water than the Red and its tributaries could handle and the resulting April-May flood created a "lake" from upstream of Fargo to the city of Winnipeg that measured 25 miles (40 kilometres) at its widest point. Grand Forks was hardest hit with most of the city under water. In the midst of this tragedy a city block caught fire, destroying eleven buildings and resulting in the iconic image broadcast around the world of flames leaping from buildings partially submerged in floodwater. (The intrepid reporting of the disaster by the *Grand Forks Herald* earned the paper a Pulitzer Prize.) Further upstream, Fargo also experienced severe flooding, as did Moorhead and East Grand Forks on the Minnesota side of the river. Winnipeg was thought to be protected by its floodway, but was spared only by a monumental effort to construct, almost overnight, a defensive wall of dikes to the south and west of the city. Even then, had there been sustained strong south winds or significant rainfall, the city would have been largely inundated. Many farms and rural residences were flooded, as was the town of St. Agathe, Manitoba, when its ring dike failed.[10]

Taking stock in the aftermath, it was clear that several things had gone wrong. Flood forecasting had failed to accurately predict the magnitude and timing of the flood peak. Most communities and rural residences did not have permanent protection for a flood of this magnitude. Some permanent works were not well maintained and this resulted in some failures of the temporary diking built on these permanent foundations. And it was now apparent after the numerous post-1950 floods that the probabilities engineers had used to design protective works in the valley no longer applied; we could expect bigger floods more often. The '97 flood became *The Flood of the Century*.

The combined damage on both sides of the border was several billion dollars; personal loss and suffering was incalculable. In the immediate wake of the tragedy the two national governments sent a reference to the IJC instructing it to analyze the root causes of the 1997 flood and make recommendations (an interim report to be filed by 31 December 1997 and the final report one year later) as to how damage from future major Red River floods could be mitigated. The commission created the International Red River Task Force, composed of experts drawn mostly from North Dakota, Minnesota, and Manitoba, to perform technical analyses; held public hearings and meetings throughout the basin; and consulted with opinion leaders at all levels of the private and public sectors. Seized with a sense of urgency the IJC was able to provide an interim report by year-end, as requested by the governments.[11]

The IJC made twenty-eight recommendations,[12] and also endorsed almost all of the recommendations of their International Red River Basin Task Force that dealt largely with technical issues. The commission's work focused on several key areas and made recommendations as to how governments should address them. The main themes of the report were as follows. First, the basin was simply not prepared for a flood of this magnitude. Huge disasters—like the inundation of Grand Forks—did occur, but even greater catastrophe, like the flooding of Winnipeg, was avoided by the narrowest of margins; and floods of this magnitude or greater can be anticipated in the future. Second, large-scale water retention in this flat basin is not feasible, and although micro-storage can help, no one solution will adequately address the risk. Third, specific additional protective measures are urgently needed for the basin's largest city, Winnipeg, to increase the level of protection; the same is true for Grand Forks and East Grand Forks, Fargo-Moorhead, and other smaller communities and rural residences. Fourth, inter-jurisdictional co-operation and integration is absolutely essential to anticipate, mitigate, and recover from the next "flood of the century," and the task force provided detailed recommendations on the ways and means to achieve this objective. And finally, governments needed to also prepare the hearts and minds of valley residents, helping them to understand the risk posed by future extreme floods and the necessity to prepare in advance for an event that could occur next year or perhaps a hundred years from now. A few years after the event the memory grows dim.

The most tangible immediate result was that the IJC's report held feet to the fire. In a highly public way it drew attention to the fact that not only was this an unprecedented catastrophe, but it could even have been much worse. Moreover, governments—national, state/provincial, and local—would have to get their collective act together to avoid future disaster. And the governments took it seriously. They collectively reported on their progress in responding to the commission's recommendations. In the United States, reclamation and recovery on both sides of the river in Grand Forks began even before the floodwaters fully receded and a new permanent diking system was constructed. Flood plain rezoning resulted in many structures being removed from high-risk areas. In Canada, a $350 million federal-provincial program raised protective dikes for rural communities and rural residences two feet above the 1997 flood level. Another cost-shared $650 million program expanded the Greater Winnipeg Floodway to provide protection from a one-in-two-hundred-and-fifty-year flood event.

These mitigation measures are without doubt the most visible outcome of the IJC's work. It is clear that funding for the expansion of the Greater Winnipeg Floodway would not have been secured without the highly visible red flag raised by the commission. Much progress was made in mapping the topography of the basin through LIDAR surveys that could detect the small elevation changes that directed the path of floodwaters, necessary knowledge in siting mitigation works. More sophisticated flood forecasting is now in place both in modeling and data collection and sharing. In 2001, as part of its International Watershed Initiative, the IJC replaced its existing engineering-oriented Red River Board with the more fully integrated and inclusive International Red River Board. This board continues to track the progress of government actions. Governments at all levels have improved, or created where they did not exist, disaster preparedness plans.

Much has been accomplished. Preparedness for the next "big one" is significantly better than it was in 1997. Much remains to be done, however.[13] The dream of institutionalizing a transnational response to flooding in the basin, through the efforts of the IJC's International Red River Board and non-government groups like the Red River Basin Commission, is a few steps closer to reality but still distant. There is co-operation and information sharing through networks of technical staff of the province and two states, but it relies more on individual relationships than formality. The issue of improved and coordinated flood forecasting between the US National Weather Service and the Province of Manitoba was raised by the IJC in its 1997 report, but there was no follow-up review. In subsequent years the two forecasts have occasionally diverged, sometimes significantly, indicating that more needs to be done.

Very little progress has been made with respect to non-structural mitigation measures. Even though usually accompanied by some form of protection, building, and rebuilding continues in the flood plain in both countries. Some research has gone into creating micro storage of water utilizing road ditches, low-lying areas, and existing wetlands, but very little has materialized on the landscape. Nonetheless, the Red River reference illustrates what the IJC perhaps does best: objective scientific analysis leading to non-partisan recommendations that benefit both countries. The work of the IJC often lays the groundwork for future co-operative action. Each situation is different of course. In the case of the Red River Valley tensions among the jurisdictions on water issues is long standing (Manitoba and Minnesota have generally co-operated in opposition to certain North Dakota water initiatives), and given that flooding is but one dimension of water management, it is unlikely that the institutionalized co-operation achieved on the Great Lakes and Columbia River basins will materialize in the valley anytime soon.

Devils Lake

The 3,810-square-mile Devils Lake watershed is located in the northeastern corner of North Dakota, in the western extremity of the Red River basin. It has no natural outlet. During drought cycles there is virtually no Devils Lake, and in prolonged wet periods a very large lake emerges. Although it has not done so for more than a millennium, it can spill over into the Sheyenne River, a tributary of the Red. Actually, except during the very wettest epochs, there are really two lakes, the larger Devils Lake and the smaller, southerly Stump Lake. When the two merge and continue to rise, spillover to the Red can occur through the west end of Stump Lake into a depression known as Tolna Coulee, and hence into the Sheyenne. This overflow will occur when the lake reaches an elevation of 1,459 feet above sea level (FSL). The lake, at the end of a periodic dry cycle, reached a low point in 1940 of just over 1,400 FSL and then over the next half-century rose some 20 feet. Then, in a mere seventeen years, from 1993 to 2010, the lake rose another 29 feet![14] Most of the agricultural development in the basin—this is a very productive region of alluvial soils—took place in the first forty years of the twentieth century, when lake levels were dropping. When wet conditions returned there was extensive drainage of more than 100,000 acres of wetlands in the 1950s.[15] On the relatively flat terrain of the basin, with no outflow, in 2010 the lake reached a peak elevation of 1,452 FSL, submerging tens of thousands of acres of productive farmland, washing over roads, and necessitating extensive diking to protect the city of Devils Lake and the Spirit Lake First Nation. The remedy for this catastrophe, if there was one, was to construct an outlet to this closed basin into the Red River basin via the Sheyenne River.

Aside from the Missouri River reservoirs in southern North Dakota, the state has few lakes of any size. Although the bane of farmers, an expanding Devils Lake has been a boon to the recreation industry. A thriving walleye fishery based on hatchery-raised fingerlings and other water-based activities have attracted large numbers of tourists, injecting about $20 million a year into the local economy. Nonetheless, the concept of an outlet had widespread support in North Dakota and in the late 1990s the North Dakota State Water Commission (NDSWC) began to promote the idea. The reaction of the Manitoba government, although certainly not unsympathetic to the impact rising lake levels were having in North Dakota, was to alert the Government of Canada that any outlet project would have the potential to negatively affect waters flowing into Canada and therefore was subject to the BWT. Specifically, the concerns centred on water quality and invasive species. Devils Lake water has sulfates, salts, and dissolved solids at levels far in excess of Manitoba water quality objectives. The Devils Lake basin has been isolated from the Red River basin for more than a millennium, and it had been artificially stocked with several fish species raised outside the Red River basin, posing the risk of transfer of non-native organisms into the Red River and Hudson Bay drainages. When Canada raised these concerns with the US State Department in 2002, even though no specific project had been proposed, Canada was presented with a proposal for a joint reference to the IJC to review the "project" and provide advice to the two governments. Canada, properly but in retrospect unwisely, responded that a reference, although ultimately desirable, was premature as there was no actual project proposal beyond the concept stage to review.[16]

When in 2003 the NDSWC rapidly advanced beyond the concept stage and into detailed design—in fact, actually initiating construction—the Government of Canada reiterated its concerns and its opinion that it was now timely, with an actual project to review, for a joint Canada-US reference to the IJC. The State Department's response was that an offer for such a reference had already been made and refused and that it considered that refusal to be final.[17] Such are the intricacies of diplomacy. Nonetheless, Canada continued to insist that the project did fall under the terms of the BWT and therefore unilateral action by a state government in those circumstances was unacceptable.

There ensued several months of negotiations involving North Dakota, Manitoba, and the two national governments aimed at satisfying the principles of the treaty without actually invoking the treaty. North Dakota, no doubt recalling the results of the Garrison reference, was adamant that there be no formal involvement of the IJC, and an intense lobbying effort was mounted by the state to convince federal officials that a reference was unnecessary and impractical. The misinformation that an "average" reference to the IJC took eight years to complete, and that without action natural overflow was "likely" and would result in a catastrophic "wall of water" roaring down the Sheyenne River, seemed persuasive. North Dakota's not unreasonable position was that this was an emergency that could only be responded to by diverting water from Devils Lake into the Red River basin. Manitoba's not unreasonable position was that a Devils Lake diversion had potential to harm Canadian waters in several ways, and should not proceed until reviewed by a neutral third party—in this case the IJC—who could determine what was required to safeguard those waters.

The result of these negotiations to develop a process was that the president's Council on Environmental Quality (CEQ), an organization established under the US National Environmental Policy Act and appointed by the president, would oversee negotiations aimed at resolving the divergent positions of Manitoba and North Dakota. As much as possible these negotiations would be led by the sub-national governments, although both Canada and the United States would play strong supporting roles. The role of the IJC was to manage a program to determine whether or not specific organisms could be identified in Devils Lake that were not present in the Red River or Lake Winnipeg, and the implications, if any, for Manitoba waters if such organisms were found. Since it was made clear at the outset that an outlet project would proceed regardless of the outcome of the CEQ-led process, negotiations focused on mitigation. On 5 August 2005, a joint Canada-US news release announced the following results:

- North Dakota will install before diversion startup a rock and gravel filter and Canada and the United States will co-operate in the design and construction of a more advanced filtration or disinfection system;
- The IJC's Red River Board will develop a shared risk-management strategy for the Red River basin for water quality and invasive species (given that this matter was being considered outside of the BWT the involvement of the IJC was unusual);
- North Dakota agrees that "it does not have such a current intention" to construct diversion of Missouri River water into Devils Lake to stabilize levels if they should drop dramatically in the future;
- And rapid bio-assessment testing will be conducted to confirm that invasive species foreign to the Red River basin are not present in Devils Lake.[18]

The news release characterized these results as "a triumph for diplomacy."[19] The project being constructed, and the subject of the negotiations, was an outlet from the west side of Devils Lake with a capacity of 100 cubic feet per second (cfs). Several months later North Dakota, without any further consultation or negotiation, increased the capacity to 250 cfs.[20] At the same time the state set in motion plans to construct a second outlet (350 cfs) from an eastern portion of the lake, more than doubling again the inflow to the Sheyenne River.[21] Even before completion of the west outlet residents along the Sheyenne opposed to the outlet ("Save the Sheyenne") initiated legal action against the project on the basis that sulfate levels in Devils Lake water exceeded the state's own limits and would therefore pollute the Sheyenne. Manitoba joined in this action. The North Dakota Department of Health then raised those limits. When the new limits proved inadequate for the increased capacity of the two outlets the state again set new numbers, more than doubling the sulfate limit over the original standard.[22] The first spring operation of the rock and gravel "temporary" filter on the west outlet resulted in the release of several small fish from Devils Lake into the Sheyenne River;[23] no action was ever taken to replace it with more advanced filtration. Again unilaterally, local authorities excavated the upper end of the Tolna Coulee so that "natural" overflow into the Sheyenne would occur at a lower level. When Manitoba raised concerns that this was neither in the spirit or the letter of the agreement reached in August 2005, a State Department representative replied that there was no "agreement," only a news release.[24] In a measure of how seriously the Government of Canada took this issue, samples from the invasive species survey languished in a federal laboratory for two years before adverse publicity forced action. Yet even today this process is portrayed in many quarters as a success, a model to be followed in the future.

There were many flaws in the Devils Lake negotiating process. First the CEQ is a political body and hardly a disinterested one. The founding principle of the BWT, and a factor in its success for both Canada and the United States, is that the two countries come to the table as equals and the IJC can provide objective advice, so valuable when seemingly irreconcilable local interests collide. Second, the process was without discipline, the result being a mere news release not apparently binding on the participants. Third, the very nature of any negotiating process usually involves inequality—inequality of resources, or information, or leverage. In this case it was the inequality of geography. Because water flows downhill the upstream jurisdiction, in the absence of restraint, could do as it pleased while the downstream jurisdiction could do nothing in response.

The tragedy here was not that there were negotiations rather than formal recourse to the BWT. It is inevitable that negotiation will take the place of dispute resolution under the treaty, and that has in fact been the case for some time. Nor was it the fact that North Dakota acted unilaterally to construct, expand, and operate projects with potential transboundary impacts. It was inevitable given the desperate situation, the animosity created by the Garrison Diversion reference, and the lack of discipline in the negotiating process. Something had to be done. But had there been more clarity, North Dakota's intentions could have been discussed in the negotiations and when the state proceeded—and that was inevitable—it might have been with a more co-operative and less embittered Manitoba. Nonetheless, what many consider a deeply flawed process has attracted partisans. The US State Department, perhaps because a negotiating process potentially offers more leverage than the dispute-resolution mechanism under the BWT, has offered this as a model for resolving future issues. Officials of the state of North Dakota have certainly been satisfied with the results.

This is as clear an example as one could find of irreconcilable interests. Whether or not any outlet or combination of outlets could "solve" Devils Lake flooding (and the Government of Manitoba contended that it could not) was irrelevant. In a situation where a significant number of citizens (there are 22,000 in the Devils Lake basin) are suffering harm, it is not an option for a democratically elected government to say, "We can't do anything." Action is required. No one argued that there was no potential for harm to Manitoba waters but, as the North Dakota government argued, the probability of harm was vanishingly small while the necessity to act was overwhelming; and the Manitoba government countered that the risk was finite and if it occurred the harm could be catastrophic. North Dakota was getting the benefits, while Manitoba was assuming the risk, however large or small. Neither position is unreasonable.

Could a more formal process under the BWT have produced a different result? It is inconceivable, given the distrust of such a process in North Dakota and given the very strong influence of both the state government and the North Dakota Congressional delegation in Washington, that agreement could have been reached on an IJC reference once the project had momentum since the political climate that favoured it in 2002 had passed. And what would a better result have looked like? An outlet to attempt to relieve the Devils Lake flooding was going to be built and Manitoba and Canada should have realized it at a much earlier stage. Had they done so some form of IJC involvement might have been possible (evidenced by the State Department's 2002 offer), thus preserving the integrity of the treaty. It may have resulted in a more systematic approach that incorporated at least some measures to reduce the risk to Canadian waters. Even more importantly it might have diffused some of the tension surrounding water issues that has plagued relations between North Dakota and Manitoba for several decades. Ironically, after the passage of more than a decade, neither jurisdiction's hopes and fears have been realized, at least not yet. As of this writing (2019) the lake level stood at just under 1,450 FSL, much as it was in 2010.[25] The outlets have managed to marginally reduce the level of the lake but have suffered operational constraints because of channel capacity and water quality concerns in the Sheyenne River. And the potential downstream disaster feared by Manitoba (the IJC technical study was able to demonstrate that parasites and pathogens harmful to Manitoba waters were not detectable in Devils Lake) has failed to materialize. But the enmity remains.

Northwest Area Water Supply Project

A number of small communities in the northwest quadrant of North Dakota draw their water supplies from groundwater. The quality of this water has never been particularly good, and although not a health concern, some parameters regularly exceed US Environmental Protection Agency drinking water standards. The Garrison Diversion vision of the mid-1970s included a project to divert Missouri River water to Minot, from where it would be distributed to these rural North Dakota communities. The project was included in both the 1986 Garrison Diversion Unit Reformulation Act and the 2000 Dakota Water Resources Act (DWRA) under the name of the Northwest Area Water Supply Project (NAWS). The Joint Technical Committee (JTC) established by the US-Canada Consultative Group (CG) following up the IJC Garrison report, had for several years been examining issues related to inter-basin water transfers, including the NAWS project, and unfortunately by 1999 the two countries had come to an impasse regarding what constituted adequate filtration and treatment of water prior to its transfer from the Missouri to the Hudson Bay basin. In 2001 as authorized under the DWRA, the US Bureau of Reclamation finalized plans for the NAWS project that did not include the water treatment recommended by the Canadian Section of the JTC (or in fact any water treatment) and subsequently obtained a declaration from the US secretary of state—without consultation with the Government of Canada—that the project as presented complied with the BWT. The bureau then released a final Environmental Impact Statement (EIS) as required under the US National Environmental Policy Act (NEPA), followed by a Finding of No Significant Impact that was appealed by both Canada and Manitoba as permitted under the bureau's NEPA process.[26] The appeals were rejected and construction of the first phase of the project, working back from Minot, was completed in 2002.

At this point it appeared that a situation had arisen not envisaged in the BWT. One government had declared that a project complied with the treaty while the other claimed it did not—and the former was unwilling to discuss the matter. The Government of Manitoba decided that if the treaty was not the vehicle for serious consideration of its concerns then perhaps NEPA was, and subsequently filed a legal challenge to the project in US District Court in Washington, DC, in October 2002.[27] Subsequently the Government of Canada, the US National Wildlife Federation, the Minnesota Center for Environmental Advocacy, the Missouri Coalition for the Environment, the Minnesota Conservation Foundation, and the South Dakota Wildlife Federation all filed memoranda as *Amici Curiae* in support of Manitoba's position.

The essence of the challenge was that the project clearly fell under the terms of the BWT (admitted in the declaration of the US secretary of state that the project complied with the BWT), thus the bureau was obligated to include possible effects in Canada as part of the project EIS. Moreover, legal precedent established that an EIS under NEPA must include consideration of alternatives to the preferred project, and that the bureau's EIS was deficient in these regards. Therefore an injunction halting further construction was sought until these deficiencies have been remedied.

In 2005 District Court Judge Collyer ruled that the bureau's EIS was indeed deficient in those respects raised by Manitoba and issued an injunction against any further construction on any portion of the NAWS project associated with diverting Missouri River water across the basin divide.[28] After further legal process the bureau filed an amended EIS that Manitoba again asserted did not address the specifics of potential harm to Canadian waters in any substantial way, nor did it present a credible analysis of alternatives. In 2010 Judge Collyer again ruled against the bureau.[29]

This unprecedented intervention by Manitoba in a US domestic legal process was never intended to permanently stop the project. Rather it was to gain legal recognition of the point that if a project in the US portion of one of the boundary waters basins has potential for impacting Canadian waters then an assessment of that potential is required and that assessment needs to be science based and not simply a pro forma and unilateral declaration, as was the case with NAWS. It was also the hope that such an assessment would point to the need for the degree of water treatment that the Canadian Section of the JTC had put forward as satisfying the second recommendation of the IJC Garrison report of 1977. NEPA does not provide the authority to either approve or reject projects. Once the procedural requirements of the act are met then the federal agency responsible for the project makes the final decision on whether or not to proceed. It is clear that at some point the Bureau of Reclamation will meet the NEPA requirements and that it most certainly will then complete the project. In fact, although the legal process is not yet complete, a 2017 decision by the US District Court does give that clearance pending appeals. (Subsequently the Bureau of Reclamation and the Province of Manitoba signed a memorandum of understanding. The province will not pursue further legal action; the project will proceed with water treatment at source and at Minot; the bureau will include Manitoba as an advisory participant in project operation.)

At the end of all of this, at least fifteen years will have passed since the first phase of the project was constructed. It remains to be seen whether or not the installed treatment will meet the standards endorsed by Canada, although it is clear that there will be significantly more attention paid to reducing risks to Canadian waters than was the case for the original NAWS design. And the US Federal Court has laid down a significant precedent respecting the need to perform a legitimate assessment of project impacts in Canada in transboundary basins. In the meantime, the drinking water quality of several North Dakota communities continues to be sub-standard. Legal fees and increasing project costs due to the construction delay probably exceed the cost of even the most expensive water treatment. Had the IJC been called upon by the national governments to provide advice on this matter at the outset, there is little doubt that these communities would have been enjoying NAWS water for a decade or more. The question of whether or not the commission would have recommended the degree of treatment desired by Canada is moot, but in any event its recommendations would have been compelling and, given past experience, likely accepted by the governments. Court is the last resort and the last place you want to resolve water disputes.

Conclusion

These four cases—the use of article ix of the BWT to resolve a dispute; the use of the IJC's highly credible investigative and advisory role to help sustain government action to respond to a disaster; and two cases in which the IJC might have played a prominent role but instead were dealt with by other means with results that seem to have deepened the discord between Manitoba and North Dakota—can present a rather negative picture of cross-border water relations. One might infer that the BWT and the role of the IJC under the treaty is in decline in this region. That would be misleading. Minnesota, North Dakota, and Manitoba continue to work co-operatively on the International Red River Board, one of the more successful IJC watershed boards. Water quality objectives are in place and monitored at the border; an early warning system for notifying all parties of any potential water quality impacts has functioned successfully for many years; the three jurisdictions have agreed on a nutrient reduction target; and the jurisdictions work closely with stakeholders in the province and both states. In short, the working relationship between operational personnel is excellent. On the Souris River that flows into the Red through the Assiniboine, a 1948 IJC reference resulted in a departure from the normal "50/50" formula for sharing water. The commission recommended that North Dakota be required to pass at least 20 cfs flow to Manitoba in open water season except during periods of "drought" when the state is not required to pass any flow. This "interim" measure has been operative since 1952. Although this seemed to favour North Dakota it really reflected the erratic flow regime of the Souris. In spite of the wide degree of discretion in determining drought conditions the province and the state have been able to co-operate in managing the Souris without friction. In the late 1980s North Dakota cost-shared (with the US Army Corps of Engineers and the Province of Saskatchewan) water storage on the Souris in Saskatchewan to reduce flood risk to the downstream city of Minot. Since this impacted the river in both countries an international agreement was required, and Manitoba and North Dakota participated in negotiations led by the US Army Corps of Engineers that resulted in an agreement satisfactory to all parties. Ongoing co-operative management of the Souris continues through the IJC's International Souris River Board.

These workaday operations under the BWT are sometimes overshadowed by the more newsworthy "conflicts" that arise from time to time, but they should not be forgotten. The conflicts are dictated by geography—Manitoba literally, and uniquely, downstream from everyone; North Dakota with abundant water on its southern border that is isolated by the Missouri-Red drainage divide from the arid remaining two-thirds of the state; and Minnesota, whose water interests tend to focus to the northeast (Lake Superior and Rainy River–Lake of the Woods) and south (Mississippi)—and that won't change. What remains to be seen is whether the BWT and the IJC will in the future be confined to a more restrictive operational niche or whether they can also play a meaningful role in the evolving process of transboundary water negotiations.

Notes

1. Gary L. Pearson, "History of Missouri River Diversion in North Dakota" (unpublished manuscript, no date).
2. Ibid.
3. The International Joint Commission, "Transboundary Implications of the Garrison Diversion Unit" (Ottawa: IJC, 1977).
4. Ibid.
5. Robert V. Oleson, Manitoba Boundary Waters Office, personal communication, April 2018.
6. Pearson, "History of Missouri River Diversion"; Garrison Diversion Conservancy District, "History and Federal Legislation," available at http://garrisondiv.org/about/HistoryFederalLegislation/.
7. Ibid.
8. Garrison Diversion Conservancy District, "Red River Valley Water Supply Project," available at http://garrisondiv.org/programs/rrv_water_supply_project/.

9   Robert W. Passfield, "Duff's Ditch: The origins, Construction and Impact of the Red River Floodway," *Manitoba Historical Society* (2001–2), http://www.mhs.mb.ca/docs/mb_history/42/duffsditch.shtml.

10   *Red Sea Rising—the Flood of the Century* (Winnipeg: Winnipeg Free Press, 1997).

11   The International Joint Commission, Red River Basin Task Force, "Red River Flooding: Short-term Measures" (Ottawa: IJC, Dec. 1997).

12   The International Joint Commission, "Living With The Red: A Report to the Governments of Canada and the US on Reducing Flood Impacts in the Red River Basin" (Ottawa: IJC, Nov. 2001).

13   The International Joint Commission International Red River Board, "Flood Preparedness and Mitigation in the Red River Basin" (Ottawa: IJC, 2003).

14   North Dakota State Water Commission, "Devils Lake Flood Facts" (Bismark: NDSWC, April 2010).

15   US Fish and Wildlife Service—DL Wetland Management District, "Flooding in the Devils Lake and Red River Valley Watersheds: A Complex Situation—A Comprehensive Solution" (USF&WS issue paper, 2011).

16   Norman Brandson and Robert R. Hearn, "Devils Lake & Red River Basin," in *Water Without Borders? Canada, the United States, and Shared Waters*, ed. Norman, Cohen, and Bakker (Toronto: University of Toronto Press, 2013); Roland Paris, "The Devils Lake Dispute between Canada and the United States: Lessons For Canadian Government Officials" (Ottawa: Centre for International Policy Studies, University of Ottawa, Feb. 2008).

17   Paris, "The Devils Lake Dispute."

18   Government of Canada, "Joint Canada-US Declaration on the Devils Lake Diversion Project" (Government of Canada news release, 5 August 2005).

19   Ibid.

20   North Dakota Office of the State Engineer—Water Development Division, "Application to Drain No. 3457I" (Approved 26 October 2009).

21   ND State Water Commission, "Project Development—DL Flood Mitigation," SWC.nd.gov.us/projectdevelopment.

22   North Dakota Department of Health, "Notice of Intent to Adopt Administrative Rule, July 15, 2009"; ND Administrative Code, Chapter 33-16-02.1.

23   David L. Glatt, Chief Environmental Health Section, North Dakota Department of Health, personal communication, August 2006.

24   Robert V. Oleson, MB Boundary Waters Office, personal communication, April 2018.

25   US Geological Survey, "Devils Lake Gauge 05056500, Water Year Summary" https://waterdata.usgs.gov/nd/nwis/uv?site_no=05056500.

26 Government of Manitoba, "Comments on the draft Supplemental Environmental Impact Statement for the Northwest Area Water Supply—History of Manitoba's Involvement in the Project," (Winnipeg: 10 September 2014).

27 *Government of the Province of Manitoba v. Norton*, 398 F. Supp. 2d 41 (DDC 2005).

28 Ibid.

29 *Government of the Province of Manitoba v. Norton*, 691 F. Supp. 2d (DDC 2018).

8

The International Joint Commission's Unique and Colourful Role in Three Projects in the Pacific Northwest

Richard Moy and Jonathan O'Riordan

The International Joint Commission (IJC) has a long and colourful history in the Pacific Northwest. There are always questions by the US and Canadian governments regarding the appropriate role the IJC should play in resolving issues in international river basins between the two countries. The following three, very different cases illustrate that the IJC can be very creative in defining innovative approaches for assisting governments. The strength of the IJC is that it brings together the best minds from governments, academia, and the private sector on both sides of the border to build a sturdier bridge to enhance the flow of science and objective data analysis across it. This process allows the IJC to be very successful in achieving consensus.

The role of the IJC in each of these cases is quite different. First, in the Ross Dam controversy, the IJC facilitated the resolution of a very contentious issue that had been festering for over forty years on the Skagit River. Second, the IJC developed the technical and policy foundation for the 1961 Columbia River Treaty (CRT). Lastly, in the Sage Creek Coal Reference, the IJC conducted an environmental assessment and defined the impacts of a proposed coal mine in Canada on the Flathead River, near the international border, and made creative recommendations to governments.

In the Skagit decision, the City of Seattle developed a long-term plan for raising Ross Dam in stages on the Skagit River to produce additional hydroelectricity to meet Seattle's future electrical needs. British Columbia did not want the dam raised, as it would back up water into the province. The IJC facilitated the resolution of this difficult dispute and arrived at a very creative "win-win" solution that benefited both Seattle and British Columbia without raising the dam. The decision has been called "the paper dam" solution.[1] The controversy was so intense that it contributed to a change of government in British Columbia and nearly reached the United States Supreme Court.[2]

Between 1944 and 1960, the governments sought the IJC's expertise and objectivity to develop the technical and policy foundation for providing flood control and enhancing hydro-power production on the Columbia River. The primary goals of the CRT were met: the construction of the three dams in British Columbia and Libby Dam in the United States with the United States paying most of the costs of construction. As the CRT can now be terminated by either party after 2024 with ten years notice, there are ongoing discussions on what a future or revised treaty should look like. The issues and concerns of today are different than those defined in the original treaty over sixty years ago. A new vision, direction, and principles of operations are needed for the Columbia River system. Both parties to the treaty have signaled that restoring ecosystem values throughout the Columbia Basin should be included in the negotiations.

The IJC process and outcomes of the Sage Creek Coal Reference in the Flathead River drainage of British Columbia in the mid-1980s set a precedent for addressing water quality and other environmental impacts based on the interpretation of article iv of the Boundary Waters Treaty (BWT). Article iv includes the following sentence: "Boundary waters and waters flowing across the boundary shall not be polluted on either side to the injury of health or property on the other." The binational technical process used by the IJC shows its strength and value in providing science-based recommendations to governments. More importantly, the IJC's 1988 recommendations became the guiding light for a number of initiatives undertaken by both Canadian and US citizen groups and their governments to protect the ecological integrity of the entire Flathead River Basin.

A common theme binds two of these three cases—that of building resilience in international watersheds through supporting and restoring healthy ecosystems. In both the Flathead and Skagit there was a strong desire to preserve the ecological integrity of the watershed. Although the CRT was completed in 1961, before scientists truly understood the value of protecting the ecological health of the basin, the renegotiated treaty will need to balance the needs of the environment against the other requirements and uses.

The Skagit River and the High Ross Dam Controversy

Basin Description

The Skagit Valley is a very special place because of its unique location and natural amenities. It is a three-hour drive from both Vancouver, British Columbia, and Seattle, Washington. The rather pristine valley stretches across the international border and is a favourite region for fishing, camping, hiking, and canoeing. The powerful Skagit River rises in British Columbia, west of the Cascade Mountains, and after flowing about 28 miles crosses the international border into the state of Washington. The river continues for another 135 miles in Washington before discharging into the Pacific Ocean through the Strait of Juan de Fuca.

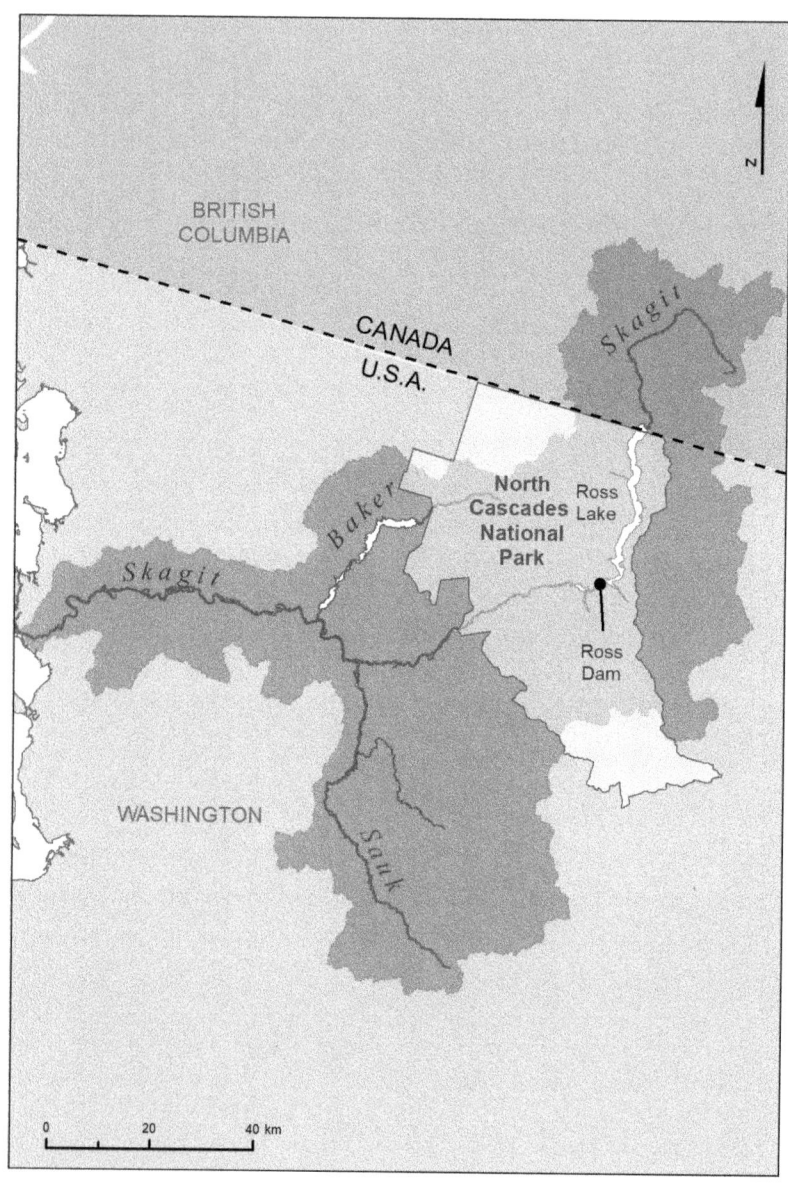

FIGURE 8.1. Skagit River Basin and Ross Lake.[3] J. Glatz, Western Michigan University Libraries.

The IJC's History

The IJC had a long and contentious history of raising Ross Dam on the Skagit River in the state of Washington. The history dates back to 1906, when Seattle City Light (Seattle Light) became interested in developing the Skagit River's hydro-power potential to provide electricity to meet the growing demands of Seattle. Starting with the Gorge and Diablo Dams, Ross Dam was to follow in a series of staged developments. To begin the process, the City of Seattle applied to the US Federal Power Commission (now re-named the Federal Energy Regulation Commission, or FERC) for initial authorization to construct Ross Dam in 1926. Knowing land in the Skagit Valley of British Columbia would be inundated within the enlarged reservoir, Seattle Light acquired the former Whitworth Ranch, the only privately owned land in the Skagit Valley of British Columbia in 1929. British Columbia placed a Crown Reserve on all remaining lands within the BC portion of the basin in 1930. Informal negotiations began between Seattle and British Columbia on the purchase of the Crown lands. After a number of years of discussions without success, the negotiations were finally suspended in 1939.

Seattle began the construction of Ross Dam in 1937, reaching a height of 475 feet (145 metres). Then, in 1941, pursuant to article iii of the BWT, Seattle submitted an application to the IJC to obtain the authority to raise Ross Dam to its full designed height in stages for the generation of additional electrical power. Seattle needed permission from the IJC as the enlarged dam's reservoir footprint would extend into British Columbia. The final dam height would increase the reservoir area in British Columbia nearly ten-fold.[4] Before issuing the order the IJC held a two-hour hearing on the project in Seattle on 12 September 1941. At that time, the Canadian Skagit was little known and very inaccessible, as the Silver-Skagit road had not yet been built. Seattle Light described the project and informed the IJC that it was urgently needed to meet the power demands for producing armaments for the Second World War. Since the dam was in Washington, far more American government agencies (43) were notified of the hearing, as compared to those from Canada (12).[5]

The few Canadian officials that attended the hearing had not heard details of the proposal. There was substantial confusion as to whether the land to be flooded was owned by the Crown or privately owned in British Columbia. Victor Meek, controller of the Dominion Water and Power Bureau, provided Canada's only official comment. He indicated that he was representing the Canadian government's Department of External Affairs and had no statement to make at this time, but indicated that the government would provide comments later, after he and others had had a chance to study the details of the project. External Affairs, however, never provided comments.[6]

On 27 January 1942, the IJC issued its Order of Approval that granted the City of Seattle the authority to raise Ross Dam to its full height of approximately 130 feet (39.6 metres) (called the High Ross Dam).[7] The enlargement would substantially increase Seattle's ability to produce peaking power and would reduce the city's dependence on the more expensive peaking power from the Bonneville Power Administration.[8]

The raised dam could flood an additional 4,475 acres (2,217 hectares) in British Columbia. The issue of compensating the province for the flooded acres was not resolved in the IJC's Order of Approval, but was a condition of the order. Figure 8.2 below illustrates the difference between the proposed High Ross Dam and the lower dam height.

In 1947, the BC Legislature passed the Skagit Valley Lands Act, which authorized the provincial cabinet to negotiate an agreement with the City of Seattle that would allow the upper BC portion of the Skagit Valley to be flooded by Seattle Light for its exclusive use. By 1952, a tentative agreement was reached. It allowed Seattle to flood the Skagit Valley for ninety-nine years in exchange for a single cash payment of $255,508 and the clearing of the reservoir basin of trees.[10]

In 1953, the provincial government was toppled and the new premier, W. A. C. Bennett began his twenty-year reign. He decided to delay the signing of the agreement. The Seattle City Council, however, went ahead and ratified the $255,508 agreement in May 1953 and proceeded to raise the dam 65 feet (19.81 metres) to a height of about 540 feet (160 metres), which in turn would flood about 494 acres (200 hectares) within British Columbia. This phase of construction would allow the dam to be easily raised to its final designed height. The province said nothing. However, in 1953 the Social Credit Party obtained a majority in the BC Parliament and suddenly informed Seattle that the proposed compensation agreement

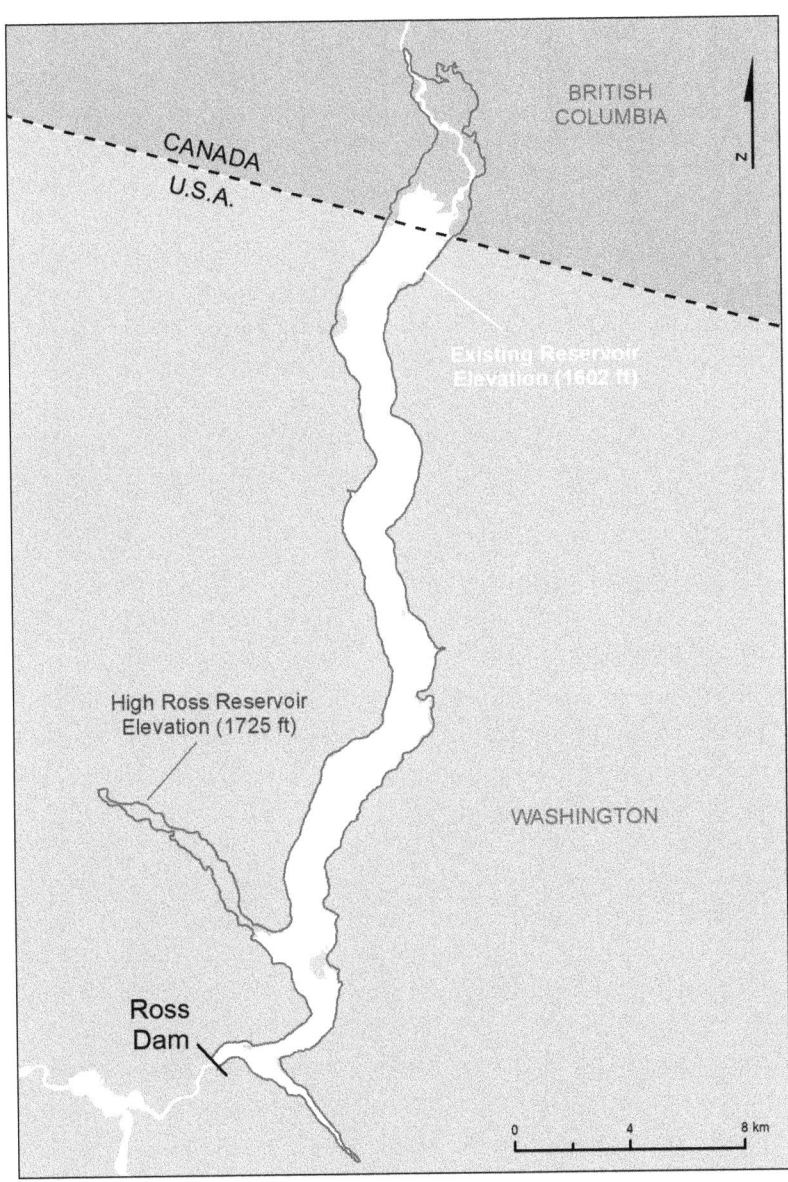

FIGURE 8.2. High Ross Dam Reservoir compared to the existing Ross Dam Reservoir.[9] J. Glatz, Western Michigan University Libraries.

was no longer acceptable. This was due in part to the influence of General A. G. L. McNaughton, the Canadian co-chair of the IJC. He realized that the value of the stored water behind Ross Dam was considerably more than that offered by the City of Seattle.[11] His assessment was based, in part, on his involvement with the IJC's technical storage studies that were being undertaken for the CRT.

The compensation controversy reached a peak in April 1954, when Seattle and the US Section of the IJC proposed that British Columbia be compelled to accept the $255,508 offer as full and complete compensation for the flooding of its lands. The province countered that no agreement had been signed.[12] General McNaughton even went as far as stating that Seattle Light's flooding of BC lands violated Canadian sovereignty and the IJC's own 1942 Order of Approval. It is understandable that the US and Canadian commissioners could not reach a majority to enforce the compensation agreement. British Columbia, however, did agree to accept $5,000 per annum as an interim settlement for the flooding of the 494 acres.

In 1958, Seattle Light made its final attempt to have the IJC impose a settlement on British Columbia, but was again rebuffed. The province decided to postpone further negotiations with Seattle Light until after the CRT was finalized, as it wanted to assure itself a fair share of the downstream benefits for compensation of lands that would be flooded in the province under a new treaty.

In 1967, British Columbia finally agreed to an annual rental fee of $34,566.21 (or its equivalent in power at a price of 3.75mill/kwh) and taxes of about $10,000 per year. And in return, Seattle Light gained the right to build Ross Dam to its full designed height and to flood a total of 5,189 acres (2,101 hectares) of land in British Columbia.[13] Seattle Light would also be required to clear the reservoir basin before flooding, replace any inundated segments of the existing road, and pay stumpage and royalties for timber removed during the clearing. All work had to be done by provincial residents. Seattle began to pay the annual rental fee and taxes until Bennett's Social Credit government was replaced in 1972, and British Columbia decided to reject the agreement and cease accepting Seattle's payments. Many in the province and the Canadian Section of the IJC felt that Seattle Light received too good of a deal.

With the annual rental agreement in hand, Seattle Light formally applied to the US Federal Power Commission (FPC) in 1970 for the final authorization required to raise Ross Dam to its full and final elevation. The hearings were held in 1974 by the FPC and they were contentious, with strong Canadian opposition. Both Canada and British Columbia argued against any additional flooding into the province. Based on the evidence provided, the FPC ruled in favour of Seattle Light's application to raise the dam to its full height in July 1977. It is interesting to note that in the United States, the issue of the High Ross Dam was a localized issue, but in Canada, it became both a provincial and national issue.[14]

Prior to the late 1960s, there was little opposition to the dam in both the United States and Canada. But because of increased environmental sensitivity in British Columbia and the state of Washington, opposition became more prevalent. The environmental movement gained strength and opposition to the High Ross Dam began to crystalize on both sides of the border. With strong pressure from British Columbia, Jack Davis, the Canadian minister of environment, sought and obtained an IJC reference from the two national governments asking the IJC to re-examine the case.[15] The reference requested that the IJC "investigate the environmental and ecological consequences in Canada of the raising of the Ross Lake to an elevation of 1,725 feet (525.8 meters) above mean sea levels, taking into account relevant information about environmental and ecological consequences elsewhere on the Skagit River, and measures being taken or planned to protect and enhance the environment in these areas." However, the reference stated that any recommendations made could not be "inconsistent with the commission's Order of Approval dated January 27, 1942," and the agreement reached between the City of Seattle and British Columbia on 10 January 1967. In other words, the outcome of this reference would not allow the IJC to alter its January 1942 Order of Approval giving the City of Seattle the authority to raise Ross Dam to its final height. Before beginning the environmental assessment, the IJC held three days of public hearings on the reference in Vancouver, Canada, and Bellingham, Washington.

Based on information from the hearings and its own assessment, the IJC submitted its environmental assessment report to the governments on 17 December 1971.[16] In preparing the assessment, the IJC compared the base case with no enlarged Ross Dam against changes that would occur if the dam was raised to its final height. The IJC began to believe that raising Ross Reservoir to its full elevation could impact the valley floor and its riparian environment. Based on the environmental assessment, and the public comments received, the commission began to question its original position over raising Ross Dam to its full designed height, but it could not change its decision without violating the terms of its original 1942 Order of Approval, as noted in the 7 April 1971 reference letter to the IJC from the national governments.

In the early 1970s, the volatility of the issue increased in Canada. On 2 November 1973, the House of Commons passed a unanimous resolution stating its "unalterable and unanimous opposition to the flooding of the Canadian Skagit Valley." This was relayed to the US government by the Canadian secretary of state for external affairs. Prime Minister Pierre Trudeau even raised the issue with President Gerald Ford in 1974, and the House of Commons reaffirmed unanimously its earlier resolution in 1977.[17]

The stage was set for the final negotiations. Seattle had followed all the appropriate procedural requirements in developing its long-term plans for additional power-generation capacity on the Skagit River, and it was in a very strong position for a number of reasons. First, it had the 1942 IJC Order of Approval that gave it the authority to raise the dam to its full height. Second, Seattle had the 1967 compensation agreement that was signed by British Columbia and upheld by the IJC for the lands that would be inundated by the raised dam, and which Seattle complied with for a number of years until its payments were no longer accepted by British Columbia. Third, the FPC licence gave Seattle the authority to raise the dam. And lastly, the opponents to raising the dam lost their appeal in the US courts.[18]

British Columbia felt that if Seattle proceeded with construction, it would consider it to be a "hostile" act against a friendly neighbour.[19] However, the province realized it was in a very difficult position because Seattle had all the appropriate authorizations to proceed. The province could not unilaterally repudiate the 1967 agreement that it signed without adequate restitution to Seattle.

On 14 August 1980, the BC government again asked the IJC to annul or rescind its 1942 Order of Approval for High Ross Dam.[20] In response, the IJC invited "interested persons" to respond by 17 December 1981. Seattle Light and the US State Department filed legal arguments contesting British Columbia's position, and urging the IJC to uphold its original 1942 ruling and order. The Canadian and provincial governments continued their objections to the High Ross Dam, noting the unanimous resolution by the House of Commons and the discussions between Prime Minister Trudeau and President Ford. A large percentage of the comments received by the IJC from US and Canadian citizens were now in opposition to raising Ross Dam over the impacts to the environment. As noted earlier, the real turning point on raising Ross Dam to its final height was the strong local opposition in both Washington and British Columbia over environmental concerns.

As the IJC began to consider the comments and what to do next, two of the three Canadian commissioners resigned and all President-Carter-appointed US commissioners were immediately fired by the newly-elected president, Ronald Reagan.[21]

The Final IJC Solution

The long and unsuccessful six-year period (1974–80) of bilateral negotiations had left both sides frustrated and mistrustful.[22] With the new commissioners in place, the IJC visited British Columbia in December 1981 and made it clear to the province that it should not make the mistake of simply assuming that the commission would agree with its request to stop Seattle from raising Ross Dam to its final designed height. The IJC then delivered a similar message in Seattle. The commissioners let Seattle know that even though it might have the legal authority to raise the dam, it would be difficult for the city to move forward with construction, and it would not dismiss British Columbia's request. The IJC wanted to find a solution that would be both equitable and durable for both sides.[23]

In response to the province's request, the IJC issued a rather innovative Supplemental Order on 28 April 1982.[24] In it, the IJC made it clear that British Columbia's request and arguments presented in its August 1980 filing did not constitute sufficient grounds to persuade the new commissioners to grant the relief sought by the province. Further, the order stated that the Skagit Valley in British Columbia should not be flooded beyond its current level, provided that appropriate compensation should be provided to the City of Seattle for the loss of the valuable and reliable source of electric power that would have resulted from raising the dam to its full designed height. In the order, the IJC took "an extra ordinary action" by ordering Seattle to maintain the low level of the Skagit River at the international border for a period of one year from the date of the 1982 Supplemental Order. Further, the order defined the membership and duties of a Special Board.[25] The composition of the board was very important. It was to be composed of two members from the commission who served as co-chairs, and two non-governmental experts. The IJC also invited representatives of the US State Department and the Canadian Department of External Affairs, the Province of British Columbia, and the City of Seattle to nominate a representative to be a member of the board. This board was required to coordinate, facilitate, and review on a continuing basis those activities directed at achieving a negotiated and acceptable agreement between the city and province and to provide status reports regarding such progress to the commission every four months.[26] Having the national representatives on the board was critically important as the final resolution of the issue would require a commitment by both federal governments to implement the final solution.[27]

When board representatives first met in Washington, DC on 10 March 1982, neither side trusted the other. Most expected another round of talks that circled the wagons around a number of intractable issues between Seattle and British Columbia over raising or not raising Ross Dam. However the new commissioners recently appointed by President Reagan had a different view on how to approach the negotiations. US commissioner Keith Bulen's opening remarks set the tone for the negotiations. He made it clear that the commission expected a different outcome. And if the negotiators could not come to an agreement, the commissioners would rule "not as Americans and Canadians" but in the best interest of both countries and no one in the room could predict the outcome. In other words, the IJC threatened to force a solution on the province and city that might not make either side happy. This strong statement forced both sides to the negotiating table. Further, it laid out a one-year timeline within which a negotiated deal had to be reached.

The year-long negotiations were tough, and they were almost terminated on several occasions. A critically important first step was the appointment of a team of special technical advisors: Douglas J. Gordon and George T. Berry. Both had impeccable credentials.[28] They were able to provide expert and impartial technical and economic advice to the IJC, and they prepared the 2 April 1982 Gordon/Berry Report for the commission. The report calculated the final construction costs and the additional electric output that would have been generated from a High Ross Dam. The report settled a number of economic and technical assumptions and conclusions that had been in dispute.[29] This data was used to inform Seattle on how much it would need to pay British Columbia (based on Seattle's costs to raise the dam to its designed height), and in return the amount of electrical power British Columbia would need to provide to Seattle if the dam was not raised. The technical information was absolutely key to the final solution. Further, the IJC had to continually push the board to complete its work, as the alternative would not be acceptable to either side.[30]

To maintain the momentum for the year-long negotiations, the IJC oversaw each round of talks.[31] In the end, the IJC functioned in exactly the way it is supposed to: it took politics, which had stalled the dam controversy for decades, out of the equation, thereby enabling a technically sound plan to be put together that was acceptable to all parties involved. The IJC played a new role as a neutral power broker that it had been unwilling to take on previously. Further, the IJC encouraged the key local BC and City of Seattle representatives to take more responsibility in finding a viable solution.

The "Paper Dam" Agreement

On 14 April 1983, BC environment minister Stephen Rogers and Seattle mayor Charles Royer announced details of a framework agreement that was reached between British Columbia and the City of Seattle for the resolution of the long-standing Skagit Valley/Ross Dam dispute.[32] The agreement met both the needs of both parties. The agreement had four key components. First, no further flooding of the Skagit Valley would be allowed, and in return British Columbia would supply Seattle with the amount of electricity that would have been generated if Ross Dam had been raised to its full height. Second, there was a clearly defined termination option. Third, a very creative Environmental Endowment Commission and funding source would be created to develop and manage the Ross Dam/Skagit Valley area for recreation and environmental conservation.[33] Lastly, a treaty would be required to bind the parties to the agreement.

Taking into account how long the issue had dragged on, the speed and manner in which the High Ross Dam controversy came to an end is remarkable. In this rare case, and as noted earlier, the IJC took politics out of the equation, which the authors feel can be one of the commission's strengths.[34] Another important reason for this success is the active involvement of local experts, who had a better understanding of the issues and the need for resolution.[35] Similar to the IJC's International Watershed Initiative program, transboundary disputes are more easily resolved when local leaders and stakeholders are involved in the decision-making process.

Leaders on both sides of the controversy thought the agreement was fair. President Ronald Reagan noted that it was "constructive and ingeniously settled."[36] Canada's minister of external affairs and the US secretary of state said it could serve as a model for resolving future transboundary disputes.

The IJC issued a Supplemental Order dated 18 January 1984 terminating its January 1942 Order of Approval that would have allowed Seattle Light to raise Ross Dam to its designed height.[37] The framework agreement became the key provisions included in the 1984 treaty. The United States and Canada entered into the treaty that ended the High Ross Dam controversy on 2 April 1984. Without the treaty, the agreement would probably have failed.[38]

Recently, the BC government approved clear-cut logging in accordance with provincial forest and range practices legislation in an unprotected mineral claim area in the upper Skagit Valley. Although there have been attempts to buy out the existing mineral claims and include them in the surrounding protected areas, none of these initiatives has been concluded. The logging approval involves 39,000 cubic metres of timber on 67 hectares of lands. The strong objections to the logging approvals by the governor of Washington, the mayor of Seattle, and many others on both sides of the border illustrates the continued interest in protecting the ecological integrity of the Skagit Valley. These are the same environmental values identified over three decades ago during the IJC intervention process.[39]

Columbia River Treaty

The Columbia River Basin

The Columbia River is the fourth largest river in North America with an average discharge of 265,000 cfs (cubic feet per second; 7,500 cubic metres per second) and annual average volume of 198 maf (million acre-feet), with its head waters originating in both the United States and Canada (see Figure 8.3 below). The total area of the basin is 260,676 square miles (668,400 square kilometres). Approximately 15 per cent of the basin is in Canada and 85 per cent is in the United States. By comparison, the volume of water produced in the Columbia is more than eight times the run-off from the Colorado. As the water flows to the Pacific, the river is second only to the Missouri-Mississippi River System in terms of annual run-off. The steep gradient and high volumes of water of the Columbia are the primary reasons why the Columbia River has the largest hydroelectric generation capacity of any river system in North America.

Historically, hydro-power has been one of the most inexpensive and most efficient sources of electricity in the region. The United States realized this in the 1930s and began constructing hydro-power dams to produce hydro-power, control floods, and to meet the other authorized purposes within its portion of the basin.[40] The chief builders of these large dam projects were the US Army Corps of Engineers and the US Bureau of Reclamation.

The primary concern with the US storage and hydro-power system in the Columbia River Basin is that the highest demand for electricity occurs in the wintertime, when river flows are generally lower. However, the higher river flows occur in the late spring and early summer, when the demand for power is the lowest. At that time, there was not enough stored water in the US portion of the Columbia River to balance river flows with electrical demands. The United States clearly recognized that some of the best storage sites were located in the Kootenai River drainage of British

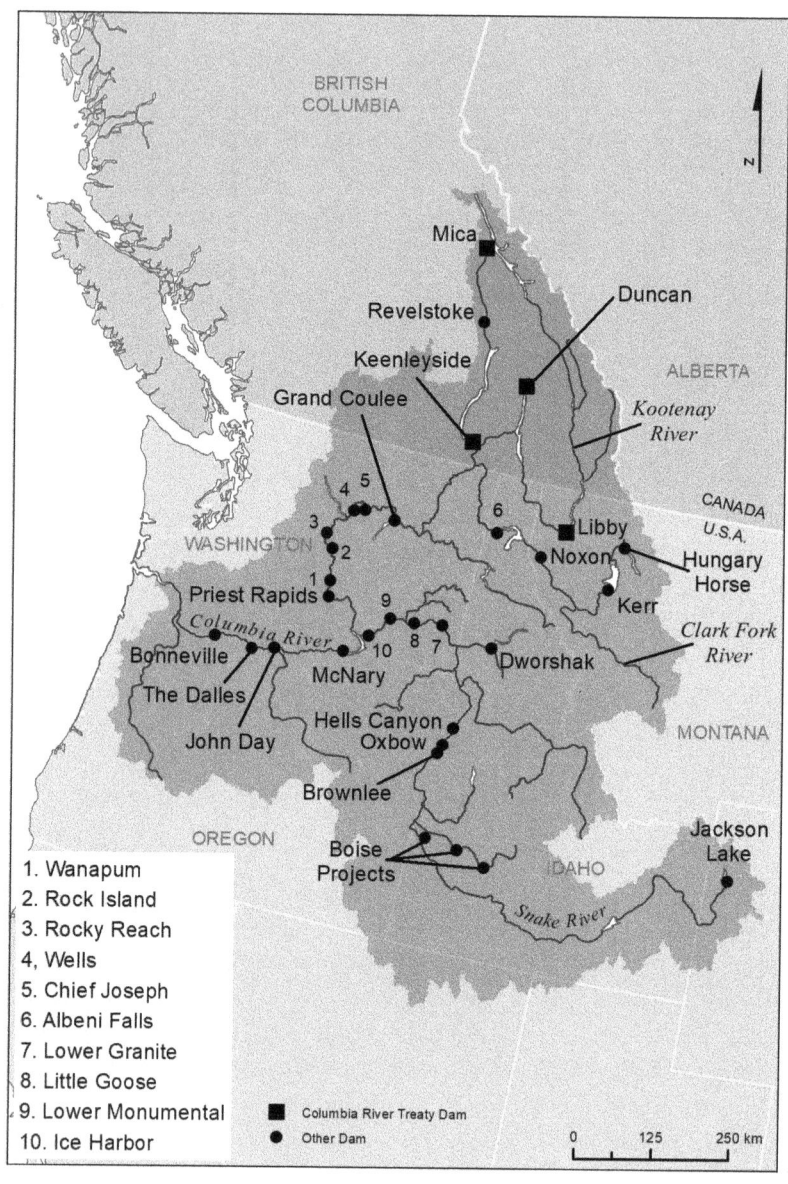

FIGURE 8.3. The Columbia River Basin.[41] J. Glatz, Western Michigan University Libraries.

Columbia. Just as important, both countries needed the additional storage to control and mitigate floods. For these reasons, the United States approached Canada to begin discussions on the potential for additional Kootenai River storage in British Columbia as a means to optimize hydro-power production and flood control. Other important uses that could benefit from additional Canadian storage include irrigation, fisheries, navigation, and recreation.

The IJC's Role in Developing the CRT

Before formal negotiations could begin, the two countries needed technical information on viable storage sites and guiding principles to support the implementation of a treaty. Accordingly, the two national governments asked the IJC to develop the technical information for a treaty in a reference letter dated 9 March 1944.[42] The reference requested that the commission:

> determine whether in its judgment further development of the water resources of the river basin would be practicable and in the public interest from the point of view of the Governments, having in mind (A) domestic water supply and sanitation, (B) navigation, (C) efficient development of water power, (D) the control of floods, (E) the needs of irrigation, (F) reclamation of wet lands, (G) conservation of fish and wildlife, and (H) other beneficial public purposes.

Even though the reference letter identified a number of beneficial uses, the primary focus was to improve hydro-power production and to control floods through co-operative development of Kootenai River infrastructure. To accomplish this, the IJC established the International Columbia River Engineering Board to review existing technical reports and to conduct required engineering and other types of investigations. To assist the IJC, Canada conducted seven engineering studies on possible dam sites in British Columbia. Based on all the technical information, the IJC reported that Canada could provide 15.5 maf of additional storage at three different BC locations: 7 maf at Mica Dam, 7.1 maf at Keenleyside, and 1.4 maf at Duncan. The IJC also considered the construction of Libby Dam in the United States. Canada had to agree to the construction of Libby, as this dam would inundate 42 miles (67.6 kilometres) into the province.[43]

The then chief of the US Army Corps of Engineers for the Columbia, General Itschner, and the Canadian IJC co-chair, General McNaughton, had differing views for the future operations of the Columbia River system and the basic principles of administrating the power arrangements.[44] The United States wished to integrate the operations of the Canadian storage and generation into the US system as an extension of the Bonneville Power Administration, and to be under its effective control. McNaughton, however, held the view that the waters in Canada belonged to Canada under the 1909 BWT and that the Canadian government would maintain independent operations of its storage, but in close co-operation with United States under guiding principles that would be defined in a treaty.

Canada also wanted to make sure that it received some form of compensation from the United States for the construction of storage sites—more than just paying for the cost of construction. General McNaughton realized that compensation for the BC land inundated by the reservoirs understated the true monetary value of the additional storage. He also felt the real value of these reservoirs in British Columbia was in the extra hydro-power that could be generated downstream in the United States, plus the reduction of flood damages.[45]

Based on the results of the technical investigations, in January 1959 the two national governments returned to the IJC and asked it to now develop the guiding principles for a treaty based on the benefits from the co-operative use of stored waters and electrical interconnection within the Columbia River system and how best to apportion the benefits for flood control and hydro-power.[46] To prepare this special report, the IJC formed a special working group to review the technical studies and to consider how the benefits from co-operative development and management of the Columbia River could be shared equitably between the two countries based on the BWT and results from the technical investigations. The principal benefits to the United States are the additional water stored in British Columbia, which would enhance hydro-power production in the United States and reduce flood damages. In return, Canada would receive financial compensation from the United States.

On 29 December 1959 the IJC proposed to the two federal governments three categories of apportionment principles: general, power, and flood control. The IJC defined three guiding principles for general operations, seven power principles, and six flood control principles.[47] All the principles were based on equitable sharing of the benefits attributable to the proposed storage reservoirs. But the details of these principles would have to be worked out as part of the actual treaty negotiations. The three general principles guided the selection of projects that would best improve the international co-operation for flood control and power enhancement in the Columbia River Basin. The seven "power principles" provided guidance for determining and sharing power benefits from the co-operative use of upstream storage that allows for changing conditions over time in power needs. The six "flood principles" defined sharing flood control benefits applicable to the Kootenai River downstream from Bonners Ferry, Idaho, and the lower main stem of the Columbia River.

Based on the IJC's technical studies and guiding principles, the two governments held nine negotiation sessions between February 1959 and January 1961. The treaty was signed by President Dwight Eisenhower and Prime Minister John Diefenbaker in January 1961. The two governments ratified and implemented the treaty in 1964, as it took British Columbia and the Canadian government another three years to agree on the appropriate administrative protocol for selling downstream power benefits to the United States and to transfer the rights, responsibilities, and implementation authority from the Canadian government to the Province.

During the negotiation sessions for the treaty, the IJC continued to provide technical and other types of advice to the governments.

Effects of Treaty Implementation

The four treaty dams provided an additional 20 maf of storage, or the equivalent of one-third of the total storage capacity of the Columbia River system. The CRT and co-operative operation of its dams improved the timing of river flows by capturing additional high spring flows and releasing the water more gradually over the summer, fall, and winter months.[48]

The four entities responsible for implementing the provisions of the treaty are BC Hydro for Canada and British Columbia, and the

Northwestern Division of the US Army Corps of Engineers and the Bonneville Power Administration for the United States. The treaty also established a Permanent Engineering Board to monitor and report on the results under the treaty and to assist in reconciling any differences concerning technical and operational matters that might arise. The Engineering Board consists of four members: two appointments by the US secretaries of the army and energy, and one each by the Province of British Columbia and the Canadian federal government.[49]

The treaty gave the United States incremental power and flood control benefits plus more water for recreation, irrigation, fishery, and other beneficial uses. However, there were adverse impacts in the United States, primarily on certain fish species,[50] and loss of small portions of land upstream of Libby Dam in the United States. It is important to note that the Grand Coulee Dam was constructed prior to the treaty and it effectively blocked passage of Columbia River salmon upstream of the dam. Overall, the coordinated storage and regulation of flows between the United States and Canada improved US hydro-power production by about 10 per cent. Besides power benefits, the United States has received significant flood control benefits as it has not suffered a serious overbank flood flow since the construction of the storage projects. This translates to billions of dollars' worth of protection of municipal, industrial, and agricultural lands—even though the protection is only partial. In the event of a huge flood, the United States could still see significant flood damage, as has been experienced in other regions of North America.

Under the CRT, British Columbia received half of the incremental downstream power benefits, but sold them off for the first thirty years—which turned out to be of less value than what the power benefits should have been. The biggest hydro-power benefit to British Columbia is not even considered in the treaty: generation at Mica and Revelstoke Dams.[51] However, there were significant economic, environmental, and social impacts as entire communities and many farms were dislocated when the Canadian dams were built, resident sport fisheries were reduced, and there was a loss of riparian and wildlife habitats and forests.[52] Some 231 square miles of valley bottom land was flooded. All these impacts were experienced without the benefit of environmental assessments and consultations with Indigenous Peoples.

The treaty negotiators agreed that the United States and Canada would share these power benefits equally. Canada's portion of downstream power benefits is called the Canadian Entitlement. These benefits are calculated annually according to a complex method negotiated by the treaty's authors, but which is generally recognized as now being out of date under current power supply conditions. The Canadian Entitlement is not solely a US federal responsibility, but it also includes the additional US power that is generated from five non-federal hydro-power dams on the Columbia River, which accounts for 27 per cent of the Canadian Entitlement. The Canadian Entitlement does not also include the effects of Libby Dam operations, which provide about 200 average-megawatts of additional power benefits downstream in Canada.[53]

British Columbia sold the first thirty years of the Canadian Entitlement to a consortium of utilities in the United States for $254 million and received its share of the predetermined US flood control benefits for the first sixty years for $64 million. British Columbia used these funds to finance the construction of the three treaty dams in the province. Upon completion of the dams, Canada and British Columbia continued to receive the Canadian Entitlement based on the sharing of power revenues on all US hydro-power projects. The entitlement value has varied over time, and depending on the market value of the incremental power, averages approximately $120 million annually.[54]

Under the CRT, article xvi says that a dispute or difference that arises may be referred by either government to the IJC for a decision. If the IJC does not render a decision within three months of the referral, or within such other period as may be agreed upon by the two federal governments, either country may submit the dispute to arbitration by providing written notice to the other country. However, no referrals have ever been sent to the IJC for resolution.

The existing CRT has provided both countries with enormous benefits. While the IJC hasn't been part of the implementation, its technical studies and its guiding principles for the treaty in the 1940s and '50s really set in motion the great working arrangement that has existed for over fifty-five years between the US and Canadian governments.

An enormous amount of thought has gone into what should be included in a new or revised CRT. Most of the ideas outlined below are presently being used by the IJC in other transboundary basins, including the Great Lakes. The national governments may wish to consider them in their negotiations of the CRT. They include:

1. Expand the focus of the treaty from optimizing power and flood control to include ecosystem-based management that balances the needs of power generation and flood control with the many ecosystem functions. Take a more holistic view for managing the basin as if no borders existed.

2. Rethink the governance structure for the basin to include local community leaders, Tribal/First Nation representatives, and key stakeholders. For example, the strength of the IJC's International Watershed Boards and Great Lakes Water Quality Board is that local leaders and stakeholders can help drive agendas and decision-making. This new governance structure should be used both in negotiating a new or revised treaty and for implementing the final CRT.

3. Address the needs of a changing climate and focus on mitigating the impacts of extreme weather conditions of floods, droughts, and wildfires. Build in an adaptive management process that addresses our changing climate. Further, the existing infrastructure in the Columbia many not be sufficient to control extreme floods in the future, as we have seen recently on Lake Ontario and in Houston, Texas. More effort is needed to protect the riparian corridor and to remove structures from within the flood plain.

4. Create and fund a binational science panel, similar to the IJC's Great Lakes Science Advisory Board, to assess the existing and required science on the river ecology and determine the best way to: a) re-establish a more natural

flow regime; b) recover the wild salmon fishery; and c) protect and improve riparian and aquatic habitats while at the same time optimizing hydro-power generation and flood control.

IJC Reference on a Proposed Sage Creek Coal Mine in the BC Flathead River Basin

The Flathead Valley sits within a larger international landscape known as the Crown of the Continent,[55] a roughly 18-million-acre transboundary region that straddles the Continental Divide in southeast British Columbia, southwest Alberta, and northwest Montana. The Crown is one of those few large natural eco-regions in North America that has built-in natural resiliency and the capacity to respond to a changing climate. The entire upper Flathead Valley (called the North Fork of the Flathead River in the United States) is a critical wildlife corridor and habitat for large ungulates and carnivores and for this reason is considered by many wildlife biologists and environmental organizations as the "heart" of the Crown. The BC Flathead River riparian corridor is over half a mile wide in some places and very rich in aquatic and terrestrial species. Much of the watershed straddles the border and is protected through parks and conservation areas, even though most of the Canadian portion of the Flathead is unprotected. There is also a complex historical web of Indigenous communities that lived and hunted in this region, including the Ktunaxa nation in Canada and Salish and Kootenai tribes in the United States.

By acts of the Canadian Parliament and the US Congress in 1932, Waterton-Glacier National Parks became the world's first international peace park. Indeed, Glacier-Waterton is both an icon and a model for the many other international peace parks established around the world in subsequent years. As well, Glacier and Waterton Lakes National Parks have each been designated a World Heritage Site and Biosphere Reserve. The waters of the North Fork of the Flathead River have been classified as Class A-1, which is Montana's highest water quality classification that includes a non-degradation standard.[57]

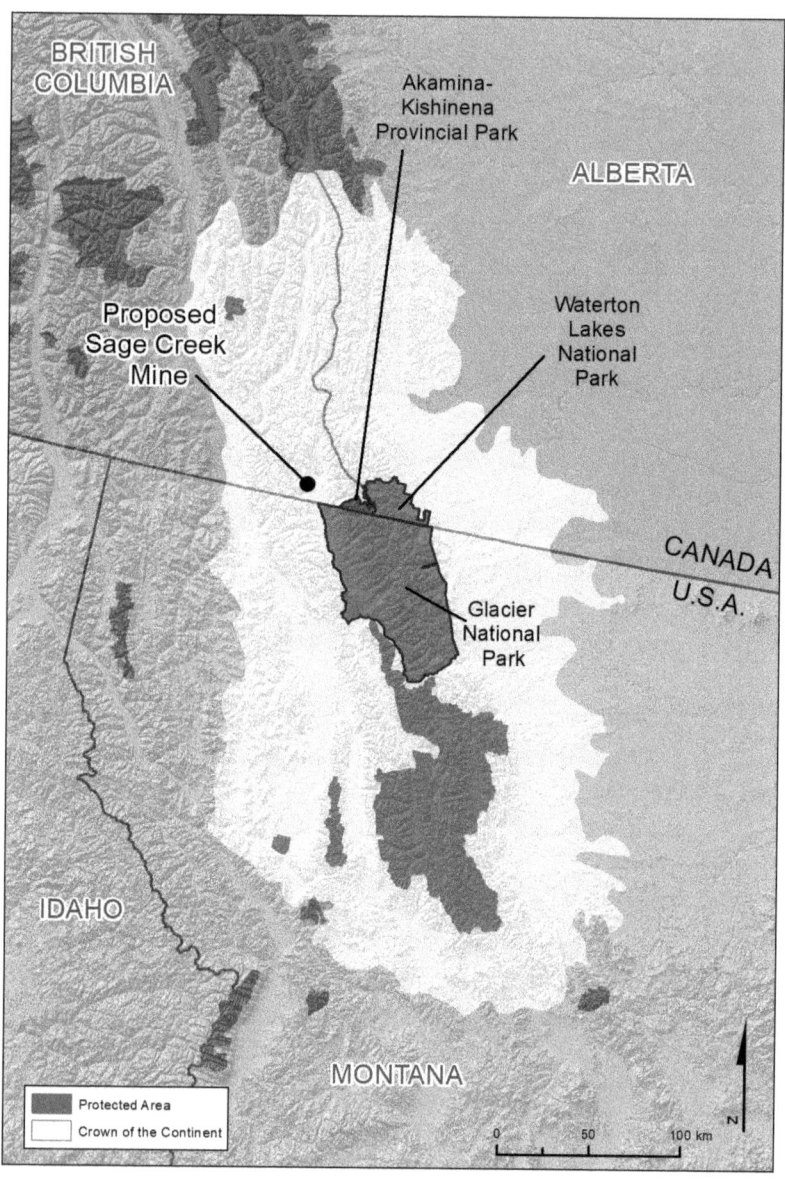

FIGURE 8.4. Crown of the Continent Eco-region.[56] J. Glatz, Western Michigan University Libraries.

In the 1980s, the upper Flathead Valley of British Columbia was very remote. The primary uses of the valley were hunting, fishing, and the limited harvest of timber. To this day, there are no permanent residences in the Flathead Valley of British Columbia.

The Proposed Sage Creek Coal Mine

Sage Creek Coal Limited, a subsidiary of Rio Algom Mines of Toronto began exploring the coal deposits in the Cabin Creek region of the BC Flathead Valley in 1980. The mine site would be located about 6 miles (9.66 kilometres) north of the US-Canada border and cover over 7,000 acres (2,832 hectares). The company proposed to mine 2.4 million tons (2.2 million tonnes) per year of thermal coal for a 21-year period with the option of a 20-year extension from two large hills adjacent to and between Howell and Cabin Creeks, two tributaries that flow directly into the Flathead River.[58] The mine would create two large open pits that would straddle Howell and Cabin Creeks. Six major waste dumps would surround the two creeks. A 230 kilovolt transmission line would be built to the mine site. Coal would be processed on site and hauled on a newly constructed paved road to Morrissey and shipped by rail to the BC coast for transportation overseas. The mine would be operated 24 hours a day, 365 days per year.

In February 1984, the BC government granted Sage Creek Coal Limited "approval-in-principle" to begin preparing detailed development and implementation plans for the mine site. These plans would be subject to an environmental assessment process where mitigation actions are determined.

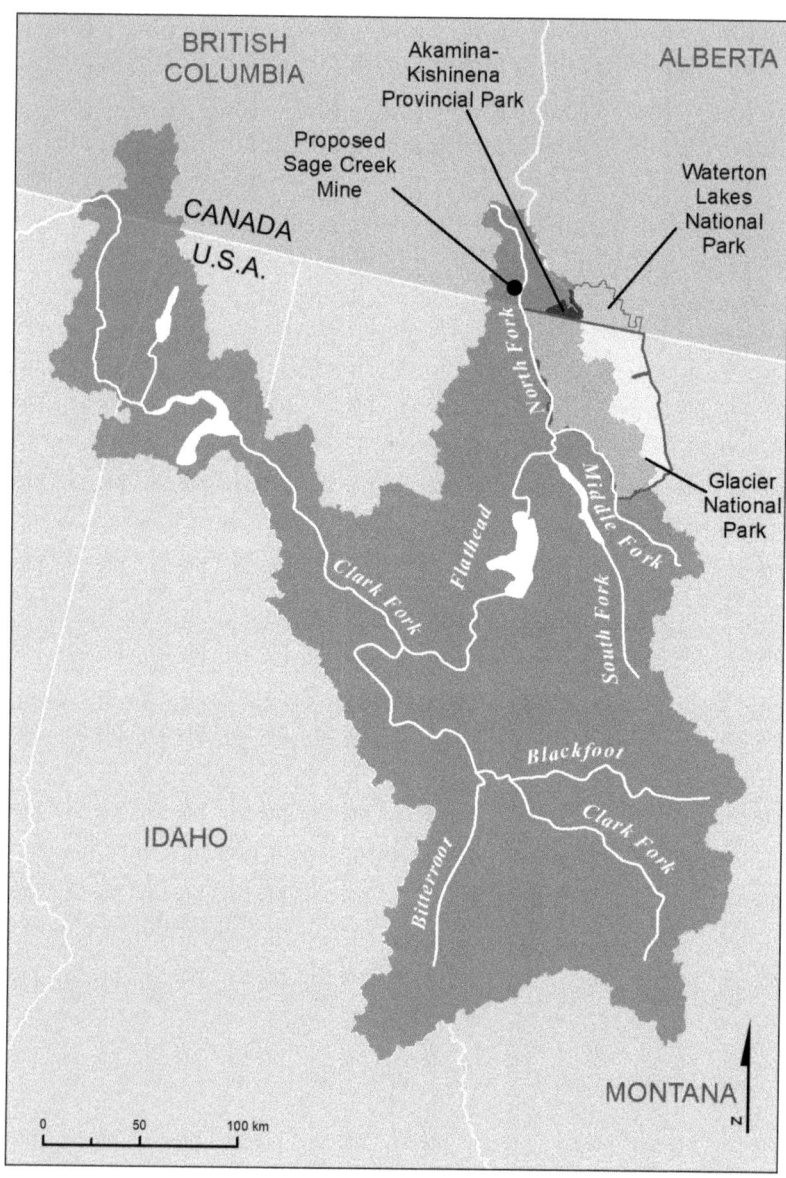

FIGURE 8.5. Location of the proposed Sage Creek coal mine within the Flathead River Basin.[59] J. Glatz, Western Michigan University Libraries.

The Reference Letter to the IJC

Due to concerns about the potential environmental degradation and transboundary pollution from the mine, the US and Canadian governments in separate, but identical, reference letters stated the following:

> Pursuant to Article IX of the Boundary Waters Treaty, the governments requested the IJC to examine into and report upon the water quality and quantity of the Flathead River, relating to the transboundary water quality and quantity implications of the proposed coal mine development on Cabin Creek in British Columbia near its confluence with the Flathead River and to make recommendations which would assist governments in ensuring that the provisions of Article IV of the said treaty are honoured.[60]

In this case, External Affairs Canada and the US Department of State invoked both articles iv and ix of the BWT. The governments further requested that the IJC examine and report on the potential impacts of the mine on the local fishery and other fisheries dependent on the waters of the Flathead River and its tributaries, Howell and Cabin creeks; the biological resources; current water uses (including water-dependent uses such as recreation); and other matters as the commission may deem appropriate and relevant to water quality and quantity at the border and downstream if the mine was constructed.

The Flathead River International Study Board Assessment Process

Based on the above reference, the IJC established the Flathead River International Study Board (henceforth "Study Board") in April 1985. It consisted of six members and two secretaries divided equally between the two countries. The Study Board created six binational science committees involving over fifty scientists. The authors of this chapter were the US secretariat and the BC representative on the Study Board. The reference investigations took almost three years.

The Study Board created a well-thought-out approach for assessing the potential mine impacts. It appointed four primary binational technical committees of experts: the Mine Development Committee, the Water Quality and Quantity Committee, the Biological Resources Committee, and a Water Uses Committee. Each committee consisted of six to eight members divided equally between the two countries. The Mine Development Committee was asked to assess the potential water quality and quantity impacts within the mine site and effluent discharges from the site. During the initial stage of the process, the other three committees were requested to establish the baseline condition within Howell and Cabin Creeks and the Flathead River downriver into Flathead Lake. After the Mine Development Committee defined the effluent discharges from the proposed mine site, the Water Quality and Quantity Committee determined the changes to water quality and quantity in Howell and Cabin Creeks and the Flathead River. The Biological Resources Committee then assessed the impacts of these changes on the aquatic, riparian, and terrestrial ecosystems. Lastly, the Water Uses Committee used the above information to calculate the effects on recreation and tourism.[61] Two additional binational committees were created by the Study Board: the Limnology Task Fork and the Water Quality Subcommittee. The Limnology Task Force determined whether the increase in nitrates and phosphorous from the mine site would have a deleterious effect on Flathead Lake. It concluded that effects would be "imperceptible."[62]

The Water Quality Subcommittee described the salient physical, chemical, and biological characteristics of water required to protect and maintain certain sensitive water quality conditions in the Flathead River system.[63] The criteria were developed to assess the potential effects of mine effluents and other contaminates on human uses (i.e., drinking water, recreational fishing, and esthetic experience) and aquatic uses such as bull trout and western cutthroat fish species and other forms of aquatic life.

To make their assessment, the Study Board and technical committees developed two cases to define the impacts.[64] The "optimal" case assumed the mine applied state-of-the-art environmental control technology and would be in complete compliance with the BC mine regulatory requirements. The second case, called the "adverse" case, assumed the mine would experience occasional failures and not meet the provincial regulatory requirements at all times. It is interesting to note that during the two-and-a-half-year Flathead mine assessment process, a number of waste dumps in the existing operating coal mines in the Elk Valley failed, and more concerning, a settling pond from one of the Elk Valley mines (Line Creek), which was designed to withstand a hundred-year flood, failed after a ten-year high flow. As stated by both the Biological Resources and Water Quality and Quantity Committees, these failures indicated that the adverse case was more realistic than the optimal case as a basis for the Study Board's final conclusions.[65]

Study Board and Committee Findings

The Study Board and its technical committees encountered two major problems in meeting the terms of reference.[66] First, the detail in the proposed mine plan was not adequate to develop reliable, quantitative predictions of impacts on water quality, water quantity, or biological resources at the mine site, at the international boundary, and downriver into Flathead Lake. Second, the baseline data required to assess the impacts of the proposed mine were either not available or were inadequate in the Flathead and Elk River drainages. Therefore, the Study Board and its technical committees had to use their best professional judgment to develop findings rather than basing them on actual data. Initially, the Study Board and committees were asked to use, for comparison, the water quality effluent and downstream data available from the existing five metallurgic mines in the Elk and Fording River drainages. These mines are in the same basic stratigraphy and rock types of the coal-bearing sequence in the Flathead River Basin, although specific features of geologic structure and of topography are different. Many of the Elk River Basin mines have been operational since before the 1950s. However, little or no water quality data were available from them.

The requirement that all members of the IJC's binational technical committees participate in their "personal and professional" capacity and not in their "official" capacity became very evident during the two-and-a-half-year technical committee process.[67] For example, the Water Quality and Quantity Committee felt that the impacts of effluent discharges would be far more severe than that suggested by the Mine Development

Committee. Further, both the Water Quality and Quantity and Biological Committees did not believe that the optimal case was realistic, noting that operating mines in the adjacent Elk River drainage in southeast British Columbia exceeded provincial regulations.

Based on the results from the four primary technical committees, the Study Board reported that the mine would create significant impacts to the spawning habitat of endangered bull trout. They concluded that while there would be no impacts to water quantity at the international border, there could be significant impacts within the mine site as the two open pit mines would have to pump groundwater from them, thus dewatering both streams.[68] It is questionable if these boards could have made these statements if their members were acting in their "official" capacity as government representatives rather than in their "personal" capacity.

Within the mine site, water quality could be substantially impacted. The Study Board felt there could be significant increases in localized sediment, turbidity, water temperature, phosphorous, nitrate, and ammonia levels. Dissolved oxygen could decrease to harmful levels. Because of the lack of data, however, the Study Board and technical committees could not tell for certain if the concentrations of phosphorous, total dissolved solids, and pH would change significantly, nor could the board assess the impacts from increased selenium and other heavy metals.

Using the above information, the Study Board felt the biota at the border and for some distance downstream would be impacted. Algae biomass would increase significantly and more frequently, both locally and for some distance downstream of the border, and it was determined that there would be a detrimental impact to benthic macro-invertebrates.[69] The Biological Resources Committee concluded that the bull trout and cutthroat would be virtually eliminated from Howell and Cabin Creeks.[70] Consequently, the Study Board concluded that these fish populations would be drastically reduced.

Upon hearing about the potential environmental impacts and experience of non-compliance in the BC regulatory process, the two federal governments asked the IJC to direct the Study Board to determine whether the identified impacts could be mitigated and what would be the costs. After further analyses, the Study Board reported that many of the impacts could not be mitigated because no viable technology existed and/or the mitigation requirements were not economically feasible.[71]

Public Hearings

The IJC held two public hearings in Cranbrook, British Columbia, and two in Kalispell, Montana, on the findings in the Study Board and technical committee report. Only one submission supported the mine. The primary reasons for the strong opposition was related to the adverse water quality affects to the fisheries, including the bull trout and westslope cutthroat, and to Glacier National Park, the Wild and Scenic Flathead River, and Flathead Lake. The submission by Montana governor Ted Schwinden reflects the general consensus shared by the US audience:

> I want to emphasize that Montana's concerns really go beyond the constraints of the Treaty and the Reference. The [Study] board's findings in reality have escalated rather than alleviated the concerns of Montanans for the Glacier-Waterton International Peace Park, for the natural integrity of the North Fork of the Flathead River and for threats to the very rich tourism opportunities of this special area shared by our two countries.[72]

After the evening public hearing in Kalispell, the two authors of this chapter developed (on a beer napkin) a possible prospectus for the upper Flathead drainage based on establishing an International Conservation Reserve Initiative (ICR).[73] The prospectus became the guiding light for future negotiations for protecting the Flathead drainage from mining in British Columbia and Montana. A number of its ideas were included in the final memorandum of understanding between Montana and British Columbia.

The IJC's Report to Governments

Based on the Study Board's findings and the public hearings, the IJC stated in its report to the two federal governments:

There are a number of impacts associated with the development of the mine that could affect spawning and rearing habitats for bull trout and cutthroat trout in Cabin and Howell creeks. These include toxic levels of nitrogen compounds in groundwater, increases in filamentous algae smothering spawning areas, increases in sediment concentrations and deposited sediments, possible reductions in dissolved oxygen, alternations to surface or ground water flow and changes in water temperature.[74]

The IJC asked the US and Canadian governments to consider the ICR proposal, along with the Skagit Environmental Endowment Fund and Commission structure, as possible management frameworks for the future of the BC Flathead.[75]

Based on the above findings and public hearings, the commissioners unanimously agreed to the following three recommendations in its report to governments:

1. [That] the mine proposal as presently defined and understood not be approved:

2. That the mine proposal not receive regulatory approval in the future unless and until it can be demonstrated that:

   a. The potential transboundary impacts identified in the report of the Flathead River International Study Board have been determined with reasonable certainty and would constitute a level of risk *acceptable to both Governments* [emphasis added]; and

   b. The potential impacts on the sport fish populations and habitat in the Flathead River system would not occur or could be fully mitigated in an effective and assured manner; and

3. The Governments consider, with the appropriate jurisdictions, opportunities for defining and implementing compatible, equitable and sustainable

development activities and management strategies in the upper Flathead River basins.[76]

The recommendations were based on article iv of the BWT, which states that "boundary waters and waters flowing across the boundary shall not be polluted to the injury of health or property of the other." British Columbia did not accept the recommendation, as it would have allowed the United States veto power over new mine developments that could potentially impact US waters. In 1989, Sage Creek Coal Limited voluntarily withdrew the Cabin Creek mining proposal.

Did the IJC make the Right Decision?

During the IJC assessment process, British Columbia and the coal mining companies indicated that no selenium data were available from the existing Elk River coal mines. Effluent from all five of these open pit metallurgic coal mines flow into the Elk River, which in turn flows into Lake Koocanusa—a transboundary reservoir.

Over the past twenty years, effluent discharge data from the Elk River mountaintop coal mines showed significantly elevated concentrations of selenium, cadmium, nitrates, and sulfates.[77] For example, water quality downstream of the existing Elk River mines showed nitrate concentrations were 3,000 times higher, sulfates 400 times higher, and selenium up to 70 times higher as compared to the upper Flathead River and the Elk River above the existing Elk River mines.[78] Further, the Flathead River has over 4 times the number of algae species as compared to the mine-impacted streams, indicating that the sensitive species were eliminated due to pollution from these mines.

Selenium is a concern due to its ability to bio-magnify in aquatic food chains and to accumulate in the tissues and eggs of higher trophic species. Recent studies have shown that selenium has severely reduced westslope cutthroat reproductive success by up to 54 per cent in the upper Fording River (the Fording is a tributary of the Elk River).[79] Furthermore, fish data from the 2008–13 period in the Montana portion of Koocanusa Reservoir showed increases in heavy metals in fish tissue for the seven species of fish studied, including Endangered Species Act–listed species. Some fish showed increases of selenium in fish tissue of up to 70 per cent over the five-year period.[80]

In early 2016, a number of new open pit coal mines were in the BC permitting process, as well as large-scale expansions at existing mines in the Elk Valley. Four expansions have been permitted even though the selenium-mitigation technology at Teck Coal's treatment plant initially failed and the plant has been shut down several times since it began operations in late 2014. In 2017, Teck discovered that the treatment plant was releasing a more bio-available form of selenium into the environment, making selenium more readily available to aquatic life and fish. Monitoring downstream of the treatment plant showed increasing concentrations of selenium in westslope cutthroat and aquatic insects, to such a degree that Teck suspend operations. To date, no technology has demonstrated the ability to successfully treat the contamination draining from the mines, including toxic heavy metals and nutrients.

In support of the above findings, Carol Bellringer, the BC auditor general reported in 2016 that the provincial mine regulators have neglected to comply and enforce the province's mine and environmental regulations for over a decade.[81] The two-year investigation paid particular attention to the Elk Valley coal mines north of Montana's Lake Koocanusa. "We found almost every one of our expectations for a robust compliance and enforcement program within the [Ministry of Energy and Mines] and the [Ministry of Environment] were not met," Auditor General Bellringer wrote in the introduction to the report. Recently, the three Indigenous Tribes that make up the Council of the Ktunaxa Nation in the United States and Canada, along with all eight US senators from Montana, Idaho, Washington, and Alaska, have also raised similar concerns over BC's existing and future mine pollution into US waters.[82]

The Movement toward Protection

After twenty-two years and seven new mining proposals in the BC Flathead for coal, gold, coal-bed methane, and phosphate, the IJC's third recommendation ultimately prevailed. The final decision to protect the watershed was based on the outstanding universal values of the transboundary Flathead. Premier Campbell of British Columbia and Governor Schweitzer of Montana negotiated and signed on 18 February 2010 a historic and visionary agreement entitled *MOU and Cooperation on Environmental Protection, Climate Action and Energy between the Province of BC and the State of Montana*. The agreement calls for the state and province to work together to implement many of the ICR provisions, including the banning of mining in the US and BC portions of the Flathead River drainage. As part of the agreement, Cline Mining Company would be compensated for its expenditures associated with its approved exploration plans. Thanks in part to Gary Doer, at that time, the Canadian ambassador to the United States, funds were raised by Nature Conservancy of Canada to retire the mine application.

Finally in 2011, British Columbia passed the Flathead Watershed Area Conservation Act with parallel legislation passed by the United States Congress (the North Fork Watershed Protection Act) in March 2014 to protect the Flathead River in British Columbia and the North Fork of the Flathead in Montana from any future mining and oil and gas activity. The ecological integrity will be protected for generations, unlike the Elk River, where selenium and other mine contaminates will continue to leach for centuries through Elk River mountain valleys filled with hundreds of feet of waste rock.

It is clear that the IJC's scientific-based process and recommendations to governments for the Sage Creek mine site were appropriate. These recommendations were the foundation for the long and arduous process that ultimately led to the protection of the North Fork of the Flathead drainage from mining. The watershed is to remain one of the most pristine of the drainages shared by two countries in North America. After over twenty years of contentious conflict, the IJC's vision for this basin finally became a reality. However, the work is not done. Like in the many other international watersheds, a transboundary institutional structure needs to be put in place to implement many of the other provisions in the *2010 MOU and Cooperative Agreement*. Consideration should also be given to the IJC's recommendation to governments for including the IJC's ideas from the proposed International Conservation Reserve and the Skagit Environment Endowment and Commission (SEEC). [83]

Conclusion

These three cases clearly illustrate the breath of the IJC's ability to use innovative approaches for assisting governments in their resolution. When the IJC steps away from political agendas and uses the best scientists and professionals from its staff, academia, the private sector, and governments from both countries—all working in their personal and professional (as opposed to official) capacities—solutions to disputes are more readily found. Without political agendas, the IJC can become more creative, can use science more effectively, and is more capable to assist governments resolve almost any issue. These three cases are good examples.

The resolution of the High Ross Dam controversy was rather innovative in that the IJC found a viable compromise without raising Ross Dam. It is conflict resolution at its best. The three key lessons learned are: involve local negotiators, not folks from afar; listen to local stakeholders and leaders concerning their knowledge of the issue and watershed; and lastly, make sure you have a sound scientific foundation of data and knowledge available for resolution. Just as important, the IJC's creation and recommendation of the SEEC and its funding source for the Skagit watershed has had many wonderful benefits. It has successfully improved the ecological health of the watershed and recreational opportunities for many.

The IJC provided governments with the technical and policy foundation for the 1964 CRT. Over the past twenty-five years the IJC has gained valuable experience with a number of innovative tools that clearly has benefited its work in other transboundary basins and the Great Lakes. These innovations may be helpful in defining a new or revised treaty.

The Sage Creek Coal Reference process was a creative, science-based process in which one layer of data was used to build the next layer of information until all potential impacts could be assessed. Like the Skagit, the third IJC recommendation that asked governments to consider a new and innovative management regime for the Flathead finally came to fruition. This 1988 recommendation became the cornerstone for preserving the ecological integrity of the Flathead from mining.

The relationship between British Columbia and the IJC has been rather contentious since the Sage Creek Coal Reference. Specifically, British Columbia did not like, nor did it accept, the IJC's recommendations on the

Sage Creek Coal Reference, especially the second recommendation, which gave the United States veto power over new BC mine proposals that could negatively impact waters flowing into the United States. British Columbia realized that it may not be able to meet this standard for new mines, or for that matter from existing mine expansions (e.g., Kootenai River).

British Columbia agreed to the Sage Creek Coal Reference because it appeared to have been satisfied with the outcomes of both the Ross Dam dispute on the Skagit River and the 1964 CRT. Further, the province had a better understanding and control of the technical data that was available to conduct the proposed Sage Creek mine assessment.

These three cases illustrate that the IJC needs to continually evaluate and improve adaptive management strategies to address a changing climate and to develop and use innovative tools for restoring ecological functions to international watersheds. It is hoped that current policy-makers in both national governments will realize this evolving capacity and continue to engage the commission in key boundary water issues in the Pacific Northwest.

Notes

1. The "paper dam" phrase was originally used by then US secretary of energy Donald P. Hodel, a past CEO of the Bonneville Power Administration, as part of his rationale for supporting the IJC's solution to the Ross Dam dispute.

2. Jackie Krin and Marion Marts, "The Skagit High Ross Controversy: Negotiation and Settlement," 26 *Nat Resources J.* 261, (1986), 261–2.

3. US data was derived from the National Atlas of the United States of America. Data for the map was also derived from: B. Lehner, K. Verdin, and A. Jarvis, "New global hydrography derived from spaceborne elevation data," *Eos, Transactions, AGU* 89, no. 10 (2008): 93–4; WWF/ HydroSHEDS, https://www.hydrosheds.org/; information licensed under the Open Government Licence—British Columbia: Freshwater Atlas Lakes, https://catalogue.data.gov.bc.ca/dataset/freshwater-atlas-lakes, and Freshwater Atlas Rivers, https://www2.gov.bc.ca/gov/content/data/open-data/open-government-licence-bc.

4. William Ross and Marion Marts, "The High Ross Dam Project: Environmental Decisions and Changing Environmental Attitudes," *Canadian Geographic* 19 (1975): 221–34.

5. Thomas C. Perry, *Excerpts from a Citizen guide to the Skagit Valley, IV: History of the High Ross Controversy* (Run Out Skagit Spoiler Committee, 1981).

6   International Joint Commission, "Transcript of hearing on High Ross Dam held at Seattle, Washington ," 12 September 1941, 9–13.

7   International Joint Commission, *In the Matter of the Application of the City of Seattle for Authority to Raise the Water Level of the Skagit River Approximately 130 feet at the International Boundary between the United States and Canada: Order of Approval*, Docket 46, 27 January 1942.

8   Kirn and Marts, "The Skagit-High Ross Controversy," 265.

9   US data was derived from the National Atlas of the United States of America. Data for the map was also derived from: B. Lehner, K. Verdin, and A. Jarvis, "New global hydrography derived from spaceborne elevation data," *Eos, Transactions, AGU* 89, no. 10 (2008): 93–4; WWF/ HydroSHEDS, https://www.hydrosheds.org/; information licensed under the Open Government Licence—British Columbia: Freshwater Atlas Lakes, https://catalogue.data.gov.bc.ca/dataset/freshwater-atlas-lakes, and Freshwater Atlas Rivers, https://www2.gov.bc.ca/gov/content/data/open-data/open-government-licence-bc.

10 Perry, *Excerpts from a Citizen guide to the Skagit Valley*, IV.

11 Ibid.

12 Ibid.

13 Lieutenant-Governor in Council, Order No. 103. Agreement between British Columbia and the City of Seattle, Victoria, BC, 19 January 1967.

14 Jackie Kirn and Marion Marts, *The Skagit-High Ross Controversy: Negotiations and Settlement*, 26 Nat Resources J. 2611986, pgs. 265–9.

15 International Joint Commission, *National governments Letter of Reference to the IJC requesting the IJC determine the environmental and ecological consequences of raising Ross Lake in the Skagit Valley to elevation 1725*, Docket 71, 7 April 1971.

16 International Joint Commission, *IJC's Report to National governments, Environmental and Ecological Consequences of Raising Ross Lake in the Skagit Valley to Elevaton1725*, Docket 91 (1971).

17 Perry, *Excerpts from a Citizen guide to the Skagit Valley*, IV.

18 Kirn and Marts, *The Skagit-High Ross Controversy*, 267–9.

19 Ibid., 268.

20 Province of British Columbia, Request in the Application, International Joint Commission, Ottawa and Washington, DC, 6 February 1981.

21 Interestingly, the firing of existing US commissioners when a new president takes office has rarely occurred in the long history of the IJC.

22 Kirn and Marts, *Skagit-High Ross Controversy*, 270.

23 Ibid., 267–9.

24 International Joint Commission, *In the matter of the Application of the City of Seattle for authority to raise the water level of the Skagit River approximately 130 feet at the*

international boundary between the United States and Canada, Supplementary Order, Docket 46, 28 April 1982.

25　Later the Special Board was renamed the Joint Consultative Group to emphasize that it was an advisory rather than a decision-making entity.

26　International Joint Commission, *In the matter of the Application of the City of Seattle for authority to raise the water level of the Skagit River approximately 130 feet at the international boundary between the United States and Canada, Supplementary Order,* Docket 46, 28 April 1982.

27　Kirn and Marts, *The Skagit-High Ross Controversy,* 271–2.

28　Mr. Gordon and Mr. Berry were recently retired chief executive officers of Ontario Hydro and the Power Authority of the State of New York, respectively.

29　Kirn and Marts, *The Skagit-High Ross Controversy,* 270–3.

30　Ibid., 273.

31　L. Keith Bulen, "Statement of the International Joint Commission," 10 March 1982, General Memoranda, vol. 2, box 56, Docket 46, IJC.

32　Province of British Columbia Ministry of Environment and City of Seattle Office of the Major, Joint News Release, Skagit Details Released (14 April 1983).

33　The SEEC is a very creative approach to ensure the preservation and protection of the natural and cultural resources, wildlife habitat, and recreational opportunities of the Upper Skagit Watershed. Under the SEEC, an Endowment Fund was established and is administered by a sixteen-member commission consisting of an eight-person Canadian delegation appointed by the premier of British Columbia and an eight-person US delegation appointed by the mayor of Seattle. Over its thirty-year history, the SEEC has evolved to where it has had a greater focus on education, ecosystem management, recreation, and land-management efforts.

34　Before a newly appointed commissioner can become active, he or she must take an oath to abide by and follow the terms of the 1909 Boundary Waters Treaty and not to represent their respective governments. The commission is to be an independent advisor to both national governments.

35　Philip Van Huizen, *Development, Politics, and Environmental Controversy in the Canadian-U.S. Skagit Valley* (PhD diss., University of British Columbia, June 2013).

36　"B.C. treaty settles Seattle dispute," *Spokane* [WA] *Chronicle,* 28 June 1984.

37　International Joint Commission, *In the Matter of the Application of the City of Seattle for Authority to Raise the Water Level of the Skagit River Approximately 130 feet the International Boundary between the United States and Canada; Supplemental Order,* Docket 46, 18 January 1984.

38　Kirn and Marts, *The Skagit-High Ross Controversy,* 277.

39　Joe Foy, co-executive director, Wilderness Committee, "Save the Skagit," 29 January 2019, *https://www.wildernesscommittee.org/publications/save-skagit.*

40 John Harrison, "Columbia River History," *Northwest Power and Conservation Council*, 31 October 2008, https://www.nwcouncil.org/.

41 US data was derived from the National Atlas of the United States of America. Data for the map was also derived from: B. Lehner, K. Verdin, and A. Jarvis, "New global hydrography derived from spaceborne elevation data," *Eos, Transactions, AGU* 89, no. 10 (2008): 93–4.

42 International Joint Commission, *Columbia River Reference letters from the national governments*, Docket 51R, 8 and 9 March 1944; International Columbia River Engineering Board Report to the International Joint Commission: *United States and Canada; Water Resources of the Columbia River Basin*, with VI Appendices, Docket 51, April 1959.

43 The reservoir behind Libby Dam has a rather unique name—Lake Koocanusa—a composite formed from the following three terms: *Koo*tenai, *Can*ada, and *USA*.

44 See McNaughton, "The Proposed Columbia River Treaty," *International Journal* (March 1964).

45 McNaughton had been a chief advocate of an all-Canadian St. Lawrence Seaway in the 1950s, and the failure of this scheme was a major contributor to his all-Canadian position on Columbia developments. See Daniel Macfarlane, *Negotiating a River: Canada, the US, and the Creation of the St. Lawrence Seaway* (Vancouver: UBC Press, 2014), 215.

46 International Joint Commission, *Reference Letters from national governments*, Docket 51, 28 and 29 January 1959.

47 International Joint Commission, *Principles for Determining and Apportioning Benefits from Cooperative Use of Storage of Waters and Electrical inter-connections within the Columbia River System*, Docket 51, 29 December 1959.

48 Harrison, "Columbia River History."

49 Ibid.

50 The white sturgeon has been significantly impacted by Libby Dam and the species is listed as endangered under the US Endangered Species Act.

51 John Shurts, Northwest Power and Conservation Council, personal communication, February 2018.

52 Robert W. Sandford, Deborah Harford, and Jon O'Riordan, *The Columbia River Treaty: A Primer* (Victoria, BC: Rocky Mountain Books), 2014.

53 Harrison, "Columbia River History."

54 Province of British Columbia, "What is the Canadian Entitlement?" engage.gov.bc.ca/columbiarivertreaty.

55 The name "Crown of the Continent" was first coined by conservationist George Bird Grinnell in the late 1800s.

56 US data was derived from the National Atlas of the United States of America; contains information licensed under the Open Government Licence—Canada; National Parks and National Park Reserves of Canada Legislative Boundaries:

https://open.canada.ca/data/en/dataset/9e1507cd-f25c-4c64-995b-6563bf9d65bd; contains information licensed under the Open Government Licence—British Columbia; BC Parks, Ecological Reserves, and Protected Areas:

https://catalogue.data.gov.bc.ca/dataset/bc-parks-ecological-reserves-and-protected-areas.

57 Jim Posewitz and Dan Kimball, *Special Designations Applicable to the North Fork of the Flathead River*, appendix 9.8 of the *Flathead River International Study: Board Report*, June 1988.

58 International Joint Commission, *Flathead River International Study, Mine Development Committee Technical Report*, December 1986.

59 US data was derived from the National Atlas of the United States of America; contains information licensed under the Open Government Licence—Canada; National Parks and National Park Reserves of Canada Legislative Boundaries:

https://open.canada.ca/data/en/dataset/9e1507cd-f25c-4c64-995b-6563bf9d65bd; contains information licensed under the Open Government Licence—British Columbia; BC Parks, Ecological Reserves, and Protected Areas:

https://catalogue.data.gov.bc.ca/dataset/bc-parks-ecological-reserves-and-protected-areas; B. Lehner, K. Verdin, A. Jarvis, "New global hydrography derived from spaceborne elevation data," *Eos, Transactions, AGU* 89, no. 10 (2008): 93–4.

60 International Joint Commission, *National Governments Reference letters to the IJC*, Docket 110R, 12 December 1984 and 15 February 1985.

61 International Joint Commission, *Flathead River International Study Board Report*, July 1988.

62 International Joint Commission, *Flathead River International Study, Limnology Task Force Report on Flathead Lake, MT*, December 1986.

63 International Joint Commission *Flathead River International Study, Water Quality Criteria Subcommittee Technical Report*, May 1987.

64 International Joint Commission, *Flathead River International Study Board Report*, July 1988.

65 Ibid.

66 Ibid.

67 Ibid.

68 Ibid.

69 Ibid.

70 International Joint Commission, *Flathead River International Study, Biological Resources Committee Technical Report*, October 1987.

71 International Joint Commission, *Flathead River International Study, Board Supplementary Report*, 30 June 1988.

72 International Joint Commission, *Sage Creek Coal Mine Public Hearings Transcript*, vol. 2, *Flathead River Study, Montana governor Schwinden's Testimony*, 22 September 1988, p. 50.

73 Jim Posewitz, the US co-chair of the International Study Board, flushed out the prospectus on the ICR. The prospectus proposed that the "approval-in-principle" for the Sage Creek mine would be allowed to expire and the province would retire the existing coal leases in the upper Flathead and in return the United States would make funds available to retire the leases. Each nation would endow the ICR with a million dollars to be held in a common trust and a binational board of directors would be appointed by British Columbia and Montana to oversee the implementation of the ICR. The objectives of the ICR would be similar to the Biosphere Reserve Program with a focus on conservation and research. The ICR would be formalized into a binding agreement such as a treaty, similar to the one developed by the governments as part of the Skagit decision.

74 International Joint Commission, *Impacts of a proposed Coal Mine in the Flathead River Basin*, Docket 110, December 1988

75 Ibid.

76 The recommendations were drafted by the Honorable Davey Fulton, Canadian IJC commissioner and co-chair from British Columbia (1986–92), who was previously a justice of the BC Supreme Court and a leader of the Progressive Conservative Party of Canada.

77 Richard F. Hauer and Erin K. Sexton, *Transboundary Flathead River: Water Quality and Aquatic Life Use*, Rocky Mountains Cooperative Ecosystems Study Unit, 4 March 2013.

78 Lindsay McIvor, *Permit 107517 Environmental Monitoring Committee 2017 Public Report*, Teck Coal Ltd. (2017).

79 Dennis A. Lemly, *Review of Environment Canada's Teck Coal Environmental Assessment and Evaluation of Selenium Toxicology Tests on Westslope Cutthroat Trout in the Elk and Fording River in Southeast British Columbia*, Expert Report, 25 September 2014. https://www.teck.com/responsibility/sustainability-topics/water/water-quality-in-the-elk-valley/.

80 "Selenium Concentrations in Lake Koocanusa Resident Fish," memo from Trevor Selch, Montana Department of Fish, Wildlife and Parks, to Tracy Stone Manning, Montana Department of Environmental Quality, 30 September 2014.

81 Carol Bellringer, auditor general of British Columbia, *An Audit of Compliance and Enforcement of the Mining Sector*, May 2016, https://www.bcauditor.com/pubs/2016/audit-compliance-and-enforcement-mining-sector.

82 In March 2019, the three Indigenous transboundary Tribes of the Council of the Ktunaxa Nation sent a letter to the Honourable George Heyman, BC minister of environment and climate change strategy, Montana governor Steve Bullock, and

Idaho governor C. L. Otter raising concerns over BC selenium pollution into the transboundary Lake Koocanusa (note, the letter was not dated). On 13 June 2019, all eight US senators from Montana, Idaho, Washington, and Alaska sent a letter to the Honorable John Horgan, premier of BC, concerning the potential environmental and economic impacts to the Pacific Northwest and Alaska resulting from large-scale hardrock and coal mine activities in BC.

83 The IJC's International Watershed Initiative (IWI) is an ecosystem-based approach for addressing transboundary watershed issues. The IWI for the Rainy and Lake of the Woods watershed is a good example of a very effective governance structure. This institutional arrangement and the use of IWI guiding principles would be beneficial for addressing existing and future watershed issues in the Flathead River drainage of British Columbia and Montana.

SECTION 3

GREAT LAKES–ST. LAWRENCE BASIN

9

The International Joint Commission and Great Lakes Water Levels

Murray Clamen and Daniel Macfarlane

The magnitude of the Great Lakes water system, comprised of Lakes Superior, Michigan, Huron, Erie, and Ontario, is difficult to appreciate, even for those who live in the basin. The lakes are the largest system of fresh surface water on earth, covering more than 94,000 square miles, draining more than twice as much land area, and holding an estimated 6 quadrillion gallons of water. Including its outflow, the St. Lawrence River, the lakes are surrounded by part of eight US states and two Canadian provinces, containing more than one-tenth of the population of the United States and one-quarter of the population of Canada. Some of the world's largest concentrations of industrial capacity are located in this region. The lakes have been a significant part of the physical and cultural heritage of North America and have provided water for consumption, transportation, power, recreation, ecosystem services, and a host of other uses.

For most of the twentieth century, governance of the Great Lakes–St. Lawrence basin revolved around the International Joint Commission (IJC), which was created by the Boundary Waters Treaty in 1909. Although in terms of governance there are literally thousands of local, regional, and special-purpose governing bodies with jurisdiction for some management aspect of the basin or the lakes, the IJC is of particular importance in the Great Lakes. Primarily, water governance and environmental diplomacy issues in the basin centre on water quantity (e.g., lake levels), water quality (e.g., pollution), and biomass issues (e.g., fisheries and invasive species). In spite of their size, the Great Lakes are sensitive to the effects of a wide range of pollutants, including those from the air. Growing public concern about the deterioration of water quality, especially in the 1960s, led governments to respond with the signing of the first Great Lakes Water Quality Agreement in 1972 (and subsequent agreements, protocols, and annexes) to protect and restore the lakes. However, for the first half of its existence the IJC was generally much more concerned with apportioning water resources. These included water levels and diversions in and out of the Great Lakes (see the map of diversions included in chapter 17 of this volume). Water level variations, both annual and seasonal, are based mainly on precipitation and run-off, and long-term trends have resulted in both high and low water periods over the last century of recorded data. Limited regulation of flows from Lake Superior into the St. Marys River, from Lake Erie into Lake Ontario via the Niagara River, and from Lake Ontario into the St. Lawrence River, are the responsibility of the IJC.

This chapter examines the historical evolution of transboundary IJC water governance in the Great Lakes basin over the course of the twentieth century. The management of Great Lakes water has been examined by scholars from various fields, though with a heavy emphasis on water quality and fisheries/invasives issues. However, this chapter will focus on water quantity—that is, water levels as affected by diversions, canals and navigation improvements, hydroelectric developments, remedial works, consumptive uses, and natural causes (and the scientific understanding of these causes).

Great Lakes governance is, on the one hand, difficult and fragmented because of the various jurisdictions. However, the IJC, though certainly not perfect, has provided a unique means of addressing transboundary problems and adjudicating between various interests. In fact, a comparison of the IJC's first hundred years of operation shows that its behaviour, role, and function has changed significantly over time, not only in general but in relation to governance of the Great Lakes–St. Lawrence basin. Indeed, flexibility has been one of the hallmarks of the IJC. At the same time, the successes of the IJC, and the concomitant high regard for it as an organization, are, we argue, more of a post–Second World War, or even a post-1965, development. The history of the IJC reveals an initial half-century of mixed results, followed by a period lasting from the 1940s to the 1960s of partisan politics resulting in large-scale endeavours with dubious environmental impacts, followed by a period of more noticeable success continuing nearly to the turn of the twenty-first century, if not all the way to the present.

Pre-IJC Water Levels

A number of diversions and alterations of water levels had taken place before the Boundary Waters Treaty of 1909, though they had next to no impact on the Great Lakes in terms of water levels.[1] The Erie, Oswego, and Welland Canals were built in the 1820s and '30s to circumvent Niagara Falls, and subsequently improved numerous times over the nineteenth century. The Erie Canal connected the Niagara River with the Albany River, then to New York Harbour. The Welland Canal, through its various iterations and routes, connected Lake Erie with Lake Ontario. Both were essentially intra-basin water transfers, which meant that the water stayed within the Great Lakes–St. Lawrence basin, as opposed to inter-basin transfers, which move water into a different water basin.[2] Beginning in the late nineteenth century, other connecting channels in the Great Lakes basin, particularly the St. Marys, St. Clair, and Detroit Rivers, were dredged and reconfigured for navigation (and for hydro-power production in the case of the St. Marys River and rapids). This cumulatively lowered lake levels slightly by expanding the volume of water these channels held, though without diverting water out of the basin. A great deal more engineering work of this type was performed in connecting channels over the course of the twentieth century. Deep-draught channels were etched into the Detroit River and Lake St. Clair, for example, which involved removing islands and parts of islands, while also creating new land masses such as dikes and training walls. The scale of this reconfiguration only accelerated after the opening of the St. Lawrence Seaway to accommodate larger vessels. By 1968, over 46,200,000 cubic metres of material was removed from the bottom of the Detroit River alone, while some 4,050 hectares of underwater area was covered by dredge spoils.[3] Consequently, in the twenty-first century there were accusations that the greater depth and flow rate of the St. Clair River–Lake St. Clair–Detroit

River stretch caused lower water levels on the upper lakes, particularly the interconnected Lakes Michigan and Huron.

One of the first large-scale diversions from the Great Lakes began in the late nineteenth century and was completed in 1900: the Chicago Sanitary and Ship Canal, which enables the Chicago (or Illinois) Diversion. This stands as the first major alteration of the twentieth century to Great Lakes water levels. Moreover, it was a project that took water out of the Great Lakes basin on a large scale. It reversed the flow of the Chicago River *away* from Lake Michigan, and thus out of the Great Lakes watershed, eventually to the Mississippi, in order to provide sewage disposal for the city of Chicago as well as navigation (and small-scale hydro production). However, plans for this canal to serve as a deep-draught navigation route from Chicago to the Gulf of Mexico using the Mississippi River never really materialized. Since the Chicago Sanitary and Ship Canal lowered the water levels in the Great Lakes–St. Lawrence system, it received opposition from Canada and other US states bordering Lake Michigan. Ottawa protested many times in subsequent decades, as did other US Great Lakes states, but this diversion was not subject to the Boundary Waters Treaty (BWT) since it predated it and the diversion was entirely within the United States, as is Lake Michigan (and there is indirect evidence that one of the main reasons for leaving Lake Michigan levels out of the BWT was that Illinois was unwilling to have the Chicago Diversion subject to the treaty).[4] Well into the second half of the twentieth century the Chicago Diversion was a major sticking point in environmental diplomacy concerning other water developments in the Great Lakes–St. Lawrence basin, particularly discussions about developing the Niagara and St. Lawrence Rivers.

Among other features, the Boundary Waters Treaty of 1909 settled the outstanding issues of Niagara Falls, Sault Ste. Marie, and the St. Mary and Milk Rivers, and created the IJC, which held its first meeting in Washington, DC, on 10 January 1912. Securing the agreement was a significant coup for Canada, since the much more powerful United States was agreeing to a commission within which the two countries were equal. The development of Niagara Falls was the single most important issue bringing the two nations to the table, for without Niagara the International Waterways Commission (IWC) would not likely have taken place, and without that, the Boundary Waters Treaty almost certainly would not have occurred;

rather than a wider settlement for general principles along border waters, a series of discrete agreements, or continued disagreement, for individual waterbodies might well have occurred.

The first few IJC cases (or dockets) did not involve the Great Lakes–St. Lawrence basin. In its third docket, the Canadian and US governments referred levels of Lake of the Woods (which is divided between Minnesota, Ontario, and Manitoba) to the IJC, later resulting in a treaty.[5] The fourth docket, in 1912, was about the general pollution of boundary waters, mostly in the Great Lakes basin (covered in the Benidickson chapter in this volume). In 1914 the IJC approved the building of the binational Compensating Works (a sixteen-gate structure with eight gates on each side of the boundary) in the St. Marys River (near Sault Ste. Marie), and hydro-power plants are near the shore in each country. At the same time, the IJC established the first of its joint boards, the International Lake Superior Board of Control, to regulate the water levels and flows of Lake Superior.[6]

The St. Lawrence

Negotiations for a St. Lawrence deep waterway and hydroelectric project dated back to the 1890s—in fact, the deep waterway was a factor leading to the Boundary Waters Treaty—but it took over half a century for an agreement.[7] This megaproject was both a hydroelectric project (power dams) and a navigation project (locks and canals), with the former submitted to the IJC by the governments for approval, while the latter was agreed to via a separate Canada-US agreement. Since the upper St. Lawrence River is a border water, under the BWT the concurrence of both countries and the IJC is necessary to change its water levels. Canada and the United States signed St. Lawrence diplomatic agreements in 1932 and 1941, but neither received congressional consent, in part because of railway, coal, and East Coast port interests.[8] In the immediate post–Second World War years a variety of economic and defence factors brought further pressure to bear on a St. Lawrence seaway and power project: in particular, the ability of a deep waterway to transport the recently discovered iron ore deposits from the Ungava district in Labrador and northern Quebec to the steel mills of the Great Lakes.

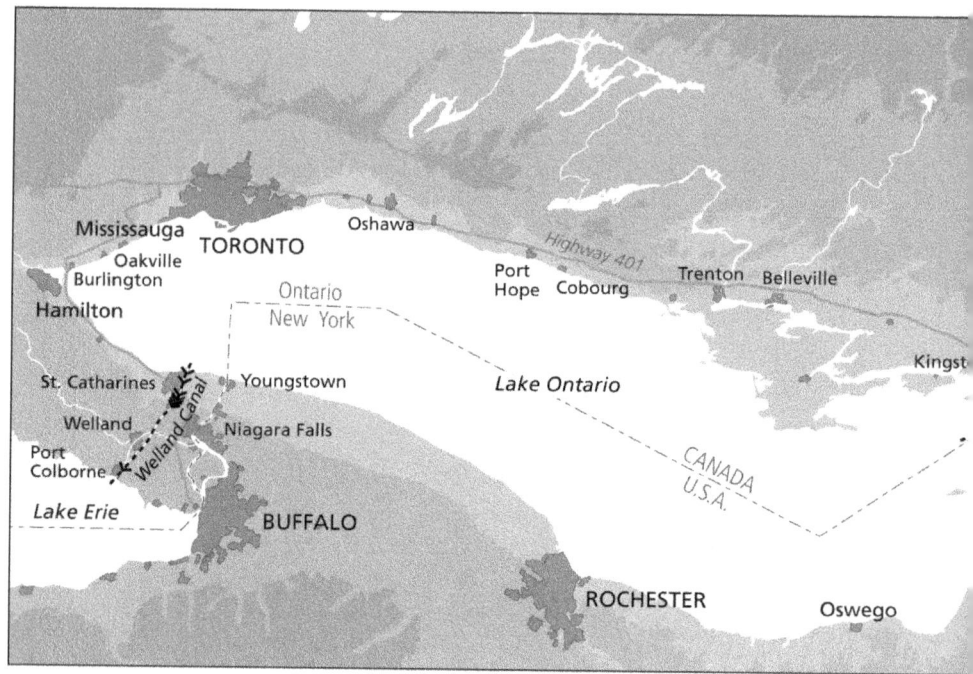

FIGURE 9.1. Map of the St. Lawrence Seaway. Map by Eric Leinberger, used with the permission of UBC Press.

Canada attempted to pursue an all-Canadian seaway, but the United States blocked a solely Canadian waterway, which was deemed to be inimical to American economic and security interests. In the early 1950s the IJC approved the plans for a transnational St. Lawrence power project and created the International St. Lawrence River Board of Control.[9] Then, through a 1954 bilateral Canada-US agreement, Canada reluctantly acquiesced in the construction of a joint seaway with the United States.

The construction of the St. Lawrence Seaway and Power Project had an enormous environmental and social impact on the St. Lawrence basin. It required a massive manipulation of the river and its environs, as part of a process that Daniel Macfarlane labels *negotiated* high modernism.[10] In excess of 210 million cubic yards of earth and rock—more than twice that of the Suez Canal—were moved through extensive digging, cutting, blasting, and drilling, using a litany of specialized equipment and

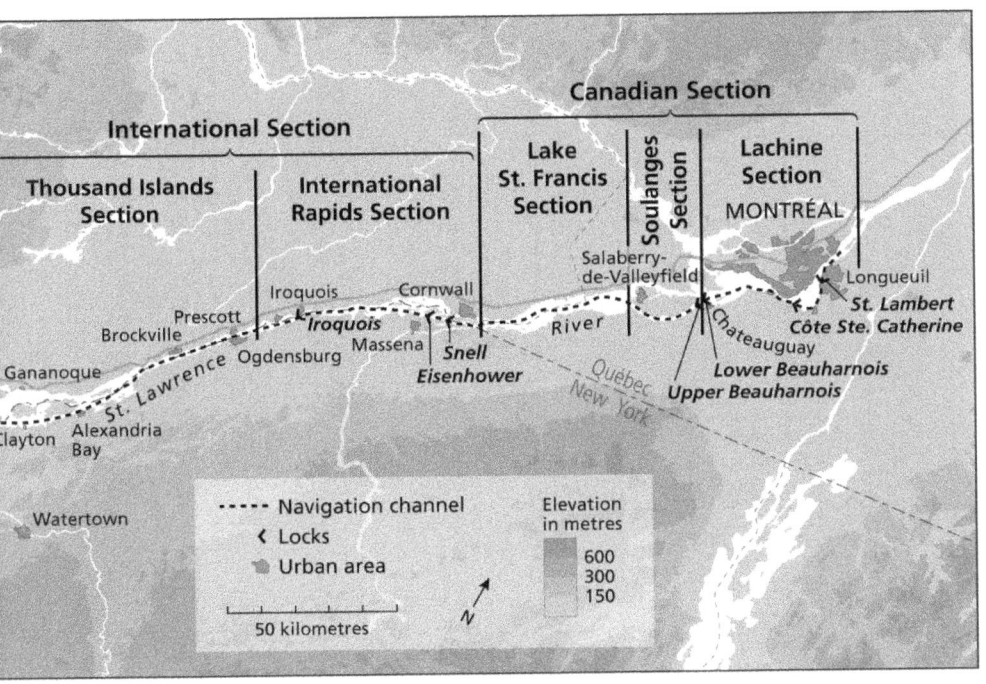

enormous machines. The St. Lawrence power project required three dams in the international stretch of the St. Lawrence between Ontario and New York: the Moses-Saunders powerhouse, the Long Sault spillway dam, and the Iroquois control dam. These dams created Lake St. Lawrence, which inundated some 20,000 acres of land on the Canadian side, along with another 18,000 acres on the US shore. On the much more heavily populated Canadian side, 225 farms, 7 villages, and 3 hamlets (often referred to as the Lost Villages), part of an eighth village, 18 cemeteries, around 1,000 cottages, and over 100 kilometres of the main east-west highway and main line railway were relocated. So as not to create navigation and other difficulties in the new lake, *everything* had to be moved, razed, or flattened, including trees and cemeteries.

The bill for the entire project was over $1 billion. Despite toll revenue the Seaway was never able to be self-financing, as traffic on the Seaway

FIGURE 9.2. St. Lawrence Seaway lock across from Montreal. Used with permission of Library and Archives Canada.

never came anywhere close to predictions. Environmental issues were of virtually no concern to the various agencies and governments involved and any potential side effects were generally considered necessary collateral damage. On top of reconfiguring a river basin, the waterway allowed invasive species to come in via the ballast water of vessels.[11]

Measures to regulate Lake Ontario water levels had been part of the IJC's engineering plans for the St. Lawrence power project, but the issue of Lake Ontario levels was turned into a separate IJC docket in the early 1950s after shore owners complained about the effects of fluctuating water levels. Thus, as part of the St. Lawrence dual project engineers had to establish a "river profile" and develop a "method of regulation" for the St. Lawrence River and Lake Ontario. The "method of regulation" referred to the levels between which the water would be maintained by dams and control works in order to meet prescribed goals. The main future users of the St. Lawrence Seaway and Power Project at the time it was designed—power production, navigation, shoreline property, and downstream interests—wanted different minimum and maximum water levels or varying ranges of stages (i.e., difference between high and low levels), and pleasing everyone seemed impossible.

The engineering goal between 1954 and 1959 was to maintain the water levels at an average that equated to "natural levels," but also to improve on nature by removing the extremes of high and low flows in order to create a predictable and orderly river and lake. "Natural" was defined as that which had existed in the nineteenth century before the first human alterations to water levels—i.e., what existed before Canada installed the Gut Dam in the St. Lawrence River between Galops and Adams islands in the early twentieth century. Yet establishing exactly what constituted a "state of nature" was problematic from the outset. Not only did representatives of the two countries disagree upon the historic impact of the Gut Dam, partly for partisan reasons, but it was also difficult to find information regarding the natural levels to use as a baseline. There were concerns that past measurements were unreliable, a problem that exacerbated by the geological phenomenon of earth tilt, as well as a 1944 earthquake centred between Cornwall and Massena. Indeed, engineering studies were showing that natural factors must have played a much larger role in the recent rise in Lake Ontario water levels than had anthropogenic factors (i.e., diversions into the Great Lakes basin).

Along the way, there were many engineering miscalculations, assumptions, compromises, and partisan preferences. Part of the problem stemmed from the faith that the engineers placed in their models. The experts essentially admitted behind closed doors that they did not know what natural conditions were, and in many ways were guessing. Granted, hydraulic engineers have always used incremental "cut and try" methods. They kept revising the method of regulation and debating what the water levels should be kept at—ultimately, the idea of 248 feet "as nearly as may be" prevailed. In July 1956 the IJC issued a supplementary order directing that Lake Ontario levels be maintained between 244 and 248 feet, again adding the "as nearly as may be" rider. Yet soon after, method 12-A-9 was replaced by another method, 1958-A. The method that stood for over half a century was arrived at, and was titled 1958-D (eventually the qualifier "with deviations" was incorporated). The precise technical differences between these methods are not important here—rather, it is the frequency of changes and the decision-making manner that are noteworthy because they betray how messy and reactive the process of regulating the river levels actually was. As will be discussed below, a new method of regulation was finally enacted in 2017.

Ogoki–Long Lac Diversions

These two diversions are technically separate but they are often considered together because they both divert into Lake Superior water that originally drained north to James Bay. Combined, they constitute the largest anthropogenic diversion into the Great Lakes basin, putting in roughly the same amount of water as the Chicago Diversion takes out. Ontario had first proposed these dual diversions in the 1920s as part of diplomatic discussions about Niagara Falls and other Great Lakes–St. Lawrence water issues. In 1940, the federal governments did conclude an arrangement, through exchanges of notes, for Ontario to use water diverted from the Albany River basin into the Great Lakes for power generation, chiefly on the Niagara Frontier.

The Long Lac Diversion, completed in 1941, connects the headwaters of the Kenogami River with the Aguasabon River, which naturally discharges into Lake Superior about 250 kilometres east of Thunder Bay, Ontario. The Ogoki Diversion, completed in 1943, connects the upper portion of the Ogoki River to Lake Nipigon and from there flows into Lake Superior, 96 kilometres east of Thunder Bay. These diversions were primarily developed to generate hydroelectric power.[12] Article iii of the 1950 Niagara River Diversion Treaty (see below) provides that waters diverted by Long Lac and Ogoki shall continue to be governed by diplomatic notes. This arrangement provides flexibility in operation because no diversion amounts are specified, but initial use at Niagara Falls was to be 5,000 cubic feet per second (cfs). The actual diversion rates vary frequently (maximum and minimum annual combined diversions have been about 8,000 cfs and 2,500 cfs, respectively) so the governments continue to use the constant figure of 5,000 cfs as a pragmatic way to calculate shares instead of actual diversion amounts as permitted by the notes. Although the diversions are controlled by Canada, examples of mutual co-operation occurred in 1952, 1973, and 1985 when, in response to a request by the United States, Canada reduced or stopped both diversions in an attempt to alleviate problems created by high lake levels. The amount of water diverted into Lake Superior by these diversions is reported by Ontario Power Generation (formerly Ontario Hydro) to the IJC through its International Lake Superior Board of Control.

These diversions increase the mean level of each of the Great Lakes: Lake Superior by 6.4 centimetres (0.21 feet); Lakes Michigan-Huron by 11.3 centimetres (0.37 feet); Lake Erie by 7.6 centimetres (0.25 feet); and Lake Ontario by 6.7 centimetres (0.22 feet).[13] Together they have had significant local environmental effects on fish spawning areas and habitat as a result of the original construction and operation of diversion structures on the main stem rivers, the construction and alteration of diversion channels, the creation of reservoirs, the greatly altered flow regimes, and the use of waterways for log transportation. As is usually the case when water is manipulated on a large scale in the Great Lakes–St. Lawrence basin, particularly for hydroelectric developments, Indigenous Peoples bear the brunt of the direct impacts since they historically utilized sites conducive to hydroelectric developments—thus it is possible to discern a pattern of "hydraulic imperialism" on the part of North American governments.

Niagara Falls

Niagara Falls was itself another major water issue that had been included in the half-century of St. Lawrence Seaway discussions.[14] Large-scale hydroelectric production and distribution from a central station had its birth at Niagara Falls in the late nineteenth century. By the 1920s, there were multiple hydro-power stations operating on both sides of Niagara. Water was diverted away from the Horseshoe and American Falls (the two main cataracts that make up Niagara Falls) in order to supply the various power houses. Before the end of the nineteenth century public concerns were raised about the aesthetic impact of decreased water levels on the Falls, as well as the industry that crowded the shoreline to take advantage of the water power.

Both the American Burton Act (1906) and the Boundary Waters Treaty put restrictions on the amount of water that could be diverted away from the Falls. In response to public worries about the scenic grandeur and diversions, Canada and the United States formed the International Niagara Board of Control in 1923, followed by a Special International Niagara Board in 1925. In an interim report that utilized photographs and aerial surveys, the Special International Niagara Board proposed the use of weirs (submerged barriers) designed to strategically divert water from the middle part of the Horseshoe Falls to the edges. This would improve the appearance of the crestline, both in quantity and colour. Based on the Special International Niagara Board's interim report, the Niagara Convention and Protocol was signed in 1929 by both countries. However, this Niagara convention was not able to make it through the US Senate.

In 1931 the Special International Niagara Board released a report titled "Preservation and Improvement of the Scenic Beauty of the Niagara Falls and Rapids." The report examined whether it was the height, width, volume, colour, or lines that made Niagara such a spectacle. The report's sections on water colour were fascinating, and a special "telecolorimeter" was developed to test for the desired "greenish-blue" colour, which was considered superior to the whitish colour resulting from a thin flow over the precipice. The excessive mist and spray at Horseshoe Falls was considered a turn-off since it obscured the view and, unsurprisingly, got people wet. The denuded bare rock at the flanks of the Horseshoe Falls was labelled as one of the greatest detriments to the visual appeal, and erosion threatened to ruin the symmetry of the Falls (the lip receded upstream several feet per year). The report concluded that a sufficiently distributed volume of flow, or at least the "impression of volume," which would create an unbroken crestline, was most important.

The board therefore recommended that the riverbed above Niagara Falls, and the Falls themselves, be manipulated in order to apportion the necessary volume of water to achieve the desired effect. Remedial works, in the form of submerged weirs and excavations, would achieve that while allowing for increased power diversions. Such measures had been included in the failed 1932 Great Lakes Waterway Treaty and the 1941 St. Lawrence executive agreement. During the Second World War the two countries agreed that the limits on the amount of water diverted at Niagara Falls

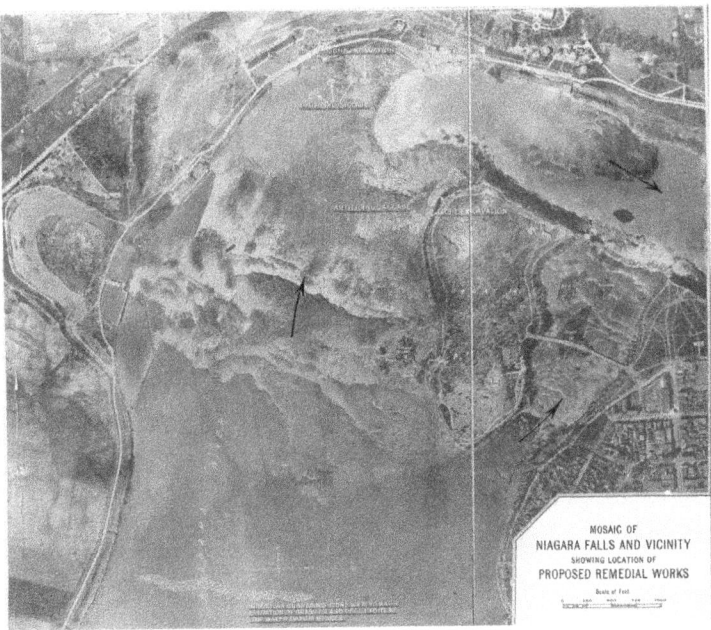

FIGURE 9.3. Proposed Niagara Remedial Works. Library and Archives Canada.

for war-time needs could be temporarily increased. Subsequently, further withdrawals were allowed during the war, rising to a total diversion of 54,000 cfs for Canada and 32,500 cfs for the United States (out of a total river flow of about 200,000 cfs). Canada and the United States agreed to split the cost of constructing a stone-filled weir—a submerged dam—above the Falls, which would raise the water level in order to facilitate greater diversions without an apparent loss of scenic beauty.

What were initially wartime diversions continued on an indefinite—and technically illegal—basis after the end of the Second World War. The two countries separated the Niagara diversion issues from the repeatedly stalled St. Lawrence negotiations, and the Niagara River Diversion Treaty was signed in February 1950. This Canadian-American accord called for further remedial works, to be approved by the IJC, and virtually equalized water diversions while restricting the flow of water over Niagara Falls to no less than 100,000 cfs during daylight hours of what was deemed the tourist season (8 a.m. to 10 p.m. from April to mid-September, and from

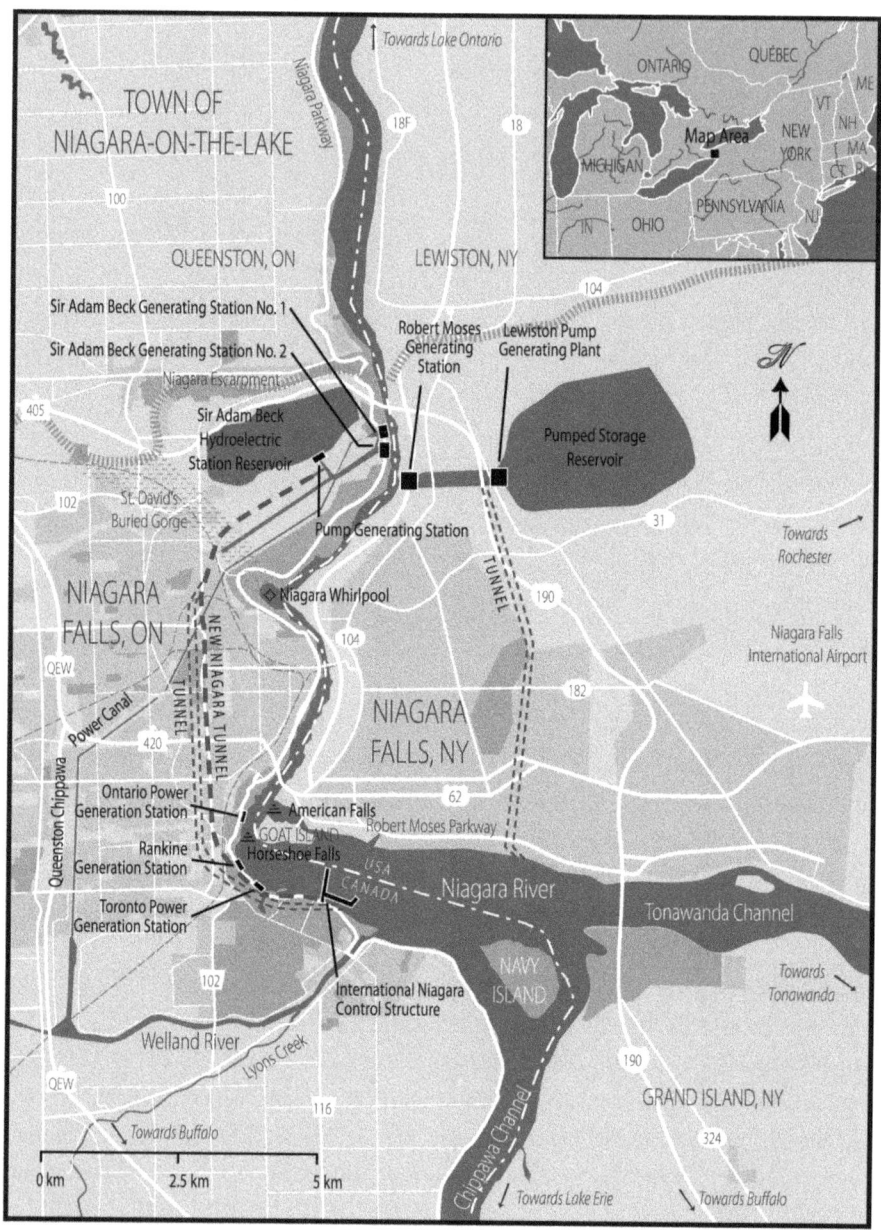

Figure 9.4. Niagara waterscape. Map by Rajiv Ravat, Anders Sandberg, and Daniel Macfarlane.

8 a.m. to 8 p.m. during the fall), and no less than 50,000 cfs during the remainder of the year. This worked out to Canada and the United States together taking about one-half of the total flow over the Falls during tourist hours, and three-quarters the remainder—and majority—of the time.

IJC engineering studies showed that, without remedial works, the diversions authorized in the 1950 treaty would have a very negative impact on the scenic beauty of the area: the Chippawa–Grass Island Pool level would drop by as much as four feet, exposing areas of the riverbed, lowering levels on Lake Erie, turning the American Falls into an unsightly spectacle, and greatly reducing the appearance of the flanks of the Horseshoe Falls.[15] In 1953 reports by the IJC and its International Niagara Falls Engineering Board, the objectives remained basically the same as they had been in the 1920s and '30s: to ensure the appearance of an unbroken and satisfactory crestline while allowing for the diversion of water for power production. A 1,550 foot control dam was built from the Canadian shore, parallel to and about 225 feet downstream from the weir built in the 1940s, featuring 13 sluices (5 more were soon added) equipped with control gates. The purpose of this structure was to control water levels and spread out the water, both for appearance and because flows concentrated in certain places caused more erosion damage. The diverted water went to the hydroelectric stations downstream. To create a better distribution of flow and an unbroken crestline, 64,000 cubic yards of rock were excavated on the Canadian flank, and 24,000 cubic yards on the American flank. To compensate for erosion, crest fills (55 feet on the Canadian shore and 300 feet on the American side) shrunk the Horseshoe Falls, with the reclaimed edges fenced and landscaped in order to provide prime public vantage points.

The Ontario and New York public power utilities, with the blessing of the IJC, soon tried to further increase the amount of water diverted from the Niagara River. But public opposition proved too big of an obstacle. Then local interests in Niagara Falls, New York, began a public relations effort of sorts to "save" the American Falls (and increase tourism to the American side). This campaign to preserve and enhance the American Falls formally began in 1965 and stretched into the 1970s; ultimately, the IJC and involved governments decided not to remove the talus at the bottom of the smaller Niagara waterfall and let "nature take its course."[16] This represented a significant shift in philosophy and approach, from both the IJC and the hydraulic engineering profession.

The various water control works installed in the Niagara River, along with other channel modifications such as bridge piers, channel filling, and shoreline reclamation, collectively constrict the river and raise the level of Lake Erie in the neighbourhood of half a foot.[17] Currently, the IJC's International Niagara Board of Control monitors operation of the control works by the power entities, Ontario Power Generation and the New York Power Authority, under an IJC directive.

Chicago Redux

Because of its importance in the history of Great Lakes diversions, we now return to the issue of the Chicago Diversion through the Sanitary and Ship Canal at Chicago, which is not subject to the Boundary Waters Treaty since it predated the 1909 accord. This diversion consists of three components: 1) water supply withdrawn directly from Lake Michigan for domestic and industrial purposes and then discharged into the Illinois River as treated sewage; 2) run-off that once drained to Lake Michigan but is now diverted to the Illinois River; and 3) water diverted directly from Lake Michigan into the Illinois River and canal system for navigation and dilution purposes in the Chicago area.

The Chicago Diversion was effectively limited by a 1930 US Supreme Court decision to 3,200 cfs on an annual basis. The United States appealed for an extension due to worries that low water levels would threaten public health conditions in Chicago, as financial difficulties stemming from the Depression had caused work to cease on sewage disposal work. Capping the Chicago Diversion had also figured prominently in Niagara and St. Lawrence Seaway negotiations over the first half of the twentieth century (in fact, the Chicago Diversion may have indirectly killed US legislative approval of the 1932 St. Lawrence treaty). At several times in the 1950s, the Chicago Diversion was allowed to be increased temporarily. In 1967, a US Supreme Court ruling put the diversions back to 3,200 cfs. In the 1980s, the Corps of Engineers looked at tripling the volume of the diversion, and then the State of Illinois requested the diversion be upped to 10,000 cfs. In the 1990s, it turned out that Chicago was often exceeding the diversion limit, though sometimes by accident; that was apparently taken care of, and the diversion has of late been kept within its legislated bounds. According to the IJC, the diversion reduces the mean level of Lakes Michigan and Huron by 6.4 centimetres (0.21 feet), Lake Erie by 4.3 centimetres (0.14 feet), and Lake Ontario by 3.0 centimetres (0.10 feet).[18] Although the average diversion rate remains constant, the potential for increases remains a concern for Canada and those living nearby in the United States who could be impacted by higher water levels or velocities.

Current debate about the Chicago Diversion tends to focus on it as a vector for invasive species—Asian carp specifically. There is a long history of foreign organisms entering the Great Lakes basin, both before and after the creation of the St. Lawrence Seaway. Since the 1950s, the majority of pernicious, accidentally introduced species—such as zebra and quagga mussels—have arrived via the ballast water of Seaway vessels. But now the looming worry in terms of invasives is that Asian carp will enter the Great Lakes basin through the Chicago Sanitary and Ship Canal.[19] Biodiversity and invasive species are an issue that the IJC has not addressed for most of its history, though Annex 6, which addresses aquatic invasive species, was added to the Great Lakes Water Quality Agreement in 2012, along with other annexes on contemporary concerns such as climate change.

Understanding Great Lakes Water Levels

Levels in the Great Lakes have always fluctuated under the influence of natural forces, including the major ones of precipitation and evaporation and also winds, barometric pressure, ice jams, glacial rebound, aquatic weed growth, and, to some extent, tides. There are of course long-term fluctuations, seasonal fluctuations, and short-term fluctuations due to storms, winds, and pressure changes. Humanity has progressively intervened in the natural regime of the Great Lakes system, including the direct regulation of Lakes Superior and Ontario, dredging in the connecting channels, diversions, and consumptive uses. Over the last century, scientific understanding of "natural" lake levels has itself fluctuated.

The vast surface area of the Great Lakes, combined with the natural restrictions of their connecting channels, makes it possible for the system to cope with huge water supply variations while maintaining water level fluctuations of one to two feet in any one year. Depending on which lake one considers, the maximum range of water level fluctuations has only been about four to seven feet in the 150 years since records have been kept. Older records are not as accurate as current observations, since both countries did not develop a wide network of level gauges until the early twentieth century. By the First World War the Canadian Hydrographic Service had installed 27 automatic gauges in the Great Lakes–St. Lawrence basin, though only 11 were open year-round (by 1926 there were 40 Canadian gauges open year-round).[20] The US Army Corps of Engineer's Lake Survey was busy doing the same. Even with these improvements, which were primarily aimed at benefitting navigation, the limited dispersal of gauges as well as their technological limitations meant that knowledge about water levels was still subject to a great deal of uncertainty. Nonetheless, gauges, soundings, and charting were necessary for establishing the baseline information upon which later engineering manipulations could be based. It is clear that, by the immediate post–Second World War period, at least some engineers and government experts had a solid understanding of the natural causes of Great Lakes fluctuations.

Long-term fluctuations occur over periods of consecutive years and have varied dramatically since water levels have been recorded for the Great Lakes. Continuous wet and cold years cause water levels to rise. Conversely, consecutive warm and dry years cause water levels to decline. The Great Lakes system experienced extremely low levels in the late 1920s, mid-1930s, in the mid-1960s, and in the early 2000s. Extremely high water levels were experienced in the 1870s, early 1950s, early 1970s, mid-1980s, mid-1990s, and currently. While various cycles of low and high water levels follow a variable schedule that is not entirely predictable, climate change already seems to be introducing even more uncertainty into these cycles. In the early 2000s Lakes Michigan and Huron experienced record lows, but now *all* the lakes, including Lake Ontario, are now experiencing record highs.

Over the last fifty years, the IJC has completed several reference studies on Great Lakes water level issues. In 1964, when water levels were very low, the governments asked the IJC whether it would be feasible to maintain the waters of all the Great Lakes at a more constant level. This study was completed in 1973, when lake levels had risen to record highs. The

IJC then advised the governments in its 1976 report "Further Regulation of the Great Lakes" that the high costs (economic and environmental) of engineering further regulation of Lakes Michigan and Huron could not be justified by the benefits.[21] The same conclusion was reached during another IJC study in 1983 on regulating outflows, specifically from Lake Erie.

In 1985, the IJC submitted its report under a reference on consumptive uses and diversions—especially the effects of existing diversions into and out of the Great Lakes system, as well as on the possibility of adjusting these diversions to help regulate water levels. Prior to this IJC study, consumptive use (e.g., agriculture, bottled water, and pop) had not been considered significant because the volume of water in the system is so large. The study concluded that climate and weather changes affect lake levels far more than existing anthropogenic diversions and uses, and it recommended that governments not consider the manipulation of existing diversions to either raise low levels or decrease high levels. In 1986, during a period of record high water levels, governments asked the IJC to examine and report on methods to alleviate the adverse consequences of fluctuating water levels in the Great Lakes–St. Lawrence River basin. The IJC's final recommendations, delivered in its 1993 report (when the high levels had receded), included a range of actions such as promoting shoreline management measures; a recommendation that five as well as three lake regulation not be further considered; establishing a binational information centre; and improving data gathering and analysis.

Primarily as a result of public outcry over a proposal to export water from Lake Superior by tanker in 1999, governments asked the IJC to examine and report on how the consumptive use and removal of water, diversions, and management and policies regarding water resources affect the levels, flows, and sustainability of water supplies in transboundary basins. Governments are using the findings, conclusions, and recommendations of the IJC's 2000 and 2004 reports as they address the many issues related to water use in the Great Lakes basin. The governments asked the IJC to review its recommendations again at ten-year intervals unless conditions dictate a more frequent review. The governments have not responded to the IJC's recommendation that they consider adopting a plan of work for the IJC on the rest of the border beyond the Great Lakes.

Large Diversion Threats

As the ability to move water long distances expanded in the last half of the twentieth century, so too did the threat of large-scale transfers. As a result, a number of major diversions at several locations on the North American continent have been propounded over the past decades.[22] There is a perception in the Great Lakes basin of a need for water elsewhere, especially in the arid US Southwest. However no major diversion from the Great Lakes basin is under formal consideration at the present time, and none of these concepts is currently proposed or endorsed by any government directly involved in the management of the water. Two schemes in particular have received some attention over the years and are noted briefly below.

The Great Recycling and Northern Development (GRAND) canal concept was first advocated in 1959 by Thomas Kierans. In this proposal, James Bay was to be diked, creating a freshwater lake, the waters of which could be diverted/recycled to the Great Lakes and on to the western United States and even Mexico. Stepped pumping and flow control structures would be required in the transmission system. The distribution system from the Great Lakes would include new two-way channel and pump transfer arrangements connecting the major rivers that drain the mid-continent and the Canadian Prairies. Reliable estimates of costs and benefits have never been available, although Kierans estimated the costs would be $79 billion with a construction time of eight years. While a few officials, such as former Quebec premier Robert Bourassa, asserted that the proposal would have multiple economic and other benefits, most argue that the direct costs are astronomical and that the project is likely to have devastating and irreversible ecological effects.

The North American Water and Power Alliance (NAWAPA) scheme was first presented in 1963 by Ralph M. Parsons and Co., a firm of engineering consultants. It involved diverting water from major rivers in Alaska, British Columbia, and the Yukon to a reservoir in the Rocky Mountain Trench. From there it would be redirected for consumption in the western United States and Canada. In 1963 NAWAPA's total cost was estimated at about $100 billion with construction taking about twenty years. Hostile public reaction and the question of feasibility quashed the idea in its infancy and, as far as can be determined, the scheme is not now being seriously considered by any government or proponent.

Recent Charters, Annexes, and Agreements

Water management in the Great Lakes basin is governed by a network of legal regimes, including international instruments and customs, federal laws and regulations in both Canada and the United States, the laws of the eight Great Lakes states and the provinces of Ontario and Quebec, and the rights of Indigenous Peoples under Canadian and US laws.[23] A number of diversion threats were mainly within US borders, and resulting legal and legislative steps to prevent such diversions were thus internal US matters that were not subject to IJC approval. In 1985, the eight states and two provinces bordering the Great Lakes–St. Lawrence basin adopted a new policy resolution: the Great Lakes Charter. The purpose of the Great Lakes Charter, which was a non-binding, good-faith agreement, was to provide the opportunity for basin-wide management. Any plan proposed in any Great Lakes state or province that involved major consumptive use or diversion had to give prior notice to, and seek approval from, all other states and provinces. However, as noted above the charter was not binding, and holes soon appeared. For example, the possibility of bulk exports out of the Great Lakes basin surfaced, as did the transfer of water to smaller communities in the United States straddling or just outside of the Great Lakes basin.[24]

The 2001 annex to the charter committed the parties to develop binding regulations to ensure no net loss to the waters through diversion or consumption or through adverse impacts on water quality, with a commitment to ensuring public input. In 2005 the Great Lakes–St. Lawrence River Basin Sustainable Water Resources Agreement (a non-binding agreement that included Ontario and New York) was inked; it was the international companion to the binding Great Lakes–St. Lawrence River Basin Water Resources Compact, which exclusively involved American jurisdictions and came into effect in 2008. These new agreements, which do not involve the IJC, ban new or increased water diversions out of the Great Lakes–St. Lawrence basin, with some strictly regulated exceptions.[25] The states and provinces also pledged to use a consistent standard to review proposed uses of basin water and a decision-support system to manage withdrawals. In addition, each state and province is to develop and implement a water conservation and efficiency program. The Council of Great Lakes Governors serves as secretariat to the Great Lakes–St. Lawrence River Basin Water Resources Regional Body and the Great Lakes–St. Lawrence River Basin Water Resources Council, both of which were created to coordinate implementation and follow-through of the agreement and compact.

Another legal issue that has been raised is whether international trade obligations, in particular the relevant World Trade Organization agreements, including the General Agreement on Tariffs and Trade, as well as the Canada–United States Free Trade Agreement and the Canada–United States–Mexico North American Free Trade Agreement (NAFTA), might affect water management in the Great Lakes basin and, in particular, commodify water. The IJC, in its 2000 and 2004 reports, concluded that international trade agreements do not prevent the governments of the United States and Canada from protecting water as it resides in the Great Lakes and their tributary rivers and streams if there is no discrimination against persons from other countries and undue expectations are not created. The governments of Canada and the United States supported this conclusion. However, because the IJC believed some concern still remained in the public's opinion, the commission recommended that the governments need to make a greater effort to clarify this issue for the public, including continuing to demonstrate that future trade agreements will not affect the ability of governments to protect water resources like the Great Lakes. The current draft of the new United States-Mexico-Canada Agreement, intended to replace NAFTA, contains a chapter on the environment; what this will mean for the Great Lakes–St. Lawrence ecosystem is difficult to predict at this point.

The IJC is now in the process of transitioning, in a way, to a new approach under the Boundary Waters Treaty. For approximately the last fifteen years, the IJC has been developing its International Watershed Initiative (IWI) as a new means of transboundary governance that allows for flexibility. The IJC is well positioned to contribute to effective, multi-layered, adaptive governance. The development of the IWI, and the creation of international watershed boards, illustrate the fact that the IJC (and transboundary water governance in general) is at a crossroads in terms of meeting the environmental challenges of the twenty-first century within the framework of the 1909 Boundary Waters Treaty. After a century of addressing many issues arising under the treaty, the evolution to international watershed boards by the IJC is one of the new concepts in transboundary environmental governance and holds great promise to help "prevent and resolve" transboundary disputes between Canada and the United States in the next century. Successful implementation is requiring the IJC to reconsider the Boundary Waters Treaty's essential purpose, as well as new and emerging natural-resource management trends in and between the United States and Canada.

St. Lawrence–Lake Ontario Levels Revisited

As far back as the 1990s, in response to recommendations in IJC board reports and growing public dissatisfaction with Plan 1958-D and the IJC Order of Approval, the IJC seriously began investigating the regulation of water levels and flows in the Lake Ontario–St. Lawrence River system. After a number of false starts the IJC finally received approval and funds from both governments to begin a five-year, $20 million study in December 2000. However this government approval and funding was predicated on an IJC commitment to *not* make any changes without the concurrence of both governments. An IJC study board was appointed and reported in May 2006. In 2008, after considering the study board's report, the IJC invited comment on a proposed new order and regulation plan known as Plan 2007, which was based on one of the three options recommended by the study board.

But Plan 2007 received widespread opposition and the commissioners decided something new was needed. In 2009 a working group was established with senior officials appointed by the two federal governments and the sub-federal governments of New York, Ontario, and Quebec. This was a clear indication that some political as well as technical and scientific expertise would be needed to resolve this matter. Of the many regulation plans developed, the working group determined that a variation of a plan called Bv7, resulting in more natural flows and lake levels, was preferable. The group worked to refine this plan, which the IJC then developed into Plan 2014 (hoping it would be implemented by that year). The existing plan (Plan 1958-D with deviations) unnaturally compressed water levels and harmed coastal ecosystems, impacts which were not understood when the project was initially approved. Plan 2014 aimed to help restore plant diversity and habitat for fish and wildlife by allowing more natural variability in water levels while continuing to moderate extreme high and low levels. After seeking public input, and further IJC study, Plan 2014 was approved in December 2016 and enacted the following month.[26] Unfortunately, the initiation of Plan 2014 coincided with record precipitation throughout the Lake Ontario–St. Lawrence basin, in both 2017 and 2019, which resulted in extreme flooding on Lake Ontario, the Ottawa River, and the upper St. Lawrence River. Residents on the south shore of Lake Ontario were outspoken in their criticism of the new regulation plan; but these criticisms are mostly misplaced, since in instances of extreme natural supply any method of regulation can have only a minimal impact on water levels and flooding would take place regardless.

Conclusion

Legal scholar Marcia Valiante identifies a number of factors that have enabled the successful management of Great Lakes water quality and quantity, most of which are reflections of the IJC's role: equality; common vision and common objectives; different scales of action; strong scientific foundation; active community participation; good governance mechanisms; accountability and adaptability; partnerships; binationalism.[27] However, while those conclusions may be valid for the period from the 1960s to the present, the first half-century of the IJC's existence do not warrant many of these positive assessments.

As this chapter has shown, the IJC's behaviour, role, and function in terms of Great Lakes governance has changed significantly over time. Up to about the time of the Second World War, the IJC focused mainly on apportioning water resources, with mixed results. A number of large-scale endeavours, during which the politicization of the IJC was apparent, characterized the two postwar decades. Beginning with notable successes, such as facing Great Lakes water pollution, the IJC transitioned into a period—which arguably continues to the present—in which it has successfully dealt with a wide range of issues. The IJC's flexibility and anticipatory ability, the trust it has engendered among the public and activist groups, combined with its invocation of scientific and engineering expertise, give it a unique character and quality that resists easy theoretical generalization. The IJC continues to blend aspects of the bureaucratic and post-bureaucratic models, though it has increasingly moved toward the latter. Likewise, the IJC has displayed elements of both a capacity-building and regulatory institution. It also stands as an example of "fragmented bilateralism" and the "rational-legal authority" approach to international relations. While the history of the IJC does not fully support the sub-state actor hypothesis, the future of Great Lakes governance (Great Lakes–St. Lawrence River Basin Water Resources Council) may well run in that direction.

Looking to the future, although the historical perspective provided in this chapter demonstrates the importance of utilizing scientific expertise through the IJC, we also should be cautious about the extent to which the two nations should even be attempting to "manage" extremely large and complex ecosystems such as the Great Lakes, particularly given uncertainty about the future impacts of climate change on water levels in the basin. History shows that there are always unintended consequences, and often these are as bad, or worse, than the original problem.

Notes

1. On Canadian-American border waters generally, see Lynne Heasley and Daniel Macfarlane, *Border Flows: A Century of the Canadian-American Water Relationship* (Calgary: University of Calgary Press, 2016). For an overview of border hydro developments, see Daniel Macfarlane, "Fluid Relations: Hydro Developments, the International Joint Commission, and Canada-U.S. Border Waters," in *Towards Continental Environmental Policy? North American Transnational Environmental Networks and Governance*, ed. Peter Stoett and Owen Temby (Albany: SUNY Press, 2017).

2. Note that the Erie and Oswego Canals did take a small amount of water out of the Great Lakes basin.

3. D. H. Bennion and B. A. Manny, "Construction of shipping channels in the Detroit River—History and environmental consequences," *US Geological Survey Scientific Investigations Report* (Washington: US Geological Survey Scientific Investigations Report 2011–5122), https://pubs.usgs.gov/sir/2011/5122/. On the Detroit River, see

also John Hartig, *Waterfront Porch: Reclaiming Detroit's Industrial Waterfront as a Gathering Place for All* (Lansing: Michigan State University Press, 2019); Ramya Swayamprakash, "Dredge a River, Make a Nation Great: Shipping, Commerce, and Territoriality in the Detroit River, 1870–1905," *Michigan Historical Review* 45, no. 1 (Spring 2019): 27–46.

4   See Daniel Macfarlane and Lynne Heasley, "Fish, Water, and Oil: The Chicago River as a Transnational Matrix of Place" in *City of Lake and Prairie: Chicago's Environmental History*, ed. Kathleen Brosnan, Will Barnett, and Ann Keating (Pittsburgh: University of Pittsburgh Press, forthcoming).

5   On this region see Jamie Benidickson, *Levelling the Lake: Transboundary Resource Management in the Lake of the Woods Watershed* (Vancouver: UBC Press, 2019).

6   On the environmental history of Lake Superior, see Nancy Langston, *Sustaining Lake Superior: An Extraordinary Lake in a Changing World* (New Haven, CT: Yale University Press, 2017).

7   This section on the St. Lawrence Seaway and Power Project is derived from Daniel Macfarlane, *Negotiating a River: Canada, the US, and the Creation of the St. Lawrence Seaway* (Vancouver: UBC Press, 2014).

8   The 1941 St. Lawrence accord was actually an executive agreement, and it was a comprehensive St. Lawrence–Great Lakes agreement that covered many transborder water bodies in the basin.

9   This was not the first time that the IJC had formed a board or investigation on a St. Lawrence issues—e.g., a dam at Waddington, New York, and the Massena Power Canal attracted the IJC's attention around the time of the First World War.

10 Daniel Macfarlane, "Negotiated High Modernism: Canada and the St. Lawrence Seaway and Power Project," in *Made Modern: Science and Technology in Canadian History*, ed. Edward Jones-Imhotep and Tina Adcock (Vancouver: University of British Columbia Press, 2018).

11 On invasive species, see Jeff Alexander, *Pandora's Locks: The Opening of the Great Lakes-St. Lawrence Seaway* (Lansing: Michigan State University Press, 2009); Dan Egan, *The Death and Life of the Great Lakes* (New York: Norton, 2017).

12 In the case of the Long Lac Diversion the transportation of the pulpwood logs southward was also a minor consideration—aspects of this diversion had actually begun operating in the late 1930s for the purposes of moving wood.

13 International Joint Commission, *Great Lakes Diversions and Consumptive Uses: Final Report* (1985).

14 Information in this section is derived from Daniel Macfarlane, "Creating a Cataract: The Transnational Manipulation of Niagara Falls to the 1950s," in *Urban Explorations: Environmental Histories of the Toronto Region*, ed. C. Coates, S. Bocking, K. Cruikshank, and A. Sandberg (Hamilton, ON: L. R. Wilson Institute for Canadian Studies-McMaster University, 2013); Daniel Macfarlane, " 'A Completely Man-Made and Artificial Cataract': The Transnational Manipulation of Niagara Falls,"

15   *Environmental History* 18, no. 4 (October 2013): 759–84; and a forthcoming book on Niagara Falls by Macfarlane.

15   The method of regulation was later revised because it became apparent that the operation of the Niagara remedial works and levels in the Chippawa–Grass Island Pool lowered Lake Erie levels by a few centimetres.

16   See Daniel Macfarlane, "Saving Niagara from Itself: The Campaign to Preserve and Enhance the American Falls, 1965–1975," *Environment and History* 25, no. 4 (November 2019): 916-943.

17   Frank F. Quinn, "Anthropogenic Changes to Great Lakes Water Levels," *Great Lakes Update* 136 (1999): 3.

18   IJC, 1985.

19   Andrew Reeves, *Overrun: Dispatches from the Asian Carp Crisis* (Toronto: ECW Press, 2019).

20   O. M. Meehan (edited by William Glover and David Gray), "The Canadian Hydrographic Service: From the time of its inception in 1883 to the end of the Second World War," *The Northern Mariner/Le marin du Nord* 19, no. 1 (January 2004): 1–158.

21   International Joint Commission, International Great Lakes Levels Board, *Report on Further Regulation of the Great Lakes* (1976).

22   IJC, 1985.

23   IJC, "Protection of the Great Lakes Report," February 2000.

24   Peter Annin, *Great Lakes Water Wars*, 2nd ed. (Washington, DC: Island Press, 2018).

25   Exceptions include communities that straddle the water basin divide that will use the diverted water for public water supply purposes, potentially having to return it to the basin. On the charter/agreement and its history, see Daniel Macfarlane and Noah Hall, "Transborder Water Management and Governance in the Great Lakes-St. Lawrence Basin," in *Transboundary Environmental Governance Across the World's Longest Border*, ed. Stephen Brooks and Andrea Olive (East Lansing: Michigan State University Press, 2018).

26   In the summer of 2013, the IJC invited public comment and convened public hearings on the proposed Plan 2014. The vast majority of stakeholders were supportive of Plan 2014 and the new order with the exception of a group of a few hundred shoreline property owners based in New York State and their local political leaders. In June 2014 the IJC then submitted a report to governments summarizing its fourteen-year effort to study improved management of water levels and flows in the Lake Ontario–St. Lawrence River system. The report recommended Plan 2014 and working with the governments in the basin to develop adaptive management as an important tool for improving management of the Lake Ontario–St. Lawrence River regulation plan. In similar letters dated 6 December 2016, both governments concurred with the IJC's proposals. The IJC appointed a new International Lake Ontario–St. Lawrence River Board and charged it with implementing the new order and directive. See Murray Clamen and Daniel Macfarlane, "Plan 2014: The Historical Evolution of Lake Ontario-

St. Lawrence River Regulation," *Canadian Water Resources Journal/Revue canadienne des ressources hydriques* 43, no. 4 (December 2018): 416–31

27 Marcia Valiante, "Management of the North American Great Lakes," in *Management of Transboundary Rivers and Lakes*, ed. O. Varis, C. Tortajada, and A. K. Biswas (Berlin: Springer, 2008): 258–60.

10

The International Joint Commission and Air Pollution: A Tale of Two Cases

Owen Temby and Don Munton

Over recent decades the International Joint Commission (IJC) has gradually but completely dropped out, or been pushed out, of the bilateral air pollution governance business. The only air pollution reference the commission received from the Canadian and American governments after 1975 assigned it a token bureaucratic role in the implementation of the 1991 Air Quality Agreement. The IJC's International Air Quality Advisory Board (IAQAB), which once managed an ongoing suite of tasks, became formally inactive in 2012.

To understand the demise of the IJC's role in air pollution during the past few decades we need to understand what it has done in the past and we need to understand its traditional functions. With the Boundary Waters Treaty (BWT) as its basis, the commission has five official functions: arbitral, administrative, quasijudicial, investigatory, and monitoring. Canada and United States have never requested the IJC to function as an arbitrator. They perhaps came close to doing so in one of the cases we consider here (the Trail smelter case). Most often, however, both governments have shown a preference for settling disputes through direct government-to-government negotiations. The IJC's administrative functions have always been minor in scope and importance. The "quasi-judicial" function, under article viii of the BWT, has mostly been seen in the IJC's authority to pass upon cases (or "applications") involving "the use or obstruction or diversion" of waters along the boundary. Much, perhaps most, of the commission's work from its inception to approximately the Second World War involved its quasijudicial authority to approve applications for "remedial or protective works or any dams" affecting boundary waters.[1] These mostly concerned local boundary issues. Such tasks no longer occupy the bulk of the commissioners' time. The dams are mostly built.

The IJC also receives "references." Article ix of the BWT empowers the commission, on request by governments, to conduct investigations and develop recommendations to governments. In contrast to the IJC's applications work, the references have often involved major Canada-US issues, such as Columbia River development and Great Lakes water pollution. The Great Lakes reference became what former commissioner and Canadian cochair Arnold Heeney called "this greatest of the Commission undertakings"; it may have planted the seeds of the IJC's demise.[2]

A change in roles and government perceptions of the commission began in 1972 with the Great Lakes Water Quality Agreement (GLWQA) and the roughly concurrent formalization of the IAQAB. In the GLWQA, Canada and the United States mandated the IJC to act both as an independent "watch dog" and a facilitator in implementing the GLWQA, which the commission attempted to do, albeit with mixed success. These new roles proved contentious to elements in both governments and led to a growing political reluctance to give the IJC new air pollution references. The IJC's watch dog function in air pollution arguably reached an apex in November 1978, when both governments responded to the IJC's recommendation for a long-range air pollution transport research task force to examine the emerging problem of airborne deposition in the Great Lakes region. However, concerns about IJC overreach in air pollution matters had been developing. The governments opted to exclude the IJC from acid rain research and from any involvement with the Bilateral Research Consultation Group on the Long-Range Transport of Air Pollutants. After a decade of conflict between Canada and the United States over acid rain finally gave way to co-operation in the form of the 1991 Air Quality Agreement, the IJC was denied a meaningful role in its implementation.

Instead, Canada and the United States created an alternative, intergovernmental committee and gave the IJC only a token reporting role.

The cases we examine here, the Trail smelter and the Detroit and St. Clair River areas cases, represent the two major IJC investigations into air pollution issues since the commission's inception. Both resulted from references. The fact that no other major issues have been subject to references reflects the reluctance of the two countries to use the IJC to address transboundary air pollution. While the Trail case has received considerable attention from historians and legal scholars, much less has been paid to the politics of transboundary air pollution in the Detroit and St. Clair River areas. There are lessons to be learned from comparing the two cases.[3] Doing so clarifies the limitations to, and potential benefits of, binational air pollution governance.

Case 1: Trail Smelter Dispute

The Trail smelter air pollution case grew out of complaints that sulphur dioxide emissions from a smelter in Trail, British Columbia were damaging farmlands and trees in the state of Washington. It arguably remains, after almost a century, the most widely known case worldwide of resolving an international environmental dispute. It is certainly one of the *loci classici* of international law, and a prominent part of the canon.[4] It was also the first Canada-US air pollution problem the two governments handed the IJC. References to the case abound—but interpretations vary and, on closer examination, misunderstandings exist. We argue here that the IJC was more important to the resolution of the Trail case than most accounts suggest.

Non-ferrous smelters were first established in Trail and in nearby Northport, in Stevens County, Washington, in the mid-1890s.[5] Both used ores from local mines and both were US-owned. The Northport facility operated for about a decade as a copper smelter. Then, after a short closure from 1908 to 1915, the facility briefly reopened to produce lead. Never a large or prosperous operation, it closed permanently in 1921. Its operation and its closure had substantial impacts on the local economy as well as agricultural production.

While in operation as a copper smelter, the Northport facility relied on open-air heap roasting, emitting approximately fifteen tons of sulphur dioxide per day.[6] Local farmers took the smelter owners to court, claiming damages to crops and trees. In response, the company purchased "smoke easements" covering 8,000 acres from fifty farmers, thus implicitly acknowledging its liability. The affected farms were mostly in the immediate Northport area but extended north to the boundary with Canada.

In 1906, just before the Northport facility closed down for the first time, a new company purchased the existing smelter in Trail and various small nearby mines. The Consolidated Mining and Smelting Company (later, Cominco) soon set about expanding smelter operations, based in large part on the new and soon-to-be massive Sullivan Mine in Rossland, British Columbia.[7] The Canadian Pacific Railway bought Consolidated shares and built a railway spur into Trail, thus promoting the Canadian smelter. Consolidated then developed an innovative process to recover its rich lead and zinc supplies. The zinc smelting process adopted involved first turning sulphide ores into zinc sulphate through roasting and then using electrolysis to create "slab zinc."[8] The overall process gave off sulphur dioxide and weak sulphuric acid.

The smelter itself was then, and is still, located in Trail, above the banks of the Columbia River, about seven miles "as the crow flies" from the fabled 49th parallel.[9] It is only slightly further as the river waters flow, through a curving valley, into the United States. Barely nineteen miles by road southward from Trail lies Northport, Washington.[10] From Trail to beyond the international border, the Columbia Valley is bounded by mountains up to 4,500 feet above sea level. The valley is thus in places more of a gorge. Under prevailing wind conditions, it effectively funnels smelter emissions southwards toward the boundary and then into Stevens County in Washington State. Bench lands line much of both sides of the Columbia River south of the boundary. In the early twentieth century, small farms occupied some of these deforested benches on the US side.

As did the emissions of its counterpart in Northport, sulphur dioxide from the Consolidated smelter originally led to local protests. The protests began around 1917, not coincidentally after the Trail plant significantly increased lead and zinc production to meet the growing demands of the First World War. Increased production, of course, led to more emissions of sulphur dioxide and higher concentrations. Total emissions rose from about 10,000 tons of sulphur dioxide per month in 1916 to about 20,000 tons in 1926, a doubling in a decade.[11]

The original Trail smelter smoke stacks were 150 feet high, not enough to disperse the fumes adequately to avoid local air pollution. As had its American counterpart, Consolidated offered financial compensation to those affected in the Trail area and purchased farmland in the Canadian part of the Columbia Valley. (In modern economic jargon, it was "internalizing" what was an "externality.") In the mid-1920s, it also built two new, taller smokestacks, over 400 feet in height, in an effort to disperse the pollutants more "effectively."[12]

Around 1925, a few years after the Washington State smelter had closed permanently and as the Canadian plant expanded, complaints over "fumes" and crop damage attributed to Trail began to mount in Northport. Some people in Stevens County came to blame the higher Consolidated smoke stacks for pushing the sulphur dioxide further down the Columbia.[13] The company investigated and concluded the complaints were not without merit. Its response was to offer compensation to affected parties, and some American farmers accepted these offers. The company also looked into buying up farms in the area—as it had in British Columbia—but was prevented from doing so by Washington State laws against foreign ownership of land. Increasingly angered, Northport area farmers began organizing against the damage caused by the Trail smelter. Their group, the Citizens' Protective Association, refused to take Consolidated's limited compensation and the farmers soon gained the attention of state and national politicians.

International Joint Commission Reference, 1928–31

After receiving the "fumigation" complaints from the citizens and voters in Washington State, the American government pressed Canada for a joint IJC reference to investigate the problem, under article ix of the BWT.[14] Ottawa concurred in 1928. Although the United States and Canada had asked the IJC to investigate boundary water pollution problems in 1912, the Trail case would the first time they had involved the commission in a transboundary air pollution issue. It would not be the last.

The governments requested the IJC to examine and report on 1) the extent to which property in Washington State had been damaged by fumes from the Trail smelter; 2) the appropriate amount of compensation to American interests for these damages; and 3) the impact of future operations of the smelter. Notably, the governments did not explicitly seek recommendations on how to reduce emissions or how to prevent further damage. They did, however, invite the commission to make recommendations on other problems "arising from drifting of fumes" as the IJC deemed appropriate.

The investigation was deliberate and thorough. Given that the commission itself had a small staff and lacked air pollution expertise, the National Research Council of Canada (NRC) assisted the IJC investigation. The NRC made available scientists and other experts, including F. E. Lathe and Morris Katz. Lathe was an experienced metallurgist and knew smelters, having worked previously at facilities in Grand Forks, British Columbia and Sudbury, Ontario. By the early 1930s, he was the head of NRC's research division. Katz was an engineer by training who was becoming an international expert on air pollution and sulphur dioxide emissions in particular. The Canadian federal government also assigned to the investigation A. W. McCallum, a forest pathologist with the Canadian Department of Agriculture. McCallum had assisted with some earlier Sudbury-area forest damage studies before turning to Trail.[15] These and other scientists provided a range of sophisticated and innovative technical services. Regular ground-based air quality monitors were supplemented with atmospheric monitoring of sulphur dioxide concentrations through portable sampling devices carried by aircraft. Tree rings were studied to determine growth patterns, both inside and outside the possibly affected areas. Conifer needles were analyzed to provide a "history" of fumigations. And plants were grown under experimental conditions to assess the impact on them of varying levels of sulphur dioxide. Although McCallum, Katz, Lathe, and other Canadians would dispute some of the American claims for damages in the Trail case, they did ultimately agree the smelter fumes were having a significant impact on farms and trees in the Columbia River basin south of the international boundary and downwind from Trail smelter.[16]

The IJC commissioners held meetings in Northport in 1928 and Nelson, British Columbia, in 1929 at which they received various briefs. They also met twice in Washington, DC, to consider preliminary findings. In early 1930, they heard presentations on the scientific investigation and arguments about the claimed damages.

The IJC delivered its final report to the governments in February 1931, a remarkable feat given the complexity of the situation. The commission found the Trail smelter at fault for polluting American territory. It estimated past damages in the American part of the Columbia Valley and damages that would accrue up to the end of December 1931 at US$350,000. This key decision was not so much a scientific finding as a political compromise. Northport-area farmers had been demanding $750,000. Consolidated had acknowledged some liability but its preference was to pay minimal or no compensation. The amount awarded was thus strikingly close to the mid-point between American claims and the company's offer.

Not surprisingly, the farmers and others were unhappy with the recommendation. Estimating the extent of the damage that was due to the Trail smelter's emissions, and calculating the appropriate size of the indemnity, were, however, problematic. A 1913 report by the US Department of Agriculture had found that a significant portion of the land in the Columbia Valley was "unsuited for agricultural purposes, either because it is too stony, too rough, too steep, or a combination of these factors."[17] The valley had also been hit by severe drought in late 1920s and a massive wildfire had nearly wiped out forests in the area. As one historian suggested, Northport citizens, who had lost their own smelter, had then "turned upon their hated rival to the north with a fury that bordered on paranoia."[18] That some damage had been done by Trail smoke was certain, but there were also some disputable American claims.

With respect to the last question in the original reference to the IJC, the commissioners took it upon themselves to address the matter of remediation, albeit modestly. They recommended Consolidated be required to complete the control measures it was undertaking (as of 1931) or was planning to undertake to prevent further damage to the United States. The remedies ranged from dispersing smelter emissions through the use of high smokestacks, to collecting sulphur dioxide exhaust gases and extracting the elemental sulphur to produce sulphuric acid or fertilizer, to varying smelter operations according to wind and weather conditions (that is, cutting production when wind and weather conditions were likely to exacerbate transboundary pollution). Ultimately all of these approaches came into effect in Trail.

Consolidated proceeded in good faith to lower emissions. It opened three sulphuric acid plants in 1931, as well as an ammonia and ammonium sulphate unit. The company began extracting steadily increasing amounts of elemental sulphur and sulphuric acid from its various processes. These changes had a dramatic impact. In the three years from 1930 to 1932 sulphur dioxide emissions declined by fully two-thirds.[19] Although annual emissions increased briefly from 1933 to 1935, they declined again when additional facilities for capturing sulphur within the zinc smelter and various gases in the lead smelter started up in 1936–7. By 1939, the plant was capturing more sulphur than it was sending into the atmosphere and was emitting less sulphur dioxide than in 1932.

By 1934, Consolidated's Elephant Brand synthetic fertilizers were a commercially successful side venture. Harmful wastes had become saleable products. Indeed, fertilizers were soon more than merely profitable. After zinc prices dropped during the Depression, Consolidated's revenues from fertilizer sales and acid recovery exceeded revenues from zinc production.[20] Almost a century ago, it had learned that pollution control can be good for business. Consolidated had reason to thank its critics in beleaguered Northport, although it may never have taken the occasion to do so.

The Arbitration Convention, 1935

Under pressure from Washington State and its political allies in Congress, the US federal government rejected the IJC's proposed compensation figure. For Consolidated, that meant the proposed compensation deal was a dead letter. Ottawa attempted to move on. The State Department, too, may well have hoped the Trail dispute would blow away. Some top State Department officials had been generally in favour of accepting the 1931 IJC report.

New fumigation incidents in 1933 and 1934 then rekindled the protests from Stevens County. After President Franklin D. Roosevelt stepped in, the Canadian government relented. In early 1935 diplomats on both sides drafted what became a formal international convention on how to resolve the conflict.[21] The "Convention for Settlement of Difficulties Arising from Operation of Smelter at Trail, BC" established a three-person arbitral tribunal and charged it with addressing the following questions:

1. Whether damage caused by the Trail Smelter in the State of Washington has occurred since the first day of January, 1932, and, if so, what indemnity should be paid therefor?
2. In the event of the answer to the first part of the preceding question being in the affirmative, whether the Trail Smelter should be required to refrain from causing damage in the State of Washington in the future and, if so, to what extent?
3. In the light of the answer to the preceding Question, what measures or régime, if any, should be adopted or maintained by the Trail Smelter?
4. What indemnity or compensation, if any, should be paid on account of any decision or decisions rendered by the Tribunal pursuant to the next two preceding Questions?[22]

At least as notable as the issues to be addressed by the Trail tribunal were those not to be addressed. The two governments did not request the tribunal to revisit the questions originally given to the IJC in 1928 or take a second look at fume damage prior to 1932. In particular, they did not mandate that the tribunal reconsider the matter of the $350,000 indemnity recommended by the commission. The first article of the bilateral convention merely required Canada to arrange payment of the $350,000 indemnity. What that article did not explicitly acknowledge, but what it clearly showed, was that the United States had thereby belatedly accepted this key recommendation of the IJC report, the same one it had initially rejected. The Government of Canada, acting on behalf of the Trail smelter owners, forwarded the $350,000 payment in late 1935.

The tribunal's mandate focused almost entirely on damage that may have been caused by smelter fumes since January 1932 and on possible compensation for this damage. The 1935 convention, therefore, did not permit the tribunal to consider events and conditions prior to January 1932 or to re-examine the IJC's earlier scientific findings for that period. And, needless to say, it did not do so. The 1931 IJC report was thus not at all passed over; *it was accepted* as the basis for the arbitration. Whether or not these crucial details were fully explained to the disgruntled residents of Stevens County is unclear. What is clear is that the US government officials soon secured not only their support for creating the tribunal but also their promise to support its conclusions.

Trail Smelter Arbitration, 1935-8

According to the 1935 convention, the arbitral tribunal was to comprise three "jurists of repute," one selected by Canada, one by the United States, and one (who could be neither American nor Canadian) selected jointly by the two governments. Those selected could not have had any previous involvement with the Trail issue. That prohibition, of course, ruled out anyone involved in the IJC report. The convention also authorized each country to hire a scientist to assist the tribunal. Washington named Dr. Reginald Dean, a Missouri metallurgist who would later become the assistant director of the US Bureau of Mines. Ottawa chose Robert Swain, a chemistry professor at Stanford University in California who had previously studied cases of sulphur fumigation in the American West.

The two experts arranged for studies into recent fume damage. This research included monitoring of air pollution, meteorological conditions in the Columbia Valley and the atmospheric dispersion of pollutants, experiments on the impact of sulphur dioxide fumigations on crops, and summaries of existing knowledge of the effects of fumes on trees. The scientific work was, however, less extensive than that done under the IJC reference. Dean and Swain presented their evidence to the tribunal at a series of meetings during 1937.

In a 1938 preliminary report the tribunal assessed an additional indemnity totalling $78,000 for damage to land and crops between January 1932 and October 1937. The award was not large and was once again much less than American farmers had sought. The tribunal rejected numerous other US claims, including those for tree damage, reduced real estate values in Northport, and the costs of scientific research conducted since the IJC investigation. The tribunal also did not accept any US claims that depended on what was then called the "invisible injury" thesis—concerning plant damage that was not readily apparent from external observation. In the end, it was not persuaded by the limited evidence presented in support of this thesis.

The tribunal also rejected an American claim for interest on the $350,000 settlement originally proposed by the IJC in 1931. Washington's counsel argued interest payments were due because Canada had not paid the indemnity until 1935. The tribunal members presumably had not forgotten the US government had itself refused to approve the IJC report in 1931 and rejected the settlement amount as inadequate. Making a claim for interest due to the "late payment" of an award one had initially rejected would seem to be grounds for a counter charge of inciting irony.

Final Trail Smelter Arbitration Decision, 1941

The tribunal's final decision in 1941 was lengthy, yet contained little that was new. It repeated much material from its own 1938 preliminary report. Large sections of the 1941 judgement also comprised carefully considered, fully referenced legal arguments as to why specific US claims were not accepted. For example, the three jurists devoted more than nine pages, including citations of numerous cases, to their reasons for denying a US request that the tribunal reconsider the compensation decision it had made in 1938. Their reasons were mostly legal and procedural rather than substantive. The overall decision was thus lengthy because of its many negative findings, not despite them. The tribunal may have felt the need to justify fully its rejection of so many American claims. Notably, the tribunal also concluded the United States had failed to provide adequate evidence of any fume damage to crops or trees between October 1937 and October 1940. That decision would effectively put an end to the matter of transboundary damages.[23]

In 1938, the tribunal had ordered a strict operating regime on a three-year trial basis. It capped emissions from the Trail smelter during the agricultural growing season, from April through September, to 100 tons per day. The regime also required a special cap of 5 tons per hour during growing season daylight hours, when sulphur dioxide concentrations downwind in the Columbia Valley exceeded 1 part per million. This cap was to be maintained until concentrations fell below 0.5 parts per million. The 1941 final report made this operating regime permanent.

The significant new feature of the 1941 tribunal decision was its statement of the principle of international environmental law that has ever since attracted so much attention to the case. Known as the "Trail smelter principle," it declared that "no State has the right to use or permit the use of its territory in such a manner as to cause injury by fumes in or to the territory of another or the properties or persons therein, when the case is of serious consequence and the injury is established by clear and convincing evidence."[24] The principle made Canada "responsible in international law for the conduct of the Trail Smelter" and therefore Canada was required to ensure the smelter continue to "refrain from causing any damage through fumes in the State of Washington."[25]

The above account of the three stages of the Trail smelter case suggests two generalizations. First, the role of the international arbitral tribunal has been overstated in many existing accounts. Second, the role of the IJC has been understated. We will return to these points in the conclusion to this chapter.

Case 2: Detroit and St. Clair River Areas Air Pollution

The Detroit and St. Clair Rivers flow south, comprising a strait connecting Lake Huron and Lake Erie, and forming the US-Canadian border in the area (see Figure 10.1). Given the considerable industrial activity in "Motor City" (Detroit) and "Chemical Valley" (Sarnia), both rivers are heavily traversed and heavily polluted. The rivers also represent sites where air pollution leaves one national jurisdiction and regulatory regime and invades lungs and property of a neighbouring country. The IJC's involvement in this area came from investigations resulting from three references of broadening scope and scale.

The first reference, which occurred in 1949, saw Canada and the United States ask the IJC to investigate the problem of smoke from steam

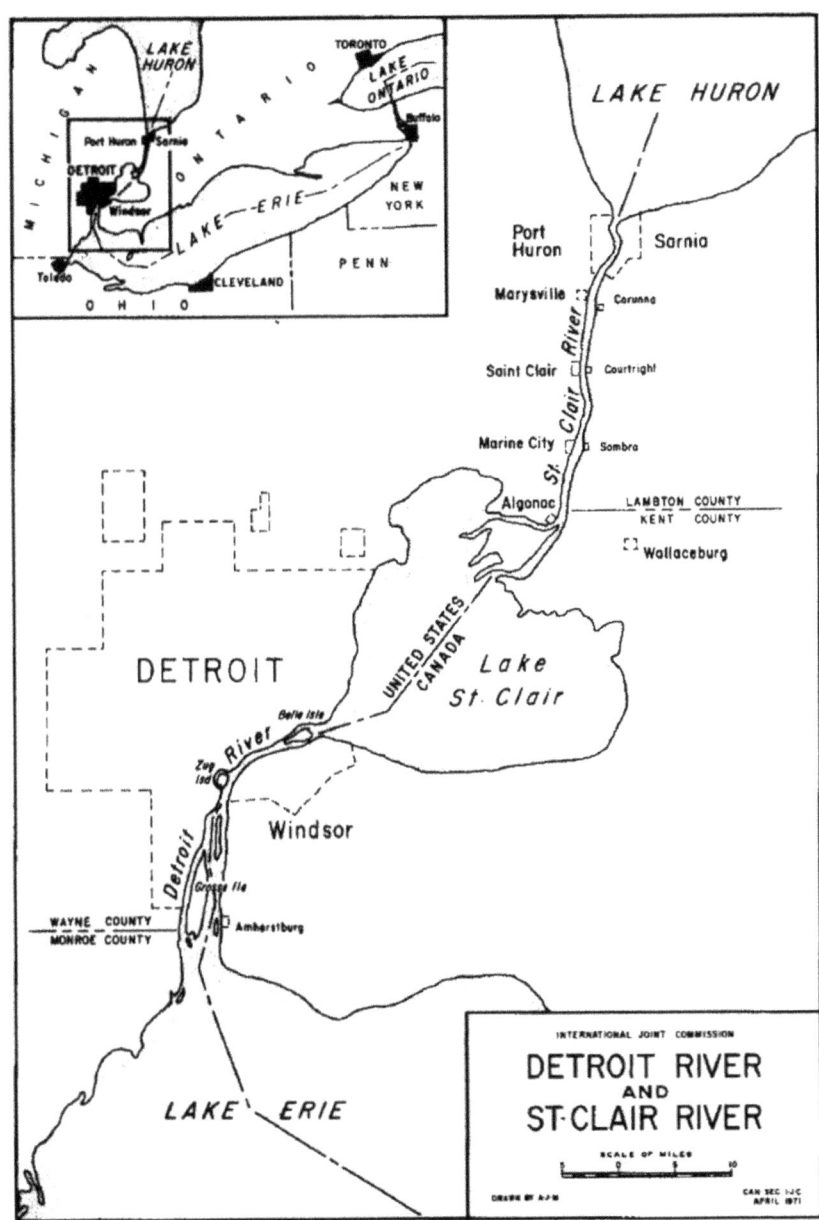

FIGURE 10.1. Detroit–St. Clair River area. IJC, *Transboundary Air Pollution: Detroit and St. Clair River Areas*, p. ii.

freighters plying the Detroit River.[26] For fifteen years, the Canadian government had complained about the dirty air from Detroit's industries. It even claimed that the maximum pollutant concentration on Canadian territory exceeded the maximum found in Northport during the Trail smelter dispute.[27] However, the reference's narrow terms limited the IJC to making recommendations to reduce pollution from the freighters only. In their 1952 interim report, the commissioners argued that the reference's terms diverted attention from the main air pollution sources, and they asked that it be amended to be more inclusive. No action was taken initially as a result of this request. The final 1960 report concluded that the transboundary air was heavily polluted from both sides of the boundary, and it singled out Detroit's Zug Island industrial area as an especially heavy source of particulates travelling across the river to Windsor. But the IJC merely recommended that the two governments adopt specific smoke emissions objectives for the freighters. The following year, in 1961, the governments authorized the IJC to maintain surveilance on these sources. Thanks to the switch from solid to liquid fuel occuring in the shipping industry at the time, the relevant authorities on both sides of the border were able to tighten standards throughout the decade. In 1966 the IJC asked the government for permission to end its work under the reference.[28] By then, the next reference, with a more appropriate scope, was underway.

1966 Reference on Detroit-Windsor and Port Huron–Sarnia Pollution

In the September 1966 reference on Detroit-Windsor and Port Huron–Sarnia air pollution, the governments posed the following questions:

1. Is the air over and in the vicinity of Port Huron-Sarnia and Detroit-Windsor being polluted on either side of the International Boundary by quantities of air contaminants that are detrimental to the public health, safety or general welfare of citizens or property on the other side of the International Boundary?

2. What sources are contributing to this pollution and to what extent?

3. What preventative or remedial measures would be most practicable from economic, sanitary, and other points of view?
4. What is the probable total cost of implementing the measures?[29]

The air pollution issues in the two regions were more discrete than suggested by their close geographic proximity or the wording of the reference. The investigation was actually two separate inquiries, one for each of the two tranboundary urban areas. Because the text of a reference submitted to the IJC is, by tradition, identical for the two countries, it is generally difficult to divine what led the governments to submit a given reference. In the case of the 1966 reference, it appears the decision to undertake investigations in each of the two urban areas was a compromise.

The US side of the Detroit River contained numerous metallurgical industries and large coal-fired power plants.[30] During the period of the IJC investigation, Metropolitan Detroit had more than 4,700 manufacturing firms and 35 per cent of the US automobile manufacturing industry. The prevailing winds transported the pollution from the Detroit area to Windsor. A 1963 study by the Canadian and Ontario governments seeking to determine the effects of transboundary pollution on the air quality on the Canadian side of the Detroit River found that the levels of iron concentrations were as high as the worst levels found in the United States. Particulary noteworthy was the sullied air in Windsor downwind of the Zug Island industrial area, home of Great Lakes Steel, the region's largest producer of airborne particulates.[31] Windsor, with less than one-tenth the population of Detroit, yet with substantial industry nevertheless, was the overwhelming net recipient of pollution. In 1964, the city government of Windsor asked the Canadian government to take action to limit the flow.[32] Given the disproportionate characteristics of the transboundary air pollution problem, it is no surprise that the previous reference was so limited. But the fact that Sarnia was beginning to receive attention for its bad air opened the door to a reference examining both areas, with one ostensive offender in each country.

Sarnia–Port Huron had many of the ingredients to become Trail II: a large industrial installation on the border producing an air pollution problem asymmetrically in relation to its neighbour. And Sarnia's bad air was unprecedented, like the size of the petrochemical complex producing much of it. The airborne polluton emitted by Sarnia's polluters, and the chemical waste they released into the St. Clair River, remains one of North America's greatest untold environmental disasters. To provide context for the reference, here is a brief overview.[33]

Sarnia is located on the St. Clair River, at the southern tip of Lake Huron, directly across from Port Huron, Michigan, and south of Point Edward, Ontario. It was a picturesque site during the 1960s. Most of the city's professional buildings were located on two streets (Christina and Front) within two blocks of the shore. The city's 54,000 residents reaped a substantial economic benefit from its industry.[34] Sarnia's median income was $101 per week in 1961, the highest in Ontario. By comparison, Toronto, then Canada's second largest urban area, had a median income of $81. By 1967, Sarnia's weekly wage had risen further, to $139 per week—the highest in Canada.

This wealthy population was sandwiched between two heavy polluters. Located on the southern end of Sarnia, Chemical Valley was one of a kind: there was no other petrochemical complex of its size and concentration in North America—a fact frequently repeated by industry representatives arguing that no other place could be used to benchmark Sarnia's pollution.[35] It consisted of ten firms at the beginning of the decade, twelve by the end, employing around 7,000 workers.[36] They included a Canadian Crown corporation (Polymer Corp.), multinational corporations (e.g., Dow Chemical, Shell), and privately held domestic firms. These companies experimented with and produced a variety of petrochemical products: solvents, ammonia, polyurethane, plastics (and its many antecedents, such as styrene), glycol, rubber, latex, chlorine, fiberglass, and others.[37] It was clear to all that they also produced a lot of air pollution. Dow released chlorine gas, for example, and might have released ammonia and chemicals involved in the manufacture of plastics (such as benzol and ethylene), but no statistics were made public on this.[38] The amount of energy needed to power these industrial facilities meant that coal-fired industrial boilers used by the firms also produced a lot of sulphur dioxide and dark smoke.[39]

At the other end of the city, fewer than two miles north of Chemical Valley, was Holmes Foundry. This maker of engine casting blocks and brake linings was a family-owned enterprise that had been at its location for nearly fifty years. It was also one of Sarnia's heaviest polluters, releasing airborne smoke and soot derived from its manufacturing processes. Technically, because Holmes Foundry was on the northwest corner of Christina and Exmouth Streets, it was located in Point Edward. This small detail is mostly irrelevant, though. Holmes Foundry employed seven hundred people and was financially troubled. It struggled to survive after going into receivership in 1966. Neither town was going to burden Holmes Foundry's owners by requiring it to install expensive abatement equipment.[40]

All research into the problem of industrial pollution in Sarnia was conducted by Chemical Valley's research arm, the St. Clair River Research Committee (SCRRC). It was created in 1952 by three Chemical Valley firms (Imperial Oil, Polymer Corporation, and Dow Chemical of Canada) to forestall regulatory measures toward air pollution then under consideration by the Sarnia government. By 1964 it counted eleven members—all of the Chemical Valley firms, plus Holmes Foundry.[41] Each of these eleven firms represented one voting member on the SCRRC; the Ontario Department of Health (DOH) was the twelfth voting member and was privy to the SCRRC's proprietary data on the city's ambient pollution levels.[42] The SCRRC's task was to study air and water pollution from the Chemical Valley companies, to "recommend to company management corrective action where warranted," and to "publicize all committee activities and thereby maintain good public relations for the benefit of the participating industries."[43] Thus, as Lorne Robb, SCRRC chairman and an executive at the Ethyl Corporation of Canada, explained in August 1965 to Sarnia's city council: "[The SCRRC's] terms of reference are to study and not to police member industries. This is being done on a voluntary basis. The industries take it upon themselves to correct their mistakes and they finance their efforts."[44]

In practice, however, the SCRRC did not monitor air and water quality in Sarnia. It contracted this work to the Ontario Research Foundation (ORF), a private research firm.[45] The ORF maintained several pollution monitors throughout Sarnia and Chemical Valley, measuring ambient levels of sulphur dioxide, hydrogen sulphide, particulate matter, and oxidants (e.g., nitrogen oxides, ground-level ozone, and chlorine). The fact that it did not measure emissions from polluting firms enabled the SCRRC to claim that the city's ambient pollution problems originated elsewhere. All data gathered by the ORF in Sarnia and paid for by the SCRCC was the SCRRC's intellectual property, even though it was reported to the DOH on a monthly basis.[46] Thus, the DOH knew the air quality measurements in Sarnia but could not share this information with the public, which received only that information disseminated by the SCRRC. Dr. E. R. Morton, a chemist at DuPont Canada who took over as the SCRRC chairman in 1966, explained that the industries' reason for secretiveness was that the information is "too prone to misinterpretation by the unsophisticated."[47] Before the IJC's investigation, the SCRRC and Lambton Industrial Society (its successor) maintained that, while air pollution was a problem in Sarnia, it was not a threat to public health since it was "essentially under control" and well within provincial guidelines for those chemicals for which guidelines were issued.[48]

In August 1965, the mayor of Port Huron, Donald Wismer, publicly called for a joint committee to investigate the problem of air pollution from Sarnia.[49] The negative attention was sufficient for the SCRRC to release a lengthy press statement asserting that "industrial air pollution is not a cause for alarm in the Sarnia area," providing evidence and quotes from the director of the regional government public health agency backing this up, and explaining the organization's role in monitoring pollution. It claimed the press release was necessary due to "recent allegations that air pollution from industry in the Sarnia area is serious and poses a health hazard."[50] Yet Port Huron's residents continued complaining, as did its mayor, and by early-to-mid-1966, they received considerable press coverage.[51] News of the IJC investigation arrived as an unpleasant surprise to Sarnia's city council and business leaders. They resolved to co-operate in the hope of improving the city's reputation, and with the stated intention of clearing the city's name.[52]

To conduct the investigation, the IJC formed the St. Clair–Detroit Air Pollution Board, consisting of civil servants from federal, state (Michigan), and provincial (Ontario) governments. The board held public hearings in June 1967 in Windsor and Port Huron, and in March 1971 in Detroit and

Sarnia. As the investigation progressed, the board submitted semi-annual reports, with the near-complete January 1971 report serving as the basis for hearings the following March.[53] Afterwards, in 1972, the IJC produced and distributed its final report.

The report showed that sources in the Detroit area produced about ten times as much sulphur dioxide and particulate matter as those in the Windsor area. More importantly, it claimed to have found "unequivocal evidence that air contaminants originating in the industrial complex of Detroit do move across the International Boundary into the Windsor area."[54] The evidence showed that pollution (particulates and sulphur dioxide) from Detroit exceeded Ontario's ambient standards, while pollution travelling from Windsor to Detroit made up a small fraction of the allowed pollution in Michigan under the US Clean Air Act.

Sarnia–Port Huron was a different story. And the findings about pollution transport in that area revealed an important reason why Sarnia–Port Huron did not turn out to be Trail II. The predominant wind direction is north and south along the river (and the international border). The main meteorological problem worsening the area's bad air was frequent temperature inversions, which held the pollution where it was produced. In other words, Chemical Valley's main victims were Sarnians, not the habitants of Port Huron. The report noted this, saying, "the high level of pollution in Sarnia is, to a large extent, attributable to emissions originating in that jurisdiction."[55] Port Huron received particulates, sulphur dioxide, and "odours" from Sarnia, but these were more than offset by the US production of pollution on the St. Clair River south of Port Huron and Sarnia (in Marysville and St. Clair) by coal-fired power plants. Sarnia's contribution to Port Huron's particulate levels, for example, in a region of eight and a half square miles, totalled only one-third of what was allowed under US ambient standards. Furthermore, the report stated that "outside of this section of Port Huron the transboundary flow of particulates from Canadian sources to the United States was rather insignificant."[56]

The IJC made two main recommedations. First, governments should establish binational ambient air quality objectives on sulphur dioxide, particulate matter, and odours for the two border zones covered by the reference. This was naive, but not particularly controversial. It was consistent with the contemporaneous trend of surrendering air pollution policy to higher authorities. The six years after the reference was submitted was a period of substantial air pollution policy developement. The 1970 US Clean Air Act created National Ambient Air Quality Standards and policy instruments for regulating polluters. In 1967, Ontario passed a statute giving the province the authority to regulate air pollution, and taking away from the cities the competency that had been given in an earlier statute. This was in response to industry lobbying the provincial government for provincial standards to prevent the further balkinization of air pollution regulations.[57] Plus, municipalites wanted to prevent industrial flight to air pollution havens. In 1967 Sarnia's elected leaders lobbied Ottawa for national emissions standards. The 1971 Canadian Clean Air Act eventually provided non-binding guidelines. Sarnia's mayor, Paul Blundy, specifically requested binational standards so that Sarnia would not need to fear losing industry if it faced increased scrutiny from provincial regulators.

Second, the IJC recommended that the governments create a binational air pollution board for the "coordination of surveillance, monitoring the implementation of programs, reporting and making recommendations to government . . . and such other duties related to the air quality in the vicinity of the Detroit River and St. Clair River areas as may be required."[58]

Outcomes, and a Subsequent Detroit and St. Clair River Areas Reference

The regional air quality improvements following the early 1971 findings were substantial—for example, the total amount of suspended particulates in the two transboundary regions were reduced from more than 950,000 tons per year in 1971 to less than 440,000 in 1975.[59] Sarnia's unwanted experience in the limelight during the late 1960s appears to have provoked a series of modernizations at several Chemical Valley facilities.[60] Yet the transboundary region's overall reductions did not come close to achieving the IJC's recommended air quality objectives.

The more transparent outcome of the IJC investigation and recommendations was a binational resolution, passed at the August 1971 Governors and Premiers Great Lakes Conference, to create a Michigan-Ontario air pollution control committee for the purpose of formulating a binational control program. The Michigan-Ontario Transboundary Air

Pollution (MOTAP) Committee, formed in 1973, "included many of the working level air pollution specialists of jursidictions in the Michigan-Ontario transboundary region who were compiling information and reporting continuously on the development of control strategies and state of compliance of pollution sources with emission limitations."[61] It produced a report that year detailing "the objectives and methods of cooperation."[62] The report led to the signing of a memorandum of understanding (MOU) by Michigan and Ontario, in November-December 1974, to achieve the IJC's recommended ambient air quality objectives by the end of 1978. In the MOU, the governments of Michigan and Ontario pledged to work co-operatively through their newly created MOTAP Committee and, consisent with the second IJC recommendation above, suggested the two national governments "request the International Joint Commission to assume responsibility for monitoring progress of implementing programs for the control of air pollution in the transboundary area."[63]

The result of the MOU request was a third and final reference on air pollution in the Detroit and St. Clair River areas. The June-July 1975 reference directed the IJC to report annually on Michigan's and Ontario's progress in meeting the objectives of the 1974 MOU (namely, the IJC's recommended air pollution objectives and the MOU's deadline for achieving them). To do this, the IJC created the International Ontario-Michigan Air Pollution Board (IOMAPB) the following year.[64] Its annual reports used data mostly from the MOTAP Committee.

History has revealed that the air quality objectives set in the United States and Canada during the early 1970s were overly optimistic. The states in the American midwest, for example, remained out of compliance with the US Clean Air Act's National Ambient Air Quality Standards for well over a decade. This was mirrored in the inability of Michigan and Ontario to adequately reduce their emissions. Suspended particulate levels in the tranboundary region remained unchanged for the rest of the decade after the 1975 reference. The IJC's ambient objectives—as well as Michigan's federal air quality standards for particulates—were far out of reach.[65] In its 1979 report on Michigan-Ontario air pollution (which covered progress to the end of the MOU's 1978 deadline) the IJC noted that particulates had "the highest levels concentrated in downtown Sarnia."[66] This was tactful language describing an ongoing environmental disaster only tenuously within the IJC's scope due to the meteorological conditions and wind patterns at play. In Lambton County (where Sarnia is located), sulphur dioxide emissions increased or stayed the same each year for the rest of the decade, through 1980.[67]

In the early 1980s, however, the region was suffering deindustrialization. Many factories closed, especially old and inefficient ones. Energy consumption declined precipitously.[68] The IOMAPB reckoned that, when an economic rebound restored the region's manufacturing base, new facilities would be built according to modern pollution abatement regulations.[69] In a final report trumpeting its accomplishments in quickly bringing the region close to compliance with the ambient objectives, the IJC declared the board's work done and disbanded it in January 1984. Yet this final report also highlighted the need for additional work outside the narrow scope of the reference:

> In the Commission's opinion, reporting on trends and programs for the orginal three pollutants in the Reference does not represent an adequate picture of the state of the atmospheric environment in the Michigan-Ontario transborder region. Rather, they convey an incomplete picture of environmental quality. Reporting their successful control in isolation suggests that air pollution problems of international concern do not exist in the region. In fact there is a need to direct more attention to a wider range of air pollutants particuarly toxic and hazardous substances.[70]

In September 1988, purportedly in response to public outcry in Canada over the construction of a solid waste incinerator in Detroit, the United States and Canada requested that the 1975 reference be reactivated with a new focus on air toxics. The IJC formed a new regional air pollution board (the International Air Pollution Advisory Board for the Detroit-Windsor/Port Huron–Sarnia Region) to investigate. It conducted public hearings in March 1991, undertook a study examining the presence of a range of toxic chemicals (ones listed in US and Canadian air pollution statutes for which the board could find data), and produced a report, released in February 1992. The report's nineteen recommendations called, in essence, for more monitoring of the presence of toxic chemicals and resulting health costs within the geographic scope of the reference.[71] It was an anticlimactic and nebulous end to the Detroit and St. Clair River areas case, a succession of references that were at times ill-suited for the considerable problems that inspired them—intially for Detroit-Windsor, and later for Sarnia. More important, it was also the end of the two countries' use of the IJC to investigate and provide recommendations on transboundary air pollution.

The Case of Acid Rain, 1970s–91

Our foregoing "tale of two cases" conspicuously omits a third, more contemporary air pollution issue between Canada and the United States. Acid rain was the most prominent such issue during the late 1970s and '80s, especially in Canada. Scientists in both countries researched its effects, officials held bilateral talks, and the two governments eventually signed an agreement aimed at controlling emission sources. But the IJC played virtually no role in these efforts. Washington and Ottawa made sure of that.

The governments coordinated acid rain research during the late 1970s and '80s through an ad hoc Canada-US body, the Bilateral Research Consultation Group, not through the independent IJC. The governments made no formal reference to the commission for a report or recommendations. When they eventually concluded the bilateral Air Quality Agreement (AQA) in 1991, they created another intergovernmental body, the Canada-US Air Quality Committee (AQC) to coordinate and evaluate implementation of the AQA. They also gave the IJC not the task of assessing their efforts—as they had done in the earlier Great Lakes Water Quality Agreement—but the ignominious task of collecting and summarizing public comments on the AQC's biennial reports. It collected a total of four comments on the AQC's 2012 report and three comments, all emailed, on the 2014 report.

Why did the governments studiously ignore the IJC and keep it out of acid rain developments? As mentioned, the governments gave the IJC a watchdog role in the 1972 Great Lakes Water Quality Agreement—a sort of continuing formal reference. They also ensured the commission had adequate staff to undertake this new responsibility and supported the establishment of a regional office in the Great Lakes basin. Over the course of the 1970s, however, an uneasy, even testy, relationship developed between the commissioners and government officials. It was evident in unusual public exchanges of letters over issues that were by themselves relatively unimportant and now long since forgotten—particularly the placement of an ice boom on the St. Mary's River and the procedures for notification concerning construction of a Saskatchewan power plant.[72] The governments were in general concerned about the apparent activism the commission was showing and perhaps about it challenging the governments' perogatives.

The IAQAB also engaged in several watchdog-type activities outside the Detroit and St. Clair River areas, leading the governments to conclude it, too, had overstepped its authority.[73] In one notable incident, the IAQAB conducted an investigation into pollution from an aluminum plant in upstate New York, and in particular its effects on the nearby cattle industry on tribal land that spans both sides of the border. After a public consultation meeting, the IAQAB recommended bilateral and domestic policy action to address the problem. In response, in October 1978, the governments compelled the IJC to limit strictly the IAQAB's role to one of alerting the governments about issues, not investigating those issues on the board's own initiative. But the damage to the IJC's reputation had already occurred.

In an edited volume on the acid rain dispute published in 1985, before the AQA negotiations began in earnest, Paul Kinscherff dismissed the IJC as a policy actor of much potential impact. He asserted the organization's perceived activism had undermined its credibility to such a great extent, at least within the two national governments, that both of them now opposed involving the commission in any politically sensitive environmental issues.[74]

The intergovernmental nature of the AQC ensures, by its design, that it will exhibit no such activist tendencies. The result is that there is no independent review of the regular reports on the AQA's implementation. One of the authors of this chapter wrote, a decade ago, that the AQC reports reflected, not objective evaluations of governmental programs to meet the provisions of the AQA, but rather binational "collusion" between the environmental and other agencies of the two countries. The two governments wanted above all to avoid embarrassment over lagging policies to meet commitments they themselves had made in the 1991 agreement.⁷⁵ The IJC had become a casualty of that concern.

Conclusion

The IJC's history as a binational organization important in air pollution policy is a tale of two cases. The Trail smelter dispute, and Detroit and St. Clair River areas air pollution are the cases for which it can be credibly argued that the IJC performed a substantial role in influencing institutional processes. Assessing the role of the IJC in the Trail smelter case requires that we recognize three independent, albeit related, stages in the dispute resolution process: the first stage comprising the IJC investigation and the commission's 1931 report, the second stage consisting of the negotiation and signing of the 1935 Canada-US convention, and the third stage involving the international tribunal and its two formal arbitration decisions (1938 and 1941).

There is a tendency in the historical and even more voluminous legal literature on the Trail smelter case to focus on the third of these three stages. It is the tribunal that is most often credited with finding that "Canada was responsible for damage in Washington State caused by [the smelter] fumes" and finding "the Canadian government liable for damages of $350,000."⁷⁶ These notions are simply historically incorrect. They wrongly credit the tribunal with conclusions and proposals actually taken previously by the IJC, and relegate the IJC to a minor and perhaps negligible role in resolving the Trail conflict.

Contrary to common belief, the IJC commissioners, not the international tribunal, first found Canada responsible for environmental damage caused by Trail smelter fumes. The commissioners also established the initial and larger indemnity ($350,000) of the two financial settlements that Canada eventually came to pay for its pollution. As noted above, both were key recommendations of the IJC's 1931 report to the governments. Moreover, both Canada and the United States explicitly agreed in 1935 that Canada was liable for damages and agreed on an indemnity, the amount of which was exactly what the IJC had recommended four years earlier. These points became the key substantive provisions of the bilateral convention that created the international tribunal. Canada had already paid the $350,000 settlement before the tribunal even got underway.[77] The additional, relatively small damage claims from Americans later approved by the tribunal itself covered only small fumigation incidents after 1932. The tribunal also notably rejected most of the US claims for further compensation. The role of the arbitral tribunal in deciding Trail compensation issues was thus a relatively minor one.

As our examination of the three stages shows, the 1935 bilateral Canada-US agreement on the 1931 IJC recommendations was the key to resolving the Trail smelter dispute. The role of the well-known arbitral tribunal was secondary. We would argue, in fact, that the Trail case was one of the major success stories of the IJC during its first century of operation.

The Detroit and St. Clair River areas case provides another example (albeit, less commonly studied) of the IJC's influence in air pollution policy. Although the IJC subsequently claimed that its 1972 report (and findings, released the previous year) spurred the governments in both transboundary regions to apply pressure for pollution reductions, it is difficult to disentangle the IJC's influence from regulatory processes already underway, such as the programs under the 1970 US Clean Air Act.[78] To the extent these pollution-reducing changes were in response to bad press (as opposed to changes that were underway anyway), the IJC investigation was one among several sources applying pressure. Toronto's two major newspapers and the Canadian Broadcasting Corporation fed the flames with their own investigations condemning Chemical Valley.[79] The IJC's role in spotlighting the problem with quantitative data probably helped. Thanks to the study, the Michigan and Ontario governments had vastly better data with which to design pollution abatement programs than did other heavily polluted areas in the two countries. It was the first report on the region's pollution to accurately describe the extent of the problem, its sources, the patterns of transboundary transport, and to contextualize these findings in terms of each country's air pollution standards. It broke the grip that the SCRRC had on information about the problem, and thus one of the organization's main forms of control.

Less clear is the effectiveness of the 1970s binational air control program aimed at achieving the IJC's recommended air quality objectives, including the third Detroit and St. Clair River areas air pollution reference and activities of the IOMAPB. Plausibly, the IJC's influence in bringing about air pollution relief was outweighed by the effects of the region's economic upheaval during the early 1980s. At least the IOMAPB coordinated the dissemination of reliable data to track progress. At any rate, by the time the IJC's work under the 1975 Detroit-Windsor and Port Huron–Sarnia reference ended in 1984, the IJC had effectively run its course as an important player in air pollution policy debates addressing transboundary air pollutants.

The way the governments dealt with the acid rain case, by working around the IJC, evidences the commission's diminished role in binational air pollution governance. Even its institutional alternative, the AQC, shows little recent activity, despite being tasked with implementing a binational treaty. The AQA's last annex (for ground-level ozone) occurred twenty years ago. Its long-discussed annex on particulates has not been completed and appears shelved. As of summer 2019, the AQC has not released its 2018 biennial progress report, despite the requirement under article viii of the AQA that it do so. Thus, the diminution of the IJC's importance in transboundary air pollution issues has occurred within the context of a general decline in support for binational air pollution governance. Given that each country's air is much cleaner than in the past (thanks mostly to domestic regulations and techological advancements in polluting industries), and the evident lack of demand for binational institutions, it is possible that US-Canada air pollution goverance has mostly run its course for the forseeable future.

Notes

1   For discussions of the law and practice of the quasi-judicial aspect of the commission's work, see Robert A. MacKay, "The International Joint Commission between The United States and Canada," *American Journal of International Law* 22, no. 2 (1928): 292–318; Louis Mortimer Bloomfield and Gerald Francis FitzGerald, *Boundary Waters Problems of Canada and the United States: The International Joint Commission 1912–1958* (Toronto: Carswell, 1958); and Charles B. Bourne, "Canada and the Law of International Drainage Basins," in *Perspectives on International Law and Organization*, ed. R. St. J. Macdonald, G. L. Morris, and D. M. Johnston (Toronto: University of Toronto Press, 1974), 468–99.

2   Arnold D. P. Heeney, "Pollution in Boundary Waters" (Address to the Canadian Institute on Pollution Control meeting, Ottawa, ON, 25 October 1965).

3   For a recent overview of the air polluton references (albeit neither an in-depth nor critical one) see Jason Buhi and Lin Feng, "The International Joint Commission's Role in the United States-Canada Transboundary Air Pollution Control Regime: A Century of Experience to Guide the Future," *Vermont Journal of Environmental Law* 11, no. 1 (2009): 107–44.

4   See, for example, Cesare Romano, "International Dispute Settlement," in *The Oxford Handbook of International Environmental Law*, ed. Daniel Bodansky, Jutta Brunnée, and Ellen Hey (Oxford: Oxford University Press, 2007), 1036–56. The Trail Smelter case is the second-most-often cited legal case in the *Oxford Handbook*.

5   The background information in this section is largely obtained from the authoritative history provided by the Trail Smelter Arbitral Tribunal in its 16 April 1938 decision report, pages 1913–19, available in United Nations, *Reports of International Arbitral Awards: Trail smelter case, Volume III* (2006), http://legal.un.org/riaa/cases/vol_III/1905-1982.pdf.

6   Heap roasting, or roast yards, involved burning off some of the sulphur in raw ores piled up in open pits, ignited by setting logs on fire. The process took weeks and the burning ore put massive amounts of suphur dioxide fumes into the local air shed. The same technique was employed for decades by the nickel smelters outside Sudbury, Ontario, and used there long after European smelters had abandoned the harmful practice.

7   The Sullivan Mine eventually closed in 2001, almost a century after it first began production. The ore for the Trail Smelter now comes by ship and rail from Alaska—a testament to the extent of the sunk investment in the Trail operation and its efficiency. The current owner of the Trail Smelter is Teck Resources, following a merger with Cominco in 2001. Teck recently waged an unsuccessful takeover bid for INCO, owner of the Sudbury smelter, losing out to Vale, a subsidiary of a Brazilian mining company, CRVD.

8   See "Zinc smelting," at https://en.wikipedia.org/wiki/Zinc_smelting. The main use of zinc is coating steel products in order to protect against rust and corrosion.

9   One of the most important references to the IJC from Canada and the United States, in 1944, concerned possible binational development of the Columbia River for flood control and hydroelectric production. The result was the Columbia River Treaty and subsequent developments. See Neil A. Swainson, *Conflict Over the Columbia: The Canadian Background to an Historic Treaty* (Montreal: McGill-Queens University Press, 1979).

10 About 270 miles south of Northport lies the immense Hanford nuclear station, originally part of the Second World War–era Manhattan Projet, in an area highly contaminated by nuclear waste.

11 Reginald S. Dean and Robert E. Swain, "Report Submitted to the Trail Smelter Arbitral Tribunal," in US Department of Interior, *Bulletin* 453 (Washington, DC: US Government Printing Office, 1944), Figure 2, p. 19, available at https://digital.library.unt.edu/ark:/67531/metadc12613/. Two tons of sulphur dioxide is equivalent to one ton of elemental sulphur.

12 Likely the main effect, and perhaps the main purpose, of the taller stacks was to improve local ambient air quality in Trail itself, not to reduce transboundary pollution flows.

13 Meteorological studies done later of Trail emissions and of the INCO "superstack" in Sudbury suggest blaming taller stacks was likely a valid conjecture. Putting emissions higher into the atmosphere facilitated their longer-range transport.

14 Article ix stipulates in part that the parties "further agree that *any other questions or matters of difference* arising between them involving the rights, obligations, or interests of either in relation to the other or to the inhabitants of the other, along the common frontier between the United States and the Dominion of Canada, shall be referred from time to time to the International Joint Commission for examination and report" (emphasis added). See https://www.ijc.org/en/who/mission/bwt.

15 Don Munton, "Forests, Fumes and Further Studies: Environmental Science and Policy Inaction in Ontario," *Journal of Canadian Studies* 37, no. 2 (2002): 130–63.

16 Morris Katz and F. E. Lathe, "Summary," in National Research Council of Canada, *Effect of Sulfur Dioxide on Vegitation*, No. 815 (Ottawa, ON: National Research Council, 1939), 429–47.

17 Quoted by the Trail Smelter Arbitral Tribunal in "Decision," *The American Journal of International Law* 35, no. 4 (1941): 691–2.

18 Keith A. Murray, "The Trail Smelter Case: International Air Pollution in the Columbia Valley," *BC Studies* 15 (1972): 73.

19 Trail Smelter Arbitral Tribunal, "Decision."

20 Murray, "The Trail Smelter Case: International Air Pollution in the Columbia Valley."

21 The 1935 convention contained as many articles as the entire Boundary Waters Treaty—fourteen in all. Fully eleven of the articles dealt, in great detail, with the procedures by which the tribunal should operate. The text of the convention was, in other words, short on substance (with one significant exception) and long on process. Once approved by the US Senate, the convention became a formal treaty under American law.

22 Article iii of "Canada-United States: Convention for Settlement of Difficulties Arising from Operation of Smelter at Trail, B. C.," *The American Journal of International Law* 30, no. 4 (1936): 163–67, doi:10.2307/2213437.

23 Trail Smelter Arbitral Tribunal, "Decision," 708–9.

24 Trail Smelter Arbitral Tribunal, "Decision," 716. The novelty of this principle lay only in it being applied here for the first time at the international level. The principle was already part of American domestic law. Legal scholars have subsequently pointed to the limitations of the principle given that the case must be "of serious consequence" and the injury be "established by clear and convincing evidence."

25 Trail Smelter Arbitral Tribunal, "Decision," 684.

26 Letter, R. A. Lovett and Louis St. Laurent to IJC, air pollution reference, 12 January 1949, https://www.ijc.org/en/docket-61-air-pollution-reference-can-1949-01-12pdf.

27 See IJC, *Transboundary Air Pollution: Detroit and St. Clair River Areas* (Washington, DC: US Government Printing Office, 1973), https://www.ijc.org/sites/default/files/Docket%2085%201972%20Report%20to%20Gov..pdf.

28 IJC, *Termination of Commission Activities on Vessel Smoke Surveillance in the Detroit River Area under the 1949 Air Pollution Reference*, 1 March 1967, https://www.ijc.org/en/docket-61-air-pollution-final-report-1967pdf.

29 Letter, John M. Leddy and Paul Martin to IJC, air pollution reference, 23 September 1966, https://www.ijc.org/en/docket-85-port-huron-sarnia-detroit-windsor-air-pollution-can-reference-1966-09-23pdf (Canadian version), and https://www.ijc.org/en/docket-85-port-huron-sarnia-detroit-windsor-air-pollution-reference-uspdf (US version).

30 IJC, *Transboundary Air Pollution: Detroit and St. Clair River Areas*.

31 Ibid., ch. 7.

32 Testimony of W. B. Drowley at the IJC public hearings in Sarnia on joint air pollution study of Sarnia–Port Huron, 10 March 1971, Docket 85, box 118, folder 85-2-2:1, IJC, Ottawa.

33 For a lengthier account of air pollution politics in Sarnia, see Owen Temby, "Control and Suppression in Sarnia's Chemical Valley during the 1960s," *Enterprise & Society* (forthcoming).

34 Walter Stewart, "Profile of a City with Poisoned Air," *Star Weekly Magazine*, 27 January 1968.

35 Marcella Brown, "Air Pollution Said Under Control Here: Research Committee's Data Reveals Area 'On the Good Side of Things,'" *Sarnia Observer*, 17 April 1967.

36 The *Globe and Mail* called Sarnia "the most stable labour force in Canada." See Ralph Hyman, "Sarnia's Generous Giants," *Globe and Mail* (Toronto), 22 July 1961.

37 Ibid.; Coal Producers Committee for Smoke Abatement, *Report of Survey in Sarnia, Ontario*, July 1953. Box 19JA-G, Conservation and Pollution, Lambton County Archives (hereafter, LCA).

38 Stewart, "Profile of a City with Poisoned Air." The Coal Producers Committee's 1953 survey and report admitted that its brief survey was insufficient to determine the extent to which chemicals were emitted into atmosphere. At Polymer, for example, it observed "fumes and odors," and said that the "extent of air pollution from this source [is] impossible to determine without elaborate collection equipment and analysis." Coal Producers Committee for Smoke Abatement, *Report of Survey in Sarnia*.

39 Ibid.

40 Terrance Wills, "Sarnia Air Pollution: Outside Invention or Local Conspiracy?" *Globe and Mail* (Toronto), 3 January 1967.

41 The eleven firms in the SCRRC in 1964 were Cabot Carbon of Canada, Dow Chemical of Canada, Dupont of Canada, Ethyl Corporation of Canada, Fiberglass Canada, Holmes Foundry, Imperial Oil Enterprise, Allied Chemical, Polymer Corporation, Shell Canada, and Sun Oil Company. C. M. Finigan, "The St. Clair River Research

Committee: A Co-Operative Approach to Pollution Abatement," in *11th Ontario Industrial Waste Conference, Proceedings*, vol. 11 (presented at the Ontario Industrial Waste Conference, Lake of Bays, Ontario: Queen's Printer for Ontario, 1964).

42 Ibid.; Wills, "Sarnia Air Pollution."

43 Finigan, "The St. Clair River Research Committee," 75.

44 Sarnia City Council, council chamber minutes, 30 August 1965, Minute Book 38, Sarnia City Hall (hereafter SCH).

45 For an explanation of the ORF's relationship to the SCRRC, see H. G. McAdie (project director of the ORF's air pollution survey in Sarnia) to G. A. M. Thomas, 2 April 1965, loc. C500-21, roll 880, City of Sarnia Correspondence, Sarnia City Hall (hereafter CSC).

46 SCRRC press release, 13 August 1965, loc. C500-11, roll 882, CSC.

47 Wills, "Sarnia Air Pollution," 1.

48 SCRRC, *Review of Air Pollution at Sarnia*, 1966. Box 19JA-G, Conservation and Pollution, LCA.

49 H. T. Ross to R. G. Given, 27 August 1965, loc. C500-24, roll 882, CSC; "Port Huron May Join Sarnia Pollution Check," *Windsor Star*, 26 August 1965.

50 SCRRC press release, 13 August 1965.

51 See Ron Lowman, "When you Walk in Sarnia, Smog Gets in your Eyes," *Toronto Daily Star*, 7 May 1966.

52 Sarnia City Council, council chamber minutes, 3 January 1967, Minute Book 40, SCH.

53 See IJC, *Joint Air Pollution Study of St. Clair–Detroit River Areas for International Joint Commission Canada and the United States* (Washington, DC: US Environmental Protection Agency, 1971), available at https://nepis.epa.gov.

54 IJC, *Transboundary Air Pollution: Detroit and St. Clair River Areas*, 33.

55 Ibid., 56.

56 Ibid., 44

57 See Owen Temby, "Policy Symbolism and Air Pollution in Toronto and Ontario, 1963–1967," *Planning Perspectives* 30, no. 2 (2015): 271–84.

58 IJC, *Transboundary Air Pollution: Detroit and St. Clair River Areas*, 60–1.

59 IJC, *First Annual Report on Ontario-Michigan Air Pollution*, 1976, http://www.ijc.org/files/publications/ID567.pdf. The second annual report indicates that, by 1977, 118 of the 122 major point sources identified by the IJC in January 1971 implemented "compliance measures acceptable to the local jurisdictions." IJC, *Second Annual Report on Michigan-Ontario Air Pollution*, 1977, p. 7, http://www.ijc.org/files/publications/ID571.pdf.

60 Notably, Polymer Corporation's conversion from coal to natural gas, and the use of low-sulphur coal at Dow Chemical, both occuring in 1969 or 1970. These were discussed in Lorne Robb's 10 March 1971 testimony to the IJC in Sarnia, Docket 85, box 118, folder

85-2-2:1, IJC, Ottawa. Robb was the chairman of the Lambton Industrial Society's technical committee, the SCRRC's successor.

61 IJC, *Final Report Pursuant to the July 8, 1975 Reference on the State of Air Quality in the Detroit-Windsor and Port Huron-Sarnia Areas*, 1984, 2, https://legacyfiles.ijc.org/publications/ID566.pdf. See also *First Annual Report on Ontario-Michigan Air Pollution*.

62 IJC, *First Annual Report on Ontario-Michigan Air Pollution*, 22.

63 "Memorandum of Understanding on Transboundary Air Pollution Control in Southwestern Ontario-Southeastern Michigan Area," 1974, in IJC, *First Annual Report on Ontario-Michigan Air Pollution*, appendix A, 29.

64 IJC, "Directive to International Ontario-Michigan Air Pollution Board," 3 February 1976, in *First Annual Report on Ontario-Michigan Air Pollution*, 13–17. The IOMAPB should not be confused with the St. Clair–Detroit Air Pollution Board or the International Air Quality Advisory Board.

65 IJC, *Fourth Annual Report on Michigan-Ontario Air Pollution*, 1979, 1, http://www.ijc.org/files/publications/ID568.pdf.

66 IJC, *Fourth Annual Report*, 4.

67 IJC, *Annual Report on Michigan-Ontario Air Pollution*, 1982, http://www.ijc.org/files/publications/ID565.pdf.

68 For example, petroleum consumption in Michigan alone declined from over 221 million barrels in 1978 to under 139 million barrels in 1982, the lowest consumption since 1963. It never recovered to previous high points. See US Energy Information Administration, "Energy Consumption Estimates for Major Energy Sources in Physical Units, 1960–2016, Michigan," https://www.eia.gov/state/seds/data.php?incfile=/state/seds/sep_use/total/use_tot_MIa.html&sid=MI.

69 IJC, *Final Report Pursuant to the July 8, 1975 Reference*.

70 Ibid., 4. The IJC did not produce an IOMAPB annual report in 1980. Its next progress report was released late, in 1982. Similarly, it released no report in 1983. The 1982 report noted the changed political-economic context, notably reduced financial support by government for monitoring activities and lower industrial production in the region, which was beginning to reduce particulate emissions, although not appreciably.

71 IJC, *Air Quality in the Detroit-Windsor/Port Huron-Sarnia Region: A Report to the Governments of Canada and the United States Pursuant to the Reference of July 8, 1975 and letters from the Governments of September 30, 1988* (1992), https://ijc.org/sites/default/files/Docket%2099%20Final%20Report%201992.pdf

72 The exchanges over these issues are discussed in Don Munton, "Paradoxes and Prospects," in *The International Joint Commission Seventy Years On*, ed. Robert Spencer, John Kirton, and Kim Richard Nossal (Toronto: Center for International Studies, 1981), 60–97.

73 For an overview of the IAQAB's activites during this period, see the IJC's *The Annual Report 1976*, 1977, p. 21, available at http://www.ijc.org/files/publications/ID1001.pdf.

74 Paul Kinscherff, "The International Joint Commission: The Role It Might Play," in *Acid Rain and Friendly Neighbors: The Policy Dispute between Canada and the United States*, ed. Jurgen Schmandt and Hilliard Roderick (Durham, NC: Duke University Press, 1985), 174–92.

75 Don Munton, "Acid Rain Politics in North America: Conflict to Cooperation to Collusion," in *Acid in the Environment: Lessons Learned and Future Prospects*, ed. G. R. Visgilio and D. M. Whitelaw (New York: Springer, 2007), 175–201.

76 Steven Bernstein, *The Compromise of Liberal Environmentalism* (New York: Columbia University Press, 2001), 47; and Lynton Caldwell, *International Environmental Policy* (Durham, NC: Duke University Press, 1984), 151. See also Andrew Morriss, "Supporting Structures for Resolving Environmental Disputes among Friendly Neighbors," in *Acid Rain and Friendly Neighbors: The Policy Dispute between Canada and the United States*, ed. Jurgen Schmandt and Hilliard Roderick (Durham, NC: Duke University Press, 1985), 211–45; Norman J. Vig, "Introduction: Governing the International Environment," in *The Global Environment: Institutions, Law, and Policy*, ed. Norman J. Vig and Regina S. Axelrod (London: Earthscan, 1999), 15.

77 Trail Smelter Arbitral Tribunal, "Decision," 694.

78 Air pollution reduction efforts in the transboundary area covered by the 1967 reference were evaluated annually, beginning 1976, in reports mandated under the 1975 reference. In general, these reports credited the IJC's work and government programs with air pollution reductions in the transboundary region, while diverting blame—occasionally incorrectly—for shortfalls to purportedly lax domestic regulations.

79 Ryan O'Connor, *The First Green Wave: Pollution Probe and the Origins of Environmental Activism in Ontario* (Vancouver: UBC Press, 2015); Temby, "Policy Symbolism and Air Pollution."

11

Origin of the Great Lakes Water Quality Agreement: Concepts and Structures

Jennifer Read

For those whose work focuses on the Great Lakes and their ecological integrity, the image of Pierre Elliot Trudeau and Richard Millhouse Nixon smiling—or wryly grimacing?—at each other as they clasp hands over the newly signed Great Lakes Water Quality Agreement on 15 April 1972 is iconic. In the nearly fifty years since that time, water quality activities in the Great Lakes basin, whether occurring at the national, state, provincial, or even local levels, have been driven by the contents of the original agreement and its subsequent iterations.

The Great Lakes Water Quality Agreement is an executive agreement between Canada and the United State for the express purpose of improving Great Lakes water quality. As an executive agreement, it does not have treaty status and is amended by an exchange of letters; its contents are *not* ratified by the US Senate. The agreement is also a standing reference to the International Joint Commission (IJC) under the Boundary Waters Treaty of 1909.

The two countries signed the 1972 agreement in the shadow of the first Earth Day, with the purpose of reducing eutrophication-causing phosphorus inputs to the lower Great Lakes. Six years later, they broadened the scope of the agreement to reduce inputs of toxic substances and initiate an

FIGURE 11.1. Trudeau and Nixon signing the GLWQA.

ecosystem approach to managing human interaction with the lakes, expanding the agreement to all the Great Lakes. In 1987, the agreement was further revised by protocol that expanded the scope of the ecosystem approach, although it retained its specific focus on water quality, and introduced programmatic opportunities to restore water quality in identified toxic "hot spots" as well as in the open lakes.

Just as the agreement has evolved since it was signed, the 1972 document represents a single point—albeit a high point—along the trajectory of evolving scientific understanding and societal appreciation that have influenced governance arrangements and management actions related to water quality of this great binational resource since the early twentieth century. Three times between 1912 and 1972 the governments of the United States and Canada asked the IJC to determine if boundary waters were being polluted on one side of the international border to the detriment of health and property on the other, and to suggest remedial measures to address the situation. This chapter investigates the evolution of thinking about managing binational water quality as expressed in the reports or follow-up of each of these investigations, and it will demonstrate that much of what was eventually included in the agreement was developed during that 1912–72 period through the binational discussion and exchange facilitated by boundary water pollution references.[1] It also considers the question posed by the editors of this volume—Is the Boundary Waters Treaty and the IJC "a pioneering model of bilateral environmental co-operation?"—by asserting in the affirmative, that, in the balance the treaty, the processes it engendered, and its institutions, including the Great Lakes Water Quality Agreement, have enabled better bilateral relations at the operational level for water resource managers in the United States and Canada, especially in the water quality realm.

The chapter begins with a discussion of a draft binational convention, developed in the 1920s after the IJC reported on its first reference, a 1912 assignment to investigate the state of boundary waters pollution. Jamie Benidickson's chapter in this volume, "The IJC and Water Quality in the Bacterial Age," provides detail on that first reference, in the context of the contemporary public health–sanitary engineering debate—whether to treat the municipal water supply at the point of distribution or to neutralize the effluent released from a community. The convention drafted as a result of the IJC's *Pollution of Boundary Waters Report* in 1918 included several elements that were later incorporated into the 1972 agreement. Two of these will be discussed here—the inclusion of a "standing reference," and a section that set out an approach to establishing pollution control measures for commercial vessels. The chapter will then trace the evolution of binational pollution engagement in the years after the Second World War, when the Connecting Channels Reference (1946–9) and its aftermath, and the Lower Lakes Reference (1964–9), provided many familiar elements later incorporated into the agreement, including General and Specific Water Quality Objectives, an acknowledgement that priority uses for boundary waters had expanded with societal changes in the post-war era, and the development of a binational governance structure that featured equal representation from US and Canadian governments and which benefited from and fostered a larger "Great Lakes" identity among board appointees. The chapter concludes by connecting these elements, extensions of the institutions developed under the Boundary Waters Treaty and auspices of the IJC, to the comparatively successful bilateral environmental relationships we in the Great Lakes enjoy.

The Convention Manqué: Prototype

In 1912, the governments of the United States and Canada asked the IJC to undertake its first investigation along the common border—to investigate the extent, causes, and location of boundary waters pollution and to provide advice on remedial measures addressing it. Reporting in 1918, after the largest bacteriological investigation in the world to that time,[2] the IJC recommended strengthening US and Canadian efforts to address Great Lakes pollution, including expanding the commission's role and recognizing that expanded role in a further bilateral agreement between the two countries. In response, the governments asked the IJC to draft a convention that incorporated its recommendations.[3]

On the surface it appeared as if this convention would fit into a number of initiatives between the two countries that had begun with the Boundary Waters Treaty of 1909. The gradual withdrawal of the British Foreign and Colonial Offices from Canadian-American relations had helped to improve relations significantly between the two countries. The successful operation of the IJC under the Boundary Waters Treaty is just one example of growing amity. The Migratory Bird Convention in 1916 provided further impetus for co-operation over natural resource management. The success prompted the Canadian Commission of Conservation to praise the emerging "system of practical co-operation in the protection of mutual [North American] interests," and to predict that as "new occasions for parallel action arise, the difficulties should prove easier of solution in light of the successes already attained."[4]

However, managing pollution in the Great Lakes, it turned out, would not to be one of those "new occasions for parallel action"—not yet, at least. The US government was not satisfied with the initial draft convention provided by the IJC, which was linked closely to the Boundary Waters Treaty. In 1926, therefore, the United States sent a new draft, written to be independent of the treaty, to the Canadian government with the intention that, should either document require future revision, it would not also require revision of the other document.⁵ Although internal Canadian review by the affected federal departments was positive, it did not progress speedily. IJC had to remind the agencies to provide their feedback, which was completed—and all positive—by May 1928; however, communication between the two countries related to the convention lapsed until it was revived by a State Department memo to the Canadian ambassador to the United States, Vincent Massey, on 25 October 1929.⁶ Four days later, the New York Stock Exchange crashed, and soon attention shifted to fighting the Great Depression. For the time being, neither government had the energy or impetus to consider boundary waters pollution.

A quick examination of the revised draft convention, however, will demonstrate that concepts later included in the Great Lakes Water Quality Agreement were already under consideration in the binational Great Lakes well before 1972. The revised draft consisted of seven articles, intended to enforce the pollution clause in article iv of the Boundary Waters Treaty and reflecting findings and recommendations from the 1918 report.⁷ One key concept in the draft document was the idea of a "standing reference." In addition to responding to requests from either or both the US or Canadian federal governments, the draft convention provided the IJC itself with authority to "enquire and determine whether any person by act or omission is polluting or contributing to the pollution of any waters on either side of the boundary between the United States and Canada to the injury of health or property on the other side."⁸ The convention went on to lay out the processes and procedures for conducting such investigations, including authority to compel witnesses and the obligation to give anyone a hearing whose acts or omissions were under investigation. It provided details on how the IJC could access relevant technical expertise and a process for funding such investigations. It outlined the content of resulting reports, in addition to when, how, and to whom they should be made.⁹ These latter details were already established as the process by which IJC references were conducted; however, the idea that the IJC could initiate such an investigation on its own was new. It offered the IJC an additional degree of autonomy that, as noted in the introduction to this collection, had not been considered achievable when the treaty was negotiated barely twenty years prior.

The 1972 Great Lakes Water Quality Agreement granted a similar level of autonomy to the IJC. The agreement laid out very specific responsibilities for the commission, including collating, analyzing, and disseminating data and information on Great Lakes water quality, assessing the effectiveness of programs designed to improve water quality, and providing advice on how to improve programs when they fell short.[10] In addition to this ongoing role to assess agreement-implementation progress and provide program advice, the agreement also empowered the IJC to "at any time make special reports to the Parties, to the State and Provincial Governments and to the public concerning any problem of water quality in the Great Lakes System."[11] These elements together have been interpreted as a "standing reference" because they empower the commission to undertake water-quality-related investigations without requiring them to be initiated by either federal government.[12]

Another idea incorporated into the 1972 agreement was initially introduced as a result of the first pollution reference—the idea that commercial vessels should be regulated in order to manage the pollution they discharged into the system. As directed under the first pollution reference from the two governments in 1912, the IJC's 1918 report outlined the sources and extent of existing pollution between Rainy River in the west and the St. Lawrence River in the east, and offered the commission's carefully considered recommendations for remedial measures. Unsurprisingly, the investigation found that the connecting channels, mouths of rivers, and other near-shore areas close to municipalities were heavily polluted by raw sewage. Surprisingly, however, they also found that commercial vessels discharging sewage and foul ballast water were a serious cause of pollution in the middle of otherwise pristine lakes. The navigation channels, for example, could be traced right down the middle of a lake by following the trail of polluted water.[13] As a result, pollution from commercial vessels easily crossed the international border from one side to the potential injury of health and property on the other because shipping channels typically trace the international border or are located in close proximity. This situation clearly violated the Boundary Waters Treaty and yet had not even been considered an issue when the treaty was negotiated.

As a result of the 1912 pollution investigation, the IJC recommended the US and Canadian governments develop common approaches to address vessel pollution.[14] When given the opportunity to incorporate this recommendation into the draft convention, the IJC proposed that it be given a significant role related to managing commercial vessels. This included the responsibility to define the size and type of vessels requiring sewage, bilge, and ballast water treatment, and equipment to prevent oil discharge. While the IJC would not have direct regulatory authority over commercial vessels, the convention proposed that compliance with IJC guidelines be required in order to acquire a commercial operating licence.[15]

The 1972 agreement did not give the IJC responsibility for developing measures to reduce or control vessel pollution. However, it did commit the parties to the agreement to doing this together in a way that produced "compatible regulations" that would govern design, construction, and operations of commercial vessels, and ensure that garbage, sewage, waste water, oil, and other "hazardous polluting substances" were not discharged from them into the Great Lakes.[16] The international "water highway" of the Great Lakes was being polluted by one of the key sectors for which the Boundary Waters Treaty had been negotiated—commercial navigation—and that clearly needed to end.

Although initially inviting the IJC to draft the convention in order to implement its 1918 recommendations, the US and Canadian governments seemed to lose interest in the document by the end of the 1920s. That can be attributed, in part, to the widespread adoption of chlorine in municipal water systems, which led to a precipitous decline in water-borne illnesses from drinking water, and an accompanying reduction in political pressure to do something about pollution in the Great Lakes and inland waters. The province of Ontario, for example, experienced a 20 per cent reduction in cases of water-borne typhoid fever during the middle years of the 1920s, when most municipalities with surface source water implemented chlorination.[17] The Great Depression and Second World War served to further divert interest from Great Lakes water quality, and it was only after the war that thoughts returned to the convention.

The 1930s and '40s, in the meantime, witnessed a continuing decline in water quality throughout the Great Lakes basin. During the Depression, building sewerage systems was well beyond the means of most communities in the region.[18] The onset of the Second World War diverted resources, which might have otherwise been allocated to pollution control infrastructure, into the massive industrial expansion of the war effort. By the end of the war, the region was home to rapidly growing industrial communities that, in many cases, lacked even the basic infrastructure to control municipal and industrial pollution. This was especially true for the St. Clair–Detroit River system, the southern Lake Erie shoreline between Toledo and Cleveland, the Niagara River, and the north shore of Lake Ontario between Hamilton and Oshawa. The connecting channels and lower lakes—Erie and Ontario—bore the brunt of the wartime and postwar expansion.

The Connecting Channels Reference: Familiar Concepts and Structures Emerge

In 1946 the United States and Canada again sent the IJC a reference to investigate boundary waters pollution, asking the commission to investigate the state of the connecting channels—the St. Clair River, Lake St. Clair, and the Detroit River. Later that year the two governments added the St. Marys River, from Lake Superior to Lake Huron. And in 1948 they added the Niagara River to the connecting channels pollution reference. Between 1946 and 1949, then, the IJC undertook a second comprehensive water quality survey of these waters, closely following the methods it had developed in the initial pollution reference in 1912. This enabled the commission to provide a close comparison of the state of the waters between the early and mid-twentieth century.

A short overview of the study and its findings will provide important context for the remaining discussion of the emergent concepts and governance structures finally incorporated into the Great Lakes Water Quality Agreement. The sixty-one communities under investigation along the connecting channels had a combined population of just over 3.5 million. Of those, 96 per cent had sewerage service and 86 per cent of that sewage had primary treatment. In the 1940s, primary treatment consisted of settling out the solids and then disinfecting the effluent before releasing it. Despite this relatively large extent of sewage treatment, the investigation found that bacteria levels were three to four times higher in 1946 than when they had last been tested in 1913. Clearly, primary treatment was not sufficient to safeguard raw water quality.[19]

While the IJC's 1918 pollution report had made only passing reference to industrial pollution, focused as it was on municipal waste (i.e., raw sewage), by 1946 the volume of pollution in the St. Clair–Detroit River system from industrial sources surpassed the amount of human waste entering the waters. After the Second World War, the average daily discharge of effluent from industries was more than 2 billion gallons, while municipalities released the comparatively smaller amount of 750 million gallons each day. However, the effect of the combined effluent on the biological functioning of the rivers amounted to that of a population twice the size of the number of people then living along the rivers.[20] In addition to the large amounts of suspended solids and oils, 13,000 pounds of phenols, 8,000 pounds of cyanides, and 25,000 pounds of ammonium compounds also entered the two rivers. Taking cyanide as an example: 8,000 pounds a day would result in a concentration of a little more than 8 micrograms per litre (µg/l).[21] A recent (2007) analysis by the World Health Organization noted that the US Environmental Protection Agency (EPA) reported that the "mean cyanide concentration in most surface waters in the USA is less than 3.5 µg/l," and that "levels are higher only in limited areas."[22] The influx of industrial wastes to the St. Clair and Detroit Rivers in the postwar era was approximately twice that routinely found in surface waters today.

General and Specific Water Quality Objectives

Given the preliminary results of the connecting channels survey, the IJC asked the technical experts conducting it to develop a list of Water Quality Objectives. These were intended to establish benchmarks against which the nature and extent of pollution could be assessed over time, and toward which municipalities, industries, and the states and province could work in reducing pollution. In April 1948, therefore, the IJC adopted Objectives for Boundary Waters Control. The objectives were divided into two categories. The first category, General Objectives, related to overall water quality and was intended to ensure that all effluent released into boundary waters, whether from municipal sewerage systems, industrial processes, or stormwater, was of high enough quality that it not interfere with established or desired uses of boundary waters.[23] The second category, Specific Objectives, identified very explicit maximum loads for specific pollutants.

For example: domestic sewage and ship effluent should have a concentration of no more than 2,400 *B. coli* per 100 ml of water prior to dilution in the open waters; the class of industrial chemicals called phenols should be at no higher concentration than 5 parts per billion after dilution.[24]

The idea of setting General and Specific Water Quality Objectives, first adopted in the late 1940s as a result of the Connecting Channels Reference, proved to be an important concept that was later incorporated into the Great Lakes Water Quality Agreement in 1972. Similar to the 1940s, the General Objectives laid out in the agreement were high-level, aspirational statements for the quality of boundary waters, and included the idea that they should not be polluted with human-introduced materials that were harmful to human, animal, or aquatic life, that might form "putrescent or otherwise objectionable sludge deposits." Likewise, human activities should not introduce debris such as oils, scums, and "other floating materials" in quantities sufficient to reduce aesthetic values, or introduce a nuisance taste, odour, or colour. Finally, human-introduced nutrients should not be in such concentrations that they encourage aquatic weeds or algae to grow.[25]

Specific Objectives in the 1972 agreement identified levels of individual substances, or physical effects, that both sides agreed were either a minimum or maximum desired limit for a given portion of the boundary waters "taking into account the beneficial uses of the water that the Parties desire to secure and protect."[26] With foresight, the negotiators of the agreement recognized that Specific Objectives were likely to change over time as new substances were identified, as new evidence suggested that earlier maximum or minimum levels were no longer sufficient, or as unanticipated issues arose. As a result, the Specific Objectives were placed in an annex to the agreement. This was meant to provide greater flexibility, with the parties agreeing to revisit the Specific Objectives periodically per the consultation and review provisions laid out in the agreement.[27]

Conflicting Uses: Updated and Revised Order of Precedence

The IJC presented its initial findings about the state of the connecting channels during public hearings held in communities on both sides of the St. Clair, Detroit, and Niagara Rivers in the summer and fall of 1948 and again in 1949. These meetings were attended by industrial and municipal officials, representatives of interested non-governmental organizations, and citizens from the communities in which the hearings were held. The hearings confirmed that the public was quite aware of the deplorable state of the connecting channels. They also highlighted a growing conflict between long-accepted uses of the water, such as for disposal of sewage and industrial waste, and emerging uses requiring much better ambient water quality. One of the more sensitive of these uses was for tourism. The immediate postwar period saw an explosion in the use of beaches and riverside parks along the connecting channels. This was the beginning of a huge outdoor recreation boom fueled by unprecedented postwar economic growth, which spread across almost every income level and social group in the Great Lakes basin. This general prosperity, combined with the greater mobility provided by private cars and the growth of highways, allowed more people to get away from their urban and suburban homes for vacations and weekend car trips.

The understanding of potentially conflicting uses of boundary waters and how they might be affected by both reduced water quality and quantity, had evolved in complexity through the century. The Boundary Waters Treaty gave the IJC authority to approve the "use, diversion or obstruction" (i.e., the available amount) of boundary waters only if the proposed activity did not materially interfere with any use above it in the established order of precedence of uses. The order of precedence, laid out in article viii of the treaty, was as follows: first, domestic and sanitary uses; second, navigation, including diverting water into canals to go around waterfalls and rapids; and third, power and irrigation. Article viii dealt strictly with water quantity and was intended to ensure that enough water was available for the established uses, not that it be of an appropriate quality. When the IJC reported on its first pollution report in 1918, the idea that one use of the Great Lakes—navigation—was in conflict with another use—municipal water supply—due to the impact on water *quality* represented the first evolution in thinking. Thus it was an important transition when the IJC reported on its initial pollution reference indicating that water quality was also an important consideration.

By the Connecting Channels Reference in the late 1940s, the conflict between these competing uses was even more heightened. Tourism was second only to the auto industry in Michigan and the third-most important economic activity in Ontario. The commissioners learned during public hearings that polluted boundary waters would have significant economic repercussions if it meant tourists went elsewhere as a result.[28] The commission therefore asserted in its 1951 report that, in general, all effluent released into boundary waters, whether from municipal sewerage systems, industrial processes, or stormwater, needed to be of sufficient quality that it not interfere with established or desired uses of boundary waters.

In its 1951 *Report of the International Joint Commission United States and Canada on the Pollution of Boundary Waters*, the commission proposed an expanded and updated list of priority, or desired, uses. In addition to municipal and sanitary uses, the IJC added industrial applications to the most important uses, or most sensitive in terms of water quality. This was because many industrial processes, such as food processing and chemical production, required very high raw water quality. Navigation remained the second-most important use; the commission then named fish and wildlife, swimming, recreation, and "other riparian activities" to the final group, which had previously included only irrigation and power. This expanded list was the IJC's acknowledgement of the growing importance of outdoor recreation and a societal appreciation for aesthetic concerns. These more sensitive uses of boundary waters were given weight against the health and economic uses originally identified in the treaty.[29]

While not directly enumerating a new order-of-precedence list, the 1972 agreement clearly prioritized more-sensitive uses of water over less-sensitive needs, based on water quality. For example, the definition of Specific Water Quality Objectives stated that allowed levels of substances or physical effects would take "into account the beneficial uses of the water that the Parties desire to secure and protect." Further, the General Objectives identified aesthetic and ecological benefits such as aquatic life and waterfowl. Aesthetics were also called out when the Parties committed to avoid "putrescent or otherwise objectionable sludge deposits," "unsightly or deleterious" floating materials, or anything causing nuisance colour, odour, or taste, and excessive nutrients causing algal blooms or aquatic weed growth. Health and well-being rounded out the priority list. The General Objectives aspired to avoid substances at concentrations harmful to humans, animals, or aquatic life.[30] It is difficult to draw a more direct comparison between the uses implied in the agreement and those stated outright in the treaty, given the former's focus on water quality alone. However, it is clear that by 1972 there were many more broadly recognized competing uses for the Great Lakes than there had been in 1909.

New Structures Emerge: Binational Pollution Boards

The IJC's 1951 connecting channels report concluded that those responsible for generating pollution should be required to meet the cost of cleaning it up and that the United States and Canada had adequate legislative authorities to accomplish this. In order to achieve the necessary focus on water quality that would ensure the application of these authorities, the IJC also asked that it be authorized to establish and supervise "boards of control" for boundary water quality. The boards would ensure that the Water Quality Objectives were met through the adoption and implementation of the 1951 report's recommended remedial measures. These boards were likely envisaged to operate similar to the water quantity boards of control for several of the Great Lakes, as described in Clamen and Macfarlane's chapter in this volume. The boards of control were responsible for maintaining water at IJC-designated levels by regulating and coordinating the operation of hydroelectric power canals, compensating works, and navigation locks at these locations. Similarly, the IJC anticipated that the proposed water quality boards would identify municipalities, businesses, and individuals whose actions contravened the Water Quality Objectives, allowing the IJC to inform those in violation about expected remedial measures. If actions to improve water quality were not taken promptly after the offender was informed, the commission would notify the responsible government authority with recommended corrective action(s).[31]

In November 1951, the US and Canadian governments authorized the IJC to establish and maintain supervision of boundary water pollution and the remedial measures necessary to control it. The commission promptly appointed permanent, binational Technical Advisory Boards on Pollution Control for the connecting channels, comprised primarily of the state, provincial, and federal agency personnel who had conducted the connecting channels pollution reference. While oversight of these boards represented an expansion of the IJC's current duties, it did not approach the level of authority the IJC had requested in the 1918 pollution report and incorporated into the draft convention. Nor, in the end, were the bodies called "boards of control." This decision appears to have been an acknowledgement of potential political barriers to the IJC attaining additional authorities.[32]

The idea of technical advisory boards, consisting of representatives of the pollution management agencies from the affected jurisdictions, was a natural outgrowth of the way the IJC conducted investigations sent to it by the two governments. Lacking large technical staffs with which to conduct involved, binational investigations, the IJC had determined very early in its existence that the best way to carry out a reference was to second the necessary expertise from the state, provincial, and federal agencies whose jurisdictions were touched by the study. The commission strove for jurisdictional parity in numbers from the beginning as well. This configuration was IJC standard operating procedure, so much so that many state and provincial agency personnel found themselves almost continuously on IJC study boards or appointed to the technical advisory boards in the post–Second World War era. For example, A. E. Berry from Ontario served on the connecting channels study board, was appointed Ontario's representative to the Technical Advisory Boards on Pollution Control, and later provided advice to the IJC from retirement as it set up the lower lakes pollution study in the 1960s.[33] The configuration of the technical advisory boards was therefore determined from IJC practices established at the outset of its binational work.

This board structure, balanced according to national and jurisdictional representation, was subsequently incorporated into the 1972 agreement. The negotiators identified two key functions for which the IJC required additional support, and they developed separate advisory boards to provide it. The first group, designed to "assist in the exercise of the powers and responsibilities assigned" to the IJC under the agreement, was named the Great Lakes Water Quality Board. This board's membership consisted of equal numbers of representatives of the US and Canadian governments representing the signatory parties to the agreement—the US EPA and Environment Canada—as well as from each of the states, and the province of Ontario. The second group, a Research Advisory Board, was also appointed to provide advice to the commission on important gaps in knowledge on which the IJC, in turn, could advise the parties. It, too, was comprised of equal numbers of US and Canadian appointees.[34] These groups provided opportunities to build regular, binational working relationships as the agreement was implemented.

Binational Working Relationships: The Key to Success

When other regions on the globe that share water and other common pool resources look at the governance and historical co-operation in the Great Lakes basin, they are often envious. It is challenging for those whose day-to-day professional life involves working across jurisdictions in the Great Lakes region to fully appreciate the value of sustained binational engagement here, but it cannot be underestimated. In the introduction to this collection, Clamen and Macfarlane ask if the Boundary Waters Treaty and its primary institution, the IJC, provide a pioneering model of bilateral co-operation. As they note, the discussion of IJC's role, as reflected in the literature, provides "disparate and competing" interpretations of the treaty's and the commission's saliency. However, on the whole, the treaty, the processes it engendered, and its institutions, including the agreement, have enabled better bilateral relations at the operational level for water resource managers in the United States and Canada, especially in the water quality realm.

With antecedents in the 1912 pollution reference, and the Connecting Channels and Lower Lakes References in the 1940s and '60s, respectively, parity of US and Canadian representation and regular interaction of all parties—state and federal—was codified into the joint institutions outlined in the 1972 agreement. This included not just the advisory boards, but also the Great Lakes Regional Office located, after much debate, in Windsor, Ontario. The IJC's professional Great Lakes staff was also recruited in equal numbers from each country, similar to the binational complexion of the Water Quality Board and the Research Advisory Board. Binational parity extended to assignments of board secretaries—one each from the US and Canadian technical staff—and the tradition that the office directorship is a four-year, term-limited appointment that rotates between US and Canadian candidates.[35]

This binational parity and engagement did not appear out of nowhere, nor did it evolve in isolation. For example, other regional institutions addressing the shared resources of the Great Lakes, such as the Great Lakes Fishery Commission and the Great Lakes Commission, were important inter-state and binational forums for otherwise parochial resource managers, policy-makers, and public officials to interact and engage with colleagues from jurisdictions spanning the region. However, the IJC was the first such body to operate with jurisdictional parity and, arguably, set the stage for these other organizations. And while some communication and collaboration with the agencies immediately adjacent to a state or province could be anticipated in normal resource management operations, these broader regional forums offered regular opportunities for people from one end of the region to meet and learn from their counterparts at the other end of the basin and from across the international boundary.[36]

For the Great Lakes water quality community involved in IJC activities between 1950 and 1972, there were many joint efforts, such as participating at meetings of the Technical Advisory Boards on Pollution Control, and working on the Lower Lakes Reference given the commission in 1964. Additional opportunities arose from the ongoing water quality work, such as briefing and accompanying state and provincial political leaders to the 1970 governors and premiers summit on the emerging Great Lakes agreement. All these activities provided formal and informal opportunities for members of this relatively small community to meet and talk, to share common experiences, work together to solve common challenges, and generally evolve a perspective that was more regional and "Great Lakes" in scope, than state or provincially focused.

This broader Great Lakes perspective is considered an important element of the initial effectiveness and success of the IJC's Water Quality

Board. When asked to comment on the experience of being on, or working with, the initial Water Quality Board, several regional leaders identified three keys to the board's success. These are the fact that board members were senior appointees who regularly attended meetings, and who were capable of making commitments on behalf of their agencies; strong technical support from both seconded agency staff and IJC staff in the Great Lakes regional office; and perhaps most important, the board member's commitment to the greater good of the Great Lakes. Leaders recalled the "overriding commitment" on the part of board members that they "were there to protect the lakes and everyone [on the Water Quality Board] wanted to do that."[37] This binational structure therefore worked like a positive feedback loop—senior, committed people deliberated on the strong technical work of a series of sub-committees, considered the actions that would be necessary to address problems identified by the sub-committees, and committed their governments to undertaking those actions.

Conclusion

Signing the 1972 Great Lakes Water Quality Agreement was clearly a landmark event in the United States–Canada relationship. It was the first time president and prime minister committed to address the water quality woes of the Great Lakes as a joint endeavour worthy of executive-level agreement. We should not be tempted, however, to view it in isolation and consider it the pinnacle of our two countries' interactions in Great Lakes water quality. Instead, we can see that the 1972 agreement reflects all that went before and is foundational to what has occurred since.

The agreement incorporated important concepts and structures that were initially proposed after the first pollution reference and subsequently evolved over the twentieth century. It also institutionalized inter-state/provincial and federal interactions, the value of which was clear from the number and type of inter-state/provincial and federal interactions that occurred through the Connecting Channels and Lower Lakes References, as well as through appointment and participation on the Technical Advisory Boards on Pollution Control. These are the kinds of opportunities and processes that will be beneficial to sustain or revive going forward. Opportunities for agency personnel to formally and, more importantly, informally interact with each other in person, is key to sustaining a larger, supra-state or national "Great Lakes" identity. The value of these kinds of meetings in fortifying a shared commitment to the larger Great Lakes basin, its ecological and economic health, cannot be overstated. In the end, the many entities with responsibility for protecting and enhancing Great Lakes water quality will benefit from this shared vision.

Notes

1. This chapter is based on previously unpublished research, as well as nearly twenty years' worth of work on water quality issues and binational governance on both sides of the border. See Jennifer Read, "Addressing 'A quiet horror': The Evolution of Ontario Pollution Control Policy in the International Great Lakes, 1909–1972" (PhD diss., University of Western Ontario, 1999).

2. See Jamie Benidickson, "The IJC and Water Quality in the Bacteriological Age" (chapter 3 in this volume). The assessment that this was the largest bacteriological investigation comes from Mary Durfee and Susan T. Bagley, "Bacteriology and Diplomacy in the Great Lakes, 1912–1920" (paper presented at the biennial meeting of the American Society for Environmental History, Baltimore, MD, 6–9 March 1997).

3. International Joint Commission (IJC), Library and Archives (Ottawa), Docket 4-3-1:1, IJC to the Secretary of State for External Affairs and the Secretary of State, 6 October 1920, 1–6.

4. Government of Canada (Canada), Commission of Conservation. *Conservation* VIII (October 1919), 41.

5. IJC, Docket 4-3-1:1, Frank B. Kellog to His Majesty's Ambassador at Washington, 8 February 1926.

6. Canada, Department of External Affairs, vol. 2644, file pocket 2871-40C, T. M. Patterson, Chronological Review of Negotiations re. Proposed Convention between Canada and the United States with respect to the Pollution of Boundary Waters and Waters Flowing Across the Boundary from August 1, 1912 to October 25, 1929," 1 October 1937, 8–12.

7. Ontario Archives (OA), Water Resources Branch, ACC 1988-89/059, box 27, file 7858-1, vol. 1, L. J. Burpee, "Memorandum for Mr. Magrath," no date, 6; and "Confidential memorandum for Mr. Magrath," no date, 8.

8. Library and Archives (LAC), IJC Docket 4-3-1:1, "Draft of a Convention to Prevent the Pollution of Boundary Waters Between Canada and the United States, 1926," Article II.

9. Draft Convention, Article II. Hereafter, "Convention."

10. Canada-United States. "Agreement between the United States and Canada on Great Lakes Water Quality," Article VI, 1, a-d, 15 April 1972. Hereafter, "Agreement."

11 Agreement, Article IV, 3.

12 Agreement, Article VI, 3. The "standing reference" concept is widely discussed among "old guard" Great Lakes folks, usually over beer after a long day at a conference, and specifically identified in Allan Schwartz, "The Management of Shared Waters: Watershed Boards Past and Future," in *Bilateral Eco-politics: Continuity and Change in Canadian-American Environmental Relations*, ed. Phillipe LePrestre and Peter Stoett (Routledge: London, 2006), 133–44.

13 IJC, *Final Report of the International Joint Commission on the Pollution of Boundary Waters Reference* (Washington, DC: Government Printing Office, 1918), 51–2.

14 Ibid., 28.

15 Convention, Article V.

16 Agreement, Article V, Annexes 3 and 4.

17 Ontario Board of Health, *Forty-fifth Annual Report of the Department of Health Ontario, Canada for the year 1925* (Toronto: King's Printer, 1927), 14, and Department of Health, *Third Annual Report of the Department of Health Ontario, Canada for the Year 1927* (Toronto: King's Printer, 1928), 44.

18 In Ontario the provincial Department of Health lost a significant amount of personnel, which affected its ability to evaluate and approve water and sewerage system construction projects and oversee operation of plants that did exist. See, for example, Ontario Department of Health, *Report of the Board of Health*, "Division of Sanitary Engineering" (Toronto: King's Printer, 1932–6 inclusive).

19 IJC, *Report of the International Joint Commission United States and Canada on the Pollution of Boundary Waters* (Washington, DC: Government Printing Office, 1951), 18–19.

20 Ibid.

21 Don Scavia, personal communication, 25 February 2019.

22 World Health Organization, *Cyanide in Drinking Water: Background document for the development of WHO Guidelines for Drinking-water Quality* (Geneva, CH: WHO Press, 2007), 3.

23 Ibid., 18.

24 Ibid. 18–19; IJC, Docket 54-3-1:4 "Correspondence – 1948," internal IJC document, "Phenols."

25 Agreement, Article II.

26 Agreement, Article I.

27 Agreement, Article III, and Annex 1.

28 IJC, Docket 54-2-2:1 "Transcript of Hearings in Detroit, 28 June 1948," 165–7, and Docket 54-2-2:10 "Transcript of Hearings – Windsor and Sault Ste. Marie, Ontario 19-22 November 1948, vol. 2," 418.

29 *Pollution of Boundary Waters* (1951), 18. Specific complaints about tainted flavours and odours came from municipal drinking water system operators as well as processed food and distilling industries, especially those with water intakes downstream of Sarnia, Ontario. See IJC, Docket 54-2-2:1 "Transcript of Hearings in Detroit, 28 June 1948," 29–33, and Docket 54-2-2:9 "Transcript of Hearings in Windsor, 17-18 November 1948, vol. 1," 130–5, 154–5, 228–30, 233. and 245–6.

30 Agreement, Article III.

31 *Pollution of Boundary Waters* (1951), 21–2.

32 In writing the 1951 report, the commissioners referred to the "reasons which impelled the Governments not to take action which had been indicated in the draft treaty (convention) proposed by the commission after the first investigation [into] pollution." Unfortunately, they did not elaborate on specific reasons. And I was unable to find any additional insights in IJC and federal memoranda related to the 1926 convention. This discussion during an executive session in 1953 is the only clear indication that there may have been political reasons for letting the convention lapse. See IJC, Docket 54-2-5:1 "Executive Session, Ottawa, Canada, 8 October 1953," 33.

33 LAC, MG 55/30, file 208, "1983 Interview with Dr. A. E. Berry, Public Works Engineer, Conducted by Norman Ball, Public Archives of Canada, and Robert G. Ferguson, Metropolitan Works Department, on Behalf of APWA, Ontario Chapter."

34 Agreement, Article VII.

35 John Gannon, interview with author, 1 March 2018, and J. P. Bruce, personal communication, 21 March 2018.

36 The Great Lakes Basin Commission and the Great Lakes Commission were two important political and institutional influences on the implementation of the GLWQA. They helped to maintain political and technical/governmental focus on Great Lakes issues. These institutions were particularly important in offering formal, institutional arrangements with an explicit Great Lakes basin perspective and were important in getting the US states used to working together in a collective fashion on selected basin-wide issues. Also, these institutions reinforced the bilateral perspective as Canadian federal and provincial agencies were offered observer status at these institutions and participated fully in discussions. See Jennifer Read, "An analysis of the intellectual and political influences on the *Great Lakes Water Quality Agreements* of 1972, 1978 and the 1987 Protocol," report prepared for the IJC Great Lakes Regional Office, Windsor, ON, July 2005.

37 Confidential personal communication with former IJC staff member. See also, Jack Manno, "Advocacy and Diplomacy in the Great Lakes: A Case History of Non-governmental Organization Participation in Negotiating the *Great Lakes Water Quality Agreement*," *Buffalo Environmental Law Journal* 1, no. 1 (1993), https://digitalcommons.law.buffalo.edu/belj/vol1/iss1/1/; and Lee Botts and Paul Muldoon, *The Great Lakes Water Quality Agreement: Its Past Successes and Uncertain Future* (Hanover, NH: Institute for International Environmental Governance, Dartmouth College, 1996).

12

The Great Lakes Remedial Action Plan Program: A Historical and Contemporary Description and Analysis

Gail Krantzberg

The Great Lakes and other lakes and rivers in the basin provide drinking water to millions. On both sides of the border, the basin supports multi-billion-dollar manufacturing, service, tourism, and outdoor recreation industries, as well as strong maritime transportation systems and diversified agricultural sectors. It provides the foundation for trade between Canada and the United States, equaling approximately 50 per cent of Canada's annual trade with the United States. Each year, the Great Lakes region contributes $180 billion to Canada-US trade. The Great Lakes region includes eight states (Minnesota, Wisconsin, Illinois, Indiana, Michigan, New York, Ohio, and Pennsylvania) and two Canadian provinces (Ontario and Quebec) The area is home to 107 million people, 51 million jobs, and a GDP of US$6 trillion.[1]

Degradation of environmental quality directly damages the viability and vigour of the region. The reliance of the economy on a healthy Great Lakes basin ecosystem is unequivocal and the imperative to restore ecosystem health is clear. To strive for a sustainable future, social and ecological and economic interests must be integrated. As Constanza asserts, sustainability can be defined as a balanced relationship between the

FIGURE 12.1. Location and status of the Areas of Concern. Used with permission of Binational.net.

AOC	Restrictions on fish & wildlife consumption	Tainting of fish & wildlife flavor	Degraded fish & wildlife populations	Fish tumor or other deformities	Bird & animal deformities or reproduction	Degradation of benthos	Restrictions on dredging activities	Eutrophication or undesirable algae	Restrictions - drinking water consumption, taste/odor problems	Beach Closings	Degradation of aesthetics	Added costs to agriculture or industry	Degradation of phyto- and zoo- plankton	Loss of fish and wildlife habitat
Thunder Bay						■	*2012			■	*2019	*2004		■
Nipigon Bay (Delisting Pending)		*1995		*1995		*2016	*1995	*2016			*2016			*2016
Jackfish Bay (In Recovery)			■	*2010		■	*1998							■
Peninsula Harbour	■					◆	*2012							
St. Marys River	■		■	■		■	◆	*2018		*2018	*2018			■
Spanish Harbour (In Recovery)	■		*1999			■	◆			*1999		*1999		
Severn Sound (Delisted 2003)	*2002		*2002				*2002	*2002						*2002
Collingwood Harbour (Delisted 1994)	*1994		*1994		*1994	*1994	*1994	*1994		*1994	*1994		*1994	
St. Clair River	■					■	*2018		■	*2018	*2016	*2012		■
Detroit River	■	*2014	■	◆	■	◆	*2019		*2010	*2016	*2016	*2010		■
Wheatley Harbour (Delisted 2010)	*2010		*2010				*2010	*2010						*2010
Niagara River	■		■		*2009	■	*2009	*2019		■				■
Hamilton Harbour	■		◆			■	■	■		■	■			■
Toronto and Region	■		■			*2016	*2016	■		■	◆			■
Port Hope Harbour							■							
Bay of Quinte	■		*2018			*2018	*2017	■	◆	*2019	■		■	*2018
St. Lawrence River	■		■			*2007	*2007	■	*1997	◆	*1997	*1997		■

* BUI Removed
■ BUI Impaired
◆ Projected for Removal in 2019

dynamic human economic systems and the dynamic but generally slower-changing ecological systems in which: 1) human life can continue indefinitely; 2) people can flourish, 3) cultures can develop, but within such bounds that human activities do not destroy the diversity, complexity, and function of the ecological life-support system.[2] Sustainable Great Lakes resilience requires, then, socio-ecological governance of the system.

As consumerism and industrial production are on the rise, non-renewable and renewable natural resources are being used more frequently in order to satisfy human desires. As described by de Boer and Krantzberg,

> Robert Hennigan at the Thirteenth Conference on Great Lakes Research expressed that there is a requirement for understanding and reform of the Great Lakes institutional ecosystem to establish an attainable and workable system for effective water management. Incorporation of the action elements of persuasion and education, legal action and economic incentives were noted as being particularly necessary for the success of this system.[3]

This insight still holds, and it calls on stakeholders to regard the water management issue as an integrated governance challenge and not a compilation of programs and policies applied reactively to address insults to the system.[4]

Binational Accords and Events

> *The United States of America and His Majesty the King of the United Kingdom of Great Britain and Ireland and of the British Dominions beyond the Seas, Emperor of India, being equally desirous to prevent disputes regarding the use of boundary waters and to settle all questions which are now pending between the United States and the Dominion of Canada involving the rights, obligations, or interests of either in relation to the other or to the inhabitants of the other, along their common frontier, and to make provision for the*

> *adjustment and settlement of all such questions as may hereafter arise, have resolved to conclude a treaty in furtherance of these ends, and for that purpose have appointed as their respective plenipotentiarie.*
>
> —Boundary Waters Treaty[5]

The 1909 Boundary Waters Treaty stated that "boundary waters and water flowing across the boundary shall not be polluted on either side to the injury of health or property on the other." The treaty created the International Joint Commission (IJC) to prevent and resolve disputes over the use of boundary waters and to deal with boundary tensions between the two nations. Further, article ix of the treaty goes on to specify that the IJC can investigate a specific transboundary issue under a formal request by both governments (worked out bilaterally) termed a "reference." Using this provision, the United States and Canada issued a joint reference in 1964 to the IJC to investigate pollution in Lake Erie and elsewhere on the lower lakes, perhaps as a result of the growing public and scientific concern about water pollution in North America after the Second World War.[6]

One of the earliest IJC dockets, this reference was focused on water quality, particularly on eutrophication in the lower Great Lakes (see Jamie Benidickson's chapter in this collection), and interest in water quality that intensified after the Second World War (which Jennifer Read covers in her chapter in this collection). A 1966 detailed investigation of pollution problems in Lakes Erie and Ontario and the St. Lawrence River resulted in an in-depth report on water quality and the recommendation for an international lower lakes clean-up effort focused on the role of phosphorus in eutrophication. The report eventually resulted in the signing of the Great Lakes Water Quality Agreement in 1972. The agreement coordinated an international clean-up effort to enhance the water quality of the Great Lakes. The IJC became actively involved in analyzing and disseminating information. The commission advised both governments on effectiveness of programs and provided water quality updates.

In 1978, the Canadian and US governments reviewed the agreement of 1972 and revised it to reaffirm the commitment of each country to restore and maintain the chemical, physical, and biological integrity of the Great Lakes basin ecosystem. Even more comprehensive than the original agreement, the 1978 Great Lakes Water Quality Agreement placed greater emphasis on the management of toxic substances, dredging and shipping regulations, and continuation of the phosphorus control program started in 1972.

Since 1973, the Great Lakes Water Quality Board (WQB), the principal policy advisors to the IJC, in its annual assessments of water quality, identified Areas of Concern (originally called Problem Areas) where Great Lakes Water Quality Agreement objectives have been exceeded and where such exceedance has caused or is likely to cause impairment of beneficial use or the area's ability to support aquatic life.[7]

The WQB, in its 1977 annual report, again listed the problem areas; described the nature of the problem; identified dischargers of one or more substances that were probably causing the problem; and commented on progress toward compliance with jurisdictional enforcement programs. The report also described remedial programs in the drainage basin of each problem area and progress toward meeting boundary water quality objectives. In 1983 the WQB determined that classifying Areas of Concern was difficult due to the lack of specificity of the criteria used to classify the areas and the guidelines to be used for their evaluation. This led to difficulties in data interpretation for the purpose of defining the problems and deducing trends in environmental quality. In order to overcome these difficulties, the board developed a procedure for data assessment and identification of Areas of Concern (AOC). The unique experiment in place-based remediation and protection called for in the 1987 protocol emerged directly from recommendations made by the WQB.[8]

In 1987, a protocol was signed amending the 1978 agreement. The amendments were aimed at strengthening the programs, practices, and technology described in the 1978 agreement and to increase accountability for their implementation. Timetables were set for implementation of specific programs. New annexes addressed atmospheric deposition of toxic pollutants, contaminated sediment, groundwater, and non-point sources of pollution. Annexes were also added to incorporate the development and implementation of Remedial Action Plans (RAPs) for the various AOC and Lakewide Management Plans to control critical pollutants.

Annex 2 of the 1987 Great Lakes Water Quality Agreement (GLWQA)

In 1985, the WQB reported that a clear method of measuring progress in AOC implementation or removing a place from the AOC list (known as "delisting") was absent. The WQB created a process for AOC development and implementation with categories that identify the status of the information database, ongoing programs to fill in information gaps, and the extent of remedial efforts directed at addressing specific use impairments. Hartig and Thomas pointed out that early in the program establishment, the development of RAPs represented a challenging departure from most historical pollution control efforts, where separate programs for regulation of municipal and industrial discharge, urban run-off, and agriculture run-off were implemented without considering overlapping responsibilities or whether they would be adequate to restore beneficial uses.[7] This new process called upon the talents available in a wide array of programs far beyond those traditionally associated with water pollution control, including the involvement of local communities and a wide range of agencies at all government levels. All programs, agencies, and communities affecting an AOC were to come together to work on common goals and objectives in the RAP.

The location and status of the geographic AOCs is presented in Figure 12.1. Originally, the Province of Ontario had 17 AOCs, the state of Michigan had 14, the state of Wisconsin had 4, Ohio had 4, and New York had 6; St. Louis River/Bay is the only AOC in Minnesota, Waukegan Harbor is the only AOC in Illinois, and the Grand Calumet River/Indiana Harbor is the only AOC in Indiana.

Annex 2 in the 1987 protocol identifies fourteen Beneficial Use Impairments and initiated programs to restore these uses to the Great Lakes. These are:

1. restrictions on fish and wildlife consumption;
2. tainting of fish and wildlife flavour;
3. degradation of fish wildlife populations;
4. fish tumors or other deformities;

FIGURE 12.2. RAP review process for delisting AOCs.

Legend:
- * BUI Removed (shown as *YEAR)
- ■ BUI Impaired
- ◆ Projected for Removal in 2019

AOC	Restrictions on fish & wildlife consumption	Tainting of fish & wildlife flavor	Degraded fish & wildlife populations	Fish tumor or other deformities	Bird & animal deformities or reproduction problems	Degradation of benthos	Restrictions on dredging activities	Eutrophication or undesirable algae	Restrictions – drinking water consumption, taste/odor problems	Beach Closings	Degradation of aesthetics	Added costs to agriculture or industry	Degradation of phyto- and zoo-plankton	Loss of fish and wildlife habitat
Waukegan Harbor	■				*2018	*2014				*2011		*2011	■	*2013
Grand Calumet River	■	■	■	■	■	■	■	■	*2012	■	◆	*2011		■
Clinton River	■		■			■		■	■		■	◆		■
Deer Lake	*2014				*2011			*2011						
Detroit River	■	*2013	■	■	■	■	■		*2011	■	■	*2011	*2012	■
Kalamazoo River	■		■		■	■	■			*2010				*2008
Manistique River	■				*2007		■							■
Muskegon Lake	*2013					■	*2011	■	*2013	*2015	■			■
River Raisin	■		*2015			■		*2013		*2013	*2012			*2015
Rouge River	■		■	■		■	■		■					■
Saginaw River & Bay	■	*2008	■		■	■		■	*2006	■	■		■	*2014
Torch Lake	■			*2007		■								
White Lake	*2013		*2014			*2012	*2011	*2012	*2014		*2014			*2014
St. Clair River	■	*2010		*2017	*2015	*2011		*2018	*2017	*2016	*2012	*2012		*2017
St. Marys River	■		◆	■	*2014	■				*2016	*2014			◆
Menominee River	*2018		*2019			*2017	*2017			*2011				*2019
Buffalo River	■	■	■	■	■	■	■				*2018			■
Eighteenmile Creek	■		■		■	■								
Oswego River	*2006		*2006				*2006							*2006
Rochester Embayment	■	*2018	■	*2015	■	*2017	*2019	◆	*2011	◆	■	*2011	*2016	■
Niagara River	■		■		*2016	■	■						*2015	■
St. Lawrence River	■		■		■	■								
Ashtabula River	*2014		*2014	◆		*2018	■							*2014
Black River	*2017		■	■		■	*2017			■	■			■
Cuyahoga River	*2019		■	■		■	■			■	*2018	*2015		■
Maumee River	■		■			■	■			■		*2015		■
Presque Isle				*2013		*2007								
Fox River/S Green Bay	■	■	■		■	■	■	■		■	■		■	■
Milwaukee Estuary	■		■	■	■	■	■	■			■		■	■
Sheboygan River	■		■	■	■	■		*2015	*2016		■		■	■
St. Louis River & Bay	■		*2019			■	■				*2014			■

12 | The Great Lakes Remedial Action Plan Program

5. bird or animal deformities or reproduction problems;
6. degradation of benthos;
7. restrictions on dredging activities;
8. eutrophication or undesirable algae;
9. restrictions on drinking water consumption, or taste and odour problems
10. beach closings;
11. degradation of aesthetics;
12. added costs to agriculture or industry;
13. degradation of phytoplankton and zooplankton populations; and
14. loss of fish and wildlife habitat.[9]

In the 1985 *Report on Great Lakes Water Quality*, a jurisdictional schedule for submission of RAPs was presented.[10] The jurisdictions reported that all 42 RAPs would be completed by December 1986. As was concluded at a forum for RAP coordinators in October 1986, the jurisdictions underestimated the time and resources necessary to develop RAPs.[11] As of 2019, RAPs continue to be implemented across the basin. At present the United States has delisted four AOCs: Oswego River, Presque Isle Bay, White Lake, and Deer Lake, while Canada has delisted three: Severn Sound, Collingwood Harbour, and Wheatley Harbour. Further progress is illustrated in Tables 1 and 2 (titled Table 3 in the *Progress Report of the Parties*, available at binational.net).

The Great Lakes Water Quality Agreement protocol of 2012, which is covered in more detail in this volume by Johns and VanNijnatten, re-affirmed the parties' commitment to implement RAPs under the new Annex 1, which retained the content of the Annex 2 from 1987 and added guidance of designating Areas of Concern in Recovery (which will be discussed further below). The agreement calls for the federal governments, in co-operation with state and provincial governments, to ensure the public is consulted throughout the development and implementation

FIGURE 12.3. Collingwood Harbour was designated as an AOC in 1987. Major environmental concerns in the area included nuisance growth of algae in the harbour and contaminated sediment.

> A critical component of the restoration of Collingwood Harbour was to reduce the concentration of phosphorus and control eutrophication (excessive nutrients that can cause algae growth). Technical solutions focused on optimizing phosphorous removal at the Collingwood Sewage Treatment Plant through an innovative demonstration project. The technology achieved an effluent quality comparable to that of tertiary treatment - the highest level of treatment generally used in highly sensitive ecosystems - but at less than 10% of the cost. In response to the loading reductions, the harbour is no longer eutrophic.
>
> In November 1992, a demonstration project was initiated to safely remove sediment contaminated with heavy metals using the Pneuma pump innovative dredge technology. The sediment was piped into a confined disposal facility. The successful demonstration led to a full-scale cleanup in the harbour in 1993. This rehabilitated the degraded benthic community, removed deleterious substances, and allowed the lifting of restrictions on navigational dredging. This was the first time this technology was used in North America, and the cleanup marked a crucial step towards the restoration of the harbour. The cost of the demonstration and cleanup was $635,000, and 7,300 cubic metres of contaminated sediment were removed.
>
> Actions were also taken to protect the existing 96-hectare Collingwood Wetland Complex, control the invasion of Purple Loosestrife in the wetlands, and rehabilitate fish and wildlife habitat in the harbour and the watershed. Bass and pike spawning and rearing habitat were created, habitat was improved for osprey, water birds, amphibians and reptiles, and a community volunteer network was mobilized to monitor wildlife populations. The Black Ash Creek Rehabilitation Project was designed to prevent erosion while incorporating habitat rehabilitation in a natural, bioengineering approach to bank stabilization. Fish and wildlife populations responded to the initiatives, with increased numbers being documented for the first time in more than 30 years.
>
> A strong emphasis was also placed on pollution prevention. The Greening of Collingwood became a community-based action plan targeted at pollution prevention for residents, businesses and industries. The first comprehensive "Green Home Tune-ups" in Ontario were completed in Collingwood in 1994, with the establishment of a green enterprise named the Environment Network, still very much in action.
>
> One of the most novel projects designed to raise awareness of the importance of pollution prevention was the creation of the environmental theme park ENVIROPARK. Situated in Sunset Point Park, this unique network of play structures was designed to instill in children an understanding of how everyday life has a direct impact on our environment.
>
> Following environmental monitoring, it was determined that environmental conditions in the area had been restored, and Collingwood Harbour became the first AOC to be delisted in 1994

FIGURE 12.4. Presque Isle Bay Case Study

YEAR	CRITICAL ACTIONS
2013	Presque Isle Bay is delisted from the Great Lakes Areas of Concern.
2012	Stage III of the RAP is completed—one of the final steps in delisting an AOC. While the rate of external growths remains a problem throughout Lake Erie, the rates of fish liver tumors in the bay has declined to the point where they are the same as the least impacted reference site in the Lake. For this reason, the fish tumor impairment is removed. The remaining beneficial use impairment is removed. A sediment analysis report is completed which evaluates the contaminated sediment in terms of ecological health and human health risks. The study took place between 2006 and 2009.
2007	The first beneficial use impairment is removed after studies reflect that bay sediment contains low levels of PAHs and fewer heavy metals.
2004-2007	Samples are collected at four locations near the AOC to determine if the incidence of fish tumors, both internal and external, had decreased. Results indicate a decline in tumors.
1992	The first stage of the Remedial Action Plan is published.
1991	Presque Isle Bay is listed as an Area of Concern.

of the RAPs.[12] Despite organizational and fiscal resource hurdles, there are notable advances in remediation and prevention programs. Essential elements that characterize successful initiatives include true participatory decision-making, a clearly articulated and shared vision, and focused and deliberate leadership.[13] These are discussed further below.

An Ecosystem Approach for RAP Development and Implementation

An "ecosystem approach" means an integrated set of policies and managerial practices that relate people to ecosystems of which they are part—rather than to external resources or environments with which they interact.[14] The identifying characteristics include: synthesis (integrated knowledge); a holistic perspective interrelating systems at different levels of integration; and actions that are ecological, anticipatory, and ethical in respect of other systems of nature.

Adopting an ecosystem approach would require three changes: reframing the planning problem, creating an integrative knowledge base, and institutionalizing multi-stakeholder participation in decision-making.[15] RAPs were a departure from water quality remediation plans to a watershed-based management context that would consider a broad array of human actions that affect water and ecosystem quality. Ecosystem-based action plans address remedial actions to restore degraded conditions, and would also inquire into the human dimensions that consider changing human behaviours that enable long-term functionality and sustainability of the ecosystem. Discovering such methods necessitated an integrative understanding of the watershed's biochemical-physical functions and their susceptibility to anthropogenic stresses. Kellog asserts that to be successful would necessitate collaboration of all representative jurisdictions, regulatory and resources agencies, and other stakeholders and citizens in the watershed.[16]

Hartig points out that there is no single best way to implement an ecosystem approach, since each defined AOC involves distinct physiochemical and biological factors, stakeholders, institutional frameworks, regulatory complexity, and more.[17] An implementation framework that is guided by eight criteria should include:

1. stakeholder involvement;
2. leadership;
3. information and interpretation;
4. action planning within a strategic framework;
5. human resource development;
6. results and indicators;
7. review and feedback; and
8. stakeholder satisfaction

As such, RAPs for Great Lakes AOCs are perhaps the best example of community-based environmental protection in existence.[18] Through the collaboration between public and private institutions, the RAPs apply a watershed approach to ecosystem regeneration and protection, as they progress toward the recovery of beneficial uses.

The experiment in collaboration aimed at aquatic ecosystem health, as Sproule-Jones asserts, provided an innovative approach in which resource users, regulators, and those with an interest in regenerating resilience for the local ecosystem can collaborate in service of a common purpose.[19] They promise to empower local stakeholders to determine their own solutions to ecological degradation, and open new venues for collaboration.

With the assistance of governments, residents in most AOCs formed an advisory council/committee to work with federal/state/provincial technical and scientific experts. Citizen advisory committees were used as the focal point of public involvement for RAPs in 75 per cent of the AOCs. Known in various jurisdictions as public advisory committees, basin committees, or stakeholder groups, the IJC contends that such mechanisms are the key to implementing the ecosystem approach in RAPs. In citizen advisory committees, diverse interests come to the same table to participate in the planning process in an interactive manner, advising the planning agency throughout the preparation of the RAP. These committees typically have or have had representatives from diverse community sectors, including agriculture, business, and industry, citizens-at-large, community groups, conservation and environment, education, fisheries, health, labour, municipal governments, Native peoples, shipping, tourism, and recreation.[20] Upon first examination, it is plausible that such diverse interests could result in opposing views, values, and priorities. The importance, however, of collaborative governance, as exemplified in successful RAPs, is elaborated on by Cheng and colleagues: "Collaborative governance of common-pool ecosystems and resources is expanding globally and is widely seen as contributing to the adaptive capacity of social-ecological systems. . . . Empirical research across ecosystem management contexts demonstrates how collaborative approaches can help in managing conflicts, building trust, pooling resources, building capacity, and sustaining action; collaboration is also shown to spark innovation, risk-taking, and more flexible, responsive actions because of the multiple viewpoints and resources that are leveraged through the collaborative process."[21]

Engaging stakeholder groups in the plan design minimizes the risk of future polarization.[22] Advisory committee participants possess unique knowledge and represent the interests of their particular stakeholder groups. A key premise is that community residents possess important knowledge, and can provide an informed perspective on the social impacts of the decisions.[23] The importance of involving communities in the management of water resources was one of the strongest and most consistent messages coming forward from an international conference in interjurisdictional water programs.[24] Also important is recognizing the value of traditional knowledge and the local public's anecdotal and experiential intellect. Best practices in public engagement processes use plain language to communicate clearly, are supported by commitments in institutional programs and policies, demonstrate early and often how the public input will be used, include mechanisms to resolve disputes, provide the community with access to technical experts, and celebrate successes to nurture momentum and train community leaders, thereby building capacity to sustain progress.

Jetoo and colleagues note that governance can be difficult to define as it is used in a multitude of different ways.[25] While different interpretations abound, most agree that the basic characteristic of governance is the migration of power from the central state up into supranational institutions, horizontally to non-state actors, and down to sub-national levels of government. Stakeholders have been instrumental in helping governments be more responsive to and responsible for restoring uses in AOCs. Further, stakeholders have been the primary catalyst for implementing actions that have resulted in ecosystem improvements. Such broad-based partnerships among diverse stakeholders can best be described as a step toward grassroots ecological democracy in the Great Lakes basin.[26] The collective objective is to work with governments and develop a plan to revitalize ecosystem health and implement the plan to achieve agreed-upon targets that indicate when beneficial uses are restored.[27]

Central to the successful deployment of the RAP process is clear accountability for active interventions. This is best accomplished through the open sharing of information, clear and unambiguous definition of stressors and problems (including the identification of indicators to be used in measuring when the desired state for a beneficial use is reached), agreement on the priority actions required, and the identification of who is responsible for taking what action. From this foundation, Hartig and Zarull clearly delineate the responsible institutions and individuals that can be held accountable for progress.[25]

Having been involved in RAPs since their inception, I can point to notable differences in the progress across the then (as of 1991) forty-three AOCs. The first stage for each RAP is to identify environmental problems, impaired beneficial uses, and their probable causes. This stage is for the most part complete. The second stage is to develop a recommended set of remedial actions and preventative initiatives to improve environmental quality in support of the beneficial uses. To develop focused and effective strategies to restore beneficial uses, targets need to be set by which RAP practitioners can recognize when they have met their goals surrounding beneficial uses. In some AOCs, the targets set science-based and quantitative targets whenever possible. In other cases, general statements guide the practitioners, making it difficult to recognize when success has been achieved. For example, rather than using ecosystem response indicators, selections may be based on restoration of a quantifiable measure of kilometres of riparian habitat remediated or installed. This measure does not necessarily correlate with what habitat in what quantities and in which locations are necessary to support particular fish and wildlife, whose populations or communities may be degraded due to loss of habitat. Similarly, targets that are based on management actions completed (e.g., upgrading nutrient removal from waste-water treatment plants, or removing a particular volume of contaminated sediment) miss measuring the ecological outcome of the action (such as successful control of eutrophication, or restoration of healthy benthic populations).

The above represent significantly divergent approaches across the AOCs in the preparation of Stage 2 Plans (actions necessary to restore beneficial uses) and the degree to which their implementation will actually achieve the aim of restoring beneficial uses. There remains a dichotomy between those who perceive that completing the implementation of the actions is synonymous with the restoration of beneficial uses, and those who assert that the ecosystem will take time to respond to human intervention, and that a period of recovery may well be required for beneficial uses to be restored. The interpretation of the annex varies among and within jurisdictions, and the final decision to delist an AOC—that is, declare all beneficial uses restored—carries with it significant implications depending upon the local and jurisdictional definition of restoration.

Does restoration imply returning to original conditions? Does restoration mean the restoration of function? Further, there are clearly limits to restoration. An urban river will never have the structure and function of a river in an untouched watershed remote from anthropogenic pressures. While government guidelines inform "healthy" states, stakeholder values shape the policy consideration of what is an "acceptable" delisting target.

Stakeholders in various AOCs in the United States and Canada have made considerable investments of time and money, and several well-documented and highly visible successes can be pointed to.[28] Gurtner-Zimmermann notes that the commitment of individuals who participate in the RAP process, local support for the RAP goals, and the scientific basis and sound analysis of environmental issues contribute to the positive outcomes.[29] Major successes include Collingwood Harbour, Severn Sound, and Wheatley Harbour in Ontario, and Deer Lake, White Lakes, Presque Isle Bay, and Oswego River in the United States; in each of these locations conditions have improved to the point that they are no longer considered to be AOCs. Spanish Harbour and Jackfish Bay in Ontario are

FIGURE 12.5. Severn Sound case study.

Severn Sound was designated an AOC because a review of available data indicated that water quality and environmental health were severely degraded. In particular, eutrophication—as a result of sewage treatment plant (STP) inputs, agricultural activities, and shoreline development—was especially evident in the narrowing of the sound's south shore.

What was accomplished?
The eutrophication impairment was addressed by controlling sources of phosphorus. Concentrations were addressed by reducing total phosphorus from STP discharges, upgrading private sewage systems, eliminating sewage bypasses and combined sewer overflows, and reducing inputs from agricultural sources.

The STP improvements reduced the phosphorus loads to meet RAP targets and provided considerable cost savings to the municipalities. Through the Sewage Treatment Optimization Project, the federal and provincial governments provided technical support and training for municipal operators in all 8 treatment plants in the AOC. In addition, the Ontario Ministry of the Environment and Climate Change contributed $23 Million to upgrade 4 of the 8 STPs.

The Severn Sound Urban Stormwater Strategy was developed by municipalities, and enabling bylaws have been passed to govern new construction, stormwater retrofits and sewer separation projects. Farm-level projects managed manure runoff, treated direct milk house wastes, restricted livestock access to rivers and improved crop practices.

Through conservation agreements and wetland rehabilitation projects, 411 hectares of wetlands and their associated uplands have been protected to date. In streams flowing directly into Severn Sound, 132 projects have been completed, creating vegetation buffers and linking habitat nodes. In addition, natural heritage strategies are being adopted by townships and municipalities.

The economic viability of the area has improved through upgraded infrastructure, local job creation, and cost-effective decisions assisted by RAP studies. Volunteer participation and positive media support indicate that community acceptance of the RAP principles of maintaining a healthy environment, including ensuring economic and environmental sustainability, are built into municipal plans.

The delisting of Severn Sound was facilitated by the Severn Sound Environmental Association. The organization sought to provide community-based, cost-effective environmental management for the Severn Sound area, which sustained the improvements achieved through the RAP process.

Severn Sound was officially delisted in 2003.

now recognized as being in a stage of recovery due to completion of all selected remedial actions, while monitoring continues to measure recovery of beneficial uses.

The parties have completed all remedial actions at five other AOCs: Nipigon Bay in Canada; and Sheboygan River (Wisconsin), Waukegan Harbor (Illinois), Ashtabula River (Ohio), and St. Clair River (Michigan) in the United States. With remedial work completed, these five AOCs are now being monitored to determine when the Beneficial Use Impairments have been fully addressed and delisting can occur.[30] According to the *Progress Report of the Parties*, improvements in Canadian AOCs include the elimination of 65 impairments of beneficial uses of the environment, with 81 impairments remaining.[31] In 2015, construction began on the largest contaminated sediment remediation project ever undertaken in a Canadian AOC. Through a public-private partnership, the project will clean up 700,000 cubic metres of severely contaminated sediment in the Hamilton Harbour AOC. Other accomplishments in Canadian AOCs during the 2013–16 period include improvements to approximately 4 kilometres of shoreline habitat and approximately 180 hectares of coastal wetlands and fish spawning grounds, and investments of approximately $562 million in upgrades to municipal waste-water treatment plants to significantly reduce nutrients, suspended solids, and pollutants.

In the United States, 62 impairments of beneficial uses of the environment have been removed, with 193 impairments remaining. The US Environmental Protection Agency estimates that management actions will be completed at 9 more AOCs by 2019. This pace of AOC restoration is attributed to the Great Lakes Restoration Initiative, by which federal agencies have been able to apply over $650 million in Great Lakes Restoration Initiative funding to finance RAP implementation.

Figures 12.3, 12.4, and 12.5 provide case studies in RAP achievements and successes. We can celebrate these strides forward; however, human health is still being compromised by toxic chemicals, particularly for those consuming fish that are contaminated at unsafe levels, and particularly for children exposed to contaminants in utero.[32] More aggressive action to revitalize the lakes is essential to protect the health of all their residents. The chemical, physical, and biological integrity of the Great

Lakes basin ecosystem remains threatened. It is apparent that a lack of resources and lack of inter-program coordination and co-operation still impedes progress.

Beierle and Koniski note other challenges to progress.[33] In their analysis, most stakeholder advisory committees in the RAP cases they studied did not engage the wider public in the decision-making process, and lacked socio-economically representative membership. Further, the ability of stakeholder involvement to improving environmental quality through coordinated action was unclear, as the process broke down in the implementation phase.

Environmental indicators communicate information about the environment and about the human activities that affect it. When communicated effectively, the indicator highlights problems and draws attention to the effectiveness of current policies. The target audiences are the public and the decision-makers (i.e., governments). To command their attention, indicators must be relevant, and they must communicate value. Choosing an indicator reflects a set of values that is perceived as being important.[34] The IJC's Indicators for Evaluation Task Force recommended indicators to evaluate progress under the Great Lakes Water Quality Agreement.[35] As a major initiative in fulfilling their reporting responsibility, the parties (the governments of Canada and the United States) developed a State of the Great Lakes Ecosystem reporting system. The State of the Great Lakes Ecosystem Conference (SOLEC) reports provide a framework for a broad assessment of the state of the Great Lakes. The first conference was held in October 1994.

Clearly, the basic water policy goals of swimmable, fishable, drinkable water, which emerged from SOLEC and the IJC recommendations, remain elusive in many Great Lakes communities.[36] To make matters more complicated, the IJC faces serious challenges as a transboundary institution with oversight on a non-binding international agreement. As Johns points out: "No politicians or governments in the US or Canada face serious political fallout if the commitments are not achieved or ignored."[37]

Despite stated co-operative objectives on the part of the parties, the RAP strategy exhibits problems in the implementation phase, particularly as a result of a lack of enforcement authority.[38] So while the IJC does advise the parties in developing RAPs, its advice lacks meaningful enforcement authority. A lack of accountability and responsibility among the parties and state and provincial agencies also presents significant barriers to RAP implementation. Langston asserts that despite the IJC's biennial reports (now triennial since the 2012 GLWQA protocol) to the parties that highlight lack of progress on virtual elimination of persistent toxic substances, governments continue to lag in effective action, and are purportedly using RAP development efforts as an excuse to delay implementation and action.[39]

Margerum and Robinson advise that partnerships operating at the organizational level require networks that support the flow of information and decisions across agencies. While such efforts predict improved decision-making, long-term efficiencies, and better outcomes, there are high transaction costs and the benefits often accrue only over the long term.[40] They point out that this necessitates that leaders be willing to make long-term investments and that organizations understand the need to change their culture and reward structures to support partnerships. For RAPs this is a difficult challenge if current pressures were aimed at short-term results, individual performance measures, and a focus on core organizational goals rather than collective management to attain shared goals.

Hall and colleagues provide an evaluation of the strengths of the RAP processes. To achieve the goal of restoring environmental health and qualities to the Hamilton Harbour AOC, an embayment at the western end of Lake Ontario, requires

> a dynamic process that relies heavily on research and monitoring to direct remediation efforts. Three principle means of coordinating this research and monitoring include: research and monitoring workshops; a monitoring catalogue outlining both government and nongovernment initiatives; and an annual report written by a local community group. These tools increase the effectiveness of remedial actions by: (i) improving stakeholders' ability to track trends; (ii) allowing program decision-makers to utilize adaptive management techniques to continuously modify programs based on new results; (iii) integrating interdisciplinary fields, and (iv) increasing accountability.[41]

The 2006-7 Review of the 1987 GLWQA

The IJC's Advice To Governments On Their Review Of The Great Lakes Water Quality Agreement states that "Article VII, a permanent reference under Article IX of the Boundary Waters Treaty, requires that the International Joint Commission . . . among other things, issue a biennial report concerning progress by the Parties and the state and provincial governments toward achieving the Agreement's general and specific purposes."[42] Article x requires that the parties conduct a comprehensive review of the agreement's operation and effectiveness following every third such biennial report. The IJC's *12th Biennial Report*, issued in September 2004, triggered the requirement for the review that took place in 2006 and concluded in 2007.

The reviewers, comprised of agency and non-agency staff and individuals, concluded that Annex II's stated purpose was ambiguous. Improved clarity was called for in several instances. The Agreement Review Committee drew attention to the following:

- There is ambiguity regarding whether the Annex takes an ecosystem approach or simply a water quality approach.
- There is ambiguity regarding whether the Annex focus is on the open waters only or on nearshore, inland, tributaries, and watersheds.
- Beneficial Use Impairments are poorly defined, particularly with regard to human health.
- There is a general question about the purpose of the Annex regarding whether it uses an ecosystem approach or a water quality approach.
- There is a question related to whether the Remedial Action Plans and Lakewide Management Plans are to be prepared and implemented in relation to Critical Pollutants using an ecosystem approach to the multi-media sources, pathways and distribution of this narrow group of contaminants or are they for general ecosystem management and stewardship within the Great Lakes basin?[43]

The IJC binationally canvassed citizens of the basin to gain feedback on perceived successes and deficits associated with the implementation of the GLWQA.[44] Perhaps not surprisingly, RAPs, having strong public engagement attributes, drew the most responses, and RAPs were repeatedly used as examples of shortcomings in GLWQA implementation:

> "They were probably the source of greatest hope for visible, tangible Improvement on an AOC-by-AOC level," said one retired government official who is still active in environmental issues. Many questions were raised in connection with Remedial Action Plans (RAPs). "Is the concept of RAPs fundamentally flawed?" asked one participant. "Did we not invest enough money? Were they not high priority enough? Did they not fit with other programs? Did we not manage them effectively enough? Were the local government people not involved enough?" Overall, insufficient funding, bureaucratization, inadequate or ineffective public participation, and a lack of accountability provisions were the factors most often cited.[45]

Annex 1 of the 2012 GLWQA

Almost everyone who has been involved in the RAP process has learned a lot over the past three decades. There emerged a school of thought that, under some conditions, following the full implementation of all practical remedial measures, nature may be the best source of recovery and restoration. The parties should consider recognizing "Areas of Concern in Recovery" as an interim step to delisting at sites where remedial measures have been implemented, yet the ecosystem is still recovering. Since Annex 1 now stipulates that the final step in RAPs prior to delisting is the achievement of the restoration of beneficial uses, recognizing AOCs in Recovery signals an enormous milestone in the advancement to the stage of delisting. Ongoing monitoring of the recovery is a necessary component of this designation. It is an interim designation that takes into account the difficulty in determining the limits to restoration, because there is no way of knowing the unforeseeable advances in technology, availability of resources, or public will.

Coming into effect in 2013, the 2012 GLWQA protocol adjusted the 1987 Annex 2 into the new Annex 1. According to the agreement: "For each AOC, the Parties, in cooperation and consultation with State and Provincial Governments, Tribal Governments, First Nations, Métis, Municipal Governments, watershed management agencies, other local public agencies, and the Public, shall develop and implement a systematic and comprehensive ecosystem approach to restoring beneficial use."[46] Also new to the RAP process is the allowance that "a Party may elect to identify an AOC as an AOC in Recovery when all remedial actions identified in the RAP have been implemented and monitoring confirms that recovery is progressing in accordance with the RAP. A Party shall monitor and take further action, if required, to restore beneficial uses within an AOC in Recovery."

Annex 1 of the 2012 agreement makes reference to the IJC three times:

> The Agreement requires that the governments of the US and Canada:
>
> 1. Consult with IJC to designate additional AOCs based on an evaluation of BUIs
> 2. Make RAPs available to the IJC
> 3. Solicit a review and comments from the IJC prior to the designation of an AOC in Recovery and prior to the removal of a designation as an AOC or an AOC in Recovery.[44]

The IJC is expected to provide time-sensitive comments on RAP reports, particularly as they relate to delisting and/or designation of AOCs in Recovery. The IJC is also expected to ensure that their feedback reflects state-of-the-art science as well as public input. Figure 12.2 illustrated the process for IJC review of RAP delisting reports. What remains unclear is the value added by IJC comments, given that the decision to delist remains that of the parties.

Conclusion

The IJC's reputation for impartiality can be attributed to the tradition of the six commissioners seeking consensus and rarely splitting along national lines. The commissioners do not act under instruction from or as representatives of their governments, but on behalf of the binational resource. That said, as political appointees of their own countries, they naturally carry national or party philosophies and may clash along national lines. Lemarquand emphasizes that, notwithstanding this situation, they are free from government control and meet as one body, which encourages a collegial approach to problem-solving, as opposed to the negotiation approach characteristic of commissioners acting as agents of their governments.[47] Success, asserts Lemarquand, depends on the appointment of qualified, capable, and politically perceptive commissioners. Over the years the governments have had a decidedly mixed record in appointing commissioners with those qualities, and these governments must take much of the responsibility during periods where the performance of the IJC has been somewhat inconsequential.

A major challenge for the IJC and the GLWQA is the process of bringing together a diverse cross-section of society in a neutral setting to address environmental, political, and/or societal issues in a manner that is very difficult to achieve within jurisdictional limitations, policy, or geopolitics. The committee structure under the Water Quality Board and the Science Advisory Board enables this to happen. Complex issues are addressed with members acting in their personal and professional capacity, not at the instruction of their agency. The IJC structure can successfully circumvent necessary but often cumbersome government bureaucracy, and the involvement of those holding the knowledge and expertise allows for objective, feasible, and important recommendations for action.

Annex 1 under the 2012 protocol is perhaps the most public of the GLWQA's annexes, because the activities required therein depended on the extensive involvement of interest groups and Great Lakes stakeholders. Newig and Fritsch make the point that multi-level governance has components that include "political structures and processes that go beyond the bounds of administrative jurisdictions, with the purpose of accounting for the interdependencies in societal development and political decision making which exist among geopolitical units. Systems of governance at different levels are ideally not hierarchical in a command and control sense, but rather are a blend of formally independent, yet mutually interacting governance levels."[48]

Where successful, RAPs clearly embrace the ecosystem approach. Here, the ecosystem approach is based on the man-in-system concept rather than a system-external-to-man concept,[49] where the ecosystem is composed of the interacting elements of water, air, land, and living organisms, including man. While Lee and colleagues discuss several variants of the ecosystem approach, most share a focus on the responsiveness of ecological systems to natural and human activities, and a readiness to strike a programmatic compromise between detailed understanding and more comprehensive holistic meaning. This flexible, pragmatic approach is perhaps the most productive feature for addressing Great Lakes environmental problems. Now that the parties have renegotiated a revised GLWQA it is imperative that they learn from the past: what has worked, what has not worked, and why. This would inform more successful outcomes regarding the implementation of Annex 1 and help instruct the governance mechanisms for addressing the nearshore zones in a local and regional manner under the new Annex 2.

Hartig and Law concluded that RAPs (and here one could substitute any place-based approach to ecosystem restoration) require co-operative learning that involves stakeholders working in teams to accomplish a common goal under conditions that involve positive interdependence (all stakeholders co-operate to complete a task) and individual and group accountability (each stakeholder is accountable for the final outcome).[50] Place-based types of restoration initiatives like RAPs are an unprecedented collaboration of international significant.[51] Creative, distributed governance mechanisms and new institutional arrangements are needed to stimulate and sustain advances in the clean-up of local waterways, raise public awareness of individuals' responsibilities, unite a community around a shared purpose and need, and make the lakes Great.[52]

Notes

1. See Council of the Great Lakes Region, "The Great Lakes Economy: The Growth Engine of North America," 22 August 2016, https://councilgreatlakesregion.org/the-great-lakes-economy-the-growth-engine-of-north-america/.

2. Robert Costanza, "Ecological economics of sustainability: Investing in natural capital," in *Population, Technology and Lifestyle*, ed. Robert J. A. Goodland, Herman E. Daly, and Salah El Serafy (Washington, DC: Island Press, 1992): 106–18.

3. R. C. Hennigan, "Effective Water Quality Management: Impossible Dream or Attainable Goal" (paper presented at the 13th Conference on Great Lakes Research, International Association for Great Lakes Research, Ann Arbor, Michigan, 31 March to 3 April 1970); Cheryl de Boer and Gail Krantzberg, "Great Lakes water governance: A transboundary inter-regime analysis," in *Water Governance as Connective Capacity*, ed. Peter Scholten, Nanny Bressers, and Jurian Edelenbos (Farnham, UK: Ashgate, 2013), 313–32; Environment Canada, "Great Lakes 2000 Cleanup Fund Project Summaries Report, 1997," http://www.on.ec.gc.ca/glimr/data/cleanup-project-summaries/intro.html.

4. Gail Krantzberg, Irena F. Creed, Kathryn. B. Friedman, Katrina L. Laurent, John A. Jackson, Joel Brammeier, and Don Scavia, "Community engagement is critical to achieve a 'thriving and prosperous' future for the Great Lakes–St. Lawrence River basin," *Journal of Great Lakes Research* 41, suppl. 1 (2015): 188–91.

5. Boundary Waters Treaty of 1909: Treaty between the United States and Great Britain Relating to Boundary Waters, and Questions Arising Between the United States and Canada, https://www.ijc.org/en/boundary-waters-treaty-1909.

6. Lee Botts and Paul Muldoon, *Evolution of the Great Lakes Water Quality Agreement* (Lansing: Michigan State University Press, 2005).

7. John H. Hartig and Rich L. Thomas, "Development of Plans to Restore Degraded Areas in the Great Lakes," *Environmental Management* 12, no. 3 (1988): 327–47.

8. Gail Krantzberg, Marty Bratzel, and John McDonald, "Contribution of the International Joint Commission to Great Lakes Renewal," *Great Lakes Geographer* 13 (2006): 25–37.

9. Canada-US Great Lakes Water Quality Agreement (1987), available at http://www.ijc.org/files/tinymce/uploaded/GLWQA_e.pdf.

10. International Joint Commission, *Report on Great Lakes Water Quality* (Windsor, ON: Great Lakes Water Quality Board, 1985).

11. International Joint Commission, *Report on Great Lakes Water Quality* (Windsor, ON: Great Lakes Water Quality Board, 1987).

12. Ibid.

13. Gail Krantzberg, "Keeping Remedial Action Plans on target: Lessons learned from Collingwood Harbour," *Journal of Great Lakes Research* 29 (2003): 641–51.

14 Jack R. Vallentyn and Al M. Beeton, "The 'Ecosystem' Approach to Managing Human Uses and Abuses of Natural Resources in the Great Lakes Basin," *Environmental Conservation* 1 (1988): 58–62.

15 Wendy A. Kellog, "Adopting an Ecosystem Approach: Local Variability in Remedial Action," *Planning Society & Natural Resources* 11 (1998): 465–83.

16 Ibid.

17 John H. Hartig, "Great Lakes Remedial Action Plans: Fostering Adaptive Ecosystem-Based Management Processes," *American Review of Canadian Studies* 27, no. 3 (1997): 437–58.

18 Environmental Protection Agency, "Great Lakes Areas of Concern," http://www.epa.gov/greatlakes/aoc/rap.html (accessed 11 May 2010).

19 Mark Sproule-Jones, *The Restoration of the Great Lakes: Promises, Practices, and Performances* (Vancouver: University of British Columbia Press, 2003).

20 Betsy K. Landre and Barbara A. Knuth, "The Role of Agency Goals and Local Context in Great Lakes Water Resources Public Involvement Programs," *Environmental Management* 17, no. 2, (1993): 153–65.

21 Antony S. Cheng, Andrea K. Gerlak, Lisa Dale, and Katherine Mattor, "Examining the adaptability of collaborative governance associated with publicly managed ecosystems over time: Insights from the Front Range Roundtable, Colorado, USA," *Ecology and Society* 20, no. 1 (2015): 35.

22 Misty Samya, Hendrik Snow, and Hobson Bryan, "Integrating social impact assessment with research: The case of methylmercury in fish in the Mobile-Alabama River Basin," *Impact Assessment and Project Appraisal* 21, no. 2 (2003):133–40.

23 Charles C. Harris, Erik A. Nielsen, William J. McLaughlin, and Dennis R. Becker, "Community-based social impact assessment: The case of salmon-recovery on the lower Snake River," *Impact Assessment and Project Appraisal* 21, no. 2(2003): 109–18.

24 Pollution Probe, "Managing Shared Waters" (2002), http://www.terrycollinsassociates.com/2013/managing-waters-shared-across-national-boundaries-treasury-of-papers-helps-capture-20-years-of-lessons/.

25 Savatri Jetoo, Adam Thorn, Kathryn Friedman, Sara Gosman, and Gail Krantzberg, "Governance and geopolitics as drivers of change in the Great Lakes–St. Lawrence basin," *Journal of Great Lakes Research* 4, suppl. 4 (2015): 108–18.

26 John H. Hartig and Michael A. Zarull, eds., *Under RAPs: Toward Grassroots Ecological Democracy in the Great Lakes Basin* (Ann Arbor: University of Michigan Press, 1992).

27 Gail Krantzberg, "Sustaining the Gains Made in Ecological Restoration: Case Study Collingwood Harbour, Ontario," *Environment, Development and Sustainability* 8 (2006): 413–24.

28 International Joint Commission, *The Great Lakes Areas of Concern Report* (Ottawa: IJC, 2003).

29 Arnold Gurtner-Zimmermann, "A mid-term review of Remedial Action Plans: Difficulties with translating comprehensive planning into comprehensive actions," *Journal of Great Lakes Research* 21, no. 2 (1995): 234–47.

30 *2016 Progress Report of the Parties: Pursuant to the Canada-United States Great Lakes Water Quality Agreement* (2016), available at https://binational.net/wp-content/uploads/2016/09/PRP-160927-EN.pdf.

31 Ibid.

32 Mary Turyk, Giamila Fantuzzi, Victoria Persky, Sally Freels, Anissa Lambertino, Maria Pini, Davina H. Rhodes, and Henry A. Anderson, "Persistent organic pollutants and biomarkers of diabetes risk in a cohort of Great Lakes sport caught fish consumers," *Environmental Research* 140 (2015): 335–44; Joseph L. Jacobson and Sandra W. Jacobson, "Intellectual impairment in children exposed to polychlorinated biphenyls in utero," *New England Journal of Medicine* 335 (1996): 783–9; Jack Bails, Al Beeton, Jonathan Bulkley, Michele DePhilip, John Gannon, Michael Murray, Henry Regier, and Don Scavia, "Prescription for Great Lakes ecosystem protection and restoration: Avoiding the tipping point of irreversible changes," *Healing Our Waters—Great Lakes Coalition Technical Advisory Committee* (May 2006), http://www.miseagrant.umich.edu/downloads/habitat/Prescription-for-the-Great-Lakes-08-2006.pdf; Krista Y. Christensen, Brooke A. Thompson, Mark Werner, Kristen Malecki, Pamela Imm, and Henry A. Anderson, "Levels of persistent contaminants in relation to fish consumption among older male anglers in Wisconsin," *International Journal of Hygiene and Environmental Health* 219, no. 2 (2016): 184–94.

33 Thomas C. Beierle and David M. Konisky, "What are we gaining from stakeholder involvement? Observations from environmental planning in the Great Lakes," *Environment and Planning C: Government and Policy* 19 (2001): 515–27.

34 Ibid.

35 International Joint Commission, "Indicators for Evaluation Task Force: Indicators to Evaluate Progress Under the Great Lakes Water Quality Agreement," (1996), available at the *International Joint Commission Digital Archive*, https://scholar.uwindsor.ca/ijcarchive/497.

36 Carolyn M. Johns, "The Great Lakes, Water Quality and Water Policy in Canada," in *Water Policy and Governance in Canada*, ed. Steven Renzetti and Diane P. Dupont (New York: Springer, 2017), 159–80.

37 Ibid.

38 Jill T. Hauserman, "Water, Water Everywhere, But Just How Much Is Clean? Examining Water Quality Restoration Efforts Under The United States Clean Water Act And The United States-Canada Great Lakes Water Quality Agreement," *Georgia Journal of International and Comparative Law* 43 (2015): 701–25.

39 Nancy Langston, *Sustaining Lake Superior: An Extraordinary Lake in a Changing World* (New Haven, CT: Yale University Press 2017).

40 Richard D. Margerum and Catherine J. Robinson, "Collaborative partnerships and the challenges for sustainable water management," *Current Opinion in Environmental Sustainability* 12 (2015): 53–8.

41 John D. Hall, Kristin O'Connor, and Joanna Ranieri, "2006 Progress Toward Delisting A Great Lakes Area Of Concern: The Role Of Integrated Research And Monitoring In The Hamilton Harbour Remedial Action Plan," *Environmental Monitoring and Assessment* 113 (2006): 227–43.

42 International Joint Commission, "Advice to Governments on their Review of the Great Lakes Water Quality Agreement: A Special Report to the Governments of Canada and the United States" (2006).

43 ARC Agreement Review Committee Report to the Great Lakes Binational Executive Committee: Volume 2 Review of the Canada–U.S. Great Lakes Water Quality Agreement: Final Review Working Group Reports to ARC" (2006), http://publications.gc.ca/site/archivee-archived.html?url=http://publications.gc.ca/collections/collection_2012/ec/En164-21-3-2007-eng.pdf.

44 International Joint Commission, "Consolidation of consultations" (no date), http://www.ijc.org/en/activities/consultations/glwqa/synth_5.php.

45 Ibid.

46 See "Full Text: The 2012 Great Lakes Water Quality Agreement," available at https://binational.net/2012/09/05/2012-glwqa-aqegl/.

47 David Lemarquand, "The International Joint Commission and Changing Canada-United States Boundary Relations," *Natural Resources Journal* 33 (1993): 59–91.

48 Jens Newig and Oliver Fritsch, "Environmental Governance: Participatory, Multi-Level—and Effective?" *Environmental Policy and Governance* 19 (2009): 197–214.

49 International Joint Commission, Great Lakes Research Advisory Board, *The Ecosystem Approach: Special Report to the International Joint Commission* (Windsor, ON: IJC, 1978).

50 John H. Hartig and Neeley L. Law, "Institutional frameworks to direct the development and implementation of Great Lakes remedial action plans," *Environmental Management* 18 (1994): 855–64.

51 Gail Krantzberg, "International Association for Great Lakes Research Position Statement on Remedial Action Plans," *Journal of Great Lakes Research* 23 (1997): 221–4.

52 Krantzberg, "Keeping Remedial Action Plans on target."

13

The International Joint Commission and the Evolution of the Great Lakes Water Quality Agreement: Accountability, Progress Reporting, and Measuring Performance

Debora VanNijnatten and Carolyn Johns

The International Joint Commission (IJC) is one of the world's most unique international environmental institutions. Though it was established under the 1909 Boundary Waters Treaty (BWT) primarily to resolve disputes between water users, especially in the Great Lakes–St. Lawrence basin, its role has greatly expanded into environmental and ecosystem governance. In the earliest decades after its establishment, the commission provided the Canadian and American governments with the means to investigate and understand the growing pollution problems in the Great Lakes. However, the IJC soon began to take on an environmental policy advisory role, gently pushing the parties to the treaty—the Canadian and US federal governments—toward a higher level of environmental co-operation in addressing worsening pollution in the Great Lakes basin, and also toward firmer infrastructure to support such co-operation. With the signing of the 1972 Great Lakes Water Quality Agreement (GLWQA), the IJC was given a more supportive role (and additional help in the form of advisory boards), but it also became enmeshed in monitoring and reporting on the commitments made. Over the course of successive revisions to the GLWQA in 1978, 1987, and 2012 this role in monitoring, reporting on, and assessing the performance of the parties in meeting these commitments has grown.

When discussions began in earnest over 2005 and 2006 on the third (and most recent) "renewal" of the GLWQA, it was clear that Canada and the United States had fallen behind in supporting implementation efforts under the agreement and were ill-prepared to meet new environmental challenges in the basin. The *Twelfth Biennial Report*, compiled by the IJC under the GLWQA and released in 2004, laid out a dizzying array of problems that had not been adequately addressed, and referred to the need for "a greater level of binational communication and cooperation" in order to "better face future threats and address current needs."[1] Debate immediately centred on a familiar concern: How do we better assess and spur performance by the parties in terms of meeting the General and Specific Objectives of the GLWQA?

Indeed, one of the main sections of the *2007 Review of the Great Lakes Water Quality Agreement*, which was intended to provide the parties with a starting point as they contemplated another round of revisions to the agreement, was "accountability and implementation"; this section laid out the need for "establishing specific results, designating responsible entities and improving mechanisms to hold them accountable."[2] According to the review authors, this should include "setting timelines and reporting on progress to achieve the goals of the agreement." Meanwhile, the IJC, given its responsibility for coordinating actions under the GLWQA, was citing the need for "an uncommonly strong Accountability Framework for Great Lakes' restoration and protection."[3] In another report, *Promises to Keep: Challenges to Meet*, a coalition of Great Lakes environmental non-governmental organizations recommended that a renewed agreement provide for greater "accountability for implementation."[4]

Performance was to be a key focus for the 2012 GLWQA, then, and certainly not for the first time since the original 1972 GLWQA came into effect. In fact, it has been a continuing concern. This chapter traces the evolution of water governance in the Great Lakes basin under the IJC with an emphasis on the post-1960 period, during which—as various contributors to this volume note—the commission has done its most important environment-related work. We focus in particular on efforts under successive versions of the GLWQA to set objectives, assess performance in meeting those objectives, and tighten accountability for this performance. Beginning with a brief look at the binational regime first established under the BWT and its mechanisms for joint accountability, the chapter carefully tracks the increase in the number and breadth of objectives under the GLWQA of 1972, 1978, 1987, and 2012, and the continued difficulties in terms of implementation. It also follows the attempts to hold governments accountable for meeting those objectives through ever more transparent and inclusive approaches, as well as reporting mechanisms. In the 2012 revision to the GLWQA, we see the most varied requirements yet, in terms of measuring and reporting on outcomes as well as asking governments to account for these outcomes.

In examining the various approaches and tools used by the IJC to push for new environmental objectives under the GLWQA and assess efforts by the parties to meet these objectives, the chapter also provides insights into the evolving role of the IJC itself over time. As an international organization, the IJC has worked through governmental, stakeholder, and scientific networks, both vertically across levels of government and horizontally across borders, to foster support for the IJC's oversight role and for the management objectives that have been built into the GLWQA regime. The IJC faces challenges, however, as it navigates the difficult diplomatic and policy terrain associated with "implementation oversight" (as the editors of this collection call it) of the signatory parties. Yet the IJC remains a model in terms of its ability to foster the creation of diverse policy communities that can work collaboratively at multiple governance levels to support achievement of GLWQA objectives. The side benefit is that when one avenue of action is closed, there remain other opportunities for encouraging binational action. In this way, this chapter provides support for the contention made by Murray Clamen and Daniel Macfarlane in their introduction to this volume, namely that the IJC is most certainly "an adaptable governance form."

The 1909 Boundary Waters Treaty and an Environmental Mandate for the International Joint Commission

The BWT was clearly an attempt to settle a long list of pre-existing disputes about the use (and abuse) of the waters of the Great Lakes–St. Lawrence, and other boundary waters, by explicitly shifting the basis of the legal and diplomatic framework to that of a shared perspective, where actions taken by one "High Contracting Party" were not to interfere with the use of the resource by the other party.[5] Further, the BWT subjected "treaty boundary waters," expansively defined, to a new evidence-based dispute-resolution procedure. This procedure, to be applied on a case-by-case basis and in a public manner with the involvement of stakeholders, was to be under the purview of the IJC and its commissioners and staff. The IJC was the guardian of this shared perspective on management of the lakes, the primary arbiter of disputes, and the key channel of communication between governments and between governments and the public on issues relating to the lakes. The text of the treaty was, however, unambiguous as to the hierarchy of relationships: the commission's role was to recommend solutions and, during the course of its advisory operations and dispute-resolution tasks, report to the governments. Final decisions and implementation were left to the parties themselves.

While prioritizing commercial and navigable uses in article i, the BWT also introduced a key pillar of the binational regime that would serve as the foundation for the parties to undertake joint environmental management later in the century. Article iv states that "the waters herein defined as boundary waters and waters flowing across the boundary shall not be polluted on either side to the injury of health or property on the other." The IJC thus became responsible, under the BWT, for administering a joint regime that upheld (indeed, protected) the economic uses of the basin waters yet also introduced pollution concerns; that subjected uses of basin waters to a high level of public scrutiny; and that did so in a manner that was to be consultative and evidentiary, with emphasis placed on the importance of science in managing basin waters. This reflected concerns at the state, provincial, and local levels around this time (as Benidickson details in chapter 3 of this volume); public officials were increasingly lamenting the impacts of local sewage and other wastes on waterways at the same time that scientists were determined to bring down rates of typhoid and other waterborne illnesses.

The provision in the BWT for the IJC to consider pollution impacts, and to do so in an evidence-based manner, was quickly set in motion. In 1912, the two national governments asked the IJC to investigate the pollution of boundary waters and undertake "the most expansive bacteriological examination of waters the world has ever known."[6] In his chapter, Benidickson highlights the truly joint nature of the study, which involved public health experts from both countries. The resulting report from the commission in 1918 drew attention to widespread problems stemming from sewage and ship discharges,[7] and showed that the pollution was indeed transboundary,[8] in direct violation of the BWT. It recommended that the IJC be given "the necessary jurisdiction and authority . . . to make such rules, regulations, directions and orders as in its judgment may be deemed necessary" to regulate and prohibit pollution of boundary waters.[9]

However, jurisdictions around the basin—and the parties themselves—were preoccupied from the 1920s to the 1940s with shipping, industrialization, fishing, and other economic activities—not with pollution.[10] It was not until after the Second World War that governments turned their attention more formally to pollution problems along the shared border.[11] Industrial waste, human sewage, and human-made chemicals began to have sustained ecosystem effects. Lake Erie, the shallowest of the lakes, showed serious signs of stress in the form of massive, lake-wide algal blooms (mats of algae) that severely depleted oxygen levels and resulted in the decline of several fish species and massive fish kills. Combined with major episodes of drought and water shortages, public and societal groups, including fishing, hunting, and women's groups, demanded government action.[12] Acting on references from the two federal governments in the late 1940s and '50s to investigate pollution problems at several "connecting channels" in the shared basin, the IJC conducted comprehensive physical, bacteriological, and chemical analysis of domestic and industrial wastes in these channels, and recommended that remedial measures and water quality objectives be put into place in these areas.[13] However, with the persistent inability of governments in the channels to meet the water quality objectives, and the knowledge that pollution problems were accelerating with industrial and population growth around the basin, Canada and the United States asked the IJC in 1964 to broaden its investigative scope and report on whether "the waters of Lake Erie, Lake Ontario, and the International Section of the St. Lawrence River are being polluted on either side of the boundary to an extent which is causing or is likely to cause injury to health or property on the other side of the boundary," as well as the causes of this pollution and remedial measures that could be taken.[14]

Meanwhile, public concern mounted with regard to the deterioration of water quality. Shocking events, including large-scale fish kills in Lake Erie, the Cuyahoga River in Cleveland, Ohio, catching fire in 1969 due to extremely high levels of pollutants in the water, and the contamination of the walleye fishery by mercury, all brought environmental issues to the forefront of government attention. These events stimulated citizens to push for basin-wide action by the Canadian and US governments, as well as more public accountability on the part of the parties.[15]

The final reference report submitted to the governments in 1970 by the IJC ended up serving as the basis for negotiations on a new binational agreement to address pollution in the Great Lakes (Jennifer Read addresses this in chapter 11 of this volume). The report, which built on technical and scientific work conducted by agencies in the two countries, as well as by the advisory boards and the IJC's own Interim Reports to the governments in the 1960s, found that "the increased quantity and the different composition of municipal and industrial wastes in the last two decades, as well as the residual characteristics of materials discharged into the Lakes, have led to dramatic changes in the biological condition of the Lower Great Lakes System."[16] After outlining a long list of pollution threats to the lakes—including nutrient loadings to the lakes (in particular phosphorus), eutrophication, oil and watercraft pollution, bacterial contamination and toxics such as mercury—the report concluded that "there is no doubt that contaminants entering Lake Erie and Lake Ontario from one country move across the boundary and affect the water quality in the other country."[17] Given this unambiguous conclusion, discussions turned to creating a firmer framework for environmental management in the basin, one that set clear objectives and provided the means for tracking and supporting implementation.

Performance Measurement Comes to the Great Lakes

There are increasing political pressures on governments everywhere to demonstrate that their interventions bring benefits to the environment, and these pressures have intensified as countries continue to struggle with deficits and accumulated debt. Performance measurement, rooted in the new public management models of the 1990s,[18] can be understood as the process of developing and using tools to assess progress in achieving predetermined goals. With growing global concern about water governance, especially in relation to climate change, international organizations such as the United Nations (UN), through its Sustainable Development Goals (SDGs), and the Organisation for Economic Co-operation and Development (OECD), through its water governance program, have been keenly interested in assessing and promoting better water governance and policy regimes using performance assessment. Those who practise performance measurement in environmental and water policy focus on analyzing both the objectives of the policy (i.e., are they appropriate? properly defined? achievable? ambitious enough?) as well as with how to measure results or outcomes against these objectives.[19]

Early attempts to measure ecosystem/water outcomes, beginning in the 1970s, when government mandates to protect the environment were expanding,[20] pioneered the use of "proxy" values, or "indicators," as a way of judging performance. Indicators are metrics, generally quantitative, designed to provide information on the state or condition of something and, when tracked over time, to highlight progress or change in relation to specific program objectives. *Outcome* indicators related to water are numerous; they have been developed as part of broader environmental indicators of water quality/quantity;[21] for water security;[22] for water stress;[23] for water poverty;[24] and for international assessments and comparisons.[25]

Beginning in the late 1990s, however, analysts began to differentiate between outcome indicators (e.g., for ecosystems or water systems) and *societal or program response* indicators.[26] The OECD, other international organizations, and many countries, influenced by the enhanced focus on performance management, began to develop suites of indicators and benchmarks related to measuring government *efforts* in implementation.

This new focus concentrated discussions on understanding the program, policy, and process tools being used to respond to specific ecosystem challenges, and determine whether these were sufficient to support the achievement of objectives.[27] Performance measurement using response indicators thus also involves investigation into *why* objectives may not have been met (i.e., have government entities provided sufficient program and resource support for meeting objectives?).

Debates about environmental policy performance have most recently focused on the need for indicators that provide us with more "horizontal" knowledge about the capacity to support the general aims of environmental management. These so-called *governance* indicators can help us to understand the factors that might contribute to broader performance failures—namely implementation deficiencies across programs, across sectors, and across systems. For example, do governance efforts effectively include and link those decision-makers and communities that are critical for addressing the challenges at hand? Do we have consistent and predictive information on which to base our efforts, with a view to forward-planning? What is the state of collective investment and efforts to implement agreements and policies?

These discussions about societal response and governance indicators highlight the fact that performance assessment is not just about measuring outcomes; it also has democratic roots (i.e., to what extent are governments doing what they say they are going to do and to what extent are they responsive to public concerns?). Much of the literature on the role of the IJC related to environmental quality and the GLWQA has focused on how the institution gets answers to these questions.[28] In a very general sense, accountability can operate "upward," which implies answerability to elected leaders, or "downward" to the public. Certainly, lines of accountability within the framework of binational Great Lakes institutions are more complex and cannot work as they do domestically, but the IJC is subject to both "up" and "down" accountability. It is clear that the IJC is accountable to the parties in carrying out its functions under the treaty (water apportionment and references), as well as in its reporting duties. However, the idea that the parties and the IJC should respond to public concern is firmly rooted in the 1909 BWT (as discussed above) and in successive versions of the GLWQA (as discussed in the next section). As a result of this, as Krantzberg points out (in chapter 12 of this volume), a "strong and organized public" has emerged that has helped "push for implementation and sustained momentum" in following through on ecological recovery goals, reinforcing "downward" accountability relationships.

Our discussion below of the evolution of a Great Lakes water management regime highlights several characteristics with respect to experience in the basin with performance assessment over time. First, we note that the objectives of the management regime have continued to expand under successive versions of the GLWQA, becoming both increasingly broad yet also more numerous, with the result that the measurement of outcomes has become an ever more difficult and complex task. At the same time (and somewhat perversely), the pressure to provide accountability and track governance performance has increased over the course of successive renewals of the GLWQA. In this respect, outcomes have been emphasized but so, too, has the way that decisions are made, prioritizing input from stakeholders and the scientific community, and layering additional reporting requirements and mechanisms into updated agreements. In line with this expansion of accountability requirements, the IJC's role and capacity has also grown, particularly in terms of performance assessment, but so has that of the parties. This has led, perhaps unsurprisingly, to increased tensions between the commission, which performs the accountability functions, and the parties, who are responsible for implementation. However, the IJC's ability to network with governments and communities at various levels, with a wide variety of stakeholders, and with the academic community, has supported its position in the accountability and performance regime. Valiante and colleagues refer to this as the IJC's ability to create "a binational community external to the formal regime."[29] This external accountability role has broadened in scope over the past four decades.

The 1972 Great Lakes Water Quality Agreement

In 1972, Canada and the United States committed to addressing pollution within the Great Lakes ecosystem under the umbrella of a new binational approach under the GLWQA. In light of "the grave deterioration of water quality on each side of the boundary," the agreement aimed—quite ambitiously—to "restore and enhance water quality," as well as to prevent future pollution.[30] In a manner similar to the 1909 treaty, it established the lakes as a shared "commons" and the two nations as jointly responsible stewards of this freshwater resource.

The agreement, which is an "executive agreement" between the two countries and does not bind them in the same way that the BWT does, has been described as "unprecedented in scope." Indeed, it was unique in several respects. First, it laid out basin-wide General Objectives enjoining the signatory parties to keep the waters free of putrescent, floating, or foul-smelling materials, toxic discharges, and also excessive nutrients.[31] Specific Objectives were aimed at reducing levels of nutrients, fecal coliform, dissolved solids, iron, and other pollutants in the lakes.[32] Interim objectives were also set for mercury and other heavy metals, organics, oils, and petrochemicals, as well as suspended solids.[33] Further, the parties agreed to meet within one year to set objectives for a range of other contaminants.[34] Annex 2 of the agreement contained a detailed list of objectives for phosphorus loadings from various sources.

Secondly, the parties committed to various implementation measures to meet these objectives—specifically, to put in place municipal and industrial pollution control programs and also to engage in binational co-operative programming.[35] The IJC was to support achievement of the objectives through the monitoring, collection, analysis, and dissemination of water quality data, and provision of advice based on these data.[36] Moreover, the commission would be aided by a new Great Lakes Water Quality Board (composed of senior representatives of the federal, state, and provincial governments), a Research Advisory Board (composed of research managers), and a Regional Great Lakes Office, which the IJC would administer.

Finally—and importantly for our purposes here—the 1972 agreement also provided several accountability mechanisms for tracking performance. The agreement demands consultation between the federal governments as well as periodic reviews of "the operation and effectiveness of the Agreement as a whole."[37] The IJC was mandated to report annually on progress in achieving the water quality objectives set out in the agreement,[38] as well as to report on any other matter, either as requested by the parties or any matter during "the discharge of its functions under the

Agreement."[39] In most instances, IJC reporting was to be done to the parties but also state and provincial governments.[40]

These provisions in articles 3 and 4 of the 1972 GLWQA constituted the first formal reporting requirements for the IJC. This seemed to imply that, given these reporting authorities, the IJC would also be implicated in performance assessment in terms of the follow-through on commitments made in the agreement. However, this immediately set up a tension between the authority to report on performance, which was lodged with the IJC under the 1972 agreement, and the authority to actually implement the commitments, which resided with the Canadian and American governments as the signatory parties to the GLWQA. This tension would become more apparent over time as commitments under the GLWQA increased.

In addition to these accountability requirements, article vi requested that the IJC inquire into and report on "pollution of the boundary waters of the Great Lakes System from agricultural, forestry and other land use activities."[41] The IJC established the International Reference Group on Great Lakes Pollution from Land Use Activities (PLUARG) to plan and implement the requested study, focusing its research agenda on land use and land-use practices, as well as trends and projections on land-use patterns and practices, and also provide detailed surveys of selected watersheds to determine the sources of pollutants. The final PLUARG report, released in 1978, outlined serious pollution sources and issues such as phosphorus that still plague the Great Lakes to this day; indeed, the group highlighted the need for increased action on many fronts, helping to set the stage for a renewal of the GLWQA.

The 1978 Revisions

As concerns deepened over the lack of progress in dealing with existing and new forms of pollution in the basin waters, the 1972 GLWQA was replaced by a new agreement in 1978. The US administration had not provided support for implementing commitments in the 1972 agreement and, on the northern side of the border, Canada's record of forcing industries to comply with the Specific Objectives had been disappointing.[42]

The 1978 GLWQA built upon the pillars established in the 1972 agreement, though it also introduced the more complex "ecosystem approach" into the water quality management regime, thus recognizing that "a much more systemic perspective was required to understand the problems and what might be done about them."[43] As Krantzberg notes in her chapter in this volume, an ecosystem approach also serves to institutionalize multi-stakeholder decision-making in order to consider a much broader range of human impacts on the water and ecosystem quality. Indeed, the 1978 revisions adopted a more holistic view of the "Great Lakes basin ecosystem," which included the interacting components of air, land, water, and living organisms—including humans—within the drainage basin of the Great Lakes and the international section of the St. Lawrence River. Further, the 1978 agreement called—ambitiously—for the "virtual elimination of persistent toxic substances" in the Great Lakes ecosystem by adopting a philosophy of "zero discharge" of inputs.

A list of toxic chemicals was established for priority action. More specially, new provisions were added in the 1978 agreement to address pollution from assorted land-use activities and the effect of air pollution on Great Lakes water quality. New, stricter water quality objectives were announced, in order not only to maintain but also to restore water quality in the lakes. These changes represented a broadening of the goals underlying the GLWQA regime, both in terms of the management approaches to be taken and the pollutants to be addressed, and a requisite expansion of the expectations on governments with respect to environmental and water quality in the basin. And, to meet these expectations, the parties agreed to provide financial assistance to construct waste treatment facilities[44] and to coordinate planning programs that monitor the discharge of pollutants in the Great Lakes[45]—both of which had been missing from the 1972 agreement.

New accountability provisions were also added to the 1978 agreement. First, the agreement required review of the Specific Objectives by both parties[46] and by the IJC, which was also to make "appropriate recommendations" on progress achieved.[47] In this respect, the United States and Canada were enjoined to consult on the establishment of new or stricter Specific Objectives "to protect the beneficial uses from the combined effects of pollutants," and they were also to "consult on pollutant loading rates for each lake basin so as to preserve the total Great Lakes system."[48] Also significant was the new requirement that Canada and the

United States maintain an inventory of pollution abatement requirements, complete with compliance schedules and status reports, and make it available to both the IJC and the public;[49] this was included "in order to gauge progress toward the earliest practicable completion and operation" of both municipal and industrial pollution control programs.[50] Finally, the IJC was required to report biennially to the parties—rather than on the annual basis set out in the 1972 GLWQA—on the progress made toward fulfilling the water quality objectives. This change recognized the difficulties associated with collecting appropriate data on an annual basis. In general, as the IJC itself notes, "since the 1978 revision, the International Joint Commission has served as an independent assessor of the progress made by the two governments in achieving the Agreement's objectives."[51]

The 1983 Supplement

When the revised 1978 GLWQA was signed, Rasmussen, in his analysis of the changes, expressed considerable doubt that the two governments would improve implementation under the new agreement, given the lack of commitment they had to that point exhibited in adopting enabling national legislation to support implementation of the water quality objectives set out in the agreement and providing the requisite funds for the implementation of such legislation.[52] In the United States, the Nixon administration had refused to fund needed infrastructure around the basin and, even after the 1978 revisions drew attention to continuing implementation problems, the Carter administration's record in funding Great Lakes water quality commitments was little better. Rasmussen had also noted a distinct lack of political enthusiasm for the revised agreement, which, he surmised, would translate into low levels of political will in moving forward on GLWQA commitments.

In response to the continuing inability of the parties to address the problem of the eutrophication of Lake Erie, the agreement underwent further revision in 1983 when a Phosphorus Load Reduction Supplement was added to Annex 3 of the 1978 GLWQA. As a result, detailed plans to reduce phosphorus loading to receiving waters were developed and adopted by each jurisdiction in the basin. The 1983 Supplement contained no changes in terms of accountability and performance mechanisms or indicators, yet this addition represented a growing recognition that there would need to be more accountability and reporting related to the annexes dealing with specific issues, such as this one dealing with phosphorus loadings. There was also growing pressure for more public involvement and proposals that the IJC "should make a fundamental shift in its primary role to that of an environmental watchdog, an advocate for an ecological perspective on both sides of the border."[53] Interestingly, it was noted at the time that "the occasional ambivalence of governments is certainly less significant than the general conviction among them and the public that the IJC has become an indispensable instrument for both countries."[54]

The 1987 GLWQA: New Scales of Action and Accountability

There had certainly been some signs of progress in addressing environmental problems in the Great Lakes between 1973 and 1985, as governments attempted to deal with municipal and industrial discharges. It was clear by the mid-1980s, however, that serious pollution problems remained. An estimated 57 million tons of liquid waste were being poured into the Great Lakes annually by its inhabitants, their industries, and their municipalities,[55] and the degraded state of ecosystems was well documented by scientists working at institutions like the National Water Resources Institute, Canada Centre for Inland Waters, Environment Canada, and the US Environmental Protection Agency (EPA).

In 1987 the two national governments again renewed the GLWQA with a concerted focus on the most polluted watersheds in the region. Studies conducted by the IJC prior to the renegotiation had identified forty-three "Areas of Concern," or AOCs, that were particularly problematic watersheds with serious pollution and governance challenges (see Figure 13.1). Remedial Action Plans (RAPs) were to be created for each AOC in order to address "Beneficial Use Impairments" (BUIs) (see Figure 13.2).

The agreement listed a total of fourteen BUIs that could result from various types of water pollution—heavy metals, pathogens, contaminated sediments, and toxic chemicals. In each AOC, multi-level and multi-stakeholder governance institutions were engaged to develop and implement

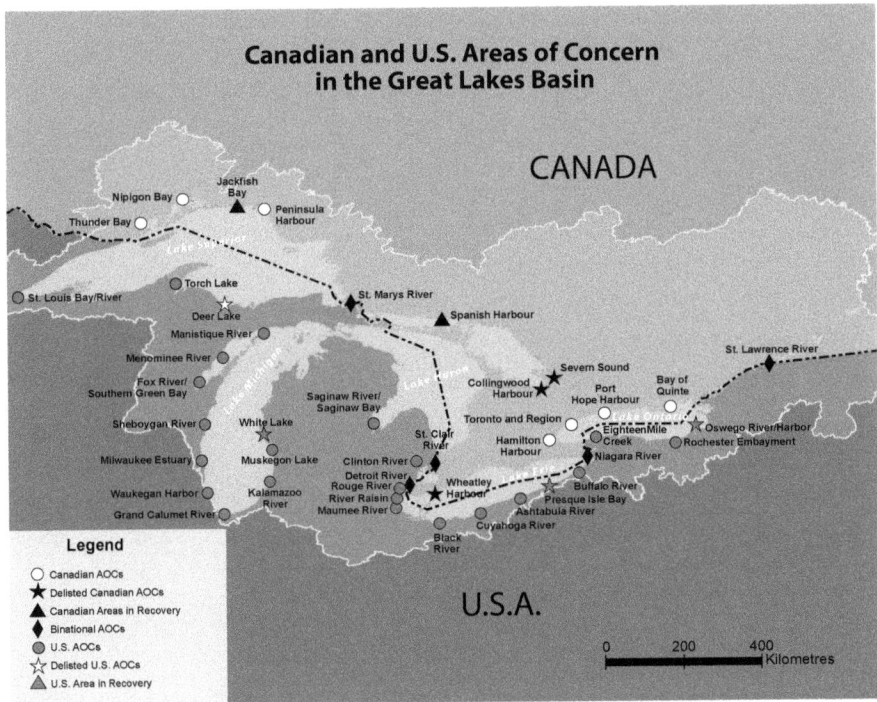

FIGURE 13.1. Areas of Concern in the 1987 GLWQA (2018). Used with the permission of Environment and Climate Change Canada.

the RAPs. BUIs were the agreed-upon indicators that must be addressed in order for an AOC to be "delisted"—the *key* metric of progress in cleaning up polluted watersheds.

The revised agreement also ushered in the development of Lakewide Management Plans (LaMPs) to address whole lake contamination by persistent toxic substances. To support these initiatives, the 1987 GLWQA was further broadened through the addition of new annexes addressing non-point contaminant sources (associated with land-use activities identified a decade earlier through PLUARG); contaminated sediment; airborne toxic substances; contaminated groundwater; and associated research and development. In addition, the expanded list of Specific Objectives, contained in the revised Annex 1, is striking when compared with the much shorter list in the original 1972 agreement.

FIGURE 13.2. Beneficial Use Impairments in Great Lakes Areas of Concern. Source: *Progress Report of the Parties* (2016), 12–13.

1. Restrictions on Fish and Wildlife Consumption
2. Tainting of Fish and Wildlife Flavor
3. Degraded Fish and Wildlife Populations
4. Fish Tumors or Other Deformities
5. Bird or Animal Deformities or Reproductive Problems
6. Degradation of Benthos
7. Restrictions on Dredging Activities
8. Eutrophication or Undesirable Algae
9. Restrictions on Drinking Water Consumption or Taste and Odor Problems
10. Beach Closings
11. Degradation of Aesthetics
12. Added Costs to Agriculture or Industry
13. Degradation of Phytoplankton and Zooplankton Populations
14. Loss of Fish and Wildlife Habitat

Accountability provisions were also tightened and decentralized. The IJC had played a critical role in the decade leading up to the 1987 agreement, and the new agreement reinforced the IJC's investigative role with specific reporting responsibilities related to the GLWQA. In effect, the IJC was given a "standing reference" and "permanent watchdog role" in the Great Lakes.[56] Biennial reporting would continue, but on the broadened range of objectives that now included AOCs and LaMPs. In fact, the language regarding the biennial report was quite strong: "This report shall include an assessment of the effectiveness of the programs and other measures undertaken pursuant to this Agreement, and advice and recommendations."[57] Performance was thus clearly in focus, particularly vis-à-vis the RAP process, which focused on tracking the delisting of BUIs in every AOC. Further, the new provision in the 1987 protocol

FIGURE 13.3. Objectives set for the 1972, 1978, 1987, and 2012 versions of the Great Lakes Water Quality Agreements. Source: *Progress Report of the Parties* (2016), 6.

1972	April 15, 1972	Prime Minister Pierre Trudeau and President Richard Nixon sign the first Canada-United States Great Lakes Water Quality Agreement (GLWQA).
		The 1972 GLWQA committed Canada and the United States to restore and enhance water quality in the Great Lakes ecosystem and established basin-wide water quality objectives and binational commitment on the design, implementation and monitoring of water quality programs.
		The focus of the 1972 GLWQA was on phosphorous loadings and visible pollution.
1978	November 22, 1978	While reaffirming and building upon the 1972 GLWQA, the 1978 GLWQA introduced the ecosystem approach to the management of Great Lakes water quality. It also called for the virtual elimination of persistent toxic substances in the Great Lakes ecosystem by adopting a philosophy of "zero discharge" of inputs and established a list of toxic chemicals for priority action.
1983	October 16, 1983	A Phosphorous Load Reduction Supplement was added to Annex 3 of the 1978 GLWQA, outlining measures to reduce phosphorous loading throughout the basin. As a result, detailed plans to reduce phosphorous loading to receiving waters were developed and adopted by each jurisdiction in the basin.
1987	November 18, 1987	The 1987 GLWQA called for: 1) the adoption of ecosystem objectives for the lakes; 2) the development and implementation of Remedial Action Plans to restore significantly degraded areas around the Great Lakes identified as Areas of Concerns; and 3) Lakewide Management Plans to address whole lake contamination by persistent toxic substances. The 1987 GLWQA was further broadened through new annexes addressing: non-point contaminant sources: contaminated sediment; airborne toxic substances; contaminated groundwater; and associated research and development.
2012	September 7, 2012	Canadian Minister of the Environment Peter Kent and United States Environmental Protection Agency Administrator Lisa Jackson sign the 2012 GLWQA.
		The 2012 GLWQA comprehensively addresses today's Great Lakes water quality issues by: 1) modernizing provisions related to excessive algae growth, chemicals, pollution from ships and scientific research; 2) incorporating new commitments to address significant challenges such as the degradation of the nearshore, the threat from aquatic invasive species and climate change, and the loss of habitat and species; and 3) strengthening provisions for governance, accountability, and engagement of government and non-government entities and the public.

FIGURE 13.4. Performance Assessment, Accountability and Reporting Mechanisms in the 1972, 1978 and 1987 versions of the Great Lakes Water Quality Agreements. Figure created by authors.

1972	Annual Report on progress in achieving Objectives to Parties and information to states/provinces
	Ability to report on any other matter "during 'the discharge of its functions under the Agreement"
1978	Biennial reporting
	Reporting by both IJC and Parties on progress achieved
	Introduction of concept of impact of pollutants on "beneficial uses" (BUIs)
	Parties required to make inventory of pollution abatement requirements with compliance schedules and status reports to IJC and public
1987	Biennial reporting on expanded range of Objectives, AOCs and LaMPs * Importance of BUIs in reporting on/delisting AOCs
	Lakewide Management Plans
	Provision to set "lake ecosystem objectives" for each Lake, along with ecosystem health indicators to assess progress towards reaching these objectives

that "lake ecosystem objectives" for each lake be established, along with "ecosystem health indicators" to assess progress toward these objectives,[58] represented a step further down the road to performance assessment, now using indicators.

If we look across the various revised agreements, Figure 13.3 highlights the changes in terms of objectives, from the original 1972 GLWQA through the 1978 and 1987 revisions. Figure 13.4 then provides our summary of alterations in the accountability and reporting regime.

Figures 13.3 and 13.4, and the discussion above, highlight two trends. First, we can see the expansion of objectives over the course of successive agreements vis-à-vis the ever longer list of pollutants and ever more annexes addressing specific problems; higher expectations embedded in new approaches such as ecosystem management and the virtual elimination of pollutants; and also the need for concerted follow-through on the BUI system (which constituted outcomes indicators) for RAPs and LaMPs. Second, alongside this broadening of programming and responsibility under the GLWQA came enhanced reporting responsibilities. Third, it is also evident that the enhanced reporting requirements were directed not only at the parties to the GLWQA (the national governments) but also to other audiences, including governments at other levels, as well as a broader range of communities, from local stakeholders, organized environmental interests, scientists, and those involved in RAP citizen advisory committees and working with LaMPs.

Accountability and Reporting by the Early 2000s

Despite the ambitious policy goals set out in the 1987 agreement, such as the commitment to virtually eliminate toxics, as well as the signing of new agreements like the 1997 Great Lakes Binational Toxics Strategy, implementation and policy efforts on the part of governments around the basin waned in the 1990s and into the 2000s. The lack of transboundary policy effort and domestic political will, were particularly evident in the slow progress cleaning up the most polluted sites on the Great Lakes.[59] Some twenty years after the 1987 and newer agreements had been established, over half of the basin's original wetlands had been lost, and miles of rivers and shoreline remained degraded.[60]

Significantly, the BUIs highlighted in the 1987 agreement had become an increasingly visible way of measuring the progress in addressing Great Lakes pollution—or, rather, the lack thereof. For each AOC, the impairments to specific beneficial uses were determined in phase 1 of the RAP, after which phase 2 would focus on restoring the beneficial uses that had been impaired. If all uses could be restored, this indicated that remediation of the AOC had been completed and ecosystem health restored. The AOC could thus be "delisted." However, by 2007, only three AOCs had been delisted (two in Canada and one in the United States),[61] and progress in the remaining AOCs and many other watersheds in the Great Lakes remained slow as pollution continued.

The State of the Great Lakes Ecosystem Conference (SOLEC) reports, released every two years between 1994 and 2008, indicated that the increasing number and imbalance of water uses continued to have negative impacts on water quality. Environment Canada and the US EPA had been leading the SOLEC assessments for the parties since 1994, when the first State of the Great Lakes report was released. In 1998, a suite of outcome indicators was introduced to allow for consistent and comprehensive assessment, as well as comparability across reporting cycles.[62] In the early 2000s, several new and re-emerging issues surfaced in the Great Lakes, including evidence of pharmaceutical chemicals; the enduring problem of the importation of invasive species;[63] the plateaued progress in addressing the "dead zone" in Lake Erie; and increasing concern about climate change and water levels.[64] Some forty years after the first GLWQA, as well as the implementation of various policy initiatives in the United States and Canada, the basic objectives of swimmable, drinkable, fishable waters had not been met, and forty of the AOCs remain the most polluted sites in the region.

In terms of performance assessment, in the decade prior to the signing of the 2012 GLWQA, binational progress reporting had virtually stopped. The last binational SOLEC jointly hosted by Environment Canada and the EPA was held in 2011, with conference presentations focusing on land-based issues that impact water quality and the health of the Great Lakes. The last SOLEC report in 2011 showed that progress had plateaued and even declined on several indicators.[65] There has not been a SOLEC or report since, and the International Association of Great Lakes Research conference, binational.net, and other forums seemed to informally replace SOLEC and scientific progress reporting.

A 2011 IJC report focusing on a twenty-five-year assessment of scientific and ecosystem indicators highlighted some successes, but also many outstanding challenges.[66] Although US legislation required reporting and the EPA continued reporting, the Canadian Senate and the Commissioner of the Environment and Sustainable Development were becoming vocal about the fact that efforts and reporting under the GLWQA had declined, and that the IJC's role in holding the parties accountable for implementation of the agreement had been undermined.[67] Moreover, the Canada-Ontario implementation agreements—which set out the roles and financing for programming on the Canadian side—were weakened and even suspended.[68]

In 2006, the IJC initiated a public consultation on the GLWQA and submitted a report to the Canadian and US federal governments expressing concerns about the lack of progress, reporting, accountability, and its own ability to fulfill its role:

> Over the years, the Commission's ability to carry out its mandate has been limited because, among other things, the governments have not followed many of the reporting requirements set out in the Agreement and have not provided all the information the Commission and the public require to evaluate progress. Shortcomings in monitoring and reporting need to be addressed in order for the Commission to be able to carry out its responsibilities more effectively.[69]

The IJC called for a new "action-oriented" agreement with "clear accountability provisions," a binational steering committee, more public involvement, and "requisite resources."[70] It also asked for "a reference in the new Agreement, pursuant to Article IX of the Boundary Waters Treaty, that gives a more clear and meaningful role to the Commission in implementing the agreement by: evaluating progress through Commission assessments, reports, and public consultations; identifying emerging issues and suggesting solutions; and facilitating collaboration among all Great Lakes basin interests."[71]

There were also calls from environmental groups and activists for an updated agreement; one report from the Alliance for the Great Lakes flagged concerns about gaps in surveillance and monitoring programs, the slow pace of moving forward with the progress indicators called for in 1987, and the need to improve research coordination and increase research funding.[72] In fact, the communities that had become increasingly involved and invested in GLWQA programming and the work of the IJC—working with the RAPs, LaMPs, water quality initiatives, and the academic community—were pushing for action to address the implementation deficits. Krantzberg (chapter 12 in this volume) also notes the key role of the Water Quality and Science Advisory Boards in fostering a collaborative environment for joint action. The result, as Clamen and Macfarlane note in the introduction to this volume, is that the IJC "increasingly incorporated transnational policy networks [and] public feedback."

Soon after the election of President Obama in 2008, change seemed to be in the offing with the announcement of a major Great Lakes environment and economy effort. The Great Lakes Restoration Initiative (GLRI), unveiled by the administration in 2009, contained an investment of $500 million (allocated over the 2010–14 period) for the basin, creating a well-funded program for state and societal actors to re-engage in Great Lakes efforts. A series of reviews and reports leading up to the BWT's and the IJC's hundredth anniversaries also fed the momentum to update the 1987 agreement. Meanwhile, scholarly observers were documenting the lack of progress on many fronts and at all levels,[73] and indicating that the parties needed to address the "implementation deficit" that existed despite numerous laws and institutions with policy mandates in the Great Lakes.[74] Finally, in 2009 it was announced by US Secretary of State Hillary Clinton and Canadian Minister of Foreign Affairs Lawrence Cannon that the two countries would renegotiate the GLWQA, last signed in 1987, with considerable input from the US EPA and Environment Canada.

The 2012 Revision and a Heightened Emphasis on Accountability and Performance Indicators

After three years of renegotiation, the new GLWQA was signed in 2012, renewing interest in policy objectives and implementation efforts. Canada and the United States significantly revised the GLWQA to strengthen and "modernize" it. Essentially, the 2012 GLWQA reflects a binational consensus that existing laws, policies, and institutions are sufficient and that, instead, the focus needs to be on improving the performance of both transboundary and domestic implementation efforts to attain better results than those achieved over the last forty years.[75]

Notable in the revised 2012 agreement, Canada and the United States have established a "comprehensive shared vision and common objectives as well as commitments to science, governance and action"[76] aimed at supporting efforts to restore and protect Great Lakes water quality and ecosystem health. As part of this vision, the 2012 revisions add the "precautionary principle," "polluter pays," and "adaptive management" as key principles and approaches guiding implementation of the agreement.[77] This expands even further the scope of responsibility the governments have taken on and also the role of the IJC in monitoring actions by all levels of government related to the General and Specific Objectives of the agreement. Something that has galvanized renewed policy efforts since the 2012 agreement was signed is the increased importance both countries have placed on engaging the broadest range of governments, interest organizations, and the public in the restoration and protection of Great Lakes water quality. The principles and approaches set out in article 4(k) now include "incorporating Public opinion and advice, as appropriate, and providing information and opportunities for the Public to participate in activities that contribute to the achievement of the objectives of this Agreement."[78] The IJC notes, on its website explaining the new agreement, that "the involvement and participation of State and Provincial Governments, Tribal Governments, First Nations, Métis, Municipal Governments, watershed management agencies, local public agencies, and the Public are essential to achieve the objectives of the Agreement."[79]

Significantly, the agreement lists "accountability" as first among its "Principles and Approaches"; here, accountability is defined as "establishing clear objectives, regular reporting made available to the Public on progress, and transparently evaluating the effectiveness of work undertaken to achieve the objectives of this Agreement."[80] Support for this focus on accountability can be found vis-à-vis the General and Specific Objectives and the annexes, several of which—such as Annex 9 on Climate Change—are new. Annex 10 on Science is a new version of a previous annex on prioritizing research that commits the parties to establishing science-based ecosystem indicators "to anticipate emerging threats and to measure progress in relation to achievement of the General and Specific Objectives of the [GLWQA]."[81] Progress reporting has become even more central to implementation—both in terms of public forums and progress reports. In addition to biannual Great Lakes Executive Committee meetings and public forums every three years, there are now three important progress reports: the Progress Report of the Parties (PRP) covers binational and domestic actions related to the implementation of the agreement; State of the Great Lakes (SOGL) reports also prepared by the parties; and the IJC's Triennial Assessment of Progress (TAP) report. In contrast to the PRP, which is organized around the annexes in the GLWQA, the SOGL indicators and the IJC TAP reports are organized according to the nine General Objectives set out in the agreement.

The first progress report on the "operationalization" of the new 2012 GLWQA was the PRP released in 2016. In addition to highlighting the actions led by the US EPA and Environment and Climate Change Canada, the report follows the structure of the 2012 agreement, addressing the progress of the parties in relation to the thirteen articles of the agreement setting forth the overall goals and "mechanics" of the agreement. The remaining sections address the progress of the parties in relation to each of the agreement's ten annexes. This report clearly outlines how the newly established implementation structures with designated actors accountable for action made significant progress in the three-year period following the new agreement. In contrast to the previous two decades, in which very limited progress was evident, the parties did make progress on several fronts.[82] One major area in this respect relates to performance indicators and recasting SOLEC into a formal SOGL report.

The SOGL report describes "basin-wide environmental trends and lake-specific conditions using ecosystem indicators." Most of the indicator work falls to the Ecosystem Indicator and Reporting (EI&R) Task Team under Annex 10. The parties have been updating and revising the suite of ecosystem (outcome) indicators previously used in SOLEC reports, using key indicators as the basis of collecting and aggregating relevant scientific information. Content from the first SOGL report was presented at the Great Lakes Public Forum in October 2016 and the technical report was released in June 2017.[83] The report focuses on nine indicators that align with the nine General Objectives in the GLWQA. The nine indicators contain forty-four sub-indicators to assess progress over time and "how the lakes are responding to management actions," including basin-wide data and lake level data to report on: current status (good, fair, poor, undetermined) and trends over time (improving, unchanging, deteriorating, undetermined). As noted in the *State of the Great Lakes 2017 Technical Report*:

Table 13.1 State of the Great Lakes 2017

Indicator	Status	Trend
Climate Change and Watersheds	Fair	Unchanging
Habitat and Species	Fair	Unchanging
Invasive Species	Poor	Deteriorating
Nutrients and Algae	Fair	Unchanging-Deteriorating
Groundwater	Fair	Undetermined
Toxic Chemicals	Fair	Unchanging-Improving
Fish Consumption	Fair	Unchanging-Improving
Drinking Water	Good	Unchanging
Beaches	Fair-Good	Unchanging

Source: *State of the Great Lakes 2017 Highlights Report*, 2017.

No one agency or organization has the jurisdiction or the capacity to monitor, manage, restore and protect an ecosystem as large as the Great Lakes so assessing the environmental conditions of the Great Lakes using ecosystem indicators involves hundreds of people from many agencies and organizations on both sides of the border. The information in this document, has been assembled with involvement from more than 180 scientists and experts from the Great Lakes community within Canada and the United States. These experts represent over 30 different agencies and organizations.[84]

The parties' first report on the state of the Great Lakes, using the new indicator suite, assessed the overall environmental condition of the lakes as "fair and unchanging." As outlined in Table 13.1, this status is evident across most of the nine General Objectives and associated indicators.

The nearly 100-page technical report is very impressive; it was followed by the 2017–19 "priorities for science and action," which guided next steps related to each of the GLWQA annexes and provided ongoing updates and reporting on binational.net. The *State of the Great Lakes 2019 Highlights Report* was released at the Great Lakes Public Forum in June

2019 and the *State of the Great Lakes 2019 Technical Report* will be released sometime in 2019, after the writing of this book.

These reporting requirements have further strengthened the accountability provisions of the agreement and, perhaps most importantly, have encouraged governments to continue to think about how progress might be measured. Indeed, both the IJC and the parties have spent considerable time and effort over the past few years developing the indicators for reporting purposes and collecting the relevant data. The IJC had also initiated work on performance measures in its 2011 report[85] by including the traditional SOLEC indicators and adding performance measures for AOCs and beaches. Further, they commissioned a report in 2013 exploring the idea of GLEEM—Great Lakes Environmental Effectiveness Metrics[86]—and organized an Indicators Workshop in 2014, where experts and stakeholders were brought together to discuss the existing ecosystem health and human health indicators, as well as potential response and program effectiveness indicators. In 2015, the IJC also tested the GLEEM approach and method related to two General Objectives outlined in the GLWQA (beaches and invasive species) using surveys of experts and stakeholders in the region to independently assess indicators, progress, and achievements.[87] However, as the parties moved ahead with their own indicators work, the IJC then seemed to take a "wait and see" approach, viewing its role as primarily to review and comment on the indicators the parties developed and made public at the Great Lakes Public Forum in October 2016.

The IJC began work on their Triennial Assessment of the Parties (TAP) report without initially having access to the PRP and SOGL reports (they were released in 2016 and 2017, respectively). Pursuant to article 7.1 (k) of the 2012 GLWQA, the IJC was also tasked with collecting and summarizing public input on PRP and SOGL reports throughout 2017. The IJC released its draft TAP report in January 2017, and after a significant public engagement and review released the final 182-page TAP report in November 2017. As noted in the report:

> The IJC commends the two federal governments for *considerable progress* they have made to accelerate the cleanup of contaminated Areas of Concern, set new loading targets for the amount of phosphorus entering Lake Erie to reduce

harmful algal blooms, and establishing the work groups and processes needed to implement the Agreement. However, the IJC finds that work needs to be increased in several key areas.[88]

While clearly acknowledging the many fronts on which the parties had made progress since implementation of the GLWQA began in 2013, including a proposed near-shore framework, accelerated restoration of contaminated AOCs, preventing any newly introduced aquatic invasive species, and improved reporting on groundwater science, the IJC stressed the need for more accountability on the basic human health goals of fishable, swimmable, drinkable waters. As noted in the report:

> The IJC also finds that the governments need to strengthen *public engagement, accountability and funding* to achieve the Agreement's objectives. Governments need to incorporate more robust public engagement into their activities, including engagement with diverse communities and Tribal, First Nations and Métis governments. Clear, time-bound targets for action are needed as are long-term aspirations for improvements in the status and trends of Great Lakes indicators against which progress can be more definitively assessed.[89]

Compared to the period before the 2012 GLWQA, progress is clearly evident when viewed in the context of the key indicators associated with the removal of BUIs and the delisting of AOCs, particularly under the US GLRI.[90] However, the IJC report also recommended that the parties set a fifteen-year goal for completing remedial actions at all AOCs, and it called on both the Canadian and US governments to properly fund these efforts, given that AOCs have been a priority since 1987. The report also underscored the need for more emphasis on accountability and indicators related to preventative actions and efforts.

Observations and Conclusions

As highlighted above, many of the environmental problems plaguing the region have been known for decades. Over forty years have passed since the public demanded action and accountability from Canadian and US governments and oversight by the IJC. In 1999, just as the parties to the GLWQA seemed to be abandoning a review of the agreement, Michael Donahue wrote that "we cannot move forward unless we are first able to look back, assess progress, evaluate performance and apply lessons learned to the balance of our journey."[91] This chapter has traced the evolution in thinking about how accountability for progress and performance has been assessed under the agreement in the period since 1960. It shows that the objectives of the GLWQA have become both more encompassing, with the integration of ecosystem, precautionary, and preventative approaches, and more specific with a lengthening list of pollutants to be addressed and indicators. Yet this examination also shows that in terms of meeting these objectives, the GLWQA has in many cases been disappointing, despite the accountability mechanisms in the agreement also becoming more numerous and varied.

The more recent efforts to embed an indicators approach into basin environmental management through the reporting function under the 2012 GLWQA represents another step up the ladder of performance assessment. However, it is important to note that, despite some significant progress by the parties in developing nine indicators and forty-four sub-indicators that align with the nine General Objectives of the agreement, the IJC has recommended refinement of some indicators as well as new indicators for future use. SOLEC served as the scientific backbone of indicator work under the GLWQA and has been subsumed within the new SOGL reporting regime that is led by the parties. The parties themselves have taken a much more active and directive role in performance reporting with the PRP and SOGL reports, but it remains to be seen if and how they will use this performance information, and whether the IJC will develop and use other performance indicators in its TAP report to assess progress under the agreement.

Under the 2012 GLWQA provisions, the parties are responsible for implementation and reporting and the IJC is responsible for overall reporting on progress under the agreement; both have focused on *outcome* indicators. The IJC and the parties have not yet moved to develop societal/program response or governance indicators. While the ecosystem and human health indicators currently in use are very important in terms of highlighting ecosystem and human health outcomes, both scholarship on water governance and international organizations such as the OECD argue that governance indicators are critical as measures of progress and for the ongoing assessment and dialogue processes in shared water basins.

Interestingly, one of the features differentiating the 2012 revision from earlier versions of the agreement, according to the IJC itself, is its focus on "enhanced governance,"[92] and the heavy emphasis it places on public and stakeholder engagement fits with this. Questions have already been raised as to how the commission and parties will know, for example, whether they have been successful in their public engagement efforts under the agreement.[93] This seems to be the next horizon for those who seek to enhance performance in maintaining and restoring environment and ecosystem health in the Great Lakes basin. At present, the sole focus on ecosystem and human health outcome indicators does not reflect the complexity and comprehensiveness now embedded in the General and Specific Objectives of the regime. Nor does it recognize the critical role that the binational community—indeed various binational communities—brought together by the IJC, in conjunction with the now very broad range of programming under the GLWQA, play in supporting implementation of GLWQA programming and in scrutinizing the effectiveness of these efforts. The aggregation of data and reporting related to the GLWQA by the parties and IJC is impressive. However, using the data beyond reporting requirements related to strategic policy, planning, and implementation priorities remains a challenge. For this, strong governance mechanisms need to be in place.

Pushing forward with the promises made in the 2012 agreement will not be easy, however. Given the policy decisions taken by the Trump administration on environmental protection, climate change, and water protection, the United States is simply not going to continue to play the leadership role vis-à-vis the Great Lakes basin that it had assumed under the Obama administration. This makes the political environment for the IJC, already sensitive, even more tricky. In this more challenging context, the commission must continue to evolve and strengthen its human and knowledge resources in order to be able to perform its traditional role of binational fact-finder. Further, the IJC will need to protect and bolster its ability to measure progress vis-à-vis the parties, rather than cede the field in terms of such key tools as indicator development and application. Yet the IJC is a dynamic organization and it displays significant strengths—in terms of in-depth research; willingness to wrestle with the longer-term focus required of adaptive management; and a real facility for working across governance scales, NGO networks, and the academic community, as well as with citizens. Perhaps more than any other contribution, the IJC's firmly rooted commitment to, and increasing expertise in, reaching outward, both across and outside of governments, in the pursuit of mutual understanding, collaborative action, and accountability, has set a productive tone for Canada-US environmental relations that reaches beyond water quality. Further, in an era in which the sub-national level has become increasingly significant not only for achieving policy outcomes, but also for building the political will to move forward, the IJC is well placed to engage and coordinate. The six new commissioners appointed to the IJC in May 2019—which include among them an Indigenous representative, several environmental activists, and a former state assemblywoman—are likely to deepen the commission's networks and reach across various communities.

The IJC is also exceedingly adept at working within changing and sensitive political contexts. Yet the key task for the commission as we move into the next hundred years will be to survive, adapt, and even thrive in turbulent times, not merely by flying below the radar but by mobilizing and operationalizing the support of diverse communities, networks, and governments to take on the difficult environmental challenges we will face in the coming decades.

Notes

1 International Joint Commission (IJC), *Twelfth Biennial Report on Great Lakes Water Quality*: Executive Summary (2004), available at: https://www.nrc.gov/docs/ML0703/ML070390585.pdf.

2 Agreement Review Committee, *Final Report to the Great Lakes Binational Executive Committee: Review of the Great Lakes Water Quality Agreement* (September 2007), http://publications.gc.ca/collections/collection_2012/ec/En164-21-1-2007-eng.pdf, p. 2.

3   IJC, *Thirteenth Biennial Report on Great Lakes Water Quality* (2006), http://publications.gc.ca/collections/collection_2011/ijc/E95-1-1-13-eng.pdf, p. 2.

4   See Alliance for the Great Lakes, Biodiversity Project, Canadian Law Association, and Great Lakes United, *The Great Lakes Water Quality Agreement. Promises to Keep; Challenges to Meet. Perspectives from Citizens in Consultation with the Great Lakes Basin's Environmental Community* (December 2006), available at: http://www.cela.ca/sites/cela.ca/files/uploads/553GLWQA_promises.pdf.

5   See, for example, article ii, which notes that "any interference with or diversion from their natural channel of such waters on either side of the boundary, resulting in any injury on the other side of the boundary, shall give rise to the same rights and entitle the injured parties to the same legal remedies as if such injury took place in the country where such diversion or interference occurs." Further, article iii states that "It is agreed that, in addition to the uses, obstructions, and diversions heretofore permitted or hereafter provided for by special agreement between the Parties hereto, no further or other uses or obstructions or diversions, whether temporary or permanent, of boundary waters on either side of the line, affecting the natural level or flow of boundary waters on the other side of the line shall be made except by authority of the United States or the Dominion of Canada within their respective jurisdictions and with the approval, as hereinafter provided, of a joint commission, to be known as the International Joint Commission."

6   IJC *Final Report of the International Joint Commission on the Pollution of Boundary Waters Reference* (Washington and Ottawa: IJC, 1918), https://www.ijc.org/sites/default/files/A62.pdf, p. 10.

7   Ibid., 18–22.

8   Ibid., 25–9.

9   Ibid., 50.

10 Murray Clamen and Daniel Macfarlane, "The International Joint Commission, Water Levels, and Transboundary Governance in the Great Lakes," *Review of Policy Research* 32, no. 1 (2015): 40–59.

11 IJC, *Annual Report for 2008: Boundary Waters Treaty Centennial Edition* (Washington and Ottawa: IJC, 2008), https://ijc.org/sites/default/files/ID1629.pdf, p. 24

12 Carolyn Johns and Mark Sproule-Jones, "Great Lakes Water Policy: The Cases of Water Levels and Water Pollution in Lake Erie," in *Canadian Environmental Policy and Politics: Prospects for Leadership and Innovation* (4th ed.), ed. Deborah VanNijnatten (Don Mills, ON: Oxford University Press, 2016), 252–77.

13 Ibid.

14 IJC, *Pollution of Lake Erie, Lake Ontario and the International Section of the St. Lawrence River* (Ottawa: Information Canada, 1971), https://scholar.uwindsor.ca/cgi/viewcontent.cgi?article=1012&context=ijcarchive, p. 3.

15 Johns and Sproule-Jones, "Great Lakes Water Policy."

16 IJC, *Pollution of Lake Erie*, 3.

17 Ibid., 37.

18 See, for example, Patrick Dunleavy and Christopher Hood, "From old public administration to new public management" *Public Money & Management* 14, no. 3 (1994): 9–16.

19 Organisation for Economic Co-operation and Development (OECD), *Measuring Results of Environmental Regulation and Compliance Assurance: Guidance for countries of Eastern Europe, Caucasus, and Central Asia* (Paris: OECD, 2009), http://www.oecd.org/env/outreach/42942944.pdf, p. 11.

20 See, for example, D. B. Tunstall, "Developing Indicators of Environmental Quality: The Experience of the Council on Environmental Quality," *Social Indicators Research* 6 (1979): 301–47, and H. Verwayen, "Social Indicators: Actual and Potential Uses," *Social Indicators Research* 14, no. 1 (1984): 1–27.

21 See, for example, Yale University's Environmental Protection Index, available at https://epi.envirocenter.yale.edu/.

22 See, for example, G. Dunn and K. Bakker, "Canadian approaches to assessing water security: An inventory of indicators" (Vancouver: University of British Columbia, 2009); D. Garrick and J. Hall, "Water Security and Society: Risks, Metrics and Pathways," *Annual Review of Environment and Resources* 39 (2014): 611–39; and E. Norman, G. Dunn, K. Bakker, D. M. Allen, and R. Cavalcanti de Albuquerque, "Water Security Assessment: Integrating Governance and Freshwater Indicators," *Water Resources Management* 27, no. 2 (2013): 535–51.

23 See, for example, Transboundary Water Assessment Programme, available http://www.geftwap.org/twap-project; United Nations, "UN Water," available at https://www.un.org/waterforlifedecade/transboundary_waters.shtml.

24 R. G. Garriga and A. Foguet, "The Water Poverty Index: Assessing Water Scarcity at Different Scales" (paper presented at Congres UPC Sostenible, Barcelona, 2015); and Caroline Sullivan, "Calculating a Water Poverty Index," *World Development* 30, no. 7 (2015): 1195–1210.

25 L. De Stefano, "International Initiatives for Water Policy Assessment: A Review," *Water Resources Management* 24 (2010): 2449–66 ; and OECD, *Water Governance in OECD Countries: A multi-level approach* (OECD Studies on Water, 2011), available at https://www.oecd.org/governance/regional-policy/48885867.pdf.

26 C. Azar, J. Holmberg, and C. Lindgren, "Socio-ecological indicators for sustainability," *Ecological Economics* 18 (1996): 89–112; F. Molle and P. Mollinga, "Water poverty indicators: Conceptual problems and policy issues," *Water Policy* 5 (2003): 529–44; and O. Ohlsson and A. R. Turton, "The turning of a screw: Social resource scarcity as a bottle-neck in adaptation to water scarcity," (Occasional Paper Series: School of Oriental and Asian Studies, Water Study Group, University of London, 1999).

27 Dunn and Bakker, "Canadian approaches to assessing water security"; and D. Kaufmann and A. Kraay, "Where are we? Where should we be going?" *World Bank Research Observer* 23, no. 1 (2008): 1–30.

28 Lee Botts and Paul Muldoon, *Evolution of the Great Lakes Water Quality Agreement* (East Lansing: Michigan State University Press, 2005); Carolyn Johns, "Transboundary Environmental Governance and Water Pollution in the Great Lakes Region: Recent Progress and Future Challenges" in *Transboundary Environmental Governance Across the World's Longest Border*, ed. Stephen Brooks and Andrea Olive (East Lansing: Michigan State University Press, 2018), 77–113. Johns and Sproule-Jones, "Great Lakes Water Policy"; Mark Sproule-Jones, *Restoration of the Great Lakes: Promises, Practices, and Performances* (Vancouver: UBC Press, 2002).

29 Marcia Valiante, Paul Muldoon, and Lee Botts, "Ecosystem Governance: Lessons from the Great Lakes" in *Global Governance: Drawing Insight from the Environmental Experience*, ed. O. Young (Cambridge, MA and London: MIT Press, 1997), 197–225.

30 Great Lakes Water Quality Agreement (GLWQA). United States and Canada. Signed at Ottawa 15 April 1972; entered into force 15 April 1972.

31 1972 GLWQA, article ii.

32 1972 GLWQA, article iii.

33 1972 GLWQA, Annex 1, sections 1 and 2.

34 1972 GLWQA, Annex 1, section 7.

35 1972 GLWQA, article v.

36 1972 GLWQA, article vi.

37 1972 GLWQA, article ix.3.

38 1972 GLWQA, article vi.3.

39 1972 GLWQA, article vi.4.

40 1972 GLWQA, article vi.3, 4.

41 1972 GLWQA, article vi.

42 Eric Rasmussen, "The 1978 Great Lakes Water Quality Agreement and Prospects for U.S.–Canada Pollution Control," *Boston College International and Comparative Law Review* 1, no. 1 (1979): 506–7.

43 George Francis, "Binational Cooperation for Great Lakes Water Quality: A Framework for the Groundwater Connection," *Chicago-Kent Law Review* 65, no. 2 (1989): 363.

44 Revised GLWQA of 1978 United States and Canada. Signed at Ottawa 22 November 1978; entered into force 22 November 1978. See article ii.b, available at https://treaties.un.org/doc/publication/unts/volume%201153/volume-1153-i-18177-english.pdf.

45 1978 GLWQA, article ii.c.

46 1978 GLWQA, article iv.2.

47 Ibid.

48 Rasmussen, "The 1978 Great Lakes Water Quality Agreement and Prospects," 511.

49 1978 GLWQA, article vi.c.

50 Ibid.

51　IJC, *First Triennial Assessment of Progress on Great Lakes Quality* (Ottawa and Washington: IJC, 2017), 6.

52　Rasmussen, "The 1978 Great Lakes Water Quality Agreement and Prospects," 520.

53　Kim Richard Nossal, "The IJC in Retrospect," in *The International Joint Commission Seventy Years On*, ed. Robert Spencer, John Kirton, and Kim Richard Nossal (Toronto: University of Toronto Press, 1981), 127.

54　Maxwell Cohen, "The Commission from the Inside," in Spencer et al., *The International Joint Commission Seventy Years On*.

55　Theodora E. Colborn, Alex Davidson, Sharon N. Green, R. A. (Tony) Hodge, C. Ian Jackson, and Richard A. Liroff, *Great Lakes, Great Legacy?* (Washington, DC: Conservation Foundation, 1990).

56　Alan M. Schwartz, "The Canada-U.S. Environmental Relationship at the Turn of the Century," *American Review of Canadian Studies: The Thomas O. Enders Biennial Issue on the State of the Canada-United States Relationship* 30, no. 2 (Summer 2002): 223.

57　Revised GLWQA of 1978 as amended by protocol on 18 November 1987. United States and Canada; signed at Ottawa 18 November 1987. See article vii.3, available at http://agrienvarchive.ca/download/GLWQ_agreement_revised_78.pdf.

58　1987 GLWQA, supplement to Annex 2.3, and Annex 11.4.

59　Sproule-Jones, *Restoration of the Great Lakes*.

60　United States Environmental Protection Agency, *State of The Great Lakes: What Is The State Of Great Lakes Coastal Wetlands?* (2006), available at https://archive.epa.gov/solec/web/pdf/coastal_wetlands.pdf.

61　Collingwood Harbour was delisted in 1994, Severn Sound in 2003 and, in the US, Oswego River was delisted in 2006. Spanish Harbour has been designated an AOC since 1999.

62　Environment Canada and United States Environmental Protection Agency, *State of the Great Lakes Report 2017* (presented at the Great Lakes Forum 4 October 2016, Toronto, ON).

63　J. Sanders and P. Stoett, "Fighting Extinction and Invasion: Transborder Conservation Efforts," in *Continental Ecopolitics: Canadian-American Relations and Environmental Policy*, ed. P. LePrestre and P. Stoett (London: Ashgate, 2006), 157–78.

64　Johns and Sproule-Jones, "Great Lakes Water Policy."

65　State of the Lakes Ecosystem Conference (2011); all documents are available at https://archive.epa.gov/solec/web/html/.

66　IJC, *15th Biennial Report on Great Lakes Water Quality* (Ottawa and Washington: IJC, 2011), available at https://www.ijc.org/en/15th-biennial-report-great-lakes-water-quality.

67　Canada, Commissioner of the Environment and Sustainable Development, Office of the Auditor General, "A legacy worth protecting: Charting a sustainable course in the Great Lakes and St. Lawrence River basin," in *Report of the Commissioner of the*

Environment and Sustainable Development (Ottawa: Minister of Public Works and Government Services, 2001), 301–14; and Canada, Commissioner of the Environment and Sustainable Development, Office of the Auditor General, "Safety of drinking water: Federal responsibilities," in *Annual Report of the Commissioner of the Environment and Sustainable Development* (2005), ch. 4.

68   Botts and Muldoon, *Evolution of the Great Lakes Water Quality Agreement*.

69   IJC, *Thirteenth Biennial Report on Great Lakes Water Quality*, 2.

70   Ibid.

71   Ibid.

72   Alliance for the Great Lakes, Biodiversity Project, Canadian Environmental Law Association, Great Lakes United, *Promises to Keep*, 5.

73   Carolyn Johns, "Transboundary Water Pollution Efforts in the Great Lakes: The Significance of National and Sub-national Policy Capacity," in *Environmental Governance on the 49th Parallel: New Century, New Approaches*, ed. Barry Rabe and Stephen Brooks (Washington, DC: Woodrow Wilson International Center for Scholars, Canada Institute, 2010), 63–82; Carolyn Johns, "Water Pollution in the Great Lakes Basin: The Global-Local Dynamic," in *Environmental Challenges and Opportunities: Local-Global Perspectives on Canadian Issues*, ed. Christopher Gore and Peter Stoett (Toronto: Emond Montgomery, 2009), 95–129; and Sproule-Jones, *Restoration of the Great Lakes*.

74   Chris McLaughlin and Gail Krantzberg, "An Appraisal of Policy Implementation Deficits in the Great Lakes," *Journal of Great Lakes Research* 37, no. 2 (2011): 390–6.

75   Johns, "Transboundary Environmental Governance."

76   IJC, "About the Great Lakes Quality Agreement" (2018), available at https://binational.net/glwqa-aqegl/.

77   Protocol Amending the Agreement Between Canada and the United States of America on Great Lakes Water Quality, 1978, as Amended on 16 October 1983, and on 18 November 1987; signed 7 September 2012; entered into force 12 February 2013. See article iv, available at https://www.ec.gc.ca/grandslacs-greatlakes/A1C62826-72BE-40DB-A545-65AD6FCEAE92/1094_Canada-USA%20GLWQA%20_e.pdf.

78   2012 GLWQA, article 4(1).

79   IJC, *About the Great Lakes Water Quality Agreement* (Ottawa and Washington: IJC, 2018).

80   2012 GLWQA, article 4.A.

81   2012 GLWQA.

82   Johns, "Transboundary Environmental Governance."

83   State of the Great Lakes 2017 reports are available at https://binational.net/2017/06/19/sogl-edgl-2017/.

84   Environment and Climate Change Canada and the US Environmental Protection Agency, *State of the Great Lakes 2017 Technical Report: Indicators to assess the status*

and *trends of the Great Lakes ecosystem* (2017), available at https://binational.net/wp-content/uploads/2017/09/SOGL_2017_Technical_Report-EN.pdf\.

85 IJC, *15th Biennial Report on Great Lakes Water Quality.*

86 J. P. Hill and D. Eichinger, *A framework for assessing the effectiveness of programs and other measures developed to address the objectives of the Great Lakes Water Quality Agreement* (Report for the International Joint Commission, 2013).

87 Carolyn Johns, Adam Thorn, and Debora VanNijnatten, "Environmental Regime Effectiveness and the North American Great Lakes Water Quality Agreement," *International Environmental Agreements: Politics, Law and Economics* 18, no. 3 (2018): 315–33.

88 IJC, "IJC calls on governments to set specific targets to accelerate Great Lakes restoration, protect drinking water and eliminate releases of untreated sewage," news release with Triennial Assessment of Progress Report, 28 November 2017.

89 Ibid.

90 Johns, "Transboundary Environmental Governance."

91 Michael Donahue, "The case for good government: Why a comprehensive review of the Great Lakes Water Quality Agreement is needed," *Toledo Journal of Great Lakes Law, Science & Policy* 2 (1999): 1.

92 IJC, *About the Great Lakes Water Quality Agreement.*

93 Great Lakes Executive Committee, meeting, June 2016.

SECTION 4

LEGACIES

14

From "Stakeholder to Rights-Holder": Re-examining the Role of Indigenous Peoples in the International Joint Commission as the Third Sovereign

Frank Ettawageshik and Emma S. Norman

Introduction

The various contributors to this volume reflect on both the accomplishments of, and the challenges faced by, the International Joint Commission. However, little has been written about how the very framework of the International Joint Commission has limited the participation of Indigenous Peoples in its governance structure, and in fact may have perpetuated a politics of omission and erasure. Certainly, the Boundary Waters Treaty (BWT) and the International Joint Commission (IJC) are products of the time in which they were created; however, it is essential to ask critical questions and reconsider the IJC through a post-colonial lens.

As the editors of this volume point out in their introduction, the signing of the BWT on 5 January 1909 was conducted between two nations—United States and Canada. However, this act, and the subsequent creation of the IJC, set the scope, tone, and trajectory of the commission as a binational agreement between two sovereign nations, rather than a multinational agreement between multiple nations. The treaty was also established through a Western legal framework, exclusive of Indigenous law.

The fact that millions of Indigenous Peoples lived along the borderland, had occupied the waterways and lands in question for thousands of years, and were (and remain) significantly impacted by the health and well-being of the waterways, was fundamentally ignored in the BWT. The fact that the Indigenous communities that were impacted by the treaty had their own legal structure and governance framework was also not considered. A deep-seated mistrust of both the Americans and the British lingered among Indigenous Peoples, the result of previous treaties ending the American War for Independence and the War of 1812. However, unlike these previous treaties, which at least acknowledged Indigenous existence and rights, there was no mention of these rights in the 1909 BWT. In fact, the IJC itself recognizes that for the first ninety years after the BWT was signed, the IJC was specifically instructed not to engage with Tribes and First Nations—the impact of which are still felt today.[1]

The omission of Indigenous Peoples from the BWT and the original formation of the IJC is unsurprising given the time in which they were created. When the BWT was negotiated and signed, a common thought was that Indigenous Peoples in North America were "vanishing Americans." At the time of the 1909 signing, the Indigenous Peoples of the United States and Canada were facing explicit governmental policies that were designed to eliminate Indigenous cultures and disrupt communities. During this era, residential schools were in full operation, families were separated, languages decimated, and significant cultural traditions such as potlatches outlawed. In fact, at this time Indigenous Peoples were not considered citizens in either the United States or Canada—and they did not have the right to vote in some US states until as late as 1954, and until 1969 in Canada (with Quebec being the final province to grant the right).

The BWT was signed in the wake of the treaties that removed Indigenous Peoples from their traditional territories in the United States and relocated them to reserves (with the guaranteed—but under-protected—access to "Usual and Accustomed" fishing and hunting areas). Devastating policies such as the US Dawes Act of 1887—which aimed to disrupt Indigenous cultures by eliminating communal governance structures and hunting and gathering practices and institutionalizing individual land-ownership and farming methods—followed these treaties.[2] Ultimately, the Dawes Act facilitated the transfer of significant portions of reservation land to non-Indigenous occupants, and it had significant impacts on the economic and cultural cohesion of Indigenous communities. In Canada, the Indian Act of 1876 had similar implications—namely the forced removal of First Nations and assimilation into non-Indigenous communities. However, the political landscape is different in Canada, where many Indigenous communities do not hold treaties. The Indian Act has been amended several times, with the most significant changes occurring in 1951 and 1985, which facilitated the removal of the act's most discriminatory sections.[3] In all of these cases, it is important to consider the impacts on the governance structure of the impacted Tribes and First Nations.

For example, during treaty time, Indigenous leaders entering into treaty negotiations had a very different relationship with the land than that of the settlers. When tribal leaders were forced to relinquish much of their traditional territory to the federal government/settlers, the tribal communities would likely have assumed that these entities would care for the land as they had. The Western idea of "ownership" was a foreign framework. Rather, Indigenous understanding of ownership entailed a responsibility to protect or care for the land and its resources. This meant that if you occupied or "owned" the land, you would care for it, protect it, and nurture it, and it would, in turn, provide for those who lived on it. In other words, you would enter into a relationship with the land, the water, and the animals. The idea of ownership, of course, had completely different implications for the Western settlers, whose economies were often based on extractive practices that focused on capital accumulation for the benefit of the individual family rather than the wider community. This world view was also instrumental in the practice of dispossessing not only Indigenous land, but impacting Indigenous ways of life.[4]

But in the intervening years, through powerful persistence, the Indigenous Peoples of North America have regained strength in numbers and have developed administrative-political institutions to better engage with, and become leaders in, the non-Indigenous world. In addition, several legal decisions have been decided in favour of supporting treaty-reserved rights for Indigenous Peoples on both sides of the Canada-US border—including U.S. v. Washington 1974 (known as the Boldt Decision), U.S. v. Michigan 1978, Lac Courte Orielles v. Voigt 1983, R v. Sparrow, 1990, 1 S.C.R. 1075 (known as the Sparrow case).[5] All of these decisions are fundamentally important cases that impacted fishing rights in the United States and Canada.

Thus, in this chapter, we examine the history of Indigenous communities' involvement in the IJC. The evolution from an "excluded role" to "invited participants" has been a slow process and is part of a wider backdrop of societal change and the politics of recognition. In an attempt to shed light on this process, we examine some critical questions: To what extent was the IJC a tool of settler colonialism? Was the IJC a product of the state's thinking, or was it quicker to incorporate Indigenous voices into its governance structures, compared with other governmental entities of the time? We explore the historical context of the lack of direct engagement with Tribes, the implications for Indigenous Peoples, and we provide a road map for the IJC to move forward.

We investigate two distinct time periods—the pre–International Watershed Initiative period (1909–99) and the post–International Watershed Initiative period (2000–present). These periods could arguably be defined as colonial and post-colonial periods, with the caveat that the process of decolonization is ongoing and much work remains. For the first period, we draw on two case studies—hydro-power projects on the Columbia River and the St. Lawrence Seaway and Power Project—to examine the tensions between state/colonial politics and Indigenous rights. In the second period, we identify other steps toward gaining a greater Indigenous voice and involvement in IJC affairs, including the establishment of Indigenous seats on some of the International Watershed Boards.

Although progress has been made, we maintain that in the "post-colonial era" the IJC needs to continue to work to reform and decolonize its own institutional body. An important step in this regard is recognizing the sovereign status of Indigenous governments; indeed, rather than treating Tribes and First Nations as "stakeholders," we argue for the IJC to treat First Nations as "rights-holders." Ultimately, transforming the IJC from a binational structure to a multinational structure would be a significant step toward acknowledging sovereign status for Indigenous Peoples and a significant step toward reconsidering the colonial structure of the IJC.

For the Love of Power: Indigenous Peoples and the IJC (1909–99)

In the early 1900s, when settler-colonial thought dominated the governance structure of North America, the idea of consulting Indigenous communities was not in the IJC's—or any other governmental agencies'—lexicon. The IJC would be called in to help mitigate issues, but these issues were viewed through the lens of state priorities. The development of hydro-power, for example, was a state priority for much of the early twentieth century. The push to harness rivers' energy was seen as a national priority, and such was wrapped up in politics and economic growth under the guise of "progress." These massive projects were framed as a way to stimulate post–Second World War economies through job creation, provide a source of "clean energy" to growing cities, control flooding, and highlight new-found engineering techniques.

Absent from these considerations, however, was the potential impact on the Indigenous communities who bore the disproportionate impacts of hydro-power development. And while Indigenous Peoples were the most negatively impacted by these projects, they had the least representation. This continues today. The role of the IJC during this era was to set up technical solutions, or to mediate issues. Although Indigenous groups were deemed "non-political" bodies, their lack of representation was, in its essence, political. It was political because the membership and purview of the IJC reified colonial practices based on settler privilege and extractive economies. This is not to say there were no calls for greater inclusion. For example, Treaty 3 First Nations specifically demanded that they be included as participants in management schemes adopted for Shoal Lake area. Tribes of the Columbia River basin have also called for greater inclusion. However, structural governance barriers continue to limit genuine and meaningful engagement.

Thus, a critical question is whether the IJC helped buttress the mindset that Indigenous groups' relationship with the Columbia River and their right to an intact ecosystem were less valued compared to modern hydro-electric projects that would—seemingly—benefit the wider (i.e., settler) society? The cases of the Columbia River and the St. Lawrence Seaway and Power Project are both important examples of how hydro-power projects moved ahead at the great expense of Indigenous Peoples and their cultures, and were an affront to both inherent and acquired rights (through treaty negotiations). A turning point, arguably, can be seen in the Great Lakes Water Quality Agreement and the International Watershed Initiative, in which Indigenous communities have become more engaged in the governance process and the shaping of outcomes.

Roll On Columbia, Roll On

On the Columbia River, the impacts of hydro-power development had—and continue to have—significant impacts on Indigenous communities (see Moy and O'Riordan's chapter in this volume). The most notable impacts include the blockage (and decimation) of salmon runs, and the displacement of Indigenous Peoples from their traditional homelands. The flooding of Celilo Falls, or Wy'am, and the waterways of the upper Columbia were perhaps the most significant losses. Wy'am was the longest continuously inhabited settlement in North America, with more than fifteen thousand years of recorded settlement.[6] The area was a significant fishing area, because of the access to salmon as they migrated upstream. Dip-net techniques were created at the falls to capture the returning salmon. The area was a place of mercantile exchange, where thousands of Indigenous Peoples from throughout the Americas came to trade their goods. Flooding this area impacted both the economies and cultural fabric of the region. It also asserted the primacy of colonial settler values over Indigenous values.

Important to note here is that the construction of dams along the Columbia was also in direct violation of the 1855 treaties between the US government and the Columbia River Tribes, according to which Tribes were guaranteed access to "Usual and Accustomed," or U and A, areas reserved for tribal fishing and hunting. Guarantee of access to U and A areas was the condition under which many Tribes signed away the majority of their landholdings. The dams were also a violation of the Royal

Proclamation of 1763, which laid down the rules of engagement with Indigenous Peoples in Canada—in particular, by assigning sovereign status to Indigenous nations (even if this was not actualized in either practice or policy). Indigenous Peoples up and down the Columbia River basin are considered Salmon People. Fishing for salmon is at the heart of cultural identity—taking the salmon runs away in essence challenges the very structure of these cultures.

As the IJC did not engage in direct dialogue with Indigenous communities during the early twentieth century, we argue that it, too, contributed to the narrative that the use of the river for hydro-power was more significant than the cultural and spiritual use of the river. That is, the benefits of power generation were perceived as more important than preserving Indigenous ways of life.

That being said, the IJC as an administrative arm of the BWT was not empowered to negotiate or work with Indigenous communities in either Canada or the United States. The separation of administrative duties between government entities arguably entrenched colonial policies and practice. In some cases, when governmental actors on the ground would be poised to work with Indigenous communities in their region, pathways of engagement did not exist. In interviews with one of authors of this chapter, IJC staff indicated that the officials who wanted to engage with Indigenous communities were—for decades—discouraged from doing so. These responsibilities were relocated to federal government agencies, such as Indigenous and Northern Affairs Canada and the US State Department. Because of this systemic division, Indigenous Peoples' calls to be included more directly in the IJC went unheeded. This lack of inclusion is deeply entrenched and will be difficult to overcome, undoubtedly requiring time and sustained effort from the IJC to make a meaningful shift.

Exacerbating any potential trust-building efforts is the fact that earlier calls for inclusion from Indigenous communities were ignored. For example, in April 1998, at a workshop in Castlegar, British Columbia, participants articulated the possible establishment of an International Watershed Board in the upper Columbia River basin. This board would function as a way to coordinate planning and decision-making functions. However, because of the limitations of the reference system and lack of political will the board did not materialize. In June 1999, Tribes and First

Nations throughout the Columbia basin again met to discuss the role of the IJC and to explore the possible establishment of an International Watershed Board. In that meeting, First Nations and tribal representatives shared that they felt that they did not have a voice in the process and were not involved in decision-making. The Indigenous communities in the Columbia basin, however, have been very successful at developing their own tribally-controlled organizations—such as the Columbia River Intertribal Fish Commission and the Upper Columbia United Tribes. Both inter-tribal organizations have been instrumental in developing regional recommendations to inform the renegotiation of the Columbia River Treaty, currently underway.[7]

Beyond the ability to negotiate or engage, the scope of the Columbia River Treaty, and the IJC's involvement in it, was indeed narrowly defined. The key focus of the treaty (and the subsequent involvement of the IJC technical processes) was on flood protection, financial distribution, and the overall operations of hydro-power facilities. This narrow focus, again, counters both an ecosystem approach and an Indigenous cultural approach, which embraces a holistic framework. It also contributes to the politics of erasure by dismantling ecological systems that support the social and economic structure of a community—in this case the Indigenous communities of the Columbia River—and this has had devastating and long-lasting impacts on the well-being of those communities. The construction of the dams were also in direct violation of the negotiated terms of the 1855 treaties between the United States and the Confederated Tribes of the Umatilla, the Confederated Tribes of Warms Springs, and the Confederated Tribes and Bands of the Yakama Nation, and the Nez Perce Tribe. Each of these treaties included provisions that secured the right to fish, both on reservation land as well as at the U and A fishing places. For example, in the Warm Springs Treaty, the following right was reserved: "The exclusive right of taking fish in the streams running through and bordering said reservation is hereby secured to said Indians, and at all other U and A stations, in common with citizens of the United States."[8]

As the Columbia River Treaty is currently undergoing renegotiation, some of these deficits have been dealt with through a regional recommendation process. Indigenous leaders and communities throughout the Columbia River basin participated in that process and influenced the recommendations aimed at modernizing the treaty. These regional recommendations include greater inclusion of Indigenous rights throughout the basin, a call for recognition of ecosystem function, and increased mechanisms to address climate change.[9] Certainly, the regional recommendations and the process by which they were made are an important step in widening the process of inclusion.

However, as the formal negotiations between Canada and the United States began, the federal parties ultimately did not invite Tribes or First Nations to participate, despite the fact that recommendations put forward were greatly influenced by Indigenous participation, and the Indigenous Peoples along the Columbia are most impacted by the changes to the river. Rather, those invited to the table included federal representatives, utility companies, and state agencies. The omission of Indigenous Peoples from the formal negotiations was a significant missed opportunity to right past wrongs; to shift from a binational to a multinational approach; and to decolonize the treaty.[10] The omission begs the question: What will it take for mechanisms rooted in colonial framings to change? Is change even possible? Or, should effort be directed at alternative, non-state mechanisms? To help answer these questions, we turn to a second historic example of a hydro-power development installed without consulting local Indigenous communities, the St. Lawrence Seaway and Power Project (which is also discussed in detail in Clamen and Macfarlane's chapter in this volume).

Mohawks and the St. Lawrence Seaway and Power Project

The St. Lawrence Seaway and Power Project is another poignant example of how Canadian and American state interests paved over Indigenous rights. In this case, the desire for hydro-power and navigation superseded Indigenous rights and title to water access, and this had devastating and long-lasting consequences for communities that for millennia had relied on the St. Lawrence River for sustenance. As a result of this controversial construction project, thousands of people were relocated. In particular, two Mohawk communities were severely impacted by the Seaway project: the Akwesasne and the Kahnawake tribal communities. These Tribes' political demarcations complicated the negotiations over the construction of the Seaway, since the Akwesasne hold reserve land both in Canada and the United States and the Kahnawake hold reserve land only in Canada. This jurisdictional fracturing impacted who would negotiate with which federal government. In addition, it severely impacted the two Tribes' relationships with each other.

The Kahnawake community lost the most land—the La Prairie dike ran parallel to the shore, effectively cutting off the community's access to the water. In the construction of the seaway, they also lost one-sixth of their 262 acres. As Daniel Macfarlane eloquently reflects, "this would be problematic for any community accustomed to river access, but it was particularly disruptive for a community that for hundreds of years based its culture and way of life on access to the river. *Kahnawake* translates as 'on the rapids,' and the seaway robbed the community not only of territory but also its meaning."[11]

This is another important example of how the drive for economic gain and power development overpowered Indigenous communities whose way of life is intricately tied to the water. The development of the Seaway not only severed access to the water, it also destroyed critically important habitat. Although the Seaway project was completed in the 1950s, the individual communities in its path continue to face issues stemming from its operation. The Akwesasne Mohawk community did not lose as much ancestral land as the Kahnawake, but it was directly downstream from the new power dam as well as the major industrial producers—and their toxins—who were attracted to the New York State side by the new supply of hydroelectricity. In the 1970s, the Akwesasne provided the IJC with a laundry list of ecological impacts resulting from the operation of the St. Lawrence Power Project, such as fish and land erosion, though these were not sufficiently addressed.[12]

However, in the twenty-first century, the consultations that led to Plan 2014, a revised method of operating the dams and controlling water levels on the upper St. Lawrence River and Lake Ontario, arguably did a better job of including Akwesasne perspectives.[13] Moreover, in 2018 the federal government and the Akwesasne arrived at a $45 million settlement to compensate the Indigenous groups for the impacts of this megaproject.

Nonetheless, changing the local aquatic and terrestrial ecosystems has torn at the cultural fabric of the community for upwards of half a century.

Opportunities Moving Forward: Contemporary Involvement of Indigenous Nations in the IJC (2000–Present)

For the majority of the IJC's existence, systemic and structural barriers have discouraged Indigenous involvement. Over the past two decades, the commission has evolved in its thinking and its engagement with Indigenous issues, as has been demonstrated by several developments. In the years since 1909, Tribes, First Nations, and Métis have fought for acknowledgement of treaty rights and Indigenous governance, resulting in many interactions with the IJC. Examples include the changes made in 1987 to the Great Lakes Water Quality Agreement, which, while not calling for any direct Indigenous involvement, nevertheless resulted in Indigenous representatives helping to develop Lakewide Action and Management Plans (LAMPs) for each of the boundary Great Lakes. One example of the widening of opportunities for Indigenous Nations' involvement with the IJC came at a meeting at Niagara-on-the-Lake, Ontario, in May 2019. At this meeting, the IJC staff arranged for a meeting of Indigenous Peoples representatives from the Midwest to the St Lawrence to talk for a day and a half about the historical IJC/Indigenous relationship and where that relationship should, and more importantly, could, go. The groups explored how to better work with Tribes and to what extent Tribes, First Nations, and Métis could use the IJC to assist in the fulfillment of their sacred duties to the natural world, the earth, fire, air, water, and all the beings who live as a part of that natural world. Chapter co-author, Frank Ettawageshik of Little Traverse Bay Bands of Odawa attended this meeting and found that while there were few if any definitive projects decided, all agreed that the meeting was a historic event that helped the parties move toward working together by recognizing the value of Indigenous science and philosophy.

On an individual level, there is no prohibition against the appointment of an Indigenous person to the IJC, or to any of its subsidiary bodies. Dr. Henry Lickers, environmental science officer with the Mohawk

Council of Akwesasne, served on the Great Lakes Science Advisory Board. Additionally, there have been other Indigenous appointments to IJC bodies. After several nominations over the past several terms, Dr. Henry Lickers became one of three commissioners appointed by the Canadian government in 2019, and the first Indigenous citizen to be appointed a commissioner in the IJC's history. This newly appointed group of commissioners will be holding a series of consultations and listening sessions throughout the United States and Canada, and as part of this outreach, they are prioritizing visiting Indigenous Nations. One of the first meetings was with the Indigenous communities of Michigan, including the twelve federally recognized Michigan Tribes, which was hosted by the Little Traverse Bay Bands of Odawa Indians. This meeting was held on 25 July 2019 at the Little Traverse Reservation in Petoskey, Michigan. Additional outreach was held on 20 July 2019 by the GLWQB Public Engagement Workgroup during the Midwest Alliance of Sovereign Tribes quarterly meeting at the Isabella Reservation near Mt. Pleasant, Michigan, hosted by the Saginaw Chippewa Indian Tribe.

In 2007, the International Upper Great Lakes Study had positions reserved for Indigenous representatives on its Public Interest Advisory Group. These positions were only partially filled due to continuing mistrust of the IJC on the part of Great Lakes First Nations communities. However, it should be noted that the 2000 IJC review of the Lake Ontario–St. Lawrence River Order did have Indigenous participation on its study board, its environmental technical work group, and in collecting and compiling information, as well as assisting with the administration of contracts and other functions. When the Great Lakes Water Quality Agreement was amended in 2012, the reconstituted Great Lakes Water Quality Board added four Indigenous representatives, two each from Canada and the United States. These positions have been continuously filled.

The Great Lakes Water Quality Board has taken significant steps toward greater inclusion and diversity within its structure. However, this intellectual opening requires constant tending through relationship-building and genuine collaboration, and trust will not come easily. One recent example that highlights the issue of the IJC's meaningful engagement with Indigenous communities comes from the account of an IJC staff member:

> The IJC has hired a contractor to do a wetlands study in the Great Lakes Basin who has attempted to reach Tribes, First Nations and Métis with very little response so far. The last I was aware ... only three had responded to their letter requesting input. The report deadline is fast approaching. There are approximately 185 Tribes and First Nations in the basin, so three is a very poor level of input. I've had several conversations with a friend of mine who has been working with the contractor to help them, but the contractor did too little too late to properly get the input they were requesting. This is a typical problem for the IJC when dealing with Tribes and First Nations.[14]

This account shows that although a desire for inclusion has materialized, a tremendous amount of work still needs to occur to bring about genuine engagement.

International Watersheds Initiative

A marked shift in the governance structure of the IJC occurred through the conception of the International Watersheds Initiative (IWI). The IWI was officially unveiled on 21 October 1997 with *The IJC and the 21st Century*.[15] That report responded to the governments' reference by identifying a series of environmental and social concerns that the countries would likely encounter in the coming years. The report also addressed the institutional challenges associated with managing dynamic environmental issues as well as the challenges associated with governmental downsizing and jurisdictional fragmentation.

The report suggested that the establishment of permanent International Watershed Boards in major transboundary basins would "provide much improved mechanisms for avoiding and resolving transboundary disputes by building a capacity at the watershed level to anticipate and respond to the range of water-related and other environmental changes."[16] Specifically, these IJC boards would adopt an integrative ecosystem approach that would involve local interests and build capacity at the watershed level to address transboundary water issues facing the Great Lakes basin in the twenty-first century. This would also provide a mechanism to address the asymmetrical governmental relations between Canada and the United States, which do not have equivalent authority or responsibilities.

These boards provide a significant opening for Indigenous representation at the board level. This is important, particularly as the previous boards had limited diversity—and certainly a lack of Indigenous representation. Specifically, the boards were tasked with:

- assessing and reporting on the state of the watershed every two years;
- employing the science necessary to make recommendations on emerging or existing issues;
- coordinating International Watershed Board activities with those of current federal, state, provincial, and local governments and NGOs; and
- providing an information network for the diverse community of interests and entities within a major transboundary watershed.

This approach differs from earlier IJC governance models as it attempts to view borders as hydrological rather than political; it includes sub-national players, and it adopts a "proactive" rather than a "reactive" approach.

Although the framing of the IWI as binational approach continues to temper the IWI's ability to connect and unify international watersheds, politically, the initiative has made great progress in asserting the need to think about long-term, preventive governance. The IJC was also very cognizant of the need to include actors at all levels of governance, while at the same time avoiding duplication.

On 10 March 1998, the Canadian minister of foreign affairs and the US secretary of state accepted the principle of International Watershed Boards. Eight months later, the governments asked for a reference—pursuant to article ix of the BWT—to:

- define the framework of the operations of the International Watershed Boards;
- recommend the location of the first board;
- identify cost of the projects;
- indicate possible sources of funding; and
- encourage the commission to utilize the existing expertise of the governments and non-governmental sources at multiple scales to complement the activities with the IWI.

Additionally, the IWI boards were designed to work with the already established IJC boards—in particular, the control boards in the specific watershed—when appropriate. However, for those regions that have not had a reference (including British Columbia and Alaska), the prospects for creating a new board are low. A guiding framework for the IWI boards is to move beyond binational discussions to embrace greater public participation. The premise behind this approach is that local people—as delineated at a watershed scale—often remain in the best position to resolve difficult transboundary environmental situations. As one senior IJC staff member reflected:

> The original Boards were not set up well to handle public participation. It can't just be two federal representatives making decisions, imposing them and telling us, 'Well, trust us. It's good for you.' This [the Watersheds Initiative] is the right decision for us.[17]

From the start, the boards were directed to have at least one meeting annually with the public to receive comments and answer questions. In some cases, this was a satisfactory approach; however, overall it represented a minimalist approach to public involvement and participation. The IJC attempted to broaden its jurisdictional scope by including "all the various levels of government and non-governmental actors" into their watershed model. This enhanced multi-jurisdictional approach placed greater emphasis on engaging local actors in the governance structure.

The current (and proposed) IWI boards show the potential for coverage along the Canada-US border. Following IJC protocol, in order for the boards to be established, political support from both countries and sub-national stakeholders is necessary. In 2005, the commission identified three existing boards that could apply the IWI concept: those of the St. Croix River (New Brunswick, Maine), the Red River (Minnesota, North Dakota, and Manitoba), and the Rainy River (Minnesota and Ontario). In 2007, the commission added a fourth pilot international board for the Souris River (Saskatchewan, Manitoba, and North Dakota).[18]

In 2007, the International St. Croix River Watershed Board became the first official International Watersheds Board, and in 2013 the International Rainy Lake of the Woods Watershed Board became the second. The Red River and Souris River Boards remain pilot IWI boards. To date, the existing International Watershed Boards have only been established where there were existing IJC boards (it is unclear if this will remain as an informal prerequisite for participation in the IWI).[19] The latest board—the International Rainy Lake of the Woods Watershed Board—has made significant progress in reframing its governance body to explicitly include Indigenous representatives—something that the previous boards had not done. This board is the first to have designated Indigenous membership, with the position currently held by Chief Brian Perrault of the Couchiching First Nation. His contribution is important, as he brings with him not only sustained knowledge of the place, but also leadership experience in both tribal and federal government. Throughout his life he guided, fished, and hunted on the lake and sounding area. He also has served for Treaty 3 Tribes, represents the ten First Nations communities in his region, and has worked for the federal government for almost two decades with Indian Affairs Canada. As of March 2016, he has served as chief of the Couchiching First Nation.

The board has also made progress in diversifying its membership, namely by designating an equal number of government and non-government members. In addition, the board emphasizes the need to have the majority of its members "living within or connected closely to the basin."[20] If the other established boards follow suit, this would represent great progress in widening the purview of the IWI to be more inclusive, and it would help work toward actualizing a post-colonial framework of transboundary governance. Gains have also been made through the Great Lakes Water Quality Board, as described below.

Great Lakes Water Quality Board

In the fall of 2016 the Great Lakes Water Quality Board (GLWQB) held a meeting in Thunder Bay, Ontario, that proved to be an important contribution to the IJC. The focus of the meeting was Indigenous rights and philosophy relating to the lakes and the natural world. Indigenous water protectors, traditional leaders, elected leaders, and other citizens of Indigenous citizens, helped to explain to the GLWQB the differences in world views that have led to disagreements in the past. The program was well received and inspired subsequent action aimed at addressing these ongoing issues.[21]

At its April 2017 meeting, the GLWQB adopted a policy for Indigenous engagement. This is an important evolution of the IJC governance model, and it lays out a model of Indigenous Peoples Engagement Principles and Practices. The context for this shift was the ambitious expectations for engagement with First Nations, Métis peoples, and Tribes in the governance and management of water quality in the Great Lakes basin that Canada and the United States had established while negotiating the Great Lakes Water Quality Agreement in 2012.

The preamble to the agreement states that "while the Parties are responsible for decision-making under this Agreement, the involvement and participation of State and Provincial Governments, Tribal Governments, First Nations, Métis, Municipal Governments, watershed management agencies, local public agencies, and the Public are essential to achieve the objectives of this Agreement." This commitment is reflected in subsequent clauses relating to the implementation of the agreement by the parties, and to the annexes.

Specifically, article 7 details the IJC's responsibilities under the agreement, and tasks the commission with engaging tribal governments, Métis, and First Nations peoples in relation to data, scientific research, and the provision of advice to the parties. Under article 8, relating to the composition and mandate of the GLWQB the agreement specifies that the board may include representatives from tribal governments, First Nations, and Métis peoples. In response, the commission's Directive to the Great Lakes Water Quality Board specifies that the Canadian members should include one member from First Nations and one from the Métis peoples, and that the US members should include two members from Tribes. The GLWQB can and should serve as an example of how people working within the constraints of Western institutions can engage deeply and genuinely with Indigenous Peoples in the Great Lakes Basin. To that end, general principles were written to guide the GLWQB's work:

1. First Nations, Métis, and Tribes are not "stakeholders." Within the distinct legal landscapes of the United States and Canada, First Nations, Métis, and Tribes hold distinct rights. This makes striving for a nation-to-nation relationship appropriate. In its work, including its deliberations, research and advice to the commission, the WQB will recognize the ways in which Tribes, Métis, and First Nations are distinct rights holders, and will act accordingly.

2. Tribes, First Nations, and Métis peoples have diverse interests, needs and concerns, distinct knowledge and ways of knowing, and their own institutions for governance. Differences also exist among the various Tribes, Métis communities, and First Nations in the basin. In its work, including its deliberations, research and advice to the commission, the WQB will recognize these interests, needs and concerns, distinct ways of knowing and institutions for governance.

The adaption of these principles is an important step in re-envisioning the governance practices of actors within the IJC, and beyond. The following are examples of practices aimed at ensuring that the GLWQB can respect these principles and the expectations established by the 2012 additions to the Great Lakes Water Quality Agreement:

1. The Agreement states that the WQB "may" include representatives from Tribal Governments, First Nations, and Métis peoples. The WQB views Indigenous representation as essential and strongly support the commission's Directive.

2. In providing advice to the International Joint Commission, the WQB will seek opportunities to highlight the distinct perspectives of Tribal, First Nations, and Métis peoples, and to account for distinct concerns among Indigenous Peoples in the Great Lakes basin.

3. In specifically seeking the advice and insight of key government and non-government actors in the basin in relation to its studies, reports, advice and other work, the WQB will ensure that Tribal, First Nations, and Métis peoples are engaged as "rights holders" rather than "stakeholders" or members of the "general public". In practice, this will involve identifying and consulting with official Tribal, First Nations and Métis representatives.

4. Public engagement and outreach are important aspects of the work of the WQB. In designing public outreach and engagement activities such as panels and presentations, the WQB will strive to ensure that the customs of Tribal, First Nations, and Métis peoples are appropriately recognized. Similarly, in designing surveys to seek the perspectives of key actors in the basin, the WQB will ensure that Tribal, First Nations, and Métis peoples are adequately represented in samples.

5. The WQB will strive to ensure that Indigenous knowledge from Tribal, First Nations, and Métis peoples are included in its work plans, research and deliberations, and advice provided to the IJC, and that this knowledge is treated appropriately according to the customs of the knowledge holders.

6. External consultants play a key role in helping the WQB deliver the work defined in its approved work plans. Terms of reference for consulting projects will be designed to reflect the principles and practices outlined in this document.[22]

In the fall of 2017, discussions were ongoing to fully implement this policy. When it was adopted, members of the GLWQB expressed hope that other IJC bodies would adopt similar policies, and that these policies would move the IJC to adopt a policy affecting all of its activities. While there remains much work to bring better engagement with Indigenous Tribes, First Nations, and Métis, the efforts of the GLWQB indicate that the IJC has come a long way since its establishment in 1909.

Conclusion and Reflections

So, to what extent has the IJC been a tool of settler colonialism? Was it a product of the state thinking of the time, or was it quicker to incorporate Indigenous voices into its governance structures, at least compared to other governmental entities of the time? Or, more specifically, was it the case that the IJC helped buttress the mindset that Indigenous groups' use of a river was unproductive compared to modern hydroelectric and water-control projects that would benefit the wider (i.e., settler) society? The answer to these questions is far from straightforward. A key consideration is that the IJC was explicitly directed to not engage with Tribes and First Nations for the first ninety years after the BWT was signed. This systemic lack of engagement for almost a century—regardless of the cause—will undoubtedly require tremendous structural work to reverse.

During that time of exclusion, individuals with the IJC did, to their credit, attempt to find ways to "work around" the policy and to consult with Indigenous communities. However, these efforts were on a limited and inconsistent basis. Could there have been more mavericks, pushing against the structure and advocating for structural change within the IJC to promote equity of representation? Of course. However, rather than dwelling on what could have been, it is more important to take the lessons from this different era and apply them productively to making changes today.

Certainly, over the past nineteen years since the "non-engagement" policy was lifted the IJC has made some steps toward reconciliation. The incorporation of Indigenous voices within the Great Lakes Water Quality Agreement, for example, was an important step in this direction, as was the increased involvement of Indigenous actors through the International Watershed Initiative. And yet action is still needed.

In both Canada and the United States, the treaty rights of Tribes, First Nations, and Métis have been upheld by numerous court decisions at all levels. Unfortunately, the need for inclusion of Indigenous representatives was not a part of the international consciousness at the time of the 1909 BWT. But the concept of only two governments having the rights and the responsibilities for the stewardship and protection of the waters and natural resources is outdated. Many conflicts need significant input from Indigenous nations if they are to be effectively resolved—indeed, in some cases, it is simply impossible to resolve these disputes without such input.

Indigenous nations have proven repeatedly that the application of traditional knowledge and technology benefits not only Indigenous citizens but all of the citizens of the boundary waters areas, and beyond. The deep and sustained place-based knowledge of Indigenous cultures can provide important context and nuanced insights into natural systems. Providing space for this knowledge to influence, ground, and impact IJC management systems (and other mainstream institutions) will provide important opportunities for improved human-natural relationships. Indigenous nations have also repeatedly demonstrated a willingness to devote time and resources toward achieving these benefits. It has often been said by Indigenous leaders that they have a sacred duty to protect the waters, and that it is not possible to protect Indigenous waters without protecting everyone's waters.

With that in mind, the IJC needs to continue its engagement with Indigenous nations and to seek ways to think, and act, beyond a two-nation system and to embrace one that will involve the full spectrum of governments whose rights and responsibilities extend across the boundary waters. Looking to the future, we offer the IJC the following suggestions for fostering Indigenous engagement:

- Consider restructuring the IJC from a binational to multinational body, one whose leadership is drawn equally from Canada, the United States, and Indigenous nations. Granted, this may require the federal governments amending the BWT. Alternatively, the possibility of working within the BWT's original structure through a series of proclamations or guiding notes, delivered under the aegis of the IJC, may prove possible, given the uncertainties (and possible pitfalls) of reopening the treaty in this current political climate. The key is to reassess the treaty through a post-colonial lens and offer suggestions for systemic changes that would include Indigenous nations on a more holistic and balanced level.

- Consider Indigenous nations as rights-holders rather than stakeholders.

- When dealing with First Nations, Métis, and Tribal governments, engage early and engage often.

- Building trust requires ongoing engagement; if done correctly it can stave off potential conflict in the future.

- Seek out at least one Indigenous representative on each side of the border for each watershed board, but recognize that that person may not be able to speak for all of the Indigenous nations that they represent.

- Recognize that multiple knowledge systems exist—this is particularly important in relationship to water.

- Refrain from seeing water as a "resource"—rather, view it as a "life source." Many Indigenous nations and communities consider water as a gift from the creator to be protected and honoured.

- Indigenous communities have a long history with water protection, and in many cultures, such as the Anishinaabe, this work often is often reserved for women "water protectors." Consider diversity of gender, as well as ethnicity, when exploring leadership positions and nominations for open positions. Although the IJC has improved gender balance over the past twenty years, this point remains important to underscore.

- Recognize that Indigenous governance systems existed prior to European settlement and the development of the IJC. These relationships were also based on contracts and treaties, although they were often recorded in oral history and ceremony rather than on paper. Take the time to learn about these prior and ongoing Indigenous-based governance structures, which are place-based and culturally relevant.
- Currently, the IJC is set up to serve in an advisory capacity under references and in a quasi-judicial capacity under applications. In the future, it is important to share the lessons learned more broadly, with governmental and non-governmental groups.

In short, empower the IJC to work within its existing structure to take small steps toward inclusion and reconciliation with Indigenous communities. However, in the long-term we support a considerable structural change from a binational to a multinational model. Although significant steps have been made in the past two decades, more work needs to occur. It is the hope of the authors that this work occurs in a timely and steadfast fashion.

Notes

1. International Joint Commission (hereafter IJC), "International Joint Commission and First Nations," PowerPoint Presentation (Ottawa: IJC, 2007).
2. General Allotment Act (or Dawes Act), Act of 8 Feb. 1887 (24 Stat. 388, ch. 119, 25 USCA 331), Acts of Forty-ninth Congress, Second Session, 1887.
3. Indian Act, S.C.1876, c. as amended by 1880, and 1894, and 1920, and 1927, and 1951, Indian Act at Can LII. 22 October 2013.

4   A. Simpson, "Settlement's secret," *Cultural Anthropology* 26, no. 2 (2011): 205–17; L. R. Simpson, "Anticolonial strategies for the recovery and maintenance of indigenous knowledge," *American Indian Quarterly* 28, no. 3–4 (2004): 373–84.

5   R v. Sparrow, 1990, 1 S.C.R. 1075; United States v. Washington. 1974. 384 F. Supp. 312 (W. D. Wash. 1974).

6   Richard White, *The Organic Machine: The Remaking of the Columbia River* (New York: Hill and Wang, 1995).

7   Alice Cohen and Emma Norman, "Renegotiating the Columbia River Treaty: Transboundary governance and Indigenous Rights," *Global Environmental Politics* 18, no. 4 (2019): 4–24.

8   Columbia River Inter-Tribal Fish Commission, "The Founding of the CRITFC" (2019), https://www.critfc.org/about-us/critfcs-founding/.

9   Ibid.

10 M. Marchand, Presentation to Vine Deloria, Jr., Indigenous Studies Class (Northwest Indian College, Lummi Nation, 2018).

11 Daniel Macfarlane, *Negotiating A River: Canada, the U.S., and the Creation of the St. Lawrence Seaway* (Vancouver: UBC Press, 2014), 126.

12 Ibid., 205–6; Daniel Macfarlane and Peter Kitay, "Hydraulic Imperialism: Hydro-electric Development and Treaty 9 in the Abitibi Region," *American Review of Canadian Studies* 47, no. 3 (Fall 2016): 380–97.

13 Murray Clamen and Daniel Macfarlane, "Plan 2014: The Historical Evolution of Lake Ontario-St. Lawrence River Regulation," *Canadian Water Resources Journal / Revue canadienne des ressources hydriques* 43, no. 4 (December 2018): 416–31.

14 The individual quoted here has requested that their name be withheld; telephone interview with authors, 31 October 2017.

15 IJC, *The IJC and the 21st Century* (Washington, DC, and Ottawa: IJC, 1997).

16 Ibid., 30.

17 Personal communication with author, 12 May 2007.

18 IJC, *Transboundary Watersheds* (Washington, DC, and Ottawa: IJC, 2000).

19 Emma S. Norman, *Governing Transboundary Waters: Canada, the United States, and Indigenous Communities* (London: Routledge, Earthscan Series of Water Resource Management, 2015).

20 IJC, "Great Lakes Water Quality Board—194th Meeting" (Thunder Bay, ON: IJC, 2016).

21 Ibid.

22 IJC Great Lakes Water Quality Board, "Indigenous Peoples Engagement Principles and Practices" (April 2017), http://ijc.org/files/tinymce/uploaded/WQB/WQB_IndigenousEngagementPolicy_20170420.pdf.

15

The Boundary Waters Treaty, the International Joint Commission, and the Evolution of Transboundary Environmental Law and Governance

Noah D. Hall, A. Dan Tarlock, and Marcia Valiante

Transboundary environmental law provides principles to address the physical harms (e.g., pollution and diminished natural resources) that spill over from one state to another. Disputes arise when intensive use or consumption of natural resources in the source state results in the externalization of the environmental costs to the neighbouring state. The facts can vary infinitely—consider the example of an upstream factory that diverts most of the river water and discharges toxic pollution just above a state boundary to an international metropolitan area with many shared economic and environmental values on both sides of the border. Physical and geographic settings, wealth disparities, differing values and cultures, and crude self-interest shape these conflicts. But the first step in resolving a dispute, and avoiding future disputes, is adopting applicable legal norms. And for over a century, the Boundary Waters Treaty (BWT) has shaped the legal norms for transboundary environmental harms.

In the years leading up to the signing of the BWT in 1909, both the United States and Canada advanced more absolutist approaches to transboundary environmental law—but from opposite directions. (The chapters in this volume by David Whorley and Meredith Denning explore this history in its deserved detail.) The United States, in the context of disputes with its southern neighbour Mexico, advanced the notion of absolute territorial *sovereignty* for using natural resources regardless of spillover harms. Canada, in its early negotiations with the United States, advanced the notion of absolute territorial *integrity* to prohibit transboundary environmental harms. Ultimately, the two countries' respective positions evolved into the balanced approach adopted and provided for in the BWT.

The Rejection and Failings of Absolutist Approaches to Transboundary Environmental Law

The shortcomings and short life of absolutist approaches to transboundary environmental law in North America was first seen in the United States' Harmon Doctrine. Disputes arose over the Rio Grande, with conflicts between the upstream American farmers and the downstream Mexican city of Ciudad Juarez. As the water use disputes escalated into a diplomatic conflict, the US secretary of state requested a legal opinion from the US attorney general as to whether the diversions in the United States that potentially affect Mexican waters violated Mexico's rights under the principles of international law.

Attorney General Judson Harmon's resulting 1895 opinion claimed that the United States was under no international legal obligation to hinder its development to protect the environment of its downstream neighbour:

> The fundamental principle of international law is the absolute sovereignty of every nation, as against all others, within its own territory. . . . No believer in the doctrine of natural servitudes has ever suggested one which would interfere with the enjoyment by a nation within its own territory of whatever was necessary to the development of its resources or the comfort of its people. The immediate as well as the possible consequences of the right asserted by Mexico show that its recognition is entirely inconsistent with the sover-

eignty of the United States over its national domain. Apart from the sum demanded by way of indemnity for the past, the claim involves not only the arrest of further settlement and development of large regions of country, but the abandonment, in great measure at least, of what has already been accomplished.[1]

The resulting principle, the so-called Harmon Doctrine, became the leading statement of the concept of absolute territorial sovereignty. However, the doctrine was practically dead on arrival. Even while advancing this absolutist approach in its dispute with Mexico, the United States backed away from it as a governing principle of international law and policy. The United States ultimately resolved the Rio Grande dispute with Mexico with a treaty "providing for the *equitable* distribution of the waters of the Rio Grande."[2] Several decades later, in testimony before the US Senate Committee on Foreign Relations, then assistant secretary of state Dean Acheson put to rest the legal arguments of Harmon's opinion: "[Harmon's opinion argued] that an upstream nation by unilateral act in its own territory can impinge upon the rights of a downstream nation; this is hardly the kind of legal doctrine that can be seriously urged in these times."[3]

Physical settings may explain both the advancement of the Harmon Doctrine and its subsequent rejection by the United States. The United States is the upstream state on the Rio Grande and most other major waterways shared with Mexico, so in that context the absolutist approach would be self-serving. But the United States is as often the downstream state on the major waterways shared with Canada, and given the reciprocal nature of the shared US-Canada waterways, the principle of absolute territorial sovereignty wouldn't look so nice on either side of the border.

While the United States was advancing absolute territorial sovereignty, Canada was advancing the counter-absolutist approach of territorial integrity. In discussions leading up to the agreement that eventually became the BWT, Canada proposed a provision forbidding any water pollution having transboundary consequences.[4] While not termed as such, this is an example of absolute territorial integrity, as it prevents an upstream state from having any transboundary pollution that affects the downstream state. If adopted, the principle would prevent any utilization of the environment or emissions in a region that is upwind or upstream of another state.

The US secretary of state rejected Canada's proposal, as it would put any upstream or upwind economic development in the United States at the mercy of the complaining downstream or downwind Canadian interests (and vice versa, from Canada's perspective). Instead, the two countries compromised on a more balanced approach ultimately incorporated into article iv of the BWT: "It is further agreed that the waters herein defined as boundary waters and waters flowing across the boundary shall not be polluted on either side to the injury of health or property on the other."[5] This language subtly but effectively rejects both absolutist approaches. Transboundary spillovers are actionable, but only based on actual harms to the downstream state's interests. And, as further described in this chapter, transboundary environmental resources must be managed to balance both economic development and environmental protection interests.

The Evolving Balanced Approach to Transboundary Environmental Law: Trail Smelter and United Nations Declarations

Transboundary environmental law continued to evolve over the subsequent century from the BWT's balanced approach. The most significant development was the Trail Smelter arbitration,[6] which "laid out the foundations of international environmental law, at least regarding transfrontier pollution."[7] It remains "the only decision of an international court or tribunal that deals specifically, and on the merits, with transfrontier pollution."[8] And, as detailed by Don Munton and Owen Temby in chapter 10 of this volume, it is central to the history of transboundary air pollution management. The facts of the dispute are best told by quoting directly from the final 1941 arbitration decision:

> In 1896, a smelter was started under American auspices near the locality known as Trail [in British Columbia, located on the Columbia River about seven miles north of the US border and Washington State]. In 1906, the Con-

solidated Mining and Smelting Company of Canada, Limited [later known as COMINCO] . . . acquired the smelter plant at Trail. . . . Since that time, the Canadian company, without interruption, has operated the Smelter, and from time to time has greatly added to the plant until it has become one of the best and largest equipped smelting plants on the American continent. In 1925 and 1927, two stacks of the plant were erected to 409 feet in height and the Smelter greatly increased its daily smelting of zinc and lead ores. This increased production resulted in more sulphur dioxide fumes and higher concentrations being emitted into the air. In 1916, about 5,000 tons of sulphur per month were emitted; in 1924, about 4,700 tons; in 1926, about 9,000 tons—an amount which rose near to 10,000 tons per month in 1930. In other words, about 300–350 tons of sulphur were emitted daily in 1930. . . . From 1925, at least, to 1937, damage occurred [to private farms and timber lands] in the State of Washington resulting from the sulphur dioxide emitted from the Trail Smelter.[9]

Canada and the United States eventually agreed to refer the Trail Smelter dispute to a three-member arbitration tribunal composed of an American, a Canadian, and an independent chair (a Belgian national was ultimately appointed).[10] The arbitration tribunal's most significant charge regarding substantive transboundary pollution principles was to decide whether the Canadian smelter should be required to cease causing damage in the state of Washington in the future, and what "measures or regime, if any, should be adopted or maintained" by the smelter, in addition to future indemnity and compensation.[11] To answer these questions, the tribunal was directed to "apply the law and practice followed in dealing with cognate questions in the United States of America as well as International Law and Practice, and shall give consideration to the desire of the High Contracting Parties to reach a solution just to all parties concerned."[12]

The arbitration tribunal's ultimate 1941 decision answering these questions became a historic precedent for international transboundary pollution law.[13] The tribunal first cited a leading international law authority: "As Professor Eagleton puts in (*Responsibility of States in International Law*): 'A State owes at all times a duty to protect other States against injurious acts by individuals from within its jurisdiction.'"[14] The tribunal supplemented this general rule with a comprehensive summary of the US Supreme Court's decisions on inter-state transboundary pollution.[15] Taking the decisions in whole, the tribunal elaborated the following substantive principle for transboundary pollution law:

> No State has the right to use or permit the use of its territory in such a manner as to cause injury by fumes in or to the territory of another or the properties or persons therein, when the cause is of serious consequence and the injury is established by clear and convincing evidence.[16]

Applying these principles to the dispute at hand, the tribunal required the Trail Smelter to "refrain from causing any damage through fumes in the State of Washington."[17] The tribunal ordered a detailed management regime and regulations for the smelter to prevent sulphur dioxide emissions at levels that cause damage to property in Washington State, and allowed future claims for damages that might occur despite the imposed management regime.[18]

Since the pioneering BWT and precedential Trail Smelter arbitration decision, numerous international declarations (non-binding pronouncements known as "soft law") have further advanced the balanced approach on the global stage. Most significantly, the balanced approach was incorporated into the United Nations Conference on the Human Environment's Stockholm Declaration of 1972, which provides in its Principle 21 that

> states have, in accordance with the Charter of the United Nations and the principles of international law, the sovereign right to exploit their own resources pursuant to their own environmental policies, and the responsibility to ensure that activities within their jurisdiction or control do not cause damage to the environment of other States or of areas beyond the limits of national jurisdiction.[19]

Principle 21 was reaffirmed in numerous other charters and declarations, most notably Principle 2 of the United Nations Conference on Environment and Development's Rio Declaration of 1992.[20] It is now widely acknowledged, as the Restatement (Third) of the Foreign Relations Law of the United States provides that

> a state is obligated to take such measures as may be necessary, to the extent practicable under the circumstances, to ensure that activities within its jurisdiction or control . . . are conducted so as not to cause significant injury to the environment of another state or of areas beyond the limits of national jurisdiction.[21]

The strength of the balanced approach is also a shortcoming—it leaves the specific obligations rather vague. States and scholars widely agree that it does not prohibit all transboundary harm any more than it immunizes polluting acts. In practice, limitations range from thresholds for actionable transboundary harms (significant or substantial) to procedural duties (due diligence) to prevent such harms. Fortunately, the thin language of the BWT has been supplemented by a rich history of the International Joint Commission's collaborative governance.

The International Joint Commission and Changed Boundary Waters Conditions

Complementing its balanced approach to transboundary environmental law, the BWT also establishes a model approach to international water resources co-operation. It provides a permanent dispute-resolution mechanism and a reference procedure, which has allowed the six-member International Joint Commission (IJC)[22] to help provinces and states adapt "the spirit of the Treaty" to new challenges to the sustainable use of the boundary waters. This section describes two examples of the IJC's adaptive capacity and its broader international influence. The first example illustrates the IJC's use of its status as an international body to influence constructively the development of a Great Lakes management regime, based largely on modern environmental principles, in both the United States and Canada. The second example illustrates the use of the reference process to foster dialogue between the State of Montana and the Province of Alberta to revisit an outdated allocation of the St. Mary and Milk Rivers and to reinforce the idea that the rivers should be shared in a manner consistent with the evolution of international water law.

The IJC and a New Ecosystem Management Model for the Great Lakes

Between 2001 and 2008, the eight Great Lakes states and two Great Lakes provinces negotiated an innovative inter-state compact, the Great Lakes–St. Lawrence River Basin Compact,[23] which complemented a series of early Canada-US initiatives to manage the Great Lakes to conserve the basin-wide ecosystem.[24] The compact makes it very difficult to divert water out of the Great Lakes–St. Lawrence watersheds (on the history of controlling water quantities in this watershed, see Clamen and Macfarlane's chapter in this volume).[25] Complementary federal and provincial legislation was also enacted in Canada.[26]

The compact is a reaction to several proposed diversions to the more arid regions of the United States or bulk water transfers to undisclosed water-short countries. This triggered concerns that states lacked the constitutional authority to prevent these diversions.[27] In Canada, there was widespread concern about the loss of Canadian sovereignty over its abundant water resources and about coming pressure for diversions to bail out the United States' profligate use of its waters.[28] Canadian nationalist greens, among others, raised the concern that a Canadian export ban, which was ultimately adopted by the federal Parliament, would be struck down as illegal under the General Agreement on Tariffs and Trade because it discriminated against non-Canadians desiring to export water, although this argument has very little support in international trade law.[29]

IJC involvement in the "diversion issue" was initially problematic because there was no treaty dispute; article iii only applies to diversions or obstructions that affect the natural level of the lakes and imposes a high burden on the country asserting a violation.[30] Therefore, the Canadian and US responses were negotiated outside the regime and superimposed over it.[31]

Politically, the compact was not a hard sell among the eight Great lakes states, but it faced serious economic and scientific challenges from outside the region, which could have made federal approval difficult. The region's stagnation and decline actually worked in favour of the compact within the Great Lakes basin. Because serious diversions are hypothetical, the problem of allocating a limited resource among competing consumptive interests did not exist as it does in many basins, including that of the St. Mary and Milk Rivers.[32] Since the value of the compact was primarily symbolic,[33] each state stood to gain politically by blocking future moves by "others" outside the region. But, any regime that prevented almost all diversions can be attacked as unfair, inefficient, irrational, and unnecessary.

The nub of the outside problem was that the compact and parallel Canadian legislation dedicate the waters of the Great Lakes–St. Lawrence basin—20 per cent of the world's freshwater supply, and 95 per cent of the United States' surface supply—almost exclusively for non-consumptive uses in a basin where only 10 per cent of the US population lives and is relatively stable or declining. Population is increasing only in Southern Ontario.[34] Given the shift of population to the more arid areas of the United States, one can legitimately ask: What is the rationale for this action, especially since all the diversion threats were and are speculative at best and highly unlikely to come to fruition for environmental and economic reasons?

The IJC was able to influence the negotiations over the compact by leveraging the reference process to address the objections to dedicating the Great Lakes primarily to in-basin, non-consumptive uses. The stars were aligned at the IJC in a way that they had not been for years. The governments of both Canada and the United States had a strong interest in the conservation of the Great Lakes and they recognized their importance as a valuable, functioning ecosystem. The Canadian and US commissioners had a strong commitment to the conservation of the Great Lakes, and both the Canadian and US sections were led by accomplished water professionals who were at home in both the technical and the policy worlds.

In 1999, the two governments agreed to an IJC reference on Great Lakes diversions. After considerable internal debate, the IJC concluded that a state-provincial effort was the best avenue to protect the lakes. There was concern that if the US federal government were to instead pre-empt state efforts, as it had the full constitutional power to do, the dedication of the Great Lakes to regional uses might be subordinated to the possibility of national (i.e., arid Western) use. The resulting 2000 report, *Protection of the Waters of the Great Lakes: Final Report to the Governments of Canada and the United States*, examined both the scientific and legal issues raised by the diversion threats and marshaled available scientific evidence to underscore the need for a strong anti-diversion regime.

The 2000 report blended a synthesis of the available science on the hydrology of the Great Lakes with economics and the emerging, and much contested, international environmental law principles, to counsel that the Great Lakes states and provinces adopt a strong anti-diversion regime. This conclusion is founded on the report's mixed scientific-economic classification of the Great Lakes as a fragile, fully allocated "non-renewable resource." Initially, the idea that the Great Lakes are fully utilized almost exclusively for non-consumptive uses is a surprising and counter-intuitive conclusion to anyone who has seen them or even looked at a map of the basin.

Resources classified as non-renewable are usually deep aquifers and mineral deposits rather than rain-fed water bodies. Rivers and lakes are classic renewable resources. Nonetheless, the Great Lakes have a fundamentally non-renewable characteristic: a long renewal time that makes them analogous to a deep aquifer. The report noted that less than 1 per cent of the lakes' total volume is renewed annually by precipitation and the levels remain relatively constant "with a normal fluctuation ranging from 30 to 60 cm (12–24 in.) in a single year."

Determining the line between a renewable and non-renewable resource is a matter of judgment, and the classification of the Great Lakes as fully allocated is a normative conclusion, which the report was careful to underscore. An allocation of a river or lake can refer either to a situation in which recognized property rights exceed the available dependable supply or to the dedication of a resource to a suite of uses to the exclusion of others. The latter, which is the case in the Great Lakes, is an economic or normative choice rather than a hydrologically constrained situation. An existing resource use mix can always be changed, as the IJC recognized, but the question is always: What are the opportunity costs that would be incurred by any change from the current allocation?

The observation that there would be opportunity costs from any change in the status quo is not *per se* a compelling argument for the maintenance of the status quo. There were many voices suggesting that more consumptive uses should be allowed because instead of costs there would be benefits from changing the status quo. Those familiar with the law of prior appropriation in the Western United States suggested that the states make a conventional allocation among the riparians to do as they wished. Some proposed a compact giving each state a share, and others, in a bow to the value of non-consumptive uses, recommended that it be constrained by a cap and trade program borrowed from the 1990 United States Clean Air Act and climate change debate.[35] Thus, the report had to take an additional step and provide a more convincing rationale for not incurring the opportunity costs of increased diversions and rejecting the lure of profitable inter-state and international water markets.

The report took this step by concluding that, not only are the Great Lakes a non-renewable resource, but they are a fragile one, and thus change involves risks. This will appear as another counter-intuitive conclusion to anyone who has seen the lakes on a stormy, windy day or remembers the concern about shoreline erosion and flooding in the mid-1980s.[36] The basis of their fragility is the fact that lake levels fluctuate according to precipitation and evaporation cycles, and even small seasonal fluctuations can have dramatic and costly consequences for the ecosystem and for the maintenance of the primary commercial, non-consumptive use of the lakes—navigation. Lake shippers, owners of pleasure-boat launching facilities, and shoreline property owners have lived with short- and long-term fluctuating levels for years.

The case for not trying to alter Great Lakes cycles is strengthened if the prospect of global climate change is factored into the mix. The report concluded that the Great Lakes are "highly sensitive to climatic variability."[37] It synthesized the various projected, but inconsistent, climate change scenarios to reach the bold conclusion that "climate change suggests that some lowering of water levels is likely to occur . . . [and] the Commission believes that considerable caution should be exercised with respect to any factors potentially reducing water levels and outflows."[38]

The precautionary principle is an evolving international environmental law norm.[39] It can be stated in hard and soft versions,[40] but the core idea is that the state has the power to limit activities that pose a risk of future harm when the available scientific evidence about the likelihood and magnitude of harm remains uncertain and inconclusive. During the George W. Bush administration, the United States opposed the precautionary principle as a European import with the dangerous potential to undermine the more rigorous scientific foundations of US environmental laws.[41]

The IJC's decision to ground the management of the Great Lakes in principles of international environmental law can be seen both directly and indirectly in the compact. First, the compact de facto recognizes that the Great Lakes are a common heritage of humankind.[42] The idea that certain resources, traditionally part of the territory of a sovereign nation—such as rain forests—are subject to duties that run to all nations has been strongly opposed by countries such as Brazil and has minimal recognition in international agreements. Nonetheless, the compact adopts the core idea that certain ecosystems should be preserved for future generations.[43] The IJC's most enduring legacy can be seen in the fact that the compact adopts the precautionary approach to management and expressly links it to climate change. Article 4.5.1(b) provides that the states must:

> Give substantive consideration to climate change or other significant threats to Basin Waters and take into account the current state of scientific knowledge, or uncertainty, and appropriate Measures to exercise caution in cases of uncertainty if serious damage may result.[44]

The IJC and the St. Mary and Milk Rivers: Small Rivers, Big Conflicts

In retrospect, the promotion of the sustainable use of the Great Lakes was relatively easy because there were few potential economic losers from so doing.[45] The same cannot be said for two rivers in Montana and the Prairie provinces of Alberta and Saskatchewan, the St. Mary and Milk Rivers. Both countries exceed their respective BWT allocations.[46] These rivers have been dedicated largely to irrigated agriculture, and strong expectations that the status quo is eternal have been built up on both sides.

Thus, change does not come easily. This section complements Timothy Heinmiller's chapter in this volume by offering an international water perspective on the ongoing efforts to achieve the equitable sharing of the two rivers.

The Milk River arises in Montana, flows into Alberta and Saskatchewan, and then back to the United States, where it eventually joins the Missouri River. The St. Mary River also arises in Montana and flows into Alberta but it continues on to Hudson Bay. At the beginning of the twentieth century, the United States proposed to divert water from the St. Mary into the Milk and Canada retaliated by beginning a diversion from the Milk into the St. Mary.[47] The dispute was initially resolved directly in the BWT. Article vi allocated 500 cubic feet per second (cfs) or so much as constitutes three-quarters of the natural flow of the Milk to the United States and the same amounts of the St. Mary to Canada. In 1921, the IJC resolved an interpretation dispute between the two countries and held that article vi prescribed an equal split of the total flow; excess flows above 500 cfs were divided equally.[48]

In response to decades of overuse, in 2003 the governor of Montana requested an IJC review of the 1921 order.[49] The IJC first formed a task force that recommended a series of management options for more equitable sharing on both sides of the border,[50] but it did not reopen the 1921 apportionment order. The IJC next suggested that the Governments of Montana and Alberta form a task force to consider collaborative, co-operative management options for the rivers.[51] A joint initiative was formed between 2008 and 2010.[52]

The initiative is continuing, but the hard sharing decisions have not yet been taken. In brief, "the United States faces an infrastructure problem because it never invested in a water efficient system while Canada . . . built a costly system to use water that it was not entitled to use."[53]

Despite the fact that Alberta and Montana have not, as of summer 2019, been able to agree on the management of the allocation of the two rivers, the IJC-inspired process has contributed positively to the development of international water law. First, the treaty and the 1921 order adopt the fundamental norm of international water law, reflected in the United Nations Convention on the Non-Navigable Uses of Water, that all riparian states have a right to make equitable and reasonable uses of transboundary rivers.[54] Second, Montana and Alberta have exceeded customary international procedural norms and the 2008 initiative can serve as a model of transboundary co-operation among riparians. Third, the IJC's 2006 report incorporated the emerging international water law norm that states may have a duty to ensure minimum environmental flows on transboundary rivers.[55] The 1921 order is naturally silent on this issue but the report concluded that the allocation "includes maintaining a 'live' stream, whether for aquatic life, esthetic or other purposes."[56] Fourth, the engagement of the states and the IJC is a good example of trust-building co-operation that advances the formal procedural norms of international water law.

Reflection on the BWT and IJC in Contemporary International Environmental Law

As already noted, as well as being of central importance in the regional Canada-US context, the BWT represents an important landmark in the evolution of international environmental law. Within North America, by establishing general principles to guide the use, obstruction, and diversion of boundary waters, the treaty set the ground rules for decision-making and dispute resolution, facilitating the development of all major projects for hydro-power, navigation, irrigation, and flood control along the border. However, by recognizing equal rights to use shared waters and by establishing a restriction on injurious pollution, the treaty also influenced the principles of international water law, and eventually environmental law more generally.

Yet for all its historical importance, the BWT was a reflection of its era—of the political, economic, and social values, and the scientific understandings, of the time; it should be obvious that those have changed dramatically over the last century, as has international law as a result. The parties have never revised the treaty to respond to or reflect such changes.[57] Rather, as needed, the parties negotiated new agreements outside of the treaty—for example, to deal with Great Lakes water quality, Great Lakes fisheries, transboundary air quality, and development of the Columbia River basin. In addition, as will be discussed further below, the practice of the IJC evolved to reflect, and in many cases advance, these changes.

Some of the differing characteristics of international water and environmental law between the early twentieth (as represented in the BWT) and twenty-first centuries include the following.

Scope

The BWT has a narrow focus on "boundary waters," which are shared waters that form the international boundary, expressly excluding tributaries to boundary waters and rivers that cross the border. Increasingly, international legal obligations address a larger frame of reference—"watercourses"[58] or watersheds and drainage basins[59] extending beyond surface water in rivers and lakes to include groundwater, wetlands, and the interacting forces on land. International obligations also now reflect the role of water systems in the protection of biodiversity, habitat, and ecosystem services such as climate and nutrient cycles, and concerns beyond pollution from sewage to those such as invasive species.[60]

Governance

The BWT is a classic international treaty between equal, sovereign states. The treaty extends limited autonomy to the IJC on decisions to approve uses and diversions,[61] but is otherwise largely hierarchical, with the national governments at the centre of decisions to refer matters to the IJC and implement the recommendations that result. In the particular context of North America, the treaty entirely excludes recognition of Indigenous sovereignty over the waters and lands affected, or even mention of Indigenous communities. Adoption of the UN Declaration on the Rights of Indigenous Peoples,[62] and calls from the courts and others to ensure such recognition and "decolonize" laws and institutions, have become more urgent in recent years.[63]

Furthermore, as the example of the state and provincial water resources agreement and compact discussed above demonstrates, much of the policy-making, management, and dispute resolution within shared ecosystems is no longer necessarily restricted to national governments. The authority, interests, and roles of sub-national polities, non-governmental organizations, local communities, business groups, and epistemic communities are expressed through both formal and informal networks and have significant influence on environmental policies and outcomes, both outside of and within traditional hierarchies.

Social Context

The BWT reflects a narrow conception of water as an economic resource. The treaty established a rigid "order of precedence" with a list of priority uses—domestic and sanitary as the first priority, followed by navigation, and then power and irrigation, with no reference to environmental or recreational interests—that reflect the needs of the time. International water law, as reflected in the UN convention and the decisions of the International Court of Justice, has come to incorporate the principle of "reasonable and equitable" use, wherein decisions about infrastructure development and the uses of shared waters are made within the particular economic, social, and environmental context.[64] At the domestic level, "environmental justice" has been recognized as an important value. At both the domestic and international levels, the relationship between health and access to water and sanitation influences policy. At the international level, recent debates about water concern whether access to water is a human right and what obligations states have to fulfill that right for their citizens, as well as what obligations water-rich regions may have to alleviate shortages in other countries in the face of global water scarcity.[65]

Governing Principles

The primary principles of the BWT are the equal right of each party to use boundary waters, and the exclusive right to exploit waters within a party's territory while prohibiting or requiring compensation for significant transboundary injury to health or property resulting from unilateral action on waters that would flow across the boundary. The latter became a fundamental principle of international environmental law, which is, as discussed above, reflected in the Stockholm and Rio Declarations and numerous multilateral treaties. However, the principles guiding national actions on water and environmental issues have broadened considerably to include: the precautionary principle, intergenerational equity, sustainable development, and the conservation and protection of biodiversity. Procedural principles that support the substantive principles include obligations to give notice, to consult, and to conduct environmental impact assessments prior to development.

The BWT is silent on how to respond to such shifts and challenges. To some extent, international law allows subsequent practice and developments in international law to be used to guide treaty interpretation.[66] These developments could be used to interpret the treaty to incorporate more contemporary values and principles into decision-making, but could not be used to revise or undermine the clear terms of the treaty itself.[67]

Conclusions

To date, much of the flexibility to respond to contemporary issues and to reflect changing values and principles in the transboundary environmental context has been due to the evolution in the role and approach of the IJC, the institution established by the treaty. In some cases, the work of the IJC through its boards, including boards of control and the boards established under the Great Lakes Water Quality Agreements, have influenced the development of international principles; in other cases, the boards have incorporated principles generated elsewhere into their scientific studies, recommendations, and management decisions.[68]

To cite just a few examples, in addition to those already discussed: The IJC's reference work on water pollution in the lower Great Lakes led directly to the parties' adoption of the Great Lakes Water Quality Agreements (1972, 1978, 1987, and 2012) and the establishment of two ongoing boards, the water quality board and the science advisory board as well as two reference groups, one on the influence of land uses on water quality and the other on the upper lakes. The work of these boards was instrumental in establishing the foundation for the concept of the Great Lakes basin as an integrated whole, for the "ecosystem approach," now widely adopted elsewhere, for including persistence and bioaccumulation in toxic chemicals management, and for the goal of the restoration of "ecological integrity." These boards have also led in recognizing the influence of airborne toxins and urban and agricultural land uses on water quality.

In all of its work in recent decades, the IJC has become a forum for input from NGOs, interested individuals, officials, and groups. In fact, the IJC has evolved from an institution only for the parties to the treaty into an institution that considers its responsibility to other public authorities and to the public.[69] IJC boards and references have developed progressive decision-making standards: for protecting against the *risk* of harm (Red River), for adding protection of habitat and environmental values as priorities (Lake Ontario), and for preventing the introduction of invasive biota across ecosystems (Garrison Diversion). Through the International Watersheds Initiative, the IJC, supported by the parties, has moved its boards beyond the narrow focus of the treaty to embrace an integrated watershed approach for existing control boards.[70] For example, in the St. Croix River watershed, the board of control, established in 1915, and the water quality board, established in 1962, were first combined into a single board and then designated as a watershed board in 2007.[71] With both this board and the International Rainy–Lake of the Woods Watershed Board, the objective is to address issues through an integrated ecosystem approach. In addition, board membership has been expanded to include local representatives and representatives of Indigenous communities.

This type of evolution in the role of an institution where the treaty text remains static is not unique to the IJC, but is common among similar long-lived international water commissions, particularly those in Europe.[72] Nevertheless, it has been essential to the ability of the existing institutions established under the treaty to adapt what has been referred to as the "spirit of the treaty" to new challenges and changing values.

The continued ability of the IJC and its boards to play this role in the future depends on many factors, including continued support from the national governments—the parties to the treaty—which has sometimes been inconsistent in the past. The framework of the treaty places limits on the degree to which the IJC may act independently to respond to bilateral disputes or new challenges. The commission has no ability to initiate a study, but must await a reference from the two governments, which may not come.[73] Moreover, the commission is subject to the parties' sometimes mercurial decisions on appointments and budget. Likewise, the IJC has no ability to implement recommendations or enforce treaty provisions, and cannot recognize Indigenous sovereignty over North American waters. This is the role of the parties.

The role of the IJC in the future may also be limited to one of support as other actors become more prominent on certain environmental and resource issues. This is best illustrated by considering the action of the states and provinces in the negotiations of the agreement and compact, in which the technical findings of the IJC's reports were used to ground negotiations that left out the treaty parties and the IJC. Nevertheless, this should not be seen as an unimportant role in transboundary water governance. Thus, even in light of these limitations, the IJC can continue to evolve and play an important role in policy development and water resource management into the future.

Notes

1. 21 U.S. Op. Att'y Gen. 274 (1895), 281–2.
2. US-Mex., *Convention Providing for the Equitable Distribution of the Waters of the Rio Grande for Irrigation Purposes* (21 May 1906), 34 Stat. 2953 (emphasis added).
3. *Hearings on Treaty with Mexico Relating to Utilization of Waters of Certain Rivers Before the Comm. on Foreign Relations* (1945), 79th Cong. 1762 (alteration in original).
4. Library and Archives Canada (LAC), Sir George C. Gibbons Papers, Vol. 14, Fol. 3.
5. Boundary Waters Treaty art. iv, 36 Stat. at 2450.
6. *Trail Smelter I*, 3 R.I.A.A. 1911 (1938); *Trail Smelter II*, 3 R.I.A.A. 1938 (1941).
7. Alexandre Kiss and Dinah Shelton, *International Environmental Law* (Ardsley-on-Hudson, NY: Transnational Publishers, 1991), 107.
8. Edith Brown Weiss, Stephen C. McCaffrey, Daniel B. McGraw, and A. Dan Tarlock, *International Environmental Law and Policy* (Boston, MA: Aspen Law and Business, 1998), 257.
9. *Trail Smelter II*, 3 R.I.A.A. at 1945 (alteration in original).
10. Convention Relative to the Establishment of a Tribunal to Decide Questions of Indemnity and Future Regime Arising from the Operation of Smelter at Trail, British Columbia, US-Can., 15 April 1935, art. ii (effective 3 Aug. 1935), 49 Stat. 3245, 3246; *Trail Smelter I*, 3 R.I.A.A. at 1911.
11. Trail Smelter Convention, art. iii, 49 Stat. at 3246.
12. Trail Smelter Convention, art. iv, 49 Stat. at 3246.
13. *Trail Smelter II* (1938), 3 R.I.A.A. 1911.
14. *Trail Smelter II* (quoting Clyde Eagleton, *Responsibility of States in International Law* [1928], 80 [internal citation omitted]).
15. *Trail Smelter II*, 1964–5.
16. *Trail Smelter II*, 1965 (alteration in original).

17   *Trail Smelter II*, 1965.

18   *Trail Smelter II*, 1966–81.

19   United Nations Conference on the Human Environment, Stockholm, SE, *Stockholm Declaration of the United Nations* (16 June 1972), 11 I.L.M. 1416, 1420.

20   United Nations Conference on Environment and Development, Rio de Janeiro, BR, *Rio Declaration on Environment and Development*, princ. 2, UN Doc. A/CONF.151/26 (June 14, 1992), 31 I.L.M. 874, 876.

21   Restatement (Third) of the Foreign Relations Law of the United States § 601(1) (1987).

22   David Lemarquand, "The International Joint Commission and Changing Canada–United States Boundary Relations," *Natural Resources Journal* 33 (1993): 62–7. For more detailed histories, see L. M. Bloomfield and G. F. Fitzgerald, *Boundary Waters Problems of Canada and the United States (the International Joint Commission 1912–1958)* (Toronto: Carswell, 1958), and A. D. P. Heeney, *Along the Common Frontier: The International Joint Commission* (Toronto: Canadian Institute of International Affairs, 1967).

23   P. L. 110–342 (2008).

24   E.g., Leonard B. Dworsky, "Ecosystem Management: Great Lakes Perspectives," *Natural Resources Journal* 33 (1993): 347. The compact was preceded by a soft law interstate agreement, the Great Lakes Charter. See Peter V. MacAvoy, "The Great Lakes Charter: Toward a Basinwide Strategy for Managing the Great Lakes," *Case Western Reserve Journal of International Law* 18 (1986): 49.

25   Noah D. Hall, "Toward A New Horizontal Federalism: Interstate Water Management in the Great Lakes Region," *Colorado Law Review* 77 (2006): 405.

26   International Boundary Waters Treaty Act, R.S.C. 1985, c. I-17 as amended by S.C. 2001, c. 40 and S.C. 2013, c. 12; Ontario Water Resources Act, R.S.O. 1980, c. O.40, as amended by S.O. 2007, c. 12; and Loi affirmant le caractere collectif des ressources en eau et favorisant une meilleure gouvernance de l'eau et des milieux associes, L.Q. 2009, c. C-6.2.

27   In the late 1970s, the US Army Corps of Engineers released a congressionally mandated study on ways to recharge the depleted Ogallala Aquifer from adjacent areas. The study did not include any proposal to construct a pipeline from Lake Superior to the High Plains, but it triggered regional fears that the water-short West would eventually ask Congress to bail it out with Great Lakes water, which held that groundwater allocated under state law was an article of commerce and thus subject to the Dormant Commerce Clause. *Sporhase v. Nebraska*, 458 U.S. 941 (1982). See also *Pennsylvania v. West Virginia*, 262 U.S. 553 (1923). Congress prohibited out-of-basin diversions without state approval in 1986, but concerns persisted. See Peter Annin, *The Great Lakes Water Wars* (Washington, DC: Island Press, 2006), 57–81, for a discussion of the reactions to feared diversions, and Maxwell Cohen, "Great Lakes Legal Seminar: Diversion and Consumptive Use," *Case Western Reserve Journal of International Law* 18, no. 1 (1986): 1–259, is a good snapshot of the diversion fears and range of legal responses in the mid-1980s.

28   Two respected Canadian academics criticized the Annex 2001 process, a precursor to the compact, as an abdication of the Canadian federal government's responsibility because it "would leave the provinces with no control over diversions in the US [and] [i]t would also give the US significant say over water-related developments in Canada." See D. W. Schindler and Adele M. Hurley, *Rising Tensions: Canada/U.S. Cross-Border Water Issues in the 21st Century* (Notes for Remarks to the Centre for Global Studies Conference on Canada/US Relations, University of Victoria, November 2004), 11.

29   Edith Brown Weiss, "Water and International Trade Law," in *Freshwater and International Economic Law*, ed. Laurence Boisson de Chazournes, Edith Brown Weiss, and Nathalie Bernasconi-Osterwalder (Oxford: Oxford University Press, 2005). The basic argument was that any regime that allowed regulated diversions was therefore a "commodification" of the lakes and could then be challenged as a disguised discriminatory trade practice. This incredible anti-commodity argument was made in litigation challenging Perrier's planned diversion of spring waters in Michigan. Opponents of the proposed extraction argued that when groundwater is used to produce commodities, the commodities could only be consumed on the overlying land. The Michigan courts rejected the argument, as groundwater law allows the use of the water for commercial purposes well beyond the tract of overlying land. *Michigan Citizens for Water Conservation v. Nestle Waters N. Am., Inc.*, 709 N.W.2d 174 (Mich. App. 2005), reversed on standing grounds, 737 N.W.2d 447 (Mich. 2007).

30   Joseph W. Dellapenna, "International Law's Lessons for the Law of the Lakes," *University of Michigan Journal of Law Reform* 40 (2007): 754–7.

31   Article 8.2.3 provides: "Nothing in this Compact is intended to affect nor shall be construed to affect the application of the Boundary Waters Treaty of 1909 whose requirements continue to apply in addition to the requirements of this Compact."

32   Ken Conca, *Governing Water: Contentious Transnational Politics and Global Institution Building* (Cambridge, MA: MIT Press, 2006), 73–80. Conca sets out the stresses that many river basins face and the barriers they pose to co-operative management among riparian states.

33   The compact does impose two real costs on the basin states. First, the straddling community's standard may block much small transfer across the basin line. Second, the compact will create pressure for the additional regulation of surface and groundwater. States such as Indiana, Illinois, Ohio, New York, and Pennsylvania have resisted the strong regulated riparianism adopted in Minnesota, Michigan, and Wisconsin. The compact was briefly held up when an Ohio state representative argued that it would erode Ohio's power to control its water resources.

34   Ontario Ministry of Finance, "Ontario Population Projections Update, 2017–2041" (2017), available at http://www.fin.gov.on.ca/en/economy/demographics/projections/.

35   42 U.S.C. § 7401 et seq., as amended.

36   Stanley A. Changnon, "Temporal Behavior of Levels of the Great Lakes and Climate Variability," *Journal of Great Lakes Research* 30 (2004): 184–200.

37   Ibid., 6.

38   Ibid., 21–2.

39 Ulrich Beyerlin, "Different Types of Norms in International Environmental Law Policies, Principles and Rules," in *The Oxford Handbook of International Environmental Law*, ed. by Daniel Bodansky, Jutta Brunée, and Ellen Hey (Oxford: Oxford University Press, 2008), 425, and Jonathan B. Wiener, "Precaution," in *The Oxford Handbook* at 597, explore the legal status of precaution.

40 The soft precautionary principle posits that a high degree of certainty about the adverse impacts of an activity is not a necessary prerequisite to limit or regulate it and is one of the foundations of international environmental law. The hard version posits that an activity should not be allowed until there is conclusive evidence that it does not cause harm. The general principle was endorsed in the 1992 Rio Declaration, Principle 15. Because crucial issues, such as who bears the burden of proof and how feedback loops should operate, remain unresolved, it remains much contested and has been criticized as incoherent and unfair. E.g., Cass Sunstein, *Laws of Fear: Beyond the Precautionary Principle* (Cambridge: Cambridge University Press, 2005); Christopher D. Stone, "Is There a Precautionary Principle?" *Environmental Law Reporter* 31 (2001): 10790, 10792; Frank B. Cross, "Paradoxical Perils of the Precautionary Principle," *Washington & Lee Law Review* 53 (1996): 851.

41 The best articulation of this position is Jonathan B. Wiener, "Whose Precaution After All? A Comment on the Comparison and Evolution of Risk Regulatory Systems," *Duke Journal of Comparative & International Law* 13 (2003): 207. Jutta Brunée, "The United States and International Environmental Law: Living with an Elephant," *European Journal of International Law* 15 (2004): 617, 628–30 places US opposition in the broader context of the fear of general principles of customary law.

42 This aspect of the compact has been addressed A. Dan Tarlock, "The Great Lakes as an Environmental Heritage of Humankind: An International Law Perspective," *University of Michigan Journal of Law Reform* 40 (2007): 995.

43 The compact does use the term "common heritage of humankind," but it recognizes that the lakes are held in trust by the states for the benefit of future generations (Article 1.3.1(a) and (f)).

44 Article 4.15.1(c) also provides that the states shall: "consider adaptive management principles and approaches, recognizing, considering and providing adjustments for the uncertainties in, and evolution of science concerning the Basin's water resources, watersheds and ecosystems, including potential changes to Basin-wide processes, such as lake level cycles and climate."

45 See note 12, *supra*.

46 US Bureau of Reclamation, "St. Mary River and Milk River Basin Study: Summary Report" (2012), 7–11.

47 Ryan P. McClane, "The St. Mary and the Milk River, Two Rivers, One Stream," *University of Denver Water Law Review* 14 (2010): 131–3; R. Halliday and G. Faveri, "The St. Mary and Milk Rivers: The 1921 Order Revisited," *Canadian Water Resources Journal* 32 (2007): 75–92.

48 Id. at 145. The 1921 order can be found in Appendix B, "International St. Mary–Milk Rivers Administrative Measures Task Force Report to the IJC" (2006), http://www.ijc.org/rel/pdf/SMMRAM.pdf.

49 Alberta irrigates 215,000 hectares from the St. Mary and "received 28.1% more than its entitlement from the St. Mary River because Montana was unable to divert and use its full share. The situation was reversed in the Milk River where Montana received 47.4% more than its entitlement because Alberta lacked physical resources to utilize its share." See, K. K. Klein, Danny G. Le Roy, Md Kamar Ali, and Tatiana Cook, "Is Water an Agricultural Trade Issue? Examining the Montana–Alberta Dispute," available at https://pdfimages.wondershare.com/forms-templates/scientific-poster-template-2.pdf.

50 International St. Mary–Milk Rivers Administrative Measures Task Force Report to the IJC (2006).

51 For a detailed discussion of the issues and possible solutions, see Michelle Morris, "Governance of the St. Mary and Milk Rivers," in *Beyond the Border: Tensions Across the 49th Parallel to the Great Plains*, ed. Kyle Conway and Timothy Patsch (Montreal: McGill-Queens University Press, 2012), 113–32.

52 Montana-Alberta St. Mary Milk River Water Management Initiative, Terms of Reference, telephone interview with Gerald Galloway (secretary US section, IJC, 1998–2003), 16 September 2008.

53 McClane, "The St. Mary and the Milk River," 156.

54 United Nations, *Convention on the Law of Non-Navigable Uses of International Watercourses*, 36 I.L.M. 700 (1997) ("UN Watercourses Convention"). Article 20 provides: "Watercourse States shall, individually and, where appropriate, jointly, protect and preserve the ecosystems of international watercourses." The need to protect aquatic ecosystems was recognized in *Case Concerning Pulp Mills on the River Uruguay (Argentina v. Uruguay)*, IJC Reports 114 (2006).

55 Josefin Gooch, *Protecting Ecological Integrity in Transboundary Watercourses: An Integrational Approach towards Implementing Environmental Flows* (PhD diss., Lund University, 2016), 64, available at https://lup.lub.lu.se/search/publication/eb2f4bfe-9045-4a5a-8e3a-36181509eb50.

56 St. Mary–Milk River Administrative Measures Task Force, Report to the IJC, 40.

57 Stephen J. Toope and Jutta Brunée, "Freshwater Regimes: the Mandate of the International Joint Commission," *Arizona Journal of International and Comparative Law* 15 (1998): 276–7.

58 The UN Watercourses Convention defines a "watercourse" as "a system of surface waters and groundwaters constituting by virtue of their physical relationship a unitary whole and normally flowing into a common terminus."

59 See, for example, UN Economic Commission for Europe, *Convention on the Protection and Use of Transboundary Watercourses and International Lakes*, www.unece.org/fileadmin/DAM/env/documents/2013/wat/ECE_MP.WAT_41.pdf, which adopts a basin-based approach to integrated water resource management, guided by the precautionary principle, polluter pays principle, and sustainable use.

60 UN, *Convention on Biological Diversity* (1992), 1760 U.N.T.S. 79, www.cbd.int/doc/legal/cbd-en.pdf.

61 As well as an adjudicatory role in article x; however, this has never been resorted to.

62 See UN General Assembly, *Declaration on the Rights of Indigenous Peoples*, GA Res. 61/295 (2007), www.un.org/esa/socdev/unpfii/documents/DRIPS_en.pdf.

63 In 2004, Indigenous leaders signed the Tribal and First Nations Great Lakes Water Accord, which states, in part: "Tribes and First Nations continue to exercise cultural and spiritual rights of self-determination and property rights within traditional territories of peoples and nations. . . . It is thus our right, our responsibility and our duty to insist that no plan to protect or preserve the Great Lakes Waters moves forward without the equal highest-level participation of Tribal and First Nations governments with the governments of the United States and Canada." In Canada, see Truth and Reconciliation Commission of Canada, *Calls to Action* (2015).

64 The UN Watercourses Convention gives less weight to existing uses and implies that "equal" might not be "equitable" in particular circumstances. Also see, International Court of Justice, *Case Concerning the Gabcikovo-Nagymaros Project (Hungary/Slovakia)*, 1997 IJC Rep. 7 (25 Sept.).

65 See, for example, the UN's Sustainable Development Goals, adopted September 2015, at the UN Sustainable Development Summit, available at https://www.un.org/sustainabledevelopment/sustainable-development-goals.

66 *Vienna Convention on the Law of Treaties* (1969), art. 31, 1155 U.N.T.S. 331, www.legal.un.org/ilc/texts/instruments/english/conventions/1_1_1969.pdf.

67 See discussion in Marcia Valiante, "How Green is My Treaty? Ecosystem Protection and the 'Order of Precedence' under the Boundary Waters Treaty of 1909," *Wayne Law Review* 54 (2008): 1525–51, in the context of the regulation of Lake Ontario.

68 The work of the IJC has been catalogued and analyzed in a mountain of academic literature. The point here is not to repeat those works but simply to note the commission's important role in keeping the transboundary regime relevant.

69 See IJC, "Guiding Principles of the International Joint Commission," at https://www.ijc.org/en/who/mission/principles/guiding-principles: "The Commission affords all parties interested in any matter before it a convenient opportunity to be heard. It promotes the engagement of state, provincial and municipal governments and other authorities in the resolution of these matters. . . . While directing its advice and assistance to governments, the Commission takes account of the need to foster public awareness of the issue in question and ensure that the public is able to contribute to the consideration and implementation of its assessments by governments."

70 See, IJC, *The International Watersheds Initiative: Implementing a New Paradigm for Transboundary Basins; Third Report to Governments on the International Watersheds Initiative* (January 2009), available at https://ijc.en/international-watersheds-initiative-implementation-new-paradigm-transboundary-basins-third-report.

71 As discussed in IJC, *The International Watersheds Initiative: From Concept to Cornerstone of the International Joint Commission, Fourth Report to Governments* (October 2015), available at www.ijc.org/files/tinymce/uploaded/IWI/IJC-IWI-EN-WEB.pdf.

72 Joachim Blatter, "Beyond Hierarchies and Networks: Institutional Logics and Change in Transboundary Spaces, *Governance: An International Journal of Policy, Administration and Institutions* 16, no. 4 (2003): 503–26.

73 For a discussion of a "retreat from bilateralism" and recent examples of avoidance of the IJC in disputes over Devil's Lake and the Trail Smelter, see Shi-Ling Hsu and Austen L. Parrish, "Litigating Canada-U.S. Transboundary Harm: International Environmental Lawmaking and the Threat of Extra-territorial Reciprocity," *Virginia Journal of International Law* 48 (2007): 1–64. See also Toope and Brunée, "Freshwater Regimes."

16

The Importance of the International Joint Commission

John Kirton and Brittaney Warren

The Boundary Waters Treaty (BWT) of 1909 and the International Joint Commission (IJC) it established have contributed to the peaceful, prosperous, and productive management of Canada–United States relations. The treaty and IJC have sometimes reflected and reinforced the key distinctive national values (DNVs) driving Canadian foreign policy as a whole. This larger legacy has been occasionally observed by those who have assessed the work of the IJC over the past century or so.[1] However, few have directly and systemically explored the IJC's place in expressing and advancing these values in Canadian foreign policy on a continental, regional, and global scale.

This chapter takes up this task. It argues that the BWT and IJC partly embodied, entrenched, and expanded several of Canada's six DNVs of anti-militarism, multiculturalism, openness, globalism, and, above all, international institutionalism, and, increasingly in recent years, environmentalism. The treaty and the institution it created initiated the continental, Canada–United States process of international institutionalism through the construction of a plethora of Canada-US joint institutions within Canada's place as an integral part of a global British Empire, and subsequently of the Commonwealth of Nations. Further, the treaty and the IJC legally and institutionally entrenched environmentalism as a core principle in the management of the intimate, disparate Canada-US relationship, and the sharing of natural resources therein, even if the IJC did not help make environmentalism a DNV in Canadian foreign policy overall. The IJC entrenched environmentalism by including in the BWT an agreement to protect human health by preventing water pollution in the Great Lakes and other transboundary waters, in the globally relevant way of science-based international co-operation. Yet after its pioneering start, the BWT's environmental principles and results soon disappeared. Indeed, the Great Lakes had been subjected to severe ecological stress—with Lake Erie briefly declared dead in the 1960s—until an environmentally revived IJC helped bring them back in the 1970s.

The IJC's pattern of permanent international institutionalism but only periodic environmentalism is partly explained by the national affirmations of these values at the highest level in both Canada and the United States. They show that Canada placed a greater emphasis than the United States on institutionalism. US national affirmations of institutionalism were low at the commencement of the BWT in 1909 then rose after the Second World War. Canada's affirmations, conversely, started high and then declined, although Canada still kept a significant lead over the United States. However, with the great exception of US president Theodore Roosevelt, there were no environmental affirmations in either country from the time the BWT was created until John F. Kennedy took office in 1963. In Canada Pierre Elliott Trudeau made the first national affirmation of the environment in 1968. Canada has taken only a slight lead in total affirmations since that time. References to the environment before the 1960s centred on the management and extraction of natural resources for economic prosperity, with no consideration of the impact of that extraction on the ecosystem.

Despite the IJC's limitations and shortcomings as an environmental institution, eighty-five years after its creation its experiences and contributions to transboundary governance of shared resources served as a referent for the creation of the expansive trilateral North American Free Trade Agreement (NAFTA) and accompanying North American Agreement on Environmental Cooperation (NAAEC), with its Commission on Environmental Cooperation (CEC) headquartered in Montreal. The IJC has since been referenced in the trilateral North American Leaders' Summit as a key institution for co-operation on environmental stewardship.[2] NAFTA, the NAAEC, and the CEC today serve as a model for incorporating environmental protection into other bilateral and multiparty global trade deals. Moreover, both the IJC and CEC have survived severe threats, most recently from US president Donald Trump's actions against the environment and international institutions. These assaults, combined with intense threats to the world's fresh water from human-driven climate change, land use, land-use change and forestry, and questions over water ownership and distribution mean the world now requires even more international and regional environmental co-operation to effectively adapt to and mitigate compounding ecological shocks, not least by ensuring that the pioneering principles on which the IJC and CEC were founded are strengthened and prevail.

To develop this argument, this chapter first outlines the concept of DNVs and the IJC's expression of several Canadian ones. Second, it examines how international institutionalism is embodied in the IJC as cause, content, and consequence. Third, it does the same for environmentalism. Fourth, it explores the IJC's legacy in North American governance, specifically in the CEC as a trilateral, transformational, contemporary expression of the international institutionalism and environmentalism embodied in the original and evolving IJC. It concludes by considering the current, even existential, stress test imposed on both bodies by Donald Trump and recommends a practical response.

Canada's Distinctive National Values

The BWT and IJC embodied, entrenched, and expanded several of Canada's six DNVs of anti-militarism, multiculturalism, openness, globalism, and, above all, international institutionalism, and, increasingly in recent years, environmentalism.

Within Canadian foreign policy, DNVs are defined as "a set of values that no other territorially organized political community in the world cares about, at least with the distinctiveness, depth, durability, and consensus that Canadians do."[3] To qualify as a DNV, a value should be constitutionally embedded from the country's start, widely and equally shared by its citizens across their other defining divides, durable in operation, deepening and expanding over time, resilient and inspiring resistance when violated and bouncing back to prevail, and distinctive in flourishing more strongly in these ways in Canada than in other consequential countries of the world. The six values that meet these criteria for Canada are antimilitarism, multiculturalism, openness, globalism, internationalism, institutionalism, and environmentalism.[4]

Since their start the BWT and IJC have expressed most of these DNVs to some degree. For anti-militarism, they helped ensure the ongoing absence of military forces unilaterally deployed and employed on the Great Lakes and other boundary waters. In doing so they built on the earlier, more traditionally siloed Rush-Bagot Agreement prohibiting conventional armaments aimed at each other's military forces. They prevented such actions against the newer, non-traditional security threats of transnational alcohol, tobacco, drugs, terrorists, and illegal migrants. Multiculturalism was a second-order benefit of anti-militarism. The IJC and BWT thus helped make the Canada-US border the world's longest undefended frontier, one that to this day is marked with bridges rather than walls.

Openness was affirmed by the IJC's bias toward equitably sharing, rather than unilaterally closing and dividing, the ecologically unified transboundary waters, and the commerce, transportation, and resulting international trade that depended on this ecological openness. The historic controversy over the Chicago water diversion and ongoing issue of diverting waters from the Great Lakes was a critical component of this.

Globalism flowed from Canada's creation as an integral part of the global British Empire. It flourished initially with the contribution of the British government to the creation of the BWT and IJC, and their reciprocal benefit in stabilizing relations between the United Kingdom and the United States as the First World War approached. Globalism intensified, with anti-militarism added, in the view of US secretary of state Elihu Root, expressed in 1913, that the BWT/IJC constituted a continental "little Hague," and of Canadian prime minister William Lyon McKenzie King's later view of these bodies as a continental model to rescue a blood-thirsty Europe and world from their recurrent wars.[56] The BWT and IJC governed an important component of an integrated global ecosystem whose global interconnectedness scientists subsequently confirmed.

International institutionalism and environmentalism, however, represent the BWT and IJC's largest and most direct relationship with Canada's DNVs.

The IJC Contribution to International Institutionalism

Canada's DNV of international institutionalism is defined as "a passion for creating international institutions to govern relations among countries and their citizens."[7] It includes the creation, improvement, and expansion of these intergovernmental institutions on a multilateral, plurilateral, regional, or bilateral scale. It flows both from a rational calculation of how best to deal with much more powerful countries, starting with the United Kingdom and the United States, and from a "sociological desire for connection, socialization, moral suasion, peer pressure and community."[8]

A key indicator of the strength of a DNV is its presence in a country's national policy address, defined as the periodic ceremonial occasion in which the highest political leader states the overall priorities of the polity. In Canada's case this is the speech from the throne that opens each new parliament, with a premium placed on the first one provided by a newly elected prime minister.

Here the DNV of international institutionalism has had a substantial place as a value that has been affirmed in a favourable way (see Appendix A). In the ten such speeches of new Canadian governments since 1945, Canada referenced international institutionalism at an overall average of +6.3 points more than the United States did in its temporally most proximate equivalent, the State of the Union address. Canada's score surpassed that of the United States in eight of the ten cases, with a lead as high as +19.9 points for John Diefenbaker in 1957. However, Canada's lead has lessened over time, from double digits before Pierre Trudeau assumed office in 1968, to a short-lived US lead under Jean Chrétien and Paul Martin, and a smaller Canadian lead under Stephen Harper and Justin Trudeau. Canada's international institutionalism has been a bipartisan affair, with (Progressive) Conservative prime ministers affirming it more strongly than Liberal Party ones. In all, international institutionalism appears confirmed as a Canadian DNV, at least relative to the United States, on a continental scale. This conclusion is sustained by the record prior to 1945 and extending back to the IJC's start.

A more specific look at the individual international organizations noted by name in Canada's throne speeches reveals several patterns (see Appendix

B). First, there is no reference to the IJC or any continental Canada-US institution at all. This confirms the widespread consensus that the IJC has operated below the "political" level in both countries, but disconfirms any view that it serves as a model or source of national pride. Second, there is a balance between broadly multilateral bodies and restricted plurilateral ones (with the evolving plurilateral to multilateral International Trade Organization and the General Agreement on Tariffs and Trade and its named liberalization rounds, and the World Trade Organization excluded from the count). Tied for first are the plurilateral Commonwealth and the multilateral United Nations, with 8 references each, closely followed by the plurilateral North Atlantic Treaty Organization (NATO), with 7. NAFTA, with 1 reference, puts Canada's trilateral institutions on the list and ahead of any absent continental Canada-US ones. Finally, there is a strong decline over time in references to international institutions, especially after the 1949–89 Cold War period, which was marked by the Diefenbaker peak of 8, and 28 overall, and into the post–Cold War 1994–2015 period, with only 4. International institutionalism is thus an enduring but declining DNV in Canada. By this measure, it is not a particularly strong contrast with a US led by Donald Trump.

However, at the foreign ministerial level, Canada's international institutionalism recently stands out. In her defining speech on Canadian foreign policy on 6 June 2017, Canada's foreign affairs minister, Chrystia Freeland, put international institutionalism in first place among the three Canadian foreign-policy priorities she set.[9] Freeland stated: "First, we will robustly support the rules-based international order, and all its institutions, and seek ways to strengthen and improve them. We will strongly support the multilateral forums where such discussions are held—including the G7, the G20, the OAS, APEC, the WTO, the Commonwealth and La Francophonie, the Arctic Council and of course NATO and the UN." In her speech she referred 28 times to 18 different international institutions. The North American Aerospace Defence Command (NORAD), and not the IJC, was the only bilateral Canada-US one on her list.

Beyond formal speeches, behaviour also shows the centrality of international institutionalism to Canada. In 1919 Canada joined the League of Nations, when the United States did not, and stayed until the bitter end. Unlike the United States and the United Kingdom, Canada never withdrew from United Nations' bodies until Prime Minister Stephen Harper withdrew Canada from the UN's Kyoto Protocol, rejected the UN Declaration on the Rights of Indigenous Peoples, and briefly removed Canada from the UN Convention to Combat Desertification (Harper's successor, Justin Trudeau, quickly brought Canada back to these bodies). Canada pioneered the Commonwealth, La Francophonie, and the G20. Harper's boycott of the Commonwealth Heads of Government Meeting in Sri Lanka was a very rare event. Due to this rarity, it is thus appropriate to call Canada one of the most well-connected countries in the world as far as international institutional involvement and invention are concerned.[10]

The IJC was established just before Canada helped turn the British Empire into the international institution of the Commonwealth with the creation of the summit-level Imperial War Council in 1917. The IJC's contribution to international institutionalism since its start should thus be assessed on a global, as well as a national Canadian and a continental Canadian-US, scale. Maxwell Cohen claims that the BWT was "far more sophisticated than perhaps any comparable piece of bilateral international machinery then existing in Western society. This would include even the successful Rhine and Danube commissions which had been functioning since the 1860s."[11] This was important because "its pioneering anti-pollution obligations all fashioned a multiple-use instrument that went beyond experience elsewhere and perhaps even beyond the full appreciation of the draftsmen themselves."[12] John Kirton notes in his outline of international institutionalism that "from an early age, Canada imposed international institutions on its much larger and then menacing neighbour—the United States—beginning with the International Joint Commission."[13]

At the start, Canada was the primary and most persistent advocate of the creation of the IJC, and it worked to secure its core objectives in the compromise that came. The IJC, and Canada within it, worked continuously, amidst major changes and global shocks. These include the First and Second World Wars, in which Canada fought from the very start while the United States remained absent from the former conflict until 1917 and the latter until 1941. They also include the reverse divide, most recently when the United States fought the wars in Vietnam from 1965 to 1975 and in Iraq starting in 2003, with Canada absent throughout. The IJC endured major changes in the overall state of the Canada-US relationship, such as the Vietnam War–bred "Nixon shock" and the US diplomatic boycott of Canada from 1972 to 1973, and the so-called Reagan revolution from 1981 to 1985.

Throughout, the IJC worked steadily with some success and setbacks.[14] At the most general level, three-quarters of its recommendations were accepted by the two governments in an overall balance that seems to have equally satisfied and benefited both. Its mandate expanded, most notably with the advent in the 1970s of the Great Lakes Water Quality Agreement (GLWQA). The GLWQA was created to deal with the declining health of the lakes, and it revealed a gap between the pollution-prevention provision of the IJC on paper and the real impacts of increased human activity on the lakes. Yet the IJC responded to this challenge and continued to function during periods when other joint continental institutions did not, notably the higher-level and more political ministerial committees on defence and economics.[15]

However, the IJC directly produced few similar institutions for specific continental geographic regions or functions in regard to water, despite recurrent recommendations to this end.[16] Nor did it regularly inspire many other enduring joint institutions of a different form and in different fields.[17] Canada and the United States did create a few more bilateral environmental bodies prior to the Second World War. Those aimed at defence production proliferated, but quickly died in 1945, to be revived in 1950 when the Korean War and Cold War arrived.[18] There also arose the Permanent Joint Board on Defence in 1940 and NORAD in 1957. The post-1940 defence-focused proliferation flowed from the pressures of overseas war, rather than the continental precedent or platform of the IJC. Despite the suggestions of the *Principles for Partnership: Canada and the United States* (known as the Merchant-Heeney Report) of 1965, proposing continental integration in energy, virtually no new joint bodies arose until the Canada-US Free Trade Agreement (CUFTA) arrived in 1989 and then NAFTA in 1994.[19]

Moreover, as a bilateral institutional partner of Canada after 1945, the United States was increasingly joined—and then exceeded after 1968—by the United Kingdom, France, Japan, and many other countries. Canada similarly emphasized plurilateral regional bodies, if ones that included the United States, across the Atlantic and the Arctic.[20] These included the environmentally-related Organisation for Economic Co-operation and Development in 1960, the North Atlantic Fisheries Organization in 1961, the International Energy Agency in 1974, and the environmentally-focused Arctic Council in 1996.

It is striking that no continental, environment-wide commission like the IJC or NORAD was ever seriously recommended, considered, or created by the two national governments, even as the intimate links among water, air, land, and animal species became scientifically clear. The Canada-US Regulatory Cooperation Council, created after the shock of the 9/11 terrorist attack on the United States, was the closest such working-level integration came. And CUFTA of 1989 was notably and controversially devoid of environmentalism—either within the agreement or alongside it—unlike NAFTA, which arrived soon after. Nor did CUFTA have any legal or institutional relationship to the IJC.

The IJC Contribution to Environmentalism

Canada's DNV of environmentalism is defined as the enduring value Canadians place on the environment as a provider of natural resources, such as water and wood, on which their life and economy depends, and their constant belief and practice that it is a common resource to be kept largely under public rather than private ownership.[21] It has been expressed in Canadians' choice, over recent decades, of global environmental protection as a priority in Canadian foreign policy; this is especially evident in the Arctic, with the creation of the Arctic Council, and in Canadians' concern with environmental security, and their consistent refusal to export bulk water on commercial terms. It is further seen in Canada's emphasis on building international environmental law and institutions, from the BWT and IJC through to the many UN instruments and institutions since 1972. It does not extend to many domestic areas, most notably in Indigenous communities, where boil-water advisories have persisted for decades.

Canada's environmentalism is grounded in the country's position as one of the globe's major possessors and custodians of critical ecological resources, some of which are geographically shared with the United States. These include Canada's location on the Atlantic, Arctic, and Pacific

Oceans, and its possession of the world's longest coastline and the world's largest body of fresh water, the Great Lakes, and "the longest water boundary in the world—from Cornwall to the Lake of the Woods—and from sharing also about 150 lakes and rivers and at least five continental watersheds crossing the boundary both ways."[22] In the January 2017 Canadian Water Attitudes Study of 2,017 adults, 91 per cent of respondents saw water as a component of Canada's national identity and 45 per cent viewed it as the country's most important natural resource.[23]

In affirmations of the value of environmentalism in their newly elected leaders' first national policy addresses since 1945, Canadians exceed Americans, but only slightly, by +1.5 points (see Appendix C). Moreover, in these 10 cases, Canada leads in 4 and the United States in 4, with a tie in 2. Canada's longest lead was in the most recent period, lasting from 2004 to 2015. Its strongest lead—of +11.4 points—came under Paul Martin. The strongest US lead came under Brian Mulroney in 1984, when he was surpassed by Ronald Reagan by +2.7 points. Environmentalism by this measure thus appears to be a shared continental value rather than a distinctively Canadian one. Indeed, for both countries it was absent from 1949 to 1963 but appeared consistently since 1968 (save for the short-lived Canadian government of Joe Clark in 1979).

This weakness in a Canadian national context may help explain why, when Canada's environmentalism rose in the 1970's, it largely bypassed the IJC and other continental bodies to go directly abroad on a plurilateral and multilateral scale. There was little apparent interaction and influence flowing between the continental and the wider worlds. To be sure, border-crossing acid rain did help inspire Joe Clark and Jimmy Carter to back Germany's Helmut Schmidt in pioneering the Group of Seven (G7) initiative in 1979 to control climate change.[24] Yet there was little impact from international environmental institutionalization on the "continent apart" back home.[25]

This gap appears most recently in Minister Freeland's speech on Canadian foreign policy.[26] Here global environmental priorities, led by climate change, came first, but continental ones were absent. She started by highlighting the "new shared human imperative—the fight against climate change first among them." She later called climate change an existential threat, applauding the 2015 Paris Agreement. Freeland also referenced the Montreal Protocol of 1987 to protect the ozone layer. Her sole continental reference was to "the acid rain treaty of the Mulroney era," with no reference at all to boundary waters or the IJC.

The IJC Contribution to North American Governance

Writing about the IJC's future in 1981, Marcel Cadieux emphasized Canada's reluctance to institutionalize its bilateral relationship with the United States and the ineffectiveness of the several ministerial-level bodies it had tried for this purpose.[27] Yet presciently and cautiously, Cadieux also noted three forces then pushing for a change: first, the growing public and government priority of environmental protection; second, the move to "third party determination" for boundary issues; and third, the willingness to accept binding arbitration.[28] The third change produced within a decade CUFTA, with its hard-won binational dispute-settlement panels for trade. The first and second changes were added half a decade later in the form of NAFTA, the companion NAAEC, and its institutional component of the CEC. All had Mexico as an equal third party and the environment as a value that was given an equal, and in some respects a priority, place.

The most pioneering of the many new NAFTA institutions created in 1994 was the Montreal-based CEC.[29] It featured an annual meeting of a ministerial council, a permanent, professional, stand-alone secretariat in Montreal, and an innovative Joint Public Advisory Committee to involve civil society in its work. It was thus born with some of the core features of the actual and evolving IJC, and those that many had recommended as IJC reforms in 1981 and beyond.[30] One was the ability to autonomously initiate independent investigations of environmental issues. NAAEC's article 13 provided the secretariat the power to "prepare a report on any other environmental matter related to the co-operative functions of [the] Agreement," although the Ministerial Council must be notified, can object by a two-thirds vote, and can prevent the report being made public.[31] Another feature was the two-thirds-majority voting provisions of the NAAEC that enabled Canada and Mexico to "out vote" the United States. The NAAEC also gave the CEC an expansive mandate, including bilateral, transboundary water, and other issues, and embedded its work in a modern ecosystem approach. Moreover, the core of NAFTA lay in its preambular principle that its trade and investment liberalization provisions had ecological enhancement as a goal.

Their similarity in a few core features suggests that the continental IJC was an active model and referent for the trilateral CEC of 1994. To be sure, the detailed historical evidence for this IJC-to-CEC pathway is unclear.[32] Yet the initiative, and the persistent, and ultimately successful, pressure to include environmental provisions in NAFTA and create the accompanying NAEEC and institutionalized CEC, came not from a highly reluctant Mexico but from the United States and Canada. The two countries' governments and their relevant components had by then acquired over eighty years of first-hand familiarity, experience, and overall satisfaction with their IJC.

Despite controversy surrounding the CEC's origins and early operation, and the ongoing efforts by national governments to control it, the CEC eventually succeeded in having an autonomous, equalizing impact on environmental outcomes within North America, and even on broader trade-environment and multilateral ones.[33] Moreover, the CEC by the end of 2018 had escaped criticism from US president Donald Trump, despite his antipathy to inherited trade agreements, to Mexico, to NAFTA, and to environmental regulations at home, on his borders, or around the world.

Surviving the Trump Stress Test

Given Trump's antipathy to environmental regulation, the start, in August 2017, of formal negotiations to modernize NAFTA, and uncertainty about US Congressional ratification of the revised Canada-US-Mexico Agreement in 2019, a key question is whether the NAFTA-NAEEC-CEC, and even the IJC, will survive, at least in their present form. It is easy to assume that with Mexico initially as the primary Trumpian target, the NAFTA regime could disappear, while leaving the remaining (and weaker) IJC as Canada's continental ecological insurance policy, along with CUFTA to cover trade. Yet Trump's persistent assault on environmental regulations and resources along and close to the Canada-US border, including in Alaska and the Arctic, call this easy conclusion into question. It is thus important to consider if and how Canada, with its DNVs of international institutionalism and continental environmentalism, along with the trade and migration component of openness, can survive and thrive amidst these Trumpian attacks. Trump's comprehensive assaults come simultaneously on the continental, trilateral, and global fronts, especially with his June 2017 decision to withdraw the United States from the UN's 2015 Paris Agreement on climate change control. Yet despite Trump's rhetoric on the Paris Agreement, in practice US representatives continue to participate and reportedly play a constructive role in climate change negotiations, including clean air and energy, as no member country can formally withdraw from the Paris Agreement until five years have passed from the day of its withdrawal submission. For the United States, this day comes only after the next US presidential election, leaving many to speculate that, should Americans elect a Democrat as president in 2020, the new administration will reverse Trump's decision and it will be as if the US had never left the Paris Agreement at all.

Since taking office in January 2017, Donald Trump's unrelenting assault on the environment has come in the form of presidential memoranda, executive orders, budget proposals, and the other instruments at his command. In contrast, since becoming Canada's prime minister in November 2015, Justin Trudeau has been strengthening environmental protection, including through the expansion of natural protected areas, although many environmentalists, Indigenous nations, and others criticize Trudeau's continuing support for fossil fuel development. Trudeau made climate change control one of his top priorities at the G7 Summit in Taormina, Italy, in May 2017, the Group of 20 (G20) Summit in Hamburg in July 2017, the G7 Summit he hosted in Charlevoix, Quebec, in June 2018, and the G20 Summit in Buenos Aires he attended in November 2018. Moreover, Canada's five priorities for the NAFTA renegotiation included "integrating enhanced environmental provisions to ensure no NAFTA country weakens environmental protection to attract investment, for example, and that fully supports efforts to address climate change."[34]

Despite the great and growing gap that has recently appeared between Canada and the United States, neither the CEC nor the IJC have yet been directly caught in the US-Canada crossfire. On the contrary, funding for the Great Lakes Restoration Initiative has thus far been maintained, if shakily, and in August 2018 Trump nominated three new commissioners to the IJC, while leaving several other posts in other key US institutions unfilled.[35] Further, the new US-Mexico-Canada Agreement and its new Agreement on Environmental Cooperation keeps the CEC intact, while also signalling potential advances in environmental protection, primarily for fisheries subsidies, and reiterating the long-standing position, seen as a Canadian priority, that weakening existing environmental provisions to create a more favourable environment for investors is "inappropriate."[36] Moreover, the powerful sub-federal constituency the IJC commands within the United States, grounded in the governors, legislators, industry, and non-governmental organizations of the Great Lakes states, could prevent some of Trump's assaults from the White House from taking effect. This politically powerful regional coalition already mobilized to counter the threatened cut in funding for the Great Lakes Restoration Initiative proposed in Trump's first budget (but those cuts are back on the table again). Within Washington, Canada's minister of the environment and climate change, Catherine McKenna, intervened directly with Scott Pruitt, the former US Environmental Protection Agency administrator, to the same end and to protect the shared continental environment more broadly.[37] Pruitt's successor, Andrew Wheeler, has since expressed, in words if not in practice, his support for the USMCA and its environmental components: "the new Environmental Cooperation Agreement expands on key elements of the USMCA and will enhance our efforts to improve air quality, reduce marine litter, and address other pressing environmental challenges."[38] Additionally, US and Canadian mayors assembled in the Great Lakes–St. Lawrence River Basin Compact Council have secured a compromise allowing the small US city of Waukesha, Wisconsin to withdraw a little water from Lake Michigan to replace the cancer-causing radium in its local supply, in return for an agreement to improve future reviews of applications for wider withdrawals.[39] While some caution is needed in recognition of the rollbacks made to environmental regulations thus far, with the pro-environment Democratic Party taking majority control of the US House of Representatives in the mid-term elections of November 2018, with that chamber having the constitutional power for appropriations, and with the traction and attention the Green New Deal has received, the IJC and CEC seem to be on safer financial ground.

Conclusion

Two weeks after scholars and policy-makers gathered at the University of Toronto in mid-June 1979 to assess the seventy-year success of the IJC, half a world away, in Tokyo, Japan, the leaders of Canada, the United States, and their G7 colleagues created the first regime to control climate change.[40] This challenge has grown far greater now. It is thus in their continental contribution to the global climate change challenge that the success of the IJC and CEC will, and should, ultimately be judged. For despite the creation of the UN Environment Program in the 1970s, there still is no World Environment Organization to resemble and act as a "little Hague" to govern the global environment, as the US secretary of state described his hopes for the IJC in 1913.[41] Nor is the IJC even close to becoming one, for its home continent, the broader region, or the world at large.

Indeed, the analysis in this chapter both confirms and qualifies the laudatory treatment that the IJC has long been given, particularly on the Canadian side. On the supportive side, the continuous, century-long strength of international institutionalism as a DNV of Canadian foreign policy is consistent with and perhaps a cause of Canada's initial desire to make the IJC a powerful body; Canada's success in securing equality between itself and the United States to offset the superior power of its southern neighbour; the inclusion of modest supranational features; its precedent for similar bodies in other fields such as the Permanent Joint Board on Defence; and, above all, its endurance amidst the many other Canada-US continental bodies that have either declined or disappeared. To this extent, the IJC thus legitimately serves as a model of the special partnership that has long been the dominant approach to how the Canada-US relationship does or should work.[42]

More specifically, the national affirmations at the highest level in the two countries' national policy addresses confirm that Canada's DNV of international institutionalism is strong and consistently stronger than that of the United States. The fact that neither country referenced the IJC in the national policy addresses of their new governments is consistent with the dominant view that the continuing success of the IJC has rested on its specialized, scientific, and depoliticized character, with its members working together in a relationship of trust to solve practical problems along a border in which the transboundary waters flow rather equally both ways.

However, this chapter also challenges the conventional wisdom, as does the introduction to this volume, that the IJC has been a pioneering model of ecological management that has inspired the global community as a whole. Indeed, there is little direct evidence that the IJC served as a referent for the more powerful, trilateral, regional environmental organization created in 1994, the CEC, let alone other global environmental-governance bodies further afield. To this day, even when Canadian prime ministers and foreign ministers highlight Canada's contribution to addressing critical global environmental challenges, such as climate change, they are silent on the contribution of the IJC. More profoundly, the absence of the IJC from this public discourse may flow from the fact that environmentalism has not been a durable DNV of Canadian foreign policy during the past century. Rather, affirmations of environmentalism in national policy addresses first appeared in the United States with Theodore Roosevelt, then disappeared for many decades, only to reappear in the 1960s with the United States again in the lead. As an international environmental institution, the best that can be said of the IJC's success is that the institution has survived when many other continental bodies disappeared. Moreover, it survived until it could be joined by the regional CEC.

Thus the IJC-CEC reform agenda at present must be a rather modest and defensive one. The immediate need is to have the IJC help protect the prosperity, health, and environment of those in Pennsylvania, Michigan, and Wisconsin who voted for Trump in 2016, and to do so in ways that make clear to them the important work done by the IJC and its supporters and stakeholders. As this could and should be done in the context of an integrated ecosystem approach, and amidst intense economy-environment-health links, the CEC could help the IJC here. This task requires the mobilization of US legislators and their voters in these three states and beyond to ensure that funds for Great Lakes water quality clean-up, the IJC, and the CEC survive Trump's erratic decision-making and relevant regulatory rollbacks.

Only then can the reform agenda turn to the ultimate challenge of protecting transboundary water from the impacts of deregulation, unsustainable resource extraction, and climate change. If it does, all North Americans should be guided by the wise words offered by a Republican US president when the BWT was being formed. In his 1909 State of the Union address, President Theodore Roosevelt began his lengthy passage on the world's forests, a crucial carbon sink and water-cycle regulator, by affirming the foundational environmental principle of intergenerational equity. He declared: "The climate has changed and is still changing. It has changed even within the last half century, as the work of tree destruction has been consummated." In describing the impact of deforestation on rainfall patterns, river flows and quality, Roosevelt concluded: "What has thus happened in northern China, what has happened in central Asia, in Palestine, in North Africa, in parts of the Mediterranean countries of Europe, will surely happen in our country if we do not exercise that wise forethought which should be one of the chief marks of any people calling itself civilized."[43]

Appendix A: Institutional References in Canadian and US National Policy Addresses

Leader	Throne Speech	% total words	State of the Union	% total words	Canada/ United States
J. Trudeau	4 December 2015	1.9 (32/1,695)	13 January 2016 B. Obama	0 (0/6,147)	+1.9
S. Harper	3 April 2006	3.1 (75/2,451)	31 January 2006 G. W. Bush	0 (0/5,435)	+3.1
P. Martin	2 February 2004	0 (0/6,270)	20 January 2004 G. W. Bush	1.0 (52/5,271)	-1.0
J. Chrétien	17 January 1994	5.0 (81/1,647)	25 January 1994 W. Clinton	8.5 (496/5,852)	-3.5
B. Mulroney	5 November 1984	9.6 (376/3,934)	25 January 1984 R. Reagan	1.2 (58/4,955)	+8.4
J. Clark	9 October 1979	12.0 (242/2,009)	23 January 1980 J. Carter	1.6 (57/3,467)	+10.4
P. E. Trudeau	12 September 1968	6.3 (188/2,963)	14 January 1969 L. B. Johnson	2.0 (80/4,135)	+4.3
L. B. Pearson	16 May 1963	15.3 (265/1,732)	14 January 1963 J. F. Kennedy	4.9 (262/5,396)	+10.4
J. Diefenbaker	14 October 1957	21.8 (292/1,337)	9 January 1958 D. Eisenhower	1.9 (93/4,929)	+19.9
L. St. Laurent	26 January 1949	15.4 (235/1,529)	5 January 1949 H. S. Truman	2.5 (86/3,398)	+12.9
Post-1945 Average	**9.0**		**Post-1945 Average**	**2.7**	**+6.3**
W. L. M. King	6 February 1936	20.0 (190/949)	3 January 1936 F. D. Roosevelt	0 (0/3,826)	+20.0
R. B. Bennett	8 September 1930	0 (0/140)	2 December 1930 H. Hoover	0 (0/4,537)	0
W. L. M. King	9 December 1926	16.7 (137/820)	7 December 1926 C. Coolidge	0 (0/10,310)	+16.7
W. L. M. King	8 March 1922	0 (0/1183)	8 December 1922 W. G. Harding	0 (0/5,749)	0
A. Meighen	26 February 1920	28.3 (260/920)	7 December 1920 W. Wilson	0 (0/2,706)	+28.3
R. Borden	15 November 1911	8.6 (61/707)	5 December 1911 W. H. Taft	2.0 (453/23,749)	+6.6
W. Laurier	20 January 1909	28.2 (307/1,087)	8 December 1909 T. Roosevelt	1.5 (297/19,418)	+26.7
Pre-1945 Average	**14.5**		**Pre-1945 Average**	**0.5**	**+14.0**
Combined Average	**11.3**		**Combined Average**	**1.5**	**+9.7**

Source: Throne Speeches: https://lop.parl.ca/ParlInfo/compilations/parliament/ThroneSpeech.aspx?Language=E. State of the Union addresses: http://www.presidency.ucsb.edu/sou.php.

Appendix B: Individual Institutional References in Canadian Prime Minister's First Speech from the Throne Post-1945

Institution	1949	1957	1963	1968	1979	1984	1994	2004	2006	2015	Total	2017
United Nations	3	2	1			1				1	8	3
NATO	1	1	2	1		2					7	3
ITO	1										1	
GATT	1										1	1
Commonwealth		4	1		1	2					8	1
Colombo Plan		1									1	
Bretton Woods				1							1	2
Kennedy Round				1							1	
Tokyo Round					1						1	
Uruguay Round							1				1	
NAFTA							1				1	1
UNESCO									1		1	
IMF											0	1
IBRD											0	1
WTO											0	3
UNGA											0	1
NORAD											0	2
G20											0	2
G7											0	2
OAS											0	1

Appendix B: Individual Institutional References in Canadian Prime Minister's First Speech from the Throne Post-1945, *continued*

Institution	1949	1957	1963	1968	1979	1984	1994	2004	2006	2015	Total	2017
APEC											0	1
La Francophonie											0	1
Arctic Council											0	1
ILO											0	1
Total	6	8	4	3	2	5	2	0	1	1	32	28

Notes: APEC = Asia Pacific Economic Co-operation; G20 = Group of 20; G7 = Group of Seven; GATT = General Agreement on Tariffs and Trade; IBRD = International Bank for Reconstruction and Development; ILO = International Labour Organization; IMF = International Monetary Fund; ITO = International Trade Organization; NAFTA = North American Free Trade Agreement; NATO = North Atlantic Treaty Organization; NORAD = North American Aerospace Defence Command; OAS = Organization of American States; UNESCO = United Nations Education, Social and Cultural Organization; UNGA = United Nations General Assembly; WTO = World Trade Organization; 2017 = Foreign Minister Chrystia Freeland's foreign policy speech on 6 June 2017; not included in total from 1949–2015.

Appendix C: Environmental References in Canadian and US National Policy Addresses

Leader	Throne Speech	% total words	State of the Union	% total words	Canada/United States
J. Trudeau	4 December 2015	15.6 (265/1,695)	13 January 2016 B. Obama	12.4 (764/6,147)	+3.2
S. Harper	3 April 2006	8.4 (206/2,451)	31 January 2006 G. W. Bush	4.8 (259/5,435)	+3.6
P. Martin	2 February 2004	12.1 (757/6,270)	20 January 2004 G. W. Bush	0.7 (37/5,271)	+11.4
J. Chrétien	17 January 1994	4.4 (72/1,647)	25 January 1994 W. Clinton	4.6 (269/5,852)	-0.2
B. Mulroney	5 November 1984	2.4 (95/3,934)	25 January 1984 R. Reagan	5.1 (251/4,955)	-2.7
J. Clark	9 October 1979	0 (0/2,009)	23 January 1980 J. Carter	4.5 (155/3,467)	-4.5
P. E. Trudeau	12 September 1968	6.7 (200/2,963)	14 January 1969 L. B. Johnson	1.3 (54/4,135)	+6.4
L. B. Pearson	16 May 1963	0 (0/1,732)	14 January 1963 J. F. Kennedy	1.3 (70/5,396)	-1.3
J. Diefenbaker	14 October 1957	0 (0/1,337)	9 January 1958 D. Eisenhower	0 (0/4,929)	0
L. St. Laurent	26 January 1949	0 (0/1,529)	5 January 1949 H. S. Truman	0 (0/3,398)	0
Post-1945 Average		5.0	**Post-1945 Average**	3.5	+1.5
W. L. M. King	6 February 1936	0 (0/949)	3 January 1936 F. D. Roosevelt	0 (0/3,826)	0
R. B. Bennett	8 September 1930	0 (0/140)	2 December 1930 H. Hoover	0 (0/4,537)	0
W. L. M. King	9 December 1926	0 (0/820)	7 December 1926 C. Coolidge	0 (0/10,310)	0
W. L. M. King	8 March 1922	0 (0/1,183)	8 December 1922 W. G. Harding	0 (0/5,749)	0
Meighen	26 February 1920	0 (0/290)	7 December 1920 W. Wilson	0 (0/2,706)	0
R. Borden	15 November 1911	0 (0/707)	5 December 1911 W. H. Taft	0 (0/23,749)	0
W. Laurier	20 January 1909	0 (0/1,087)	8 December 1909 T. Roosevelt	15 (2,899/19,418)	-15.0
Pre-1945 Average		0	**Pre-1945 Average**	2.14	-2.14
Combined Average		5.0	**Combined Average**	2.9	+0.05

Sources: Throne Speeches https://lop.parl.ca/ParlInfo/compilations/parliament/ThroneSpeech.aspx?Language=E. State of the Union addresses: http://www.presidency.ucsb.edu/sou.php.

Notes

1. Robert Spencer, John Kirton, and Kim Richard Nossal, eds., *The International Joint Commission Seventy Years On* (Toronto: Centre for International Studies, University of Toronto, 1981).

2. John Kirton, "The Intent and Evolution of the NAAEC-CEC 23 Years On" (paper prepared for the Joint Public Advisory Committee, Commission for Environmental Cooperation Forum on "NAFTA's Environmental Side Agreement: Assessing the Past, Looking Towards the Future," Chicago, 9 November 2017).

3. John Kirton, *Canadian Foreign Policy in a Changing World* (Toronto: Thomson Nelson, 2007), 20.

4. Ibid.

5. Maxwell Cohen. "The Commission from the Inside," in Spencer, Kirton, and Nossal, *The International Joint Commission Seventy Years On*, 106–123.

6. Roger Frank Swanson, *Intergovernmental Perspectives on the Canada-U.S. Relationship* (New York: New York University Press, 1978).

7. Kirton, *Canadian Foreign Policy in a Changing World*, 24–5.

8. Ibid.

9. Chrystia Freeland, "Chrystia Freeland on Canada's Foreign Policy: Full Speech," *Maclean's*, 6 June 2017, http://www.macleans.ca/politics/ottawa/chrystia-freeland-on-canadas-foreign-policy-full-speech/.

10. John Wendell Holmes and John Kirton, "Canada's New Internationalism," in *Canada and the New Internationalism*, ed. John Wendell Holmes and John Kirton (Toronto: University of Toronto Centre for International Studies, 1988); see also, Joe Clark, "Canada's New Internationalism," in Holmes and Kirton, *Canada and the New Internationalism*.

11. Cohen, "The Commission from the Inside," 108.

12. Ibid.

13. Kirton, *Canadian Foreign Policy in a Changing World*, 25.

14. Robert Bothwell, *The Penguin History of Canada* (Toronto: Penguin, 2006); Swanson, *Intergovernmental Perspectives on the Canada-U.S. Relationship*; for comparison, see William R. Willoughby, *The Joint Organizations of Canada and the United States* (Toronto: University of Toronto Press, 1979). See also Murray Clamen and Daniel Macfarlane, "The International Joint Commission, Water Levels and Transboundary Governance in the Great Lakes," *Review of Policy Research, Special Issue: Transboundary Natural Resource Governance in North America* 32, no. 1 (2015): 40–59.

15. Swanson, *Intergovernmental Perspectives on the Canada-U.S. Relationship*; see for comparison, Willoughby, *The Joint Organizations of Canada and the United States*.

16. John Carroll, "Patterns New and Old," in Spencer, Kirton, and Nossal, *The International Joint Commission Seventy Years On*.

17 Swanson, *Intergovernmental Perspectives on the Canada-U.S. Relationship*; Kal Holsti and Thomas Allen Levy, "Bilateral Institutions and Transgovernmental Relations Between Canada and the United States," in *Canada and the United States: Transnational and Transgovernmental Relations*, ed. Annette Baker Fox, Alfred O. Hero, Jr., and Joseph S. Nye, Jr. (New York: Columbia University Press, 1976).

18 John Kirton, "The Consequences of Integration: The Case of the Defence Production Sharing Agreements," in *Continental Community?* ed. Andrew Axline, James Hyndmann, Peyton Lyon, and Maureen Malot (Toronto: McClelland and Stewart, 1974), 116–36.

19 John Kirton and Raphael Fernandez de Castro, *NAFTA's Institutions: The Environmental Potential and Performance of the NAFTA Free Trade Commission and Related Bodies* (Montreal: Commission for Environmental Co-operation, 1997).

20 Kirton, *Canadian Foreign Policy in a Changing World*, 492.

21 Ibid., 23

22 Cohen, "The Commission from the Inside," 110.

23 Shawn McCarthy, "Canadians Value, Worry about Fresh Water: Poll," *Globe and Mail* (Toronto), 14 April 2017, https://www.theglobeandmail.com/news/politics/poll-says-canadians-value-worry-about-countrys-supply-of-fresh-water/article34344660/.

24 John Kirton and Ella Kokotsis, *The Global Governance of Climate Change: G7, G20 and UN Leadership* (Farnham, UK: Ashgate, 2015).

25 William T. R. Fox, *A Continent Apart: The United States and Canada in World Politics* (Toronto: University of Toronto Press, 1985)

26 Freeland, "Chrystia Freeland on Canada's Foreign Policy: Full Speech."

27 Marcel Cadieux, "The View from the Pearson Building," in Spencer, Kirton, and Nossal, *The International Joint Commission Seventy Years On*, 98–105.

28 Ibid., 103.

29 Kirton and de Castro, *NAFTA's Institutions*.

30 Spencer, Kirton, and Nossal, eds., *The International Joint Commission Seventy Years On*; Velma I. Grover and Gail Krantzberg, "Transboundary Water Management: Lessons Learnt from North America," *Review of Policy Research* 40, no. 1 (2015): 183–98.

31 Stephen Toope and Jutta Brunne, "Freshwater Regimes: The Mandate of the International Joint Commission," *Arizona Journal of International and Comparative Law* 15, no. 1 (1998): 273–87.

32 Pierre Marc Johnson and André Beaulieu, *The Environment and NAFTA: Understanding and Implementing the New Continental Law* (Washington DC: Island Press, 1995).

33 Don Munton and John Kirton, "North American Environmental Co-Operation: Bilateral, Trilateral, Multilateral," *North American Outlook* 4, no. 3 (1994): 59–86; John Kirton, "Ten Years After: An Assessment of the Environmental Effectiveness of the NAAEC," in *NAFTA @ 10: Trade Policy Research*, ed. John M. Curtis and

Aaron Sydor (Ottawa: Ministry of Public Works and Government Services Canada, 2006), 125–66; John Kirton, "Managing Canada's U.S. Relations Through NAFTA's Trade-Environment Regime," in *Bilateral Ecopolitics: Continuity and Change in Canadian-American Environmental Relations*, ed. Philippe Le Prestre and Peter Stoett (Aldershot, UK: Ashgate, 2006), 17–50; Alan Rugman, John Kirton, and Julie Soloway, *Environmental Regulations and Corporate Strategy: A NAFTA Perspective* (Oxford: Oxford University Press, 1999).

34   Chrystia Freeland, "Address by Foreign Affairs Minister on the Modernization of the North American Free Trade Agreement (NAFTA)," Government of Canada, 14 August 2017.

35   White House, "President Donald J. Trump Announces Intent to Nominate and Designate Personnel to Key Administration Posts," 27 August 2018, https://www.whitehouse.gov/presidential-actions/president-donald-j-trump-announces-intent-nominate-designate-personnel-key-administration-posts-2/.

36   Scott Vaughan, "USMCA Versus NAFTA on the Environment," *International Institution on Sustainable Development*, 3 October 2018, https://www.iisd.org/about/people/scott-vaughan/all.

37   Shawn McCarthy, "Catherine McKenna Seeks EPA head Scott Pruitt's Help to Restore Great Lakes," *Globe and Mail* (Toronto), 17 March 2017, https://www.theglobeandmail.com/news/politics/catherine-mckenna-seeks-epa-head-scott-pruitts-help-to-restore-great-lakes/article34334156/.

38   United States Environmental Protection Agency (EPA), "The United States, Mexico, and Canada Conclude Negotiations on a Trilateral Agreement on Environmental Cooperation," 30 November 2018, https://www.epa.gov/newsreleases/united-states-mexico-and-canada-conclude-negotiations-trilateral-agreement.

39   Brennan Doherty, "Canadian U.S. Mayors Drop Challenge to Lake Michigan Water Diversion," *Globe and Mail* (Toronto), 3 August 2017, https://www.theglobeandmail.com/news/national/canadian-us-mayors-drop-challenge-to-lake-michigan-water-diversion/article35880049/.

40   Kirton and Kokotsis, *The Global Governance of Climate Change: G7, G20 and UN Leadership*.

41   Cohen, "The Commission from the Inside," 106–123; John Kirton, "Generating Effective Global Environmental Governance: The North's Need for a World Environment Organization," in *A World Environment Organization: Solution or Threat for Effective International Environmental Governance?* ed. Frank Biermann and Steffen Bauer (Aldershot, UK: Ashgate, 2005), 145–72; Frank Biermann and Steffen Bauer, eds., *A World Environment Organization: Solution or Threat for Effective International Environmental Governance?* (Aldershot, UK: Ashgate, 2005).

42   Kirton, *Canadian Foreign Policy in a Changing World*, 272–4.

43   Theodore Roosevelt, "Eighth Annual Message," State of the Union address, *The American Presidency Project*.

The International Joint Commission: Continually Evolving Approaches to Conflict Resolution

Ralph Pentland and Ted R. Yuzyk

Although there are a number of disturbing signs that the past may not necessarily be prologue, historically, conflict and co-operation have always coexisted relatively successfully in the Canada-US water relationship. This reality prompted both nations to agree to the Boundary Waters Treaty (BWT) over a century ago, in 1909. The treaty has proven to be remarkably visionary in its scope. It provides for joint studies, and it establishes joint requirements for the approval of certain uses, obstructions, and diversions of waters that affect levels or flows in the other country. And despite the fact that it predated most modern environmental awareness, it contains a provision against any pollution that would result in "injury of health and property" on the other side of the boundary.

A key to the BWT's success was the establishment of the International Joint Commission (IJC). The commissioners, three from each country, are obliged to pursue the common interest of the two nations rather than a narrowly national perspective on boundary and transboundary issues. According to the BWT, the IJC has two primary functions: to approve remedial or protective works, dams, or other obstructions in boundary waters and set terms and conditions for the operation of those projects;

and to investigate and make recommendations on questions or disputes referred to it by either or both governments.[1]

In the introduction to this volume, the editors argue, quite correctly, that the BWT and IJC have not become widely accepted models for international water management outside North America. That is because the Canada-US situation is unique in at least two important respects. First, it is both hydrologically and politically relevant that Canada and the United States are both upstream and downstream states. Almost half of their shared waterways flow from the United States to Canada, and just over half flow from Canada to the United States.[2] Second, Canada and the United States share very common histories, cultures, and values across the border in specific regions. Clearly, the BWT-IJC model could not be directly transferred to, for example, the ten highly diverse nations that share the Nile River basin.

As both observers and participants in the work of the IJC over several decades, the authors of this chapter would suggest that the success of the commission relates both to the attributes directly embedded in the treaty, but also to a number of other attributes that have evolved over the past century plus, and which are continuing to evolve. In the following sub-sections we will explore ten such attributes to demonstrate that continual evolution by way of specific examples. For several of the attributes, we will refer the reader to more historical detail included in other chapters of this book. Even though the BWT and IJC models, per se, may not be directly transferrable to other continents, we would argue that many of the attributes described below would be helpful to others. Our ten specific attributes are:

1. Effective binational dispute resolution;
2. Facilitation of projects of mutual interest;
3. Consensus approach, but an ability to disagree where necessary;
4. Capacity to evolve and undertake preventative actions before an issue escalates;

5. Focus and persistence on holding governments accountable;
6. Continual learning leading to improved binational policies and practices;
7. A healthy mix of longevity and institutional flexibility;
8. Inclusive approach with the public and Indigenous Peoples;
9. Advancement of environmental performance through science; and
10. Standardization and improved data utility in boundary and transboundary basins.

While the IJC has had a long and distinguished record of achievement, there is no guarantee that it will be able to continue meeting all future challenges successfully. In the third section of this chapter, we will speculate briefly on a few of those probable challenges, and explore what additional attributes and approaches may have to be advanced to deal effectively with them.

Key Attributes and Examples

1. *Effective binational dispute resolution*

The first and perhaps most important attribute of the BWT and the IJC is *effective binational dispute resolution*. Our example is the early-twentieth-century St. Mary–Milk River dispute. (The history of this issue is discussed in more detail in chapter 4 by Timothy Heinmiller.) At the level of principle, allocation of the waters of the St. Mary–Milk basin was established within the BWT itself. But conflicts regarding the details of the allocation have been dealt with by the commission on several occasions.

The first Order of Approval regarding the actual allocation of water between the parties was developed by the IJC in 1921. A subsequent dispute in the early 1930s resulted in a re-examination of the order in the early 1930s. In 2003, the Montana governor again asked the commission to re-evaluate the order as well as the administrative procedures by which it is implemented. The commission did not reopen the order, but did appoint a task force to examine administrative matters.

There are a number of other ongoing issues that are keeping the IJC engaged. For example, there are certain infrastructure constraints impacting both countries that impede the effective utilization of their respective entitlements. A particular concern is the fact that storage, diversion, and conveyance facilities in Montana are in need of rehabilitation. Also, as climate change progresses, the commission is continually examining the impact of diminishing glaciers and snowpack in the upper watersheds on the seasonal pattern of run-off.[3]

2. Facilitation of projects of mutual national interest

Another important attribute of the IJC has been its *ability to facilitate projects of mutual advantage.* Our example is the IJC contribution to the development of the Columbia River Treaty (addressed in more detail in chapter 8 by Richard Moy and Jon O'Riordan). In 1944, the governments of Canada and the United States asked the IJC to study and report on the potential of the Columbia River system with respect to domestic water supply, navigation, hydro-power, flood control, irrigation, reclamation of wetlands, and conservation of fish and wildlife.[4]

In 1954, the International Columbia River Engineering Board reported to the IJC. Later that year, the commission made its recommendations to the two countries, outlining principles for calculating and distributing benefits that would result from the co-operative use of storages in Canada for the primary purposes of power generation and flood control in both countries. Formal bilateral negotiations began early in 1960, and by early 1961 Prime Minister Diefenbaker and President Eisenhower signed the Columbia River Treaty. In mid-1963, Canada and British Columbia signed a federal-provincial agreement regarding implementation, and in September of 1964, Prime Minister Pearson and President Johnson formally ratified the current treaty.

The CRT has a clause that it be opened for review after fifty years. Governments and operating entities are currently considering options for renegotiating the CRT. It is unclear at this time how any renegotiation of the treaty may turn out. But there are certain views already coalescing in the academic community. For example, in late April 2017, a group of twenty-four scientists and representatives of First Nations and tribes from Canada and the United States gathered at the University of California in Berkeley and made a number of interesting recommendations regarding the renegotiation, with an emphasis on science.[5] One of those recommendations suggested appointment of a binational science panel, which "could be modelled on the successful procedures developed by the International Joint Commission," to support both sovereign nations in treaty renegotiations.

3. *Consensus approach, but ability to disagree where required*

Consensus is the norm. But on a few rare occasions, the two sections of the IJC have been *unable to reach a consensus* on recommendations to forward to governments. One such example was the 1948 reference regarding existing and further uses, apportionment, conservation, control, and utilization of the waters of the Waterton and Belly Rivers, which flow from Montana into Alberta.[6]

The international issue arose when interests in Alberta proposed the construction of additional irrigation works that would permit use of the entire flow of the rivers. Canada did so based on the assumption, which turned out to be correct, that Montana was using no basin waters at the time, and had no practical prospects for using any into the foreseeable future. The United States requested the reference in an attempt to keep all future options open.

During the reference, the United States studied possibilities for diverting water via a tunnel from the two rivers for use in another basin. That so-called All-American Tunnel and Canal, which would have had to pass through a mountain, was ultimately deemed by US engineers to be infeasible. The United States then put forth a proposal that Canada should allow the United States to take its share from the Canadian portion of the nearby St. Mary River, with the cost of transportation to be borne by Canada.

Argumentation on both sides was highly legalistic. Counsel for Canada argued that article ii of the treaty was not applicable "when nature prevented actual diversion, and nothing in the treaty could give rise

FIGURE 17.1. Diversion system for St. Mary–Milk Rivers (International Joint Commission Photo Library).

to a claim such as that of the United States whereby the latter wanted Canada to surrender to it water in substitution for the other water which the United states could not use in the first place." Counsel for Alberta concurred, but also noted that the terms of reference suggested that any project recommended should be "practical in the public interest," and that in his opinion that meant not only "feasible" but "consistent with prudence and economy." Counsel for the United States argued that the Canadian position was against the spirit of the treaty and therefore "selfish." Counsel further argued that the all-American tunnel was feasible, and that it was not Canada's concern whether or not it was economically sound. In his view, if Canada was to use all of the water, that would represent "appropriation," not "apportionment."

The two sections of the commission were unable to reach a consensus, and reported separately to their respective governments in accordance with article ix of the BWT. Following appropriate consultations between the two countries, work continued on the diversion and irrigation project in Alberta. Periodically, Alberta continues to report to the IJC on operations of the resulting system.

The system in Alberta now diverts and interconnects water from the Waterton, Belly, and St. Mary Rivers (see Figure 17.1). It is the source of supply for downstream users along those rivers and for over 200,000 hectares of irrigation in the Magrath, Raymond, St. Mary River, and Taber Irrigation Districts. It is also the main supply for the 10,000 hectare Blood Tribe Irrigation Project, and supplies supplementary water for the United Irrigation District from the Waterton Reservoir.[7]

4. Capacity to evolve and undertake actions before an issue escalates

In 1997, the IJC recommended to the governments that a *watershed approach would help to better address current and emerging environmental issues* in a more holistic manner.[8] The governments responded favourably to this recommendation and an ongoing reference was provided to the commission in 1998 to develop and apply the concept that has become known as the International Watersheds Initiative (IWI). The commission under this reference has regularly reported back to governments on the progress that has been achieved through the IWI.[9]

The premise of the IWI is that local people, with focused scientific and financial assistance from IJC boards, are often best suited to resolve transboundary water issues before they escalate further into contentious binational issues. The success of the IWI is based on the application of seven principles that have become increasingly incorporated into IJC affairs over time:

1. An integrated ecosystem approach to transboundary water issues;
2. Binational collaboration;
3. Involvement of local expertise;
4. Public engagement;
5. Balanced and inclusive IJC board representation;
6. Open and respectful dialogue; and
7. An adaptive management approach.

FIGURE 17.2. Devils Lake annual peak water levels (International Joint Commission, 2015).

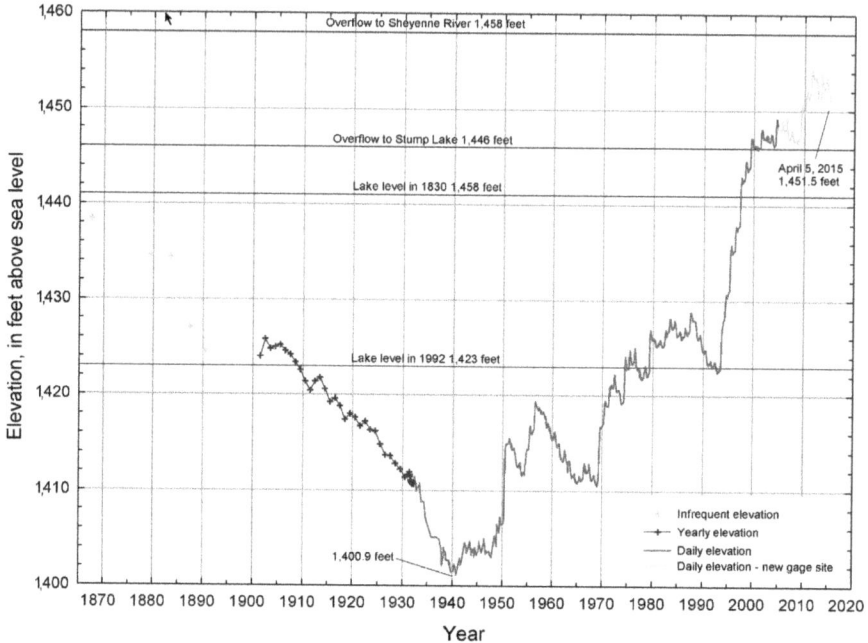

Central to this approach is the evolution of existing IJC boards to watershed boards with a broader and more inclusive mandate to achieve the above principles. To date, there are two officially designated watershed boards: the International St. Croix River Watershed Board (2007) and the International Rainy–Lake of the Woods Watershed Board (2013). A number of other IJC boards are in the process of achieving this status. The governments are generally supportive of this paradigm shift in board governance, but there are many factors that need to be considered and a dialogue needs to take place prior to making such a designation. Since 2010, there has been significant sustained funding from the two governments to support numerous IWI projects addressing transboundary issues before they escalate. Through the IWI, the commission has further increased its ability to deliver on its mandate to prevent and resolve transboundary environmental issues.

An example of how the IWI is averting a potential binational conflict relates to Devils Lake, North Dakota (discussed in chapter 7 by Norman Brandson and Allen Olson). Water levels in this closed lake system, within the Red River basin, have been rising over the last seventy-five years to the point where it is threatening to overflow and drain into the Sheyenne River, a tributary of the Red River (see Figure 17.2). In response to this, North Dakota proceeded with construction of an outlet to control the outflow. Canada was concerned that this would result in the introduction of new fish parasites and pathogens that could affect recreational fishing in the Red River system and commercial fishing in Lake Winnipeg.[10]

With IWI funding, a team of binational aquatic scientists were engaged to undertake a comprehensive, multi-year field survey of fish parasites and pathogens throughout the Red River basin. Their work concluded that the fish parasites and pathogens found in Devils Lake are ubiquitous, though much of North America's river basins and numerous vectors of entry to the basin were possible beyond the outflows from Devils Lake. Through this sound and accepted science this issue was able to be resolved.

5. Focus and persistence on holding governments accountable

Another attribute that we would like to briefly touch on is the treaty and commission's *ability to hold governments—federal, state, and provincial—accountable over long periods of time.* The specific example we would like to offer is Great Lakes–St. Lawrence diversions and consumptive use (also covered in chapter 9 by Murray Clamen and Daniel Macfarlane). Over half a century ago, public concern was already growing about a perceived trend toward lowering of Great Lakes levels and outflows, with potentially serious consequences for both economic interests and ecological integrity. These fears related to a number of factors, including increasing consumptive uses, embryonic climate change concerns, and dredging in connecting channels. But most critical from the public's perspective were proposals for both small-scale and massive southward diversions from the Great Lakes basin. Figure 17.3 shows the state of existing water diversions in the Great Lakes basin

The IJC initially became involved through a reference from the two federal governments, which was carried out between the mid-1970s and

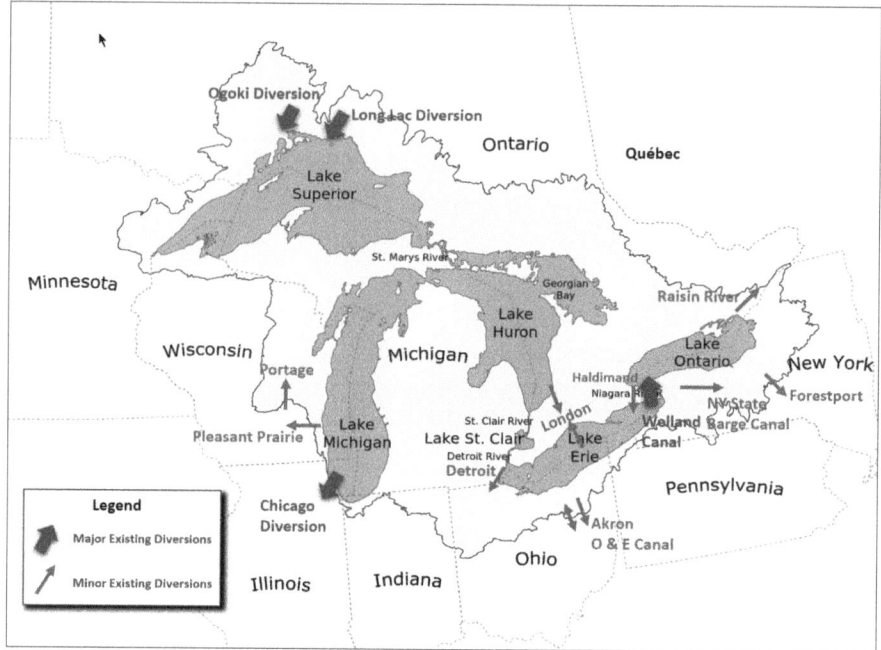

FIGURE 17.3. Existing diversions in the Great Lakes basin (Pentland and Mayer, 2015).

mid-1980s. In January of 1985, the commission released its first major report on the topic. That report called for improved information on consumptive use, and a process of notice and consultation before any new or changed diversions could be approved. The eight Great Lakes states and two Canadian provinces were closely involved in the reference, and even as the study was winding down, they had already negotiated the Great Lakes Charter, which they signed on 11 February 1985.

The federal governments and the IJC were brought back into the picture through another high-priority reference to the IJC in 1999. The IJC released its findings and recommendations in February of 2000.[11] By December of 2005, the Great Lakes governors and premiers signed the Great Lakes–St. Lawrence River Basin Sustainable Water Resources Agreement. Following ratification by the eight state legislatures and the US Congress, a parallel compact was signed into law by the US president in 2008.

In accepting the IJC's 2000 report, the two federal governments asked the commission to provide progress reports after three years and at ten-year intervals thereafter. The most recent progress report, released in 2015, was for the most part a good-news story.[12] No new inter- or intra-basin water transfer, which would have significant negative impacts on the ecological integrity of the Great Lakes, had been approved. The growth in consumptive use had been at least temporarily arrested, and international arrangements were largely in place to continue those positive trends. This continued reporting by the IJC on the progress being made by governments can be viewed as a good approach for holding governments accountable.

6. Continual learning leading to improved binational policies and practices

Prior to the early 2000s, the approach to addressing environmental issues was to undertake a large, costly study to evaluate a particular environmental concern or to conduct a periodic Review of Orders for a specific transboundary water regulating structure (i.e., dam). Considerable time and resources were expended on that particular effort, but once it was completed little or no resources were dedicated to effectively and efficiently implementing many of the recommendations. In many cases the recommendations were based on limited or disparate data, or on assumptions of how the environment might be impacted or the impacts of climate change that warranted a need for ongoing scientific evaluation.

The concept of an adaptive management approach to environmental issues was taking root in the water management field around this time and there was a proliferation of literature on this topic. Adaptive management is considered to be a planning process that provides a structured, iterative approach for improving actions through long-term monitoring, modelling, and assessment (see Figure 17.4). It is *built on continuous learning that leads to improved policies and practices over time.*

The need to implement an adaptive management approach in regulating water levels in the Great Lakes–St. Lawrence River system was a key recommendation of a major binational study.[13] The IJC embraced this recommendation and established a task force after the study to provide more details on its implementation, organizational framework, and the

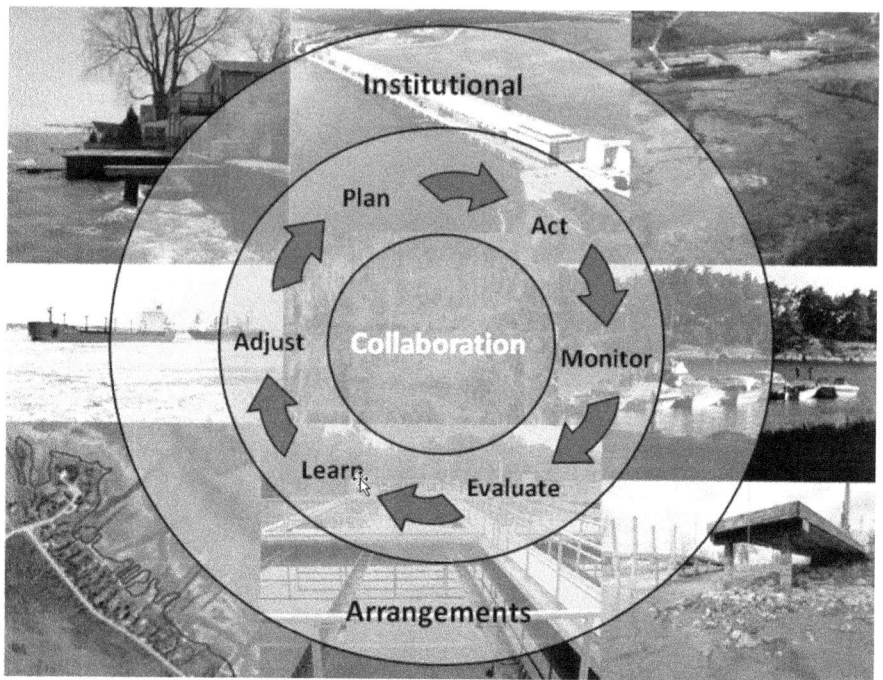

FIGURE 17.4. Adaptive management conceptual framework (International Upper Great Lakes Study Board, 2012).

resources that would be required. The task force's report was completed in 2013 and the commission provided its recommendations to governments in 2014.[14] This, in turn, resulted in the establishment of a Great Lakes–St. Lawrence River Adaptive Management Committee, which reports on an annual basis to the commission on their work plans.[15] Implementation of an adaptive management approach in the context of water-level regulation is now well established in the Great Lakes–St. Lawrence River system, and it is being pursued by IJC boards in other transboundary basins.

7. A healthy mix of longevity and institutional flexibility

The IJC has continuing jurisdiction over its Orders of Approval, and this is a mainstay of its mandate. Some orders date back a long way, such as the Lake Superior Order of Approval that goes back to 1914. As they are revised they are referred to as a Supplementary Order of Approval. There is an ongoing need to undertake a Review of Orders that have evolved over time that reflects the *longevity and institutional flexibility* of the work that the commission conducts.

Many orders are open-ended in terms of needing to be reviewed and go for long periods before a review is triggered, while others, like the Osoyoos Lake Order of Approval, has a clause that it be reviewed at a minimum of every twenty-five years.

There has been a conscious effort by the IJC and governments to review many of the long-standing orders to address evolving needs. The commission has adopted an ecosystem approach over the last twenty years that has resulted in factoring water use for the environment into any new regulation plans. The BWT has an order of precedence for water usage:

1. Sanitary/domestic,
2. Navigation, and
3. Power generation/irrigation.

To accommodate such considerations as the environment, the commission applies the principle that "no interest shall be unduly impacted" by the regulation plan. Other interests, such as riparians' (i.e., cottagers), have also been able to be accommodated under this principle.

In the last couple of decades we have seen regulation plans and subsequent orders being modified that reflect this new thrust, such as: Lake Osoyoos (2013), Lake Superior (2014), and Lake Ontario–St. Lawrence River (2016). A Review of Orders is currently underway for regulatory structures in the Souris and Rainy River basins.

8. Inclusive approach with the public and Indigenous Peoples

One of the key principles on which the commission operates is inclusiveness. It has been focusing on expanding its board membership over time to *include the public and Indigenous Peoples*, and to better engage all interests in its activities.

The past couple of decades have seen a marked change in the composition of the membership of many of the IJC boards. Previously, most of the boards were comprised solely of jurisdictional representatives from the various government agencies. This changed when the IJC presented a more inclusive vision of board governance in its landmark report to governments in 1997.[16] The governments responded favourably to the idea but wanted to see it undertaken in a thoughtful manner and in consultation with the key federal, state, and provincial jurisdictions that had long-standing membership on these IJC boards. They were particularly responsive to involving Indigenous Peoples and encouraged the IJC to reach out and engage them.

With the establishment of watershed boards (see section 4 on capacity to evolve) we are seeing this more inclusive approach being applied. We also are seeing an increase in the number of board members and numerous supporting committees or groups that help to address this broader mandate.

The International Rainy–Lake of the Woods Watershed Board that was established in 2013 provides a good example of this new governance model. The board when formed was comprised of 20 members: 11 federal, state, and provincial members; 3 from the American tribes, First Nations, and Métis; and 6 from the general public. It has since expanded to 24 members. In the interest of inclusivity, there are now 3 supporting committees or groups that report to the board: the International Water Levels Committee, the Community Advisory Group, and the Industry Advisory Group. A recent report to the IJC calls for further expansion with an Engineering and Scientific Support Committee and an International Adaptive Management Committee.[17] This is definitely a more complex organizational structure, but it does promote inclusiveness and reflects the broader focus on addressing transboundary water issues.

It is important to note that increased public, and to varying degrees Indigenous, participation is now commonplace on most of the IJC boards.

9. Advancement of environmental performance through science

The IJC relies upon shared information, establishing agreed-upon facts, and applying sound science in making its recommendations to governments. It is through this *credible and science-based approach that the commission has been able to make progress on addressing challenging binational environmental issues* and ensure the effective management of transboundary waters.

Numerous examples are available that elucidate this attribute, but we will focus on just one to make our point. The one that we have selected relates to restoring alewife, a small river herring that is important to the freshwater food chain and the transfer of marine-derived nutrients, to fishery management in the St. Croix River basin, and to the Passamaquoddy people in the region. This native fish's migration route and habitat were severely impacted when the State of Maine blocked their passage at the Woodland dam.

Recreational fishers believed that an increase in the alewife population in Spednic Lake, upstream of the Woodland dam, in the 1980s was the cause of the significant decrease in the smallmouth bass population in the lake. Through intensive lobbying the State of Maine introduced a bill to close off the fishways at the dam in 1995. Over the following years the commission worked with all the interests in the basin to develop a consensus on reopening the fishways and allowing the alewives access back to the upper parts of the basin. Central to building this case was the production of a number of scientific reports that made it clear that there were others factors that had resulted in the decline of the smallmouth bass population and that alewives were basically a scapegoat, or in this case a "red herring." The sound scientific finding and continued dialogue with all the interests made the difference in resolving this contentious environmental issue.

On 10 April 2013, the Maine Legislature passed, by an overwhelming majority, a bill to grant alewife unconstrained passage at Woodland and Grand Falls dam in the St. Croix River watershed. Ten days later, on April 22, the law came into effect.[18] Annual counts of alewife at a counting station near the mouth of the river have been slowly increasing, but numbers are a far cry from where they were in the 1980s. Nonetheless, it is a step in the right direction.

10. *Standardization and improving data utility in transboundary basins*

Undertaking water-related scientific work in transboundary basins has its challenges. Water data are collected using different methodologies and to

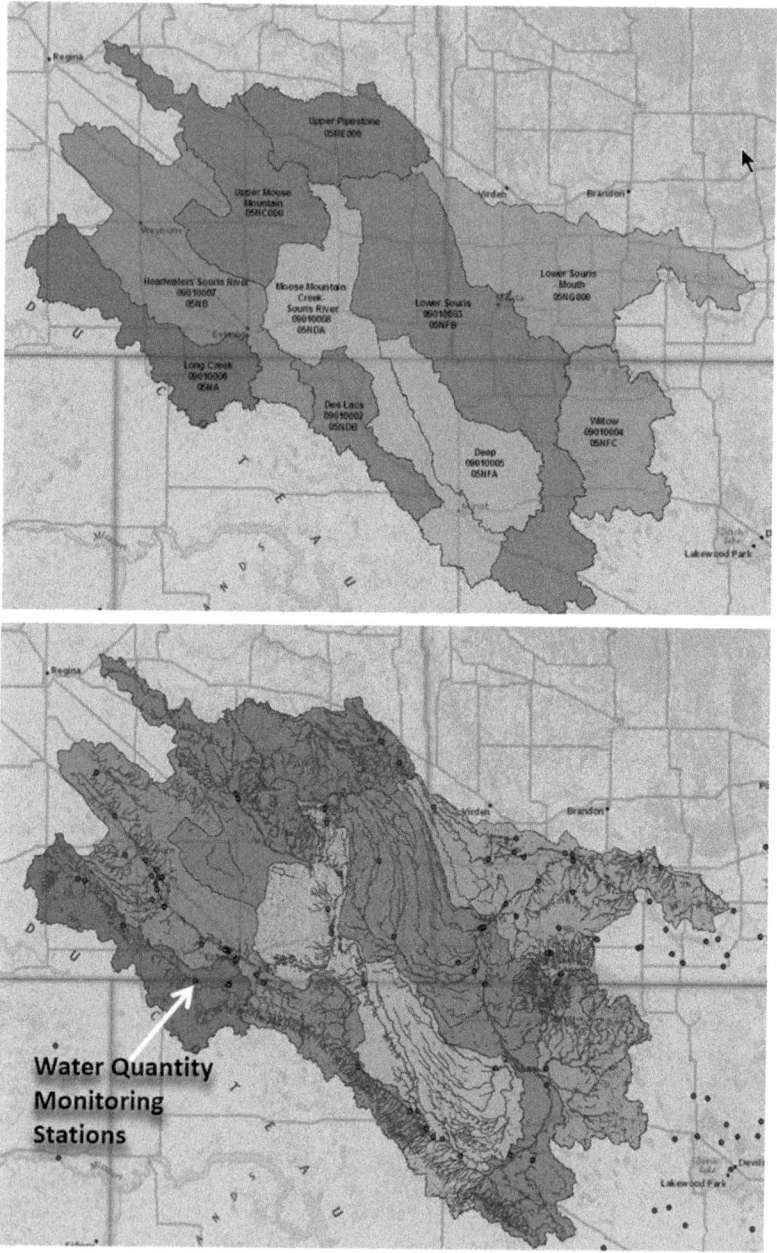

FIGURE 17.5. Harmonized data sets for Souris River basin (International Joint Commission, 2015).

varying standards in the two countries. Considerable time and funds are spent reconciling these essential data sets each time a binational study is undertaken. This prompted the commission to focus its effort on *standardizing and improving the data utility*, starting with the hydrographic data sets: river/stream/lake hydrographic features and associated drainage basin delineations.

After a 2006 pilot study produced a seamless, harmonized hydrographic data set in the St. Croix basin, the IJC determined that this work should be undertaken in all of the transboundary basins. This ambitious undertaking began in earnest in 2007 with the formation the binational Transboundary Hydrographic Data Harmonization Task Force with membership from the key federal agencies on both sides of the border that are responsible for the collection and stewardship of these important data. Figure 17.5 highlights the harmonized data sets created for the Souris River basin.

Over the past ten years this work has proceeded and harmonization of these data sets have been achieved in most of the transboundary basins, with the final thrust being on the Great Lakes–St. Lawrence River Basin. Current efforts are also focusing on the ongoing stewardship of these data with the key national agencies as these data sets become updated with improved higher-resolution data. The IJC is now beginning to reap the benefits of this extensive effort as these data sets are being applied in numerous binational studies involving hydraulic modelling and hydrological determination of net basin supplies to water quality assessments.

One example of the value of these harmonized data is the recently completed binational study of nutrient delivery in the Red–Assiniboine River basin.[19] In this study, harmonized hydrographic data formed an underlying geographical information system data layer. Efforts were also made to standardize the water quality data inputs and the sources of nutrients in the application of the SPARROW (water quality) model throughout the basin. This work provided the first comprehensive assessment of nutrient loading to Lake Winnipeg from the transboundary portion of this extensive basin. The information from this study is being used as part of ongoing effort to help reduce nutrient loading in the basin.

Looking Ahead

These ten attributes clearly reflect why the IJC has been so successful in addressing water issues and avoiding any major water conflicts along the 8,800 kilometre Canada-US border, 40 per cent of which comprises shared waters. These examples highlight the efforts that have gone on from coast to coast over the past fifty years. The forward-looking BWT is responsible for much of the success story, but the commission's ability to interpret the treaty in the context of changing times, to continually evolve, and to nonetheless remain pertinent to the governments is equally remarkable. As one looks around the world there are few, if any, other examples of such an effective transboundary water management governance relationship among different nations.

The principles outlined in the BWT have generally stood the test of time, and they continue to be as relevant today as they were a century ago.[20] However, both the water and water-related issues facing the two nations, as well as the conventional wisdom regarding governance, have continually changed. Consequently, the attributes needed to address them have had to evolve, and will no doubt continue to do so.

Early in the twentieth century, most issues related to water apportionment and water level and flow regulation, and the capacity to deal with them, increased exponentially, especially related data-collection and the sciences. In the middle of the last century, the emphasis of governments and the IJC was in support of water resource development and projects of mutual advantage. In the early 1970s this focus shifted to a large extent to addressing common environmental problems, with an ecosystem approach gaining prominence by the 1990s. In more recent years, there has been an attempt to bring economic and environmental considerations together under the banner of sustainable development. A key response in the Canada-US context has been the International Watersheds Initiative highlighted in this chapter and which focuses on addressing water-related issues in a holistic manner in a transboundary basin.

Prognostication is always a hazardous undertaking. However, there are certain trends that are now well established, both globally and in North America, that would suggest a challenging future from both institutional and water issues perspectives. One institutional trend is toward globalization of the world economy, which may or may not restrict the ability of individual nations to preserve their water resources. A second, perhaps related, trend is toward decentralization of water management decisions and a consequent attempt to build a more distributed capacity in both countries. A part of that second trend has also been a concerted effort to more fully involve the public and Indigenous Peoples in management processes.

A current troubling issue has been a steadily declining governmental-scientific capacity in both countries. This decline is compromising the IJC's ability to protect water resources because the commission relies heavily on credible scientific experts within governments to assist in binational fact-finding efforts and scientific assessments.

From an issues perspective, there is little doubt that our shared waters will increasingly be affected by global issues that are likely to intensify conflicts in shared waters. These include, for example, global energy security, climate change, exponentially escalating demands for non-renewable resources, intensifying environmental health issues, potentially widespread food or water shortages, and possibly even environmental refugees.

We would like to highlight three specific "wild cards" that could be particularly challenging in the Canada-US context in the coming decades:[21]

1. Uneven water demands: One example is the Great Lakes, specifically the Chicago Diversion, which is exempt from the state-provincial agreement prohibiting removals of water from the Great Lakes basin. A second example is in the Red River basin, where a 2005 US Bureau of Reclamation study included the option of diverting water from the shared Lake of the Woods to the US portion of the basin. Yet a third example is in the St. Mary–Milk region of the Great Plains, where US interests have been demanding a re-examination of a long-standing international water apportionment arrangement.

2. International trade agreements: The text of a proposed revised NAFTA (or USMCA) is currently being considered by the legislative authorities in Canada, the US and Mexico. The current NAFTA, as well as domestic legislation and policy in both countries discourages

inter-basin transfers of water that may damage ecological integrity, and the proposed USMCA would not change that fact. Nevertheless, unforeseen future changes in trade law, combined with other evolving issues, could conceivably influence that situation in such a way as to strain bilateral water relations.

3. Climate Change: The US population continues to migrate southward and westward, particularly to coastal regions and other parts of Texas and California. This shift in population puts citizens on a collision course with the storms, rising sea levels, and extended droughts that are associated with global warming. It is not impossible to imagine a time when the US Southwest becomes desperate for water, and political pressures intensify greatly for large-scale inter-basin transfers from the Northern Tier states, and eventually even from Canada.

Any or all of these broader issues could translate into increased conflict in boundary and transboundary basins. Nevertheless, we would not expect any appetite to renegotiate the generally successful BWT itself. Rather, we would expect the approaches to conflict resolution to continue to evolve as necessary to meet any new challenges, as they have over the past century.

With those considerations in mind, we would suggest that the IJC needs to continue focusing on its many positive attributes. In that regard, we would especially endorse further progress on the IWI. What is needed in many transboundary basins, and will increasingly be needed in the future, is the approach applied by the IWI that recognizes the complex interplay between socio-economic and environmental factors, quantity and quality concerns, and various segments of society, including Indigenous Peoples.

Also, as we have seen in the Columbia River example, society may very well begin insisting that more restorative approaches move to the forefront. Citizens in the basin—and we suspect in many other transboundary basins—are beginning to demand that natural assets be used and managed much more sustainably from an ecological-integrity perspective, that non-structural approaches be more seriously considered, and that more consideration be given to the potential of renewable energy sources. In the end, sustaining and rebuilding natural resilience may be our only real defence against the impacts of climate change. The kind of credible, binational fact-finding and sound science for which the IJC is well-known will be crucial to future successes.

While it may be controversial initially, the IJC may also have to become less constrained in expressing its views on global and continental issues such as climate change and chemicals management. Many of the continental and worldwide advances in the water sciences over the past century took place because of Canada-US efforts in shared waters. But simply letting that happen by osmosis may be insufficient in the future. A more proactive stance would be to engage with other regions around the world to advance new ideas and concepts. And finally, regarding science capacity, the IJC may have to begin looking well beyond North America for guidance if government capacity on this continent continues to decline. Other parts of the world are now surpassing North America in some respects. For example, many knowledgeable observers believe we have much to learn from the overall European approach to water management as well as to chemicals management.[22]

Notes

1. Canadian and the United States Governments, "Boundary Water Management, Two country contribution to the U.N. Water Conference Mar Del Plata, Argentina" (Ottawa: Government of Canada, 1977).

2. Noah Hall, "Transboundary Pollution: Harmonizing International and Domestic Law," *University of Michigan Journal of Law Reform*, 40 (2007): 681–746.

3. Ralph Pentland, "Comments on the International St. Mary–Milk Rivers Administrative Measures Task Force Report" (Toronto: Munk Centre, University of Toronto Occasional Paper, 2006).

4. R. Sandford, D. Harford, and J. O'Riordon, *The Columbia River Treaty: A Primer* (Victoria, BC: Rocky Mountain Books, 2014).

5. Berkeley CRT Science Advisory Group, "New Science Requirements in Support of a Modernized Columbia River Treaty" (Berkeley: University of California, Berkeley, 2017).

6. Multiple Authors, "Summaries of Dockets Numbers 1–72" (Ottawa and Washington: International Joint Commission), 177–80.

7. Alberta Government, *Water Management Operations* (Edmonton, AB: Government of Alberta, 2004).

8   International Joint Commission (IJC), *The IJC and the 21st Century* (Ottawa and Washington: IJC, 1997).

9   IJC, *Transboundary Watersheds* (Ottawa and Washington: IJC, 2000); IJC, *A Discussion Paper on the International Watersheds Initiative* (Ottawa and Washington: IJC, 2005); IJC, *The International Watersheds Initiative: Implementing a New Paradigm* (Ottawa and Washington: IJC, 2009); IJC, *The International Watersheds Initiative: From Concept to Cornerstone of the International Joint Commission* (Ottawa and Washington: IJC, 2015).

10 International Red River Board, Aquatic Ecosystem Committee, *Devils Lake–Red River Basin Parasite and Pathogens Project: Qualitative Risk Assessment Report, Report to the International Joint Commission* (Ottawa and Washington: IJC, 2011).

11 IJC, *Protection of the Waters of the Great Lakes* (Ottawa and Washington: IJC, 2000).

12 Ralph Pentland and Alex Mayer, *Review of the International Joint Commission's Report on Protection of the Waters of the Great Lakes* (Ottawa and Washington: IJC, 2015).

13 International Upper Great Lakes Study Board, *Lake Superior Regulation: Addressing Uncertainty in Upper Great Lakes Water Levels, Report to the International Joint Commission* (Ottawa and Washington: IJC, 2012).

14 International Great Lakes–St. Lawrence River Adaptive Management Task Force, *An Adaptive Management Plan for Addressing Extreme Water Levels, Report to the International Joint Commission* (Ottawa and Washington: IJC, 2013).

15 Great Lakes–St. Lawrence River Adaptive Management Committee, *Annual Work Plan Fiscal Year 2016, Report to the International Joint Commission* (Ottawa and Washington: IJC, 2015); Great Lakes–St. Lawrence River Adaptive Management Committee, *Annual Work Plan Fiscal Year 2017: Report to the International Joint Commission* (Ottawa and Washington: IJC, 2016).

16 IJC, *The IJC and the 21st Century*.

17 International Rainy and Namakan Lakes Rule Curves Study Board, *Managing Water Levels and Flows in the Rainy River Basin, Report to the International Joint Commission* (Ottawa and Washington: IJC, 2017).

18 International St. Croix Watershed Board, *Alewives and the IJC—A Short History: Report to the International Joint Commission* (Ottawa and Washington: IJC, 2013).

19 G. A. Benoy, R. W. Jenkinson, D. M. Robertson, and D. A. Saad, "Nutrient Delivery to Lake Winnipeg from the Red-Assiniboine River Basin," *Canadian Water Resources Journal* 40, no. 3 (2016): 429–47.

20 Ralph Pentland and Adele Hurley, "Thirsty Neighbours, a Century of Canada-U.S. Transboundary Water Governance," in *Eau Canada: the Future of Canada's Water*, ed. Karen Bakker (Vancouver: UBC Press, 2007): 163–84.

21 Ralph Pentland and G. W. Sherk, "Giving Our Water Away? Canadian and U.S. Water Issues in an Era of Uncertainty, Law of Water Resource Utilization: Impact of Federal Environmental Laws" (American Bar Association, forthcoming).

22 Ralph Pentland and Chris Wood, *Down the Drain: How We Are Failing to Protect our Water* (Vancouver: Greystone Books, 2013).

Conclusion

Murray Clamen and Daniel Macfarlane

In the Conclusion to their 1958 book *Boundary Waters Problems of Canada and the United States*, L. M. Bloomfield and G. F. FitzGerald wrote: "There is no doubt that the International Joint Commission has successfully discharged the high functions entrusted to it by the Boundary Waters Treaty. It has acted successfully as judge, adviser and administrator for two great neighbours during a period of unparalleled expansion when conflicts of important interests were bound to arise. In playing its triple role the Commission has developed techniques of continuous consultation which are a model for the world."[1] More than twenty years later, in the 1981 volume *The International Joint Commission Seventy Years On*, Kim Richard Nossal wrote in the concluding chapter: "It is inevitable that the IJC with its seventy-year history of problem-solving will be used to point to the success and pitfalls of utilizing bi-national mechanisms to bring to Canadian-American transboundary relations a certain civility and, over the long haul, tranquility."[2]

Both volumes were framed by their respective "issues of the day." In the case of Bloomfield and Fitzgerald, the St. Lawrence Seaway and Power Project and Niagara remedial works were just being completed, while the "unfinished tasks which stagger the imagination" included the Columbia, the Passamaquoddy, and, ultimately, the rivers of the far Northwest. For *The International Joint Commission Seventy Years On*, there were of course important issues involving the Great Lakes–St. Lawrence River basin in terms of water levels and water quality (1972 Great Lakes Water Quality Agreement) and also, for some, the question of long-range airborne acid precipitation, which "could have far-reaching implications for both the mandate of the Commission and its effectiveness"[3]—something that really never came to pass.

So here we are, almost forty years after that seventieth birthday, more than a century after the creation of the Boundary Waters Treaty (BWT) and the establishment of the International Joint Commission (IJC), trying to take another objective look back at, and consider future prospects for, this remarkable institution and the 1909 treaty that created it to provide a regime for managing transboundary and border waters between Canada and the United States. In this concluding chapter we want to reflect on what the various authors have written and also to talk about the future of the IJC. We are fortunate that the preceding chapters in this volume have been written by noted scholars, experts, and practitioners who have presented an array of viewpoints, including both the successes and failures of the organization, from which to draw conclusions. Granted, we should add the caveat that the arguments presented in this conclusion reflect only our personal opinions as co-authors of this chapter and co-editors of this collection. What do the contributions that make up this volume collectively teach us about the past of the IJC, and what are the conclusions we should draw about where it goes in the future? What will be key to the success of the IJC moving forward? Is the greatest threat to the future of the IJC likely that the Canadian and American governments will ignore it? If so, what does the IJC need to do and provide to remain, or become more, relevant?

Structure and Governance

One way to measure the success of the IJC and the BWT is the number of references and applications it has dealt with and the results, keeping in mind the overall goal or purpose is to "prevent and resolve disputes." In the case of applications it would not just be the number but also the success (or not) of projects that were applied for, built, and operated. In the case of references, it would be the number of references sent to the IJC from governments, the recommendations made by the commissioners, and then, ultimately, whether these recommendations were in fact accepted and implemented by either or both governments. While that may seem relatively straightforward, this kind of reference "score card" does not officially exist, so the only answers are for the most part impressionistic. The current perception is that most but not all IJC recommendations are accepted and acted on by governments. Another measure is the administrative responsibilities attached to the St. Mary–Milk Rivers apportionments (see the chapter by Heinmiller). Here the results appear to be quite good, except if you are in Montana, which continues to raise arguments against the current formulae. Still another measure is the ongoing recommendation and implementation cycle under the Great Lakes Water Quality Agreement (GLWQA) and its various renewals since 1972. This standing reference, dealing with one of the world's more important and precious resources, occupies about half of all the IJC's time and workload and involves a great many bureaucrats and others, yet it is difficult to determine the success or not of the GLWQA over the past almost fifty years (see the chapters by Read, Krantzberg, and Van Nijnatten and Johns).

But we also need to keep in mind that simply tallying up the number of references or applications can be misleading since the two countries tend to not send references or applications to the IJC if it doesn't appear that this is likely to produce an acceptable result for those involved. If the federal and sub-federal governments aren't in agreement about invoking the IJC and don't think utilizing the commission will produce a mutually agreeable outcome, then they simply don't utilize the IJC. Thus, good prospects for success are usually key to explaining the IJC's track record when it comes to crafting references and approving/disapproving applications that both countries are satisfied with. But, as noted earlier, this can also skew the so-called success rate of the IJC—that is, if a matter is likely to break down along national lines, then it is unlikely that both nations will agree to take the issue to the commission.

The procedural and institutional consequences of the IJC and the BWT are also relevant. For example, the IJC has evolved from a body that almost always used to call on government bureaucrats to help with references and applications into one that now seconds experts from various jurisdictions outside government such as universities, the private sector, First Nations and Tribes, non-government organizations, and civil society. And these various disciplines as well as their local knowledge have created a tremendous pool of talent from which commissioners can draw when looking for suitable candidates for IJC boards, task forces, initiatives, etc. Moreover, these members, some of whom serve for many years consecutively, form bonds with their counterparts in other jurisdictions and these spill over into areas far beyond the work of the IJC. This incalculable benefit continues to grow each year the IJC makes new appointments and, coupled with the dictum that members operate in "their personal and professional" capacity while they seek the best science-based objective advice, creates a very powerful tool that governments can call on.

Of course, it wasn't always this way—the early IJC certainly did not have these important principles and ways of working to guide it—but it evolved and, as one commentator put it, succeeded "out of sheer luck."[4] The IJC started off as an agreement between two countries aimed at the most efficient exploitation of their shared natural resources—the BWT was a conservationist agreement with a dash of preservationist mindset thrown in. The IJC's first few decades, when it was finding its feet and evolving, reflect that. In the middle third of the twentieth century, the IJC was generally captured by an engineering mentality that saw nature as something to be dominated and controlled—granted, this reflected the prevailing ethos in North American society during this period—resulting in megaprojects and hard-path water infrastructures that are now considered ecologically dubious.[5] Ironically, the first decades of the Cold War were also the IJC's heyday in terms of its prominence and influence—as we have seen, environmental diplomacy was vitally important to Canadian-American relations, and the two national governments took a strong interest and direct involvement in the IJC's activities (though the bilateral agreements on the St. Lawrence Seaway, Niagara Falls, and the Columbia River all took place outside the IJC). But this also resulted in the overt politicization of the IJC for an extended stretch, during which chairmen such as General A. G. L. McNaughton and Roger McWhorter prioritized their respective nationalist interests.

However, the megaproject era also overlapped with the studies that would produce in the 1970s what is arguably the IJC's greatest success: the Great Lakes Water Quality Agreements. Although the IJC had paid attention to water (and air) pollution since the early twentieth century, it was not until the post–Second World War period that the commission really began to take a leading role in addressing pollution (or perhaps it was more the case that the governments now took pollution concerns more seriously). It shouldn't necessarily be surprising that, once the commission became preoccupied with efforts that tended to interfere with industrial and economic expansion (and one of its main consequences—pollution), rather than fostering this expansion, the national governments have marginalized the IJC by avoiding it, reducing its funding, and ignoring its recommendations. Moreover, since the 1980s the IJC's role seems to have been reduced by the proliferation of a range of other transboundary governance mechanisms. But even if the IJC is sometimes ignored or not utilized, it often still plays an important supporting role by providing scientific knowledge and legitimacy to the policy process. Indeed, the IJC's ability to create, gather, synthesize, harmonize, mobilize, and share environmental and scientific information has only increased since the 1980s, and its reports, findings, and recommendations carry weight precisely because the IJC is widely perceived as objective, impartial, and expert.

Personnel

One can argue that it is IJC board and task force members who are in fact the real success of the IJC. Why is this so when it is commissioners who sign reports and orders and IJC staff that assists them? One of the editors of this volume served as a staff member himself for over three decades, and he can attest to the importance of commissioners and their advisers; however, if one were handing out awards for accomplishment, the members of IJC boards should be given them first. They more often than not have to find time to devote to IJC work when their employers (whoever they are) cannot sacrifice them from their day jobs. They have to spend countless hours travelling to and from meetings, often away from family, analyzing data, writing reports, and negotiating under often very difficult circumstances in tight time frames on recommendations that many times are not in conformity with the desired outcome of their respective government. This calls for real professionalism and integrity and the IJC is fortunate to have found people ready and willing to serve under such trying conditions. Without their science-based judgment, the

IJC commissioners would have little on which to base their findings, conclusions, and recommendations. Why are people willing to serve the IJC under such conditions? Certainly not because of the money—no one gets rich working for the IJC. Possibly because of the prestige—one can say they were appointed to this "illustrious" international body and put that on their resume. Some may actually want to grow professionally and take on a new challenge. Some may be altruistic and see working on Canada-US issues as being very important, especially in these days of heightened environmental sensitivity. Whatever the reason, the IJC is truly fortunate that it has continued to find good people to serve.

That is not to say that the character, background, and expertise of the appointed commissioners themselves are unimportant. While there have been few studies of this issue, aside from Stephen Brooks's work, first-hand experience would tend to suggest some relevant points.[6] The best commissioners (however that may be defined) appear to be those who are the most willing to take an open mind to what they are being called upon to adjudicate and who have, by way of their background and character, a definite willingness and even desire to seek solutions in "the common interest." Commissioners, just like the board members they appoint, operate in their personal and professional capacities and, on their appointment, take an oath to uphold the BWT. They are certainly aware of their respective governments' positions on most if not all matters before the commission and while that may guide them it does not dictate the decisions they make and the consensus they strive for.

One of the editors had the opportunity to interview some commissioners in 2012 on matters surrounding their appointments, IJC administrative issues, the successes and failures of the commission during their tenures, and key challenges ahead. Their responses present a very cogent and perceptive view that can only be obtained from having served as a commissioner. All agreed that IJC appointments are important and that governments should show care in selecting a commissioner. While certain training (legal, scientific, engineering) may be helpful, everyone pointed to other characteristics, such as being earnest and seriously dedicated to the task and concept of the IJC. Good commissioners should have the ability to ask questions, listen carefully, and talk last! Interpersonal skills and lateral thinking abilities were also mentioned. Most felt the current administrative architecture (secretariats, board structure, lead commissioners, public involvement, etc.) worked well and they opposed significant changes. The "IJC personality" has evolved over the years and is neither the chief problem nor the solution in dealing with any internal issues. Everyone agreed it will be vital to preserve the independence of the commission at all costs and that collegiality and consensus are critical. While it is healthy to make some board and task force appointments outside government circles, it is important to preserve balance so that IJC recommendations can filter back to government decision-makers and be more easily implemented. On the question of IJC relevance and importance heading into the future, everyone believed the commission will be more relevant in the coming century than the previous one.

It does not appear that any particular educational background or profession has much influence on commissioners' expertise and their ability to make decisions and work collegially with their counterparts, both from their own country and from their neighbour. And collegiality is another important point often not realized. When six people who are appointed (sometimes all at the same time but more often staggered) are asked to work together "in the common good" of both countries on water issues and broad environmental ones, it does take a special kind of person to really make this work. They must be open-minded, able to read carefully and critically and to consider scientific and other relevant facts, be open to suggestions, be willing to work with and listen to the public, be innovative yet mindful of useful precedents, and above all considerate of fellow commissioners' views and opinions. If someone has these characteristics then they likely have the makings of a good commissioner. Interestingly enough, even if not all commissioners fit this unique mould (and there have been some commissioners who have definitely not fit this mould), the IJC still manages to survive and, more often than not, to thrive. And that is due to another important part of the equation—the IJC's cadre of advisers.

In the early years of the IJC up until about the 1960s, the number and expertise of its Canadian and US Section staff in Ottawa and Washington was quite limited. In the 1970s, however, Canadian Section chair Maxwell Cohen, deciding that commissioners needed a broader base from which to draw advice than just board members and their own experience, started to expand the number and types of positions in the Ottawa office. This was met by quite a bit of criticism from the US Section, fellow Canadian commissioners, and Canadian government bureaucrats who did not see such a need. Nevertheless, Cohen persisted and managed to secure funds for several new positions. Eventually, the US Section followed suit—creating the fear among several IJC watchers of an IJC bureaucracy that would not be helpful to the overall process.

And yet now, some forty years later, a strong cadre of advisers in both sections is, and will continue to be, helpful and important. For one thing, it provides continuity and helps with the education of newly appointed commissioners when they can rely on staff who have served the organization well for so many years. Although IJC commissioners take an oath to be objective and to prioritize the wider interest, realistically an IJC commissioner is at least in part a type of appointed politician; thus, having trained and expert staff who are more removed from the pressures of partisanship is important and useful. Secondly, it has allowed, and likely will continue to allow, the IJC to take on more new work and to experiment with new techniques (GIS, computer modelling, shared vision models, etc.). Finally, it helps commissioners with outreach and liaison with governments and other players when knowledgeable and experienced advisers are in the offices and trusted by government bureaucrats and board members.

Indeed, this notion of "trust" is so important it needs to be dealt with separately. One of the co-editors of this book initially envisaged this volume being called "A similar letter, etc." because this phrase enshrined for him the notion of trust. A word of explanation is perhaps in order. When advisers in both national section offices draft letters or other IJC documents outlining a certain decision, the ending almost always says: "A similar letter has been sent to the Department of Foreign Affairs/State Department by the Secretary of the Canadian/US Section of the Commission." This signifies that both governments are being sent this identical communication. But rather than write all this out in every draft the adviser would typically put at the end "A similar letter, etc." to signify this trust—not only that the drafts would be identical when finally agreed to, signed, and sent, but that one could trust the other section to do so every time. Without this trust, which had to pervade the entire organization from top to bottom, likely nothing meaningful would ever get done.

One should also realize that the IJC is, as one adviser often said, just "one of the tools in the governmental toolbox." Governments can and often do choose which process to use depending on the issue and a wide variety of political and other factors. Sometimes the confidence the governments have in the IJC at any given time (whether it is the commissioners themselves or other factors) precludes using that institution, even if it appears to be the best tool for the job. Sometimes a sub-federal jurisdiction like a state or province may distinctly say it does not want to involve the IJC, even if both federal governments do. As we have seen, British Columbia tends to be wary of the IJC, while Ontario and New York State are sub-federal jurisdictions likely to seek IJC involvement. Sometimes the timing is off, or the cost is too high, or the proposed reference has not evolved to the point where good scientific data can be obtained.

Qualities

At the very least, the IJC has made a valuable, tangible contribution to economic prosperity (for some more than others) and environmental security (again, in selective ways) in North America, and it continues to offer a much-needed diplomatic safety valve for Canada-US relations. Some have speculated about whether the IJC model could be applied to other Canada-US natural resource questions or to other countries with boundary/transboundary issues—with the quotation opening this chapter just one such example. The authors included in this volume are of different viewpoints about whether the IJC, or certain aspects or programs of the commission, are replicable across the globe, and they differ in their optimism about the IJC's role in the twenty-first century. However, taking all the contributions to this volume collectively, we contend that the IJC is a unique governance institution between two countries that have a similar culture, language, history, and border, where no country is predominantly upstream or downstream, and that a similar treaty and organization would be difficult to create elsewhere in the world. Thus, the IJC probably isn't a replicable model. The lack of institutions or countries that have directly used the BWT and IJC as a model testify to that. Nevertheless, there are some aspects of the IJC and the BWT (including techniques, approaches, and programs) that other transboundary water-governance organizations and mechanisms use as a model, or at least borrow as best practices, including: sound science, equality, acting in a personal and professional manner, involving the public and providing opportunities to be heard, openness, flexibility, and stable funding.

Sound science is at the foundation of the IJC's work, and obviously the commission has evolved considerably over its first century as the ability of scientists and related professions has improved with advanced data gathering and analytical techniques, including modelling and computer technology. The inclusion of transboundary pollution in the 1909 BWT, even if it was a bit of an aside, seems to have been the earliest stricture ever in the world against such activity harming another political jurisdiction. The two chapters on the creation of the BWT and IJC, by Meredith Denning and David Whorley, speak to this. Jamie Benidickson's chapter suggests that the IJC's earliest pollution references in the Great Lakes area were important precedents. The GLWQAs are potentially the earliest environmental policy initiative to have incorporated an ecosystem approach, and as the wide range of chapters on the Great Lakes indicate, the GLWQAs are a program that deserves to be used as a model. Regardless of what the future brings, it is important that the IJC scientific process remains open, transparent, shared, and verifiable. Those working on IJC studies have the ability to call into question information from the opposite country and to ask that new data be collected or that existing data be discarded, depending on the circumstances. This way of working is now firmly rooted in the IJC tradition, and other countries would do well to emulate this methodology.

In a number of key respects, it is today simply much more difficult to manage environmental resources than was the case when the BWT was first signed. For example, the populations—and thus the environmental footprints—of both countries are much larger. It was much easier to come to a transborder agreement about a particular waterbody when the various stakeholders weren't consulted. Environmental knowledge, and thus expectations and beliefs about true sustainability, are also quite different. Even though uncertainty still defines many problems, scientifically we know far more than did past IJC decision-makers. But in some ways we are victims of this success—many of the "wicked" environmental problems we now have to deal with weren't even known a half-century ago.

As environmental requirements pile up, and the legacy of past pollution and mistakes becomes even greater, managing them becomes that much more difficult and complex. We have created all sorts of amazing new synthetic products, but now we have to deal with the legacy of toxins, like the emerging "forever" chemicals PFAS/PFOA. It was much easier to address point-source pollution, as the 1972 GLWQA did, than to address non-point-source pollution, which was the case for the 1978 GLWQA and subsequent iterations. Or consider the current renegotiation of the Columbia River Treaty: complex ecological and stakeholder questions that weren't at play in the early Cold War period now have to be taken into account.

The complexity of environmental governance has been a key factor in the trend toward multi-level and sub-national governance forms and approaches, which is partly related to greater emphasis on the ecosystem and the associated importance of local and multiple stakeholders. While this trend has involved a devolvement of responsibility and funding away from national-level governance bodies such as the IJC, arguably some of the greatest achievements of the IJC policy nexus include: helpful aid to the development of policy communities, state and non-state based, across various levels of governance and interaction. The IJC has never *de jure* updated its precedence of uses, though it has *de facto* incorporated industrial, recreational, and environmental elements in its decision-making, particularly since 1945. This situation has resulted in calls to update or modernize the BWT. That said, amending the terms of the treaty, particularly in the current political climate, could do more harm than good if certain interests use the opportunity to water down the BWT (pun intended). Incremental changes, with the International Watersheds Initiative as an example, may be the preferred route over altering the treaty.

In many respects, the IJC is emblematic of the history of the larger Canada-US diplomatic relationship—though with some important exceptions. Had the BWT been signed today it is difficult to imagine that it would enshrine as a central tenet equality of operation, but it has proven to be extremely valuable when IJC commissioners consider report conclusions and recommendations or when passing orders. Such equality may not be achievable between other countries wary of relinquishing sovereignty, especially if there are more than just two involved, but some sort of equality could be helpful, especially if there is power asymmetry. When

IJC commissioners as well as board and task force members act in their "personal and professional" capacity, this tends to depoliticize many situations. This is a difficult thing to imagine, let alone act upon, but this practice has and is being implemented time and time again and it helps make the IJC process successful—though not always. As a number of the chapters in this volume have demonstrated, there are numerous cases where the IJC has broken down along national lines and where different commissioners have prioritized national self-interest or otherwise not lived up to the IJC's lofty reputation (see, for example, chapters by Kenny, Moy and O'Riordan, Nossal, and Clamen and Macfarlane). In his chapter on the St. Mary–Milk basin, Timothy Heinmiller argues that the IJC has contained, if not resolved, conflict there, and Owen Temby and Don Munton's chapter on air quality shows that the IJC was instrumental to good outcomes, even if it has been marginalized as of late. This marginalization is also true in several cases on the plains, as Norman Brandson and Allen Olson show in their chapter, as well as the realm of Great Lakes water quality, though the authors of our various chapters on this subject (Read, Krantzberg, VanNijnatten and Johns, and Hall, Tarlock, and Valiante) generally paint the IJC's activities in this basin in a positive light. The synthetic overviews (section 3) also mostly frame the BWT and IJC as successful in such areas as environmental law and Canadian-American relations—though the IJC's treatment of Indigenous Peoples, even if it has been improving, has contributed to the two federal government's colonial legacy.

One cannot emphasize enough the importance of the public in the IJC's work and the value that outside voices can bring to a dispute-finding and resolution process. Someone could write a whole volume on this topic, looking at the evolution over the last century of the IJC's public consultation, involvement, communication, and methodologies, and what has worked and what has not, and why. Writing the words "and all parties interested therein shall be given convenient opportunity to be heard" directly into the BWT (article xii) placed an added emphasis on this aspect of the IJC process such that today board members are drawn from all sectors of civil society, not just government agencies (as in the past), and the IJC commissioners and advisers continually improve communication and information methodologies by taking advantage of the latest technologies and trends.

Openness, trust, and flexibility are critical characteristics, as has been noted and demonstrated in the various chapters. In chapters on the Pacific Northwest (Moy and O'Riordan); the St. Mary–Milk (Heinmiller); environmental law in the Great Lakes (Hall, Tarlock, and Valiante); Indigenous-IJC relations (Ettawageshik and Norman); Great Lakes water levels (Clamen and Macfarlane); and the long-term importance of the IJC (Kirton and Warren), the authors directly note the importance of trust (or distrust). In addition to most of these chapters, several others directly cite the importance of "flexibility" for the IJC, including those by Krantzberg, Whorley, Pentland and Yuzyk, and Read. Clearly the ability of the IJC to study and make recommendations about the need for an agreement on Great Lakes water quality, and then for governments to assign the commission ongoing oversight responsibilities in 1972 under the GLWQA—which continues through numerous updates to this day—is an indication of treaty and institutional flexibility. This is clearly demonstrated by the initiation and implementation of the International Watersheds Initiative over the last twenty years or so.

Stable funding and a commitment by the signatories to implement the BWT, as well as the creation and support of a permanent institutional mechanism (in this case the IJC) is clearly needed for success. While there is no obvious reason why six commissioners works well, history has shown that, with a few exceptions, this may be a "magic number." It allows for good dialogue, diverse opinions without unwieldy speeches and rhetoric by numerous players, gives geographic diversity from both countries, and allows for decent social interaction between commissioners of both countries outside of formal meetings, which often is a key aspect of decision-making and consensus.

The Future

We noted at the beginning of this conclusion that previous studies of the International Joint Commission were framed by the major issues of their day. As this book was in preparation between 2016 and 2019, the remarkable relationship that has existed between Canada and the United States for so many years in so many areas was being threatened, primarily but not exclusively, by disputes over trade. While a draft North American free trade agreement has been produced, the Trump administration's demonstrated penchant for reducing or eliminating environmental protections and policies, such as in the Great Lakes–St. Lawrence basin, will certainly impact border waters. However, until Trump's gutting of the Environmental Protection Agency and attempts to eliminate the Great Lakes Restoration Initiative, Canada was arguably the weaker link when comparing the two nations' environmental regulations concerning border waters; Canada needs to step its game up, regardless of what is happening south of the border.

Currently, negotiations for a new Columbia River Treaty are underway between Canada and the United States. In their chapter discussing three case studies in the Pacific Northwest, Rich Moy and Jon O'Riordan describe the role the IJC played in developing the technical and policy foundation for the original Columbia River Treaty of 1961. Borrowing from Moy and O'Riordan's suggestions for the future negotiation of the Columbia matter, which they shared separately with us, as well as Pentland and Yuzyk's chapter in this volume, we propose the following prescriptions for how the IJC can be successful in not only the transnational Columbia River basin, but along the length of the border, moving forward.

The "Shared Vision Model"

Under this approach, the IJC brings together decision-makers, experts, and stakeholders to create a system model that connects science, public preferences, and decision-making criteria. The process is very transparent. First, the IJC establishes binational technical, science-based, and stakeholder working groups that would first define the issues and options it would like to see addressed. Second, these working groups would become comfortable with the technical information and the methods used. Third, they would operate the models to show the trade-offs between the various economic values for uses and important environmental indicators. And lastly, they would make sure the process is transparent and open to the public. For example, in the Great Lakes, the IJC used this model approach to define and show the trade-offs for a number of important indicators, which included municipal and industrial water use, commercial navigation, hydro-power generation, coastal flooding, recreational boating, flood control and mitigation, and a large number of environmental indicators including wetland enhancement.

International Watershed Initiative Approach

The IJC has been taking the approach that water resources and environmental problems can best be anticipated, prevented, and resolved at the local watershed or basin level before developing into international issues. The IJC has successfully used the International Watersheds Initiative approach and its guiding principles in a number of our shared river basins.[7] In these watersheds, the IJC creates a different governance system. It brings together the best minds from academia, governments, Native American and First Nations communities, and the private sector from both countries to build the science and policy considerations in its recommendations to governments for solving cross-border issues and problems. It uses an integrated, ecosystem-based approach that recognizes the complex interrelationships within each watershed. It also develops a common database to understand the science of each watershed, including a better understanding of the aquatic, riparian, and land-based ecosystems and how anthropogenic uses affect them. Further, the IJC develops and uses compatible hydrographic and geospatial data and develops balanced water quality, hydrologic, and other ecosystem-based models. But the IJC also needs to better respect and incorporate traditional ecological knowledge and to effect reconciliation. As part of the destructive legacy of settler colonialism, and its continuing perpetuation and reverberations, First Nations and Native American communities have been disproportionately affected and burdened by hydroelectric and water-control developments—what can be termed "hydraulic imperialism."[8] Like North American societies and governments at large, the IJC will need to find ways of moving forward that both addresses past injustices and gives better voice to those who have lived within watersheds for millennia. In their chapter, Frank Ettawageshik and Emma Norman provide a range of concrete suggestions toward that end.

A Better Governance Structure

Outside of the Great Lakes–St. Lawrence basin governments may wish to consider the oversight framework in the Great Lakes Water Quality Agreement. The governments, and specifically the US EPA and Environment and Climate Change Canada, share responsibility for implementing the agreement. The IJC's role is to oversee and evaluate how well governments are doing in implementing their responsibilities under the GLWQA. The IJC's Great Lakes Water Quality Board reviews and assesses the progress of the governments in implementing the GLWQA; identifies emerging issues; and recommends strategies and approaches for preventing and resolving complex challenges facing the Great Lakes. The key strength of this twenty-eight-member binational board is that the local members push the governmental members to take appropriate actions in implementing the provisions of the agreement. The board is an effective partnership between the federal government agencies and the local stakeholders and community governments.

A Better Science Foundation

The IJC's Great Lakes Science Advisory Board is made up of two binational committees: the Science Priority Committee (SPC) and the Resource Coordinating Committee (RCC). The SPC, consisting primarily of academic research scientists from universities in both countries, identifies required research for addressing critical water quality issues. The RCC consists primarily of leaders of key federal government agencies from both countries. These agencies monitor and assess the state of water quality within the Great Lakes. These two committees within the Science Advisory Board continually work together in defining and conducting Great Lakes scientific research and comprehensive water quality and aquatic ecosystem monitoring. They provide valuable recommendations and oversight to the IJC and governments on the implementation of the agreement. A key function of the IJC liaisons with these boards is to ensure that their activities are coordinated.

Addressing a Changing Climate

Within the Great Lakes and its other international watersheds, the IJC has put a strong emphasis on refining and improving its process of "adaptive management." In the Great Lakes, the IJC has built in an adaptive management framework for reviewing and determining ways to continually improve the operations of dams in light of a changing climate, especially extreme events like flooding and drought. Flooding, as was seen recently in Lake Ontario and the upper St. Lawrence, will likely become a flashpoint given uncertainty about climate change. Thus, water quantity and lake level issues may attract a greater share of the commission's attention in the future. The IJC historically has had little involvement with the areas of biodiversity and invasive species, but considering Annex 6 of the 2012 update to the GLWQA, this is a direction in which the commission might wish to move in the future. The same can be said of micro-plastics and plastics, which could fit under the aegis of water quality.

Conclusion

The inability of the IJC to initiate or get involved in issues that commissioners believe are important, or that the IJC could help "prevent and resolve," is both a strength and a weakness. On the one hand, this has allowed the federal governments to avoid using the commission. In the last few decades, transnational environmental governance in North America has increasingly taken place outside of, and has circumscribed, the IJC: the Great Lakes–St. Lawrence Compact (and the companion agreement) is just one of the most recent and prominent examples. On the other hand, the inability to initiate applications and references has given the commission a reputation for objectivity and neutrality. The role of the individual commissioners can be extremely important here. The BWT and IJC can foster a unique collegial body that puts commissioners in a position to make the best choices for all involved, which in the last half-century has increasingly included the ecosystem. But the structure of the treaty and the commission doesn't guarantee that this collegiality and group decision-making happens—it is still up to the individual commissioners to buy into that. Looking at the past century of the IJC it is apparent that its emphasis, focus, and approach has changed over time, so to assume that the IJC of today, or of the 1970s, reflects how it has always been, would be a mistake. The upside is that the IJC can continue to change and adapt in the future.

Likely the best explanation for the IJC's success is its pragmatism and geographic position, along with its institutional structure and culture. To the extent that the IJC has worked well, it is largely because Canada and the United States share a water border where neither one is the predominant upstream or downstream riparian. Waterbodies like those in the Great Lakes basin *form* rather than *cross* the border; and even though there are many rivers where one nation is downstream from the other, there are plenty of others where that relationship is reversed, and thus each nation would have an opportunity for retribution. That is not to say that the countries have not historically engaged in linkage—there are numerous examples just within the realm of the IJC where the politics of border waters on one side of the continent are politically linked to those on the other—but that the national self-interests commonly align, while other aspects of the shared border act as shock absorbers. But if Canadian-American relations perpetually become stressed or fractured—and there are signs of that happening with Donald Trump in office—and if the atmosphere of bilateral co-operation is undermined, then an unfortunate but not impossible future direction for the IJC is drifting into irrelevancy.

In the introduction to this volume we posed the question of whether there is an "IJC myth"? The answer is a measured "yes." The IJC is not always objective or effective, it is limited in what areas it can have an impact, and it is not really seen as a direct model by the rest of the world. The era when the IJC was the most politically relevant—the 1950s and into the 1960s—is also the era when it was most politicized and advocated for destructive megaprojects. The GLWQA was, on paper, an enormous success—but the IJC's role within that agreement has been marginalized, the federal governments have proven unwilling to put the necessary money into the agreement's stipulations, and many of the problems that motivated the initial GLWQAs seem to be returning. However the IJC has also built up scientific expertise networks, is trusted by the public and in many environmentalist circles, its policy and scientific expertise lend legitimacy to its activities, and the IWI indicates that the commission is adjusting its approach.

Looking back at the first century of the IJC and BWT has allowed us to make some observations about how the IJC has changed over time, what has made it successful, and what limitations and obstacles it has faced and might face in the future. Scholars of North American history and policy, particularly in the environmental and transborder relations fields, would be wise to pay attention to the commission—as would any members of the public concerned about the environments in which they reside. There is no question that the IJC has played a significant role in the history of northern North America. Moreover, given the tricky future of climate change, the IJC is well equipped to play a significant role in the future of Canada-US border eco-politics—and we believe that it should.

Notes

1. L. M. Bloomfield and G. F. FitzGerald, *Boundary Waters Problems of Canada and the United States* (Toronto: Carswell, 1958), 63.

2. Kim Richard Nossal, "The IJC in Retrospect," in *The International Joint Commission Seventy Years On*, ed. Richard Spencer, John Kirton, Kim Richard Nossal (Toronto: Centre For International Studies, University of Toronto, 1981), 130.

3. Ibid., 126.

4. William R. Willoughy, "Expectations and Experience, in Spencer, Kirton, and Nossal, *The International Joint Commission Seventy Years On*, 39.

5. Peter H. Gleick writes of "a 'hard path' that will rely almost exclusively on centralized infrastructure to capture, treat, and deliver water supplies; and a 'soft path' that will complement the former by investing in decentralized facilities, efficient technologies and policies, and human capital. This soft path will seek to improve overall productivity rather than to find new sources of supply. It will deliver water services that are matched to the needs of end users, on both local and community scales." See Gleick, "Water Management: Soft Water Paths," *Nature* 418 (25 July 2002), https://www.nature.com/articles/418373a; Oliver M. Brandes and David B. Brooks, "The Soft Path for Water in a Nutshell," (Victoria, BC: Friends of the Earth and POLIS Project on Ecological Governance, University of Victoria, 2005).

6. Stephen Brooks "The International Joint Commission: Convergence, Divergence, or Submergence?" in *Transboundary Environmental Governance in Canada and the United States* (Washington, DC: Woodrow Wilson International Center for Scholars, Canada Institute, Occasional Paper Series, 2005), 3–18; Stephen Brooks, "The International Joint Commission: The Promise and Limits of an Ambitious Model," in *Transboundary Environmental Governance Across the World's Longest Border*, ed. Stephen Brooks and Andrea Olive (Lansing: Michigan State University Press, 2018).

7. International Joint Commisison, *The International Watersheds Inititiatve: From Concept to Cornerstone of the IJC (Fourth IWI Report to Governments)* (Ottawa/Washington: International Joint Commission, October 2015).

8. Daniel Macfarlane and Peter Kitay, "Hydraulic Imperialism: Hydro-electric Development and Treaty 9 in the Abitibi Region," *American Review of Canadian Studies* 47, no. 3 (Fall 2016): 380–97.

APPENDICES

Appendix 1: Boundary Waters Treaty

TREATY BETWEEN THE UNITED STATES AND GREAT BRITAIN RELATING TO BOUNDARY WATERS, AND QUESTIONS ARISING BETWEEN THE UNITED STATES AND CANADA

The United States of America and His Majesty the King of the United Kingdom of Great Britain and Ireland and of the British Dominions beyond the Seas, Emperor of India, being equally desirous to prevent disputes regarding the use of boundary waters and to settle all questions which are now pending between the United States and the Dominion of Canada involving the rights, obligations, or interests of either in relation to the other or to the inhabitants of the other, along their common frontier, and to make provision for the adjustment and settlement of all such questions as may hereafter arise, have resolved to conclude a treaty in furtherance of these ends, and for that purpose have appointed as their respective plenipotentiaries:

The President of the United States of America, Elihu Root, Secretary of State of the United States; and His Britannic Majesty, the Right Honourable James Bryce, O.M., his Ambassador Extraordinary and Plenipotentiary at Washington;

Who, after having communicated to one another their full powers, found in good and due form, have agreed upon the following articles:

PRELIMINARY ARTICLE

For the purpose of this treaty boundary waters are defined as the waters from main shore to main shore of the lakes and rivers and connecting waterways, or the portions thereof, along which the international boundary between the United States and the Dominion of Canada passes, including all bays, arms, and inlets thereof, but not including tributary waters which in their natural channels would flow into such lakes, rivers, and waterways, or waters flowing from such lakes, rivers, and waterways, or the waters of rivers flowing across the boundary.

ARTICLE I

The High Contracting Parties agree that the navigation of all navigable boundary waters shall forever continue free and open for the purposes of commerce to the inhabitants and to the ships, vessels, and boats of both countries equally, subject, however, to any laws and regulations of either country, within its own territory, not inconsistent with such privilege of free navigation and applying equally and without discrimination to the inhabitants, ships, vessels, and boats of both countries.

It is further agreed that so long as this treaty shall remain in force, this same right of navigation shall extend to the waters of Lake Michigan and to all canals connecting boundary waters, and now existing or which may hereafter be constructed on either side of the line. Either of the High Contracting Parties may adopt rules and regulations governing the use of such canals within its own territory and may charge tolls for the use thereof, but all such rules and regulations and all tolls charged shall apply alike to the subjects or citizens of the High Contracting Parties and the ships, vessels, and boats of both of the High Contracting Parties, and they shall be placed on terms of equality in the use thereof.

ARTICLE II

Each of the High Contracting Parties reserves to itself or to the several State Governments on the one side and the Dominion or Provincial Governments on the other as the case may be, subject to any treaty provisions now existing with respect thereto, the exclusive jurisdiction and control over the use and diversion, whether temporary or permanent, of all waters on its own side of the line which in their natural channels would flow across the boundary or into boundary waters; but it is agreed that any interference with or diversion from their natural channel of such waters on either side of the boundary, resulting in any injury on the other side of the boundary, shall give rise to the same rights and entitle the injured parties to the same legal remedies as if such injury took place in the country where such diversion or interference occurs; but this provision shall not apply to cases already existing or to cases expressly covered by special agreement between the parties hereto.

It is understood however, that neither of the High Contracting Parties intends by the foregoing provision to surrender any right, which it may have, to object to any interference with or diversions of waters on the other side of the boundary the effect of which would be productive of material injury to the navigation interests on its own side of the boundary.

ARTICLE III

It is agreed that, in addition to the uses, obstructions, and diversions heretofore permitted or hereafter provided for by special agreement between the Parties hereto, no further or other uses or obstructions or diversions, whether temporary or permanent, of boundary waters on either side of the line, affecting the natural level or flow of boundary waters on the other side of the line shall be made except by authority of the United States or the Dominion of Canada within their respective jurisdictions and with the approval, as hereinafter provided, of a joint commission, to be known as the International Joint Commission.

The foregoing provisions are not intended to limit or interfere with the existing rights of the Government of the United States on the one side and the Government of the Dominion of Canada on the other, to undertake and carry on governmental works in boundary waters for the deepening of channels, the construction of breakwaters, the improvement of harbours, and other governmental works for the benefit of commerce and navigation, provided that such works are wholly on its own side of the line and do not materially affect the level or flow of the boundary waters on the other, nor are such provisions intended to interfere with the ordinary use of such waters for domestic and sanitary purposes.

ARTICLE IV

The High Contracting Parties agree that, except in cases provided for by special agreement between them, they will not permit the construction or maintenance on their respective sides of the boundary of any remedial or protective works or any dams or other obstructions in waters flowing from boundary waters or in waters at a lower level than the boundary in rivers flowing across the boundary, the effect of which is to raise the natural level of waters on the other side of the boundary unless the construction or maintenance thereof is approved by the aforesaid International Joint Commission.

It is further agreed that the waters herein defined as boundary waters and waters flowing across the boundary shall not be polluted on either side to the injury of health or property on the other.

ARTICLE V

The High Contracting Parties agree that it is expedient to limit the diversion of waters from the Niagara River so that the level of Lake Erie and the flow of the stream shall not be appreciably affected. It is the desire of both Parties to accomplish this object with the least possible injury to investments which have already been made in the construction of power plants on the United States side of the river under grants of authority from the State of New York, and on the Canadian side of the river under licences authorized by the Dominion of Canada and the Province of Ontario.

So long as this treaty shall remain in force, no diversion of the waters of the Niagara River above the Falls from the natural course and stream thereof shall be permitted except for the purposes and to the extent hereinafter provided.

- The United States may authorize and permit the diversion within the State of New York of the waters of said river above the Falls of Niagara, for power purposes, not exceeding in the aggregate a daily diversion at the rate of twenty thousand cubic feet of water per second.

- The United Kingdom, by the Dominion of Canada, or the Province of Ontario, may authorize and permit the diversion within the Province of Ontario of the waters of said river above the Falls of Niagara, for the power purposes, not exceeding in the aggregate a daily diversion at the rate of thirty-six thousand cubic feet of water per second.
- The prohibitions of this article shall not apply to the diversion of water for sanitary or domestic purposes, or for the service of canals for the purposes of navigation.

Note: The third, fourth, and fifth paragraphs of article v were terminated by the Canada–United States Treaty of 27 February 1950 concerning the diversion of the Niagara River.

ARTICLE VI

The High Contracting Parties agree that the St. Mary and Milk Rivers and their tributaries (in the State of Montana and the Provinces of Alberta and Saskatchewan) are to be treated as one stream for the purposes of irrigation and power, and the waters thereof shall be apportioned equally between the two countries, but in making such equal apportionment more than half may be taken from one river and less than half from the other by either country so as to afford a more beneficial use to each. It is further agreed that in the division of such waters during the irrigation season, between the 1st of April and 31st of October, inclusive, annually, the United States is entitled to a prior appropriation of 500 cubic feet per second of the waters of the Milk River, or so much of such amount as constitutes three-fourths of its natural flow, and that Canada is entitled to a prior appropriation of 500 cubic feet per second of the flow of St. Mary River, or so much of such amount as constitutes three-fourths of its natural flow.

The channel of the Milk River in Canada may be used at the convenience of the United States for the conveyance, while passing through Canadian territory, of waters diverted from the St. Mary River. The provisions of

Article II of this treaty shall apply to any injury resulting to property in Canada from the conveyance of such waters through the Milk River.

The measurement and apportionment of the water to be used by each country shall from time to time be made jointly by the properly constituted reclamation officers of the United States and the properly constituted irrigation officers of His Majesty under the direction of the International Joint Commission.

ARTICLE VII

The High Contracting Parties agree to establish and maintain an International Joint Commission of the United States and Canada composed of six commissioners, three on the part of the United States appointed by the President thereof, and three on the part of the United Kingdom appointed by His Majesty on the recommendation of the Governor in Council of the Dominion of Canada.

ARTICLE VIII

This International Joint Commission shall have jurisdiction over and shall pass upon all cases involving the use or obstruction or diversion of the waters with respect to which under Article III or IV of this treaty the approval of this Commission is required, and in passing on such cases the Commission shall be governed by the following rules or principles which are adopted by the High Contracting Parties for this purpose:

The High Contracting Parties shall have, each on its own side of the boundary, equal and similar rights in the use of the waters hereinbefore defined as boundary waters.

The following order of precedence shall be observed among the various uses enumerated hereinafter for these waters, and no use shall be permitted which tends materially to conflict with or restrain any other use which is given preference over it in this order of precedence:

1. Uses for domestic and sanitary purposes;
2. Uses for navigation, including the service of canals for the purposes of navigation;

3. Uses for power and for irrigation purposes.

The foregoing provisions shall not apply to or disturb any existing uses of boundary waters on either side of the boundary.

The requirement for an equal division may in the discretion of the Commission be suspended in cases of temporary diversions along boundary waters at points where such equal division can not be made advantageously on account of local conditions, and where such diversion does not diminish elsewhere the amount available for use on the other side.

The Commission in its discretion may make its approval in any case conditional upon the construction of remedial or protective works to compensate so far as possible for the particular use or diversion proposed, and in such cases may require that suitable and adequate provision, approved by the Commission, be made for the protection and indemnity against injury of all interests on the other side of the line which may be injured thereby.

In cases involving the elevation of the natural level of waters on either side of the line as a result of the construction or maintenance on the other side of remedial or protective works or dams or other obstructions in boundary waters flowing there from or in waters below the boundary in rivers flowing across the boundary, the Commission shall require, as a condition of its approval thereof, that suitable and adequate provision, approved by it, be made for the protection and indemnity of all interests on the other side of the line which may be injured thereby.

The majority of the Commissioners shall have power to render a decision. In case the Commission is evenly divided upon any question or matter presented to it for decision, separate reports shall be made by the Commissioners on each side to their own Government. The High Contracting Parties shall thereupon endeavour to agree upon an adjustment of the question or matter of difference, and if an agreement is reached between them, it shall be reduced to writing in the form of a protocol, and shall be communicated to the Commissioners, who shall take such further proceedings as may be necessary to carry out such agreement.

ARTICLE IX

The High Contracting Parties further agree that any other questions or matters of difference arising between them involving the rights, obligations, or interests of either in relation to the other or to the inhabitants of the other, along the common frontier between the United States and the Dominion of Canada, shall be referred from time to time to the International Joint Commission for examination and report, whenever either the Government of the United States or the Government of the Dominion of Canada shall request that such questions or matters of difference be so referred.

The International Joint Commission is authorized in each case so referred to examine into and report upon the facts and circumstances of the particular questions and matters referred, together with such conclusions and recommendations as may be appropriate, subject, however, to any restrictions or exceptions which may be imposed with respect thereto by the terms of the reference.

Such reports of the Commission shall not be regarded as decisions of the questions or matters so submitted either on the facts or the law, and shall in no way have the character of an arbitral award.

The Commission shall make a joint report to both Governments in all cases in which all or a majority of the Commissioners agree, and in case of disagreement the minority may make a joint report to both Governments, or separate reports to their respective Governments.

In case the Commission is evenly divided upon any question or matter referred to it for report, separate reports shall be made by the Commissioners on each side to their own Government.

ARTICLE X

Any questions or matters of difference arising between the High Contracting Parties involving the rights, obligations, or interests of the United States or of the Dominion of Canada either in relation to each other or to their respective inhabitants, may be referred for decision to the International Joint Commission by the consent of the two Parties, it being understood that on the part of the United States any such action will be by and with the advice and consent of the Senate, and on the part of His Majesty's Government with the consent of the Governor General in Council. In each case so referred, the said Commission is authorized to examine into and report upon the facts and circumstances of the particular questions any matters referred, together with such conclusions and recommendations as may be appropriate, subject, however, to any restrictions or exceptions which may be imposed with respect thereto by the terms of the reference.

A majority of the said Commission shall have power to render a decision or finding upon any of the questions or matters so referred. If the said Commission is equally divided or otherwise unable to render a decision or finding as to any questions or matters so referred, it shall be the duty of the Commissioners to make a joint report to both Governments, or separate reports to their respective Governments, showing the different conclusions arrived at with regard to the matters or questions referred, which questions or matters shall thereupon be referred for decision by the High Contracting Parties to an umpire chosen in accordance with the procedure prescribed in the fourth, fifth and sixth paragraphs of Article XLV of the Hague Convention for the pacific settlement of international disputes, dated October 18, 1907. Such umpire shall have power to render a final decision with respect to those matters and questions so referred on which the Commission fail to agree.

ARTICLE XI

A duplicate original of all decisions rendered and joint reports made by the Commission shall be transmitted to and filed with the Secretary of State of the United States and the Governor General of the Dominion of Canada, and to them shall be addressed all communications of the Commission.

ARTICLE XII

The International Joint Commission shall meet and organize at Washington promptly after the members thereof are appointed, and when organized the Commission may fix such times and places for its meetings as may be necessary, subject at all times to special call or direction by the two Governments. Each Commissioner upon the first joint meeting of the Commission after his appointment, shall, before proceeding with the work of the Commission, make and subscribe a solemn declaration in writing that he will faithfully and impartially perform the duties imposed upon him under this treaty, and such declaration shall be entered on the records of the proceedings of the Commission.

The United States and Canadian sections of the Commission may each appoint a secretary, and these shall act as joint secretaries of the Commission at its joint sessions, and the Commission may employ engineers and clerical assistants from time to time as it may deem advisable. The salaries and personal expenses of the Commission and of the secretaries shall be paid by their respective Governments, and all reasonable and necessary joint expenses of the Commission, incurred by it, shall be paid in equal moieties by the High Contracting Parties.

The Commission shall have power to administer oaths to witnesses, and to take evidence on oath whenever deemed necessary in any proceeding, or inquiry, or matter within its jurisdiction under this treaty, and all parties interested therein shall be given convenient opportunity to be heard, and the High Contracting Parties agree to adopt such legislation as may be appropriate and necessary to give the Commission the powers above mentioned on each side of the boundary, and to provide for the issue of subpoenas and for compelling the attendance of witnesses in proceedings before the Commission before the Commission. The Commission may adopt such rules of procedure as shall be in accordance with justice and equity, and may make such examination in person and through agents or employees as may be deemed advisable.

ARTICLE XIII

In all cases where special agreements between the High Contracting Parties hereto are referred to in the foregoing articles, such agreements are understood and intended to include not only direct agreements between the High Contracting Parties, but also any mutual arrangement between the United States and the Dominion of Canada expressed by concurrent or reciprocal legislation on the part of Congress and the Parliament of the Dominion.

ARTICLE XIV

The present treaty shall be ratified by the President of the United States of America, by and with the advice and consent of the Senate, thereof, and by His Britannic Majesty. The ratifications shall be exchanged at Washington as soon as possible and the treaty shall take effect on the date of the exchange of its ratifications. It shall remain in force for five years, dating from the day of exchange of ratifications, and thereafter until terminated by twelve months' written notice given by either High Contracting Party to the other.

In faith whereof the respective plenipotentiaries have signed this treaty in duplicate and have hereunto affixed their seals.

Done at Washington the 11th day of January, in the year of our Lord one thousand and nine hundred and nine.

(Signed) ELIHU ROOT [SEAL]

(Signed) JAMES BRYCE [SEAL]

And WHEREAS the Senate of the United States by their resolution of March 3, 1909, (two thirds of the Senators present concurring therein) did advise and consent to the ratification of the said Treaty with the following understanding to wit:

"Resolved further, (as a part of this ratification), that the United States approves this treaty with the understanding that nothing in this treaty shall be construed as affecting, or changing, any existing territorial or riparian rights in the water, or rights of the owners of lands under, on either side of the international boundary at the rapids of the St. Mary's river at Sault Ste. Marie, in the use of water flowing over such lands, subject to the requirements of navigation in boundary water and of navigation canals, and without prejudice to the existing right of the United States and Canada, each to use the waters of the St. Mary's river, within its own territory, and further, that nothing in the treaty shall be construed to interfere with the drainage of wet swamp and overflowed lands into streams flowing into boundary waters, and that this interpretation will be mentioned in the ratification of this treaty as conveying the true meaning of the treaty, and will in effect, form part of the treaty;"

AND WHEREAS the said understanding has been accepted by the Government of Great Britain, and the ratifications of the two Governments of the said Treaty were exchanged in the City of Washington, on the 5th day of May, one thousand nine hundred and ten;

NOW THEREFORE, be it known that I, William Howard Taft, President of the United States of America, have caused the said Treaty and the said understanding, as forming a part thereof, to be made public, to the end that the same and every article and clause thereof may be observed and fulfilled with good faith by the United States and the citizens thereof.

In testimony whereof, I have hereunto set my hand and caused the seal of the United States to be affixed. Done at the City of Washington this thirteenth day of May in the year of our Lord one thousand nine hundred and ten, [SEAL] and of the Independence of the United States of America the hundred and thirty-fourth.

Wm. H. Taft

By the President:
P C Knox
Secretary of State

PROTOCOL OF EXCHANGE

On proceeding to the exchange of the ratifications of the treaty signed at Washington on January 11, 1909, between the United States and Great Britain, relating to boundary waters and questions arising along the boundary between the United States and the Dominion of Canada, the undersigned plenipotentiaries, duly authorized thereto by their respective Governments, hereby declare that nothing in this treaty shall be construed as affecting, or changing, any existing territorial, or riparian rights in the water, or rights of the owners of lands under water, on either side of the international boundary at the rapids of St. Mary's River at Sault Ste. Marie, in the use of the alters flowing over such lands, subject to the requirements of navigation in boundary waters and of navigation canals, and without prejudice to the existing right of the United States and Canada, each to use the waters of the St. Mary's River, within its own territory; and further, that nothing in this treaty shall be construed to interfere with the drainage of wet, swamp, and overflowed lands into streams flowing into boundary waters, and also that this declaration shall be deemed to have equal force and effect as the treaty itself and to form an integral part thereto.

The exchange of ratifications then took place in the usual form.

IN WITNESS WHEREOF, they have signed the present Protocol of Exchange and have affixed their seals thereto.

DONE at Washington this 5th day of May, one thousand nine hundred and ten.

PHILANDER C KNOX [SEAL]
JAMES BRYCE [SEAL]

Appendix 2: The Clinton-Gibbons Draft, 1907

TO

THE HONORABLE THE SECRETARY OF STATE

OF THE UNITED STATES, and

THE HONORABLE THE PRIME MINISTER

OF THE DOMINION OF CANADA:

The undersigned have the honor to most respectfully submit for your consideration the attached draft of a proposed treaty.

Dated September 24, 1907.

(Signed)　　　GEORGE CLINTON

"　　　　　　GEO. C. GIBBONS

PROPOSED TREATY CLAUSES.

ARTICLE I

WHEREAS questions have arisen and may hereafter arise involving the use and diversion of the boundary waters of the United States and Canada, and in relation to the protection of the fisheries therein, the improvement of navigable channels, the location of the boundary line, the construction of new channels for navigation, the improvement and maintenance of the levels therein, and the protection of the banks and shores of such waters; and whereas it is desirable that the rules of navigation upon navigable waters forming a part of the boundary between the United States and the Dominion of Canada, and the use of signal lights of vessels navigating said waters should be uniform, and whereas the use of said waters for power and other purposes should be regulated by joint rules of the United States and the Dominion of Canada, and such rules must be enforced by joint action of said countries; and whereas it is deemed wise by the high contracting parties, in order to settle all such questions now existing, or which may hereafter arise, and to dispose of all other matters above mentioned, that a permanent international commission be appointed with full powers in the premises: therefore the high contracting parties agree that all such questions and matters as they may arise shall be referred by them to a commission to consist of six commissioners, three to be appointed by the President of the United States, and three by His Britannic Majesty; and the high contracting parties agree to appoint the commissioners as soon after the ratification hereof as may be convenient. In case of the death, absence or incapacity of a commissioner, or in the event of a commissioner omitting or ceasing to act as such, the President of the United States, or His Britannic Majesty, respectively, shall name another person to act as commissioner in the place or stead of the Commissioner originally named.

ARTICLE II

The Commissioners shall meet in Washington at the earliest convenient time after they shall have been named, and shall, before proceeding to do any business, make and subscribe a solemn declaration that they will impartially and carefully examine and decide, to the best of their judgment and according to justice and equity, without feeling, favor or affection to their country, upon all such matters as shall be laid before them on the part of the governments of the United States and of His Britannic

Majesty, respectively, and such declaration shall be entered on the record of their proceedings.

After having organized the commissioners may meet at such times and places as they may appoint. They shall give all parties interested in matters which come before them, convenient opportunity to be heard, and may take evidence on oath when deemed necessary. They may adopt such rules of procedure as may be in accordance with justice and equity and may make such examinations in person and through agents, or employees, as they may deem advisable.

The majority of the commission shall have power to render a decision, but in case a majority do not agree, the commission shall select an arbitrator or arbitrators to whom the matters in difference may be referred and whose decision shall be final.

The Commission may employ secretaries, engineers and other assistants, from time to time as it may deem advisable. The salaries and personal expenses of the Commissioners shall be paid by their respective governments, and all other expenses, including the pay of arbitrators, shall be paid equally by the high contracting parties, who shall make proper provision therefor.

ARTICLE III

The Commission shall have the power to consider and determine all questions and matters related to the subject specified in Article I which may be referred to it by the High Contracting Parties.

The decision of the Commission upon any matters submitted to it shall be enforced by the High Contracting Parties; and for the purpose of enforcing any rules and regulations, which may be adopted by the Commission, pursuant to the powers conferred upon it by this treaty, the Commission may exercise such police powers as may be vested in it by concurrent legislation of the United States and the Dominion of Canada.

ARTICLE IV

It is agreed as follows: -

1. The expression "boundary waters" as used in this treaty includes the following described waters, to wit: Lake Superior, Michigan, Huron including Georgian Bay, St. Clair, Erie and Ontario; the connecting and tributary waters of said lakes, the river St. Lawrence from its source to the ocean; the Columbia River and all rivers and streams which cross the boundary line between the Dominion of Canada and the United States, and their tributaries.

2. All navigable boundary waters, and all canals and channels connecting the same or aiding in their navigation, now existing or which may hereafter be constructed are and shall be forever free for navigation by the citizens and subjects of both countries, ascending and descending, subject to such just rules and regulations as either of the High Contracting Parties may, within its own territory, impose, provided that such rules and regulations shall not discriminate between the citizens or subjects of the high contracting parties.

3. The right to use said waters for navigation is paramount to all other rights, except that of use for necessary domestic and sanitary purposes and the service of canals for purposes of navigation.

4. Where diversions of water are permitted for the purpose of generating power, upon waters along the line of the international boundary, the interests of navigation must be fully protected, and, as far as possible, the right to use on half of surplus waters available for power purposes shall be preserved to each country, its citizens or subjects.

5. Where diversion for irrigation is permitted the paramount right of navigation must be preserved and the rights of each country affected and of its citizens or subjects must be equitably protected.

6. The said waters must not be polluted in one country to the injury of health or property in the other.

7. No water shall be diverted from the Niagara River or from Lake Erie by way of the Niagara Peninsula in excess of 18,500 cubic feet per second in the United States, and 36,000 cubic feet per second in the Dominion of Canada, except for necessary domestic and sanitary uses, and for service of canals for purposes of navigation.

8. Solely for the purposes of this treaty, the expression "Navigable boundary waters" shall be taken to mean all such boundary waters as are subject to public use for the transportation of property, in accordance with the common law as recognized in the Dominion of Canada and in the United States; and the Commission is authorized and empowered to determine the navigability of streams, as matter of fact, when it becomes necessary to do so in matters referred to it.

9. No diversion or obstruction of boundary waters in, or by, either country, which shall materially interfere with the natural flow thereof, to the injury of the other country, or of its citizens or subjects shall be permitted without the consent of such other country.

10. The words "citizens" and "subjects" as used in this treaty shall be deemed to include individuals, corporations, joint stock companies, associations and partnerships.

ARTICLE V

The Commission is hereby empowered and directed to ascertain the boundary line between the United States and the Dominion of Canada through lakes Ontario, Erie, St. Clair, and Huron, and the waters connecting the same as laid down by the Commissioners appointed under the treaty of Ghent, as nearly as possible, and to delineate the same upon modern charts and to describe it in writing, and, so far as practical, by reference to fixed monuments which the Commission may locate and erect and which shall be so described that they can be readily found.

The Commission shall by report, signed by the Commissioners, designate the boundary line so ascertained by it and shall cause to be prepared proper maps delineating the same. They shall file their report together with such maps, in duplicate with the Secretary of State of the United States and with the Minister of Public Works of the Dominion of Canada.

The boundary line as ascertained and reported by the Commission shall be the boundary line between the United States of America and the Dominion of Canada, through the waters last above mentioned.

In case a majority of the commission shall not be able to agree on the location of the boundary line through the waters last above mentioned, in whole or in any part, they shall make joint or several reports in duplicate, to the government of His Britannic Majesty and to that of the United States, stating in detail the points on which they differ.

ARTICLE VI

AND WHEREAS it is desirable that the said Commission, when formed, shall have authority to deal with all other matters, which shall, by consent of both the contracting parties, be submitted to it for decision or which shall with such consent, be referred to it with a view to having the said Commission consider and report thereon with such recommendations as they may think advisable,

NOW THEREFORE the High Contracting Parties agree that the said Commission shall, as to all matters so referred to them for decision, have the same powers as given them with respect to the subjects mentioned in Article I of this treaty.

As to such matters as are not referred to them for decision the said commission shall consider and report upon the facts, with such recommendations as they may see fit.

In case a majority of the Commission cannot, in matters so referred to the for decision, agree upon findings, they shall appoint one or more arbitrators as provided in Article I, but as to all other subjects referred to them if the majority cannot agree upon conclusions, the views of the members shall be embodied in separate reports to be submitted to both the High Contracting Parties.

ARTICLE VII

The Commission with all its powers conferred and duties imposed by this treaty shall continue during the pleasure of both the high contracting parties; but if either of the parties desires to terminate the treaty it shall give to the other at least one year's notice in writing before doing so. For all the purposes of these articles the Dominion of Canada shall be deemed to represent His Britannic Majesty.

All reports and communications of the Commission are to be made to the Secretary of State of the United States and to the Prime Minister of the Dominion of Canada.

Appendix 3: List of IJC Commissioners

List supplied by and used with the permission of the IJC.

Commissioners of the International Joint Commission / Commissaires de la Commission mixte internationale

UNITED STATES SECTION / SECTION AMÉRICAINE

Thomas H. Carter	1911 (co-chair/co-président)
James A. Tawney	1911–1919 (1912–1914 co-chair/co-président)
Frank S. Streeter	1911–1913
George Turner	1911–1914
Obadiah Gardner	1913–1923 (1914–1923 co-chair/co-président)
Robert B. Glenn	1914–1920
Clarence D. Clark	1919–1929 (1923–1929 co-chair/co-président)
Marcus Smith	1921–1924
William Bauchop Wilson	1921–1921
Charles E. Townsend	1923–1924
Fred T. Dubois	1924–1930
Porter J. McCumber	1925–1933
John H. Bartlett	1929–1933 (co-chair/co-président)
Augustus Owsley Stanley	1933–1954 (co-chair/co-président)
Eugene Lorton	1933–1939
Roger B. McWhorter	1939–1958
Ralph Walton Moore	1939–1941
Eugene W. Weber	1948–1973
Leonard Jordan	1955–1957 (co-chair/co-président)
Douglas McKay	1957–1959 (co-chair/co-président)
Francis L. Adams	1958–1962
Edward Bacon	1960–1961 (co-chair/co-président)
Teno Roncalio	1961–1964 (co-chair/co-président)

UNITED STATES SECTION / SECTION AMÉRICAINE continued

Charles R. Ross	1962—1981
Matthew E. Welsh	1965—1970 (1966—1970 co-chair/co-président)
Christian A. Herter Jr.	1970—1975 (co-chair/co-président)
Henry P. Smith III	1973—1978 (1975—1978 co-chair/co-president)
Robert J. Sugarman	1978—1981 (co-chair/co-président)
Kenneth Curtis	1978—1979
Jean L Hennessey	1979—1981
Lawrence Keith Bulen	1981—1990
Donald Totten	1981—1990
Robert C. McEwen	1981—1989 (co-chair/co-président)
Gordon K. Durnil	1989—1994 (co-chair/co-président)
Hilary P. Cleveland	1990—1994
Robert F. Goodwin	1990—1993
Susan B. Bayh	1994—2001
Alice Chamberlin	1994—2001
Thomas L. Baldini	1994—2002 (co-chair/co-président)
Dennis L. Schornack	2002—2008 (co-chair/co-président)
Irene B. Brooks	2002—2011 (2008—2010 co-chair/co-présidente)
Allen I. Olson	2002—2010
Sam Speck	2008—2010
Lana Pollack	2010—2019
Dereth Glance	2011—2016
Rich Moy	2011—2019
Jane Corwin	2019—present/jusqu'à present (co-chair/co-president)
Robert Sisson	2019—present/jusqu'à present
Lance Yohe	2019— present/jusqu'à présent

CANADIAN SECTION / SECTION CANADIENNE

Thomas Chase Casgrain	1911—1914 (co-chair/co-président)
Henry A. Powell	1911—1928
Pierre-Basile Mignault	1914—1918
Charles A. Magrath	1915—1936 (co-chair/co-président)
William H. Hearst	1920 - 1940
George W. Kyte	1928—1940
Charles Stewart	1936—1946 (co-chair/co-président)
Joseph E. Perrault	1940—1948 (1947—1948 co-chair/co-président)
James Allison Glen	1943—1950 (1948—1950 co-chair/co-président)
Georges Spencer	1947—1957
Andrew G. L. McNaughton	1950—1962 (co-chair/co-président)
J. Lucien Dansereau	1950—1961
Donald M. Stephens	1958—1968
René Dupuis	1962—1969
Arnold D. P. Heeney	1962—1970 (co-chair/co-président)
Andy D. Scott	1968—1972
Bernard Beaupré	1969—1980
Louis J. Robichaud	1971—1973 (co-chair/co-president)
Keith A. Henry	1972—1979
Maxwell Cohen	1974—1979 (co-chair/co-président)
Jean R. Roy	1979—1981
Stuart M. Hodgson	1979—1981 (co-chair/co-président)
Charles M. Bédard	1981—1984
E. Richmond Olson	1981—1985 (1981—1982 co-chair/co-président)
James Blair Seaborn	1982—1985 (co-chair/co-président)
Pierre-André Bissonnette	1985—1989 (co-chair/co-président)
Edmond Davie Fulton	1986—1992 (1989—1992 co-chair/co-président)
Robert S. K. Welch	1986—1992
Claude Lanthier	1990—1995 (1992 to 1995 co-chair/co-président)
James A. Macaulay	1992—1995

CANADIAN SECTION / SECTION CANADIENNE *continued*

Gordon Walker	1992—1995
Pierre Béland	1995—1997 (1996—1997 co-chair/co-président)
Francis C. Murphy	1995—2000
Adèle M. Hurley	1995—1996 (co-chair/co-présidente)
Leonard H. Legault	1997—2001 (co-chair/co-president)
Robert Gourd	1998—2007
Jack P. Blaney	2001—2009
Mary M. Gusella	2001—2002 (co-chair/co-présidente)
Herb Gray	2002—2010 (co-chair/co-président)
Pierre Trépanier	2008—2012
Lyall D. Knott	2009—2013
Joseph Comuzzi	2010—2014 (co-chair/co-président)
Benoît Bouchard	2013—2017
Gordon Walker	2013—2018 (co-chair/co-président)
Richard A. Morgan	2014—2018
Pierre Béland	2019—present/jusqu'à present (co-chair/co-president)
Henry Lickers	2019—present/jusqu'à present
Merrell-Ann Phare	2019— present/jusqu'à présent

SELECTED BIBLIOGRAPHY

Alexander, Jeff. *Pandora's Locks: The Opening of the Great Lakes-St. Lawrence Seaway*. Lansing: Michigan State University Press, 2009.

Anisman, Philip. "Water Pollution Control in Canada." *Ottawa Law Review* 5, no. 2 (1972): 342–410.

Annin, Peter. *Great Lakes Water Wars*. 2nd ed. Washington, DC: Island Press, 2018.

Ashworth, William. *The Late, Great Lakes*. Detroit: Wayne State University Press, 1987.

Austin, Jacob. "Canadian-United States Practice and Theory Respecting the International Law of International Rivers: A Study of the History and Influence of the Harmon Doctrine." *Canadian Bar Review* 37, no. 3 (September 1959): 391–443.

Bankes, Nigel, and Elizabeth Bourget. "Apportionment of the St. Mary and Milk Rivers." In *Water Without Borders? Canada, the United States, and Shared Waters*, edited by Emma S. Norman, Alice Cohen, and Karen Bakker, 159–78. Toronto: University of Toronto Press, 2013.

Beach, Christopher S. "Electrification and Underdevelopment in New Brunswick: The Grand Falls Project, 1896–1930." *Acadiensis* 23, no. 1 (Autumn 1993): 60–85.

Beck, Gregor G., and Bruce Littlejohn. *Voices for the Watershed: Environmental Issues in the Great Lakes-St. Lawrence Drainage Basin*. Montreal: McGill-Queen's University Press, 2000.

Benidickson, Jamie. *The Culture of Flushing: A Social and Legal History of Sewage*. Vancouver: UBC Press, 2007.

———. *Levelling the Lake: Transboundary Resource Management in the Lake of the Woods Watershed*. Vancouver: UBC Press, 2019.

Biermann, Frank, and Steffen Bauer, eds. *A World Environment Organization: Solution or Threat for Effective International Environmental Governance?* Aldershot, UK: Ashgate, 2005.

Biermann, Frank, and Bernd Siebenhuner, eds. *Managers of Global Change: The Influence of International Environmental Bureaucracies*. Cambridge, MA: MIT Press, 2009.

Bilder, Richard. "Controlling Great Lakes Pollution: A Study in United States-Canadian Environmental Cooperation." *Michigan Law Review* 70, no. 3 (1972): 469–556.

Bloomfield, Louis Mortimer, and Gerald Francis FitzGerald. *Boundary Waters Problems of Canada and the United States: The International Joint Commission, 1912-1958.* Toronto: Carswell, 1958.

Bogue, Margaret Beattie. *Fishing the Great Lakes: An Environmental History, 1783-1933.* Madison: University of Wisconsin Press, 2000.

Bothwell, Robert. *Canada and the United States: The Politics of Partnership.* New York: Twayne Publishers, 1992.

Botts, Lee, and Paul Muldoon. *Evolution of the Great Lakes Water Quality Agreement.* East Lansing: Michigan State University Press, 2005.

Bouchier, Nancy B., and Ken Cruikshank. *The People and the Bay: A Social and Environmental History of Hamilton Harbour.* Vancouver: UBC Press, 2016.

"The Boundary Waters Treaty Centennial Symposium." *Wayne Law Review*, 54, no. 4 (Winter 2008). https://heinonline.org/HOL/Page?handle=hein.journals/waynlr54&id=1423&collection=journals&index=.

Brebner, John Bartlett. *North Atlantic Triangle: The Interplay of Canada, the United States and Great Britain.* Toronto: Ryerson Press, 1945.

Brooks, Stephen. "The International Joint Commission: Convergence, Divergence, or Submergence?" In *Transboundary Environmental Governance in Canada and the United States*, 3-18. Washington, DC: Woodrow Wilson International Center for Scholars, Canada Institute, Occasional Paper Series, 2009.

———. "The International Joint Commission: The Promise and Limits of an Ambitious Model." In *Transboundary Environmental Governance Across the World's Longest Border*, edited by Stephen Brooks and Andrea Olive, 1-30. Lansing: Michigan State University Press, 2018.

Brooks, Stephen, and Andrea Olive. *Transboundary Environmental Governance Across the World's Longest Border.* East Lansing: Michigan State University Press, 2018.

Buhi, Jason and Lin Feng. "The International Joint Commission's Role in the United States Canada Transboundary Air Pollution Control Regime: A Century of Experience to Guide the Future." *Vermont Journal of Environmental Law* 11, no. 1 (2009): 107-44.

Caldwell, Lynton. "Disharmony in the Great Lakes Basin: Institutional Jurisdictions Frustrate the Ecosystem Approach." *Alternatives* 20, no. 3 (1994): 26-31.

———. *International Environmental Policy.* Durham, NC: Duke University Press, 1984.

Carroll, John E. *Environmental Diplomacy: An Examination and a Prospective of Canadian- United States Transboundary Environmental Relations.* Ann Arbor: University of Michigan Press, 1983.

Chacko, J. C. *The International Joint Commission between the United States of America and the Dominion of Canada.* New York: Columbia University Press, 1932.

Changnon, Stanley A. "Temporal Behavior of Levels of the Great Lakes and Climate Variability." *Journal of Great Lakes Research* 30 (2004): 184-200.

Changnon, Stanley A., and Joyce M. Changnon. "History of the Chicago Diversion and Future Implications." *Journal of Great Lakes Research* 22, no. 1 (1996): 100–18.

Clamen, Murray. "The IJC and Transboundary Water Disputes: Past, Present, and Future." In *Water Without Borders? Canada, the United States, and Shared Waters*, edited by Emma S. Norman, Alice Cohen, and Karen Bakker, 159–78. Toronto: University of Toronto Press, 2013.

Clamen, Murray, and Daniel Macfarlane. "The International Joint Commission, Water Levels, and Transboundary Governance in the Great Lakes." *Review of Policy Research* 32, no. 1 (2015): 40–59.

———. "Plan 2014: The Historical Evolution of Lake Ontario St. Lawrence River Regulation." *Canadian Water Resources Journal / Revue canadienne des ressources hydriques* 43, no. 4 (December 2018): 416–31.

Colborn, Theodora E., Alex Davidson, Sharon N. Green, R. A. Hodge, C. Ian Jackson, and Richard A. Liroff. *Great Lakes, Great Legacy?* Washington, DC: Conservation Foundation, 1990.

Conca, Ken. *Governing Water: Contentious Transnational Politics and Global Institution Building*. Cambridge, MA: MIT Press, 2006.

Corbett, P. E. *The Settlement of Canadian-American Disputes: A Critical Study of Methods and Results*. Toronto: Ryerson Press, 1937.

Cosens, Barbara, ed. *The Columbia River Treaty Revisited: Transboundary River Governance in the Face of Uncertainty*. Corvalis: Oregon State University Press, 2012.

Curtis, K. M., and J. E. Carroll. *Canadian-American Relations: The Promise and the Challenge*. Toronto: DC Heath and Company, 1983.

Dealey, J. Q. "The Chicago Drainage Canal and St. Lawrence Development." *American Journal of International Law* 23, no. 2 (April 1929): 307–28.

Dellapenna, Joseph W. "International Law's Lessons for the Law of the Lakes." *University of Michigan Journal of Law Reform* 40 (2007): 754–7.

Dempsey, Dave. *On the Brink: The Great Lakes in the 21st Century*. East Lansing: Michigan State University Press, 2004.

Denning, Meredith. "Connections and Consensus: Changing Goals for Transnational Water Management on Lake Erie and Lake Ontario, 1900-1972." PhD diss., Georgetown University, 2018.

Dinwoodie, D. H. "The Politics of International Pollution Control: The Trail Smelter Case." *International Journal* 27, no. 1 (1971–2): 219–35.

Dolan, Lawrence S. "Comment on 'The St. Mary and Milk Rivers: The 1921 Order Revisited' by R. Halliday and G. Faveri." *Canadian Water Resource Journal* 32, no. 4. (2007): 335–8.

Dorsey, Kurkpatrick. *The Dawn of Conservation Diplomacy: U.S.-Canadian Wildlife Protection Treaties in the Progressive Era*. Seattle: University of Washington Press, 1998.

Dreisziger, N. F. "The Campaign to Save Niagara Falls and the Settlement of United States Canadian Differences, 1906–1911." *New York History* 55, no. 4 (October 1974): 437–58.

———. "The Great Lakes in United States-Canadian Relation: The First Stock-Taking." *Inland Seas* (Q.J. Great Lakes Historical Society) 28, no. 4 (1972): 259–71.

———. "The International Joint Commission of the United States and Canada, 1895–1920: A Study in Canadian-American Relations." PhD diss., University of Toronto, 1974.

———. "Wrangling over the St. Mary and Milk." *Alberta History* 28, no. 2 (1980): 6–15.

Durnil, Gordon. *The Making of a Conservative Environmentalist*. Bloomington: Indiana University Press, 2001.

Egan, Dan. *The Death and Life of the Great Lakes*. New York: Norton, 2017.

Fox, Annette Baker, Alfred O. Hero, Jr., and Joseph S. Nye. *Canada and the United States: Transnational and Transgovernmental Relations*. New York: Columbia University Press, 1976.

Francis, George. "Binational Cooperation for Great Lakes Water Quality: A Framework for the Groundwater Connection." *Chicago-Kent Law Review* 65, no. 2 (1989): 359–73.

Gibbons, Alan O. "Sir George Gibbons and the Boundary Waters Treaty of 1909." *Canadian Historical Review* 34, no. 2 (June 1953): 124–38.

Glazebrook, George. *A History of Canadian External Relations*. Toronto: Oxford University Press, 1950.

Gluek, Jr., Alvin C. "Pilgrimages to Ottawa: Canadian-American Diplomacy, 1903–1913." *Historical Papers* 3, no. 1 (1968): 64–83.

Graff, Maurice O. "The Lake Michigan Water Diversion Controversy: A Summary Statement." *Journal of the Illinois State Historical Society* 34, no. 4 (December 1941): 453–71.

Griffin, William. "A History of the Canadian-United States Boundary Waters treaty of 1909." *University of Detroit Law Journal* 37, no. 1 (October 1959): 76–95.

Grover, Velma, and Gail Krantzberg, eds. *Great Lakes: Lessons in Participatory Governance*. New York: CRC Press, 2012.

———. "Transboundary Water Management: Lessons Learnt from North America." *Review of Policy Research* 40, no. 1 (2015): 183–98.

Hall, Noah D. "Toward a New Horizontal Federalism: Interstate Water Management in the Great Lakes Region." *Colorado Law Review* 77 (2006): 405–56.

———. "Transboundary Pollution: Harmonizing International and Domestic Law." *University of Michigan Journal of Law Reform* 40 (2007): 681–746.

Halliday, R., and G. Faveri. "The St. Mary and Milk Rivers: The 1921 Order Revisited." *Canadian Water Resources Journal* 32, no. 1 (2007): 75–92.

Hartig, John H. "Great Lakes Remedial Action Plans: Fostering Adaptive Ecosystem-Based Management Processes." *American Review of Canadian Studies* 27, no. 3 (1997): 437–58.

———. *Waterfront Porch: Reclaiming Detroit's Industrial Waterfront as a Gathering Place for All.* Lansing: Michigan State University Press, 2019.

Hartig, John H., and Michael Zarrell. *Under RAPs: Toward Grassroots Ecological Democracy in the Great Lakes Basin.* Ann Arbor: University of Michigan Press, 1992.

Hays, Samuel P. *Conservation and the Gospel of Efficiency: The Progressive Conservation Movement, 1890–1920.* Pittsburgh: University of Pittsburgh Press, 1959.

Heasley, Lynne, and Daniel Macfarlane, eds. *Border Flows: A Century of the Canadian American Water Relationship.* Calgary: University of Calgary Press, 2016.

Heeney, Arnold D. P. "Along the Common Frontier: The International Joint Commission." *Behind the Headlines* 26, no. 5 (July 1967).

———. *Along the Common Frontier: The International Joint Commission.* Toronto: Canadian Institute of International Affairs, 1967.

Heinmiller, B. Timothy. "Multilevel Governance and the Politics of Environmental Water Recoveries." In *Multilevel Environmental Governance: Managing Water and Climate Change in Europe and North America*, edited by Inger Weibust and James Meadowcroft, 58–79. Cheltenham, UK: Edward Edgar, 2014.

———. *Water Policy Reform in Southern Alberta: An Advocacy Coalition Approach.* Toronto: University of Toronto Press, 2016.

Hilliker, John. *Canada's Department of External Affairs, Volume 1: The early years, 1909–1946.* Montreal: McGill-Queen's University Press, 1990.

Hillmer, Norman, and Jack Granatstein. *For Better or For Worse: Canada and the United States into the twenty-first century.* Toronto: Nelson, 2005.

Hsu, Shi-Ling, and Austen L. Parrish. "Litigating Canada-U.S. Transboundary Harm: International Environmental Lawmaking and the Threat of Extra-territorial Reciprocity." *Virginia Journal of International Law* 48 (2007): 1–64.

Jetoo, Savatri, Adam Thorn, Kathryn Friedman, Sara Gosman, and Gail Krantzberg. "Governance and geopolitics as drivers of change in the Great Lakes–St. Lawrence basin." *Journal of Great Lakes Research* 41 (2015): 108–18

Jockel, Joseph T. and Alan M. Schwartz. "The Changing Role of the Canada-United States International Joint Commission." *Environmental Review* 8, no. 3 (Autumn 1984): 236–51.

Johns, Carolyn. "The Great Lakes, Water Quality and Water Policy in Canada." In *Water Policy and Governance in Canada*, edited by Steven Renzetti and Diane P. Dupont, 159–80. New York: Springer, 2017.

———. "Transboundary Environmental Governance and Water Pollution in the Great Lakes Region: Recent Progress and Future Challenges." In *Transboundary Environmental Governance Across the World's Longest Border*, edited by Stephen

Brooks and Andrea Olive, 77–112. East Lansing: Michigan State University Press, 2018.

———. "Transboundary Water Pollution Efforts in the Great Lakes: The Significance of National and Sub-national Policy Capacity." In *Environmental Governance on the 49th Parallel: New Century, New Approaches*, edited by Barry Rabe and Stephen Brooks, 63–82. Washington, DC: Woodrow Wilson International Center for Scholars, Canada Institute, 2010.

———. "Water Pollution in the Great Lakes Basin: The Global-Local Dynamic." In *Environmental Challenges and Opportunities: Local-Global Perspectives on Canadian Issues*, edited by Christopher Gore and Peter Stoett, 95–129. Toronto: Emond Montgomery, 2009.

Johns, Carolyn, and Mark Sproule-Jones. "Great Lakes Water Policy: The Cases of Water Levels and Water Pollution in Lake Erie." In *Canadian Environmental Policy and Politics: Prospects for Leadership and Innovation*, 4th ed., edited by Deborah VanNijnatten, 252–77. Toronto: Oxford University Press.

Johnson, Marc Pierre, and André Beaulieu. *The Environment and NAFTA: Understanding and Implementing the New Continental Law*. Washington, DC: Island Press, 1995.

Jordan, F. J. E. *An Annotated Digest of Materials Relating to the Establishment and Development of the International Joint Commission*. Prepared for internal use of the Canadian Section of the International Joint Commission, Ottawa, 1967.

———. "Great Lakes Pollution: A Framework for Action." *Ottawa Law Review* 5 (1971): 65–9.

Keenleyside, Hugh L. *Canada and the United States: Some Aspects of the History of the Republic and the Dominion*. New York: Alfred A. Knopf Inc, 1929.

Kehoe, Terence. *Cleaning Up the Great Lakes: From Cooperation to Confrontation*. Dekalb: Northern Illinois University Press, 1997.

Kenny, James L., and Andrew Secord. "Public Power for Industry: A Re-examination of the New Brunswick Case, 1940–1960." *Acadiensis* 30, no. 2 (Spring 2001): 84–108.

Kirton, John. "Generating Effective Global Environmental Governance: The North's Need for a World Environment Organization." In *A World Environment Organization: Solution or Threat for Effective International Environmental Governance?*, edited by Frank Biermann and Steffen Bauer, 145–72. Aldershot, UK: Ashgate, 2005.

Kirton, John. *Canadian Foreign Policy in a Changing World*. Toronto: Thomson Nelson, 2007.

Kirton, John, and Raphael Fernandez de Castro. *NAFTA's Institutions: The Environmental Potential and Performance of the NAFTA Free Trade Commission and Related Bodies*. Montreal: Commission for Environmental Cooperation, 1997.

Kirton, John, and Ella Kokotsis. *The Global Governance of Climate Change: G7, G20 and UN Leadership*. Farnham, UK: Ashgate, 2015.

Krantzberg, Gail. "Keeping Remedial Action Plans on target: Lessons learned from Collingwood Harbour." *Journal of Great Lakes Research* 29 (2003): 641–51.

Krantzberg, Gail. "Renegotiating the Great Lakes Water Quality Agreement: The Process for a Sustainable Outcome." *Sustainability* 1 (2009): 254–67.

Krantzberg, Gail, Marty Bratzel, and John McDonald. "Contribution of the International Joint Commission to Great Lakes Renewal." *Great Lakes Geographer* 13 (2006): 25–37.

Krin, Jackie, and Marion Marts. "The Skagit High Ross Controversy: Negotiation and Settlement." *National Resources Journal* 26 (1986): 261–85.

La Forest, G. V. "Boundary Problems in the East." In *Canada-United States Treaty Relations*, edited by David R. Deener, 28–50. Durham, NC: Duke University Press, 1963.

Langston, Nancy. *Sustaining Lake Superior: An Extraordinary Lake in a Changing World*. New Haven, CT: Yale University Press, 2017.

Lee, Deborah H., Frank H. Quinn, Douglas Sparks, and Jean Clause Rassam. "Modification of great lakes regulation plans for simulation of maximum Lake Ontario outflows." *Journal of Great Lakes Research* 20 (1994): 569–82.

Lemarquand, David. "The International Joint Commission and Changing Canada-United States Boundary Relations." *Natural Resources Journal* 33 (1993): 59–91.

Le Prestre, Philippe, and Peter Stoett, eds. *Bilateral Ecopolitics: Continuity and Change in Canadian-American Environmental Relations*. Burlington, VT: Ashgate, 2006.

Lynde, Cornelius. "The Controversy Concerning the Diversion of Water from Lake Michigan by the Sanitary District of Chicago." *Illinois Law Review* 25, no. 3 (1930): 243–60.

Macfarlane, Daniel. " 'A Completely Man-Made and Artificial Cataract': The Transnational Manipulation of Niagara Falls." *Environmental History* 18, no. 4 (October 2013): 759–84.

———. *Negotiating a River: Canada, the U.S., and the Creation of the St. Lawrence Seaway*. Vancouver: UBC Press, 2014.

———. "Fluid Relations: Hydro Developments, the International Joint Commission, and Canada-U.S. Border Waters." In *Towards Continental Environmental Policy? North American Transnational Environmental Networks and Governance*, edited by Peter Stoett and Owen Temby, 307–33. Albany: SUNY Press, 2017.

———. "Natural Security: Canada-US Environmental Diplomacy." In *Undiplomatic History: Rethinking Canada in the World*, edited by Asa McKercher and Philip Van Huizen, 107–36. Montreal: McGill-Queen's University Press, 2019.

Macfarlane, Daniel, and Noah Hall. "Transborder Water Management and Governance in the Great Lakes-St. Lawrence Basin." In *Transboundary Environmental Governance Across the World's Longest Border*, edited by Stephen Brooks and Andrea Olive, 31–50. Lansing: Michigan State University Press, 2018.

Macfarlane, Daniel, and Peter Kitay. "Hydraulic Imperialism: Hydro-electric Development and Treaty 9 in the Abitibi Region." *American Review of Canadian Studies* 47, no. 3 (Fall 2016): 380–97.

MacKay, Robert A. "The International Joint Commission between the United States and Canada." *American Journal of International Law* 22, no. 2 (1928): 292–318.

Makepeace, Garth O. "The International Joint Commission: Determinants of Success." MA thesis, University of British Columbia, 1980.

McCaffrey, Stephen. "The Harmon Doctrine One Hundred Years Later: Buried, Not Praised." *Natural Resources Journal* 36, no. 4 (1996): 965–1007.

McClane, Ryan P. "The St. Mary and the Milk River, Two Rivers, One Stream." *University of Denver Water Law Review* 14 (2010): 131–33.

McLaughlin, Chris, and Gail Krantzberg. "An Appraisal of Policy Implementation Deficits in the Great Lakes." *Journal of Great Lakes Research* 37, no. 2 (2011): 390–6.

Melosi, Martin. *The Sanitary City: Urban Infrastructure in America from Colonial Times to the Present*. Baltimore, MD: Johns Hopkins University Press, 2000.

Minghi, Julian V. "Point Roberts, Washington: Boundary Problems of an American Exclave." In *Borderlines and Borderlands: Political Oddities at the Edge of the Nation-State*, edited by Alexander C. Diener and Joshua Hagen, 173–89. Lanham, MD: Rowman and Littlefield, 2010.

Morris, Michelle. "Governance of the St. Mary and Milk Rivers." In *Beyond the Border: Tensions Across the 49th Parallel to the Great Plains*, edited by Kyle Conway and Timothy Patsch, 113–32. Montreal: McGill-Queen's University Press.

Muldoon, Paul Robert. "The International Joint Commission and Point Roberts: A Venture into a New Area of Concern." MA thesis, McMaster University, 1983.

Munton, Don. "Acid Rain Politics in North America: Conflict to Cooperation to Collusion." In *Acid in the Environment: Lessons Learned and Future Prospects*, edited by G. R. Visgilio and D. M. Whitelaw, 175–201. New York: Springer, 2007.

———. "Forests, Fumes and Further Studies: Environmental Science and Policy Inaction in Ontario." *Journal of Canadian Studies* 37, no. 2 (2002): 130–63.

Neary, Peter. "Grey, Bryce and the Settlement of Canadian-American Differences, 1905–1911." *Canadian Historical Review* 49, no. 4 (December 1968): 357–80.

Norman, Emma S. *Governing Transboundary Waters: Canada, the United States, and Indigenous Communities*. London: Routledge, Earthscan Series of Water Resource Management, 2015.

Nossal, Kim Richard. "Institutionalization and the Pacific Settlement of Interstate Conflict: The Case of Canada and the International Joint Commission." *Journal of Canadian Studies* 18, no. 4 (Winter 1983–4): 75–87.

O'Connor, Ryan. *The First Green Wave: Pollution Probe and the Origins of Environmental Activism in Ontario*. Vancouver: UBC Press, 2015.

Paris, Roland. "The Devils Lake Dispute Between Canada and the United States: Lessons For Canadian Government Officials." Ottawa: Centre for International Policy Studies, University of Ottawa, February 2008.

Pentland, Ralph, and Adele Hurley. "Thirsty Neighbours: A Century of Canada-US Transboundary Water Governance." In *Eau Canada: The Future of Canadian Waters*, edited by Karen Bakker, 163–82. Vancouver: UBC Press, 2007.

Pentland, Ralph, and Chris Wood. *Down the Drain: How We Are Failing to Protect our Water*. Vancouver: Greystone Books, 2013.

Piper, Don Courtney. *The International Law of the Great Lakes: A Study of Canadian-United States Co-operation*. Durham, NC: Duke University Press, 1967.

Platt, Harold. "Chicago, the Great Lakes, and the Origins of Federal Urban Environmental Policy." *Journal of the Gilded Age and Progressive Era* 1, no. 2 (April 2002): 122–53.

———. *Shock Cities: The Environmental Transformation and Reform of Manchester and Chicago*. Chicago: University of Chicago Press, 2005.

Quinn, Frank H. "Anthropogenic Changes to Great Lakes Water Levels." *Great Lakes Update* 136 (1999): 1–4.

———. "The Evolution of Federal Water Policy." *Canadian Water Resources Journal* 10 (1985): 21–5.

Read, Jennifer. " 'A Sort of Destiny': The Multi-Jurisdictional Response to Sewage Pollution in the Great Lakes, 1900–1930." *Scientia Canadensis* 22–3 (1998): 103–29.

Read, Jennifer. "Addressing 'A quiet horror': The Evolution of Ontario Pollution Control Policy in the International Great Lakes, 1909–1972." PhD diss., University of Western Ontario, 1999.

Reeves, Andrew. *Overrun: Dispatches from the Asian Carp Crisis*. Toronto: ECW Press, 2019.

Riley, John L. *Once and Future Great Lakes Country: An Ecological History*. Montreal: McGill-Queen's University Press, 2013.

Ross, William, and Marion Marts. "The High Ross Dam Project: Environmental Decisions and Changing Environmental Attitudes." *Canadian Geographic* 19 (1975): 221–34.

Rousell, Stephane. *The North American Democratic Peace: Absence of War and Security Institution-Building in Canada-US Relations, 1867–1958*. Montreal and Kingston: McGill-Queen's University Press, 2004.

Sandford, Robert W., Deborah Harford, and Jon O'Riordan. *The Columbia River Treaty: A Primer*. Victoria, BC: Rocky Mountain Books, 2014.

Scarpino, Philip. "Addressing Cross-Border Pollution of the Great Lakes after World War II: The Canada-Ontario Agreement and the Great Lakes Water Quality Agreement." In *Transnationalism: Canada-United States History into the Twenty-First Century*, edited by M. D. Behiels and R. C. Stuart, 115–32. Montreal: McGill-Queen's University Press, 2010.

Spencer, Robert, John Kirton, and Kim Richard Nossal, eds. *The International Joint Commission Seventy Years On*. Toronto: University of Toronto Centre for International Studies, 1981.

Sproule-Jones, Mark. *Restoration of the Great Lakes: Promises, Practices, Performances.* Vancouver: UBC Press, 2003.

Swayamprakash, Ramya. "Dredge a River, Make a Nation Great: Shipping, Commerce, and Territoriality in the Detroit River, 1870–1905." *Michigan Historical Review* 45, no. 1 (Spring 2019): 27–46.

Tarlock, A. Dan. "The Great Lakes as an Environmental Heritage of Humankind: An International Law Perspective." *University of Michigan Journal of Law Reform* 40 (2007): 995–1020.

Tarr, Joel. *The Search for the Ultimate Sink: Urban Pollution in Historical Perspective.* Akron, OH: University of Akron Press, 1996.

Temby, Owen. "Policy symbolism and air pollution in Toronto and Ontario, 1963–1967." *Planning Perspectives* 30, no. 2 (2015): 271–84.

Temby, Owen, and Peter Stoett, eds. *Towards Continental Environmental Policy? North American Transnational Networks and Governance.* Albany: SUNY Press, 2017.

Thompson, John Herd, and Stephen J. Randall. *Canada and the United States: Ambivalent Allies.* 4th Ed. Athens: University of Georgia Press, 2008.

Toope, Stephen, and Jutta Brunne. "Freshwater Regimes: The Mandate of the International Joint Commission." *Arizona Journal of International and Comparative Law* 15, no. 1 (1998): 273–87.

Valiante, Marcia. "How Green is My Treaty? Ecosystem Protection and the 'Order of Precedence' under the Boundary Waters Treaty of 1909." *Wayne Law Review* 54 (2008): 1525–51.

—. "Management of the North American Great Lakes." In *Management of Transboundary Rivers and Lakes,* edited by O. Varis, C. Tortajada, and A. K. Biswas, 245–67. Berlin: Springer, 2008.

Valiante, Marcia, Paul Muldoon, and Lee Botts. "Ecosystem Governance: Lessons from the Great Lakes." In *Global Governance: Drawing Insight from the Environmental Experience,* edited by O. Young, 197–226. Cambridge, MA: MIT Press, 1997.

Vallentyn, Jack R., and Al M. Beeton. "The 'Ecosystem' Approach to Managing Human Uses and Abuses of Natural Resources in the Great Lakes Basin." *Envronmental Conservation* 1 (1988): 58–62.

Van Huizen, Philip. "Building a Green Dam: Environmental Modernism and the Canadian-American Libby Dam Project." *Pacific Historical Review* 79, no. 3 (2010): 418–53.

van de Kerkhof, Martijn. "The Trail Smelter Case Re-examined: Examining the Development of National Procedural Mechanisms to Resolve a Trail Smelter Type Dispute." *Utrecht Journal of International and European Law* 27, no. 73 (2011): 68–83.

Weller, Phil. *Fresh Water Seas: Saving the Great Lakes.* Toronto: Between the Lines, 1990.

Wershof, M. H. "Notes on the Jurisprudence of the International Joint Commission." Prepared for the International Joint Commission, Ottawa, 1975.

White, Richard. *The Organic Machine: The Remaking of the Columbia River.* New York: Hill and Wang, 1995.

Willman, Hildegard. "The Chicago Diversion from Lake Michigan." *Canadian Bar Review* 10, no. 9 (1932): 575–83.

Willoughby, William. "The Appointment and Removal of Members of the International Joint Commission." *Canadian Public Administration* 12, no. 3 (1969): 411–26.

———. *The Joint Organizations of Canada and the United States.* Toronto: University of Toronto Press, 1979.

———. *The St. Lawrence Waterway: A Study in Politics and Diplomacy.* Madison: University of Wisconsin Press, 1961.

Wightman, William R. *The Land Between: Northwestern Ontario Resource Development, 1800 to the 1990s.* Toronto: University of Toronto Press, 1997.

Wirth, John D. *Smelter Smoke in North America: The Politics of Transborder Pollution.* Lawrence: University Press of Kansas, 2000.

Wolfe, M. E. "The Milk River: Deferred Water Policy Transitions in an International Waterway." *Natural Resources Journal* 32, no. 1 (Winter 1992): 55–76.

Young, R. A. "Planning for Power: The New Brunswick Electric Power Commission in the 1950s." *Acadiensis* 12, no. 1 (Autumn 1982): 73–99.

CONTRIBUTORS

JAMIE BENIDICKSON teaches Canadian and international environmental law at the Faculty of Law, University of Ottawa, where he is a member of the Centre for Environmental Law and Global Sustainability. Jamie is the author of *Environmental Law* 5th (Irwin 2019), *The Culture of Flushing: A Social and Legal History of Sewage* (UBC Press, 2007) and *Levelling the Lake: Transboundary Resource Management in the Lake of the Woods Watershed* (UBC Press, 2019). His other water-related publications include "The Evolution of Canadian Water Law and Policy: Towards the Conservation of Sustainable Abundance," (2017) 13 *McGill Journal of Sustainable Development Law and Policy*, 59-108.

NORMAN BRANDSON currently consults on resource and environment issues as President of N2B. He is a member of the Forum for Leadership on Water. For the last 15 years of his career with the government of Manitoba he served as the Deputy Minister of the department of Environment and the founding Deputy Minister of the departments of Conservation and Water Stewardship; and was involved in local, inter-provincial and international water issues throughout his government service.

MURRAY CLAMEN is currently an Affiliate Professor in the department of Bioresource Engineering at McGill University and a Member of the Forum for Leadership on Water. For 35 years prior to 2011, he was employed in the Canadian Section of the International Joint Commission where he held several positions including engineering adviser and Secretary. He is the author of a number of papers, reports and presentations including a text on integrated water management with Jan Adamowski, Cory Zyla, Eduardo Ganem Cuenca, Wietske Medema, and Paul Reig titled *Integrated and Adaptive Water Resources Planning, Management, and Governance* published by WRP LLC (2014).

MEREDITH DENNING is a Junior Fellow at the Bill Graham Centre for Contemporary and International History at the University of Toronto, where she is working on a transnational history of water management on Lake Erie and Lake Ontario. She received her PhD from Georgetown University in 2018

FRANK ETTAWAGESHIK lives in Harbor Springs, Michigan. He is a citizen of the Little Traverse Bay Bands of Odawa Indians and served 14 years, ending in 2009, as the Tribes' elected Chairman. Since 2009, and currently, he is the Executive Director of the United Tribes of Michigan. He is a member of the International Joint Commission's Great Lakes Water Quality Board and the Triennial Assessment of Progress Study Board. During his nearly 45 years of public service he has held numerous Tribal, International, Federal, State and local appointed positions regarding water, climate change, environmental justice, governance, and international relations.

NOAH D. HALL is a Professor of Law at Wayne State University Law School in Detroit, Michigan. He founded the Great Lakes Environmental Law Center and has an active public interest law practice focusing on water and environmental justice. He has co-authored several of the leading books in these fields, "*Water Law: Private Property, Public Rights, and Environmental Protection*" (2018), "*Water Law*" (2017), and "*Environmental Law and Policy: Nature, Law, and Society*" (2016). In 2016, Noah was appointed Special Assistant Attorney General for the Flint water crisis investigation, and served in this role until 2019.

B. TIMOTHY (TIM) HEINMILLER is an Associate Professor in the Department of Political Science at Brock University where he researches and teaches in the areas of Canadian and comparative public policy. His research has been published in such journals as *Politics and Policy,*

Canadian Journal of Political Science, Natural Resources Journal, Review of Policy Research, and *Governance.* His most recent book is *Water Policy Reform in Southern Alberta: An Advocacy Coalition Approach,* published by University of Toronto Press in 2016.

JOHN J. KIRTON is a professor of political science at the University of Toronto, specializing in Canadian foreign policy. He was principle investigator of the Commission for Environmental Cooperation's project to assess NAFTA's environmental effects. He served from 1989 to 2005 as a member of the Foreign Policy Committee of Canada's National Roundtable on the Environment and Economy. He co-edited *The International Joint Commission Seventy Years On* (1982), authored *Canadian Foreign Policy: Theory and Practice* (2019, in Chinese) and co-authored *The Global Governance of Climate Change: G7, G20 and UN Leadership* (2015).

JAMES KENNY is an Associate Professor in the History Department, Royal Military College of Canada. He has published articles on a range of topics related to the political economy and environmental history of New Brunswick. His current research project explores political, social, and environmental factors related to Canada-US attempts to develop hydroelectricity on the St. John River in the postwar era.

GAIL KRANTZBERG is Professor with the Engineering and Public Policy Program at McMaster University offering Canada's first Master's Degree in Engineering and Public Policy. Gail completed her M.Sc. and Ph.D. at the University of Toronto in environmental science and freshwaters. She worked for the Ontario Ministry of Environment from 1988 to 2001, as Coordinator of Great Lakes Programs, and Senior Policy Advisor on Great Lakes. Dr. Krantzberg was the Director of the Great Lakes Regional Office of the International Joint Commission from 2001 to 2005. She has co-edited/authored 8 books and more than 190 scientific and policy articles on issues pertaining to ecosystem quality and sustainability. Her research interests include investigating Great Lakes governance capacity and methods to better integrate science and engineering in policy formulation and decision making.

DANIEL MACFARLANE is an Associate Professor in the Institute of the Environment and Sustainability at Western Michigan University. He is currently President of the International Water History Association (IWHA) and a Senior Fellow in the Bill Graham Centre for Contemporary International History at the University of Toronto. Daniel is the author of *Negotiating a River: Canada, the US, and the Creation of the St. Lawrence Seaway* (2014) and co-editor (with Lynne Heasley) of *Border Flows: A Century of the Canadian-American Water Relationship* (2016), is the author of a forthcoming book on the transborder history of manipulating Niagara Falls, and is working on a co-authored (with Colin Duncan) environmental history of Lake Ontario.

RICH MOY was a US Commissioner on the International Joint Commission (IJC) from 2011 to 2019. Prior to joining the IJC, he worked as a land and water consultant and was a Senior Fellow at the Center of Natural Resources and Environmental Policy at the University of Montana. For 27 years, Mr. Moy oversaw collaborative, strategic and science-based approaches to water policy, management and planning for the State of Montana. He worked on many Native American, trans-boundary and regional water issues. Other work included serving as a member and chair of the 23-member Flathead Basin Commission; directing Montana's involvement in the High Plains Research Experiment; and working as a park ranger/ecologist in Glacier National Park.

DON MUNTON was founding chair of the International Studies Program at the University of Northern British Columbia and a Fulbright Fellow, NATO Fellow and Schlesinger Fellow at the John F. Kennedy Presidential Library. He conducts research and writes in the areas of security, intelligence and environmental policy – including numerous articles on acid rain, the Canada-United States Air Quality Agreement, Great Lakes water pollution and the International Joint Commission. His books include *The Cuban Missile Crisis: A Concise History* (with David Welch), *Canadian Foreign Policy: Selected Cases* (with John Kirton), *Rethinking National Security* (with Hans Rattinger), and *Hazardous Waste Siting and Democratic Choice*.

EMMA S. NORMAN is Department Chair of the Native Environmental Science program at Northwest Indian College, located on Lummi Nation, Coast Salish Territory. Emma works alongside and with Indigenous communities to increase diversity in the STEM field and open up space for multiple ways of knowing. Her writing and teaching engages with critical geographies of space, specifically decolonizing borderlands and Indigenous water governance. She is the author of *Governing Transboundary Water: Canada, the United States and Indigenous communities*, which won the Julian Minghi award for best book in Political Geography in 2015. She is also the co-editor of *Water without Borders: Canada, the United States and Shared Waters* (with Alice Cohen and Karen Bakker), and *Negotiating Water Governance: Why the Politics of Scale Matter* (with Christina Cook and Alice Cohen).

KIM RICHARD NOSSAL is Professor of Political Studies and Director of the Centre for International and Defence Policy at Queen's University. He is the author of a number of works on Canadian foreign and defence policy, including *The Politics of Canadian Foreign Policy*, 4th ed., co-authored with Stéphane Roussel and Stéphane Paquin (2015), *Charlie Foxtrot: Fixing Defence Procurement in Canada* (2016), and *The Politics of War: Canada's Mission in Afghanistan, 2001–14*, co-authored with Jean-Christophe Boucher (2017).

JONATHAN O'RIORDAN was a senior public servant in environment and natural resource policy with the BC Provincial Government. He was a technical advisor to the IJC on the review coal mine development in the Flathead River.

ALLEN OLSON was raised on a diversified North Dakota farm approximately 3 miles from the Manitoba border, approximately 70 miles south of Winnipeg. He received his B.S.B.A in 1961 and J.D. in 1963 from the University of North Dakota in Grand Forks. Allen served as North Dakota Attorney General (1972-80) and Governor (1980-84) as well as on the International Joint Commission (2002-10).

RALPH PENTLAND is currently President of Ralbet Enterprises Incorporated, a Member of the Forum for Leadership on Water, a Board Member with LakePulse, and a Member of the Advisory Committee for Environmental Defense Canada. For 13 years prior to 1991, he was Director of Water Planning and Management in the Canadian Federal Government, where he was responsible for negotiating and administering numerous federal-provincial and Canada-US Agreements, and was the primary author of the *1987 Federal Water Policy*. Since 1991, he served as a water and environmental consultant in numerous countries, served as Canadian Co-Chairman on several IJC Boards and Committees, collaborated with several non-governmental and academic organizations, helped negotiate major intergovernmental agreements in the Great Lakes and Mackenzie Basins, and was co-author of the 2013 book *Down the Drain: How We Are Failing to Protect our Water Resources.*

JENNIFER READ is Director of the University of Michigan Water Center where she brings regional decision makers and university expertise together to address some of the biggest challenges in the Great Lakes region. Jen has held positions at the Great Lakes Commission, the Great Lakes Institute for Environmental Research at the University of Windsor, and as Assistant Director and Research Coordinator of Michigan Sea Grant. From 2008-14 Jen served as the first Executive Director of the bi-national Great Lakes Observing System, a regional node of the US Integrated Ocean Observing System (IOOS). Jen currently serves on the US IOOS federal advisory committee as well as the Environmental Information Services Working Group reporting to NOAA's Science Advisory Board, and has served on various IJC water quantity working groups.

A. DAN TARLOCK is University Distinguished Professor Emeritus, Illinois-Tech Chicago-Kent College of Law. Dan has written and consulted extensively on United States and international water management. During the 1980s and 1990s, he worked with Great Lakes governors and the IJC on a wide range of diversion-related issues.

OWEN TEMBY is an associate professor in the School of Earth, Environmental, and Marine Sciences at the University of Texas Rio Grande Valley (UTRGV). He is an environmental policy specialist with current research in air pollution and fishery policy. Before joining UTRGV Dr. Temby worked as a postdoctoral fellow at McGill University and Carleton University. He is the author of numerous articles in respected journals and editor (with Peter Stoett) of the book, *Towards Continental Environmental Policy? North American Transnational Networks and Governance* (SUNY Press, 2017). One of his recent journal articles won the Ontario Historical Society's Riddell Award for the best article of the year on Ontario History. Presently Dr. Temby serves as editor for English-language content of *Urban History Review/Revue d'histoire urbaine*.

MARCIA VALIANTE is Professor Emerita in the Faculty of Law, University of Windsor. Her teaching and research have focused on Canadian environmental law, water law and Canada-US environmental policy. She is currently Vice-Chair of the Ontario Environmental Review Tribunal.

DEBORA L. VANNIJNATTEN is Professor, Political Science and North American Studies at Wilfrid Laurier University and Associate Faculty in the Balsillie School of International Affairs. Her current research focuses on the design and application of indicators for assessing the performance of transboundary institutions and networks aimed at managing water disputes in North America.

BRITTANEY WARREN is the Director of Compliance Research and Lead Researcher for Climate Change for the G7 and G20 Research Groups, based at the Munk School of Global Affairs and Public Policy and Trinity College at the University of Toronto. Brittaney is a co-author of "G7 Governance of Climate Change: The Search for Effectiveness" in *The G7, Anti-Globalism and the Governance of Globalization* (2018), and co-author of "G20 Governance of Digitalization" in the *International Organisations Research Journal* (2018). She has a scholarly background in International Relations at the University of Toronto and in Environmental Studies at York University.

DAVID WHORLEY is the Director of Resource Management Operations at Fisheries and Oceans Canada (DFO). His work with the federal government at DFO, the Privy Council Office, Global Affairs Canada, and Environment and Climate Change Canada has included extensive involvement in Canada-US relations in the areas of joint fisheries, shared waterways, regulatory cooperation, and migratory wildlife. He has published widely on Canadian public policy and administration, and Canada-US diplomatic history.

TED R. YUZYK worked for more than 27 years on the a broad range of water programs at Environment Canada. In 2006, he left Environment Canada to become the Canadian Chair of the International Upper Great Lakes Study, a five year binational study responsible for developing a new water regulation plan. After completion of the study, he continued on at the International Joint Commission as Director of Science and Engineering until he retired in 2014. He continues to contribute his expertise to many IJC initiatives, the most current being the International Lake Champlain-Richelieu River Study.

INDEX

A

Accredited Officers, 99, 150, 152–53, 156, 163
Acid Rain, 213, 314, 335–37, 339, 492–93
Adaptive Management, 260, 275, 311, 331, 385, 417, 424, 478, 513, 517–18, 544
Agriculture, 73, 146, 147, 154, 222, 226, 258, 303, 315, 319, 323, 367–68, 372–74, 379, 382, 405, 410, 468, 473. *See also* irrigation
Air Quality Agreement (1991), 213, 313, 314, 335–36, 339
Alaska Boundary, 69, 82, 85–88, 103
Allagash River, 180–81, 183, 187, 192–93
Anderson, Chandler, 52, 58–64, 95, 97–99, 104
Arctic Council, 488, 491, 502
Areas of Concern (AOCs), 25, 368, 371, 378, 380–83, 385, 387, 388, 408–14, 420–21, 428
Ashtabula River, 373, 383
Atlantic Ocean, 43, 45, 49, 67, 215, 490–91

B

Bay of Fundy, 134, 166–67, 170, 185
Belcourt, Napoleon, 133–36
Belly River, 146, 154–55, 157–58, 160, 511, 513
Bennett, Richard Bedford, 500, 503
Bennett, William Andrew Cecil (WAC), 244, 246
Berry, George T., 251, 277
Biodiversity, 159, 301, 471–72, 545
Birch Lake, 50, 79

Boating, 1, 467, 542
Borden, Robert, 16, 500, 503
Boundary Bay, 196, 200, 208
Bourassa, Robert, 304
Bowell, Mackenzie, 134–35
Bryce, James, 5, 91–94, 97, 102
Burpee, Lawrence, 197–98
Burton Act, 296.
Bush, George W., 468, 500, 503

C

Campobello Island, 408
Canada Centre for Inland Waters, 408
Canada–United States Free Trade Agreement (CUFTA), 306, 490–91, 493–94
Canada–US Air Quality Committee (AQC), 335–36, 339
Carter, Jimmy, 249, 407, 492, 500, 503
Chemical Valley (Sarnia), 324, 328–29, 331–32, 338
Chicago Diversion, 5, 12, 40–41, 46–48, 60, 79–81, 89, 94–95, 98–99, 103, 288, 294, 300–301, 486, 525
Chrétien, Jean, 487, 500, 503
Clark, Joe, 492, 500, 503
Climate change, 99, 144–45, 156–60, 260, 261, 275, 301–3, 309, 401, 411, 414, 417, 419, 423, 440, 467–68, 485, 492, 495, 497–99, 510, 515, 517, 525–27, 544–45, 547
Clinton–Gibbons Draft, 36, 53–63, 69–70, 94–95, 98

597

Cohen, Maxwell, 11, 489, 535–36
Collingwood Harbour, 368, 374–75, 381, 428
Columbia River, 7, 12, 24, 45, 55, 165–66, 170, 175, 186, 225, 240, 253–61, 314, 316–17, 436–41, 460, 470, 510, 526, 529, 532, 542
Columbia River Treaty (CRT), 21, 193, 220, 239–41, 253–61, 340, 440, 510, 539, 542
Commission on Environmental Cooperation (CEC), 484–85, 493–97
Connecting Channels Reference (Great Lakes), 349, 354–56, 358, 361, 363
Conservation, 37–38, 77, 89, 133, 171, 180–181, 196, 205–6, 210, 252, 255, 261, 269, 306, 379, 382, 465, 472, 510–511, 532. *See also* environmentalism; preservation
Cooper, Dexter, 166–67, 177
Council of Great Lakes Governors, 306

D

Dams, 20, 77, 79, 80, 83, 99, 155, 159, 166–67, 170, 175, 177, 180–81, 183, 185, 187, 240, 253, 255, 257, 258–59, 289, 291–93, 297, 299, 314, 438, 440, 442, 507, 517, 521, 544
Deer Lake, 373–74, 381
Detroit, 76, 124, 127, 141, 203, 324–27, 330–31, 334–35
Detroit River, 12, 46, 126, 130, 287, 310, 324–38, 354–55, 357, 368, 373
Devils Lake, 22, 217, 225–31, 514–15
Diefenbaker, John, 257, 487, 488, 500, 503, 510
Diversions (water), 7, 8, 9, 21, 25, 39–49, 50–51, 54–55, 60–61, 72, 81, 83, 86, 94, 99, 151, 154, 158–59, 227–28, 286–87, 293, 297, 299, 303, 304–5, 310, 314, 357, 425, 457, 458, 464–67, 469–71, 477, 486, 511–13, 515–16

E

Eastern Tributaries, 146, 152, 155, 156, 159, 160
Ecosystem approach, 348, 377–78, 386, 388, 390, 405–6, 411, 440–45, 473–74, 494, 498, 513, 519, 524, 538, 543
Eisenhower, Dwight, 174, 187, 257, 500, 503, 510
Environment Canada (Environment and Climate Change Canada), 361, 408, 414, 416, 418, 543
Environmental assessment, 194, 239, 247, 248, 258, 263
Environmentalism, 1, 483–86, 491–98, 546. *See also* conservation; preservation
External Affairs, Department of (Canada), 93, 103–4, 168–69, 185, 243, 250, 265, 416, 536

F

First Nations, 20, 90, 170, 201, 258, 272, 280, 295, 305, 379, 388, 417, 421, Chapter 14 *passsim*, 471, 474, 480, 509, 511, 519–20, 525–26, 531, 540–41, 543
Fish, 159, 175, 181, 218, 226, 229, 258, 266, 268, 271–72, 295, 358, 372–76, 381, 383, 399–400, 410, 419, 440, 442, 515
Fish and wildlife, 217–18, 255, 308, 358, 368, 372–75, 381, 410, 510
Fisheries, 54, 59, 69, 93, 96, 168, 170, 175, 181–82, 185, 189, 201, 241, 255, 258, 263, 265–66, 269, 286, 379, 399, 434, 438–40, 470, 496, 515, 521
Flathead River, 24, 239–41, 261, 263–67, 269–71, 273, 281
Flooding, 3, 19, 28, 183, 189, 194, 221–25, 230, 240, 246–48, 251, 255–61, 308, 340, 437–38, 467, 470, 510, 542, 544
Ford, Gerald, 248–49
Forestry, 405, 485
Fraser River, 201

G

Garrison Diversion, 19, 198, 217–21, 227, 230–31, 233, 474
General Agreement on Tariffs and Trade (GATT), 306, 464, 488, 501–2
Georgia Strait, 200, 205
Georgian Bay, 55
Gibbons, George, 46, 48, 52, 54, 56, 58, 64, 89, 93, 95–99, 102–4
Gordon, Douglas J., 251, 277
Grand Coulee Dam, 19, 198, 217–21, 227, 230–31, 233, 474
Great Depression, 16, 137, 221, 300, 320, 351, 353
Great Lakes, 6, 8, 16, 17, 20, 25, 40–49, 71, 105, 116, 122, 124–36, 260, 274, 284–308, 314, 347–64, 367–90, 395–424, 464–68, 470, 484, 486, 492, 498, 516, 538, 540, 541, 544
Great Lakes basin, 19, 25, 40, 77, 98, 149, 285–95, 301–6, 309, 335, 347, 353, 357, 361, 362, 364, 367, 371, 380, 383–84, 386, 395–424, 443–44, 445, 449, 450–51, 465–67, 473, 515, 525, 546
Great Lakes Charter, 305, 476, 516
Great Lakes Restoration Initiative (GLRI), 383, 416, 421, 495–96, 542
Great Lakes Science Advisory Board, 260, 389, 415, 443, 473
Great Lakes Water Quality Agreement (GLWQA), 7–8, 9, 12, 17, 19, 20, 21, 25, 286, 301, 314, 335, 347–56, 363, 370–90, 395–97, 402–8, 410–23, 438, 443, 444, 449, 450, 452, 473, 490, 530–32, 538–39, 541, 543–46
Great Lakes Water Quality Board (GLWQB), 260, 361–63, 371–72, 389, 404, 444, 448–52, 544
Great Lakes–St. Lawrence basin, 15, 23, 24, 25, 40, 79, 286–95, 302–3, 305, 395, 465, 496, 516, 518, 523, 529, 542
Great Lakes–St. Lawrence River Adaptive Management Committee, 518
Great Lakes–St. Lawrence River Basin Water Resources Compact (Great Lakes–St. Lawrence Compact, Great Lakes–St. Lawrence River Basin Compact), 12, 305–6, 464–68, 545
Great Lakes–St. Lawrence River Basin Sustainable Water Resources Agreement, 305, 516
Great Recycling and Northern Development (GRAND), 304
Grey, Earl, 88–93, 102, 104

H

Harmon Doctrine, 21, 95, 148, 458–59
Harper, Stephen, 487, 489, 500, 503
Heeney, Arnold Danford Patrick (ADP), 198, 314
HEPCO, 16. *See also* Ontario Hydro
High Modernism, 290
Horseshoe Falls. *See* Niagara Falls
Hudson Bay, Hudson's Bay, 39, 50, 53, 145, 217, 218, 226, 231, 469
Hydro-electricity, 1, 5, 6, 7, 10, 12, 16, 20, 21, 24–25, 38, 40–41, 46–47, 50, 54–55, 59, 72, 76–77, 79, 81, 86, 94–95, 98–102, 105, 149, 165–87, 203, 209, 240, 243–44, 248, 250–51, 253, 255–59, 261, 285–96, 299–300, 357–59, 436–42, 452, 470, 472, 510, 519, 529, 542–43
Hydropower. *See* hydro-electricity

I

Illinois River, 300
Indigenous Peoples. *See* First Nations
International Air Quality Advisory Board (IAQAB), 7, 313–14, 336, 344
International Lake Superior Board of Control, 289, 295
International Niagara Board of Control, 296, 300
International Ontario–Michigan Air Pollution Board (IOMAPB), 333–34, 338–39, 344
International Passamaquoddy Engineering Board (IPEB), 175–79, 181–82, 187, 192–93

International Rainy–Lake of the Woods Watershed Board, 474, 514, 520
International Red River Board, 224, 234
International Reference Group on Great Lakes Pollution from Land Use Activities (PLUARG), 405, 409
International St. Croix River Watershed Board, 448, 514
International St. Lawrence River Board of Control, 290
International Souris River Board, 235
International trade, 306, 464, 486, 525
International Trade Organization (ITO), 488, 502
International Watershed Board(s), 9, 260, 306–7, 436, 439, 445–46, 448
International Watersheds Initiative (IWI), 25, 224, 252, 306, 436, 438, 445–49, 452, 474, 513–15, 524, 526, 541, 543, 546
International Waterways Commission (IWC), 5, 23, 35–37, 42–46, 48–53, 56–57, 62–64, 66–67, 69, 82, 89–90, 93, 102, 111, 149, 288
Invasive species, 291, 220, 226, 228–29, 286, 292, 301, 310, 411, 414, 419–21, 471
Irrigation, 218, 255, 258, 357, 358, 470, 472, 510–12. *See also* agriculture

J

Jackfish Bay, 368, 381
James Bay, 294, 304
Johnson, Lyndon B., 184–85, 205, 500, 503, 510

K

Kennebec River, 169
Kennedy, John F., 174, 183–84, 186, 484, 500, 503

L

Lake Erie, 46, 54, 55–56, 73, 77, 126, 285, 287, 295, 299–301, 303, 311, 324, 354, 370, 376, 399, 400, 407, 414, 420, 484
Lake Huron, 41, 54–55, 73, 76, 106, 126, 162, 285, 288, 295, 301–3, 324, 328, 354
Lake Michigan, 7, 40, 55, 78, 99, 106, 285, 288, 295, 300–303, 496
Lake of the Woods, 46, 50, 79, 126, 235, 281, 289, 448, 492, 525
Lake Ontario, 1–3, 10, 54–55, 73, 77, 126, 128, 136, 260, 285–87, 292–93, 295, 301–2, 308, 354, 370, 385, 400, 442, 474, 545
Lake St. Clair, 287, 354
Lake St. Lawrence, 291
Lake Superior, 10, 41, 55, 73, 76, 235, 285, 286, 289, 294–95, 301, 303, 354, 518–19
Lake Winnipeg, 215, 228, 515, 523
Lakewide Action and Management Plans (LAMPs), 25, 371, 386, 409–15, 443
Laurier, Wilfrid, 45, 52, 54, 76, 81–82, 84, 86–96, 98–102, 500, 503
Libby Dam, 258
Long Lac Diversion, 240, 256, 258–59, 278
Lower Lakes Reference, 349, 361–63

M

Martin, Paul, 487, 492, 500, 503
McKenzie King, William Lyon, 486, 500, 503
McNair, John B., 170–71
McNaughton, Andrew GL (AGL), 23, 190, 191, 246, 256, 278, 532
Merrimack River, 117–18
Métis, 388, 417, 421, 443–44, 449–54, 520. *See also* First Nations
Michigan, Government of, 330, 332–34, 338
Migratory Bird Convention, 350
Milk River, 5, 39–40, 80, 108, 157, 159, 163, 464–65, 468–70
Mississippi River, 40, 78, 235, 253, 288
Missouri River, 39, 145, 217, 219–20, 226, 228, 231–32, 235, 253, 469
Monroe Doctrine, 85
Muir, John, 37–38
Mulroney, Brian, 492, 493, 500, 503

N

National Research Council of Canada (NRC), 318
National Water Resources Institute, 408
Navigation, 1, 6, 7, 10, 12, 20, 40–41, 43, 44, 47, 51, 54–55, 60, 78–79, 81, 94, 98–99, 102, 106–107, 111, 177, 203, 255, 286–89, 291, 293, 300, 302, 352–53, 357–59, 375, 441, 467, 470, 472, 510, 519, 542
Nelson River, 39, 145
New York, Government of, 3, 18, 307, 372, 442, 537
New York Power Authority, 299
Niagara Convention and Protocol, 296
Niagara Falls, 5, 8, 38, 40–42, 46–48, 52, 55, 77, 79, 128, 140, 287–88, 294–99, 532
Niagara River, 7, 42, 55, 79, 80, 99, 106, 124, 126–29, 149–50, 286–87, 299–300, 354, 357, 368, 373
Niagara River Diversion Treaty, 8, 294, 297
Nipigon Bay, 368, 383
Nixon, Richard, 347–48, 407, 411, 490
North American Aerospace Defence Command (NORAD), 488, 490–91, 501–2
North American Agreement on Environmental Cooperation (NAAEC), 484, 493–94
North American Free Trade Agreement (NAFTA), 306, 484, 488, 490–91, 493–95, 501–2, 525
North American Water and Power Alliance (NAWAPA), 304
North Atlantic Treaty Organization (NATO), 488, 501–2
Northwest Area Water Supply Project, 217, 231–34

O

Obama, Barack, 416, 423, 500, 503
Ogoki Diversion, 294–95, 310
Ontario, Government of, 18, 327, 330, 338
Ontario Hydro, 295. *See also* HEPCO
Ontario Power Generation, 295, 300
Ontario Research Foundation (ORF), 329–30

Organisation for Economic Co-operation and Development (OECD), 401, 423, 491
Oswego River, 373–74, 381, 428
Ottawa River, 133, 308

P

Passamaquoddy Bay, 9, 165–87, 529
Passamaquoddy References, 166–70, 174, 182
Pearson, Lester B., 205, 500, 503, 510
Pennobscot River, 169
Pinchot, Gifford, 37–38
Plan 2014. *See* Regulation Plans (St. Lawrence–Lake Ontario)
Point Elliott Treaty, 201
Point Roberts, Chapter 6 *passim*
Pollution, general, 3, 4, 12, 17, 20, 25, 203, 204, 313–39, 406, 460–63, 532–33
  Air pollution, 3, 4, 12, 20, 25, 203–4, 313–39, 406, 460–63, 532–33
  Water pollution, 6, 12, 17, 20, 24, 55, 115–38, 159, 206, 229, 240, 265, 271–72, 285–86, 289, 308, 314, 317, 329, 348–60, 370–72, 375, 395, 398–400, 403–9, 411, 413–14, 417, 457, 459–60, 470–71, 473, 484, 489–90, 507, 532–33, 538–39
Port Huron, 140, 203, 326–35
Precautionary Principle, 417, 467–68, 472, 478, 479
Preservation, 37–38, 42, 96, 129, 180–81, 296, 532
Presque Isle Bay, 374, 376, 381
Progressive Era, 37, 38, 76, 131

Q

Quebec, Government of, 170, 304–5, 307
Quoddy. *See* Passamaquoddy

R

Rainy Lake, 79, 448, 478, 514, 520
Rainy River, 45–46, 50, 79, 98–99, 103, 215, 235, 352, 448, 519
Rankin Rapids, 172, 174, 177, 179–83, 187
Reagan, Ronald, 249–50, 252, 490, 492, 500, 503
Reconciliation, 452, 455, 543. *See also* First Nations
Recreation, 1, 7, 138, 174, 177, 181, 183, 196, 204–5, 210, 226, 252, 255, 258, 265–66, 274, 277, 285, 357–58, 367, 379, 472, 515, 521, 539, 542
Red River, 19, 215, 217–28, 448, 474, 515, 525
Regulation Plans (St. Lawrence–Lake Ontario), 1, 2, 307–8, 311, 342
Richelieu River, 46
Roosevelt, Franklin Delano, 167, 205, 320, 500, 503
Roosevelt, Theodore, 37–38, 81, 85, 86, 90, 92, 97, 115, 125, 130, 133, 484, 498–99, 500, 503
Root, Elihu, 5, 50, 52, 54, 55, 58–59, 61, 85, 86, 90–92, 95–102, 103, 486
Ross Dam, 239, 241–53, 274–75

S

St. Clair River, 287, 315, 324–38, 354, 357, 368, 373, 383
St. Clair–Detroit Air Pollution Board, 330, 344
St. Clair–Detroit River, 354, 355
St. Croix River, 45, 448, 474, 520–21, 523
St. John River, 45–46, 126, 165–66, 169, 173, 177, 179–80, 183–187
St. John River Engineering Board (SJREB), 171–72
St. John River Reference, 170–73
St. Laurent, Louis, 23, 169, 500, 503
St. Lawrence River, 165–66, 203, 285–86, 288–94, 303, 305, 307–8, 310–12, 352, 368, 370, 373, 400, 406, 441–42, 517–19, 523, 529, 545

St. Lawrence Seaway and Power Project, 21, 77, 174, 180, 186, 278, 287, 289–90, 292–93, 295, 300–301, 436–37, 441–42, 529, 532
St. Mary River, 39, 80, 108, 145–62, 464, 465, 468–70, 479, 511, 513
St. Mary–Milk Rivers, 5, 7, 24, 39–40, 45, 60, 80, 96, 99, 108, 143, 147–50, 154–55, 157, 159, 288, 464–65, 468–70, 479, 509, 512, 525, 531, 540–41, Chapter 4 *passim*
St. Marys River, 41, 100–101, 126, 145–46, 158, 162, 286–87, 289, 336, 354, 368, 373
Sage Creek, 146, 154–55, 163
Sage Creek Coal Reference, 239–40, 261, 275, 280
Sarnia, 140, 203, 324, 326–35, 342, 366
Sault Ste Marie, 40, 41, 46, 76–77, 80, 100, 101, 140, 288–89, 305
Science-based, 240, 274, 380, 417, 484, 520, 532–33, 542
Scientific expertise, 307, 309, 546
Severn Sound, 368, 374, 381–82, 428
Sewage, 40, 51, 55, 78, 98, 101–2, 115, 138, 202, 288, 300, 352–57, 358, 375, 382, 399, 471–72, 519
Sheboygan River, 373, 383
Sheyenne River, 225–31, 515
Shoal Lake, 437
Skagit River, 24, 206, 239–53, 274–75
Souris River, 215, 219, 234–35, 448, 519, 522, 523
Spanish Harbour, 368, 381, 428
Special International Niagara Board, 296
State Department (US), 47, 52, 58–59, 61, 80–81, 90, 94, 97, 99, 168, 184–85, 226–27, 229–30, 249–50, 265, 320, 350, 439, 536
State of the Great Lakes Ecosystem Conference (SOLEC), 384, 413–14, 418, 420, 422
Standing reference, 9, 347, 349, 351–52, 365, 410, 531
Stanley, Augustus Owsley (AO), 168–69
State of the Great Lakes (SOGL), 414, 417, 420, 422

602 Index

Strait of Georgia, 200, 205
Sub-federal governments, 307, 496, 531, 537
Sustainable development, 38, 472, 524
Swimming, 358, 384, 414, 421. *See also* recreation

T

Taft, William H., 49, 500, 503
Technology, 220, 266, 269, 272, 371, 375, 388, 453, 538
Tourism, 79, 128, 266, 269, 297, 299, 357, 358, 367, 379
Trade (general), 367, 438, 493, 494–95, 541
Traditional Ecological Knowledge, 379, 453, 543
Trail Smelter, 12, 19, 25, 203, 313, 315–24, 326, 337–38, 460–63
Transportation, 76–77, 105, 132, 170, 285, 295, 310, 367, 486
Treaty of Oregon, 200
Trudeau, Justin, 487, 489, 495, 500, 503
Trudeau, Pierre Elliott, 248–49, 347–48, 411, 484, 487, 500, 503
Truman, Harry, 168–69, 187, 500, 503
Trump, Donald, 423, 485, 488, 494–96, 498, 542, 546
Tweeddale, Reg, 172–73, 182, 186

U

Udall, Stewart, 183–85
United Nations (UN), 18, 401, 460, 488–89
United Nations Convention on the Non-Navigable Uses of Water, 469
United Nations Declaration on the Rights of Indigenous Peoples, 471, 489
United States–Mexico–Canada Agreement (USMCA), 496, 525–26
US Clean Air Act, 331–33, 338, 467
US Environmental Protection Agency (EPA), 159, 231, 355, 361, 383, 408, 411, 414, 416, 418, 496, 542–43
US Federal Power Commission (FPC), 167, 191, 193, 243, 247–48

W

War of 1812, 41, 434
Water Apportionment, 6, 17, 24, 46, 99, 143–45, 149–61, 257, 286, 296, 308, 402, 469, 511–12, 524–25, 531
Water Levels, 3, 7, 10, 77, 79, 95, 285–309, 414, 442, 467, 514–20, 524, 530, 541,
Water Pollution. *See* pollution, water; water quality
Water quality, 3, 4, 8, 10, 20, 24, 71, 115, 138, 159, 219, 220, 226, 228, 231, 233–34, 240, 261, 265–72, 285–86, 305, 308, 329, 347–49, 352–64, 370–71, 377, 382, 386, 399–401, 403–4, 406–7, 411, 414–17, 449, 470, 473, 498, 523, 526, 530, 540–41, 543–45
Water quantity, 3, 4, 20, 25, 71, 79, 119, 265–68, 285–86, 308, 357, 401, 464, 526, 545
Water treatment, 119–20, 122–30, 132, 219–20, 231, 233, 272, 353, 354, 381–83
Watershed Boards, 9, 234, 306–7, 454, 514, 520
Waterton River, 155, 158, 511, 513
Waukegon Harbor, 372–73, 383
Webster-Ashburton Treaty, 44, 51, 79, 99
Welland Canal, 77, 287
Wheatley Harbour, 368, 374, 381
White Lake(s), 373, 374, 381
World Health Organization (WHO), 355
World Trade Organization (WTO), 306, 488, 502

www.ingramcontent.com/pod-product-compliance
Lightning Source LLC
Chambersburg PA
CBHW041730300426
44115CB00022B/2968